POPULAR
MUSIC,
1980-1989

The Popular Music Series

Popular Music, 1920–1979 is a revised cumulation of and supersedes Volumes 1 through 8 of the *Popular Music* series, of which Volumes 6 through 8 are still available:

Volume 1, 2nd ed., 1950–59 Volume 5, 1920–29
Volume 2, 1940–49 Volume 6, 1965–69
Volume 3, 1960–64 Volume 7, 1970–74
Volume 4, 1930–39 Volume 8, 1975–79

Popular Music, 1980–1989 is a revised cumulation of and supersedes Volumes 9 through 14 of the *Popular Music* series, all of which are still available.

Volume 9, 1980–84 Volume 12, 1987
Volume 10, 1985 Volume 13, 1988
Volume 11, 1986 Volume 14, 1989

This series continues with:

Volume 15, 1990 Volume 17, 1992
Volume 16, 1991 Volume 18, 1993

Popular Music, 1900–1919 is a companion volume to the revised cumulations.

Other Books by Bruce Pollock

The Face of Rock and Roll: Images of a Generation

Hipper Than Our Kids?: A Rock and Roll Journal of the Baby Boom Generation

In Their Own Words: Popular Songwriting, 1955–1974

When Rock Was Young: The Heyday of Top 40

When the Music Mattered: Rock in the 1960s

ISSN 0886-442X

POPULAR MUSIC, 1980-1989

An Annotated Guide to American Popular Songs,
Including Introductory Essays, Lyricists and Composers Index,
Important Performances Index, Chronological Index,
Awards Index, and List of Publishers

A Revised Cumulation

BRUCE POLLOCK
Editor

 **Gale Research Inc.**

An International Thomson Publishing Company

I(T)P

NEW YORK • LONDON • BONN • BOSTON • DETROIT • MADRID
MELBOURNE • MEXICO CITY • PARIS • SINGAPORE • TOKYO
TORONTO • WASHINGTON • ALBANY NY • BELMONT CA • CINCINNATI OH

Bruce Pollock, *Editor*

Gale Research Inc. Staff

Allison K. McNeill, *Developmental Editor*
Marie C. Ellavich, Jolen Marya Gedridge, Camille A. Killens, *Associate Editors*
Lawrence W. Baker, *Managing Editor*

Mary Beth Trimper, *Production Director*
Deborah L. Milliken, *Production Assistant*

Cynthia Baldwin, *Product Design Manager*
Barbara J. Yarrow, *Graphic Services Supervisor*
Sherrell Hobbs, *Macintosh Artist*

Theresa Rocklin, *Manager, Technical Support Services*
Muhammad Anwar, *Programmer*
Benita L. Spight, *Data Entry Services Manager*
Gwendolyn S. Tucker, *Data Entry Supervisor*
Edgar C. Jackson, *Data Entry Associate*

∞™ This book is printed on acid-free paper that meets the minimum requirements of American National Standard for Information Sciences—Permanence Paper for Printed Library Materials, ANSI Z39.48-1984.

Library of Congress Catalog Card Number 85-653754
ISBN 0-7876-0205-1
ISSN 0886-442X

Published simultaneously in the United Kingdom
by Gale Research International Limited
(An affiliated company of Gale Research Inc.)

I(T)P™ Gale Research Inc., an International Thomson Publishing Company.
ITP logo is a trademark under license.

10 9 8 7 6 5 4 3 2 1

Contents

About the Book and How to Use It

This cumulative, revised edition updates and provides additional access to the wealth of information contained in volumes 9 through 14 of the *Popular Music* series. This unique important resource sets down in permanent and practical form a selective, annotated list of nearly 4,000 significant popular songs of the 1980s. Other indexes of popular music have either dealt with special areas, such as jazz or theater and film music, or been concerned chiefly with songs that achieved a degree of popularity as measured by the music-business trade indicators, which vary widely in reliability.

Annual Publication Schedule

The first nine volumes in the *Popular Music* series covered sixty-five years of song history in increments of five or ten years. *Popular Music, 1900–1919,* covers songs from the first twenty years of the twentieth century. Volume 10 initiated a new annual publication schedule, making background information available as soon as possible after a song achieves prominence. Yearly publication also allows deeper coverage—over five hundred songs—with additional details about writers' inspiration, uses of songs, album appearances, and more.

Indexes Provide Additional Access

Four indexes make the valuable information in the song listings even more accessible to users. The Lyricists & Composers Index shows all the songs represented in *Popular Music, 1980–1989,* that are credited to a given individual. The Important Performances Index tells at a glance which albums, musicals, films, television shows, or other media-featured songs are represented in the volume. The "Performer" category—now available for 1980–1985 for the first time—allows the user to see with which songs an artist was associated during this time period. The index is arranged by broad media category, then alphabetically by the show or album title, with the songs listed under each title. The Chronological

Index lists songs registered for copyright between 1980 and 1989 under the year of registration; songs with earlier copyright dates are listed under the year in which they were important. Finally, the Awards Index provides a list of the songs nominated for awards by the American Academy of Motion Picture Arts and Sciences (Academy Award) and the American Academy of Recording Arts and Sciences (Grammy Award). Winning songs are indicated by asterisks.

List of Publishers

The List of Publishers is an alphabetically arranged directory providing addresses—when available—for the publishers of the songs represented in *Popular Music, 1980–1989.* Also noted is the organization handling performance rights for the publisher—in the United States, the American Society of Composers, Authors, and Publishers (ASCAP) or Broadcast Music, Inc. (BMI), in Canada, the Society of Composers, Authors, and Music Publishers of Canada (SOCAN), and in Europe, the Society of European Songwriters and Composers (SESAC).

Tracking Down Information on Songs

Unfortunately, the basic records kept by the active participants in the music business are often casual, inaccurate, and transitory. There is no single source of comprehensive information about popular songs, and those sources that do exist do not publish complete material about even the musical works with which they are directly concerned. Four of the primary proprietors of basic information about our popular music are the major performing rights societies—ASCAP, BMI, SOCAN, and SESAC. Although each of these organizations has considerable information about the songs of its own writer and publisher members and has also issued indexes of its own songs, their files and published indexes are designed primarily for clearance identification by the commercial users of music. Their publications of annual or periodic lists of their "hits" necessarily include only a small fraction of their songs, and the facts given about these are also limited. ASCAP, BMI, SOCAN, and SESAC are, however, invaluable and indispensable sources of data about popular music. It is just that their data and special knowledge are not readily accessible to the researcher.

Another basic source of information about musical compositions and their creators and publishers is the Copyright Office of the Library of Congress. A computerized file lists each published, unpublished, republished, and renewed copyright of songs registered with the Office. It takes between six months and a year from the time of application before songs are officially registered (in some cases, songs have already been released before copyright registration begins). This file is helpful in determining the precise date of the declaration of the original ownership of musical works, but since some authors, composers, and publishers have been known to employ rather makeshift methods of protecting their works legally, there are songs listed in *Popular Music* that may not be found in the Library of Congress files.

Selection Criteria

In preparing the original volumes for this time period, the editor was faced with a number of separate problems. The first and most important of these was that of selection. The stated aim of the project—to offer the user as comprehensive and accurate a listing of significant popular songs as possible—has been the guiding criterion. The purpose has never been to offer a judgment on the quality of any songs or to indulge a prejudice for or against any type of popular music. Rather, it is the purpose of *Popular Music* to document those musical works that (1) achieved a substantial degree of popular acceptance, (2) were exposed to the public in especially notable circumstances, or (3) were accepted and given important performances by influential musical and dramatic artists.

Another problem was whether or not to classify the songs as to type. Most works of music are subject to any number of interpretations and, although it is possible to describe a particular performance, it is more difficult to give a musical composition a label applicable not only to its origin but to its subsequent musical history. In fact, the most significant versions of some songs are often quite at variance with their origins. Citations for such songs in *Popular Music* indicate the important facts about not only their origins but also their subsequent lives, rather than assigning an arbitrary and possibly misleading label.

Research Sources

The principal sources of information for the titles, authors, composers, publishers, and dates of copyright of the songs in this volume were the Copyright Office of the Library of Congress, ASCAP, BMI, SOCAN, SESAC, and individual writers and publishers. Data about best-selling recordings were obtained principally from three of the leading music business trade journals—*Billboard, Radio & Records,* and *Cash Box.* For the historical notes; information about foreign, folk, public domain, and classical origins; and identification of theatrical, film, and television introducers of songs, the editor relied upon collections of album notes, theater programs, sheet music, newspaper and magazine articles, and other material, both his own and that in the Lincoln Center Library for the Performing Arts in New York City.

About the Book and How to Use It

Contents of a Typical Entry

The primary listing for a song includes

- Title and alternate title(s)
- Country of origin (for non-U.S. songs)
- Author(s) and composer(s)
- Current publisher, copyright date
- Annotation on the song's origins or performance history

Title: The full title and alternate title or titles are given exactly as they appear on the Library of Congress copyright record or, in some cases, the sheet music. Since even a casual perusal of the book reveals considerable variation in spelling and punctuation, it should be noted that these are the colloquialisms of the music trade. The title of a given song as it appears in this series is, in almost all instances, the one under which it is legally registered.

Foreign Origin: If a song is of foreign origin, the primary listing indicates the country of origin after the title. Additional information may be noted, such as the original title, copyright date, writer, publisher in country of origin, or other facts about the adaptation.

Authorship: In all cases, the primary listing reports the author or authors and the composer or composers. The reader may find variations in the spelling of a songwriter's name. This results from the fact that some writers used different forms of their names at different times or in connection with different songs. "See also" references in the Lyricist & Composers Index allow readers to tie such variations together (e.g. John Cougar vs. John Mellencamp). In addition to this kind of variation in the spelling of writers' names, the reader will also notice that in some cases, where the writer is also the performer, the name as a writer may differ from the form of the name used as a performer.

Publisher: The current publisher is listed. Since *Popular Music* is designed as a practical reference work rather than an academic study, and since copyrights more than occasionally change hands, the current publisher is given instead of the original holder of the copyright. If a publisher has, for some reason, copyrighted a song more than once, the years of the significant copyright subsequent to the year of the original copyright are also listed after the publisher's name.

Annotation: The primary listing mentions significant details about the song's history—the musical, film, or other production in which the song was introduced or featured and, where important, by whom it was introduced, in the case of theater and film songs; any other performers identified with the song; first or best-selling recordings and album inclusions, indicating the performer and the record company; awards; and other relevant data. The name of a performer may be listed differently in connection with different songs, especially over a period of years. The name listed is the form of the name given in connection with a particular performance or record. Dates are provided for important recordings and performances.

Popular Music, 1980–1989

If the ultimate acceptance of the lowly song can be confirmed from the measure of its success in the two other supposedly more adult popular art-forms—television and the movies—then in the 1980s, songs arrived at an unprecedented maturity. Whether that kind of recognition brought the quality of songwriting and performance to similar new levels of artistry, or instead, only succeeded in simultaneously inflating expectations and diluting the end product, is a philosophical conundrum even several years of hindsight has not equipped me to entirely penetrate.

Suffice it to say, if only through the law of supply and demand, songs were needed and produced at an astonishing rate. If fewer of them became certified national hits, to be permanently embedded in our collective subconsciousness, more of them certainly reached their desired narrow niches—at the cafes, nightclubs, dance halls, and other lonely haunts of the underground—where their effects were easily as powerful. Moreover, as the recent succession of late night trendy 80s song compilations now suggests, the decade did at least meet the minimum challenge of any such ten-year time period, by providing the requisite several hundred or so recognizable tunes, most of them referenced in this volume, that would aid a multiplicity of marketing ventures in defining the pop cultural epoch as, variously, between the wars, after the fires, post-hippie, post-modern, proto-yippie, and the dreaded Generation X.

Even within the overwhelming cultural and technological context of a continuously televised music channel, leading to the possibility of a decade in which there could be more people watching music than listening to it, it is nevertheless comforting to note that such willful revisionism did not entirely subvert the completion of several time-honored musical cycles. The fertile 1970s undergrounds of punk and its slightly more respectable cousin New Wave sent several representatives hurtling toward the overground early in the new decade. By mid-decade, a new alternative music sprung up and would produce its own notable breakthroughs by decade's end. A number of individual songwriters and songwriting teams prospered in the flourishing art of the corporate rock tune, the overblown ballad, and the insidious R&B groove. Through its association with major hit movies, country music once again flirted with the mainstream during the early '80s, before reverting to its traditional limited formulas. Generally, if a picture was worth a thousand words (back in the old days), then a song, whether classic, newly written, a clever cover, or a ten-second snippet, was probably worth at least a half a dozen movies in the '80s, as any number of hit and cover-packed soundtrack albums will attest. At the same time, that aging beast Broadway, which was once our major supplier of extra-musical context, managed to heave forth some enduring beauties, and even offer some hope for a new generation of songwriters, if not necessarily their audience. Another aging beast, heavy metal, found solace for its trimmer cohorts on the late night music video circuit, while Michael Jackson and Lionel Richie, in 1985, spearheaded the world's first Made for MTV telethon, entitled "We Are the World."

And yet, ironically, but not so surprisingly, when the decade did produce a music revolution, television missed it. Indeed, the desolate urban back alley neighborhood bar where the churning sounds of a new kind of black protest music were erupting was hardly the appropriate sitcom setting required for television's infamous comfort zone. But the rap rhymes and hip hop rhythms that evoked the earliest days of rock and roll, with its bristling energy and colorful cast of crooked characters, its one-shot superstars, and white imitators, would all but overtake the pop landscape by decade's end, by which point television would be safely on board, honoring the once potent form with sitcoms of its own, regular time-slots, department store window displays, and incessant TV commercials to attest to its absorbing potential. In spite of this, with its melding and massaging of the past and future through ingenious sampling techniques, its assaults on suburban decorum and language, and its rampant disregard of the copyright laws, black musicians were not only rediscovering their own history, but in effect reclaiming what they never got paid for in the first place, making the rap revolution as pure a form of pop protest as any race, creed, or generation has yet managed.

By the end of the decade the song had experienced an utter schizophrenia of mood and purpose. On TV, the pictures increasingly seemed to have little or nothing to do with the words and music they accompanied, or at best, to represent but one person's idea of one particular song. On radio, fractionalized formats served to divide frustrated fans into competing factions, sub-genres, and specialties, further isolating listeners from the total experience. At the same time, the advent of the Compact Disc, while playing havoc with the sanctity of an album's original track order, resulted in the concurrent proliferation of recycled boxed sets, making it possible, if money were no object, to have the entire history—or several competing histories—of music delivered to one's doorstep overnight.

However, as the following reprinted essays—in chronological order, without the benefit of such lengthy hindsight—suggest, despite the impossible odds (and insufferable sods) and obstructing imagery, the lonely song continues to make its way, both with and against the fashions and the currents—maturity be coveted, maturity be damned—inevitably and invariably producing enough songs of style and substance and memorability each year to satisfy even the most discerning of palates.

Bruce Pollock
1994

Popular Music 1980-1984

When last considered in these pages, popular music offered indications that diversity, creativity, "a cross-cultural renaissance of form and feeling" lay just around the bend, perhaps to become evident sometime around 1986. That target date now seems but a hopeful, if not entirely unfounded, projection. The recent arrival of such joyful hybrids as the Bangles, the Hooters, R.E.M., the Three O'Clock, Cyndi Lauper, Prince, Suzanne Vega, Ferron, Claudia Schmidt, The Eurythmics, and Tears for Fears, recalls the folk/pop literacy that infused the mid-sixties to mid-seventies period with so much style and energy, briefly fueling fantasies of a new and improved sensibility of the masses—heart, soul, beat, and lyrics united in a common drive for meaning, mystery, and movement. But, as if to take the wind out of even this relatively mild heroic squall, one must take note of the overwhelming dominance (enough, in fact, virtually to define the period) of pop music's heretofore untapped visual element.

Since its advent in the summer of 1981, a cable network called MTV (Music Television), using short, filmed presentations of the latest Top 40 contenders, has changed the nature of pop music, giving it a face, legs, and dozens upon dozens of dancing feet. By removing the song from the purely aural, MTV has both enhanced and diluted the tradition. It has taken mere superstars and, with constant TV exposure and an endless variety of seductive poses, turned them into demigods (Michael Jackson, Bruce Springsteen). It has transformed successful albums into long-playing TV series, as works by Huey Lewis & The News, Z.Z. Top, Van Halen, Billy Joel, Tina Turner, and others secured renewal well beyond the usual hit song or two, producing on the average three or four singles—and videos—per LP. MTV took colorful newcomers who were gifted with the savvy and intuition to master the new rules and made them into overnight role models (Madonna, Cyndi Lauper, Boy George & Culture Club, Prince, Duran Duran).

Music videos did not exclude the many aging worthies who had performed their services to pop music song after song and yet remained unheard on radio. Unlike the Mickey Mantles and Joltin' Joe DiMaggios of yore, who could only sigh when commenting on the seven-figure contracts of today's ballplayers, pop's veterans capitalized on the new exposure to lengthen shadowy careers, in some cases exploding beyond their youthful prominence. (Examples include Tina Turner, Rod Stewart, David Bowie, John Fogerty, Olivia Newton-John, Paul McCartney, and Elton John). Black performers, however, benefitted somewhat less than their contemporaries through MTV exposure. While Lionel Richie, Michael Jackson, Prince, Donna Summer, and the Pointer Sisters made strong moves toward the mainstream (and their own variety shows someday), rhythm 'n' blues was not a priority on the videoized rock 'n' pop mix. In the movies, on network television, and on Broadway, however, the Motown sound of the Supremes, the Temptations, Smokey Robinson, and the Four Tops experienced a creative coming of age, as demonstrated with the soundtrack to *The Big Chill*, the *Motown 25th Anniversary Special*, and *Dreamgirls*.

As with the small screen, so with the large. During the 1980-1984 period there were at least forty songs from movies that occupied slots in the Top 10 of their respective years. Many movies, in fact, were little more than excuses for soundtrack albums featuring material of varying quality from big-name acts. Other movies seemed to be nothing more than elaborate and elongated soundtrack albums themselves. As in the preceding five years, rock stars, now even more primed by their experience romping through the mini-movies of the MTV realm, jumped to the silver screen much as sports stars were moving from the field to the broadcast booth, and with results that were just as erratic (Rick Springfield in *Hard to Hold*, Dolly Parton in *9 to 5*, Olivia Newton-John in *Xanadu*, Bette Midler in *The Rose*, Willie Nelson in *Honeysuckle Rose*, Debbie Harry in *Videodrome*, and Neil Diamond in *The Jazz Singer*). The songs themselves generally fared better, with tunes like "Fame," "Up Where We Belong," "Eye of the Tiger," "Chariots of Fire," "It's My Turn," "Arthur's Theme," "I Just Called to Say I Love You," and "The Rose" offering a better showcase than much of the acting on the screen. And, lest we forget, among his other accomplishments of the period, Michael Jackson made a short movie of his song "Thriller" and sold many copies of it on video cassette. Jackson's *Thriller* album, in addition to producing a record seven Top 10 singles ("Beat It," "Billie Jean," "Human Nature," "PYT," "Thriller," "The Girl Is Mine," and "Wanna Be Startin' Something"), also went on to become the largest-selling album of all time (aided and abetted, of course, by constant MTV exposure).

With such imposing media guns falling in behind the mere song, equipping it and adorning it with technical values far beyond simple words and music, it is not surprising that a discussion of the period's song output should take such a backseat to matters of image and exposure, technical expertise, and abject self-promotion. These issues all but obliterated the distinctions among singer, song, and medium. If such accoutrements as setting and scene, script and stage lighting are stripped away, to our dismay (but not quite utter shock) we find a collection of love songs as undistinguished as any produced in the preceding five-year period. Unrelentingly one-track minded, the songwriters of the era, either by professional choice or inherent creative limitations (of themselves or of the general listening populace), neither strayed too far from the norm nor caused that norm to expand in any direction. Much more creative than the songwriters of the period, for the most part, were the video directors, who had to take yet another forlorn or boasting, repentant or repulsive lyric about love and cast it, dress it up, provide it with special effects, run it through its paces, stage it, edit it, and present it to the public grossly underbudgeted and short of time. That so many of these videos were trite only reflects their source, the song. And while there may be an underground in the video realm, just as there is one in the aural realm, its work, at least through most of the period, not only failed to create an impact strong enough to ripple the status quo, but seemed, on cursory inspection, mired in traps and tricks that were in circulation back in 1961 (the Talking Heads, Laurie Anderson, and other such performance artists notwithstanding).

So, from 1980-1982, at least, stagnancy reigned. If the musical underground was fertile, few significant tendrils were pushing up through the earth for the starving fan. "Another Brick in the Wall" in 1980 offered ominous signs of impending rebellion, but the preponderance of airless drivel from the lips of Kenny Rogers, Christopher Cross, and Air Supply was enough to suffocate the remaining diehards. "All Out of Love," "Sailing," "Do That to Me One More Time," "Lady," "Lost in Love," and "Real Love" may have made the plight of wedding bands a bit easier, but provided no indication of the pop singer's power to revitalize a moment, if not an entire generation. "Tired of Toein' the Line" had some nifty rockabilly defiance; "Brass in Pocket" introduced Chrissie Hynde's sassy style to the world; "Whip It" brought to the masses the zany Devo program for salvation. The Clash, long an underground favorite, received partial due with "Train in Vain (Stand by Me)." John Lennon's return to recording with "Just Like Starting Over" was the year's biggest heartwarming story, even if the song itself was far outweighed by the sentiment.

1981 was a year cut from the same cloth. Not even the death of John Lennon could arouse our slumbering songwriters, although Lennon's former colleagues did manage to put something down on paper. George Harrison wrote "All Those Years Ago," Paul McCartney contributed "Here Today," and New York neighbor Paul Simon gave us "The Late Great Johnny Ace." In the meantime, one of the best novels of the post-War era, *Endless Love* by Scott Spencer, was being turned into a trivial movie, sporting a trivial pop theme, scripted by Lionel Richie, whose penchant for lush love songs made him the era's Paul McCartney.

Love was in the air, it was safe to say, for the entire year; not a disparaging or thought-provoking word was uttered in song. "Jessie's Girl" had a certain intensity; "Kiss on My List" captured a feeling that the duo of Hall and Oates would hang onto for the better part of the period. A trace of poignancy could be found in the quivering carcasses of "Same Old Lang Syne," "Hey Nineteen," "Hearts," and "Don't Stand So Close to Me." Often cited as the next Lennon and McCartney, the team of Difford and Tilbrook made their first appearance on the charts with "Tempted," a rather wordy but totally charming departure from the slickness otherwise prevailing.

The drought continued into another year, with 1982 offering a number one status to such warhorses as Chicago, Steve Miller, Paul McCartney and Stevie Wonder, the J. Geils Band, and Joe Cocker (in a duet with Jennifer Warnes). However, John Cougar's "Jack and Diane" was something of a documentary, "Always on My Mind" was genuinely moving, and "Key Largo" created pictures for the soul. Satire entered the scene for the first time in a long while with "Valley Girl," while social commentary started edging back into prominence, bolstered by the majesty of "Still in Saigon." Bruce Springsteen put Gary U.S. Bonds back to work with "Out of Work," launching his own one-man crusade as the king of the blue collar poets. "Pressure," "Under Pressure," "Spirits in the Material World," "Kids in America," and Prince's "1999" all gave indications that pop music might at least be coming to grips with a purpose higher than the elemental desires.

However, before such a great leap beyond could be taken, all the elements of the period would come together into a yearlong showcase. Thus, 1983 gave us movie music ("Flashdance . . . What a Feeling," "Maniac," "It Might Be You") and image-drenched MTV productions ("Total Eclipse of the Heart," "Beat It," "Do You Really Want to Hurt Me," "Hungry Like the Wolf," "All Night Long (All Night)," "Goody Two Shoes"). There was a bit of social commentary ("Undercover of the Night," "Allentown," "New Year's Day," "Rock the Casbah") and a number of significant comeback songs ("Let's Dance," "Say Say Say," "Sexual Healing," "Come Dancing"). The English techno sound, otherwise known as the New Wave, crested on the shores of hitsville ("I Ran," "Sweet Dreams (Are Made of These)," "One Thing Leads to Another," "She Blinded Me with Science"). American superstars-in-waiting garnered precious airtime ("Heart and Soul," "Uptown Girl," "Stand Back," "Little Red Corvette"). But perhaps the largest crack in complacency was made mid-year by a little band out of Georgia by the name of R.E.M. with a song called "Radio Free Europe." Beyond the simplicity of the group's instrumentation and their utter lack of television image, the symbolism of the song's title could not be ignored. R.E.M. was a little slash in the curtain hanging over pop radio. This slight tear would not perceptibly widen throughout 1983, although bands like Big Country ("In a Big Country"), U2 ("New Year's Day"), the Pretenders ("Back on the Chain Gang"), Tears for Fears ("Change"), Scandal ("Love's Got a Line on You"), and Talking Heads ("Burning Down the House") produced sounds that were as fresh as anything heard on the air since the mid-seventies.

In 1984 Bruce Springsteen personally ushered in several millenniums of popular music with one album, a yearlong tour, and the mandatory accompanying video performances. Songs like "Born in the U.S.A.," "Glory Days," "No Surrender," and "My Home Town" simultaneously resurrected the singer-songwriter as a viable entity (casting new, favorable light on contemporaries like Billy Joel, John Cougar, and Bryan Adams, and even on an abject imitator like John Cafferty) and presented Springsteen as the working-class poet, ushering in with patriotic zeal a year of American-made rock 'n' roll unequalled since the pre-Beatles heyday of the Brill Building. Performers included Huey Lewis from San Francisco, the Cars from Boston, Cyndi Lauper from New York, Madonna from Detroit, Georgia's R.E.M., and the Bangles from Los Angeles. Springsteen's songs once again fused rock energy to folk sensibilities and caught the ears of an underground ready to surface in the works of Los Lobos, The Replacements, Husker Du, and Suzanne Vega. As a result, 1984 ended on a reaffirmation of pop's best qualities, produced by a healthy crop of newcomers. And if the deacons of the songwriter elite, Bob Dylan, Joni Mitchell, Jackson Browne, Laura Nyro, Leonard Cohen, and Paul Simon, were relatively quiet, there were new voices to be heard in T-Bone Burnette, Chrissie Hynde, Sting, Richard Thompson, the resurgent Lou Reed, and Phil Collins.

Such optimism could be carried forward into the world of musical theater, but with certain reservations. Although the period sported its share of big winners *(Cats, Dreamgirls, La Cage au Folles, Nine, Little Shop of Horrors, Pump Boys and Dinettes, Sunday in the Park with George)*, 1984 was virtually bereft of noteworthy contenders for the longevity title of *A Chorus Line*. Some big songs emanated from these shows, among them "Memory," "I Am What I Am," "And I Am Telling You I'm Not Going." Andrew Lloyd Webber established himself as the heir apparent to Stephen Sondheim in productivity if not in talent. William Finn made strides toward greater recognition with *In Trousers* and *March of the Falsettos*. Craig Carnelia garnered solid notices for his talent, even if his *Is There Life after High School* failed to graduate into the black for its backers. Elizabeth Swados teamed with the political cartoonist Garry Trudeau for the mildly entertaining *Doonesbury,* while Kander and Ebb had much more success with *The Rink* for Liza Minnelli and *Woman of the Year* for Lauren Bacall. While Sondheim himself won a Pulitzer Prize for *Sunday in the Park with George,* perhaps the most interesting recognition was conferred upon Gary Portnoy and Judy Hart Angelo, authors of the score of the otherwise unheralded *Preppies,* who went on to compose the theme songs for two of television's more successful situation comedies, *Cheers* and *Punky Brewster.*

The 1980-1984 period was not especially revolutionary in the country or rhythm 'n' blues realms. The best of those breeds managed to mingle effortlessly with pop music—Randy Goodrum, Lionel Richie, Prince. At its best, country had its share of poignant if gin-soaked gems: "Wind Beneath My Wings," "Bottom of the Fifth," "Always on My Mind," "She Got the Goldmine (I Got the Shaft)." Rhythm 'n' blues, with the focus as usual on the rhythm, caught the streetbeat as ever in the form of "rap music," with Grandmaster Flash and Kurtis Blow pioneering the deejay's rhyming art and, in the case of "The Message" and "The Breaks," putting that beat into the service of some angry poetics. The re-release, then, of Gil Scott-Heron's best works on a single album took on new significance as, with the Last Poets, Scott-Heron could be termed a founder of Rap. At any rate, a listen to "The Revolution Will Not Be Televised" should be all you need to persuade you of its coiled power.

As the period ended, another significant song was released, holding much hope for 1985 as a year of idealism and purpose. Bob Geldof's "Do They Know It's Christmas" was recorded by a virtual royalty of English rock stars, the profits from the song to be donated to aid Ethiopian children. Once again, the power of the song was stepping forth, to shake the senses and move the world.

Bruce Pollock

Popular Music in 1985

Trends of protest and nostalgia, themes of sex and violence, and the demands of proliferating film and television productions combined to make 1985 a year of American song creation nearly unparalleled in history. This revival played out on several stages, not the least of which was the political arena in Washington, DC—site of so many marches and demonstrations back in the sixties, song's last such gleaming moment in the sun.

The Return of Social Concern

With an American songwriting renaissance in full flower, performers and bands occupied heartland stages, not only celebrating their own creations, but marking a national community coming together, inspired by mutually energizing music and causes. The momentum against African famine, initiated in Britain by Bob Geldof's "Do They Know It's Christmas" in 1984, crested with America's Lionel Richie-Michael Jackson anthem "We Are the World" and the simultaneous Live Aid concerts which were broadcast worldwide from London and Philadelphia. The success of Live Aid sparked benefits by performers across the musical spectrum for causes ranging from the economic crisis of U.S. farmers and the Mexican earthquake, to the epidemic of acquired immune deficiency syndrome (AIDS). Bruce Springsteen's charismatic commitment to a variety of social concerns and his former partner Steve Van Zandt's "Sun City" chant against South African apartheid set a tone for the year of high optimism, backed with a realistic, street-and-history toughened knowledge of the long haul.

Topping the year off with a sense of drama, perspective, and irony, Bob Dylan—a featured voice on "We Are the World" and a weathered and poignant presence at the Live Aid and Farm Aid concerts—released the astonishing five-record *Biograph* set. The albums collected three decades of achievement into one package and definitively proved Dylan the forefather of a generation still expanding, still preaching the surreal, jugular-piercing gospel he invented, perfected, and glorified. *Biograph* would be a much needed weapon, a soul-comforting Bible to grasp in the troubled atmosphere of threatened censorship that arose out of Washington.

In the capital a group formed by the wives of several members of the federal government demanded Congressional hearings on the lyrics of rock 'n' roll. The Parents Music Resource Center (PMRC) proposed a labelling system analagous to the "PG" (parental guidance suggested) used in the film industry as a way to protect adolescents from the suggestive words of popular records. Their testimony was challenged by that of such musicians as Frank Zappa, former leader of the legendary Mothers of Invention, and Dee Snider of the deliberately outrageous Twisted Sister. The drama of the hearings and the threat to the heart and soul of rock 'n' roll seemed to arouse many songwriters into producing their best work.

Love, Patriotism, and Other Themes

Closer to the middle of the road, pop music continued to perform its more traditional function as purveyor of platitudes, palliative to the masses, offering an abundance of love songs for throbbing hearts teenaged and older. These transitory odes had no greater purpose than to commemorate a time or a place, a chance encounter or a last embrace with a catchy tune and greeting-card poetics. Yet even these efforts exhibited a higher level of intelligence and intensity, etching the place more firmly in the consciousness, making the last embrace all the more sensuous for its finality. Sophistication in setting and emotion enhanced the work of stock players and packaged teen idols.

George Michael's efforts with Wham!, "Careless Whisper" and "Wake Me Up Before You Go Go," respectively the number one and number three songs of the year according to *Billboard* magazine, evinced a nightclub chic worlds removed from the discos of Brooklyn popularized by the Bee Gees, John Travolta, and the movie *Saturday Night Fever* in the previous decade. The torchy tramp portrayed by Madonna and scripted by the writers of her hits "Like a Virgin" (Tom Kelly and Billy Steinberg) and "Crazy for You" (John Bettis and Jon Lind) was a quantum leap in sleaze-tease quotient and in witty self-knowledge beyond any number of girl-as-victim, singer-as-puppet, and woman-as-loser songs of the past thirty years. In "I Want to Know What Love Is" Mick Jones, surely one of rock's consummate craftsmen, dared to ask a question most of his dutifully resigned contemporaries would have preferred not to contemplate, even as they earned their livings batting out tepid soap operatic approximations.

Throughout the rest of the year's most honored and best-selling songs, themes of pride and confidence range across a terrain sprinkled with three-minute epitomes of philosophizing, psychological insight, political fury, sexual heat, sociological snippets, and just plain unbridled ebullience. The convergence of the nationalism promoted by the Reagan administration, the 1984 Olympics in Los Angeles, and such pop culture icons as actor Sylvestor Stallone's *Rambo,* with the musical influence of Bruce Springsteen's landmark 1984 album, *Born in the U.S.A.,* continued to shape popular songs from John Cougar Mellencamp's "Small Town" to Charlie Daniels's "Amber Waves of Grain." Even commercials caught the beat, exemplified by the revitalized Chrysler Corporation's slogan, "The pride is back, born in America." An apt credo for a patriotic year, even though a blatant ripoff on a neo-Springsteenian theme. So it goes.

While these songs were designed to draw enthusiastic agreement, others—intentionally or not—drew criticism. Gays alleged that Mark Knopfler's "Money for Nothing" was a slur. Others took offense at Prince's graphic description of female anatomy in "Sugar Walls," given steamy life by Sheena Easton . . . or at Madonna's enthusiastic acceptance of greed—a sore point in a year of Yuppies—in "Material Girl". . . or at David Lee Roth's sexist interpretation of the Beach Boys' classic "California Girls." Many more, however, were moved by Lionel Richie's tribute to the late Marvin Gaye, "Missing You," as sung by Diana Ross, or by "Nightshift," a tune from Lionel's old group, the Commodores, in which they honored Gaye and Jackie Wilson as well. Those on the side of sentiment couldn't help but applaud the success of Julian Lennon, son of the murdered former Beatle, when "Valotte" and "Too Late for Goodbyes" were released on these shores. "We Built This City" by the Starship (formerly Jefferson Starship) inspired some to proclaim a restoration of the long missing power of rock. Other writers demonstrated that power in different ways. Corey Hart's "Never Surrender," John Parr's "St. Elmo's Fire (Man in Motion)," "We Belong," by Pat Benatar, and "Everybody Wants to Rule the World," by Tears for Fears, all espoused a more personal credo of self-realization by ordeal, a coming of age through psychic growth. And, you could dance to them.

Songs from Films

As usual, movie assignments, holding the possibility of the venerable Academy Award rather than the more common Grammy and sometimes offering superior inspiration from the material being filmed, prompted songwriters to some of the finest efforts of the year. Although "St. Elmo's Fire (Man in Motion)," by John Parr and David Foster, inexplicably failed to gain a nomination, Stephen Bishop, a vocalist for "It Might Be You," the theme from *Tootsie* nominated in 1982, returned to the circle of the nominees, as a writer, with "Separate Lives" from

White Nights. "Say You, Say Me," from the same film (and not a musical, at that) earned Lionel Richie one of his two nominations, the other coming for "Miss Celie's Blues (Sisters)," which he wrote with Rod Temperton and Quincy Jones for *The Color Purple.* "The Power of Love," from *Back to the Future,* was a smash for Huey Lewis & The News, as well as drawing an Oscar nomination. "Surprise, Surprise" was added to the score of the film version of the Broadway musical *A Chorus Line* by writers Hamlisch and Kleban especially to secure a nomination as best original song. It did—surprise, surprise.

Although this completes the list of Academy Award nominees, it by no means defines the extent of quality songs debuting in movie soundtracks in 1985. At least a dozen tunes ascended to the upper reaches of the pop charts, propelled by the multi-media boost only a feature-length movie showcase (with the requisite music video trailer) can provide. *Beverly Hills Cop* had three such tunes: "The Heat Is On," "Neutron Dance," and "Axel F." In addition to "The Power of Love," "St. Elmo's Fire," and "Separate Lives," these movie songs hit the top of the pops: "Don't You Forget about Me," from *The Breakfast Club;* "Rhythm of the Night," from *The Last Dragon;* "That's What Friends Are For," originally used in the 1982 flick *Nightshift;* and Bryan Adams's re-released "Heaven," which premiered in *A Night in Heaven.* The rock group Duran Duran contributed its first soundtrack for the James Bond spy movie *A View to a Kill,* while Tina Turner had a featured role in the futuristic fantasy *Mad Max Beyond Thunderdome,* for which she also recorded "We Don't Need Another Hero."

Songs on Television

Lacking Hollywood's diversity, the primary contribution of the small screen—television—to popular music remained its showcasing of music videos, both on special all-music cable channels like MTV (Music Television) for rock and VH1 (Video Hits One) for adult contemporary songs and on weekly shows on network and independent stations. However, one series, not ostensibly a music show, emerged as virtually a sixty-minute slot for a rock 'n' roll soundtrack each week. *Miami Vice* did, in fact, yield a hit album in 1985. This highly glamorized detective show revived certain rock chestnuts, notably "In the Air Tonight," by Phil Collins. More obscure items integrated into the action took on a cachet not unlike that preferred by *Saturday Night Live* in its heyday. Prime-time exposure boosted hit singles twenty to thirty points on the *Billboard, Cash Box,* and *Variety* charts, as the Monkees and the Partridge Family had learned all too well when they had weekly shows in an earlier decade. *Miami Vice* went the situation comedies of the sixties one better in its marriage of television and song, however. Glenn Frey's song "Smuggler's Blues" was the basis for an entire episode of the show, with Frey himself as a featured character. This use recalled the film version of Arlo Guthrie's picaresque ballad "Alice's Restaurant" in the late sixties and the album, rock opera, film, and ballet appearances of the Who's *Tommy.* Frey was just one of many stars who made appearances on *Miami Vice,* but his was successful enough that the producers succumbed to the characteristic drive of television moguls to make too much of a good thing and they brought him back a second time. The show's two-hour premier episode in the fall of 1985 featured Frey's debut of his song "You Belong to the City." It had no trouble cracking radio play lists nationwide.

Theatrical Songs

Unfortunately, Broadway and its legendary local commodity, musical theater, had no such luck and apparently little intent to mine the music video format so successfully exploited by television and films. This despite the fact that two of its more successful endeavors of the year were composed by writers who had previously had Top 40 songs. Rupert Holmes ("The Pina Colada Song") wrote *The Mystery of Edwin Drood,* based on an unfinished Charles Dickens novel. Roger Miller ("King of the Road") was the country bumpkin who turned Mark Twain's *Huckleberry Finn* into *Big River.* Other than these two admittedly less-than-sensational productions, Broadway had little material to make into a music video. Andrew Lloyd Webber's *Song and Dance* rehashed old material. Charles Strouse's *Mayor* was a topical revue of interest to the fans and foes of Ed Koch, but unlikely to have much appeal outside the New York City area. Masterly Stephen Sondheim had no new material produced, but was represented by two monumental album releases. A four-record boxed set reprising his career was, for another audience, an event on a par with Dylan's release of *Biograph.* Fans of the musical also appreciated the all-star concert recording of Sondheim's 1972 classic score, *Follies.* The composer also contributed a rewrite of his "Putting It Together" to Barbara Streisand's long awaited and very successful *Broadway Album.*

Perhaps the most intriguing project cooking these days in the realm of the musical is one that did exploit the music video concept. Authors Tim Rice (who has been the hit single route before, with "Jesus Christ, Superstar" and "I Don't Know How to Love Him" from his musical *Jesus Christ, Superstar)* and Benny Anderson and Bjorn Ulvaeus (the male half of the Swedish supergroup ABBA) found they had a hit U.S. single with "One Night in Bangkok" from *Chess* well before the show even opened in its native England. The exotic imagery of the video for the song may have boosted its appeal and whetted appetites for the entire musical. Perhaps other Broadway producers will consider this marketing device in the future.

Rhythm 'n' Blues, Country, and Folk Songs

Although both rhythm 'n' blues (also known as black music or dance music) and country music must be counted as forbears of today's popular music, they differ greatly in how they are relating to mainstream music just now. The most popular black musicians are also the most popular music makers and songwriters for a general audience. Lionel Richie, Stevie Wonder, Ashford and Simpson, Bobby Womack, Sade, Kool & The Gang, Prince, Billy Ocean, the Pointer Sisters—all project a universal style that transcends genre. Moreover, the subject matter of rhythm 'n' blues—the many manifestations of sexual adrenalin—only ensures the timelessness of the message, while the sass and pizazz of the dance club, with new songs issued as fast as new steps are created and new catch phrases ushered into the slanguage of the street, give the music a drive and urgency that attracts artists of different hues. Most dance hits emanate from independent record companies, confirming the grassroots nature of this genre, the hot-off-the-presses aspect of the territory, where the music strikes the body first, before it gets civilized into the button-down brain of pop. Where else but on the r 'n' b side could you come up with 1985's two local favorites that made it nationwide (Rocking Sidney's "My Toot Toot" from Louisiana and "Roxanne, Roxanne" from the streets of New York City)?

The country heritage of rock 'n' roll extends just as far back and just as deep. Hank Williams inspired Bob Dylan. Buddy Holly, Carl Perkins, Elvis Presley, Johnny Cash, and Jerry Lee Lewis are major rockabilly influences still felt three decades later. What did Tin Pan Alley ever have that Tennessee's Felice and Boudleaux Bryant didn't? Yet in 1985 country music was a virtual world unto itself, symbolized by Ronnie Milsap's best-selling "Lost in the Fifties." The country neighborhood this year is a place we've been to many times before, the candy store still selling baseball cards of the Brooklyn Dodgers. Unfailingly realistic, if not downright depressing in their lyrical concerns, country songwriters continue to churn out titles like these: "Drinkin' and Dreamin'," "She's Single Again," "Some Fools Never Learn," "Meet Me in Montana," "She Keeps the Home Fires Burning." Content to grow old with their audiences, established country musicians are giving away the turf to rock-inspired newcomers like the Long Ryders, Green on Red, R.E.M., Jason & The Scorchers, and the Dream Syndicate. These groups have also rediscovered the folk sensibility till now buried on the dirt roads of the sixties.

Some of the best songs written in 1985 come out of this latent sensibility. Suzanne Vega released an album chock full of them: "Freeze Tag," "Small Blue Thing," "Marlene on the Wall," and others. Vega is a graduate of Barnard College at Columbia University and an alumna, if you will, of the *Fast Folk Musical Magazine,* a recorded periodical that gives voice to a community still dedicated to practicing the fine art of the folk song. Bob Franke's devastating "For Real" also comes from this tradition. Other evidence of its persistence is the Roches' rendition of Mark Johnson's ethereal "Love Radiates Around." Richard and Linda Thompson, once the king and queen of folk music, now patrol individual domains. Richard's "She Twists the Knife Again" and Linda's "One Clear Moment" give adequate testimony to the mastery they both maintain. The Los Angeles folk scene produced "Song for the Dreamers," written by Dan Stuart and Steve Wynn. Finally, Dylan's *Biograph* set unearthed enough treasures to keep folk fans occupied through the millennium, among them the legendary "Percy's Song" and the equally historic "I'll Keep It with Mine."

Other songwriters mined different veins of experience to produce quality material, ranging from the gritty wordplay of John Hiatt ("She Said the Same Thing to Me") to the other worldly chants of Kate Bush ("Running Up That Hill"). Marshall Crenshaw continued to refine his minimalist approach with "Little Wild One," while Paul Westerberg of the Replacements had to maximize his talents for big label bucks now in hand. His efforts yielded "Here Comes a Regular" and the quirky "Swingin' Party." After writing for Cyndi Lauper in 1984, Eric Bazilian and Rob Hyman put out their own album as the Hooters, featuring pungent and resounding works like "Where Do the Children Go." Talking Heads' David Byrne was at his most accessible in "And She Was." From television's *Saturday Night Live,* musician Paul Shaffer—whose "Honey (Touch Me with My Clothes On)" with SNL veteran Gilda Radner remains one of the best love songs ever—assisted comedian Billy Crystal with "You Look Marvelous," one of his funniest efforts. And, last of all, old Lonesome Don Henley, formerly of the Eagles, gave us perhaps the year's best song, "The Boys of Summer." Oddly enough, this anguished and totally real ballad managed to hit the top of the charts and received two Grammy nominations.

We could well be on the brink of another Golden Age. Tune in next year.

—Bruce Pollock

Popular Music in 1986

No doubt about it, in 1986 popular music—rock 'n' roll included—grew up. In substance and presentation, most of the music that was released and won audience acceptance assumed a maturity of voice, instrumentation, mood, message, and overall musicality only available to those with a deeper experience in life, love, and the rigors of the music business—or to those directly influenced by their "elders." While country music lyrics traditionally have dwelt on soap operatic themes of everyday life (and, in fact, this year "Friends and Lovers," a tune first heard on a daytime serial, gained national number one status), in 1986 all the other enduring forms of contemporary song voiced the thoughts, dreams, aspirations, and ideals of persons above the voting and drinking age. A songwriting community fully in possession of its wits and wisdom offered not just lip service, but the book, score, and lyrics for a grown-up radio play without end.

Rock 'n' roll held the teenaged audience, though probably ninety percent of its practitioners are at least a decade older than seventy-five percent of their fans. New Age music, the instrumental hybrid of folk, jazz, pop, and classical strains, attracted well-to-do stereo connoisseurs whose average age is exceeded only by their salaries. In both fields, nevertheless, as in every other musical genre, the hackneyed and acned sentiments once required to touch a mass nerve faded like the bloom of youth, as songwriters looked inside and outside for inspiration and began writing for their peers. If some of the concepts expressed went over the heads of the commonest denominators, for the most part listeners displayed admirable cleverness in deciphering the wordplay at their ears. For the slightly more sophisticated listener, the musical experience, song for song, had not been any better, more various, or more heated since the years 1965 to 1967, a period widely regarded by critics as nirvana for a radio-ridden generation that has been bereft ever since.

There may be many interesting sociological reasons why the mood of the music should have shifted quantum gears in 1986. The Baby Boom generation, who finished out their school years and marched off to—or against—the war in Vietnam during the late sixties, matured into a prime market for advertisers. That was certainly a real, if crassly pragmatic, cause for music catering to their tastes. Nor should the view of 1986 as an evolutionary flowering of seeds planted throughout the eighties, the sound of a decade coming into earshot, be discounted. The artists nurtured in silence through some of those notoriously lean years suddenly exploded their grenades of truth and beauty in tandem, pushed by the higher level of competition into a higher level of work. As Suzanne Vega told me, "It's one thing to be inspired by Dylan; it's another to be competing with him on the same record chart."

Linking the Decades

Not only were sons and daughters competing with their musical parents, but several generations were out and about, the old gaining new respect from the young in a startling reversal of everything sacred in pop culture. We had songs from the fifties and sixties all over movies in the eighties ("Earth Angel" in *The Karate Kid, Part 2,* "Wild Thing" in *Something Wild,* "Blue Velvet," "Jumping Jack Flash," and "Soul Man" in movies of the same titles). We had groups of the eighties writing songs for groups of the sixties as they reunited in the eighties (the Mosquitoes wrote "That Was Then, This Is Now" for the Monkees). We had songwriters in the eighties writing sixties-based music for sixties-influenced bands (Prince wrote "Manic Monday" for the Bangles). We had songs of the sixties given new meaning through their use in feature films and television shows of the eighties that were set in the sixties ("Stand by Me" in the movie of the same name; "Runaway" as the theme for television's *Crime Story*; the Beatles' remake of the Isley Brothers chestnut "Twist and Shout" earned a new lease on charts when the song was performed in *two* movies—by the Beatles in *Ferris Bueller's Day Off* and by Rodney Dangerfield in *Back to School*). We had stars of the fifties gaining new found celebrity with new songs in new movies (Little Richard's "Great Gosh a Mighty" from *Down and Out in Beverly Hills*). And, finally, we had hit songs in the eighties borrowing refrains from songs of the sixties and even borrowing the original singer for an updated reprise (Ronnie Spector did a guest vocal on Eddie Money's "Take Me Home Tonight," uttering timeless lines from "Be My Baby").

Writers from the Past Return to Form

If such groups as the Monkees and the Ronettes were primarily tools of recurring nostalgia, the resurgence of artists and songwriters from the halcyon decade of song as art was no marketing whim or plaster of paris quickie reproduction job. These were people still in the prime of creative life, encouraged by the marketplace to be sure, but using the friendly atmosphere to showcase works of depth, not calcified recreations of old formulas. In other words, they had their second chance, and they didn't muff it.

Paul Simon, coming off a disappointing half-decade, delivered his finest work since his Grammy-winning *Still Crazy After All These Years* album of 1976. With "The Boy in the Bubble," "Graceland," and "You Can Call Me Al," each inspired by the infectious rhythms of South Africa, he re-established himself as among the generation's most creative resources. Peter Townshend, now a novelist, offered a searing interpretation of "After the Fire," while James Taylor's cool fire was in evidence on "Only One." Steve Miller ("I Want to Make the World Turn Around") and Eric Clapton ("It's in the Way That You Use It") both used the blues to make striking contemporary statements. Such stalwarts of the first progressive rock era of the early seventies as Steve Winwood ("Higher Love"), Peter Gabriel ("Sledgehammer"), Van Morrison ("In the Garden"), Genesis' Mike Rutherford ("All I Need Is a Miracle"), and the Moody Blues ("Your Wildest Dreams") brought new energy and meaning to their long-awaited 1986 projects.

A more American sound was rekindled by Tom Scholz's "Amanda," which marked Boston's first effort in seven years; Steve Walsh's "All I Wanted" for Kansas; Lou Reed's "No Money Down"; and the Martin Page-Bernie Taupin composition, "These Dreams," which hoisted Heart to the top of the charts. In one of pop music's more appropriate pairings, the once ghoulishly notorious Alice Cooper emerged to help pen "He's Back" for the horror film *Friday the 13th, Part 6*. Meanwhile, Bob Dylan, perhaps the generation's greatest songwriter, labored through four somewhat odd matches as he tried to follow up the success of his 1985 collective album *Biograph*. He collaborated with characters as disparate as pop lyricist Carole Bayer Sager ("Under Your Spell"), actor-playwright Sam Shepherd ("Brownsville Girl"), ultimate rapper Kurtis Blow (a guest vocal on "Street Rock"), and Tom Petty (a largely successful tour, which featured much harmonic interplay and promises new material in 1987). In other years, activities like this, whether tongue-in-cheek or possessed of other-worldly significance, might have prompted an interpretive tome or two to determine their effect on the world as we know it. In 1986 few paid Dylan's digressions much notice. Far more impressive was Jackson Browne, another lone and anguished voice from the introspective period of the late sixties and early seventies. His "Lives in the Balance" took advantage of media exposure on the television show *Miami Vice* and some timely governmental follies to make its point about Nicaragua.

The Return of the Message

Topical music, once strictly the domain of the folksinger, and protest music, once strictly the sound of the sixties, made a remarkable return in radio playable forms ranging from the countrified jazz of Bruce Hornsby's "The Way It Is," to the punkified rock 'n' roll of the Ramones' "My Brain Is Hanging Upside Down (Bonzo Goes to Bitburg)." The charitable efforts begun by Bob Geldof's "Do They Know It's Christmas" and Americanized by Lionel Richie and Michael Jackson's "We Are the World" were continued in 1986 by Marc Blatte and Larry Gottleib. With John Carnes they wrote "Hands Across America," the theme for the only moderately successful cross-country hand-clasping day in May. With Alan Monde they also transformed a patriotic Chrysler car commercial into a patriotic Kenny Rogers tune, "The Pride Is Back." Representing the charitable voice of young America, heavy metal's Ronnie Dio, Vivian Campbell, and Jimmy Bain finally recorded "Stars," which featured a thirteen-man guitar solo. Proceeds from the record went to the African Famine Relief Fund.

Drugs were the big domestic issue, especially cocaine, which received comment in songs by Bob Seger ("American Storm"), Paul Laurence ("Strung Out"), and Mitch McDowell and Owen Cray ("Crack Killed Applejack"). Teenage sex came under scrutiny from Madonna ("Papa Don't Preach") and Preston Glass and Narada Michael Walden ("We Don't Have to Take Our Clothes Off"), taking another point of view for Jermaine Stewart. Paul Simon's "Homeless" struck a nerve in many an inner city, though its inspiration was miles away. Joni Mitchell introduced a tune about America's favorite boast—"Number One"—at the Amnesty International Conspiracy of Hope concert in June. And John Cougar Mellencamp's highly popular "Rain on the Scarecrow" addressed issues brought to national attention at Farm Aid II a month later.

Bruce Springsteen, a man whose entire career virtually spells integrity, was the signal artist of 1986. His five-record live album with the E-Street Band rivaled Dylan's *Biograph* in length and intensity, if not in undiscovered gems. Its first release, a pointed rendition of the Whitfield-Strong "War," prompted the re-release of the Edwin Starr original a few weeks later.

If Springsteen was the man of the hour, capping another herculean tour with a marriage ceremony, the year was otherwise dominated by women. Just the fact that Michael Jackson, star of the biggest-selling album in history, became known in 1986 as Janet Jackson's brother would have made this a remarkable year for female artists. Janet's *Control* album approached Michael's spectacular sales and supplied her with significant songwriter credits ("Nasty" and "What Have You Done for Me Lately" are two of the tunes she co-wrote with her producers). Anita Baker's "Sweet Love" was a major smash, evoking comparisons to Sarah Vaughan. Some of the brightest stars of 1985 continued to produce excellent material, from Sade ("The Sweetest Taboo" and "Never as Good as the First Time") to Madonna ("Live to Tell" from the movie *At Close Range*) to Cyndi Lauper ("Change of Heart," co-written with sixties veteran Essra Mohawk). Valerie Simpson and Nick Ashford provided the compelling title tune for Patti Labelle's album *There's a Winner in You.* Marie Burns's "I Wonder Who's Out Tonight" served as a theme for a television documentary on women, *After the Sexual Revolution.* And perhaps the most poignant performance was given by newcomer Whitney Houston reviving "The Greatest Love of All," a Linda Creed-Michael Masser song from the 1977 film *The Greatest.* The record reached number one shortly after Creed succumbed to a long battle with cancer.

Masser contributed another tune ("All at Once") to Houston's smashing debut success, while men like Terry Britten and Lyle Graham ("Typical Male" for Tina Turner), Tom Kelly and Billy Steinberg ("True Colors" for Cyndi Lauper), Jules Shear and Liam Sternberg ("If She Knew What She Wants" and "Walk Like an Egyptian," respectively, for the Bangles), Jonathan Richman (whose "Roadrunner" was rediscovered by Joan Jett), and Robbie van Leeuven (whose "Venus" was retouched by Bananarama) all profited immensely from the increased recognition of female artists in 1986.

On a purely songwriting level, the year belonged neither to the Boss or the ladies, but to a couple of cool dudes from Minneapolis named James Harris (Jimmy Jam) and Terry Lewis. These proteges of Prince graduated from the Time to a year that could be envied by the fluent songmasters of Motown (Holland-Dozier-Holland) or Muscle Shoals (Hayes-Porter) at their nimblest. With seeming effortlessness they wrote and produced a mini-chart full of the year's top smashes. They gave Human League their first touch of humanity with "Human." They furthered Robert Palmer's comeback efforts with "I Didn't Mean to Turn You On." As previously noted, they helped Janet Jackson achieve her own recognition. Their "Tender Love" boosted the career of the Force M.D.'s. Harris and Lewis also scored with "Saturday Love" for Cherelle and "The Finest" for S.O.S.

Black Music

Black artists accounted for six of the top seven spots on the year-end charts, ten of the top twenty. But the impact of black music was more than merely commercial. From the plucky success of "Rumors," to the suave raps of "The Rain," to Run DMC's assault on the halls of classic rock with a remake of "Walk This Way," black music dominated and energized the cityscape. In the dance clubs, "House Music" challenged "Go-Go Music" as the prevailing street beat. Though Prince's second foray into the world of film, *Under the Cherry Moon*, was beaten down by the critics, its big song, "Kiss," survived to take its place in pop history. More successful was the rap and sports connection—recalling the rock and wrestling phenomenon of 1985—with Melvin Owens, Barry Lloyd, and company's two efforts, "The Super Bowl Shuffle" for the Chicago Bears and "Dr. K" for Mets pitcher Dwight Gooden.

Country Songs

Long a dormant field for creative experimentation, country music at last began turning over the reins to a new generation. With fellows like Dwight Yoakum ("Guitars, Cadillacs, Etc., Etc.") and Steve Earle ("Guitar Town"), the instrument of choice could not be more apparent—nor could the rebellious link to rock 'n' roll. Lyle Lovett emerged as a major new singer/songwriter with songs like "An Acceptable Level of Ecstasy." "Love at the Five and Dime," recorded by Kathy Mattea, marked new visibility for the skills of Nanci Griffith, who went on to make her major label debut early in 1987. Country's current queen, Reba McEntire, was not worried. Her renditions of "Whoever's in New England," by Kendall Franceschi and Quentin Powers, and "Little Rock," by Pat McManus, Bob DiPiero, and Gerry House, represent the country tradition at its unwavering best. Newcomer Randy Travis quickly made songwriters feel as if he'd been around for years, making instant standards out of "On the Other Hand," by Paul Overstreet and Don Schlitz, and "1982," by James Blackmon and Carl Vipperman.

Music in the Theater

For yet another year, however, the terrain on and off Broadway was less fertile than the country field. Some major established names came and went in the space of disastrous opening nights (Stephen Schwartz-Charles Strouse's *Rags*, Joe Raposo's *Raggedy Anne*). The Marvin Hamlisch-Howard Ashman *Smile* survived less than two months after its belated opening. Ashman was far more successful with the new tune he wrote with Alan Menken for the filmed version of *Little Shop of Horrors*, "Mean Green Mother from Outer Space." As sung by Levi Stubbs of the Four Tops the song was nominated for an Academy Award. The rare big Broadway win was achieved by *Me and My Girl*, a revival from 1937. Pleasurable Off Broadway originals included *Nunsense* and *Olympus on My Mind.*

As 1987 dawned Broadway was still awaiting Tim Rice's *Chess,* Andrew Lloyd Webber's *Starlight Express,* and the operatic *Les Miserables,* as well as *Out of the Woods,* the latest Sondheim effort, signaling the advent of one of the lushest years in recent history. Whether anything lasting—or even singable—will spring from that particular crop remains to be seen—and heard.

Film Songs

Hollywood's link to the earlobes of America is at present much more noticeable and commanding. Not only did the movies produce their share of number one pop songs (the Academy Award-winning "Take My Breath Away" from *Top Gun* and "Glory of Love" from *The Karate Kid, Part 2*), but they accounted for more than their share of songs destined to be among the year's enduring gems. Kris Kristofferson's haunting "The Hawk" received a bravura performance by Marianne Faithfull in *Trouble in Mind.* The dance record of the year came from the pen of David Byrne and was performed by Byrne with Celia Cruz, the Salsa queen, on the soundtrack of *Something Wild.* Randy Newman's affably quirky view of life surfaced in *9½ Weeks* with Joe Cocker's remake of "You Can Leave Your Hat On." Suzanne Vega lent a touch of melancholy to *Pretty in Pink* with "Left of Center," while Carly Simon lent a touch of class to *Heartburn* with "Coming Around Again." "Blood and Roses" was featured in *Dangerously Close* and "Modern Woman" in *Ruthless People,* launching albums by newcomers the Smithereens and veteran Billy Joel, respectively.

Music on Television

But film didn't have the only franchise on career-making in 1986. Exhibiting more muscle than at any time since *Welcome Back, Kotter* provided John Sebastian relatively easy access to the top of the charts in 1976, television's powerful intimacy was exploited in a variety of ways. The soaps gave us "Friends and Lovers." *Miami Vice's* Don Johnson gave us "Heartbeat," which he then turned into a made-for-home-video movie. Not to be outdone, *Moonlighting's* Bruce Willis recorded and scored with a version of "Respect Yourself" by year's end. The *Moonlighting* theme itself, written by Lee Holdridge and Al Jarreau and sung by Jarreau, could be a likely candidate for chart status. And, finally, *Moonlighting's* producers borrowed another page from *Miami Vice* when they made Billy Joel's "Big Man on Mulberry Street" the basis of an entire episode.

Michael Jackson's first two songs since the *Thriller* album were premiered as part of a television special for the Disney Channel. The Frank Wildhorn-Brian Potter tune "Don't Look in My Eyes" received special showcasing when it was sung by Kenny Rogers on the soundtrack of a film clip showing the profile of a stricken Wade Boggs, the Red Sox third baseman, as the New York Mets celebrated their improbable World Series victory at Shea Stadium. Another song used to great emotional effect on television in 1986 was Billy Vera's "At This Moment." Released as a single in 1981, the recording went nowhere, but the tune was used in a key 1985 double episode of *Family Ties* and thereafter functioned as the themesong of Alex's doomed love affair. When it was used again in 1986, listener reaction literally forced the record back on the market and ultimately up to the top of the charts.

Looking Ahead

With all this retronicity abounding in every quarter, a good popsong-ologist, no matter how personally gratified, would rightfully have to fear for the future, the ever-gyrating ball of change upon whose axis the fate of popular music dips and sways. Not to worry. Drawing influences not only from the airwaves, but also in the rarified air where visionaries alone wander, new artists and groups were plentiful and fully grown in 1986. From the smoky blues of Simply Red ("Holding Back the Years") to the earthier rhythms of the Fabulous Thunderbirds ("Tuff Enuff") and the Georgia Satellites ("Keep Your Hands to Yourself") to the folk flavors of R.E.M. ("Fall on Me" and "Cuyahoga") and Richard Thompson ("Nearly in Love"), the roots of rock were never more artfully contemporized. And in songwriters like Bob Walkenhorst of the Rainmakers ("Let My People Go Go"), Karl Wallinger of World Party ("All Come True"), Grant Hart of Husker Du ("Sorry Some-how"), Rob McGinty of the Woodentops ("Love Affair with Everyday Livin'"), and Pat MacDonald of Timbuk 3 ("Just Another Movie"), the moment was never more fittingly conveyed. MacDonald summed it up on the debut album *Welcome to Timbuk 3* with his unexpected and quirky hit "The Future's So Bright, I Gotta Wear Shades."

—Bruce Pollock

Popular Music in 1987

Extending and deepening the forms and content that made the 1985-1986 period of songwriting so exhilarating, 1987 offered little that was downright daring or outright revolutionary, yet it extended this particular song heyday another year through its diversity and overall strength. If nothing took over the year the way patriotic pride and the threat of censorship did 1985 or the sudden unilateral maturation of pop did 1986, this year at least enlarged upon the prevailing themes with grace and taste. With the wheel already re-invented, all-weather radials were now affixed to some fine motor vehicles. And while in good creative weather like this there could be no real losers (unlike the late 1970's, when disco reigned, or the early 1980's, when MTV called the tune), some definite winners did emerge in this year of steady, unspectacular growth.

Broadway, long as dormant an urban landscape as country music has been a rural one, suddenly found itself turning green as Spring and green as money, sprouting tendrils called *Starlight Express, Les Miserables,* and *Phantom of the Opera,* which in turn sprouted long lines at the ticket window and much optimism for the future. At the same time, after 1986, when the average age of the pop song purveyor seemed as if it must have been thirty-five plus, the under twenty-one (in many cases the under eighteen) crowd made bold moves to reclaim some emotional turf with the drive and energy for which the teen age is known. These elements were previously weak links in the creative chain, but abundance stretched across 1987 in a nearly unbroken horizon of songwriting excellence.

Remakes and Comebacks

It is ironic, however, in a year when the raucous sounds of adolescent rebellion dominated the radio waves—from the abject defiance of "You Gotta Fight for Your Right to Party" and the blatant sexism of "Girls, Girls, Girls" and "Talk Dirty to Me," to the more uplifting yet no less threatening sentiments contained in "Wanted Dead or Alive" and "The Final Countdown"—that by far the year's most interesting development was the preponderance of remakes from the fifties and early sixties. Never an entirely moribund genre, in 1987 revivals proved a remarkably fecund resource; and the amazing number of artists on the comeback trail, with weathered voices fully restored, offered implicit and explicit messages of renewal and hope intact.

For the most part these artists attached the accrued goodwill of their previous images to current works of sophisticated and pointed content. Robbie Robertson ("Sweet Fire of Love"), the Grateful Dead ("Touch of Grey"), Elton John ("Candle in the Wind"), Cher ("I Found Someone"), Stevie Wonder ("Skeletons"), Fleetwood Mac ("Seven Wonders"), and George Harrison ("When We Was Fab") found the atmosphere quite receptive to their newly-minted personas, often nothing more than last year's model with a spiffy paint job, or, in the case of the Grateful Dead, a dab of Grecian Formula. Robbie Robertson's work was perhaps the most advanced and eloquent of the comeback pack, revealing with songs like "Sonny Got Caught in the Moonlight" and "Fallen Angel" a sure poetic voice even stronger than his earthy odes as a member of the Band. And Cher's comeback was certainly a multi-media event, including, besides an album, twin bravura performances in the films *Suspect* and *Moonstruck* that once again reclaimed for her the inside track position as the generation's hippest natural.

Other comebacks now in the 1987 record books included those by Natalie Cole ("Jump Start"), Brian Wilson ("Let's Go to Heaven in My Car"), Pink Floyd ("Learning to Fly"), Roger Waters ("Radio Waves"), Aerosmith ("Dude Looks Like a Lady"), Squeeze ("Hourglass"), Richard Carpenter ("Something in Your Eyes"), and the Pet Shop Boys ("What Have I Done to Deserve This"); the latter two recordings were enhanced by the voice of Dusty Springfield, who was herself making a comeback. Of course, there was also the highly touted return of Michael Jackson, whose previous album, *Thriller,* was merely the biggest seller of all time. Despite predictable hits from the new release ("The Way You Make Me Feel," "Bad," "I Can't Stop Loving You"), the overwhelming critical reaction was disappointment. Maybe it was simply that *Bad* was no *Thriller,* or that Jackson should have taken the rest of the decade off before coming back. In any case, with these and other familiar faces and voices all clattering and colliding on radio and television screens, listeners were treated to thirty years of pop music history nearly every time they switched on the dial.

And if the performer of preference wasn't at the moment available, you could always count on a contemporary remake of one of their classic oldies to fill the bill. Like standards from pop's most pre-eminent era, the thirties and forties, rock songs from the fifties and sixties became the chestnuts of 1987, whose viability in a multitude of cross-media formats assured them a life well beyond the limits heretofore assumed. Thus, television's zany kids' show host PeeWee Herman sang "Surfin' Bird" in an Annette Funicello/Frankie Avalon nostalgia flick, *Return to the Beach,* and the animated pitchmen California Raisins reprised their television commercial remake of "I Heard It Through the Grapevine," surely one of the more convoluted journeys back to the hitsville of any title in song history (the popular country song "Hymne," formerly a wine commercial, pales in comparison, as does the ride Genesis took to the top of the charts on "Tonight, Tonight, Tonight," courtesy of its incessant use as a beer commercial).

On the other side of the coin of commerce, much controversy was caused by the use of the Beatles' "Revolution" to sell running shoes, while George Harrison's "Something in the Way She Moves" was hardly noticed as an aid to moving cars. We had rock ballads turned into country songs in three-part harmony ("To Know Him Is to Love Him," as sung by the trio of Linda Ronstadt, Dolly Parton, and Emmylou Harris); we had classic neo-rhythm 'n' blues turned into moviestar camp ("Little Darlin'" as sung by Warren Beatty and Dustin Hoffman in the box office disaster *Ishtar*). Also in 1987 we had a pop chanteuse who remade one of her own hits from the sixties ("As Tears Go By," by Marianne Faithfull) and a modern vintage singer who remade a tune that had already been remade a couple of other times and, like her predecessors, saw it reach number one (Kim Wilde, whose version of "You Keep Me Hanging On" joined the original by the Supremes and the later edition by the Vanilla Fudge as chart-toppers). The otherwise obscure sixties songwriter Denny Cordell experienced a rare daily double when two of his tunes were revived and shared the same top ten ("I Think We're Alone Now," and "Mony Mony"). Finally, we had an obscure flipside of a fifties top ten single not only become a number one song itself, but serve as the title to the hit movie that launched its revival ("La Bamba").

New Songwriters Emerge

Yet with all this seemingly regressive activity, by far the strongest mark on the landscape of 1987 was made by the new generation of songwriting voices asserting themselves with uncommon individuality. While songwriting outfits like U2 ("With or Without You," "I Still Haven't Found What I'm Looking For"), REM ("The One I Love," "It's the End of the World As We Know It and I Feel Fine"), and Los Lobos ("The Hardest Time," "One Time One Night") had all produced quality works before, this was a year that found them all breaking through to new levels of popular awareness, an accomplishment made all the more admirable by the lack of commercial compromise on the part of any of these groups. Meanwhile, pushing the creative envelope even wider, new artists in bands named Firetown, 10,000 Maniacs, Crowded House, and Camper Van Beethoven more than kept the promise implicit in the works of their brethren and forbears, with songs like "Verdi Cried," "Heart Country," "Don't Dream It's Over," and "Joe Stalin's Cadillac," respectively. Add Julie Brown's properly dyspeptic "The Homecoming Queen's Got a Gun," Andy White's Dylanesque "Reality Row," and Mojo Nixon's antic "Elvis Is Everywhere" and you might have the groundwork for the first wave of remakes of the year 2007.

In 1987 even the established songwriters of the day were stretching toward new plateaus of experience. Bruce Springsteen, known for his boyish boardwalk bravado, turned "The Tunnel of Love" into his own harrowing metaphor of the marital state. Mose Allison, long a droll treasurehouse of emotional information, had a different perspective on the situation in "Puttin' up with Me," while John Hiatt, coming closer to his own in 1987, nailed the issue shut with "Learning How to Love You." If Loudon Wainwright in "I Eat Out" and Prince in "House-quake" were content to explore familiar quirky terrain, John Cougar Mellencamp was not afraid to reveal a sentimental side in "Cherry Bomb." Julie Gold wrote one of country music's finest songs of the year, "From a Distance," for Nanci Griffith, who wrote another, "Beacon Street," for herself. And when writers weren't reaching inside for material, they were drawing material from some of the year's biggest events and issues.

Headlines into Songs

Surely 1987 will be thought of as the year in which children in jeopardy kept us in almost constant turmoil, from the girl in the well in Texas to the one who survived the airline crash in Detroit to the one who didn't survive the beatings of her parents in New York City. Songwriters took appropriate note: Suzanne Vega's "Luka," Natalie Merchant's "What's the Matter Here," and "Dear Mr. Jesus" by Powersource all gave trenchant musical voice to the subject of child abuse. The AIDS epidemic prompted a re-examination of attitudes on sexuality that ad hoc censorship groups could never attain. As usual, rap groups, the cutting edge urban troubadours, delivered the message at its most basic level in songs like "Go See the Doctor," by Kool Moe Dee, written during a visit to a walk-in clinic, and "Protect Yourself," by the Fat Boys, which debuted on the television sex discussion show hosted by Dr. Ruth Westheimer. Even in country music, as far from rap as north is from the south, precautions were the rule, as epitomized by "I Want to Know You Before We Make Love," the hit for Conway Twitty. But since the sex drive is what causes popular music's turntable to turn, there were those who instinctively resisted even the most eminently plausible admonishments. In 1987 they paid a stiff price. George Michael's "I Want Your Sex" was widely regarded as irresponsible (it hit the top of the charts anyway); "Walk with an Erection," a parody of 1986's "Walk Like an Egyptian," so outraged the original copyright owners that permission to record it was denied (it was released anyway); and Luther Campbell's rather blatant "We Want Some Pussy" resulted in the arrest of a record store clerk merely for ringing up its sale (she was later cleared of the charges). On a lesser though no less dramatic moral scale, songs of the religious experience made news, ranging from Andy Partridge's existential atheism in "Dear God," to Tammy Faye Bakker's essential egotism in "The Ballad of Jim and Tammy," alluding, of course, to the precipitous fall of the Bakkers' television ministry, a subject the Hooters addressed in "Satellite" and Ray Stevens convincingly questioned in "Would Jesus Wear a Rolex." Only Stevie Nicks' heartfelt remake of "Silent Night" seemed to restore the lustre of traditional religion.

Some of the year's best songs were of the sort that might have been termed to protest music back in the early sixties. In 1987 they were pop songs: Sting's eerie "They Dance Alone," U2's chilling "Where the Streets Have No Name," Timbuk 3's "All I Want for Christmas," a pointed anti-war toys lament, Steven Van Zandt's raucous "Trail of Broken Treaties," and the moving re-release of "Biko," the song penned by Peter Gabriel that inspired the 1987 movie *Cry Freedom*.

Film Music

With soundtrack albums complete with anthemic closing rock finales now as obligatory and entrenched a moviegoer item as popcorn, once again in the battle of the screens the silver easily outdid the tube as haven for both abject filler and the unearthed gem. That few connoisseurs otherwise would have heard Neil Young's "We've Never Danced," but for Martha Davis's version on the soundtrack album of *Made in Heaven* may seem argument enough for those devoted to the genre. Far more in the majority were the viewers of films like *Dirty Dancing* and *Beverly Hills Cop 2,* who composed a good deal of the listening crowd that made "I've Had the Time of My Life," and "She's Like the Wind," from the former, and "Shakedown" and "Cross My Broken Heart," from the latter into some of the year's biggest sellers. With success like that, who needed musicals?

Songs from the Theater

Broadway did. If in the past two seasons you could count on the fingers of one mitten the number of original Broadway musical mega-hits, 1987 made up not only for the years past, but gave promise, at least in several theaters, of filling seats throughout the remainder of the decade. The man most responsible for this revival was the English composer Andrew Lloyd Webber, whose *Evita, Cats,* and *Jesus Christ, Superstar,* had done much to keep the musical alive, if barely breathing, for the past decade. In 1987 he brought forth *Starlight Express* and *Phantom of the Opera,* both road tested in England and chart-tested with singles and LP packages. *Starlight*'s album consisted of modern popstars not associated with the show offering interpretations of its tunes ("Only You," "I Am the Starlight"); the cast album of *Phantom* produced several large hits in England, among them "Music of the Night" and "All I Ask of You." These recordings provided readymade audiences for each show's opening night. (*Phantom* did not officially open until early in 1988, but tickets had been selling for most of the preceding year.) Another hugely successful epic imported from abroad was *Les Miserables,* eventually sporting both an American and an English cast album for its memorable songs, including "On My Own" and "I Dreamed a Dream." On top of that, our own Stephen Sondheim was back on the boards with another of his complex, metaphorical tales, *Into the Woods,* from which the title tune and "Agony" deserve special mention.

In addition to the obvious winners of the season, some promising names either arrived on the scene (Douglas J. Cohen with *No Way to Treat a Lady*) or continued compiling credentials for a major breakthrough (Craig Carnelia once again garnered fine notices for "She Was K.C. at Seven," from *3 Postcards,* and "Privacy," from the much-heralded *No Frills Revue.*) And at year's end John Kander and Fred Ebb revived their *Flora, the Red Menace* with previously unheard material like "The Kid Herself." In all this, the fact that the Tim Rice opus *Chess* would at last be opening in 1988, seemed to lose a lot of its once game-saving significance.

Country and Folk Music

Nashville, however, could have used a home run in 1987. The much-heralded 1986 infusion of new blood down those old mill streams, with fully developed young superstars like Dwight Yoakum, Steve Earle, Holly Dunn, Lyle Lovett, Nanci Griffith, and Randy Travis taking center stage, proved primarily an interesting ruse designed to provide new outlets for the same established songwriting teams. Works by Paul Overstreet and Don Schlitz ("Forever and Ever Amen"), Sonny LeMaire and J. P. Pennington ("She's Too Good to Be True"), and others, while as polished as anything either the left coast or the right might have produced, hardly qualified as a revolution or anything more than a two-base hit. More interesting was the line many of the best country performers were crossing into folk music, a territory where expression might be just a bit freer. Lyle Lovett ("God Will") and Nanci Griffith ("Ford Econoline," "There's a Light Beyond These Woods, Mary Margaret") traversed those borders with ease. John Prine crossed from folk to country with "Let's Talk Dirty in Hawaiian" and "Out of Love." Wendy Waldman came to Nashville via Los Angeles with her work on "Fishing in the Dark"; Ian Tyson came down from Canada with some excellent tunes ("Summer Wages," "Navajo Rug"); country/ folk living legend Townes Van Zandt provided inspiration with "For the Sake of the Song." The English folk troupe Fairport Convention reconvened with "Close to the Wind" and Richard Thompson's revived "Meet on the Ledge." Slightly more sophisticated tastes could find all the sustenance they needed in songs by Loudon Wainwright ("Hard Day on the Planet," "The Back Nine") and Christine Lavin ("Another Woman's Man"). Richie Havens, a major folk voice of the sixties, was briefly given a reprieve from singing commercials and put back behind some quality material like John Martyn's "I Don't Wanna Know" and his own "Simple Things."

Rhythm 'n' Blues

In 1987 the world of rhythm 'n' blues was far from simple. From the streets to the penthouses, careers tumbled and shook with the seismic intensity of a typical week in Los Angeles. If Michael Jackson's new album was tainted with a bit too much of his semi-private persona, Whitney Houston, having none, was able to survive similar lackluster notices, largely through the strength of ballads by some of pop song's reigning royalty: Michael Masser and Will Jennings ("Didn't We Almost Have It All") and Billy Steinberg and Tom Kelly ("So Emotional"). Last year's songwriting princes, Jimmy Jam and Terry Lewis, could only muster "Fake" for their 1987 resume, while Prince himself rebounded from his disastrous movie, *Under the Cherry Moon,* with surprisingly good reviews for his autobiographical documentary, *Sign o' of the Times,* especially for its music —"U Got the Look," "I Could Never Take the Place of Your Man." While the soul queens Aretha Franklin and Natalie Cole were both on the scene making interesting noises this year, new pretenders to their throne emerged in the persons of Lisa Lisa ("Lost in Emotion") and Jody Watley

("Looking for a New Love," "Still a Thrill"). Smokey Robinson made a comeback in 1987 ("Just to See Her"), but the crooning turf was in no danger of being swiped from Freddie Jackson ("Jam Tonight," "I Don't Want to Lose Your Love").

By far the most pleasing development to cross from the rhythm 'n' blues sanctuary into the wider world was the emergence of Robert Cray. With "Smoking Gun" and "Right Next Door Because of Me," Cray brought a taste of the blues back not only to rhythm 'n' blues and to the radio waves, but to the arena concert stages of America and subsequently to the upper quarter of the charts, with the ghosts of Muddy Waters and Robert Johnson, Son House and Lightning Hopkins nodding in the wings. In a world where a bluesman, even one as slick and refined as Cray, can reign as king of the hill, even for a little while, anything is possible.

Popular Music in 1988

The power of the popular song to identify a time and place and to move a mass audience to action is directly related to its access to media coverage. In 1961 and '62, with the mass media witnessing a youth movement Twisting into egoistic life at the Peppermint Lounge in New York City, a generation was born, and borne into headline history. What was brewing underground when the camera's eye started to focus on the heaving throngs—the idealistic crush of Baby Boom, civil rights- and war-protesting, young, college-dropout singer/songwriters of the urban folk movement in Greenwich Village and other left-leaning campus centers across the country—rose to the surface of public consciousness and swept across the record charts within a year or two. By 1965, altered by the chemically inspired rhythms of a generation not only imbued with a sense of mission and of itself, but bolstered by a media scrapbook any superstar of the era would have coveted, the folk sounds of protest coalesced into a frantic underscore for a tumultuous decade.

In the mid-1970's, after the pendulum of alternate culture had swung back into the faces of its proponents, knocking them not only out flat, but flat out of the front pages of the nation's press, once again the notion of audience as focal point for the musical identity of an era, the generation as the star, emerged through the reinvention of the discotheque. Under the dulling drumbeat a quietude reigned; in those days a new twist on the prevailing rhythm was a momentous event. The pumping and preening masses in the mirrored caves of night drew out the television cameras and the journalists' pens again, and the "Me Generation" was christened.

Ideals may have been exorcised from the popular music of the disco era, but the underground aspect reasserted its standards in the protest cycles dubbed Punk and New Wave, which anticipated the song's eventual return to power. In the 1980's this return has taken place, aided by yet a third national medium (TV news and movies being the other two), one that offered instant dissemination of the pop message to an audience much wider than any lowly bopper of the sixties or seventies could have imagined. Or, rather, probably one that the prescient rock 'n' roll advocates of the time had imagined all too well, and in the eighties finally got going. With the invention in 1981 of MTV, "We Are the World" replaced mere generational rallying points.

The Power of the Medium and the Message

In 1988 music's power for change, while immense, was nearly inseparable from the power of the tube itself, the utter self-consciousness television's very presence imposes on the worthiest of cause-mongers and the crassest of salesmen alike. Now, with every move blasted around the world, the crass, the idealistic, and the mundane appear in successive images that draw no distinctions between them and offer no clues as to which is which. And while some night call this democracy, since every viewer is free to shift by remote control to another channel, this intermarriage of medium and message, of content and commercial, has ominous echoes of the disco era, when an audience was dulled into a similar stupor. But where the disco dancer at least had to go out to perpetrate his mindless writhing, the MTV generation need not move a muscle. Now the tube provides it all, from the sitcom soundtracks of *The Wonder Years, Thirtysomething,* and *Almost Grown,* to the mixed bag compilations of obscure oldies, contemporary rejects, and the occasional hit single that help to sell the movies on HBO and the Movie Channel.

If the original MTV song videos were little more than advertisements to sell a product—the artist's current album—now even that goal is being turned on its head, first with rock's most golden oldies being used to sell sponsors' products between videos, and lately with the artists themselves willingly offering their wares to Coke or Pepsi or Michelob, making themselves part of the commodities' sales package from the start. Thus, with current pop and rock 'n' roll so comfortably ensconced in the board rooms and on the television screens of America at a time when money is so blatantly the drug of choice among the trendy, the popular song has finally arrived at a kind of pinnacle of respect far removed from where it all began on the streets more than thirty years ago.

Given this situation, the underground source, which historically has produced all of popular music's most convincing changes and interesting growth spurts has been hard pressed to offer an alternative to this McDonaldization of the American sensibility, one that while difficult and shocking enough to be banned from MTV, would also be meaningful and melodically recognizable enough still to pass as music.

And if this worthy challenge has as yet to produce an obvious heir in 1988, it was still a year in which songwriters gave us nothing if not our money's worth.

Songs and Artists of the Past Return

In the absence of revolution, then, there were storylines aplenty, new faces and telling odes, and moments of real power, too. Who could deny the heartwarming saga of "What a Wonderful World," reemerging behind a battle scene in the movie *Good Morning Vietnam,* to visit the American pop charts twenty years after its initial failure on these shores? Who could dispute the irony of the Beach Boys' return to number one with "Kokomo," during the same period of time when their creative as well as spiritual voice for so many years, Brian Wilson, was foundering with "Love and Mercy" from his long-awaited solo album? Other lost voices came sobbing back from the void. Neil Young rejoined Crosby, Stills, and Nash, for "American Dream"; Little Feat, minus their late leader, Lowell George, bravely told of "Hangin' on to the Good Times"; Led Zeppelin's legendary tandem, Robert Plant and Jimmy Page (both with solo works this year), collaborated on a tune tellingly entitled "The Only One"; Keith Richards, tired of waiting for the Rolling Stones to tour again, issued "Take It So Hard" on his own album; the Traveling Wilburys united Roy Orbison with Bob Dylan and Tom Petty, George Harrison and Jeff Lynne, for a brief taste of glory on "Handle with Care," before Orbison passed away. James Brown returned to active funk with "I'm Real," but was jailed soon after. Phil Collins repaid an emotional debt to an early rock influence by collaborating with Motown legend Lamont Dozier on a Grammy-winning tune entitled "Two Hearts" from the movie *Buster.*

The Mood of the Music

If Bobby McFerrin's pseudo-philosophical ode, "Don't Worry, Be Happy," from the movie *Cocktail,* seemed to set a simpleminded tone for this election year, the true tone of darkness underneath the bright superficial colors was more nearly exemplified by Tracy Chapman's unsettling "Fast Car"; the Christians' melancholy "Ideal World"; Guns N' Roses' abrasive "Welcome to the Jungle"; UB40's loping reggae interpretation of "Red, Red Wine"; the morality play of Full Force's "Thanks for My Child."

Generations of Folk Inspiration

Responding, perhaps, to the "Don't Worry, Be Happy" regime, under which most of the year's songs were content to be regarded as frivolous, singer/songwriters of the folk school, both new and vintage, students and teachers, made 1988 a particularly fruitful year. Bruce Springsteen revived Bob Dylan's "Chimes of Freedom"; the works of Woody Guthrie, Dylan's idol, were showcased with a variety of interpretations on a landmark album; Dylan collaborated with the Grateful Dead's Robert Hunter on "Sylvio"; Leonard Cohen delivered "I'm Your Man"; Randy Newman struck an autobiographical lode in "New Orleans Wins the War" and "I Want You to Hurt Like I Do" and hit a generational nerve with "It's Money That Matters." James Taylor described turning forty with pride and precision in "Baby Boom Baby"; Patti Smith was particularly trenchant and evocative in "People Have the Power"; Joni Mitchell, stark and moving with "Lakota" and "The Tea Leaf Prophecy (Lay Down Your Arms)"; Karla Bonoff, poignant in "Goodbye My Friend"; Steve Forbert, touchingly optimistic in "As We Live and Breathe."

Two relative newcomers joined the folkie ranks this year with works as fully formed as those of their elders: Fred Small ("Diamonds of Anger," "Scott and Jamie") and Rod MacDonald ("Sanctuary") confronted various world situations with awesome verbal power. But for the most part, the younger breed of folk students has been plying their trade in a less linear and didactic fashion, constructing affecting songs from found objects, synthesizing moods of extreme disaffection with playful but pointed satire. Tracy Chapman's "Talkin' 'Bout a Revolution" may have been the most overt of this genre, but it was written back in 1982. More typical of today's ambiguity is Edie Brickell's "What I Am," "Nothing But Flowers" by the Talking Heads, "Eden Alley" by Timbuk 3, the savage wordplay of "Purple Toupee" and "Kiss Me Son of God" by They Might Be Giants, Michelle Shocked's winsome "Anchorage," Sinead O'Connor's brooding "Mandinka," the neo-psychedelia of "Eye of Fatima, Part I" by Camper Van Beethoven, the compellingly eerie "Under the Milky Way" by the Church, Kate Bush's personal triumph of pleasure and pain, "This Woman's Work," from the movie *She's Having a Baby,* and the Godfathers' bleak mantra, "Birth, School, Work, Death.

Country Music's Traditions

Ostensibly dealing with the same subjects, country music in 1988 treated each with a deference and respect for tradition only age and hard knocks could provide. For "Streets of Bakersfield," Dwight Yoakum joined his hero, Buck Owens, in a song by Homer Joy; erstwhile rebel daughter Rosanne Cash paid tribute to her daddy, Johnny, in "Tennessee Flat Top Box"; Nanci Griffith also hailed the older generation with "Love Wore a Halo (Back Before the War)" and the land itself in "Gulf Coast Highway"; that "Honky Tonk Moon" was revered by Dennis O'Rourke in a song by Randy Travis; and love's redemptive power was celebrated in any number of tunes, most notably K. T. Oslin's "Hold Me." By far, what Nashville holds in strongest reverence is its songwriting community. This year Glen Campbell showcased the works of his former collaborator, Jimmy Webb ("Lightning in a Bottle"); Cajun star Jo-el Sonnier gave the nod to folk/rock legend Richard Thompson ("Tear Stained Letter"); and Kim Carnes exhibited an exemplary taste for John Prine ("Speed the Sound of Loneliness"). And the regulars of Tin Pan Alley South did the club proud for yet another year as evidenced by "Never Mind" (Harlan Howard), "What She Is (Is a Woman in Love)" (Bob McDill), "Strong Enough to Bend" (Don Schlitz), and "When You Say Nothing at All" (Paul Overstreet). The only irregular of the lot, Lyle Lovett ("She's No Lady," "If I Had a Boat," "L.A. Country"), has become so eclectic of late, mixing Mose Allison blues with big-band jazz and traces of rockabilly, that he may soon be ridden out of Nashville on the rail of a huge crossover hit song.

The Diversity of Black Music

Crossover has been the name of the game in the black music field for many years. In fact, ever since rockabilly's earliest forays into this territory to find some new rhythms for its blues, you could say the beat of black music (no matter what limiting name you put over the genre) has been the primary beat of popular music, pure and simple. Thus, there was a contradiction implied in using the term "black music" in 1988 to describe such disparate artists as Whitney Houston ("One Moment in Time") and Prince ("Alphabet Street"), Michael Jackson ("The Man in the Mirror") and Terrence Trent D'Arby ("Sign Your Name"), cerebral folkie Tracy Chapman ("Baby Can I Hold You") and ascendant heavy metal guitar star Vernon Reid's Living Colour ("Open Letter to a Landlord"). Even white pop idol turned soul crooner George Michael ("Father Figure," "Kissing a Fool") has found a place on the black charts, which earlier had been home to such artists as Hall and Oates and Elton John. With hip hop and house music, rap and reggae, black music has certainly not lost touch with the street rhythms that have always sustained it, its essential dancability; but this year, rap in particular must be said to have come of age, and not because of its acceptance as a Grammy category. Though what surface charm rap may have is primarily the product of its blatant self-promotion—a kind of updated "Duke of Earl" braggadocio made universal—this year's rappers like Ice-T ("Colours") and D.J. Jazzy Jeff ("Parents Just Don't

Understand") put more than a token effort behind developing a social consciousness. Seeing themselves as heroes beyond question, now they've accepted a status as role models that causes them to lash out against the drugs and violence that stereotype the world of the street they portray.

A Poor Year for Musical Theater

One street on which the violence is usually metaphorical—for the most part done by critics upon purported works of art—is Broadway, where the musical is still an endangered species, despite last year's bumper crop. In fact, the high point of 1988's theater season could be said to be the release of various original cast albums of shows mounted in or before 1987: *Into the Woods* ("Hello Little Girl"), *Sarafina* ("Sarafina"), *Oil City Symphony* ("Iris"), and *The Gospel at Colonus* ("Now Let the Weeping Cease"). Both *Les Miserables* ("On My Own," "I Dreamed a Dream") and *Chess* ("One Night in Bangkok," "I Know Him So Well") existed on record well before their official 1988 New York opening nights. For Brian Gari, the composer of *Late Night Comic* ("Clara's Dancing School"), that cast album's successful release more than six months after his show's dismally brief Broadway run might have brought a small measure of redemption. This route may somewhat salvage Peter Allen's star vehicle, *Legs Diamond* ("All I Wanted Was the Dream"), which had many more preview performances than legitimate nights on the boards after the scathing reviews came in. 1989's forthcoming *Goya* by Maury Yeston, composer of *Nine,* took the antecedent recording strategy even further, setting up the play with the Barbra Streisand-Don Johnson hit single, "Til I Loved You," the first of several tunes to be extracted from the album of songs from the show. The only musical of note in 1988 to open on Broadway to favorable reviews and then live to see its cast album appear in the same year, was the double bill *Romance, Romance* by Barry Harman and Keith Herrmann ("Goodbye Emil," "Words He Doesn't Say").

Revivals Spark Soundtrack Albums

If Broadway has become the refuge for the revival in recent years, from *Me and My Gal* to *The King and I,* by 1988 the movie soundtrack album became the virtual Old Age Rest Home and Hall of Fame for rock 'n' roll singles of a certain vintage and cachet, or for remakes of same. In addition to the aforementioned "Wonderful World," the *Good Morning Vietnam* soundtrack offered us hits by Wayne Fontana & The Mindbenders, the Vogues, and the Searchers, as well as "Liar Liar" by the Castaways, which Debbie Harry redid in *Married to the Mob.* A second soundtrack album from *Dirty Dancing* gave new life to the

Contours' classic, "Do You Love Me," written by Motown's founder himself, Berry Gordy. John Cougar Mellencamp confirmed his roots with a rendition of Buddy Holly's "Rave On" in *Cocktail,* where the Georgia Satellites plucked "Hippy Hippy Shake" from obscurity. "Under the Boardwalk" was a perfect Bette Milder vehicle in *Beaches,* while Phil Collins' *Buster* sported not only the award-winning "Two Hearts," but his remake of Carole Bayer Sager's "Groovy Kind of Love." The killer of the lot had to be a tossup between Slayer's update of "In a Gadda-da-Vida," from *Less Than Zero,* and Judas Priest's revivified "Johnny B. Goode," from the movie bearing its name.

Other Revivals

Outside the soundtrack realm, Cheap Trick redid "Don't Be Cruel"; Tiffany transmogrified "I Saw Him (Her) Standing There"; Michael Bolton did the definitive blue-eyed soul version of "(Sittin On) The Dock of the Bay"; Darlene Love presided over the maturation of "He's Sure the Man I Love," the Barry Mann-Cynthia Weil tune that started out in life as "He's Sure the Boy I Love" (a song Love was never credited for singing as the voice of the Crystals back in 1962); Kylie Minogue brought the Goffin-King classic, "The Locomotion," to the top of the charts for a record-breaking third time; and Ringo Starr matched up perfectly to the Disney standard "When You Wish Upon a Star," from an album called *Wake Up,* which paired several artists of today with Disney tunes of the past.

But the most significant remake of 1988 has to be that of Mr. Johnny B. Goode himself, Chuck Berry. With a documentary film, an autobiography, and at year's end a boxed edition of his best work, the legend has been laid open for inspection in three mediums. To say his work has stood the test of time comes close to minimizing its impact. As an influence, as an inspiration, Chuck Berry, like rock 'n' roll itself, is here to stay.

Popular Music in 1989

For a decade that started out with the promise of an abundant future, with MTV (Music Television) set to offer a multiplicity of pictures to go with the diverse sounds, the eighties ended on a note of extreme fragmentation, with each sparring genre of pop having its own radio stations, sub-sects, hairstyles, buzzwords, superstars, instrumentation, audience, and images. Advancing into the nineties, the mass audience has been split by age, by race, by geography, by taste, even by neighborhood, more so than at any time in pop history. And while this kind of cultlike, standoffish attitude may not in and of itself preclude individual songwriting milestones, it does make them more localized, marginal, and less likely to achieve the national audience that allows a masterwork to be recognized and endure.

Where once broad-based enthusiasm for the Beatles marked a pop cultural revolution, today's New Kids on the Block are strictly a teenage phenomenon, one of teenaged girls, for that matter. The male teens by far prefer bands like Metallica, the booming sounds of heavy metal rather than the unctuous dance rhythms of the Top 40. The division between rhythm and blues and country music, long a matter of black and white, has filtered down to the high school level, where rappers and devotees of roots rock patronize separate water fountains. Thus, what was once a music that brought the races and the sexes together now separates them as never before, making it that much easier to divide and conquer youth culture and dissipate the moral fervor and fever that once brought forth social upheavals.

Songs still being songs, though, even when they are just that, must satisfy the impulse for expression, however limited, as well as the marketplace. And if, in 1989, we must look at the year in terms of sub-sects instead of tidal movements, there is still a certain statistical glory accruing to the reigns of those who for the moment nearly transcended these limitations.

Popular Music in 1989

Dance Music Holds Widest Appeal

Songs made for dancing constituted perhaps the dominant pop sub-genre this year. These beat-predominated, heavily produced works ushered in a possible second coming of disco, surely an ominous sign for the pop community as a whole, but an entirely welcome one for the mostly sub-teen female adherents of this music. For, while rock was reclaimed in the late eighties by youth, from the hardening arteries of the greybeards from past decades who dominated the mid-eighties' charts, in 1989 pre-teens succeeded in grabbing the top of the charts from their older brothers and sisters, fashioning a mini-generation gap. A largely faceless cast of studio creations named Roxette ("The Look," "Listen to Your Heart," "Dangerous"), Seduction ("Two to Make It Right"), and Milli Vanilli ("Girl, I'm Gonna Miss You," "Girl, You Know It's True") joined the more visually distinctive Janet Jackson ("Miss You Much," "Rhythm Nation," written in collaboration with Jimmy Jam and Terry Lewis) and Paula Abdul ("Straight Up," "It's Just the Way That You Love Me," "Forever Your Girl," "Cold Hearted"), Janet's former choreographer, at center stage. With their safe, danceable, romantic comic book lyrics and processed, repetitive sound, their new, "lite disco" tunes did much to turn radio in the latter half of 1989 into one repeating band of irrelevant, recycled wall-paper.

A Big Year for Ballads

In a time lacking a focus...a generational imperative...a rabid and effective underground thrust, the big ballad has a greater chance of making a sustained impact. Sentimentality fills our collective need for outsized emotional displays. Ironically, this year's biggest ballads were both revivals from the earlier part of the decade. The Larry Henley and Jeff Silbar tune "Wind Beneath My Wings" had been recorded, in the authors' own estimation, upwards of a hundred times before Bette Midler sang it in the movie *Beaches*. Nearly every singer of any repute with an album slot to fill did a take on the song, recalling the heyday of Tin Pan Alley, when tunes with similar appeal underwent such a multiplicity of interpretations as a matter of course. Today, this 1981 copyright stands out not only as an example of the resilience of the timeless big ballad at its zenith, but as an indictment of the unimagina-tive singers and producers who would rather choose to be the ninety-ninth and one hundredth cover of one particularly apt melody than encourage a spirit of musical enterprise where three or four singers might cover twenty-five worthy tunes.

Immensely aiding the cause of "Wind Beneath My Wings," which even its authors had thought played out by the time Midler performed it, was its prominence in the movie, where a multi-million dollar budget cast it in a light unavailable to its previous assayers. This is not to denigrate the tune, winner of two Grammys for 1989, or its number-one-seller rendition, only to indicate that even the most meritorious of songs can moulder for years without a showcase befitting its worth.

Such is the case with the Barry Mann-Cynthia Weil-Tom Snow tune "Don't Know Much" that was turned into a mini-operetta this year by Linda Ronstadt and Aaron Neville. The ballad, written in 1980, was last heard under the title "All I Need to Know," when it was recorded by Bette Midler in 1983, at that time hardly denting the consciousness of the radio audience. As Ronstadt and Midler are two in a dwindling field of interpretive singing, it would be nice to think that these two songs suggest that there are more such gems tucked away in the catalogues of other, less established songwriters, and that if other singers would venture further, they might find them.

A case in point is Tom Waits's fine, evocative "Downtown Train," a tune that showed up in the late eighties as a single from albums by Patty Smythe and Mary Chapin Carpenter. But it didn't register with the populace until Rod Stewart wrapped his leather lungs around it in 1989, for a long stay at the top of the charts.

Perhaps not the biggest, but certainly one of the finest ballads of the year came from the pen of Mike Rutherford, a graduate of the supergroup Genesis, who had been overshadowed by the great success of former bandmate Phil Collins. Written about the death of Rutherford's father, "The Living Years" was one of the few 1989 songs actually to be about anything of substance, and it was a particularly apt representative of the thirtysomething generation even as they were rapidly losing most of their places on the hit parade.

Another ballad that shows signs of enduring to become a standard part of many a singer's repertoire is Julie Gold's "From a Distance," which Nanci Griffith brought to her audience in 1987; Judy Collins gave it the official folk/art stamp on her most recent release. Singer-songwriter Kath Bush made her own special contribution with "This Woman's Work." Originally debuting in the movie *She's Having a Baby* and revived on the British artist's album *The Sensual World*, it is one of her finest performances on record.

Popular Music in 1989

New and Established Pop Stars Shape the Trends

Into the void of established superstars for the pre-teen set, who need such icons thrust down their throats at regular intervals like vitamins (with Menudo gone by the wayside and Donny Osmond grown up), stepped New Kids on the Block. This group of earnest, endearing Boston performers filled the mandatory bill, securing lifetime bank accounts for their members (or for their producer, Maurice Starr) with insidiously hummable ditties like "You Got It (the Right Stuff)," "This One's for the Children," "I'll Be Loving You Forever," "Cover Girl," and "Hangin' Tough," that provided squeaky clean, yet romantic fuel for the dreams of the increasingly sought after pre-teen female market. The sales potential of that market was fully exploited by New Kids' albums, singles, videos, concerts, and even dolls.

An artist with a considerably less wholesome image, Madonna, maintained her popularity in 1989 despite the moral whitewashing of the times. Defying the year's prevailing wisdom, she continued her quest for a place in showbiz legend without capitulating to the matrons of polite society so rampant in the fields of artistic discourse this year. When she was exorcised from her multi-figure contract with Pepsi-Cola because of the supposed religious and/or racial overtones of her video rendition of "Like a Prayer," the first single from her new album, Madonna perhaps unintentionally struck a blow for artistic detachment of church and state, of the artist from the green hand of the corporation. She breezed through the remainder of the year, striking the top of the charts with her accustomed regularity, with tunes like "Express Yourself" and "Cherish."

Also aided by the big screen, Prince righted his faltering career with a collection of dance tracks for the vaunted *Batman* project ("Batdance," "Partyman," and "Scandalous"). Yet, as incongruous as his involvement in such a high-gloss, establishment movie seemed to some, to others it only signified his ultimate detachment from the centers of Black music power. In fact, it reconfirmed at the same time, and perhaps completed, his emergence as a force unto himself, a field of one, whirling, intuitive, and unpredictable.

The Dimensions of the Black Music Scene

In the reaches of Black music where rhythm and blues meets the street, rap had another banner year, moving that much closer to general establishment acceptance, and thus its own demise as a relevant, underground take on the mood of the common man. Nonetheless, for an underground form, its impact was indisputable, as Tone Loc's "Wild Thing," the largest selling single of all time, except for "We Are the World," can attest. (And speaking of "We Are the World"...could "Wild Thing" be more different from that plea for universal spiritual brotherhood? Not since the days when Pat Boone battled Elvis Presley for the soul of pop music have we had such a provocative debate.)

If streetwise chants like "Bust a Move" and "Funky Cold Medina" managed to occupy the high visibility rungs of the pop charts, fraternizing with the likes of Janet Jackson and Martika, it was left for more threatening types like Public Enemy, with "Fight the Power" from the film *Do the Right Thing*, to keep rap in its proper role, as a voice of the powerless, gaining from its constituency a force in numbers as in spirit that could overthrow, if nothing else, the complacency of the rest of the pop community. But Public Enemy, perhaps stepping over the bounds of prejudice and license, ended the year mired in charges of anti-Semitism. Less controversial, but easily just as necessary an evolution for rap has been the addition of a social conscience to go with its stream of consciousness. With name players like Chuck D., Flavor Flav, MC. Lyte, and Heavy D, the Stop the Violence movement raised upwards of $50,000 for the National Urban League. Their warning of "Self Destruction" helped to battle illiteracy, crime, and a variety of other social ills, including rap's own bad reputation.

Enjoying another renaissance year on the pop charts, Black music in its more traditional forms produced some solid statements, from the fresh street sounds of Neneh Cherry ("Buffalo Soldiers," "Kisses on the Wind") to the heavy rock breakthrough of Living Colour, led by guitarist Vernon Reid ("Cult of Personality"), to the nostalgia engendered by some great, updated rhythm and blues ("The Ten Commandments of Love" by Howard Hewitt, "Goodnight My Love" by El DeBarge, and "If You Don't Know Me by Now," the Gamble and Huff classic of the seventies, redone by the multi-hued group Simply Red). Angela Winbush established herself as a top songwriter and singer with "Spend the Night" for the Isley Brothers and "It's the Real Thing" for herself. Frankie Beverly's return with Maze was well worth the wait, bringing Donna Allen's rendition of "Joy and Pain" and Maze's success with "Can't Get Over You." The O'Jays also made a fine comeback with "Have You Had Your Love Today."

By far the most encouraging songwriting development in Black music of 1989 was the full fruition of the Antonio "L. A." Reid and Kenny "Babyface" Edmunds team (often in collaboration with Daryl Simmons). They mounted a hot streak of Jimmy Jam and Terry Lewis-like proportions with hits for Bobby Brown ("On Our Own," "Rock Witcha"), Karyn White ("Superwoman," "Love Saw It," "The Way You Love Me," "Secret Rendezvous"), Sheena Easton ("The Lover in Me"), and the Boys ("Dial My Heart"), as well as for Babyface himself ("Tender Lover," "It's No Crime").

Warren and Hiatt Lead Pop Writers

On the pop side of the dial, clearly this year's credit for most productive pen goes to Diane Warren, who had a calendar filled with assignments from most of the top rock groups in need of a hit single and a notebook filled with appointments with most of the top collaborators in the songwriting business, including Bryan Adams and Jim Vallance ("When the Night Comes" for Joe Cocker), Albert Hammond ("It Isn't, It Wasn't, It Ain't Never Gonna Be" for Aretha Franklin and Whitney Houston, and "Through the Storm" for Aretha and Elton John), and last year's holder of this title, Desmond Child himself ("Just Like Jesse James" for Cher). On her own, Warren added to her little black book of top ten clients the private numbers of Bad English ("When I See You Smile"), Milli Vanilli ("Blame It on the Rain"), and Chicago ("Look Away") and had her songs in such films as *Tap* ("All I Want Is Forever") and *License to Kill.*

Among male writers, John Hiatt, who has long been considered the songwriter's songwriter, finally came into his own as the singer's songwriter, a tribute not only to his work ethic and quality but to the various interpretations his work has engendered, almost unheard of in this specialized age. He helped put the blind Canadian blues guitarist Jeff Healey on the map with "Angel Eyes," brought funky Bonnie Raitt over the comeback hump with the Grammy-winning "Thing Called Love," gained a prominent slot on country queen Emmylou Harris's latest release with "Icy Blue Heart," scored with retro rocker Marshall Crenshaw with "Someplace Love Can't Find Me," penned the Grammy-nominated "She Don't Love Nobody" for the Desert Rose Band, and provided the meritorious *Will the Circle Be Unbroken, Vol. II* project with one of its finest moments, "One Step Over the Line."

Country Heartbreak

In country music the biggest news was also the saddest—the deaths of stalwarts Keith Whitley and Roy Orbison. Whitley succumbed to alcohol and Orbison to the rigors of an ancient heart, but both went out on the court, as it were. They were on the charts at the time they died,

Whitley with the prophetic "I Wonder Do You Think of Me" and Orbison with the jaunty "You Got It." Among the survivors, Clint Black had an almost legendary year, coming up with the top two country songs of the year, "Better Man" and "Killin' Time," both written with Hayden Nicholas. From the aforementioned *Will The Circle Be Unbroken, Vol. II* came "You Ain't Goin Nowhere," the Dylan tribute and remake by former Byrds Roger McGuinn and Chris Hillman. While that duet was notable, by far the duo of the year honors belonged to the Williams boys, Hank and Hank Jr., who were united electronically on the elder's previously unreleased demo of "There's a Tear in My Beer." Another noteworthy duet occurred when Nanci Griffith tapped Phil Everly to sing backup on "You Made This Love a Teardrop," one of the many fine tunes on the latest album from a consistently high quality singer and songwriter.

Folk and Other Non-Commercial Genres

Good songwriting for its own sake is more a province of folk music, where there was once again a preponderance of finely honed tunes with an eye not on the charts but on the heart. Students of the serious lyric should find indispensable the effort of Fast Folk Magazine, an organization devoted to presenting an ongoing study of the folksinger's art, where the seminal works of Nanci Griffith, Suzanne Vega, and Tracy Chapman were first showcased. Highlights of their sixth anniversary album include Frank Christian's "Three Flights Up" and Christine Lavin's "Realities." The mellow record label Windham Hill entered this arena in 1989 with a sampler that contains many folk gems, like "Insanity Street" (Lillie Palmer), "Legacy" (Pierce Pettis), "Men and Women" (Uncle Bonsai), and "My Father's Shoes" (Cliff Eberhardt). Other veteran artists made the scene again, as guitarist Leo Kottke returned to vocalizing with his usual bent flair in "Jack Gets Up" and Eric Andersen reflected upon his beatnik roots in the haunting "Ghosts upon the Road." The Washington Squares, representing a younger generation of beatniks, celebrated one of their forebears' archetypal anti-heroes with their ode to "Neal Cassady." Two excoriating portraits of the performer's life and lifestyle came from the poison pens of Loudon Wainwright ("Harry's Wall") and Bob Dylan ("What Was It You Wanted"). Novelist Larry McMurty's son James came forth with a finely realized first novel of an album, highlighted by the drolly sociological and pointedly observant "I'm Not from Here"; the Indigo Girls made an intense debut ("Close to Fine"); and "Crossroads" showed Tracy Chapman survived her sophomore year on a major label with her soul intact.

Across the spectrum of hip from folk music, the sub-genre variously known as "post-modern," "New Wave," "punk," "cow-punk," "post-punk," and "avante garde," proved itself just as unabashedly uninterested in the commercial, except for positions on its own charts, which are compiled from the cult and college radio stations who service this educated, young, affluent, malcontented audience, too musically tasteful for heavy metal, too grammatically proficient for rap. This is where groups with tongue-in-cheek monikers like Camper Van Beethoven ("All Her Favorite Fruit," "Across the Borderline") and the Dead Milkmen ("Punk Rock Girl") rule, and XTC ("Mayor of Simpleton") is God— although the group would disclaim that mantle as they did with last year's irreverent "Dear God." Bob Mould ("Brasilia Crossed with Trenton") emerged from the ashes of Husker Du, while the Replacements ("Talent Show") continued on their quirky path. The forerunners of this genre were once referred to in a punk classic as "The Blank Generation"; the descendants have now been similarly dubbed by Matt Johnson of The The as "The Beat(en) Generation."

It is from underground precincts like post-modern, folk, rap, and thrash, where in lieu of certified hit singles, favorite album cuts take on a life all their own, that artists who work the fringes of musical sainthood without selling out to dance or romance may take a decade or more to achieve mainstream success. Elvis Costello built further this year on his rarified status ("God's Comic," "Satellite"); Stan Ridgway ("A Mission in Life"), Robyn Hitchcock ("Madonna of the Wasps"), and Skid Roper and Mojo Nixon ("Debbie Gibson Is Pregnant with My Two-Headed Love Child") may be several years away. Not known as a proving ground for great literary minds, the heavy metal sub-genre of thrash has nevertheless produced much of the protest music of the late eighties, with Metallica's Grammy-winning "One" a more than apt representative. It is an anti-war song based on the novel *Johnny Got His Gun* by Dalton Trumbo. Extending the concept of the decade-long album cut lifespan, Eric Kaz broke through this year, when his twenty-year-old "Cry Like a Rainstorm, Howl Like the Wind" became the title song for Linda Ronstadt's new album. Nearly two decades earlier, she had made his "Love Has No Pride" a staple of the folk/pop repertoire.

Comebacks by a Variety of Performers

Like much of the decade, 1989 was another year in which many long forgotten or semi-retired icons of the past shook off the dust of idleness to put another album together in the hopes of rekindling memories of their own heydays and their audiences'. The perennially squabbling Rolling Stones were the most successful, not only financially, but artistically as well ("Mixed Emotions," "Rock and a Hard Place"), although Bonnie Raitt, winner of four Gammys ("Nick of Time," "Thing Called Love"), wasn't complaining either, finally having the career year people had been predicting for her since the mid-seventies. Neil Young found his old craggy voice ("Rockin' in the Free World"); Dion ("King of the New York Streets") proved he'd never lost his. Paul McCartney's songwriting pairing with Elvis Costello ("Veronica," "My Brave Face") had some people thinking of his days alongside the late John Lennon. Laura Nyro continued her by now established pace of producing an album every five years ("Broken Rainbow"), but this time she accompanied it with some notable live performances. In a sort of belated mid-life crisis, Carole King (City Streets") left the safety of her piano bench for the uncharted world of the electric guitar. 1989 also marked the too long awaited returns to major label action of Rickie Lee Jones ("Horses," written with Walter Becker, another recent underachiever) and the Roches ("Mama Drama").

Broadway's Music on Record and Stage

Perhaps reflecting a generational shift in musical predilections, away from the adolescent bombast of rock, the processed palaver of pop, and in general the anti-establishment fervor of folk, rap, thrash, and the other forms of underground entertainment, those above a certain age this year found great comfort in appreciating the sophisticated turns of phrase and melody favored by proponents of the Broadway sound. Propelled by Liza Minnelli's surprising success on the pop charts of 1989 with her remake of Stephen Sondheim's "Losing My Mind" (from *Follies*), more attention and notoriety were given the much-maligned showtune than at any time certainly in this decade, and possibly even further back. The discovery of some lost Jerome Kern manuscripts in a New Jersey warehouse became a media event, which led to a special concert production his 1919 musical *Sitting Pretty*. A rare Frank Loesser tune, "The Wind Blows Through My Window" was given a public hearing after years of obscurity, by no less knowledgeable a singing duo than his widow and his daughter. Veteran writers Richard Maltby and David Shire opened an extremely well-received revue that was a compilation of their life's work (*Closer than Ever*); John Kander and Fred Ebb commandeered an evening of their own, in which they previewed the title tune from their bound-for-Broadway venture, *Kiss of the Spider Woman*. When pop stylists like Michael Feinstein and Harry Connick Jr. routinely pack the poshest boites from Park Avenue to Palm Beach, it was not surprising that an old chestnut like "Makin' Whoopee" should receive not one but two new, high visibility renditions: Rickie Lee Jones and Dr. John recorded it on the latter's new album; and Michelle Pfeiffer made a stunning debut as a singer with her bravura performance of it in the movie *The Fabulous Baker Boys*.

In the midst of this revival of interest in the form, Broadway found itself bursting with song this year. In a decade singularly bereft of American classics, two shows that opened in 1989 promised to rewrite that libretto for the 1990's: Cy Coleman's *City of Angels* and *Grand Hotel*, with new songs by Maury Yeston of *Nine* fame. And while the ignominious out-of-town shutdown of *Annie 2* and the quick dismissal of Elizabeth Swados's well-meaning *The Red Sneaks* suggest that any optimism may well be short-lived, there is also a busy Off-Broadway underground at work, showcased in 1989 in such vibrant works as *Buzzsaw Berkeley* by Michael John La Chiusa, *Showing Off* by Douglas Bernstein and Denis Markell, Joseph Papp's long awaited production of Joe Orton's *Up against It*, with music by Todd Rundgren, and Tim Finn's *Romance in Hard Times* to help mitigate the threat.

Film and Television Showcase Songs

As *Beaches* once again has shown us with "Wind Beneath My Wings," there is just no substitute for the movies as the decade's strongest purveyor of a pop song to its widest possible audience. By now multiple artist soundtrack compilation albums routinely accompany films and generate many hit songs. Witness "On Our Own" from *Ghostbusters,* "Rock On" from *Dream a Little Dream*, "In Your Eyes" from *Say Anything*, "After All" from *Chances Are*, "Iko Iko" from *Rain Man*, "Let the River Run" from *Working Girl*, "Surrender to Me" from *Tequila Sunrise*, "Buffalo Stance" from *Slaves of New York*, "Batdance" from *Batman*, etc. But in 1989 movie music's big step forward came with *The Little Mermaid*, an old-fashioned movie musical, with songs expressly written for it ("Kiss the Girl," "Under the Sea") by Alan Menken and Howard Ashman, previously noted for their collaboration on *Little Shop of Horrors*. Hollywood marked the occasion by bestowing the Academy Award for Best Original Song on "Under the Sea."

On the smaller screen, with the demise of *Miami Vice*, once an unparalleled song showcasing entity, the available slots for original prime time songs are all but nil, aside from the stultifying predictability of the MTV video realm. Only the occasional variety special for Kenny Rogers or Dolly Parton and the inevitable opening theme for debuting sitcoms or adventure series offer an opportunity. While far from approaching the heyday of this form, when people like John Sebastian, Sonny Curtis, and Jose Feliciano routinely turned in small gems for *Welcome Back, Kotter, The Mary Tyler Moore Show,* and *Chico and the Man,* respectively, the curiously abbreviated but nevertheless compelling themes for *Dear John* and *Empty Nest,* Bill Medley's spirited rendition of Steve Dorff's "Doin' It the Best I Can" from *Just the Ten of Us,* and Roberta Flack's introduction to *The Hogan Family,* suggest a moderate comeback of substance for a much underappreciated genre. By far the strangest development in this field, however, occurs on one network's Friday schedule, where the successive theme songs for *Full House, Family Matters,* and *Perfect Strangers* have all been written by the same team of Jesse Fredericke and Bennett Salvay.

Top 40 Roundup

While dance music and rap and the occasional big ballad predominated on the Top 40 of 1989, reducing the form to pre-teen fodder for the most part, the stray noteworthy tune did manage now and then to filter into the mass public ear. If Richard Marx ("Satisfied," "Right Here Waiting," "Angelina") has earned his hard-won knack for the ersatz emotionalism necessary to capture mass attention, surely Tom Petty's triumphant year ("I Won't Back Down," "Runnin' Down a Dream") was as satisfying as it was surprising. Fine Young Cannibals brought reggae rhythms to the top of the charts with "She Drives Me Crazy" and "Good Thing." Martika's Suzanne Vega-ish "Toy Soldiers" was in substance an anti-war statement. Don Henley's "The End of the Innocence" evoked his previous masterwork, "The Boys of Summer." Debbie Gibson's growth as an artist, writer, and producer ("Lost in Your Eyes," "Electric Youth") separated her from most of her peers. The Cure ("Love Song"), the B-52s ("Love Shack"), R.E.M. ("Stand"), and Love and Rockets ("So Alive") climaxed lengthy ascents from the post-modern underground, while "What I Am," by Edie Brickell and New Bohemians, launched from that realm, achieved its popularity without such protracted dues-paying.

In the end, the most provocative moment of the Top 40 year, and the year in general, may have been provided by Billy Joel and his use of recent history as subject matter for "We Didn't Start the Fire." The firestorm of praise and criticism for his effort not only made him an item in such serious media as *Newsweek* and a subject of study in the junior high schools of America, which adopted the song as a kind of sing-along syllabus, it gained him this year's coveted opening slot on the Grammy Awards presentation. The number did not win him a Song of the Year Award, but it accomplished something far more difficult and rewarding: it got the world's attention to coalesce around a tune for the first time in ages—good, bad, or indifferent, pretty powerful stuff at that.

A

(You're Puttin') A Rush on Me
Words and music by Timmy Allen and Paul Laurence.
Willesden Music, Inc., 1987/Bush Burnin' Music.
Best-selling record by Stephanie Mills, from the album *If I Were Your Woman* (MCA, 87).

Above and Beyond
Words and music by Harlan Howard.
Tree Publishing Co., Inc., 1959, 1987.
Best-selling record in 1989 by Rodney Crowell from *Diamonds and Dirt* (Columbia, 88).

Abracadabra
Words and music by Steve Miller.
Sailor Music, 1982.
Best-selling record by The Steve Miller Band from *Abracadabra* (Capital, 82).

Absolute Beginners (English)
Words and music by David Bowie.
Jones Music Co., 1986.
Introduced by David Bowie in the film *Absolute Beginners* (86).

An Acceptable Level of Ecstasy
Words and music by Lyle Lovett.
Michael H. Goldsen, Inc., 1986/Lyle Lovett, 1986.
Introduced by Lyle Lovett on the album *Lyle Lovett* (MCA/Curb, 86).

Ace in the Hole
Words and music by Paul Simon.
Paul Simon Music, 1980.
Introduced by Paul Simon on *One Trick Pony* (Warner Brothers, 80) and in the film *One Trick Pony* (80).

Ace in the Hole
Words and music by Dennis Adkins.

1

Sweet Tater Tunes, 1989.
Best-selling record by George Strait from *Beyond the Blue Neon* (MCA, 89).

Achin' to Be
Words and music by Paul Westerberg.
NAH Music, 1989.
Introduced by The Replacements on *Don't Tell a Soul* (Sire, 89).

Act Naturally
Words by Vonie Morrison, music by Johnny Russell.
Blue Book Music, 1963.
 Revived by Buck Owens and Ringo Starr on the album *Act Naturally* (Capitol, 89). Former Beatle Starr had a hit with this song in 1965; the 1989 duet was recorded at England's Abbey Road studio made famous by the Beatles.

Action Jackson
Words and music by Bernadette Cooper.
Spectrum VII, 1988/Lorimar Music Corp., 1988.
Introduced by Madame X in the film and on the soundtrack album *Action Jackson* (Lorimar, 88).

Addicted
Words and music by Cheryl Wheeler.
Bug Music, 1987/Amachrist Music, 1987/Penrod & Higgins, 1987.
Best-selling record by Dan Seals from *Rage On* (Capitol, 88).

Addicted to Love (English)
Words and music by Robert Palmer.
Bungalow Music, N.V., 1986/Polygram International, 1986.
Best-selling record by Robert Palmer from the album *Riptide* (Atlantic, 86). The band Van Halen often jammed on this song during soundchecks on their 1986 tour. Nominated for Grammy Awards, Record of the Year, 1986, and Song of the Year, 1986.

Addicted to You
Words and music by Gerald Levert and Eddie Levert.
Ensign Music, 1988/Willesden Music, Inc., 1988/Trycet, 1988.
Best-selling record by Levert from *Just Coolin'* (Atlantic, 88.)

A.D.I./The Horror of It All
Words and music by Anthrax.
Happy Trails, 1986/Anthrax Music, 1986.
Revived in 1988 by Anthrax in the film *Return of the Living Dead, Part II* and on its soundtrack album (Island, 88).

Adios
Words and music by Jimmy Webb.

White Oak Songs, 1987.
Performed by Linda Ronstadt on *Cry Like a Rainstorm, Howl Like the Wind* (Elektra, 89).

Adult Education
Words and music by Daryl Hall, John Oates, and Sara Allen.
Fust Buzza Music, Inc., 1983/Hot Cha Music Co., 1983/Unichappell Music Inc., 1983.
Best-selling record by Daryl Hall and John Oates from *Rock 'N Soul, Part 1* (RCA, 84).

Affair of the Heart (Australian)
Words and music by Rick Springfield, Blaise Tosti, and Danny Tate.
Vogue Music, 1983/Polygram International, 1983.
Best-selling record by Rick Springfield from *Living in Oz* (RCA, 83).

Africa
Words and music by David Paich and Jeffrey Porcaro.
Hudmar Publishing Co., Inc., 1982/Rising Storm Music, 1982.
Best-selling record by Toto from *Toto IV* (Columbia, 82).

After All (Love Theme from *Chances Are*)
Words and music by Tom Snow and Dean Pitchford.
Snow Songs, 1988/Pitchford, 1988/Triple Star Music, 1988.
Cher teamed with Peter Cetera, former lead singer of Chicago, to perform this song on the soundtrack of the film *Chances Are* (album by Geffen, 89); it was her first recorded duet since the days of Sonny and Cher. The song was also featured on her album *Heart of Stone* (Geffen, 89). Nominated for an Academy Award, Best Original Song, 1989.

After All These Years
Words by Fred Ebb, music by John Kander.
Fiddleback, 1983/Kander & Ebb Inc., 1983.
Introduced by Male Chorus in *The Rink* (84).

After All This Time
Words and music by Rodney Crowell.
Granite Music Corp., 1988/Coolwell Music.
Best-selling record by Rodney Crowell from *Diamonds and Dirt* (Columbia, 88). Won a Grammy Award, and Country Song of the Year, 1989.

After the Fall
Words and music by Steve Perry and John Friga.
Twist & Shout Music, 1982.
Best-selling record by Journey from *Frontiers* (Columbia, 83).

After the Fire (English)
Words and music by Pete Townshend.
Atlantic Recording Corp., England, 1985/Bejubop, England, 1985/Eel
Pie Music, 1985.
Best-selling record by Roger Daltrey from the album *Under a Raging
Moon* (Atlantic, 85). Revived in 1986 by Pete Townshend on *Deep
End Live* (ATCO). Townshend's commentary on the Ethiopian famine
was introduced on his Brixton, England concert video, which
precededthe album.

Against All Odds (Take a Look at Me Now) (English)
Words and music by Phil Collins.
EMI Golden Torch Music, 1984/WB Music, 1984/Hit & Run Music.
Best-selling record by Phil Collins (Atlantic, 84). Introduced in the film
and soundtrack *Against All Odds* (84). Nominated for an Academy
Award, Best Song, 1984; a Grammy Award, Song of the Year, 1984.

Against the Wind
Words and music by Bob Seger.
Gear Publishing, 1980.
Best-selling record Bob Seger from *Against the Wind* (Capitol, 80).

Ages of You
Words and music by Peter Buck, Bill Berry, Mike Mills, and Michael
Stipe.
Night Garden Music, 1986.
Introduced by R.E.M. on the album *Live for Life* (I.R.S., 86). This was
culled from a compilation disk, the profits of which were intended for
cancer research.

Agony
Words and music by Stephen Sondheim.
BMG Songs Inc., 1986/WB Music/Rilting Music Inc.
Introduced by Chuck Wagner and Robert Westenberg in the musical
Into the Woods, which opened on Broadway in 1987.

Ah, Men
Words and music by Will Holt.
Lemon Tree Music, Inc., 1981.
Introduced by Company of *Ah, Men* (81).

Ai No Corrida (English)
Words and music by Chaz Jankel and Kenny Young.
Full Keel Music, 1980.
Best-selling record by Quincy Jones from *The Dude* (A&M, 81).
Nominated for a Grammy Award, Rhythm 'n' Blues Song of the
Year, 1981.

Ain't Even Done with the Night
Words and music by John Cougar Mellencamp (pseudonym for John Mellencamp).
Full Keel Music, 1980.
Best-selling record by John Cougar from *Nothing Matters & What If It Did* (Riva, 81).

Ain't Misbehavin'
Words by Andy Razaf, music by Fats Waller and Harry Brooks.
Mills Music Inc., 1929/Chappell & Co., Inc., 1929/Razaf Music, 1929.
Revived in 1986 by Hank Williams, Jr. on the album *Five-O* (Warner Bros.).

Ain't No Cure for Love (Canadian)
Words and music by Leonard Cohen.
Stranger Music Inc., 1986.
Performed by Jennifer Warnes on the album *Famous Blue Raincoat,* (Cypress, 86), a collection of works written by the gifted Canadian songwriter-novelist-poet, Leonard Cohen.

Ain't No Road Too Long
Words and music by Waylon Jennings.
Waylon Jennings Music, 1985.
Introduced by Waylon Jennings and the Sesame Street muppet character Big Bird in the film *Follow That Bird.*

Ain't Nobody
Words and music by David Wolinski.
Full Keel Music, 1983.
Best-selling record by Rufus with Chaka Khan from *Live - Stompin' at the Savoy* (Warner Brothers, 83). Nominated for a Grammy Award, Rhythm 'n' Blues Song of the Year, 1983.

Ain't Nothin' Goin' on But the Rent
Words and music by Gwen Guthrie.
Dum Di Dum, 1986.
Best-selling record by Gwen Guthrie from the album *Good to Go Lover* (Polydor, 86).

Ain't Nothin' in the World
Words and music by Joe Nettlesby and Terry Coffey.
Chicago Brothers Music, 1989.
Best-selling record by Miki Howard from *Miki Howard* (Atlantic, 89).

Ain't She Something Else
Words and music by Jerry Foster and Bill Rice.
Polygram International, 1985.
Best-selling record by Conway Twitty from the album *Don't Call Him a Cowboy* (Warner Bros., 85).

Alive and Kicking (English)
Words and music by Simple Minds.
Colgems-EMI Music, 1985.
Best-selling record by Simple Minds from the album *Once upon a Time*
(A & M, 85).

All American Cowgirl
Words and music by Bobby Braddock.
Tree Publishing Co., Inc., 1987.
Introduced by Renee Wilson (Capitol, 89). The song was a winner in
the 'You Can Be a Star' contest in Nashville.

All American Girls
Words and music by Narada Michael Walden, Lisa Walden, Allee
Willis, and Joni Sledge.
Walden Music, Inc., 1981/Gratitude Sky Music, 1981/Irving Music Inc.,
1981/Kejoc Music, 1981/Baby Shoes Music, 1981.
Best-selling record by Sister Sledge from *All American Girls* (Atlantic,
81).

All at Once
Words by Jeffrey Osborne, music by Michael Masser.
Almo Music Corp., 1983/March 9 Music, 1983/Prince Street Music,
1983.
Best-selling record by Whitney Houston in 1986 from the album
Whitney Houston (Arista, 85).

All Come True (English)
Words and music by Karl Wallinger.
Polygram International, 1986.
Introduced by World Party on the album *Private Revolution* (Chrysalis,
86). The songwriter was previously a member of the Waterboys.

All Cried Out
Words and music by Full Force.
Willesden Music, Inc., 1986/My My Music, 1986/Careers Music Inc.,
1986.
Best-selling record by Lisa Lisa and Cult Jam in 1986 from the album
Lisa Lisa and Cult Jam with Full Force (Columbia, 85).

All Fired Up
Words and music by Kerryn Tolhurst, Pat Giraldo, and Myron
Grombacher.
Chrysalis Music Group, 1988.
Best-selling record by Pat Benatar from *Wide Awake in Dreamland*
(Chyralis, 88).

All Her Favorite Fruit
Words and music by Victor Krummenacher, Greg Lisher, David

Lowery, and Chris Pedersen.
Camper Van Beethoven Music, 1989.
Introduced by Camper Van Beethoven on *Key Lime Pie* (Virgin, 89).

All I Ask of You (English)
Words by Andrew Lloyd Webber, Charles Hart, and Richard Stilgoe.
Colgems-EMI Music, 1987/Really Useful Music, 1987.
Introduced by Sarah Brightman in the London production of the musical
   The Phantom of the Opera, which opened on Broadway early in
   1988. Performed on the cast album by Steve Barton; the song reached
   the top ten in England. This song was revived by Barbara Streisand
   on *Till I Loved You* (Columbia, 88).

All I Have to Do Is Dream
Words and music by Boudleaux Bryant.
Acuff-Rose Publications Inc., 1958.
Revived by Andy Gibb and Victoria Principal (Polygram, 81).

All I Need
Words and music by Clifton Magness, Glen Ballard, and David Pack.
Yellow Brick Road Music, 1984/MCA, Inc., 1984/Art Street Music,
   1984.
Best-selling record by Jack Wagner from *All I Need* (Warner Brothers,
   84).

All I Need Is a Miracle (English)
Words and music by Mike Rutherford and Christopher Neil.
Hit & Run Music, 1985.
Best-selling record by Mike & The Mechanics in 1986 from the album
   Mike & The Mechanics (Atlantic, 85). Mike Rutherford is one of the
   founding members of Genesis.

All I Need to Know (Don't Know Much)
Words by Cynthia Weil and Tom Snow, music by Tom Snow and Barry
   Mann.
ATV Music Corp., 1980/Mann & Weil Songs Inc., 1980/Braintree
   Music, 1980/Snow Music, 1980.
Introduced by Bill Medley (Liberty, 81). Best-selling record by Bette
   Midler on *No Frills* (Atlantic, 83).

All I Need to Know, see **Don't Know Much.**

All I Want
Words and music by Zack Smith, Patty Smyth, and Benji King.
EMI-Blackwood Music Inc., 1984.
Introduced by Scandal on *Warrior* (Columbia, 84).

All I Want for Christmas
Words and music by Pat MacDonald.

Mambadaddi, 1987/I.R.S. Music, 1987.
Introduced by Timbuk 3 (I.R.S., 87). Proceeds from this protest against
war toys were donated to the campaign to eliminate such toys.

All I Want Is Forever
Words and music by Diane Warren.
Realsongs, 1988.
Best-selling record in 1989 by James 'J.T.' Taylor and Regina Belle
from the film and soundtrack album *Tap* (Epic, 88). This was one of
many of the year's hits written by the prolific Warren.

All I Wanted
Words and music by Steve Walsh and Steve Morse.
Dangling Participle, 1986/Hard Fought, 1986/Stark Raving, 1986.
Best-selling record by Kansas from the album *Power* (MCA, 86).
Songwriter Steve Morse is one of the rock world's most highly
lauded guitarists.

All I Wanted Was the Dream
Words and music by Peter Allen.
Irving Music Inc., 1988.
Introduced by Peter Allen in *Legs Diamond* the roundly criticized
Broadway debut for the former song and dance man.

All My Ex's Live in Texas
Words and music by Sanger D. Shafer and Lyndia J. Shafer.
Acuff Rose Music, 1986.
Best-selling record in 1987 by George Strait, from the album *Ocean
Front Property* (MCA, 86). Nominated for a Grammy Award,
Country Song of the Year, 1987.

All My Life
Words and music by Karla Bonoff.
Seagrape Music Inc., 1986.
Revived in 1989 by Linda Ronstadt on *Cry Like a Rainstorm, Howl Like
the Wind* (Elektra, 89). Always one of the writer's staunchest
supporters, Ronstadt here chose a tune from Bonoff's 1988 album,
New World.

All My Rowdy Friends (Have Settled Down)
Words and music by Hank Williams, Jr.
Bocephus Music Inc., 1981.
Best-selling record by Hank Williams, Jr. from *The Pressure Is On*
(Elektra, 81).

All My Rowdy Friends Are Coming over Tonight
Words and music by Hank Williams, Jr.
Bocephus Music Inc., 1984.
Best-selling record by Hank Williams, Jr. from *Major Moves* (Warner

Bros, 84). Nominated for a Grammy Award, Country Song of the
Year, 1984.

All Night Long
Words and music by Joe Walsh.
Wow and Flutter Music Publishing, 1980.
Best-selling record by Joe Walsh (Full Moon, 80).

All Night Long (All Night)
Words and music by Lionel Richie, Jr.
Brockman Enterprises Inc., 1983.
Best-selling record by Lionel Richie from *Can't Slow Down* (Motown,
    83). Nominated for Grammy Awards, Record of the Year, 1983, and
    Song of the Year, 1983.

All of My Love
Words and music by Raymond Calhoun, Aldyn St. Jon, and Ronnie
    Wilson.
Day Ta Day, 1989/Rajaca, 1989/Good Choice Music, 1989.
Best-selling record by The Gap Band from *Round Trip* (Capitol, 89).

All of You (Spanish)
English words by Cynthia Weil, music by Tony Renis and Julio Iglesias.
Elettra Music, 1984/Ewald Corp., 1984/Dyad Music, Ltd., 1984/
    Braintree Music, 1984.
Best-selling record by Julio Iglesias and Diana Ross from *1100 Bel Air
    Place* (Columbia, 84).

All out of Love (Australian)
Words and music by Graham Russell.
BMG Music, 1980.
Best-selling record by Air Supply from *All out of Love* (Arista, 80).

All over the World (English)
Words and music by Jeff Lynne.
EMI-Blackwood Music Inc., 1980.
Best-selling record by ELO from the film and soundtrack to *Xanadu*
    (MCA, 80).

All Right
Words and music by Christopher Cross.
BMG Songs Inc., 1983.
Best-selling record by Christopher Cross from *Another Page* (Warner
    Brothers, 83).

All She Wants to Do Is Dance
Words and music by Danny Kortchmar.
WB Music, 1984/Woody Creek Music, 1984.

Best-selling record by Don Henley from the album *Building the Perfect Beast* (Geffen, 85).

All the Children in a Row
Words by Fred Ebb, music by John Kander.
Fiddleback, 1983/Kander & Ebb Inc., 1983.
Introduced by Liza Minnelli in *The Rink* (84).

All the Love in the World (English)
Words and music by John Spinks.
MCA, Inc., 1986.
Best-selling record by The Outfield from the album *Play Deep* (Columbia, 86).

All the Right Moves
Words and music by Tom Snow and Barry Alfonso.
WB Music, 1983/Sprocket Music, Inc., 1983/Warner-Tamerlane Music, 1983/Rewind Music, Inc., 1983.
Best-selling record by Jennifer Warnes and Chris Thompson (Casablanca, 83). Introduced in the film *All the Right Moves* (83).

All This Love
Words and music by Eldra DeBarge.
Jobete Music Co., 1982.
Best-selling record by DeBarge from *All This Love* (Gordy, 83).

All This Time
Words and music by Tim James and Steve McClintock.
George Tobin, 1988.
Best-selling record in 1989 by Tiffany from *Hold an Old Friend's Hand* (MCA, 88).

All This Time
Words and music by Tim James and James McClintock.
George Tobin, 1988.
Introduced by Tiffany on *Hold an Old Friend's Hand* (MCA 88).

All Those Years Ago (English)
Words and music by George Harrison.
Zero Productions, 1981.
Best-selling record by George Harrison from *Somewhere in England* (Dark Horse, 81). Written as a tribute to John Lennon.

All Through the Night
Words and music by Jules Shear.
Juters Publishing Co., 1982.
Best-selling record by Cyndi Lauper from *She's So Unusual* (Portrait, 84).

All Time High (English)
Words by Tim Rice, music by John Barry.
EMI-Blackwood Music Inc., 1983/United Lion Music Inc., 1983.
Introduced by Rita Coolidge in the film and soundtrack album
    Octopussy (83).

All Walk Alone
Words and music by Karla Bonoff and Michael Ruff.
Seagrape Music Inc., 1988/Ruff Mix Music, 1988.
Introduced by Karla Bonoff on *New World* (Gold Castle, 88). This cut
    marked a return to form by one of the 70's foremost singer-
    songwriters.

All You Own
Words and music by Jake Meyer and Scott Bricklin.
Bricksongs, 1986.
Best-selling record by Bricklin from the album *Bricklin* (A & M, 86).

All You Zombies
Words and music by Rob Hyman and Eric Bazilian.
Dub Notes, 1982/Human Boy Music, 1982.
Best-selling record by The Hooters from the album *Nervous Night*
    (Columbia, 85).

Allentown
Words and music by Billy Joel.
Joelsongs, 1981.
Best-selling record by Billy Joel from *The Nylon Curtain* (Columbia,
    83).

Allergies
Words and music by Paul Simon.
Paul Simon Music, 1981.
Best-selling record by Paul Simon from *Hearts and Bones* (Warner
    Brothers, 83).

Almost Paradise... Love Theme from *Footloose*
Words by Dean Pitchford, music by Eric Carmen.
Ensign Music, 1984.
Best-selling record by Mike Reno and Ann Wilson (Columbia, 84).
    Introduced in the film and soundtrack album *Footloose* (84).

Almost Saturday Night
Words and music by John Fogerty.
Greasy King Music Inc., 1975.
Best-selling record by Dave Edmunds from *Twargin* (Swan Song, 81).

Alone
Words and music by Billy Steinberg and Tom Kelly.

Sony Tunes, 1987/Denise Barry Music, 1987.
Best-selling record by Heart from the album *Bad Animals* (Capitol, 87).
Introduced by the authors on an obscure album called *1-10*. After a
rewrite, Heart brought it to number one.

Along Comes a Woman
Words and music by Peter Cetera and Mark Goldenberg.
BMG Songs Inc., 1984/Music of the World, 1984/Fleedleedee Music,
1984/MCA, Inc.
Best-selling record by Chicago from the album *Chicago XVII* (Warner
Bros., 85).

Along for the Ride ('56 T-Bird)
Words and music by Danny O'Keefe and Bill Brawn.
Bicameral Songs, 1985/Slavetone Music.
Introduced by John Denver on the album *One World* (RCA, 86).

Alphabet Street
Words and music by Prince Rogers Nelson.
Controversy Music, 1988.
Best-selling record by Prince, from *Lovesexy* (Paisley Park, 88).

Always
Words and music by Jonathan Lewis, David Lewis, and Wayne Lewis.
Jodaway Music, 1987.
Best-selling record by Atlantic Starr, from the album *All in the Name of
Love* (Warner Bros., 87). This ballad has become an instant wedding
classic.

Always Have Always Will
Words and music by Johnny Mears.
Texican Music Co., 1986/Dixie Stars Music, 1986.
Best-selling record by Janie Fricke from the album *Black & White*
(Columbia, 86).

Always on My Mind
Words and music by Johnny Christopher, Wayne Thompson, and Mark
James, words and music by The Pet Shop Boys.
Sebanine, 1971.
　　　　Revived by Willie Nelson from *Always on My Mind* Originally
recorded by Elvis Presley, 1972. Revived in 1988 by The Pet Shop
Boys on *Introspective* (EMI-Manhattan, 88), as part of an Elvis
Presley tribute. Became a hit in England before crossing the Atlantic.
Won Grammy Awards. Nominated for a Grammy Award, Record of
the Year, 1982.

Always Something There to Remind Me
Words by Hal David, music by Burt Bacharach.

Casa David, 1964/New Hidden Valley Music Co., 1964.
Revived by Naked Eyes from *Naked Eyes* (EMI-America, 83).

Always the Sun (English)
Words and music by The Stranglers.
Plumbshaft Ltd., England, 1987/EMI Music Publishing, 1987.
Best-selling record by The Stranglers, from their album *Dreamtime*
(Columbia, 87).

Am I Blue
Words by Grant Clarke, music by Harry Akst.
WB Music, 1929.
Revived by George Strait on the album *Ocean Front Property* (MCA).

Amanda
Words and music by Tom Scholz.
Hideaway Hits, 1986.
Best-selling record by Boston from the album *Third Stage* (MCA, 86).
The first release in six years from this seventies' supergroup
masterminded by technical wizard Tom Scholz.

Amber Waves of Grain
Words and music by Merle Haggard and Freddy Powers.
Mount Shasta Music Inc., 1985.
Introduced by Merle Haggard on the album *Amber Waves of Grain*
(Epic, 85). Song deals with plight of the American farmer.

America
Words and music by Neil Diamond.
Stonebridge Music, 1980.
Best-selling record by Neil Diamond (Capitol, 81). Introduced in the
film & soundtrack album *The Jazz Singer*.

America Is
Words by Hal David, music by Joe Raposo.
Casa David, 1985/Jonico Music Inc.
Introduced by B. J. Thomas. The song was written for the centennial of
the Statue of Liberty.

American Dream
Words and music by Neil Young.
Silver Fiddle, 1987.
Best-selling record by Crosby, Stills, Nash, & Young from *American
Dream* (Atlantic, 88). Yet another reunion album by this oft-
dismembered group, this marked Neil Young's first recording with
them since *Deja Vu* in 1970.

American Heartbeat
Words and music by Frank Sullivan and Jim Peterik.

Holy Moley Music, 1982/Rude Music, 1982/WB Music, 1982/Easy
   Action Music, 1982.
Best-selling record by Survivor from *Eye of the Tiger* (Scotti Brothers,
   82).

American Made
Words and music by Robert DiPiero and Pat McManus.
Music City Music, 1982/EMI Music Publishing, 1982.
Best-selling record by The Oak Ridge Boys from *American Made*
   (MCA, 83).

American Me
Words and music by Thom Schuyler and Fred Knobloch.
Colgems-EMI Music, 1987/BMG Songs Inc., 1987/Writer's Group
   Music, 1987/Lawyer's Daughter, 1987.
Introduced by Schuyler, Knoblock & Overstreet, from their album *SKO*
   (MTM, 87). The song was later customized by the authors for the use
   of 24 major league and 17 minor league baseball teams.

American Music
Words and music by Parker McGee.
Ensign Music, 1982.
Best-selling record by The Pointer Sisters from *So Excited* (Planet, 82).

American Storm
Words and music by Bob Seger.
Gear Publishing, 1986.
Best-selling record by Bob Seger & The Silver Bullet Band from the
   album *Like a Rock* (Capitol, 86). This song is a commentary on the
   cocaine crisis and was inspired by Bob Woodward's book *Wired* on
   the death of comedian John Belushi.

Amnesia and Jealousy (Oh Lana)
Words and music by T-Bone Burnette and Larry Poons.
Black Tent Music, 1983.
Performed by T-Bone Burnette in *Attack of the Killer B's* (Warner
   Brothers, 83).

Ana Ng
Words and music by They Might Be Giants.
They Might Be Giants Music, 1988.
Introduced by They Might Be Giants, a duo composed of John
   Vosburgh and John Linnell, on the album *Lincoln* (Restless, 88). A
   love song as skewed as it's title.

Anchorage
Words and music by Michelle Shocked.
Polygram Songs, 1988.

Introduced by Michelle Schocked on *Short Sharp Shocked* (Mercury, 88).

And I Am Telling You I'm Not Going
Words by Tom Eyen, music by Henry Krieger.
Dreamgirls Music, 1981/Dreamette's Music, 1981/Tom Eyen's Publishing Co., 1981.
Best-selling record by Jennifer Holliday (Geffen, 82). Introduced in *Dreamgirls* (82).

And She Was
Words and music by David Byrne, music by Chris Frantz, Tina Weymouth, and Jerry Harrison.
Index Music, 1985/Bleu Disque Music, 1985.
Introduced by The Talking Heads on the album *Little Creatures* (Sire, 85).

And So It Goes (with Everything But Love)
Words and music by Paul Overstreet and Don Schlitz.
MCA Music, 1989/Don Schlitz Music, 1989/Writer's Group Music, 1989/Scarlet Moon Music, 1989.
Performed by John Denver on *Will the Circle Be Unbroken, Vol. II* (Universal, 89), the landmark followup to the first *Circle* LP, from an all-star lineup of country and bluegrass musicians.

And the Beat Goes On
Words and music by Leon Sylvers, Steven Shockley, and William B. Shelby.
Portrait/Solar Songs Inc., 1980/Rosy Publishing Inc., 1980.
Best-selling record by The Whispers from *The Whispers* (Solar, 80).

And The Cradle Will Rock
Words and music by Eddie Van Halen, David Lee Roth, Alex Van Halen, and Michael Anthony.
Diamond Dave Music, 1980.
Best-selling record by Van Halen from *Women and Children First* (Warner Brothers, 80).

And We Danced
Words and music by Rob Hyman and Eric Bazilian.
Human Boy Music, 1984/Dub Notes.
Introduced by The Hooters on the album *Nervous Nights* (Columbia, 85).

And When She Danced (Love theme from *Stealing Home*)
Music by David Foster, words by Linda Thompson-Jenner.
Warner-Tamerlane Music, 1988/Air Bear, 1988/Linda's Boys Music, 1988.

Introduced by Marilyn Martin and David Foster from the movie *Stealing Home* (Atlantic, 88).

Angel
Words and music by Madonna and Steve Bray.
WB Music, 1984/Bleu Disque Music, 1984/Webo Girl, 1984/Black Lion, 1984.
Best-selling record by Madonna in 1985 from the album *Like a Virgin* (Warner Bros., 84).

Angel
Words and music by Angela Winbush.
Angel Notes Music, 1987.
Introduced by Angela Winbush on her album *Sharp* (Mercury, 87), which was the rhythm 'n' blues songwriter's first solo effort. She previously recorded as a member of Rene and Angela.

Angel
Words by Steven Tyler, words and music by Desmond Child.
Aero Dynamic Music, 1987/Desmobile Music Inc., 1987/EMI-April Music, 1987.
Introduced by Aerosmith in *Permanent Vacation* (Geffen, 87).

Angel Eyes
Words and music by John Hiatt and Fred Koller.
Lillybilly, 1988/Bug Music, 1988/Lucrative, 1988.
Best-selling record in 1989 by the Jeff Healey Band from *See the Light* (Arista, 88).

Angel Flying Too Close to the Ground
Words and music by Willie Nelson.
Willie Nelson Music Inc., 1979.
Best-selling record by Willie Nelson from the film and soundtrack *Honeysuckle Rose* (Columbia, 81).

Angel in Blue
Words and music by Seth Justman.
Center City Music, 1981/Pal-Park Music, 1981.
Best-selling record by The J. Geils Band from *Love Stinks* (EMI-America, 82).

Angel in Disguise
Words and music by Earl Thomas Conley and Randy Scruggs.
EMI-April Music, 1983/EMI-Blackwood Music Inc., 1983/Full Armor Publishing Co., 1983.
Best-selling record by Earl Thomas Conley (RCA, 84).

Angel of Harlem (Irish)
Words by Bono (pseudonym for Paul Hewson), words and music by U2.

Polygram International, 1988.
Best-selling record in 1989 by U2, from *Rattle and Hum* (Island, 88).
  This song was dedicated to the late blues singer Billie Holiday.

Angel of Music (English)
Words by Charles Hart, music by Andrew Lloyd Webber.
The Really Useful Group, 1987/Polygram International, 1987.
Introduced by Sarah Brightman and Janet Devenish on the London cast
  album of *The Phantom of the Opera* (Polydor, 88), which opened on
  Broadway early in 1989.

Angel of the Morning
Words and music by Chip Taylor.
EMI-Blackwood/Feist & April Music, 1967.
Revived by Juice Newton from *Juice* (Capitol, 81).

Angelia
Words and music by Richard Marx.
Chi-Boy, 1989.
Best-selling record by Richard Marx from *Repeat Offender* (EMI, 89).

Angeline
Words and music by James McMurtry.
Short Trip Music, 1989.
Introduced by by James McMurtry on *Too Long in the Wasteland*
  (Columbia, 89).

Angelyne
Words and music by Bruce Springsteen.
Bruce Springsteen Publishing, 1986.
Performed by The Nitty Gritty Dirt Band on the album *Hold On*
  (Warner Bros., 86).

Animal (English)
Words and music by Steve Clark, Phil Collen, Robert John 'Mutt'
  Lange, and Rick Savage.
Calloco, 1987/Zomba Music, 1987.
Best-selling record by Def Leppard, from their album *Hysteria*
  (Mercury, 87).

Another Brick in the Wall
Words and music by Roger Waters.
Unichappell Music Inc., 1979.
Best-selling record by Pink Floyd from *The Wall* (Columbia, 80).

Another Day in Paradise (English)
Words and music by Phil Collins.
WB Music, 1989/Hit & Run Music, 1989.

Best-selling record by Phil Collins from *But Seriously* (Atlantic, 89).
Backing vocals by David Crosby.

Another Honky Tonk Night on Broadway
Words and music by Milton Brown, Steve Dorff, and Snuff Garrett.
Peso Music, 1982/Wallet Music, 1982.
Best-selling record by David Frizzell & Shelly West (Warner/Viva, 82).

(You Don't Need) Another Lover
Words and music by George McFarlane, Gardner Cole, and Campsie.
Almo Music Corp., 1988/Warner-Tamerlane Music, 1988/Sizzling Blue
Music, 1988.
Best-selling record by Giant Steps from *The Book of Pride* (A & M,
88).

Another One Bites the Dust (English)
Words and music by John Deacon.
Queen Music Ltd., 1980.
Best-selling record by Queen from *The Game* (Elektra, 80).

Another Part of Me
Words and music by Michael Jackson.
Mijac Music, 1987/Warner-Tamerlane Music, 1987.
Introduced by Michael Jackson in *Captain Eo*, a short film that
premiered at Disneyland for an audience of invited press. This is one
of two new songs written by Jackson, the first since the phenomenal
success of *Thriller* in 1983. Best-selling record in 1988 by Michael
Jackson from *Bad* (Epic, 87).

Another Sleepless Night
Words and music by Charlie Black and Rory Bourke.
Chappell & Co., Inc., 1981.
Best-selling record by Anne Murray from *Where Do You Go When You
Dream* (Capitol, 82).

Another Tricky Day (English)
Words and music by Pete Townshend.
Towser Tunes Inc., 1981.
Introduced by The Who on *Face Dances* (Warner Brothers, 81).

Another Woman's Man
Words and music by Christine Lavin.
CL-2, 1987/Rounder Music, 1987.
Performed by Christine Lavin on her album *Another Woman's Man*
(Philo, 87), this song formed part of a treatise on modern marriage
and divorce.

Another World
Words and music by John Leffler and Ralph Schuckett.

Fountain Square Music Publishing Co. Inc, 1987.
Best-selling record by Crystal Gayle and Gary Morris. Introduced as the theme for the TV series *Another World.* Recorded by Gayle on her album *What If We Fall in Love* (Warner Bros., 87).

The Anti-Sex Backlash of the 80's
Words and music by Margaret Roche, Terre Roche, and Suzzy Roche. Deshufflin' Inc., 1989.
Introduced by The Roches on *Speak* (Paradox, 89).

Any Day Now
Words by Bob Hilliard, music by Burt Bacharach.
The Bourne Co., 1962/New Hidden Valley Music Co., 1962.
Revived by Ronnie Milsap on *Inside Ronnie Milsap* (RCA, 82).

Any King's Shilling (English)
Words and music by Declan MacManus.
Plangent Visions Music, Inc., London, England, 1986, 1989.
Introduced by Elvis Costello on *Spike* (Warner Bros., 89).

Any Love
Words and music by Luther Vandross and Marcus Miller.
Uncle Ronnie's Music, 1988/Sunset Burgundy Music, Inc., 1988/MCA Music, 1988.
Best-selling record by Luther Vandross from *Any Love* (Epic, 88). Nominated for a Grammy Award, Rhythm 'n' Blues Song of the Year, 1988.

Any Way You Want It
Words and music by Steve Perry and Neil Schon.
Weed High Nightmare Music, 1979.
Best-selling record by Journey from *Departure* (Columbia, 80).

Anyone Can Be Somebody's Fool
Words and music by Nanci Griffith.
Wing & Wheel Music, 1987.
Introduced by Nanci Griffith on *Little Love Affairs* (MCA, 87).

Anyone Who Had a Heart
Words by Hal David, music by Burt Bacharach.
Casa David, 1963/New Hidden Valley Music Co., 1963.
Revived by Luther Vandross on his album *Give Me the Reason* (Epic, 86).

Anything For You
Words and music by Gloria Estefan.
Foreign Imported, 1987.
Best-selling record in 1988 by Gloria Estefan & Miami Sound Machine, from *Let It Loose* (Epic, 88).

Appalachian Memories
Words and music by Dolly Parton.
Velvet Apple Music, 1983.
Introduced by Dolly Parton on *Burlap and Satin* (RCA, 83).

Appetite (Irish)
Words and music by Paddy McAloon.
EMI-Blackwood Music Inc., 1985.
Introduced by Prefab Sprout on the album *Two Wheels Good* (Epic, 85).

The Apple Doesn't Fall
Words and music by Fred Ebb, music by John Kander.
Fiddleback, 1983, 1900/Kander & Ebb Inc., 1983.
Introduced by Liza Minnelli and Chita Rivera in *The Rink* (84).

The Apple Stretching
Words and music by Melvin Van Peebles.
Yeah Inc., 1981.
Introduced by Melvin Van Peebles in *The Waltz of the Stork* (82).

The Arbiter (I Know the Score) (English-Swedish)
English words and music by Tim Rice, Bennie Anderson, and Bjorn
    Ulvaeus.
MCA, Inc., 1985.
Introduced by Bjorn Skifs (RCA, 85). From the musical *Chess*.

Arc of a Diver (English)
Words and music by Steve Winwood and Vivian Stanshall.
Island Music, 1980/Alley Music, 1980.
Best-selling record by Steve Winwood from *Arc of a Diver* (Island, 81).

Are the Good Times Really Over
Words and music by Merle Haggard.
Shade Tree Music Inc., 1980.
Best-selling record by Merle Haggard from *Big City* (Epic, 82).

Are We Ourselves (English)
Words and music by Cy Curnin, Jamie West-Oram, Dan K. Brown, and
    Adam Woods.
Colgems-EMI Music, 1984/EMI Music Publishing, 1984.
Best-selling record by The Fixx from *Phantoms* (MCA, 84).

Are You Ever Gonna Love Me
Words and music by Chris Waters, Tom Shapiro, and Holly Dunn.
Cross Keys Publishing Co., Inc., 1989/Terrace Entertainment Corp.,
    1989/Lawyer's Daughter, 1989.
Best-selling record by Holly Dunn from *Blue Rose of Texas* (Warner
    Bros., 89).

Are You on the Road to Lovin' Me Again
Words and music by Deborah Kay Hopp and Bob Morrison.
Southern Nights Music Co., 1979.
Best-selling record by Debby Boone (Warner Brothers, 80).

Are You Single
Words and music by Stephen Washington, George Curtis Jones,
    Starleana Young, Philip Fields, and Jennifer Ivory.
Red Aurra Publishing, 1981/Lucky Three Music Publishing Co., 1981.
Best-selling record by Aurra from *Send Your Love* (Salsoul, 81).

Armed and Dangerous
Words and music by Maurice White, Martin Page, and Garry Glenn.
EMI Golden Torch Music, 1986/Saggifire Music, 1986/Zomba Music,
    1986/Martin Page Music, 1986/WB Music, 1986/Silver Sun
    Publishers, 1986/Silver Sun Music/EMI Music Publishing.
Introduced by Atlantic Starr in the film *Armed and Dangerous* (86) and
    on the soundtrack album (Manhattan, 86).

Armegeddon It (English)
Words and music by Steve Clark, Phil Collen, Robert John 'Mutt'
    Lange, Rick Savage, and Joe Elliot.
Bludgeon Riffola Music, 1987/Zomba Music, 1987.
Best-selling record by Def Leppard, from *Hysteria* (Mercury, 87).

Arthur's Theme (The Best That You Can Do)
Words by Carole Bayer Sager, words and music by Christopher Cross
    and Peter Allen, music by Burt Bacharach.
WB Music, 1981/Warner-Tamerlane Music, 1981/Polygram
    International, 1981/Woolnough Music Inc., 1981/Begonia Melodies,
    Inc., 1981/Unichappell Music Inc., 1981.
Best-selling record by Christopher Cross. Introduced in the film &
    soundtrack album (Warner Bros., 81) *Arthur* (81). Won an Academy
    Award, and Best Song, 1981. Nominated for Grammy Awards,
    Record of the year, 1981, and Song of the Year, 1981.

As Days Go By
Words and music by Jesse Fredericke and Bennett Salvay.
Introduced by Jesse Fredericke as the theme for the 1989 television
    show *Family Matters*.

As Long as I'm Rockin' with You
Words and music by Bruce Channel and Kieran Kane.
Old Friends Music, 1981/Cross Keys Publishing Co., Inc., 1981.
Best-selling record by John Conlee (MCA, 84).

As Long as We Got Each Other
Words and music by John Bettis, music by Steve Dorff.
WB Music, 1985.

21

Introduced by B. J. Thomas on the television series *Growing Pains* (85).
Revived in by Steve Do rff and Friends, Thomas and Dusty
Springfield (Reprise). It was also recorded by Louis Mandrell and
Eric Carmen.

As Tears Go By (English)
Words and music by Mick Jagger, Keith Richards, and Andrew Loog
Oldham.
Essex Music, Inc., 1964/Westminster Music, Ltd., 1964.
Revived in 1987 by Marianne Faithfull on her album *Strange Weather*
(EMI, 87); the same artist had used the song to launch her career in
1964, when Mick Jagger wrote it for her.

As We Live and Breathe
Words and music by Steve Forbert.
Geffen Music, 1988/Rolling Tide Music, 1988.
Introduced by Steve Forbert on *Streets of This Town* (Geffen, 88).

Ashes to Ashes (English)
Words and music by David Bowie.
Fleur Music, 1980/Jones Music Co., 1980.
Introduced by David Bowie on *Scary Monsters* (RCA, 80).

At This Moment
Words and music by Billy Vera.
WB Music, 1981/Vera Cruz Music Co., 1981.
Performed by Billy & The Beaters in a 1985 two-part episode of the
television series *Family Ties* in which the character of Alex, played
by Michael J. Fox, meets his true love, played by Tracy Pollan. The
song was revived the following season whenever Alex thought of the
girl after their break-up. It was released as a single on Rhino Records
in 1986. A version recorded live in Los Angeles in 1981 was on the
album *The Best of Billy Vera & The Beaters* (Rhino); it also made the
1981 charts as a single released by the now defunct Japanese label
Alta.

Athena (English)
Words and music by Pete Townshend.
Towser Tunes Inc., 1982.
Best-selling record by The Who from *It's Hard* (Warner Brothers, 82).

Atlanta Blue
Words and music by Don Reid.
Statler Brothers Music, 1984.
Best-selling record by The Statler Brothers from *Atlanta Blue* (Mercury,
84).

Atlantic City
Words and music by Bruce Springsteen.

Bruce Springsteen Publishing, 1982.
Introduced by Bruce Springsteen in *Nebraska* (Columbia, 82).

Atomic Dog
Words and music by George Clinton, Garry Shider, and David Spradley.
Bridgeport Music Inc., 1982.
Best-selling record by George Clinton from *Computer Games* (Capitol,
    83).

Attack Me with Your Love
Words and music by Larry Blackmon and Kevin Kendricks.
All Seeing Eye Music, 1985/Larry Junior Music, 1985/King Kendrick
    Publishing, 1985.
Best-selling record by Cameo from the album *Single Life* (Polygram,
    85).

The Authority Song
Words and music by John Cougar Mellencamp.
Full Keel Music, 1983.
Best-selling record by John Cougar Mellencamp from *Uh-Huh* (Riva,
    84).

Automatic
Words and music by Brock Walsh and Mark Goldenberg.
Music of the World, 1983/MCA, Inc., 1983.
Best-selling record by The Pointer Sisters from *Break Out* (Planet, 84).

Axel F
Music by Harold Faltermeyer.
Famous Music Corp., 1985.
Introduced in the film and soundtrack album *Beverly Hills Cop* (85).
    Best-selling record by Harold Faltermeyer (MCA, 85).

B

B-Side of Life
Words and music by Pat MacDonald.
Mambadaddi, 1989/I.R.S. Music, 1989.
Introduced by Timbuk 3 on *Edge of Allegiance* (IRS, 89).

Babooshka (English)
Words and music by Kate Bush.
Kate Bush Music, Ltd., London, England, 1980/EMI Music Publishing, 1980.
Introduced by by Kate Bush in *Never Forever* (EMI, 80).

Baby Blue
Words and music by Aaron Barker.
Muy Bueno Music, 1988/Bill Butler Music, 1988.
Best-selling record by George Strait from *If You Ain't Lovin' You Ain't Livin'* (MCA, 88).

Baby Boom Baby
Words and music by James Taylor.
Country Road Music Inc., 1988.
Introduced by James Taylor on *Never Die Young* (CBS, 88).

Baby Bye Bye
Words and music by Gary Morris and James Brantley.
WB Music, 1984/Gary Morris Music, 1984.
Best-selling record by Gary Morris from the album *Anything Goes* (Warner Bros., 85).

Baby Can I Hold You
Words and music by Tracy Chapman.
Purple Rabbit Music, 1987.
Introduced by Tracy Chapman on her album *Tracy Chapman* (Elektra, 88).

Baby, Come to Me (English)
Words and music by Rod Temperton.

Almo Music Corp., 1981.
Best-selling record by Patti Austin and James Ingram from *Every Home Should Have One* (Qwest, 82).

Baby Come to Me
Words and music by Narada Michael Walden and Jeffrey Cohen.
Gratitude Sky Music, 1989/Virgin Music, 1989/Penzafire Music, 1989/WB Music.
Best-selling record by Regina Belle from *Stay with Me* (Columbia, 89).

Baby Don't Forget My Number (German-English)
English words and music by Frank Farian, Franz Reuter, Brad Howell, and Roger Dalton.
FMP Songs, Berlin, Germany, 1988/Ed. Intro, Berlin, Germany, 1988/ MCA Music, 1988.
Best-selling record by Milli Vanilli from *Girl, You Know It's True* (Arista, 89).

Baby Fall Down
Words and music by T-Bone Burnette.
Bug Music, 1983.
Introduced by T-Bone Burnette on *Proof Through the Night* (Warner Brothers, 83).

Baby Grand
Words and music by Billy Joel.
Joelsongs, 1986.
Introduced by Billy Joel on the album *The Bridge* (Columbia, 86). This song is a tribute to singer Ray Charles, who performed it in a duet with Joel.

(You're So Square) Baby, I Don't Care
Words and music by Jerry Leiber and Mike Stoller.
Budson Music, 1957.
Best-selling record by Joni Mitchell from *Wild Things Run Fast* (Geffen, 82).

Baby I Lied
Words and music by Deborah Allen, Rory Bourke, and Rafe Van Hoy.
Posey Publishing, 1982/Unichappell Music Inc., 1982/Van Hoy Music, 1982.
Best-selling record by Deborah Allen from *Cheat the Night* (RCA, 83). Nominated for a Grammy Award, Country Song of the Year, 1983.

Baby I Love Your Way (English)
Words and music by Peter Frampton.
Almo Music Corp., 1975/Nuages Artists Music Ltd.
Revived in 1988 by *Will to Power* (Epic, 88) as part of a medley with the southern rock epic 'Free Bird.'

Baby I'm Hooked (Right into Your Love)
Words and music by Cedric Martin and Van Ross Redding.
Carollon Music Co., 1983/Van Ross Redding Music, 1983.
Best-selling record by Con Funk Shun from *Fever* (Mercury, 83).

Baby I'm Yours
Words and music by Steve Wariner and Guy Clark.
Steve Wariner, 1988/EMI-April Music, 1988/GSC Music, 1988.
Best-selling record by Steve Wariner from *I Should Be with You* (MCA, 88).

Baby, It's the Little Things, also known as **Little Things**
Words and music by Bill Barber.
Reynsong Music, 1985.
Best-selling record by The Oak Ridge Boys from the album *Step on Out* (MCA, 85).

Baby Jane
Words and music by Rod Stewart and Jay Davis.
Rod Stewart, 1983/Anteater Music, 1983.
Best-selling record by Rod Stewart from *Body Wishes* (Warner Brothers, 83).

Baby Love
Words and music by Steve Bray, Regina Richards, and Mary Kessler.
Polygram International, 1985/Regina Richards, 1985/Deutsch/Berardi Music Corp., 1985/Maz Appeal, 1985.
Best-selling record by Regina from the album *Curiosity* (Atlantic, 86). Co-author Bray, who has written many of Madonna's hits, was a drummer in Regina's previous band, Regina and the Red Hots. Regina plans to revert to her full name by the next album - a trend spearheaded by John Cougar Mellencamp and Elvis Costello (born Declan McManus).

Baby Plays Around (English)
Words and music by Declan Macmanus and Cait O'Riordan.
Plangent Visions Music, Inc., London, England, 1988, 1989.
Introduced by Elvis Costello on *Spike* (Warner Bros., 89).

Baby's Got a Hold on Me
Words and music by Josh Leo, Jeff Hanna, and Bob Carpenter.
Warner-Chappell Music, 1986/Mopage, 1986/Warner-Refuge Music Inc., 1986/Moolagenous, 1986.
Best-selling record by the Nitty Gritty Dirt Band, from their album *Hold On* (Warner Bros., 86).

Baby's Got a New Baby
Words and music by Fred Knobloch and Dan Tyler.
A Little More Music Inc., 1987/Sharp Circle, 1987/EMI Music

Publishing, 1987/BMG Songs Inc.
Best-selling record by Schuyler, Knobloch & Overstreet, from their
album *SKO* (MTM, 87).

Baby's Got Her Blue Jeans On
Words and music by Bob McDill.
Hall-Clement Publications, 1984.
Best-selling record by Mel McDaniel from the album *Let It Roll*
(Capitol, 85). Nominated for a Grammy Award, Country Song of the
Year, 1985.

Baby's Gotten Good at Goodbye
Words and music by Tony Martin and Troy Martin.
Co-Heart Music, 1989/Muy Bueno Music, 1989.
Best-selling record by George Strait from *Beyond the Blue Neon* (MCA,
89).

Back and Forth
Words and music by Kevin Kendricks, Tomi Jenkins, Nathan Leftenant,
and Larry Blackmon.
All Seeing Eye Music, 1986/Polygram Music Publishing Inc., 1986/
Better Days Music, 1986/Polygram Songs, 1986.
Best-selling record by Cameo, from the album *Word Up* (Atlanta
Artists, 86).

Back in Baby's Arms
Words and music by Bob Montgomery.
Talmont Music Co., 1987.
Introduced by Emmylou Harris on the soundtrack of the 1987 film
Planes, Trains, and Automobiles; released on the soundtrack album
(Hughes/MCA, 87).

Back in Black (English)
Words and music by Angus Young, Malcolm Young, and Brian
Johnson.
E. B. Marks Music Corp., 1980.
Best-selling record by AC/DC from *Back in Black* (Atlantic, 81).

Back in Buffalo
Words and music by Leo Kottke.
Round Wound Sound, 1989/Bug Music.
Introduced by Leo Kottke on *My Father's Face* (Private Music, 89), this
is a rare vocal song from the master guitarist.

Back in Stride
Words and music by Frankie Beverly.
Amazement Music, 1985.
Best-selling record by Maze featuring Frankie Beverly from the album
Can't Stop the Love (Capitol, 85).

Back in the High Life Again (American-English)
Words by Will Jennings, music by Steve Winwood.
F.S. Ltd., England, 1986/Willin' David, 1986/Blue Sky Rider Songs,
   1986.
Best-selling record by Steve Winwood, from his album *Back in the High
   Life Again* (Island, 86). Nominated for a Grammy Award, Record of
   the Year, 1987.

The Back Nine
Words and music by Loudon Wainwright.
Snowden Music, 1986.
Introduced by Loudon Wainwright, from the album *More Love Songs,*
   (Rounder, 87); marks a return to form the noted, autobiographically
   inclined folk balladeer, in which he likens his life to a game of golf.

Back on the Chain Gang (English)
Words and music by Chrissie Hynde.
MCA Music, 1982.
Best-selling record by The Pretenders from *Learning to Crawl* (Sire,
   83).

Back to Life (English)
Words and music by Romeo.
Law Music, England, 1989/Virgin Music, 1989/Virgin Songs, 1989/WB
   Music, 1989.
Best-selling record by Soul II Soul from *Keep on Movin'* (Virgin, 89).
   Featuring Caron Wheeler.

Back to Paradise (American-Canadian)
Words and music by Neil Geraldo, Jim Vallance, and Bryan Adams.
Calypso Toonz, 1987/Irving Music Inc., 1987/Big Tooth Music Corp.,
   1987/Chrysalis Music Group, 1987/TCF, 1987.
Best-selling record by 38 Special, from the movie *Revenge of the Nerds*
   (87); also released on the soundtrack album (A & M, 87).

Back Where You Belong (Canadian)
Words and music by Gary O'Connor.
EMI-April Music, 1983.
Best-selling record by 38 Special from *Tour De Force* (A & M, 84).

Backstrokin'
Words and music by Bill Curtis and John Flippin.
Clita Music, 1980.
Best-selling record by Fatback from *Hot Box* (Spring, 80).

Bad
Words and music by Michael Jackson.
Mijac Music, 1987/Warner-Tamerlane Music.
Best-selling record by Michael Jackson, from his album of the same title

(Epic, 87); this was a long-awaited follow-up to the record-breaking success of Jackson's *Thriller*.

Bad Boy
Words and music by Larry Dermer, Joe Galdo, and Rafael Vigil.
Foreign Imported, 1985.
Best-selling record by Miami Sound Machine in 1986 from the album *Primitive Love* (Epic, 85).

Bad Influence
Words and music by Robert Cray and Mike Vannice.
Calhoun Street, 1983.
Introduced by Eric Clapton on his album *August* (Duck, 86). Noted blues singer-guitarist Clapton significantly aided the career of author Cray, also a blues artist, when he took up this song.

Bad Medicine
Words and music by Jon Bon Jovi, Richie Sambora, and Desmond Child.
Bon Jovi Publishing, 1988/New Jersey Underground, 1988/Polygram Music Publishing Inc., 1988/Desmobile Music Inc., 1988/EMI-April Music, 1988.
Best-selling record by Bon Jovi, from *New Jersey* (Mercury, 88).

Bad News from Home
Words and music by Randy Newman.
Twice As Nice Music, 1988.
Introduced by Randy Newman on *Land of Dreams* (Reprise, 88).

Ballad for D
Words and music by Peabo Bryson, Roberta Flack, and Ira Williams.
Peabo Bryson Enterprises, Inc., 1981/WB Music, 1981/Very Every Music, Inc., 1981/Budson Music, 1981.
Introduced by Peabo Bryson in the film *Bustin Loose*, 1982. Dedicated to Donny Hathaway.

Ballad of Gary Hart
Words and music by Tom Paxton.
Accabonac, 1988.
Introduced by Tom Paxton on *Politics* (Flying Fish, 88). The master satirist here takes aim at one of the more notorious candidates in the Democratic presidential primaries.

The Ballad of Jim and Tammy
Words by Tammy Faye Bakker, music by Tom T. Hall.
Unichappell Music Inc., 1987.
Introduced by Tammy Faye Bakker (Sutra, 87). By re-using the music to 'Harper Valley PTA' (see *Popular Music, 1920-1979*), Bakker

offered her side of the scandal that ousted herself and her husband from their evangelical empire.

Ballerina Girl
Words and music by Lionel Richie, Jr.
Brockman Enterprises Inc., 1986.
Best-selling record by Lionel Richie, from his album *Dancing on the Ceiling* (Motown, 86).

Balloon Man (English)
Words and music by Robyn Hitchcock.
Two Crabs, England, 1987.
Introduced by Robyn Hitchcock on *Box of Frogs* (A & M, 88).
    Although a cult figure in England for his droll lyrics, Hitchcock has yet to strike a chord with a large American audience.

The Banana Boat Song, see Day-O.

Band of the Hand (Hell Time Man!)
Words and music by Bob Dylan.
Special Rider Music, 1986.
Introduced by Bob Dylan in the film *Band of the Hand* (86) and performed on the soundtrack album (MCA, 86).

Bar Room Buddies
Words and music by Snuff Garrett, Clifton Crofford, Steve Dorff, and Milton Brown.
Peso Music, 1980/Bar Cee Music, 1980/Warner-Tamerlane Music, 1980.
Best-selling record by Clint Eastwood with Merle Haggard (Elektra, 80).
    Introduced in the film *Honky Tonk Man* (80).

Batdance (From *Batman*)
Words and music by Prince (pseudonym for Prince Rogers Nelson).
Controversy Music, 1989.
Best-selling record by Prince from the film and soundtrack album *Batman* (Warner Bros., 89).

Battle Lines
Words by Hal Hackaday, music by Richard Kapp.
Introduced by Beth Fowler in the 1987 musical *Teddy and Alice*. All of the songs in this musical were adapted from marches by John Philip Sousa.

Battleship Chains
Words and music by Terry Anderson.
Tomata du Plenti, 1986.
Best-selling record by The Georgia Satellites, from their self-titled album (Elektra, 86). The author is a member of NRBQ, often fondly referred to as 'America's bar band.'

Bayou Boys
Words and music by Frank Meyers, Troy Seals, and Eddy Raven.
Morganactive Music, 1989/You and I Music, 1989/WB Music, 1989/
Two-Sons Music, 1989/Ravensong Music, 1989.
Best-selling record by Eddy Raven from *Temporary Sanity* (Universal,
89).

Be Good to Yourself
Words and music by Steve Perry, Jonathan Cain, and Neal Schon.
Street Talk Tunes, 1986/Rock Dog Music, 1986/Frisco Kid Music, 1986.
Best-selling record by Journey from the album *Raised on Radio*
(Columbia, 86).

Be Italian
Words and music by Maury Yeston.
Yeston Music, Ltd., 1975.
Introduced by Kathi Moss in *Nine* (Musical, 82).

Be Near Me (English)
Words and music by Martin Fry and Mark White.
10 Music Ltd., England, 1985/Neutron Music, England, 1985/EMI-
Virgin, 1985.
Best-selling record by ABC from the album *How to Be a Billionaire*
(Polygram, 85).

Be One
Words and music by Bill Lee.
New Version Music, 1987.
Introduced by Phyllis Hyman in the film and on the soundtrack album
School Daze (EMI-Manhattan, 88).

Be Still My Beating Heart (English)
Words and music by Sting (pseudonym for Gordon Sumner).
Magnetic Music Publishing Co., 1987/Reggatta Music, Ltd., 1987/Illegal
Songs, Inc., 1987.
Best-selling record in 1988 by Sting, from *Nothing Like the Sun* (A &
M, 87). Nominated for a Grammy Award, Song of the Year, 1988.

Be There
Words and music by Allee Willis and Franne Golde.
Ensign Music, 1987/Off Backstreet Music, 1987/Franne Gee, 1987/
Rightsong Music, 1987.
Best-selling record by The Pointer Sisters, from the film and soundtrack
album *Beverly Hills Cop II* (MCA, 87).

Be Your Man
Words and music by Jesse Johnson.
Almo Music Corp., 1985/Crazy People Music/Almo Music Corp., 1985.

Best-selling record by Jesse Johnson's Revue from the album *Jesse Johnson's Revue* (A & M, 85).

The Beach Boys Medley
Words and music by Brian Wilson.
Best-selling record by The Beach Boys (Capitol, 81). Consists of 'Good Vibrations,' 'Help Me, Rhonda,' 'I Get Around,' 'Shut Down,' 'Surfin' Safari,' 'Barbara Ann,' 'Surfin' USA,' and 'Fun Fun Fun.'

Beacon Street
Words and music by Nanci Griffith.
Wing & Wheel Music, 1987.
Introduced by Nanci Griffith, from the album *Lone Star State of Mind* (MCA '87).

The Beast in Me
Words and music by Eric Kaz and Marvin Morrow.
EMI-April Music, 1985/Kaz Music Co., 1985.
Introduced by The Pointer Sisters in the film *Heavenly Bodies* (85).

Beast of Burden (English)
Words and music by Mick Jagger and Keith Richards.
Colgems-EMI Music, 1978.
Revived by Bette Midler from *No Frills* (Atlantic, 84).

The Beat(en) Generation (English)
Words and music by Matt Johnson.
ID Music Ltd., 1989/Virgin Songs, 1989.
Introduced by The The from *Mind Bomb* (Epic, 89). This song was inspired by a painting by Andrew Johnson, the author's late brother.

Beat It
Words and music by Michael Jackson.
Mijac Music, 1982/Warner-Tamerlane Music, 1982.
Best-selling record by Michael Jackson from *Thriller* (Epic, 83). Won a Grammy Award, and Record of the Year, 1983. Nominated for a Grammy Award, Song of the Year, 1983.

Beat of a Heart
Words and music by Zack Smith, Patty Smyth, and Keith Mack.
EMI-Blackwood Music Inc., 1984/Keishmack Music.
Best-selling record by Scandal featuring Patty Smyth in 1985 from the album *Warrior* (Columbia, 84).

The Beat of Black Wings
Words and music by Joni Mitchell.
Crazy Crow Music, 1988.
Introduced by Joni Mitchell on *Chalk Mark in a Rainstorm* (Geffen, 88).

The Beatles' Movie Medley
Words and music by John Lennon and Paul McCartney.
Performed by The Beatles (Capitol, 82).

Beat's So Lonely
Words and music by Charlie Sexton and Keith Forsey.
Unicity Music, Inc., 1985/Swindle Music, 1985/Sextunes Music, 1985.
Best-selling record by Charlie Sexton from the album *Pictures for Pleasure* (MCA, 86).

Beatstreet
Words and music by Melvin Glover and Reggie Griffin.
Hargreen Music, 1984/Sugar Hill Music Publishing, Ltd., 1984.
Best-selling record by Grand Master Flash & The Furious Five with Mr. Ness and Cowboy (Sugarhill, 84). Introduced in the film and soundtrack album *Beatstreet* (84).

Beaujolais
Words and music by Kurt Neumann and Sammy Llanas.
Lla-Mann, 1989.
Introduced by The BoDeans on *Home* (Reprise, 89).

Beautiful
Words and music by Stephen Sondheim.
WB Music, 1981.
Introduced by Barbara Byrne and Mandy Patinkin in *Sunday in the Park with George* (83).

Beautiful Music
Words by William Dumaresq, music by Galt MacDermott.
Introduced by Debra Byrd & Co. in *The Human Comedy* (83).

Beautiful You
Best-selling record by The Oak Ridge Boys (MCA, 81).

Because the Night
Words and music by Patti Smith and Bruce Springsteen.
Ramrod Music, 1978/Bruce Springsteen Publishing, 1978.
Revived in 1986 by Bruce Springsteen on the album *Bruce Springsteen & The E Street Band Live, 1975-1985* (Columbia, 86). Also featured on *Cover Me* (Rhino, 86) where it is sung by Patti Smith, who had the original hit.

Beds Are Burning (Australian)
Words and music by Midnight Oil.
Sprint, 1987/Warner-Tamerlane Music, 1987.
Best-selling record in 1988 by Midnight Oil, from the album *Diesel and Dust* (Columbia, 87).

Beep a Freak
Words and music by Rudolph Taylor, Lonnie Simmons, and Charles Wilson.
Temp Co., 1985.
Best-selling record by The Gap Band from the album *Gap Band VI* (RCA, 85).

Before You Sing
Words and music by Jack Hardy.
Jack Hardy Music, 1987.
Introduced by The Roches on *Fast Folk Sixth Anniversary Issue* (Fast Folk, 89), this song was adapted from a theatrical work by Hardy.

Behind the Wall
Words and music by Tracy Chapman.
EMI-April Music, 1983/Purple Rabbit Music, 1983.
Introduced by Tracy Chapman, on *Tracy Chapman* (Elektra, 88). The song details a scene of urban terror.

Behind the Wall of Sleep
Words and music by Pat DiNizio.
Famous Monsters Music, 1986/La Rana, 1986.
Introduced by the Smithereens on the album *Especially for You* (Enigma, 86).

Being with You
Words and music by William Robinson.
Bertam Music Co., 1981.
Best-selling record by Smokey Robinson from *Being with You* (Tamla, 81).

Believe It or Not, see The Theme from *The Greatest American Hero*.

Beneath Still Waters
Words and music by Dallas Frazier.
Acuff-Rose Publications Inc., 1967.
Best-selling record by Emmylou Harris from *Blue Kentucky Girl* (Warner Brothers, 80).

The Best
Words and music by Mike Chapman and Holly Knight.
Mike Chapman Publishing Enterprises, 1989/Knighty Knight, 1989/All Nations Music, 1989.
Best-selling record by Tina Turner from *Foreign Affairs* (Capitol, 89).

The Best Man in the World
Words and music by John Barry, Ann Wilson, Sue Ennis, and Nancy Wilson.

Famous Music Corp., 1986/Ensign Music, 1986.
Introduced by Ann Wilson in the film *The Golden Child* (86).

The Best of Me
Words and music by David Foster, Jeremy Lubbock, and Richard Mars.
Air Bear, 1983/Nero Publishing, 1983/Hollysongs, 1983.
Introduced by David Foster and Olivia Newton-John on the album
    David Foster (Atlantic, 86).

The Best of Times
Words and music by Dennis DeYoung.
Almo Music Corp., 1981/Stygian Songs, 1981.
Best-selling record by Styx from *Paradise Theater* (A & M, 81).

The Best of Times
Words and music by Jerry Herman.
Jerryco Music Co., 1983.
Introduced by George Hearn, Elizabeth Parrish & Cast in *La Cage Au
    Folles* (83).

Best of Times
Words and music by Peter Cetera and Patrick Leonard.
Fall Line Orange Music, 1988/Johnny Yuma, 1988.
Best-selling record by Peter Cetera from *One More Story* (Full Moon,
    88). The former lead singer of Chicago has kept pace with the success
    of his old group.

Bette Davis Eyes
Words and music by Donna Weiss and Jackie DeShannon.
Plain & Simple Music Corp., 1975/Donna Music Publishing Co., 1975.
Best-selling record by Kim Carnes from *Mistaken Identity* (EMI-
    America, 1981).

Better Be Home Soon (New Zealand)
Words and music by Neil Finn.
Roundhead, 1988.
Best-selling record by Crowded House, from *Temple of Low Men*
    (Capitol, 88).

Better Love Next Time
Words and music by Steve Pippin, Larry Keith, and Johnny Slate.
Warner House of Music, 1980.
Best-selling record by Dr. Hook from *Sometimes You Win* (Capitol, 79).

A Better Man
Words and music by Clint Black and Hayden Nicholas.
Howlin' Hits Music, 1988.
Best-selling record by Clint Black from *Killin' Time* (RCA, 89). Black
    recorded the number one and two top country songs of 1989; this was

number one. Nominated for a Grammy Award, Country Song of the Year, 1989.

Between Blue Eyes and Jeans
Words and music by Kenneth McDuffie.
Hall-Clement Publications, 1984.
Best-selling record by Conway Twitty from the album *Don't Call Him a Cowboy* (Warner Bros., 85).

Between the Sheets
Words and music by Christopher Jasper, Ernest Isley, Marvin Isley, Ronald Isley, Rudolph Isley, and O'Kelly Isley.
EMI-April Music, 1983/Bovina Music, Inc., 1983.
Best-selling record by The Isley Brothers from *Between the Sheets* (T-Neck, 83).

Between Trains
Words and music by Robbie Robertson.
Medicine Hat Music, 1983.
Introduced by Robbie Robertson in the film and soundtrack album *The King of Comedy* (83).

Big City
Words and music by Dean Holloway and Merle Haggard.
Shade Tree Music Inc., 1981.
Best-selling record by Merle Haggard from *Big City* (Epic, 82).

Big Country
Words and music by Bruce Gowdy, Billy Sherwood, and Peter Aykroyd.
Making Betts Music, 1988/Swirling Vortex, 1988/Music Corp. of America, 1988/MCA Music, 1988/Forest Music, 1988.
Introduced by Joe Walsh in the film and on the soundtrack album *The Great Outdoors* (Atlantic, 88).

Big Dreams in a Small Town
Words and music by Dave Robbins, Vern Stephenson, and Tim Dubois.
WB Music, 1988/Warner-Tamerlane Music, 1988/Uncle Beave Music, 1988/Bunch of Guys Music, 1988.
Best-selling record in 1989 by Restless Heart from *Big Dreams in a Small Town* (RCA, 88).

Big Fun
Words and music by Ronald Bell, Curtis Williams, Clifford Adams, James Taylor, Michael Ray, Charles Smith, George Brown, Robert Mickens, Eumir Deodato, and Robert Bell.
Delightful Music Ltd., 1982/Double F Music, 1982/WB Music.
Best-selling record by Kool & The Gang from *As One* (De-Lite, 82).

37

Big Log (English)
Words and music by Robert Plant, Robbie Blunt, and Jezz Woodruffe.
EMI-April Music, 1982.
Best-selling record by Robert Plant from *The Principle of Moments* (Es
Paranza, 83).

Big Love
Words and music by Lindsay Buckingham.
Now Sounds Music, 1987.
Best-selling record by Fleetwood Mac, from the album *Tango in the
Night* (Warner Bros., 87). Soon after album's release, Buckingham
left the band to resume his solo career.

Big Man on Mulberry Street
Words and music by Billy Joel.
Joelsongs, 1986.
Introduced by Billy Joel on the album *The Bridge* (Columbia, 86). The
text of the song was the basis for an episode of the popular television
series *Moonlighting.*

Big Ole Brew
Words and music by Russell Smith.
Tintagel Music, Inc., 1980/Bad Ju Ju Music, 1980.
Best-selling record by Mel McDaniel (Capitol, 82).

The Big Sky (English)
Words and music by Kate Bush.
Screen Gems-EMI Music Inc., 1985.
Introduced by Kate Bush on the album *Hounds of Love* (EMI-America,
85).

Big Time (English)
Words and music by Peter Gabriel.
Cliofine, 1986/Hidden Pun, 1986.
Best-selling record by Peter Gabriel, from the album *So* (Geffen, 86).
The artist and album were voted best of the year in many annual
polls, including that in *Rolling Stone* magazine.

Big Train from Memphis
Words and music by John Fogerty.
Wenaha Music Co., 1984.
Recorded by Class of '55 (American, 86), a group consisting of Rick
Nelson, Dave Edmunds, Johnny Cash, Jerry Lee Lewis, Carl Perkins,
and Roy Orbison. Introduced by John Fogerty on the album
Centerfield (Warner Bros., 85).

Big Wheels in the Moonlight
Words and music by Bob McDill and Dan Seals.
Polygram International, 1988/Pink Pig Music, 1988/Ranger Bob Music,

1988.
Best-selling record in 1989 by Dan Seals from *Rage On* (Capitol, 88).

Bigger Stones
Words and music by Paul Kamanski.
Paul Kamanski Music, 1985.
Best-selling record by The Beat Farmers from the album *Tales of the New West* (Rhino, 85).

(The) Biggest Part of Me
Words and music by David Pack.
Rubicon Music, 1980.
Best-selling record by Ambrosia from *One-Eighty* (Warner Brothers, 80).

Biko (English)
Words and music by Peter Gabriel.
Hidden Pun, 1983.
Revived in 1987 by Joan Baez on her album *Recently* (Gold Castle). The noted folksinger and activist of the 1960's chose this song about the South African black leader murdered in 1977 to initiate her comeback. Composer Gabriel also re-released his own rendition (Geffen, 87), proceeds from which went to the International Defense and Aid Fund for South Africa and to the Africa Fund. Biko was also the subject of the film *Cry Freedom,* released in 1987.

Billie Jean
Words and music by Michael Jackson.
Mijac Music, 1982/Warner-Tamerlane Music, 1982.
Best-selling record by Michael Jackson from *Thriller* (Epic, 83). Won a Grammy Award, and Rhythm 'n' Blues Song of the Year, 1983. Nominated for a Grammy Award, Song of the Year, 1983.

The Birds
Words by William Dumaresq, music by Galt MacDermott.
Introduced by Rex Smith and Leta Galloway in *The Human Comedy* (83).

Birth, School, Work, Death (English)
Words and music by Godfathers.
Introduced by The Godfathers on the album *Birth, School, Work, Death* (Epic, 88), this cut became a New Wave anthem of disaffection.

Birthday Suit
Words and music by Rhett Lawrence and Dean Pitchford.
TSP Music, Inc., 1989/Triple Star Music, 1989.
Best-selling record by Johnny Kemp from the film and soundtrack album *Sing* (Columbia, 89).

Bit by Bit (Theme from *Fletch*)
Words by Frannie Golde, music by Harold Faltermeyer.
MCA, Inc., 1985/Franne Golde Music Inc., 1985/Rightsong Music,
  1985/Kilauea Music, 1985.
Best-selling record by Stephanie Mills (MCA, 85). Introduced in the
  film and soundtrack album *Fletch* (MCA, 85).

Bitter Fruit
Words and music by Steve Van Zandt.
Little Steven Music, 1987/Blue Midnight Music.
Introduced by Little Steven on his album *Freedom--No Compromise*
  (Manhattan, 87), with guest vocalist Ruben Blades. This song,
  dedicated to the plight of migrant workers, highlighted the album of
  neo-protest music by the former guitarist in Bruce Springsteen's E
  Street Band.

Black and Blue
Words and music by Eddie Van Halen, Alex Van Halen, Sammy Hagar,
  and Michael Anthony.
Yessup Music Co., 1988.
Best-selling record by Van Halen, from *OU812* (Warner Bros., 88).

Black Limousine (English)
Words and music by Mick Jagger, Keith Richards, and Ron Wood.
Colgems-EMI Music, 1981/Screen Gems-EMI Music Inc., 1981.
Introduced by The Rolling Stones on *Tattoo You* (Rolling Stones, 81).

Black Sheep
Words and music by Daniel Darst and Robert Altman.
Al Gallico Music Corp., 1983/Algee Music Corp., 1983/John Anderson
  Music Co. Inc., 1983.
Best-selling record by John Anderson from *All the People are Talkin'*
  (Warner Brothers, 83).

Blame It on the Rain
Words and music by Diane Warren.
Realsongs, 1989.
Best-selling record by Milli Vanilli from *Girl, You Know It's True*
  (Arista, 89).

Blessed Are the Believers
Words and music by Charlie Black, Rory Bourke, and Sandy Pinkard.
Chappell & Co., Inc., 1981/Unichappell Music Inc., 1981/Rhythm Ranch
  Music, 1981.
Best-selling record by Anne Murray from *Where Do You Go When You
  Dream* (Capitol, 81).

Blizzard of Lies
Words and music by David Frishberg and Samantha Frishberg.

Swiftwater Music, 1982.
Introduced by David Frishberg in *The David Frishberg Songbook, Volume Two* (Omnisound, 83).

Blood and Fire
Words and music by Amy Ray.
Godhap Music, 1988/Virgin Songs, 1988.
Introduced by Indigo Girls on *Indigo Girls* (Epic, 89). The potent folk/
rock group from Georgia had help on vocals from R.E.M.'s Michael
Stipe on this song.

Blood and Roses
Words and music by Pat DiNizio.
Famous Monsters Music, 1986/La Rana, 1986.
Introduced by the Smithereens on the album *Especially for You*
(Enigma, 86). Featured in the film *Dangerously Close* (86).

Bloody Mary (Australian)
Words by Steve Kilbey, music by The Church.
Funzalo Music, 1987/Bug Music, 1987/MCA Music, 1987.
Introduced by The Church on *Starfish* (Arista, 88).

Blue Eyes (English)
Words by Gary Osborne, music by Elton John.
Intersong, USA Inc., 1982.
Best-selling record by Elton John from *Jump Up* (Geffen, 82).

Blue Hotel
Words and music by Chris Isaak.
Chris Isaak Music Publishing, 1987.
Introduced by Chris Isaak on his album, also called *Chris Isaak* (Warner
Bros., 87). This was one of six Isaak cuts showcased on the television
series *Private Eye;* the rockabilly sound of his material suited the
atmosphere of this detective show set in Los Angeles in the 1950's.

Blue Jean (English)
Words and music by David Bowie.
Jones Music Co., 1984.
Best-selling record by David Bowie from *Tonight* (EMI-America, 84).

Blue Moon with Heartache
Words and music by Rosanne Cash.
Atlantic Music Corp., 1982/Hotwire Music, 1982.
Best-selling record by Rosanne Cash from *Seven Year Ache* (Columbia,
82).

Blue Rider
Words and music by Chris Williamson.

Bird Ankles Music, 1982.
Introduced by Chris Williamson on *Blue Rider* (Olivia, 82).

Blue Spanish Sky
Words and music by Chris Isaak.
Chris Isaak Music Publishing, 1989.
Introduced by Chris Isaak on *Heart-Shaped World* (Reprise, 89). In the
    year of Roy Orbison's passing, Isaak emerged as his heir apparent.

Blue Velvet
Words and music by Bernie Wayne and Lee Morris.
Vogue Music, 1951.
Revived in 1986 in the film *Blue Velvet*. Bobby Vinton's best-selling
    1963 rendition of the song was a favorite of the film's director.

The Blues
Words and music by Randy Newman.
Six Pictures Music, 1983.
Best-selling record by Randy Newman and Paul Simon from *Trouble in
    Paradise* (Warner Brothers, 83).

Blues for the River
Words and music by Rod MacDonald.
Blue Flute Music, 1988.
Introduced by Rod MacDonald on *White Buffalo* (Mountain Railroad,
    88).

Blues Is King
Words and music by Marshall Crenshaw.
Colgems-EMI Music, 1985/House of Greed Music, 1985.
Introduced by Marshall Crenshaw on the album *Downtown* (Warner
    Bros., 85).

Blues Power (English)
Words and music by Eric Clapton and Leon Russell.
Skyhill Publishing Co., Inc., 1980.
Best-selling record by Eric Clapton from *Blues Power* (RSO, 80).

Bluest Eyes in Texas
Words and music by Dave Robbins, Vern Stephenson, and Tim DuBois.
WB Music, 1987/Uncle Beave Music, 1987/Warner-Tamerlane Music,
    1987/Bunch of Guys, 1987/Tim DuBois Music, 1987.
Best-selling record in 1988 by Restless Heart, from *Wheels* (RCA, 87).

Bobbie Sue
Words and music by Wood Newton, Daniel Tyler, and Adele Tyler.
Warner House of Music, 1981/WB Gold Music Corp., 1981/Chappell &
    Co., Inc., 1981.

Best-selling record by The Oak Ridge Boys from *Bobbie Sue* (MCA, 82).

Bobby Jean
Words and music by Bruce Springsteen.
Bruce Springsteen Publishing, 1984.
Introduced by Bruce Springsteen on *Born in the U.S.A.* (Columbia, 84).

Body Language (English)
Words and music by Freddie Mercury.
Queen Music Ltd., 1982.
Best-selling record by Queen from *Hot Space* (Elektra, 82).

Body Talk
Words and music by Stephen Pearcy, Warren DeMartini, and Juan Croucier.
Ratt Music, 1986/Time Coast Music, 1986/Rightsong Music, 1986.
Introduced by Ratt in the film *The Golden Child* (86) and on the album *Dancing Undercover* (Atlantic, 86).

Bon Bon Vie
Words and music by Sandy Linzer and Lawrence Russell Brown.
Unichappell Music Inc., 1980/Featherbed Music Inc., 1980/Lar-Bell Music Corp., 1980.
Best-selling record by T. S. Monk from *House of Music* (Mirage, 81).

Bonnie Jean (Little Sister)
Words and music by David Lynn Jones.
Mighty Nice Music, 1983/Hat Band Music, 1983.
Introduced by David Lynn Jones on the album *Hard Times on Easy Street* (Mercury, 87).

Boomtown Blues
Words and music by Bob Seger.
Gear Publishing, 1982.
Introduced by Bob Seger on *The Distance* (Capitol, 82).

Bop
Words and music by Jennifer Kimball and Paul Davis.
Michael H. Goldsen, Inc., 1985/Web 4 Music Inc., 1985/Sweet Angel Music, 1985.
Best-selling record in 1986 by Dan Seals from *Won't Be Blue Anymore* (EMI-America, 85). Won a Country Music Association Award, and Single of the year, 1986.

The Border
Words and music by Russ Ballard and Dewey Bunnell.
Russell Ballard, Ltd., Middlesex, England, 1983/EMI-April Music, 1983/

Poison Oak Music, 1983.
Best-selling record by America from *Your Move* (Capitol, 83).

Borderline
Words and music by Reginald Lucas.
Likasa Music, 1983.
Best-selling record by Madonna from *Madonna* (Warner Brothers, 84).

Borderline
Words and music by Victor Krummenacher, Greg Lisher, David
  Lowery, and Chris Pedersen.
Camper Van Beethoven Music, 1989.
Introduced by Camper Van Beethoven on *Key Lime Pie* (Virgin, 89).

Born in the U.S.A.
Words and music by Bruce Springsteen.
Bruce Springsteen Publishing, 1984.
Best-selling record by Bruce Springsteen from *Born in the U.S.A.*
  (Columbia, 84). Nominated for a Grammy Award, Record of the
  Year, 1985.

Born to Be My Baby
Words and music by Jon Bon Jovi, Richie Sambora, and Desmond
  Child.
Bon Jovi Publishing, 1988/New Jersey Underground, 1988/Polygram
  Songs, 1988/Desmobile Music Inc., 1988/EMI-April Music, 1988.
Best-selling record in 1989 by Bon Jovi from *New Jersey* (Mercury, 88).

Born to Be Wild
Words and music by Mars Bonfire.
Music Corp. of America, 1968.
Revived in 1987 by The Cult, from the album *Electric* (Electric).
  Following the success of their revival, the songwriter, John Kay,
  released a comeback album of old material.

Born to Boogie
Words and music by Hank Williams, Jr.
Bocephus Music Inc., 1987.
Best-selling record by Hank Williams, Jr., from the album of the same
  title, (Warner/Curb, 87).

Born to Run
Words and music by Paul Kennerley.
Irving Music Inc., 1981.
Best-selling record by Emmylou Harris from *Cimarron* (Warner
  Brothers, 82).

Born Yesterday
Words and music by Don Everly.

Tropicbird, 1986.
Introduced by The Everly Brothers on the album *Born Yesterday* (Mercury, 86).

The Bottle
Words and music by Gil Scott-Heron.
Brouhaha Music, 1976.
Revived by Gil Scott-Heron in *The Best of Gil Scott-Heron* (Arista, 84).

Bottom of the Fifth
Words and music by Porter Wagoner and Michael Pearson.
Break Every Rule Music, 1982.
Introduced on *Viva* by Porter Wagoner (Warner Brothers, 83).

The Bottomless Lake
Words and music by John Prine.
Big Ears Music Inc., 1979/Bruised Oranges, 1979.
Introduced by John Prine on the album *Aimless Love* (Oh Boy, 85).

Boulevard
Words and music by Jackson Browne.
Swallow Turn Music, 1980.
Best-selling record by Jackson Browne from *The Pretenders* (Asylum, 80).

Boy from New York City
Words and music by John Taylor.
Trio Music Co., Inc., 1964.
Revived by Manhattan Transfer from *Mecca for Moderns* (Atlantic, 81).

The Boy in the Bubble (American-South African)
English words and music by Paul Simon, music by Forere Motlobeloa.
Paul Simon Music, 1986.
Introduced by Paul Simon on the album *Graceland* (Warner Bros., 86).
   The melody is based on original roots music of South Africa.

Boy with a Problem (English)
Words and music by Elvis Costello, words by Chris Difford.
Plangent Visions Music, Inc., London, England, 1982/Almo Music Corp., 1982.
Introduced by Elvis Costello in *Imperial Bedroom* (Columbia, 82).

The Boy with the Thorn in His Side (English)
Words and music by Morrissey (pseudonym for Tommy Morrissey).
Morrissey/Marr Songs Ltd., England, 1986/Warner-Tamerlane Music, 1986.
Introduced by The Smiths on the album *The Queen Is Dead* (Sire, 86).

45

Boys Night Out
Words and music by Timothy B. Schmidt, Will Jennings, and Bruce
   Gaitsch.
Jeddrah Music, 1987/Blue Sky Rider Songs, 1987/Willin' David, 1987/
   Edge of Fluke, 1987/Wild Gator Music.
Best-selling record by Timothy B. Schmidt, from the album *Timothy B.*
   (MCA, 87), marking a return by a former member of the Eagles.

The Boys of Summer
Words and music by Don Henley and Mike Campbell.
Cass County Music Co., 1984/Wild Gator Music.
Best-selling record in 1985 by Don Henley from the album *Building the
   Perfect Beast* (Geffen, 84). Nominated for Grammy Awards, Record
   of the Year, 1985, and Song of the Year, 1985.

Brand New Life
Words and music by Larry Carlton and Robert Kraft.
Belfast Music, 1985/Overboard Music, 1985.
Introduced by Steve Wariner as the theme song of television series
   Who's the Boss?

Brand New Lover
Words and music by Marshall Crenshaw.
Belwin-Mills Publishing Corp., 1980/MHC Music, 1980.
Performed by Marshall Crenshaw on *Marshall Crenshaw* (Warner
   Brothers, 82).

Brand New Lover (English)
Words and music by Peter Burns, Michael Percy, Timothy Lever, and
   Steven Coy.
Dead or Alive Music Ltd., England, 1986/Latebound, England,
   1986/WB Music, 1986.
Best-selling record by Dead or Alive, from the album *Mad, Bad, and
   Dangerous to Know* (Epic, 86). The same group was responsible for
   the 1985 dance record of the year, 'You Spin Me Round.'

Brand New World
Words by Stephen Schwartz, music by Charles Strouse.
Charles Strouse Music, 1986/Grey Dog Music, 1986.
Introduced by Teresa Stratas in the 1986 Broadway musical *Rags*. The
   presence of opera star Stratas failed to prevent this musical about
   immigrants arriving in turn-of-the-century New York from closing
   after only a few performances.

Brasilia Crossed with Trenton
Words and music by Bob Mould.
Granary Music, 1989.

Introduced by Bob Mould in *Workbook* (Virgin, 89), the first solo effort from an underground legend with Husker Du.

Brass in Pocket (I'm Special) (English)
Words and music by Chrissie Hynde and James Honeyman Scott.
MCA, Inc., 1979.
Best-selling record by The Pretenders from *The Pretenders* (Sire, 80).

Brave Companion of the Road
Words and music by Nanci Griffith.
Irving Music Inc., 1989/Ponder Heart Music, 1989.
Introduced by Nanci Griffith on *Storms* (MCA, 89).

Break It to Me Gently
Words and music by Diane Laupert and Joe Seneca.
MCA Music, 1961.
Revived by Juice Newton from *Quiet Lies* (Capitol, 82).

Break My Stride
Words and music by Matthew Wilder and Greg Prestopino.
Streetwise Music, 1983/Buchu Music, 1983/No Ears Music, 1983.
Best-selling record by Matthew Wilder from *I Don't Speak the Language* (Private, 83).

Breakaway
Words and music by Jackie DeShannon and Sharon Sheeley.
EMI Unart Catalogue, 1983.
Introduced by Gail Davies in the film *Sylvester*.

Breakaway
Words and music by Tom Zanes and Rob Friedman.
Copyright Control, 1989.
Introduced by The Del Fuegos on *Smoking in the Fields* (RCA, 89).

Breakdance (American-German)
English words by Irene Cara and Bunny Hull, music by Giorgio Moroder.
WB Music, 1983/Carub Music, 1983/Alcor Music, 1983/Brassheart Music, 1983.
Best-selling record by Irene Cara from *What a Feelin'* (Geffen, 84).
Introduced in the film *Breakdance* (84).

Breakdown Dead Ahead
Words and music by Boz Scaggs and David Foster.
BMG Songs Inc., 1980/Foster Frees Music Inc., 1980/Irving Music Inc., 1980.
Best-selling record by Boz Scaggs from *Middle Man* (Columbia, 80).

Breakfast in Bed (English)
Words and music by Donnie Fritts and Eddie Hinton.
EMI-April Music, 1988/Ruler Music Co., Inc., 1988.
Introduced by UB40 with Chrissie Hynde on *UB40* (A & M, 88).

Breakin' Away
Words and music by Al Jarreau, Thomas Canning, and Jay Graydon.
Al Jarreau Music, 1981/Desperate Music, 1981/Garden Rake Music,
  Inc., 1981.
Best-selling record by Al Jarreau from *Breakin' Away* (Warner Brothers,
  82).

Breakin'... There's No Stopping Us
Words and music by Ollie E. Brown and Jerry Knight.
Ollie Brown Sugar Music, Inc., 1984/Almo Music Corp., 1984/Crimsco
  Music, 1984.
Best-selling record by Ollie and Jerry (Polydor, 84). Introduced in the
  film and soundtrack album *Breakin'* (84).

Breaking Us in Two (English)
Words and music by Joe Jackson.
Almo Music Corp., 1982.
Best-selling record by Joe Jackson from *Night and Day* (A & M, 83).

Breakout (English)
Words and music by Swing Out Sister.
EMI-Virgin, 1987.
Best-selling record by Swing Out Sister, from the album *It's Better to
  Travel* (Mercury, 87).

The Breaks
Words and music by James Moore, Lawrence Smith, Kurt Walker,
  Robert Ford, and Russell Simmons.
Neutral Gray Music, 1980/Funk Groove Music Publisher Co., 1980.
Best-selling record by Kurtis Blow from *Kurtis Blow* (Mercury, 80).

The Breakup Song (They Don't Write 'Em)
Words and music by Greg Kihn, Steve Wright, and Gary Philips.
Rye-Boy Music, 1981.
Best-selling record by The Greg Kihn Band from *Rockihnroll*
  (Beserkley, 81).

Breath Away from Heaven
Words and music by George Harrison.
Ganga Publishing Co., 1987/Zero Productions, 1987.
Introduced by George Harrison on the soundtrack of the film *Shanghai
  Surprise,* which was financed by ex-Beatle Harrison. He also
  performed the song on his album *Cloud Nine* (Dark Horse, 87).

Breathless
Words and music by Otis Blackwell.
Sea Foam Music Co., 1958/Unichappell Music Inc., 1958.
Revived by X on *Under the Big Black Sun* (Elektra, 82). Performed in the film *Breathless* (82).

Brilliant Disguise
Words and music by Bruce Springsteen.
Bruce Springsteen Publishing, 1987.
Best-selling record by Bruce Springsteen, from the album *Tunnel of Love* (Columbia, 87).

Bring Back Nelson Mandela
Words and music by Hugh Masekela.
Kalahari Music, 1987.
Introduced by Lelita Khumalo and company in the black South African musical *Sarafina*, whch played on Broadway in 1988; original cast album released by RCA, 1989.

Bring on the Loot
Words and music by Gary Portnoy and Judy Hart Angelo.
Koppelman Family Music, 1983/Bandier Family Music, 1983/Yontrop Music, 1983/Judy Hart Angelo Music, 1983/R. L. August Music Co., 1983.
Introduced by Dennis Bailey in *Preppies* (83).

Bringin' on the Heartbreak (English)
Words and music by Steve Clark, Pete Willis, and Joe Elliott.
Zomba Music, 1981.
Best-selling record by Def Leppard from *High N' Dry* (Mercury, 81 and 84).

Broken Glass
Words and music by Claudia Schmidt.
Pragmavision Music, 1982.
Introduced by Claudia Schmidt on *Midwestern Heart* (Flying Fish, 82).

The Broken Pianolita (Brazilian)
English words by Robert Wright and George Forrest, music by Heitor Villa-Lobos.
Revived by John Raitt in the 1987 production of the operetta *Magdelena*, staged in New York City to celebrate the one-hundredth anniversary of composer Villa Lobos's birth. Raitt was in the original 1948 production as well, which closed after 88 performances because of a musicians' strike. This song was dropped after opening night, however. The lyricists also collaborated on 'Stranger in Paradise,' among others.

Broken Rainbow
Words and music by Laura Nyro.
Luna Mist Music, 1989.
Introduced by Laura Nyro in *Live at the Bottom Line* (Cypress, 89),
　which brought the artist back after a five-year absence.

Broken Wings (American-English)
Words and music by Richard Page, Steven George, and Robert John
　'Mutt' Lang.
Warner-Tamerlane Music, 1985/Entente Music, 1985.
Best-selling record by Mr. Mister from the album *Welcome to the Real
　World* (RCA, 85).

Brothers
Words and music by Hugh Blumenfeld.
Hugh Blumenfeld, 1987.
Introduced by Hugh Blumenfeld on *Fast Folk Sixth Anniversary Issue*
　(Fast Folk, 89).

Brothers in Arms (English)
Words and music by Mark Knopfler.
Chariscourt Ltd., 1985/Almo Music Corp., 1985/Virgin Music Ltd.,
　1985.
Introduced by Dire Straits on the album *Brothers in Arms* (Warner
　Bros., 85).

Brownsville Girl
Words and music by Bob Dylan and Sam Shepard.
Special Rider Music, 1986.
Introduced by Bob Dylan on the album *Knocked Out Loaded* (Columbia,
　86). Co-writer Shepard is an accomplished playwright and actor.

Bruce
Words and music by Rick Springfield.
Vogue Music, 1981.
Best-selling record by Rick Springfield from *Beautiful Feelings*
　(Mercury, 84).

Buffalo Stance (English)
Words and music by Neneh Cherry, Booga Bear, Phil Ramacon, and
　Jamie Morgan.
Virgin Music, 1989/Warner-Chappell Music, 1989/Warner-Tamerlane
　Music, 1989/Copyright Control, 1989.
Best-selling record by Neneh Cherry from *Raw like Sushi* (Virgin, 89).
　Introduced in the film *Slaves of New York* (Virgin, 89).

Built to Last
Words and music by Jerry Garcia and Robert Hunter.

Ice Nine Publishing Co., Inc., 1989.
Introduced by The Grateful Dead on *Built to Last* (Arista, 89).

Burn Rubber on Me
Words and music by Lonnie Simmons, Charley Wilson, and Rudolph
Taylor.
Temp Co., 1980.
Best-selling record by Gap Band from *The Gap Band* (Mercury, 81).

Burnin' a Hole in My Heart
Words and music by Skip Ewing, Mike Geiger, and Woody Mullis.
Acuff-Rose Publications Inc., 1988/Milene Music, 1988.
Best-selling record in 1989 by Skip Ewing from *The Coast of Colorado*
(MCA, 88).

Burnin' for You
Words and music by Donald Roeser and Richard Meltzer.
B. O'Cult Songs, Inc., 1981.
Best-selling record by Blue Oyster Cult from *Fire of Unknown Origin*
(Columbia, 81).

Burnin' Old Memories
Words and music by Larry Boone, Gene Nelson, and Paul Nelson.
BMG Music, 1989/Warner-Tamerlane Music, 1989/Believe Us or Not
Music, 1989/Screen Gems-EMI Music Inc., 1989.
Best-selling record by Kathy Mattea from *Willow in the Wind* (Mercury,
89).

Burning Down the House
Words and music by David Byrne, Chris Frantz, Jerry Harrison, and
Tina Weymouth.
Index Music, 1983.
Best-selling record by Talking Heads from *Speaking in Tongues* (Sire,
83).

Burning Heart
Words and music by Frankie Sullivan and Jim Peterik.
Holy Moley Music, 1985/Rude Music, 1985/Famous Music Corp., 1985/
Easy Action Music, 1985.
Best-selling record by Survivor (Scotti Bros., 85). Introduced in the film
and soundtrack album *Rocky IV*.

Burning Love
Words and music by Dennis Linde.
Combine Music Corp., 1972.
Introduced by Elvis Presley, this song was revived in 1987 by Doctor
and the Medics on the album *Burning Love* (IRS).

Bust a Move
Words and music by Marvin Young, Matt Dike, and Michael Ross.
Varry White Music, 1989/Young Man Moving Music, 1989.
Best-selling record by Young M.C. from *Stone Cold Rhymin'* (Delicious
  Vinyl, 89). Won a Grammy Award, and Rap Song of the Year, 1989.

Busted
Words and music by Harlan Howard.
Tree Publishing Co., Inc., 1982.
Best-selling record by John Conlee from *John Conlee's Greatest Hits*
  (MCA, 82).

But You Know I Love You
Words and music by Mike Settle.
Devon Music, 1968.
Best-selling record by Dolly Parton from *9 to 5 and Odd Jobs* (RCA,
  81).

By Now
Words and music by Don Pfrimmer, Charles Quillen, and Dean Dillon.
Hall-Clement Publications, 1981/Polygram International, 1981.
Best-selling record by Steve Wariner (RCA, 81).

C

C-I-T-Y
Words and music by John Cafferty.
John Cafferty Music, 1985.
Best-selling record by John Cafferty and The Beaver Brown Band from
the album *Tough All Over* (Scotti Bros., 85).

Cadillac Car
Words by Tom Eyen, music by Henry Krieger.
Dreamgirls Music, 1981/Dreamette's Music, 1981/Tom Eyen's
Publishing Co., 1981.
Introduced by Ben Harney, Cleavant Derricks, and Obba Babatunde in
Dreamgirls (81).

Cadillac Ranch
Words and music by Bruce Springsteen.
Bruce Springsteen Publishing, 1980.
Introduced by Bruce Springsteen in *The River* (Columbia, 80).

Cajun Moon
Words and music by Jimmy Rushing.
Hall-Clement Publications, 1985/Ricky Scaggs, 1985/Polygram
International, 1985.
Best-selling record by Ricky Skaggs from the album *Live in London*
(Epic, 86).

California Girls
Words and music by Brian Wilson.
Irving Music Inc., 1965.
Revived by David Lee Roth on the album *Crazy from the Heat* (Warner
Bros., 85).

Call It Love
Words and music by Rusty Guilbeau, Bill Crain, Richard Lonow, and
Jim Messina.
Atlantic-Gibron Music, 1989/Storky Music, 1989/Jasperilla Music Co.,

1989/Frankly Scarlett Music, 1989/Music of the World, 1989/Could Be Music, 1989.
Best-selling record by Poco from *Legacy* (RCA, 89).

Call Me (German)
English words and music by Giorgio Moroder and Debbie Harry.
Ensign Music, 1980/Cookaway Music Inc., 1980.
Best-selling record by Blondie (Chrysalis, 80). Introduced by Blondie in the film *American Gigolo* (80). Featured on *The Best of Blondie* (Chrysalis, 81).

Call Me
Words and music by Randy Muller.
All Nations Music, 1981.
Best-selling record by Skyy from *Skyy Line* (Salsoul, 82).

Call Me (English)
Words and music by Peter Cox and Richie Drummie.
ATV Music Corp., 1985.
Introduced by Go West on the album *Go West* (Chrysalis, 85).

Call Me Mr. Telephone
Words and music by T. Carrasco.
MCA, Inc., 1985.
Best-selling record by Cheyne (MCA, 85).

Call to the Heart
Words and music by Gregg Guiffria and David Eisley.
Kid Bird Music, 1984/Herds of Birds Music Inc., 1984/Greg Guiffria Music, 1984/Frozen Flame Music, 1984.
Best-selling record by Guiffria from the album *Guiffria* (MCA, 85).

Calling America (English)
Words and music by Jeff Lynne.
EMI-April Music, 1986.
Best-selling record ELO from *Balance of Power* (Epic, 86).

Calling You
Words and music by Bob Telson.
Otis Lee Music, 1988.
Introduced by Javetta Steele in the film and soundtrack album *Bagdad Cafe* (Island, 88). Nominated for an Academy Award, Song of the Year, 1988.

Can I Let Her Go
Words by Hal Hackaday, music by Richard Kapp.
Introduced by Len Cariou in the 1987 musical *Teddy and Alice*. This ballad was adapted from 'The March of the Thunderer' by John Philip Sousa.

Can U Read My Lips
Words and music by Arthur Zamora, Michael Carpenter, and Eric Strickland.
Looky Lou Music, 1989/Bright Light Music, 1989.
Best-selling record by Z'Looke from *Take U Back to My Place* (Orpheus, 89).

Can You Help Me
Words and music by Jesse Johnson.
Almo Music Corp., 1985/Crazy People Music/Almo Music Corp., 1985.
Best-selling record by Jesse Johnson's Revue from the album *Jesse Johnson's Revue* (A & M, 85).

Can You Stand the Rain
Words and music by James Harris, III and Terry Lewis.
Flyte Tyme Tunes, 1988.
Best-selling record in 1989 by New Edition from *Heart Break* (MCA, 88).

Candle in the Wind (English)
Words by Bernie Taupin, music by Elton John.
Dick James Music Inc., 1973/Polygram Music Publishing Inc., 1973.
Revived in 1987 by Elton John on his album *Live in Australia with the Melbourne Symphony Orchestra* (MCA). He had originally recorded the song, which was inspired by the life and death of Marilyn Monroe, in 1973 on *Yellow Brick Road.*

Candy
Words and music by Larry Blackmon and Tomi Jenkins.
All Seeing Eye Music, 1987/Polygram Music Publishing Inc., 1987/ Better Days Music, 1987/Polygram Songs, 1987.
Best-selling record by Cameo, from the album *Word Up* (Polygram, 86).

Candy Girl
Words and music by Maurice Starr (pseudonym for Larry Johnson) and Michael Jonzun.
Boston International Music, 1982/Warlock Music, 1982.
Best-selling record by New Edition from *Candy Girl* (Streetwise, 83).

Can't Even Get the Blues
Words and music by Rick Carnes and Thomas William Damphier.
Warneractive Songs, 1982/King Coal Music Inc., 1982.
Best-selling record by Reba McEntire (Mercury, 82).

Can't Fight This Feeling
Words and music by Kevin Cronin.
Fate Music, 1984.
Best-selling record by REO Speedwagon from the album *Wheels Are Turning* (Epic, 85).

Can't Get over You
Words and music by Frankie Beverly.
Amazement Music, 1989.
Best-selling record by Maze featuring Frankie Beverly, from *Silky Soul* (Warner Bros., 89).

Can't Get There from Here
Words and music by William Berry, Peter Buck, Mike Mills, and Michael Stipe.
Unichappell Music Inc., 1985.
Best-selling record by R.E.M. from the album *Fables of the Reconstruction* (I.R.S., 85).

Can't Hardly Wait
Words and music by Paul Westerberg.
NAH Music, 1987.
Introduced by The Replacements, from the album *Pleased to Meet Me* (Sire, 87).

Can't Keep a Good Man Down
Words and music by Robert Corbini.
Sabal Music, Inc., 1984.
Best-selling record by Alabama from the album *40 Hour Week* (RCA, 85).

Can't Live Without 'em Blues
Words and music by Jack Herrick and Tommy Thompson.
On the Trail Music, 1986/Southern Melody Music, 1986.
Introduced by The Red Clay Ramblers as musical accompaniment to Sam Shepard's 1985 production of his play *Lie of the Mind*. Was used on the subsequent album (Sugar Hill, 86).

Can't Stay Away from You
Words and music by Gloria Estefan.
Foreign Imported, 1987.
Best-selling record in 1988 by Gloria Estefan & Miami Sound Machine, from *Cut It Loose* (Epic, 88).

Can't Stop My Heart from Loving You
Words and music by Jamie O'Hara and Kieran Kane.
Cross Keys Publishing Co., Inc., 1987/Tree Publishing Co., Inc., 1987/ Kieran Kane, 1987.
Best-selling record by The O'Kanes, from the album *The O'Kanes* (Columbia, 87).

Can't Stop the Girl (English)
Words and music by Linda Thompson.
Linda Thompson, England, 1985/Firesign Music Ltd., England, 1985/ Chappell & Co., Inc., 1985.

Best-selling record by Linda Thompson from the album *One Clear Moment* (Warner Bros., 85).

Can't We Try (Canadian)
Words and music by Dan Hill and B. Hill.
EMI-April Music, 1987/A Question of Material, 1987/Scoop, 1987.
Best-selling record by Dan Hill and Vonda Sheppard, from the album *Can't We Try* (Columbia, 87). Canadian balladeer Hill wrote this song with his wife.

Can'tcha Say (You Believe in Me)
Words and music by J. Green, Tom Scholz, and Brad Delp.
Hideaway Hits, 1987/Perceptive, 1987.
Best-selling record by Boston, from the album *Third Stage* (MCA, 87).

The Captain of Her Heart (German)
German words and music by Kurt Maloo and Felix Haug.
Z-Music, Switzerland, 1985/Almo Music Corp., 1985.
Best-selling record by Double from the album *Blue* (A & M, 86). The song was a big hit in West Germany, France, England, Canada, and Switzerland before crossing over to the United States.

Caravan of Love
Words and music by Earnest Isley, Marvin Isley, and Christopher Jasper.
EMI-April Music, 1985/IJI, 1985.
Best-selling record by Isley/Jasper/Isley from the album *Caravan of Love* (CBS Associated, 85). Revived in 1987 by the Housemartins, whose a cappella version went to number one in England, but was not included on their album. (Go Discs, 87).

Careless Whisper (English)
Words and music by George Michael and Andrew Ridgeley.
Chappell & Co., Inc., 1984.
Best-selling record by Wham! featuring George Michael, from the album *Make It Big* (Columbia, 84).

Caribbean Queen (No More Love on the Run)
Words and music by Keith Diamond and Billy Ocean.
Willesden Music, Inc., 1984/Zomba Music, 1984.
Best-selling record by Billy Ocean from *Suddenly* (Jive, 84). Nominated for a Grammy Award, Rhythm 'n' Blues Song of the Year, 1984.

Carrie (Swedish)
English words and music by Joey Tempest and M. Michael.
Screen Gems-EMI Music Inc., 1986.
Best-selling record by Europe, from the album *The Final Countdown* (Epic, 86).

Carry the Torch
Words and music by Paul Davis and Doug Erikson.
Flip 'n' Dog, 1987.
Introduced by Firetown, from the album *In the Heart of the Heart Country*, (Atlantic, 87). When originally released on an independent extended-play record, the song was hailed by critics, resulting in a deal with a major label.

Cars (English)
Words and music by Gary Numan.
London, 1979.
Best-selling record by Gary Numan from *The Pleasure Principle* (Atco, 80).

Casanova
Words and music by Reggie Calloway.
Calloco, 1987/Hip-Trip Music Co., 1987.
Best-selling record by Levert, from the album *The Big Throwdown* (Atlantic, 87). Nominated for a Grammy Award, Rhythm 'n' Blues Song of the Year, 1987.

Cat People (Putting out Fire) (English-German)
English words and music by David Bowie and Giorgio Moroder.
MCA, Inc., 1982/Music of the World, 1982.
Best-selling record by David Bowie from *Let's Dance* (Backstreet/MCA, 82). Introduced in the film *Cat People* (82).

Catch Me (I'm Falling)
Words and music by Jade Starling and Whey Cooler.
Genetic, 1987.
Best-selling record by Pretty Poison, from the album *Hiding Out* (Virgin, 87); also on the soundtrack of the film *Hiding Out.*

Cathy's Clown
Words and music by Don Everly and Phil Everly.
Acuff Rose Music, 1960.
Revived in 1989 by Reba McEntire on *Sweet 16* (MCA, 89).

Caught up in the Rapture
Words and music by Garry Glenn and Diane Quander.
WB Music, 1986/DQ Music, 1986.
Best-selling record by Anita Baker from the album *Rapture* (Elektra, 86). Co-writer Quander plays keyboards in Baker's touring band.

Caught up in You
Words and music by Jeff Carlisi, Jim Peterik, Richard Barnes, and Frankie Sullivan.
Rocknocker Music Co., 1982/Easy Action Music, 1982/WB Music,

1982.
Best-selling record by 38 Special from *Special Forces* (A & M, 82).

Causing a Commotion
Words and music by Madonna and Steve Bray.
WB Music, 1987/Polygram International, 1987/Bleu Disque Music, 1987/Lost in Music, 1987.
Best-selling record by Madonna, from the album (Sire, 87) and film *Who's That Girl?*, in which she starred.

Celebration
Words and music by Ronald Bell, Charles Smith, George Brown, Robert Bell, James Taylor, Eumir Deodato, Robert Mickens, Earl Toon, and Dennis Thomas.
Delightful Music Ltd., 1980/WB Music, 1980/Second Decade Music, 1980.
Best-selling record by Kool & The Gang from *Celebrate* (DeLite, 80).

Celestial Soda Pop
Music by Ray Lynch.
Introduced by Ray Lynch on the album *Deep Breakfast* (MusicWest, 86), this popular instrumental received heavy play on 'new age' radio, programming much in vogue with stressed-out yuppies.

Centerfield
Words and music by John Fogerty.
Wenaha Music Co., 1984.
Best-selling record by John Fogerty from the album *Centerfield* (Warner Bros., 85).

Centerfold
Words and music by Seth Justman.
Center City Music, 1982/Pal-Park Music, 1982.
Best-selling record by J. Geils Band from *Freeze-Frame* (EMI-America, 82).

Centipede
Words and music by Michael Jackson.
Mijac Music, 1984.
Best-selling record by Rebbie Jackson from *Centipede* (Columbia, 84).

Central Park Ballad
Words and music by Charles Strouse.
Charles Strouse Music, 1985.
Introduced by Keith Corran and Ilene Kristen in the Off Broadway musical *Mayor* (85), based on New York City's Mayor Ed Koch.

Century's End
Words and music by Donald Fagen and T. Meher.

U/A Music, Inc., 1988/Freejunket Music, 1988.
Introduced by Donald Fagen in the film and on the soundtrack album of Bright Lights, Big City (Warner Bros, 88). Nominated for a Grammy Award, Best Song for a Film or TV, 1988.

Chains of Love (English)
Words and music by Vince Clarke and Andy Bell.
Sonet Publishing Ltd., London, England, 1988/Emile, London, England, 1988.
Best-selling record by Erasure from *The Innocents* (Sire/Reprise, 88).

The Chair
Words and music by Hank Cochran and Dean Dillon.
Tree Publishing Co., Inc., 1971/Larry Butler Music Co., 1971/EMI-Blackwood Music Inc., 1971.
Revived by George Strait on the album *Something Special* (MCA, 85).

Change of Heart
Words and music by Essra Mohawk (pseudonym for Sandy Hurvitz) and Cyndi Lauper.
Stone and Muffin Music, 1986/Rella Music Corp., 1986.
Best-selling record by Cyndi Lauper from the album *True Colors* (Portrait, 86). Co-writer Mohawk was also known as Uncle Meat in the sixties when she performed as a back-up singer for Frank Zappa & The Mothers of Invention.

Change of Heart
Words and music by Naomi Judd.
Caseyem Music, 1984/Kentucky Sweetheart Music, 1984.
Best-selling record in 1989 by The Judds from *The Judds' Greatest Hits* (RCA, 88).

Change with the Changing Times
Words and music by Peter Holsapple.
Holsapple, 1987/I.R.S. Music, 1987.
Introduced by The dBs, from the album *The Sound of Music* (IRS, 87).

Changes
Words by Martin Charnin, music by Charles Strouse.
Introduced by Danielle Findley in *Annie 2,* the sequel to the same team's *Annie.* The expensive production was panned during its 1989 out-of-town tryouts and the Broadway opening planned for 1990 was postponed.

Changin' Luck
Words and music by Bill Payne, Fred Tackett, and Craig Fuller.
Little Music, 1988/Feat Music, 1988.
Introduced by Little Feat on *Let It Roll* (Warner Bros., 88). Minus the

late Lowell George, Little Feat put out a successful reunion album in 1988.

Changing
Words by Gretchen Cryer, music by Nancy Ford.
Valando Group, 1973.
Introduced by Marcia Rodd in the 1973 Broadway musical *Shelter*.
  Revived in 1989 by lyricist-performer Gretchen Cryer in her cabaret
  act, *Back in My Life*.

Channel Z
Words and music by B-52s.
Man Woman Together Now Music, 1989/Irving Music Inc., 1989.
Introduced by The B-52s on *Cosmic Thing* (Reprise, 89), this song
  offers a quirky pop comeback by the group that gave us 'Rock
  Lobster' and 'Private Idaho.'

Chariots of Fire (Race to the End)
Music by Vangelis, words by Jon Anderson.
WB Music, 1981.
Best-selling records by Melissa Manchester from *Hey Ricky* (Arista, 81)
  and Vangelis (Polydor, 82). Introduced by Vangelis in the film and
  soundtrack album *Chariots of Fire* (81). Nominated for a Grammy
  Award, Record of the Year, 1982.

Charlie's Medicine
Words and music by Warren Zevon.
Zevon Music Inc., 1982.
Introduced by Warren Zevon in *The Envoy* (Asylum, 82).

Cheating in the Next Room
Words and music by George Henry Jackson and Robert Alton Miller.
Muscle Shoals Sound Publishing Co., Inc., 1982.
Best-selling record by Z.Z. Hill (Malaco, 82).

Check It Out
Words and music by John Cougar Mellencamp.
Riva Music Ltd., 1987.
Best-selling record in 1988 by John Cougar Mellencamp from *The
  Lonesome Jubilee* (Mercury, 88).

Cherish
Words and music by Ronald Bell, Charles Smith, Robert Bell, James
  Taylor, George Brown, Curtis Williams, and James Bonneford.
Delightful Music Ltd., 1984.
Best-selling record by Kool & The Gang from the album *Emergency*
  (De-Lite, 85).

Cherish
Words and music by Madonna and Patrick Leonard.
WB Music, 1989/Bleu Disque Music, 1989/Lost in Music, 1989/Johnny
  Yuma, 1989.
Best-selling record by Madonna from *Like a Prayer* (Sire, 89).

Cherry Bomb
Words and music by John Cougar Mellencamp.
Full Keel Music, 1987.
Best-selling record by John Cougar Mellencamp, from the album *The
  Lonesome Jubilee* (Polygram, 87).

Chestnuts Roasting on an Open Fire, see The Christmas Song.

Cheyene
Words and music by Scott Kempner.
Prince of the Bronx Music, 1987.
Introduced by The Del Lords on *Based on a True Story* (Enigma, 88).

Chicago, Illinois
Words by Leslie Bricusse, music by Henry Mancini.
EMI Variety Catalogue, 1981/Stage & Screen Music Inc., 1981/EMI
  Variety Catalog, Inc., 1981/Henry Mancini Enterprises, 1981.
Introduced by Lesley Ann Warren in the film *Victor, Victoria* (82).

Children and Art
Words and music by Stephen Sondheim.
WB Music, 1981.
Introduced by Bernadette Peters in *Sunday in the Park with George*
  (83).

Children of the Revolution (English)
Words and music by Marc Bolan.
Wizard, Bahamas, 1986.
Revived in 1986 by Violent Femmes on the album *The Blind Leading
  the Naked* (Slash/Warner Bros., 86). The late Marc Bolan was the
  leader of the influential glitter rock band T-Rex, now defunct.

Children of the Wild Word
Words and music by John O'Hara.
Cross Keys Publishing Co., Inc., 1988.
Introduced by Michael Martin Murphey on *River of Time* (RCA, 88).

Children's Crusade (English)
Words and music by Sting (pseudonym for Gordon Sumner).
Magnetic Music Publishing Co., 1985/Reggatta Music, Ltd., 1985/Illegal
  Songs, Inc., 1985.
Introduced by Sting on the album *The Dream of the Blue Turtles* (A &
  M, 85).

Chimes of Freedom
Words and music by Bob Dylan.
WB Music, 1964.
> Revived by Bruce Springsteen in 1988 on *Chimes of Freedom* (Columbia, 88).

China Girl (English)
Words and music by Iggy Pop and David Bowie.
Bug Music, 1977/James Osterberg Music, 1977/Jones Music Co., 1977/ Fleur Music, 1977.
Featured on *Let's Dance* by David Bowie (EMI-America, 83).

Chiseled in Stone
Words and music by Vern Gosdin and Max D. Barnes.
Hookem Music, 1987/Hidden Lake, 1987.
Best-selling record by Vern Gosdin from *Chiseled in Stone* (Columbia, 88). Nominated for a Grammy Award, Country Song of the Year, 1988.

Christie Lee
Words and music by Billy Joel.
Joelsongs, 1983.
Introduced by Billy Joel on *An Innocent Man* (Columbia, 83).

Christmas (Baby Please Come Home)
Words and music by Phil Spector, Ellie Greenwich, and Jeff Barry.
Mother Bertha Music, Inc./Trio Music Co., Inc.
Revived in 1987 by U2 for the album *A Very Special Christmas* (A & M), proceeds from which were donated to the Special Olympics. The song was originally record by Darlene Love, who sings back-up on the more recent version.

Christmas in America
Words and music by Dolly Parton.
Velvet Apple Music, 1989.
Introduced by Kenny Rogers on *Christmas in America,* an album that was the basis for a later television special.

Christmas in Hollis
Words and music by Joseph Simmons, D. McDaniels, and Jason Mizell.
Protoons Inc., 1987/Rush Groove Music, 1987.
Introduced by Run DMC on the album *A Very Special Christmas* (A & M), this song offers a rap treatment of holiday sentiments.

The Christmas Song, also known as **Chestnuts Roasting on an Open Fire**
Words and music by Mel Torme and Robert Wells.
Edwin H. Morris, 1946.
Revived in 1988 by Natalie Cole in the film *Scrooged* and on its

soundtrack album (A & M, 88). Cole's father, Nat 'King' Cole, had made this song his signature tune.

Church of the Poison Mind (English)
Words and music by Roy Hay, Jon Moss, Michael Craig, and George O'Dowd.
Virgin Music, 1983.
Best-selling record by Culture Club from *Colour by Numbers* (Epic, 83).

The Church on Cumberland Road
Words and music by Bob DiPiero, John Scott Sherrill, and Dave Robbins.
Little Big Town Music, 1987/American Made Music, 1987/Trevcor Music, 1987.
Best-selling record by Shenandoah from *The Road Not Taken* (Columbia, 89).

Circle
Words and music by Edie Brickell, music by Kenny Withrow.
Geffen Music, 1986/Withrow Publishing, 1986/Edie Brickell Songs, 1986.
Introduced by Edie Brickell & New Bohemians on *Shooting Rubberbands at the Stars* (Geffen, 88).

Circle in the Sand
Words and music by Ellen Shipley.
Future Furniture, 1987/Shipwreck, 1987.
Best-selling record in 1988 by Belinda Carlisle, from *Heaven on Earth* (MCA, 87).

Circles
Words and music by Wayne Lewis and David Lewis.
Almo Music Corp., 1982/Jodaway Music, 1982.
Best-selling record by Atlantic Starr from *Brilliance* (A & M, 82).

City Drops (into the Night)
Words and music by Jim Carroll, Steve Linsley, and Brian Linsley.
Earl McGrath Music, 1980.
Introduced by Jim Carroll in *Catholic Boy* (Atlantic, 80).

City of Crime
Words and music by Peter Aykroyd, Dan Aykroyd, and Pat Thrall.
Swirling Vortex, 1987/Applied Action, 1987/Enthralled, 1987.
Introduced by Dan Aykroyd and Tom Hanks in the film and on the soundtrack album *Dragnet* (China/Chrysales, 87).

City of New Orleans
Words and music by Steve Goodman.
Turnpike Tom Music, 1970.

Revived by Willie Nelson from *City of New Orleans* (Columbia, 84).
Won a Grammy Award, and Country Song of the Year, 1984.

City Streets
Words and music by Carole King.
Lushmole Music, 1989.
Introduced by Carole King on *City Streets* (Capitol, 89), a comeback
attempt that failed.

Clara's Dancing School
Words and music by Brian Gari.
Tenacity Music, 1987/Foxborough Music, 1987.
Introduced by Teresa Tracy in the 1988 musical *Late Nite Comic* Sung
by Julie Budd on the album *Late Nite Comic* (Original Cast, 88).
Sung by Robin Shipley in the revue *Damned If You Do.*

Close My Eyes Forever (English)
Words and music by Lita Ford and Ozzy Osbourne.
Lisabella Music, 1988/Virgin Music, 1988.
Best-selling record in 1989 by Lita Ford (with Ozzy Osbourne), from
Lita (RCA, 88).

Close to the Wind (English)
Words and music by Stuart Marson.
Misty River Music Ltd., England, 1987.
Performed by Fairport Convention on the album *In Real Time (Live '87)*
(Island, 87).

Closer Than Close
Words and music by Terry Price.
Sloopus, 1986/EMI-Gold Horizon Music Corp., 1986.
Best-selling record by Jean Carne from the album *Closer Than Close*
(Atlantic, 86).

Closer Than Friends (English)
Words and music by Bernard Jackson and David Townsend.
Colgems-EMI Music, 1988.
Best-selling record in 1989 by Surface from *Second Wave* (Columbia,
88).

Closer to Fine
Words and music by Emily Saliers.
Godhap Music, 1988/Virgin Songs, 1988.
Best-selling record by The Indigo Girls from *Indigo Girls* (Epic, 89).

Closest Thing to Perfect
Words and music by Michael Omartian, Bruce Sudano, and Jermaine
Jackson.
EMI Golden Torch Music, 1985/All Nations Music, 1985/EMI-Gold

Horizon Music Corp., 1985/Black Stallion County Publishing, 1985/
Soft Summer Songs, 1985.
Best-selling record by Jermaine Jackson from the album *Jermaine
Jackson* (Arista, 85). Featured in the film and soundtrack album
Perfect (85).

Cloudbusting (English)
Words and music by Kate Bush.
Screen Gems-EMI Music Inc., 1986.
Introduced by Kate Bush on the album *The Whole Story* (EMI-America,
86).

The Clown
Words and music by Brenda Barnett, Charles Chalmers, Sandra Rhodes,
and Wayne Carson Thompson.
Mammoth Spring Music, 1981/Rose Bridge Music Inc., 1981.
Best-selling record by Conway Twitty (Elektra, 82).

Club Paradise
Words and music by Jimmy Cliff.
Island Music, 1986.
Introduced by Jimmy Cliff and Elvis Costello in the 1986 film *Club
Paradise* and on the soundtrack album (Columbia, 86).

Code of Silence
Words and music by Billy Joel and Cyndi Lauper.
Joelsongs, 1986.
Introduced by Billy Joel and Cyndi Lauper on the album *The Bridge*
(Columbia, 86).

Cold Blooded
Words and music by Rick James.
Stone City Music, 1983.
Best-selling record by Rick James from *Cold Blooded* (Gordy, 83).

Cold-Hearted
Words and music by Elliott Wolf.
Elliott Wolff Music, 1989/Virgin Music, 1989.
Best-selling record by Paula Abdul from *Forever Your Girl* (Virgin, 89).

Cold Hearts/Closed Minds
Words and music by Nanci Griffith.
Wing & Wheel Music, 1987.
Introduced by Nanci Griffith on the album *Lone Star State of Mind*
(MCA, 87).

Colored Lights
Words and music by Fred Ebb and John Kander.

Fiddleback, 1983/Kander & Ebb Inc., 1983.
Introduced by Liza Minnelli in *The Rink* (84).

Colors
Words and music by Ice-T, words and music by Africa Islam.
Colgems-EMI Music, 1988/Rhyme Syndicate Music, 1988.
Introduced by Ice-T in the film and on the soundtrack album *Colors*
(Warner Bros., 88).

The Colors of My Life
Words by Michael Stewart, music by Cy Coleman.
Notable Music Co., Inc., 1980.
Introduced by Jim Dale and Glenn Close in *Barnum* (80).

The Colour of Love
Words and music by Wayne Braithwaite, Barry Eastmond, Billy Ocean,
and Jolyon Skinner.
Zomba Music, 1988.
Best-selling record by Billy Ocean, from *Tear Down These Walls* (Jive,
88).

Come As You Are
Words and music by Peter Wolf and Tim Mayer.
Pal-Park Music, 1987.
Best-selling record by Peter Wolf, former lead singer of the J. Geils
Band, from the album *Come As You Are* (EMI, 87).

Come Back to Me
Words by John Doe and Exene Cervenka.
Eight/Twelve Music, 1982.
Introduced by X in *Under the Big Black Sun* (Elektra, 82).

Come Back with the Same Look in Your Eyes (English)
Words and music by Don Black, music by Andrew Lloyd Webber.
Dick James Music Ltd., London, England, 1986.
Performed by Bernadette Peters on the album *Song and Dance - The
Songs* (RCA/Red Seal, 86) - a collection of songs introduced by
Peters in the Broadway musical *Song and Dance*.

Come Dancing (English)
Words and music by Ray Davies.
Davray Music, Ltd., London, England, 1983.
Best-selling record by The Kinks from *State of Confusion* (Arista, 83).

Come from the Heart
Words and music by Suzanna Clark and Richard Leigh.
EMI-April Music, 1989/GSC Music, 1989/Lion Hearted Music, 1989.
Best-selling record by Kathy Mattea from *Willow in the Wind* (Mercury,
89).

Come Go with Me
Words and music by C. E. Quick.
Gil Music Corp./Fee Bee Music.
Revived by The Beach Boys from *M.I.U. Album* (Warner Brothers, 82).

Come Go with Me
Words and music by Lewis Martinee.
Panchin, 1987.
Best-selling record by Expose, from the album *Exposure* (Arista, 87).

Come in Planet Earth (Are You Listening)
Words and music by Karen Taylor-Good and Kent MacDonald.
Bil-Kar, 1988/Giraffe Tracks, 1988.
Introduced by Karen Taylor-Good as the theme song for the Planet
    Earth Project. Winner of an international award from SESAC.

Come on Eileen (English)
Words and music by Kevin Rowland, Jim Paterson, and Kevin Adams.
Colgems-EMI Music, 1982/EMI-April Music, 1982.
Best-selling record by Dexy's Midnight Runners from *Too-Rye-Ay*
    (Mercury, 83).

Come on In (You Did the Best You Could)
Words and music by Rick Corles and George Green.
Dejamus Inc., 1986/Full Keel Music, 1986.
Best-selling record by the Oak Ridge Boys from the album *Seasons*
    (MCA, 86).

Comin' in and out of Your Life
Words and music by Richard Parker and Bobby Whiteside.
Emanuel Music, 1981/Koppelman Family Music, 1981/Jay Landers
    Music, 1981/Bandier Family Music, 1981/Bobby Whiteside Ltd.,
    1981/R. L. August Music Co., 1981.
Best-selling record by Barbra Streisand from *Memories* (Columbia, 81)

Coming Around Again
Words and music by Carly Simon.
C'est Music, 1986/Famous Music Corp.
Best-selling record by Carly Simon from the film *Heartburn* (86).

Coming Home
Words and music by Tom Keifer.
Evesongs Inc., 1988/Chappell & Co., Inc., 1988.
Best-selling record in 1989 by Cinderella from *Long Cold Winter*
    (Mercury, 88).

Coming to America
Words and music by Nile Rodgers and Nancy Huang.
Ensign Music, 1988/Warner-Tamerlane Music, 1988/Smokin' Dog,

1988.
Best-selling record by The System, from the film and on the soundtrack of *Coming to America* (Atco, 88).

Coming Up (English)
Words and music by Paul McCartney.
MPL Communications Inc., 1980/Welbeck Music Corp., 1980.
Best-selling record by Paul McCartney from *McCartney II* (Columbia, 80).

Common Man
Words and music by Sammy Johns.
Lowery Music Co., Inc., 1981/Legibus Music Co., 1981/Captain Crystal Music, 1981.
Best-selling record by John Conlee from *John Conlee's Greatest Hits* (MCA, 83).

Complicated Girl
Words and music by Michael Steele and David White.
EMI-Blackwood/Feist & April Music, 1988/Bangophile Music, 1988/ Warner-Tamerlane Music, 1988/Ashdale Music, 1988.
Introduced by The Bangles on *Everywhere* (Columbia, 87).

Conga
Words and music by Enrique Garcia.
Foreign Imported, 1985.
Best-selling record by Miami Sound Machine in 1986 from the album *Primitive Love* (Epic, 85).

Congratulations
Words and music by Traveling Wilburys.
Copyright Control, 1988.
Introduced by The Traveling Wilburys on *Traveling Wilburys Volume I* (Wilbury, 88). This unique folk/rock family effort evokes the past glory of the form.

Controversy
Words and music by Prince Rogers Nelson.
Controversy Music, 1981.
Best-selling record by Prince from *Controversy* (Warner Brothers, 82).

Cool It Now
Words and music by Vincent Brantley and Rick Timas.
All Nations Music, 1984.
Best-selling record by New Edition from *New Edition* (MCA, 84).

Cool Love
Words and music by Cory Lerios, David Jenkins, and John Pierce.
Irving Music Inc., 1981/Pablo Cruise Music, 1981/Almo Music Corp.,

1981.
Best-selling record by Pablo Cruise from *Reflector* (A & M, 81).

Cool Night
Words and music by Paul Davis.
Web 4 Music Inc., 1981.
Best-selling record by Paul Davis from *Cool Night* (Arista, 81).

Cool Part 1
Words by Dez Dickerson, music by Prince Rogers Nelson.
Tionna Music, 1981.
Best-selling record by The Time from *The Time* (Warner Brothers, 82).

Cool Places
Words and music by Ron Mael and Russel Mael.
EMI-April Music, 1983.
Best-selling record by Sparks and Jane Wiedlin from *Sparks in Outer Space* (Atlantic, 83).

Coolsville
Words and music by Laurie Anderson.
Difficult Music, 1989.
Introduced by Laurie Anderson on *Strange Angels* (Warner Bros., 89), more avant-garde poetry from the performance artist.

Copperhead Road
Words and music by Steve Earle.
Lorimar Music Corp., 1987/Duke of Earle, 1987.
Introduced by Steve Earle on *Copperhead Road* (Uni, 88).

Copperhead Road
Words and music by Steve Earle.
Goldline Music Inc., 1987/Duke of Earle, 1987.
Introduced by Steve Earle on *Copperhead Road* (Uni, 88).

The Corvette Song, see **The One I Loved Back Then.**

Could I Have This Dance
Words and music by Wayland Holyfield and Bob House.
Tree Publishing Co., Inc., 1980/Polygram International, 1980.
Introduced in the film and soundtrack album *Urban Cowboy* (80). Best-selling record by Anne Murray (Capitol, 80).

Could've Been
Words and music by Lois Blaisch.
George Tobin, 1987.
Best-selling record by Tiffany, from the album *Tiffany* (MCA, 87).

Count Me Out
Words and music by Vincent Brantley and Rick Timas.

New Generation Music, 1985.
Best-selling record by New Edition from the album *All for Love* (MCA, 85).

Count Your Blessings
Words and music by Nicholas Ashford and Valerie Simpson.
Nick-O-Val Music, 1986.
Best-selling record by Ashford and Simpson from the album *Real Love* (Capitol, 86). The song was also performed during a nightclub scene on the television show *The Equalizer.*

Country Boy
Words and music by Tony Colton, Ray Smith, and Albert Lee.
Polygram International, 1977.
Best-selling record by Ricky Skaggs from the album *Country Boy* (Epic, 85).

A Country Boy Can Survive
Words and music by Hank Williams, Jr.
Bocephus Music Inc., 1981.
Best-selling record by Hank Williams, Jr. from *The Pressure Is On* (Elektra/Curb, 82).

Country Girls
Words and music by Troy Seals and Eddie Setser.
Warner-Tamerlane Music, 1984/WB Music, 1984/Two-Sons Music, 1984.
Best-selling record by John Schneider from the album *Too Good to Stop Now* (MCA, 85).

Cover Girl
Words and music by Maurice Starr.
Maurice Starr Music, 1988/EMI-April Music, 1988.
Best-selling record by New Kids on the Block, the hottest teen group in many years, from *Hang Tough* (Columbia, 89).

Cover Me
Words and music by Bruce Springsteen.
Bruce Springsteen Publishing, 1984.
Best-selling record By Bruce Springsteen from *Born in the U.S.A.* (Columbia, 84).

Coward of the County
Words and music by Roger Bowling and Billy Edd Wheeler.
Sleepy Hollow Music, 1979/Billy Edd Wheeler.
Best-selling record by Kenny Rogers from *Kenny* (United Artists, 80).

The Cowboy Rides Away
Words and music by Sonny Throckmorton and Casey Kelly.

Cross Keys Publishing Co., Inc., 1984/Tight List Music Inc., 1984.
Best-selling record by George Strait from the album *Does Fort Worth Ever Cross Your Mind?* (MCA, 84).

Cowboys and Clowns
Words and music by Steve Dorff, Snuff Garrett, Larry Herbstritt, and Gary Harju.
Peso Music, 1980/Bar Cee Music, 1980/Warner-Tamerlane Music, 1980/WB Music, 1980/Senor Music, 1980/Billy Music, 1980.
Best-selling record by Ronnie Milsap from *Milsap Magic* (RCA, 80).

Crack Killed Applejack
Words and music by Mitch McDowell and Cray Owen.
Jobete Music Co., 1986/Gentle General, 1986.
Introduced by General Kane on the album *In Full Chill* (Gordy, 86). This rap song about a high school basketball star who falls victim to the street drug crack was inspired by the death of the college athlete Len Bias. The song was originally entitled 'Death Lives in the Rover House.'

Crazay
Words and music by Jesse Johnson.
Almo Music Corp., 1986.
Best-selling record by Jesse Johnson (featuring Sly Stone) from the album *Shockadelica* (A & M, 86). The writer is a former member of The Time, proteges of Minneapolis legend Prince.

Crazy
Words and music by Kenny Rogers and Richard Marx.
Lionsmate Music, 1984/Security Hogg Music, 1984.
Best-selling record by Kenny Rogers from the album *What About Me* (RCA, 85).

Crazy (Australian)
Words and music by Andy Qunta, Jan Davies, and Bob Kretschmer.
EMI-April Music, 1987/Almo Music Corp., 1987/Rondor Music Inc., 1987.
Best-selling record in 1988 by Icehouse, from *Man of Colours* (Chryaslis, 87).

Crazy About Her (English)
Words and music by Rod Stewart, Duane Hitchings, and Jim Cregan.
Rod Stewart, 1988/Intersong, USA Inc., 1988/Full Keel Music, 1988.
Best-selling record in 1989 by Rod Stewart, from *Out of Order* (Warner Bros., 88).

Crazy Arms
Words and music by Chuck Seals and Ralph Mooney.
Champion Music, 1956/Tree Publishing Co., Inc./Manitou-Champion.

Revived in 1989 by Jerry Lee Lewis on the soundtrack of the movie based on his rise to fame and subsequent scandal, *Great Balls of Fire,* where he was portrayed by Dennis Quaid. A soundtrack album for the film was released by Polydor.

Crazy for You
Words by John Bettis, music by Jon Lind.
Warner-Tamerlane Music, 1983/WB Music, 1983/Deertrack Music, 1983.
Best-selling record by Madonna. Introduced by Madonna in the film and soundtrack album *Vision Quest.* (Geffen, 85).

Crazy for Your Love
Words and music by James P. Pennington and Sonny LeMaire.
Careers Music Inc., 1984/Tree Publishing Co., Inc., 1984/Pacific Island Music, 1984.
Best-selling record by Exile from the album *Kentucky Hearts* (Epic, 85).

Crazy from the Heat
Words and music by David Bellamy and Don Schlitz.
Bellamy Brothers Music, 1987/Don Schlitz Music, 1987.
Best-selling record by The Bellamy Brothers, from the album *Crazy from the Heart* (MCA/Curb, 87).

Crazy in the Night (Barking at Airplanes)
Words and music by Kim Carnes.
Moonwindow Music, 1985.
Best-selling record by Kim Carnes from the album *Barking at Airplanes* (EMI-America, 85).

Crazy Man Michael (English)
Words and music by Richard Thompson and Dave Swarbrick.
Sparta Music, London, England, 1987/Island Music, 1987.
Performed by Fairport Convention, from the album *In Real Time (Live '87)* (Island, 87). Co-author Thompson is a former member of this legendary English folk group.

Crazy World
Words by Leslie Bricusse, music by Henry Mancini.
EMI Music Publishing, 1981/Stage & Screen Music Inc., 1981/Henry Mancini Enterprises, 1981.
Introduced by Julie Andrews in *Victor, Victoria* (81).

Crazy World
Words and music by Michael Rupert and Jerry Colker.
Introduced by Mara Getz and Michael Rupert in the 1987 musical *Mail,* produced in Los Angeles and scheduled for Broadway in 1988. The same authors previously scored off Broadway with *Three Men Naked from the Waist Down.*

73

Creatures of Love
Words and music by David Byrne.
Index Music, 1985/Bleu Disque Music.
Introduced by The Talking Heads on the album *Little Creatures* (Sire, 85).

Creepin'
Words and music by Stevie Wonder.
Jobete Music Co., 1974/Black Bull Music, 1974.
Rhythm 'n' Blues by Luther Vandross in the album *The Night I Fell in Love* (Epic, 85).

Criminal (Theme from *Fatal Beauty*)
Words and music by Sylvester LeVay and Tom Whitlock.
WB Music, 1987/Levay, 1987.
Introduced by Shannon in the film *Fatal Beauty;* also appears on its soundtrack album.

Crimson and Clover
Words and music by Peter Lucea and Tommy James.
Big Seven Music Corp.
Revived by Joan Jett & The Blackhearts from *I Love Rock and Roll* (Boardwalk, 82).

Cross My Broken Heart
Words and music by Steve Bray and Tony Pierce.
Famous Music Corp., 1987/Polygram International, 1987.
Best-selling record by The Jets from the film and soundtrack album *Beverly Hills Cop II* (MCA, 87).

Crossroads
Words and music by Tracy Chapman.
Purple Rabbit Music, 1989/EMI-April Music, 1989.
Introduced by Tracy Chapman on *Crossroads* (Elektra, 89).

Cruel Summer (English)
Words and music by Tony Swain and Steve Jolley.
In A Bunch Music, London, England, 1983/Red Bus Music Ltd., London, England, 1983/MCA, Inc., 1983.
Best-selling record by Bananarama from *Bananarama* (London, 84).

Crumblin' Down
Words and music by John Cougar Mellencamp and George Michael Green.
Full Keel Music, 1983.
Best-selling record by John Cougar Mellencamp from *Uh-Huh (Riva, 83)*.

Crush on You
Words and music by Jerry Knight and Aaron Zigman.
Almo Music Corp., 1986/Crimsco Music, 1986/Irving Music Inc., 1986.
Best-selling record by The Jets from the album *The Jets* (MCA, 86).

Cry (English)
Words and music by Kevin Godley and Lol Creme.
Man-Ken Music Ltd., 1985.
Best-selling record by Godley and Creme from the album *The History Mix Volume I* (Polygram, 85).

Cry
Words and music by Churchill Kohlman.
Mellow Music Publishing Co., 1951.
Revived in 1986 by Crystal Gayle on the album *Straight to the Heart* (Warner Bros., 86). This was once a hit for Johnny Ray.

Cry (English)
Words and music by Phillip Cilia and Christopher Duffy.
EMI-Blackwood Music Inc., 1989.
Best-selling record by Waterfront from *Waterfront* (Polydor/Polygram, 89).

Cry Baby Cry (English)
Words and music by John Lennon and Paul McCartney.
Northern Songs, Ltd., England, 1968/Maclen Music Inc., 1968.
Introduced by The Beatles on *The White Album* (Capitol, 68), the song was revived by Richard Barone on *Cool Blue Halo* (Passport, 87).

Cry, Cry, Cry
Words and music by John Scott and Don Devaney.
Sweet Baby Music, 1987/Music City Music, 1987.
Best-selling record in 1988 by Highway 101 from *Highway 101* (Warner Bros., 87).

Cry Freedom
Music by George Fenton and Jonas Gwangwa.
MCA, Inc., 1987.
Introduced by George Fenton and Jonas Gwangwa in the film and on the soundtrack album of *Cry Freedom* (MCA, 87). Nominated for an Academy Award, Best Original Song, 1987; a Grammy Award, Best Song for Film or TV, 1988.

Cry Like a Rainstorm
Words and music by Eric Kaz.
Glasco Music, Co., 1970.
Revived in 1989 by Linda Ronstadt on *Cry Like a Rainstorm, Howl Like the Wind* (Elektra, 89).

Cry Little Sister (Theme from *The Lost Boys*)
Words and music by Mike Mainieri and Gerard McMann.
Warner-Tamerlane Music, 1987/Hot Corner, 1987/WB Music, 1987.
Introduced by Gerard McMann, from the film and soundtrack album *The Lost Boys* (Atlantic, 87).

Cry Myself to Sleep
Words and music by Paul Kennerley.
Irving Music Inc., 1986.
Best-selling record by The Judds from the album *Rockin' with the Rhythm* (RCA/Curb, 86).

Cry Out
Words and music by L. Ron Hubbard.
Introduced by Edgar Winter on *Mission Earth*. The tune was written in 1986 by the late founder of Scientology.

Crying
Words and music by Roy Orbison and Joe Melton.
Acuff-Rose Publications Inc., 1961.
Revived by Don McLean from *Chain Lightning* (Millennium, 81).

Crying My Heart Out over You
Words and music by Jerry Organ, Louise Certain, Carl Butler, and Gladys Stacey.
Cedarwood Publishing Co., Inc., 1959.
Best-selling record by Ricky Scaggs from *Waiting for the Sun to Shine* (Epic, 82).

Cuban Slide (English)
Words and music by Chrissie Hynde and James Honeyman Scott.
Welbeck Music, 1980/MCA, Inc., 1980.
Introduced by The Pretenders on *The Pretenders* (Sire, 81).

Cult of Personality
Words and music by Vernon Reid, Will Calhoun, Cary Glover, and Muzz Skillings.
Dare to Dream Music, 1987/Famous Music Corp., 1987.
Best-selling record in 1989 by Living Colour from *Vivid* (Epic/E.P.A., 88). Appearing as the opening act on the Rolling Stones' 1989 tour helped this black band break the color barrier in hard rock.

Cum on Feel the Noize (English)
Words and music by Noddy Holder and Jim Lea.
Barn Music, London, England, 1972.
Revived by Quiet Riot from *Metal Health* (Pasha, 83).

Cupid
Words and music by Sam Cooke.

ABKCO Music Inc., 1961.
Revived by The Spinners from *Love Trippin'* (Atlantic, 80).

The Curly Shuffle
Words and music by Peter Quinn.
Swing Tet Publishing, 1983.
Best-selling record by Jump 'n' The Saddle (Atlantic, 83). Song is based on the antics of The Three Stooges.

Curves
Words and music by Preston Glass and Narada Michael Walden.
Bellboy Music, 1985/Gratitude Sky Music, 1985.
Introduced by Siedah Garrett in the film and soundtrack album *Vision Quest* (Geffen, 85).

Cutie Pie
Words and music by Albert Hudson, Theodore Dudley, Dave Roberson, Gregory Green, Jonathan Meadows, Terry Morgan, and Glenda Hudson.
Duchess Music Corp., 1982/Perk's Music, Inc., 1982.
Best-selling record by One Way from *Who's Foolin' Who* (MCA, 82).

Cuyahoga
Words and music by Bill Berry, Peter Buck, Mike Mills, and Michael Stipe.
Night Garden Music, 1986.
Introduced by R.E.M. on the album *Life's Rich Pageant* (I.R.S., 86).
This song is about the same river in Cleveland once immortalized by Randy Newman in 'Burn on, Big River.'

Cynical Girl
Words and music by Marshall Crenshaw.
Belwin-Mills Publishing Corp., 1982/MHC Music, 1982.
Introduced by Marshall Crenshaw in *Field Day* (Warner Brothers, 83).

D

Da Butt
Words and music by Marcus Miller and Mark Stevens.
MCA Music, 1987/Sunset Burgundy Music, Inc., 1987/Toosie, 1987.
Introduced by E. U. in the film and soundtrack album of *School Daze*.
  Best-selling record (EMI-Manhattan, 88), it also inspired a major
  dance craze in 1988.

Daddy's Come Home
Words and music by Steve Van Zandt.
Blue Midnight Music, 1980.
Featured on *Dedication* by Gary U.S. Bonds (EMI-America, 83).

Daddy's Hands
Words and music by Holly Dunn.
Uncle Artie, 1986.
Best-selling record by Holly Dunn from the album *Holly Dunn* (MTM,
  86). Nominated for a Grammy Award, Country Song of the Year,
  1986.

Damn Good
Words and music by David Lee Roth and Steve Vai.
Diamondback Music Co., 1987/Sy Vy Music, 1987.
Introduced by David Lee Roth on *Skyscraper* (Warner Bros., 88).

Dance Floor
Words and music by Roger Troutman and Larry Troutman.
Troutman's Music, 1982.
Best-selling record by Zapp from *Zapp II* (Warner Brothers, 82).

Dance Hall Days (English)
Words and music by Jack Hues.
Warner-Tamerlane Music, 1983.
Best-selling record by Wang Chung from *Points on the Curve* (Geffen,
  84).

Dance Little Sister (English)
Words and music by Terence Trent D'Arby.
Virgin Music, 1987/Young Terrence, 1987.
Best-selling record in 1988 Terence Trent D'Arby from *The Hardline According to Terence Trent D'Arby* (Columbia, 87). Won a Grammy Award, and Best New Artist, 1987.

Dance Wit' Me
Words and music by Rick James.
Stone City Music, 1982.
Best-selling record by Rick James from *Throwin' Down* (Gordy, 82).

Dancin' Cowboys
Words and music by David Bellamy.
Bellamy Brothers Music, 1980/Famous Music Corp., 1980.
Best-selling record by The Bellamy Brothers (Warner Brothers, 80).

Dancin' Your Memory Away
Words and music by Eddie Burton and Thomas Grant.
Barnwood Music, 1981.
Best-selling record by Charly McClain (Epic, 82).

Dancing in the Dark
Words and music by Bruce Springsteen.
Bruce Springsteen Publishing, 1984.
Best-selling record by Bruce Springsteen from *Born in the U.S.A.* (Columbia, 84). Nominated for a Grammy Award, Best Record of the Year, 1984.

Dancing in the Sheets
Words by Dean Pitchford, music by Bill Wolfer.
Famous Music Corp., 1984/Ensign Music, 1984.
Best-selling record by Shalamar from *HeartBreak* (Columbia, 84). Introduced in the film and soundtrack album *Footloose* (84). Nominated for a Grammy Award, Rhythm 'n' Blues Record of the Year, 1984.

Dancing in the Streets
Words and music by William Stephenson and Marvin Gaye.
Jobete Music Co., 1964/Stone Agate Music, 1964.
Revived by Mick Jagger and David Bowie (EMI-America, 85). All proceeds from this 1985 recording were donated to fight famine in Africa and the United States.

Dancing on the Ceiling
Words and music by Lionel Richie, Jr. and Carlos Rios.
Brockman Music, 1986.
Best-selling record by Lionel Richie from the album *Dancing on the Ceiling* (Motown, 86).

Dancing with Myself (English)
Words and music by Billy Idol and Tony James.
Chrysalis Music Group, 1980.
Best-selling record by Billy Idol and Generation X from *Don't Stop*
(Chysalis, 81). Revived by Billy Idol (Chrysalis, 84).

Danger Zone (American-German)
English words and music by Giorgio Moroder and Tom Whitlock.
Famous Music Corp., 1986.
Best-selling record Kenny Loggins from the soundtrack album of the
film *Top Gun* (Columbia, 86), easily the soundtrack album of the
year.

Dare Me
Words and music by Sam Lorber and Dave Innis.
WB Music, 1985/Bob Montgomery Music Inc., 1985/Dave Innis Music,
1985.
Best-selling record by The Pointer Sisters from the album *Contact*
(RCA, 85).

Dark Eyes
Words and music by Bob Dylan.
Special Rider Music, 1985.
Introduced by Bob Dylan on the album *Empire Burlesque* (Columbia,
85).

Darlene
Words and music by Mike Geiger, Woody Mullis, and Ricky Rector.
Acuff Rose Music, 1988/Milene Music, 1988/It's on Hold, 1988.
Best-selling record by T. Graham Brown, from *Come As You Were*
(Capitol, 88).

Day by Day
Words and music by Rob Hyman, Eric Bazilian, and Rick Chertoff.
Dub Notes, 1985/Human Boy Music/Hobbler Music.
Best-selling record by the Hooters in 1986 from the album *Nervous
Night* (Columbia, 85).

Day in--Day Out (English)
Words and music by David Bowie.
Jones Music Co., 1987.
Best-selling record by David Bowie, from the album *Never Let Me
Down* (EMI, 87).

Day-O, also known as **The Banana Boat Song**
Words and music by Irving Burgess and William Attaway.
Cherry Lane Music Co., 1955, 1983.
Revived in 1988 by Harry Belafonte in the film and soundtrack
Beetlejuice (Geffen, 88).

Daydream Believer
Words and music by John Stewart.
Screen Gems-EMI Music Inc., 1967.
Revived by Anne Murray from *I'll Always Love You* (Capitol, 80).

Days Gone By
Words by P. G. Wodehouse and Guy Bolton, music by Jerome Kern.
Polygram International, 1924.
Revived by Beverly Lambert in the 1989 production of the musical
    Sitting Pretty.

D.C. Cab
Words and music by Richard Feldman, Rich Kelly, and Larry John
    McNally.
Unicity Music, Inc., 1983/Broadcast Music Inc., 1983.
Best-selling record by Peabo Bryson (MCA, 84). Introduced in the film
    D.C. Cab (84).

De Do Do Do, De Da Da Da (English)
Words and music by Sting (pseudonym for Gordon Sumner).
Blue Turtle, 1980/Criterion Music Corp., 1980.
Best-selling record by The Police on *Zenyatta Mondatta* (A & M, 80).

Dead Giveaway
Words and music by Joey Gallo, Marquis Dair, and Leon F. Sylvers, III.
Portrait/Solar Songs Inc., 1983/Solar, 1983.
Best-selling record by Shalamar from *The Look* (Solar, 83).

Dear God (English)
Words and music by Andy Partridge.
EMI-Virgin, 1987.
Best-selling record by XTC, from the album *Skylarking* (Geffen, 86);
    although it was not on the original U.S. version of the album, it was
    added to later pressings after generating controversy for the
    agnosticism of its lyrics and achieving high sales as a twelve-inch
    single in the U.S. (it had been released as a B-side in England).

Dear John
Words and music by John Sullivan.
Introduced by Wendy Talbot as the theme for *Dear John,* the television
    series.

Dear Mr. Jesus
Words and music by Richard Klender.
Klenco, 1986.
Introduced by by PowerSource, from the album *Shelter from the Storm*
    (PowerSource, 86). Featuring the voice of nine-year-old Sharon Batts,
    this poignant song deals with the compelling issue, child abuse.

Debbie Gibson Is Pregnant (with My Two-Headed Love Child)
Words and music by Mojo Nixon.
Muffin Stuffin, 1988/La Rana, 1988.
Introduced by Mojo Nixon and Skid Roper on *Root Hog or Die*
(Enigma, 89). With this song the satirists followed up last year's
'Elvis Is Everywhere' by taking on another cultural icon.

Dedicated to the One I Love
Words and music by Lowman Pauling and Ralph Bass.
Duchess Music Corp., 1957.
Revived by Bernadette Peters in *Now Playing* (MCA, 81).

Deep Inside My Heart
Words and music by Randy Meisner and Eric Kaz.
Nebraska Music, 1980/EMI Unart Catalogue, 1980/Glasco Music, Co.,
1980.
Best-selling record by Randy Meisner from *One More Song* (Epic, 80).

Deeper Love
Words and music by Diane Warren.
Realsongs, 1987.
Introduced by Meli'sa Morgan on the soundtrack of the film *The Golden
Child* and its album (Capitol, 87).

Deeper Than the Holler
Words and music by Paul Overstreet and Don Schlitz.
Scarlet Moon Music, 1988/Screen Gems-EMI Music Inc., 1988/Don
Schlitz Music, 1988/MCA Music, 1988.
Best-selling record in 1989 by Randy Travis from *Old 8 X 10* (Warner
Bros., 88).

Deeper Understanding (English)
Words and music by Kate Bush.
Kate Bush Music, Ltd., London, England, 1989/Screen Gems-EMI
Music Inc., 1989.
Introduced by Kate Bush on *The Sensual World* (Columbia, 89).

Deja Vu
Music by Isaac Hayes, words by Adrienne Anderson.
Rightsong Music, 1978.
Best-selling record by Dionne Warwick from *Dionne* (Arista, 80).

Delirious
Words and music by Prince Rogers Nelson.
Controversy Music, 1982.
Best-selling record by Prince from *1999* (Warner Brothers, 83).

Der Kommissar (German)
German words by Falco, English words by Andrew Piercy, music by

Robert Ponger.
Chappell & Co., Inc., 1983.
Best-selling record by After the Fire from *ATF* (Epic, 83).

Desert Moon
Words and music by Dennis De Young.
Grand Illusion Music, 1984.
Best-selling record by Dennis De Young from *Desert Moon* (A & M, 84).

Desire
Words and music by Barry Gibb, Robin Gibb, and Maurice Gibb.
Stigwood Music Inc., 1979.
Best-selling record by Andy Gibb from *After Dark* (RSO, 80).

Desire (Irish)
Words by Bono (pseudonym for Paul Hewson), music by U2.
Polygram International, 1988.
Best-selling record by U2 from the film and soundtrack album *Rattle and Hum* (Island, 88).

Desperado Love
Words and music by Michael Garvin and Sammy Johns.
Tree Publishing Co., Inc., 1986/Lowery Music Co., Inc., 1986.
Best-selling record by Conway Twitty from the album *Fallin' for You for Years* (Warner Bros., 86).

Desperados Waiting for a Train
Words and music by Guy Clark.
Chappell & Co., Inc., 1973/World Song Publishing, Inc., 1973.
Revived by Waylon Jennings, Willie Nelson, Johnny Cash, and Kris Kristofferson on the album *The Highwayman* (Columbia, 85).
Nominated for a Grammy Award, Country Song of the Year, 1985.

Detox Mansion
Words and music by Warren Zevon and Jorge Calderon.
Zevon Music Inc., 1987.
Introduced by Warren Zevon on the album *Sentimental Hygiene* (Virgin, 87). The song details Zevon's struggle toward recovery from alcoholism.

Devil Inside (Australian)
Words and music by Andrew Farriss and Michael Hutchence.
MCA Music, 1987.
Best-selling record in 1988 by INXS in *Kick* (Atlantic, 87).

Dial My Heart
Words and music by L. A. Reid (pseudonym for Antonio Reid), Babyface (pseudonym for Kenny Edmunds), and Daryl Simmons.

84

Kear Music, 1988/Hip-Trip Music Co., 1988.

Best-selling record in 1989 by The Boys, from *Messages from the Boys* (Motown, 88). 1989 was another banner year for the songwriters.

Diamonds
Words and music by Jimmy Jam (pseudonym for James Harris, III) and Terry Lewis.
Flyte Tyme Tunes, 1987.
Best-selling record by Herb Alpert, featuring Janet Jackson as lead singer; from the album *Keep Your Eye on Me* (A & M, 87).

Diamonds of Anger
Words and music by Fred Small.
Pine Barrens Music, 1987.
Introduced by Fred Small on *I Will Stand Fast* (Flying Fish, 88). The song deals with racial unrest in South Africa.

Diamonds on the Soles of Her Shoes (American-South African)
English words and music by Paul Simon and Joseph Shabalala.
Paul Simon Music, 1986.
Best-selling record by Paul Simon, from the album *Graceland* (Warner Bros., 86), which won a Grammy Award as best album of the year. In the album Simon adapted many elements of South African street music and here collaborated with a noted musician from that country.

Did It in a Minute
Words and music by Daryl Hall, Sara Allen, and Janna Allen.
Hot Cha Music Co., 1981/Fust Buzza Music, Inc., 1981/Unichappell Music Inc., 1981.
Best-selling record by Daryl Hall and John Oates from *Private Eyes* (RCA, 82).

Didn't I (Blow Your Mind)
Words by Thom Bell and William Hart, music by Thom Bell.
Bellboy Music, 1970/Mighty Three Music, 1970.
Revived in 1989 by New Kids on the Block on *Hangin' Tough* (Columbia, 89).

Didn't We Almost Have It All
Words by Will Jennings, music by Michael Masser.
Prince Street Music, 1987/Willin' David, 1987/Blue Sky Rider Songs, 1987.
Best-selling record by Whitney Houston, from the album *Whitney* (Arista, 87). Nominated for a Grammy Award, Song of the Year, 1987.

(I Just) Died in Your Arms (English)
Words and music by Nick Eede.
EMI-Virgin, 1987.

Best-selling record by Cutting Crew, from the album *Broadcast* (Virgin, 87).

Diggin' up Bones
Words and music by Paul Overstreet and Al Gore.
Writer's Group Music, 1986/Scarlet Moon Music, 1986/Sawgrass Music, 1986/Lawyer's Daughter, 1986.
Best-selling record by Randy Travis from the album *Storms of Life* (Warner Bros., 86).

Digging Your Scene (English)
Words and music by Robert Howard.
BMG Songs Inc., 1986.
Best-selling record by The Blow Monkeys from the album *Animal Magic* (RCA, 86).

Dinner with Gershwin
Words and music by Brenda Russell.
WB Music, 1987/Geffen Music, 1987/Rutland Road, 1987.
Best-selling record Donna Summer, from the album *All Systems Go* (Geffen, 87). This was one of a number of releases marking the fiftieth anniversary of the death of songwriter George Gershwin, among them, new recordings of his musicals *Let Them Eat Cake* and *Of Thee I Sing* and opera star Kiri Te Kanawa's album *Kiri Sings Gershwin* (Angel/EMI), which made use of original orchestrations newly discovered in a Secaucus, New Jersey, warehouse.

Dirty Diana
Words and music by Michael Jackson.
Mijac Music, 1987/Warner-Tamerlane Music, 1987.
Best-selling record in 1988 by Michael Jackson, from *Bad* (Epic, 87).

Dirty Laundry
Words and music by Don Henley and Danny Kortchmar.
Woody Creek Music, 1982.
Best-selling record by Don Henley from *I Can't Stand Still* (Asylum, 82).

Dirty Movies
Words and music by Eddie Van Halen, Alex Van Halen, David Lee Roth, and Michael Anthony.
Van Halen Music, 1981/Diamond Dave Music.
Introduced by Van Halen on *Fair Warning* (Warner Brothers, 81).

Discretion
Words and music by Chandler Travis.
Party Music (USA), 1987.
Introduced by The Incredible Casuals on *That's That* (Rounder, 88).

Disneyland
Words by Howard Ashman, music by Marvin Hamlisch.
Chappell & Co., Ltd., London, England, 1986/Red Bullet Music, 1986.
Introduced by Jodi Benson in the 1986 Broadway musical *Smile*. The show was based on the non-musical film of the same title released in 1975.

Divine Emotion
Words and music by Narada Michael Walden and Jeffrey Cohen.
Gratitude Sky Music, 1988/When Worlds Collide, 1988.
Introduced by Narada Michael Walden, who is better known as a producer, in the film and soundtrack album *Bright Lights, Big City* (Reprise, 88).

Dixie Road
Words and music by Don Goodman, Mary Ann Kennedy, and Pam Rose.
Southern Soul Music, 1981/Window Music Publishing Inc., 1981.
Best-selling record by Lee Greenwood from the album *Streamline* (MCA, 85).

Dixieland Delight
Words and music by Ronnie Rogers.
Sister John Music, Inc., 1982/Maypop Music, 1982.
Best-selling record by Alabama from *The Closer You Get* (RCA, 83).

Do Deny
Words and music by Robert Hunter.
Ice Nine Publishing Co., Inc., 1987.
Introduced by Robert Hunter, lyricist for The Grateful Dead, on *Liberty* (Relix, 88).

Do I Do
Words and music by Stevie Wonder.
Jobete Music Co., 1981/Black Bull Music, 1981.
Best-selling record by Stevie Wonder from *Stevie Wonder's Original Musicquarium* (Tamla, 82). Nominated for a Grammy Award, Rhythm 'n Blues Song of the Year, 1982.

Do Me Baby
Words and music by Prince Rogers Nelson.
Controversy Music, 1986.
Best-selling record by Meli'sa Morgan from the album *Do Me Baby* (Capitol, 86).

Do They Know It's Christmas (Irish)
Words and music by Bob Geldof and Midge Ure.
Chappell & Co., Inc., 1984.
Best-selling record by Band-Aid (Columbia, 84). Proceeds were donated

to aid Ethiopian children. Group was composed of British rock all-stars.   **Revived by** Kylie Dinosur, Bananarama, Cliff Richard, Technotronic, Wet Wet Wet, Chris Rea and other in the U.K.

Do What You Do, also known as **Why Do You (Do What You Do)**
Words and music by Ralph Dino and Larry DiTomaso.
Unicity Music, Inc., 1980.
Best-selling record by Jermaine Jackson from *Jermaine Jackson* (Arista, 84).

Do Ya'
Words and music by K. T. Oslin.
Wooden Wonder, 1987.
Best-selling record by K. T. Oslin, from the album *80's Ladies* (RCA, 87).

Do Ya (English)
Words and music by Jeff Lynne.
EMI-Blackwood Music Inc., 1974/Sugartown Music, 1974.
Revived in 1989 by Ace Frehley on *Trouble Walkin'* (Megaforce/Atlantic, 89).

Do You Believe in Love (English)
Words and music by Robert John 'Mutt' Lange.
Zomba Music, 1982.
Best-selling record by Huey Lewis & The News from *Picture This* (Chrysalis, 82).

Do You Get Enough Love
Words and music by Bunny Sigler and Kenny Gamble.
Assorted Music, 1986/Henry SueMay Music.
Best-selling record by Shirley Jones from the album *Always in the Mood* (Manhattan, 86).

Do You Hear What I Hear
Words and music by Noel Regney and Gloria Shayne.
Regent Music, 1962, 1979.
Revived in 1987 by Whitney Houston on the album *A Very Special Christmas* (A & M), this song was originally a best-seller for Bing Crosby. Co-author Regney also wrote the English lyrics for the 1963 hit by the Singing Nun, 'Dominique'.

Do You Love Me
Words and music by Berry Gordy, Jr.
Jobete Music Co., 1962.
Revived in 1987 by The Contours in the film *Dirty Dancing* and on its second soundtrack album *More Dirty Dancing* (RCA, 87). The Motown single became a bestseller in 1988.

Do You Really Want to Hurt Me (English)
Words and music by Roy Hay, Jon Moss, Michael Craig, and George O'Dowd.
Virgin Music, 1982.
Best-selling record by Culture Club from *Kissing to Be Clever* (Epic, 83).

Do You Remember
Words and music by Gary William Friedman and Will Holt.
Bussy Music, 1983/Devon Music, 1983/Hampshire House Publishing Corp., 1983/Lemon Tree Music, Inc., 1983.
Introduced by Ted Thurston and Company of *Taking My Turn* (83).

Do You Remember Rock and Roll Radio
Words and music by Douglas Colvin, John Cummings, and Jeff Hyman.
Bleu Disque Music, 1979/Taco Tunes Inc., 1979.
Introduced by The Ramones on *End of the Century* (Sire, 79).

Do You Wanna Go to Heaven
Words and music by Curly Putman and Bucky Jones.
Tree Publishing Co., Inc., 1980/Cross Keys Publishing Co., Inc., 1980.
Best-selling record by T. G. Sheppard (Warner Brothers, 80).

Do You Wanna Touch Me (English)
Words and music by Gary Glitter and Mike Leander.
Music of the World, 1973.
Best-selling record by Joan Jett & The Blackhearts from *I Love Rock and Roll* (Boardwalk, 82).

The Doctor
Words and music by Tom Johnston, Charlie Midnight, and Eddie Schwartz.
Windecar Music, 1989/EMI-Blackwood Music Inc., 1989/Janiceps, 1989/High Frontier, 1989.
Best-selling record by The Doobie Brothers from *Cycles* (Capitol, 89).

Doctor! Doctor! (English)
Words and music by Thomas Bailey, Alanah Currie, and Joe Leeway.
Zomba Music, 1984.
Best-selling record by The Thompson Twins from *Into the Gap* (Arista, 84).

Dr. Feelgood
Words and music by Mick Mars and Nikki Sixx.
Motley Crue, 1989/Sikki Nixx, 1989/Mick Mars, 1989.
Best-selling record by Motley Crue from *Dr. Feelgood* (Elektra, 89).

Dr. K
Words and music by Melvin Owens and Lloyd Barry.

Port St. Joe, 1986/Vine Street Music, 1986.
Introduced by 'Dr. K,' baseball player Dwight Gooden, with the 'MCL' Rap Machine (Vine St., 86).

Doggin' Around, see Stop Doggin' Me Around.

Dogs
Words and music by Stanard Ridgway (pseudonym for Stanard Funston).
Mondo Spartacus Music, 1989/Illegal Songs, Inc., 1989/Criterion Music Corp., 1989.
Introduced by Stan Ridgway on *Mosquitos* (Geffen, 89).

Doing It All for My Baby
Words and music by Phil Cody (pseudonym for Phil Feliciato) and M. Duke.
Polygram International, 1986/Zookini, 1986/Vogue Music, 1986/Bob-a-Lew Music, 1986.
Best-selling record by Huey Lewis & The News, from the album *Fore!* (Chrysalis, 86); this was the fifth top-ten single from the album.

Doing It the Best I Can
Words by John Bettis, music by Steve Dorff.
John Bettis Music, 1988.
Performed by Bill Medley as the theme song for the television series *Just the Ten of Us,* this song was also featured on the album *Steve Dorff & Friends* (Reprise, 88).

Domino Dancing (English)
Words and music by Nick Tennant and Chris Lowe.
Cage Music Ltd., England, 1988/10 Music, 1988/Virgin Music, 1988.
Best-selling record by The Pet Shop Boys, from *Introspective* (EMI, 88).

Dominoes
Words and music by Robbie Nevil, Barry Eastmond, and Bobby Hart.
MCA Music, 1986/Bobby Hart Music, 1986.
Best-selling record by Robbie Nevil, from the album *Robbie Nevil* (Manhattan, 86).

Donna
Words and music by David Johansen.
Buster Poindexter, Inc., 1978.
Introduced by David Johansen on *Live It Up* (Blue Sky, 82).

Don't Ask Me Why
Words and music by Billy Joel.
Impulsive Music, 1980/EMI-April Music, 1980.
Best-selling record by Billy Joel from *Glass Houses* (Columbia, 80).

Don't Be Afraid of the Dark
Words and music by Dennis Walker.
Calhoun Street, 1988.
Introduced by Robert Cray on *Don't Be Afraid of the Dark* (Mercury, 88).

Don't Be Cruel
Words and music by Babyface (pseudonym for Kenny Edmunds), L. A. Reid (pseudonym for Antonio Reid), and Daryl Simmons.
Kear Music, 1988/Hip-Trip Music Co., 1988.
Best-selling record by Bobby Brown, from *Don't Be Cruel* (MCA, 88). Nominated for a Grammy Award, Rhythm 'n' Blues Song of the Year, 1988.

Don't Be Cruel
Words and music by Otis Blackwell and Elvis Presley.
Elvis Presley Music, 1956/Unart Music Corp., 1956/Unart-Unart, 1956.
Revived in 1988 by Cheap Trick on *Lap of Luxury* (Epic).

Don't Call Him a Cowboy
Words and music by Deborah Kay Hupp, Johnny McRae, and Brian Morrison.
Southern Nights Music Co., 1984.
Best-selling record by Conway Twitty from the album *Don't Call Him a Cowboy* (Warner Bros., 85).

Don't Call It Love
Words by Dean Pitchford, music by Tom Snow.
Pzazz Music, 1985/Snow Music, 1985.
Best-selling record by Dolly Parton from the album *Real Love* (RCA, 85).

Don't Close Your Eyes
Words and music by Donnie Purnell, Robert Halligan, Jr., and John Palumbo.
Cookies Music, 1988/Oppornockity Tunes, 1988/Ellymax Music, 1988/Willesden Music, Inc., 1988/Zomba Music, 1988.
Best-selling record by Kix from *Blow My Fuse* (Atlantic, 89).

Don't Close Your Eyes
Words and music by Bob McDill.
Polygram International, 1988.
Best-selling record by Keith Whitley, from *Don't Close Your Eyes* (RCA, 88).

Don't Come Around Here No More
Words and music by Tom Petty and Dave Stewart.
Gone Gator Music, 1985/Blue Network Music Inc., 1985.

Best-selling record by Tom Petty & The Heartbreakers from the album *Southern Accents* (MCA, 85).

Don't Come Inside My Head
Words and music by Elizabeth Swados.
EMI-Blackwood Music Inc., 1987.
Introduced by by Maribel Lizardo in the 1987 musical *Swing.*

Don't Cry (English)
Words and music by John Wetton and Geoffrey Downes.
WB Music, 1983/Island Music, 1983.
Best-selling record by Asia from *Alpha* (Geffen, 83).

Don't Cry for Me Argentina (English)
Words by Tim Rice, music by Andrew Lloyd Webber.
Off Backstreet Music, 1975.
Best-selling record by Festival from *Evita* (RSO, 80).

Don't Disturb This Groove (English)
Words and music by Mic Murphy and David Frank.
Science Lab, 1987.
Best-selling record by The System, from the album *Don't Disturb This Groove* (Capitol, 87).

Don't Do Me Like That
Words and music by Tom Petty.
Skyhill Publishing Co., Inc., 1979.

Don't Dream It's Over (Australian)
Words and music by Neil Finn.
Roundhead, 1987.
Best-selling record by Crowded House, from their album *Crowded House* (Capitol, 87). This song made a breakthrough single for singer-author Finn, who earlier had some fine efforts with Split Enz.

Don't Fall Apart on Me Tonight
Words and music by Bob Dylan.
Special Rider Music, 1983.
Introduced by Bob Dylan on *Infidels* (Columbia, 83).

Don't Fall in Love with a Dreamer
Words and music by Kim Carnes and Dave Ellingson.
Appian Music Co., 1980/Almo Music Corp., 1980/Quixotic Music Corp., 1980.
Best-selling record by Kim Carnes and Kenny Rogers from *Gideon* (United Artists, 80). Also featured, on *Kenny Rogers' Greatest Hits* (Likely, 80), *Twenty Greatest Hits* (Likely, 83) and *Duets* (Likely, 84).

Don't Fight It
Words and music by Kenny Loggins and Steve Perry, words by Dean Pitchford.
Milk Money Music, 1982/Lacy Boulevard Music, 1982/Warner-Tamerlane Music, 1982/Body Electric Music, 1982.
Best-selling record by Kenny Loggins with Steve Perry from *High Adventure* (Columbia, 82).

Don't Forget Your Way Home
Words and music by Ed Hunnicutt and John Raymond Brannen.
Tapadero Music, 1985/Young Beau Music, 1985.
Introduced by Reba McEntire on the album *Have I Got a Deal for You* (MCA, 85).

Don't Get Me Wrong (English)
Words and music by Chrissie Hynde.
MCA, Inc., 1986.
Best-selling record by The Pretenders from the album *Get Close* (Sire, 86).

Don't Give Up (English)
Words and music by Peter Gabriel.
Cliofine, 1986/Hidden Pun, 1986.
Introduced by Peter Gabriel and Kate Bush on the album *So* (Geffen, 86).

Don't Go
Words and music by Marlon Jackson.
Vabritmar, 1987.
Best-selling record by Marlon Jackson, from the album *Baby Tonight* (Capitol, 87).

Don't Go to Strangers
Words and music by J. D. Martin and Russell Smith.
MCA Music, 1986.
Best-selling record by T. Graham Brown; from the album *I Tell It Like It Used to Be* (Capitol, 86).

Don't It Make You Wanna Dance
Words and music by Rusty Weir.
Prophecy Publishing, Inc., 1980.
Introduced by Bonnie Raitt in the film and soundtrack album *Urban Cowboy* (80).

Don't Know Much, also known as **All I Need to Know**
Recorded by Bette Midler in 1983 and Bill Medley in 1981, this big ballad was revived by Linda Ronstadt and Aaron Neville on *Cry Like a Rainstorm, Howl Like the Wind* (Elektra, 89). Nominated for a Grammy Award, Song of the Year, 1989.

Don't Know What You Got (Till It's Gone)
Words and music by Tom Keifer.
Chappell & Co., Ltd., London, England, 1988/Evesongs Inc., 1988.
Best-selling record by Cinderella, from *Long Cold Winter* (Mercury, 88).

Don't Let Go
Words and music by Jesse Stone.
Roosevelt Music Co., Inc., 1957.
Best-selling record by Isaac Hayes from *Don't Let Go* (Polydor, 80).

Don't Let Go the Coat (English)
Words and music by Pete Townshend.
Towser Tunes Inc., 1981.
Best-selling record by The Who from *Face Dances* (Warner Brothers, 81).

Don't Let It End
Words and music by Dennis De Young.
Stygian Songs, 1983/Almo Music Corp., 1983.
Best-selling record by Styx from *Kilroy was Here* (A & M, 83).

Don't Let Me Be Misunderstood
Words and music by Bennie Benjamin, Sol Marcus, and Gloria Caldwell.
Bennie Benjamin Music, Inc., 1964/Chris-n-Ten Music, 1964.
Revived in 1986 by Elvis Costello on the album *King of America* (Columbia, 86).

Don't Look Any Further
Words and music by Franne Golde, Dennis Lambert, and Duane Hitchings.
Full Keel Music, 1984/Franne Golde Music Inc., 1984/Vandorf Songs Co., 1984/Rightsong Music, 1984.
Best-selling record by Dennis Edwards from *Don't Look Any Further* (Gordy, 84).

Don't Look Back (English)
Words and music by David Steele and Roland Gift.
Virgin Music, 1989.
Best-selling record by Fine Young Cannibals from *The Raw and the Cooked* (IRS, 89).

Don't Look in My Eyes
Words and music by Frank Wildhorn and Brian Potter.
Jobete Music Co., 1984/Chrysalis Music Group, 1984/Scaramanga Music, 1984.
Performed by Kenny Rogers on the album *The Heart of the Matter* (RCA, 86). This song was featured in wrap-up coverage of the 1986 World Series as the soundtrack for a clip showing a despondent Wade

Boggs of the losing Boston Red Sox in the dugout while the New York Mets celebrated their victory.

Don't Lose My Number (English)
Words and music by Phil Collins.
Hit & Run Music, 1985.
Best-selling record by Phil Collins from the album *No Jacket Required* (Atlantic, 85).

Don't Make It Easy for Me
Words and music by Earl Thomas Conley and Randy Scruggs.
EMI-April Music, 1983/EMI-Blackwood Music Inc., 1983/Full Armor Publishing Co., 1983.
Best-selling record by Earl Thomas Conley (RCA, 84).

Don't Make Me Over
Words by Hal David, music by Burt Bacharach.
Blue Seas Music Inc., 1962/Jac Music Co., Inc., 1962.
Revived in 1989 by Sybil on *Sybil* (West Plateau, 89).

Don't Make Me Wait for Love
Words and music by Preston Glass, Narada Michael Walden, and Walter Afanasieff.
Bellboy Music, 1986/Gratitude Sky Music, 1986.
Best-selling record by Kenny G., with vocal by Kenny Williams, from the album *Duotones* (Arista, 87).

Don't Mean Nothin'
Words and music by Richard Marx and Bruce Gaitsch.
Chi-Boy, 1987/Edge of Fluke, 1987.
Best-selling record by Richard Marx, from the album *Richard Marx* (Manhattan, 87). Co-author and performer Marx is an accomplished studio musician.

Don't Pay the Ferryman (English)
Words and music by Chris DeBurgh.
Irving Music Inc., 1982.
Best-selling record by Chris DeBurgh from *The Getaway* (A & M, 83).

Don't Push It Don't Force It
Words and music by Leon Haywood.
Jim-Edd Music, 1979.
Best-selling record by Leon Haywood from *Naturally* (20th Century, 80).

Don't Rock the Boat
Words and music by Bill Simmons.
Hastings Music Corp., 1988/Jig-a-Watt Jams, 1988.

Best-selling record by Midnight Star (featuring Ectasy), from *Midnight Star* (Solar, 88).

Don't Run Wild
Words and music by Dan Zanes, Tom Lloyd, and James Ralston.
Of the Fire Music, 1985.
Introduced by The Del Fuegos on the album *Boston, Mass* (Slash, 85).

Don't Rush Me
Words and music by Alexandra Forbes and Jeff Franzel.
Almo Music Corp., 1987.
Best-selling record by Taylor Dayne, from *Tell It to My Heart* (Arista, 88).

Don't Say Goodnight (It's Time for Love) - Parts 1 & 2
Words and music by Ernest Isley, Ronald Isley, Marvin Isley, Rudolph Isley, Christopher Jasper, and O'Kelly Isley.
Bovina Music, Inc., 1980/EMI-April Music, 1980.
Best-selling record by The Isley Brothers from *Go All The Way* (T-Neck, 80).

Don't Say No Tonight
Words and music by Ronnie Broomfield and McKinley Horton.
Philly World Music Co., 1985.
Best-selling record by Eugene Wilde from the album *Serenade* (Philly World, 85).

Don't Shed a Tear
Words and music by Eddie Schwartz and Rob Freidman.
High Frontier, 1987/EMI-Blackwood/Feist & April Music, 1987/Wood Monkey Music, 1987/Little Life Music, 1987.
Best-selling record in 1988 by Paul Carrack, from *One Good Reason* (Chrysalis, 87).

Don't Shut Me Out
Words and music by Kevin Paige.
Paige by Paige Music, 1989/Chrysalis Music Group, 1989.
Best-selling record by Kevin Paige from *Kevin Paige* (Chrysalis, 89).

Don't Stand So Close to Me (English)
Words and music by Sting (pseudonym for Gordon Sumner).
Blue Turtle, 1980/Criterion Music Corp., 1980.
Best-selling record by The Police from *Zenyatta Mondatta* (A & M, 81).

Don't Stop Believin'
Words and music by Steve Perry, Neal Schon, and Jonathan Cain.
Twist & Shout Music, 1981.
Best-selling record by Journey from *Escape* (Columbia, 81).

Don't Stop the Music
Words and music by Lonnie Simmons, Alisa Peoples, and Jonah Ellis.
Total X Publishing Co., 1980/Blackwell Publishing, 1980.
Best-selling record by Yarbrough and Peoples from *The Two of Us*
(Mercury, 81).

Don't Take It Personal (English)
Words and music by David Conley, Derrick Colter, and David
Townsend.
Colgems-EMI Music, 1989/Multi Culler Music, 1989.
Best-selling record by Jermaine Jackson from *Don't Take It Personal*
(Arista, 89).

Don't Take My Mind on a Trip
Words and music by Gene Griffin.
Cal-Gene Music, 1989/Donril Music, 1989.
Introduced by Boy George on *High Hat* (Virgin, 89). The colorful
crooner's long-awaited return was more successful on the black charts
than the pop charts.

Don't Talk to Strangers (Australian)
Words and music by Rick Springfield.
Vogue Music, 1982.
Best-selling record by Rick Springfield from *Success Hasn't Spoiled Me
Yet* (RCA, 82).

Don't Tell Me Lies (English)
Words and music by Dave Glaspar and Marcus Lillington.
Virgin Music, 1988.
Best-selling record in 1989 by Breathe from *All That Jazz* (A & M, 88).

Don't Underestimate My Love for You
Words and music by Steve Diamond, Steve Dorff, and Dave Loggins.
MCA, Inc., 1985/Diamond House, 1985/Dorff Songs, 1985/Leeds Music
Corp., 1985/Patchwork Music, 1985/Warnerbuilt, 1985.
Best-selling record by Lee Greenwood from the album *Streamline*
(MCA, 86).

Don't Wait on Me
Words and music by Harold Reid and Don Reid.
American Cowboy Music Co., 1980.
Best-selling record by The Statler Brothers from *Years Ago* (Mercury,
81).

Don't Wanna Be Like That (English)
Words and music by Joe Jackson.
Almo Music Corp., 1979.
Introduced by Joe Jackson on *I'm the Man* (A & M, 79).

Don't Wanna Lose You
Words and music by Gloria Estefan.
Foreign Imported, 1989.
Best-selling record by Gloria Estefan from *Cuts Both Ways* (Epic, 89).

Don't Want to Know If You Are Lonely
Words and music by Grant Hart.
Husker Music, 1986.
Introduced by Husker Du on the album *Candy Apple Grey* (Warner
    Bros., 86).

Don't Waste Your Time
Words and music by Jonah Ellis.
Temp Co., 1984.
Best-selling record by Yarbrough and Peoples from *Be a Winner* (Total
    Experience, 84).

Don't We All Have the Right
Words and music by Roger Miller.
Tree Publishing Co., Inc., 1988.
Best-selling record in 1988 by Ricky Van Shelton, from *Wild Eyed
    Dream* (Columbia, 87).

Don't Worry Baby
Words and music by Brian Wilson and Roger Christian.
Irving Music Inc., 1964.
Originally written for the Ronettes as a follow-up to 'Be My Baby,' the
    song was rejected by them. Revived in 1988 by the Beach Boys and
    the Everly Brothers for the film *Tequila Sunrise* and its soundtrack
    album (Capitol, 88).

Don't Worry Be Happy
Words and music by Bobby McFerrin.
ProbNoblem Music, 1988.
Featured in the film *Cocktail* and on its soundtrack album (Elektra, 88),
    this recycling of the Meier Baba credo was a best-seller for Bobby
    McFerrin (EMI-Manhattan, 88). It was also the first a capella record
    to reach the top of the charts. Won a Grammy Award, 1988.

Don't Worry 'bout Me Baby
Words and music by Deborah Allen, Bruce Channel, and Kieran Kane.
Music of the World, 1981/Old Friends Music, 1981/Posey Publishing,
    1981/Cross Keys Publishing Co., Inc., 1981.
Best-selling record by Janie Fricke (Columbia, 82).

Don't You (Forget About Me)
Words and music by Keith Forsey and Steve Schiff.
MCA, Inc., 1985/Music of the World, 1985.

Best-selling record by Simple Minds (A & M, 85). Featured in the film and the soundtrack album *The Breakfast Club* (85).

Don't You Ever Get Tired (of Hurting Me)
Words and music by Hank Cochran.
Tree Publishing Co., Inc., 1964.
Best-selling record by Ronnie Milsap from *Stranger Things Have Happened* (RCA, 89).

Don't You Get So Mad
Words and music by Jeffrey Osborne, Michael Sembello, and Donald Freeman.
Almo Music Corp., 1980/March 9 Music, 1980/Gravity Raincoat Music, 1980/Haymaker Music, 1980/Warner-Tamerlane Music, 1980.
Best-selling record by Jeffrey Osborne from *Stay with Me Tonight* (A & M, 83).

Don't You Know What the Night Can Do (English)
Words by Will Jennings, music by Steve Winwood.
F.S. Ltd., England, 1988/Warner-Tamerlane Music, 1988/Willin' David, 1988/Blue Sky Rider Songs, 1988.
Originally a beer commercial, this song became a best-seller for Steve Winwood, from his album *Roll with It* (Virgin, 88).

Don't You Want Me (English)
Words and music by Jo Callis, Phil Oakey, and Adrian Wright.
Virgin Music, 1981/WB Music, 1981.
Best-selling record by Human League from *Dare* (A & M/Virgin, 82).

Don't You Want Me
Words and music by Franne Golde, D. Bryant, and Jody Watley.
Bellboy Music, 1987/Gratitude Sky Music, 1987.
Best-selling record by Jody Watley, from the album *Jody Watley* (MCA, 87); this was the first solo effort from Watley, a former member of Shalamar.

Double Dutch Bus
Words and music by Frankie Smith and William Bloom.
Frashon Music Co., 1980/Front Wheel Music, Inc., 1980/Wimot Music Publishing, 1980.
Best-selling record by Frankie Smith from *Children of Tomorrow* (WMOT, 81).

Down on Love
Words and music by Mick (Foreigner) Jones and Lou Gramm.
Somerset Songs Publishing, Inc., 1984/Little Doggies Productions Inc., 1984/Colgems-EMI Music, 1984.
Best-selling record by Foreigner from the album *Agent Provocateur* (Atlantic, 85).

Down on the Farm
Words and music by John Greenebaum, Troy Seals, and Eddie Setser.
Make Believus Music, 1985/WB Music, 1985/Two-Sons Music, 1985/
  Warner-Tamerlane Music, 1985.
Introduced by Charley Pride (RCA, 85). Song about the plight of
  modern day farmers presaged 'Farm Aid' benefit concert to raise
  money for farmers several months later, whch starred Willie Nelson,
  Bob Dylan, and others.

Down on up to Me
Words and music by Dave Pirner.
LFR Music, 1988/Tomata du Plenti, 1988/Almo Music Corp., 1988.
Introduced by Soul Asylum on *Hang Time* (Twin Tone, 88).

Down to My Last Broken Heart
Words and music by Chick Rains.
Tree Publishing Co., Inc., 1980/Chick Rains Music, 1980.
Best-selling record by Janie Fricke (Columbia, 81).

Down to the Bone
Words and music by Dan Stuart and Steve Wynn.
Poison Brisket Music, 1985/Hang Dog Music, 1985.
Introduced by Danny and Dusty on the album *The Lost Weekend* (A &
  M, 85).

Down Under (Australian)
Words and music by Colin Hay and Roy Strykert.
EMI-Blackwood Music Inc., 1982.
Best-selling record by Men at Work from *Business as Usual* (Columbia,
  82).

Downtown Life
Words and music by Daryl Hall, John Oates, Rich Iantosca, and Sarah
  Allen.
Hot Cha Music Co., 1988/Careers Music Inc., 1988/Fust Buzza Music,
  Inc., 1988/Delightful Music Ltd., 1988.
Best-selling record by Hall and Oates, from *Ooh Yeah* (Artista, 88).

Downtown Train
Words and music by Tom Waits.
Jalma Music, 1985.
Introduced by Tom Waits in the movie *Down by Law* ('86). Revived in
  1987 by Patty Smythe in the album *Never Enough* (Columbia) and
  Mary Chapin Carpenter in the album *Hometown Girl* (Columbia, 87).
  Revived in 1989 by Rod Stewart on *Storyteller* (Warner Bros., 89).

Dragnet
Music by Earl Schuman.
EMI Music Publishing, 1953, 1981/Dragnet Music.

Rhythm 'n' Blues Art of Noise in the film and on the soundtrack album *Dragnet* (China/Chrysalis, 87).

Dream Warriors
Words and music by George Lynch and Jeff Pilson.
Megadude, 1987/E/A Music, 1987.
Introduced by Dokken in the movie *A Nightmare on Elm Street, Part 3*, (87). Featured on their album *Back for the Attack* (Elektra, 87).

Dreamer (English)
Words and music by Roger Davies and Roger Hodgson.
Almo Music Corp., 1974/Delicate Music, 1980.
Best-selling record by Supertramp from *Crime of the Century* (A & M, 80).

Dreamin'
Words and music by Lisa Montgomary, Geneva Paschal, and Michael Forte.
Jobete Music Co., 1988/Depom Music.
Best-selling record in 1989 by Vanessa Williams, from *The Right Stuff* (Wing, 88). This success gave the former Miss America a foothold on a new career.

Dreaming (English)
Words and music by Alan Tarney and Leo Sayer.
ATV Music Corp., 1980/Chrysalis Music Group, 1980.
Best-selling record by Cliff Richard from *I'm No Hero* (EMI-America, 80).

Dreaming (English)
Words and music by OMD.
Virgin Music, 1988.
Best-selling record by Orchestral Maneuvers in the Dark, from *The Best of OMD* (A & M, 88).

Dreams
Words and music by Eddie Van Halen, Michael Anthony, Sammy Hagar, and Alex Van Halen.
Yessup Music Co., 1986.
Best-selling record by Van Halen from the album *5150* (Warner Bros., 86).

Dreams
Words and music by Sammy Llanas and Kurt Neumann.
Lla-Mann, 1987/Intersong, USA Inc., 1987.
Best-selling record by The BoDeans, from *Outside Looking in* (Reprise, 88).

Dreamtime (American-English)
Words and music by Daryl Hall and John Beeby.
Anxious, England/Hallowed Hall, 1986/Red Network Music/Warner-Tamerlane Music.
Best-selling record by Daryl Hall from the album *Three Hearts and the Happy Ending Machine* (RCA, 86). This was Hall's first solo effort since *Sacred Songs*.

Dreamtime (English)
Words and music by The Stranglers.
Plumbshaft Ltd., England, 1986/CBS Songs Ltd., 1986.
Introduced by The Stranglers, on the album *Dreamtime* (Epic, 87).

Dress You Up
Words and music by Peggy Stanziale and Andrea LaRusso.
House of Fun Music, 1984.
Best-selling record by Madonna in 1985 from the album *Like a Virgin* (Warner Bros., 84).

Dressed for Success (Swedish)
English words and music by Per Gessle.
Jimmie Fun, 1989.
Best-selling record by Roxette from *Look Sharp!* (EMI, 89).

Drifter
Words and music by Don Pfrimmer and Archie Jordan.
Pi-Gem Music Publishing Co., Inc., 1980/Polygram International, 1980.
Best-selling record by Sylvia from *Drifter* (RCA, 81).

Drink with Me to Days Gone By (French-English)
English words by Herbert Kretzmer, French words and music by Alain Boublil, music by Claude-Michel Schonberg.
Alain Boublil Music Ltd., 1980, 1986.
Introduced by Anthony Crivello and company in the 1987 Broadway production of *Les Miserables*.

Drinkin' and Dreamin'
Words and music by Troy Seals and Max D. Barnes.
Two-Sons Music, 1985/Blue Lake Music, 1985/WB Music, 1985.
Best-selling record by Waylon Jennings from the album *Turn the Page* (RCA, 85).

Drive
Words and music by Ric Ocasek.
Lido Music Inc., 1984.
Best-selling record by The Cars from *Heartbeat City* (Electra, 84).

Drivin' My Life Away
Words and music by Eddie Rabbitt, Even Stevens, and David Malloy.

Debdave Music Inc., 1980/Briarpatch Music, 1980.
Best-selling record by Eddie Rabbitt from *Horizon* (Elektra, 80).
Nominated for a Grammy Award, Country Song of the Year, 1980.

Dude (Looks Like a Lady)
Words and music by Steven Tyler, Joe Perry, and Desmond Child.
Aero Dynamic Music, 1987/Desmobile Music Inc., 1987/EMI-April
Music, 1987.
Best-selling record by Aerosmith, from the album *Permanent Vacation*
(Geffen, 87). The song was nearly called 'Cruisin' for the Ladies,' but
returned to this, its original title, in a rewrite.

Dumb Things (Australian)
Words and music by Paul Kelly.
Australian Mushroom, Australia, 1987.
Introduced by Paul Kelly on the album *Under the Sun* and featured in
the 1988 Australian film *Young Einstein,* the song was also used in
the 1989 film *Look Who's Talking.*

Dungeons and Dragons
Words by Michael Champagne, music by Elliot Weiss.
Bittersuite Co., 1987.
Introduced by Joy Franz in the 1987 musical *Bittersuite.*

Dynamite
Words and music by Andy Goldmark and Bruce Roberts.
Nonpariel Music, 1984/Broozertoones, Inc., 1984.
Best-selling record by Jermaine Jackson from *Jermaine Jackson* (Arista,
84).

E

Early in the Morning
Words and music by Charles Wilson, Rudolph Taylor, Lonnie Simmons, and Robert Palmer.
Temp Co., 1982.
Best-selling record by The Gap Band from *The Gap Band IV* (Total Experience, 82). Revived in 1988 by Robert Palmer on *Heavy Nova* (EMI, 88).

Earn Enough for Us (English)
Words and music by Andy Partridge.
EMI-Virgin, 1986.
Introduced by XTC on the album *Skylarking* (Geffen, 86).

Earth Angel
Words and music by Jesse Belvin.
Dootsie Williams, Inc., 1954.
Revived in 1986 by New Edition in the film *Karate Kid, Part 2* and on the album *Under the Blue Moon* (MCA, 86). This original do-wop classic is, one of the first rock 'n' roll hits.

Easier to Love
Words by Richard Maltby, music by David Shire.
Fiddleback, 1984/Long Pond Music, 1984/Progeny Music, 1984/Revelation Music Publishing Corp., 1984.
Introduced by James Congdon in *Baby* (83).

Easy
Words and music by Pat MacDonald and Barbara K. MacDonald.
Mambadaddi, 1987/Atlantic Music Corp., 1987/I.R.S. Music, 1987.
Introduced by Timbuk 3 in *Eden Alley* (I.R.S., 88).

Easy Lover (English)
Words and music by Philip Bailey, Phil Collins, and Nathan East.
Sir & Trini Music, 1984/New East Music, 1984/Hit & Run Music, 1984.

Best-selling record by Philip Bailey with Phil Collins from the album *Chinese Wall* (Columbia, 85).

Eat It
Words and music by Michael Jackson, words by Al Yankovic.
Mijac Music, 1984, 1982/Warner-Tamerlane Music, 1984.
Best-selling record by Weird Al Yankovic from *Weird Al Yankovic in 3-D* (Rock 'n' Roll, 84). Parody of Michael Jackson's 'Beat It.'

Ebony and Ivory (English)
Words and music by Paul McCartney.
MPL Communications Inc., 1982.
Best-selling record by Paul McCartney and Stevie Wonder from *Tug of War* (Columbia, 82). Nominated for Grammy Awards, Record of the Year, 1982, and Song of the Year, 1982.

Eden Alley
Words and music by Pat MacDonald and Barbara K. MacDonald.
Mambadaddi, 1987/I.R.S. Music, 1987/Atlantic Music Corp., 1987.
Introduced by Timbuk 3 on *Eden Alley* (I. R. S., 88).

The Edge of Heaven (English)
Words and music by George Michael (pseudonym for Georgios Kyriaku Panayiotou).
Morrison Leahy, England, 1986/Chappell & Co., Inc., 1986.
Best-selling record by Wham! from the album *Music from the Edge of Heaven* (Columbia, 86).

Edge of Seventeen
Words and music by Stephanie Nicks.
Welsh Witch Publishing, 1981.
Best-selling record by Stevie Nicks from *Bella Donna* (Modern, 82).

867-5309/Jenny
Words and music by Alex Call and James Keller.
Tutone-Keller Music, 1982/New Daddy Music, 1982.
Best-selling record by Tommy Tutone from *Tommy Tutone 2* (Columbia, 82).

Eight Miles High
Words and music by Gene Clark, David Crosby, and Jim McGuinn.
Tickson Music, 1966.
On their 1987 album *Never Before* (CBS), the song's originators, the Byrds, offered an alternate version of this milestone folk-rock title.

Eighteen and Life
Words and music by Snake (pseudonym for Dave Sabo) and Rachel Bolan.

New Jersey Underground, 1989.
Best-selling record by Skid Row from *Skid Row* (Atlantic, 89).

Eighteen Wheels and a Dozen Roses
Words and music by Paul Nelson and Gene Nelson.
Warner-Tamerlane Music, 1987/Believe Us or Not Music, 1987/Screen Gems-EMI Music Inc., 1987.
Best-selling record in 1988 by Kathy Mattea from *Untasted Honey* (Mercury, 87).

80's Ladies
Words and music by K. T. Oslin.
Wooden Wonder, 1987.
Best-selling record by K. T. Oslin, from the album *80's Ladies* (RCA, 87). Nominated for a Grammy Award, Country Song of the Year, 1987.

Election Day (English)
Words and music by Nick Rhodes, Roger Taylor, and Simon LeBon.
BIOT Music Ltd., London, England, 1985.
Best-selling record by Arcadia from the album *So Red the Rose* (Capitol, 85).

Electric Avenue (English)
Words and music by Eddy Grant.
Greenheart Music, Ltd., London, England, 1982.
Best-selling record by Eddy Grant from *Killer on the Rampage* (Portrait, 83). Nominated for a Grammy Award, Rhythm 'n' Blues Song of the Year, 1983.

Electric Blue (Australian)
Words and music by Ian Davies and John Oates.
SBK-Australia, Australia, 1987/EMI-April Music, 1987/10/10, 1987.
Best-selling record in 1988 by Icehouse, from the album *Man of Colours* (Chrysalis, 87).

Electric Youth
Words and music by Deborah Gibson.
EMI-April Music, 1988/Possibilities Publishing, 1988.
Best-selling record by Debbie Gibson from *Electric Youth* (Atlantic, 89).

Elizabeth
Words and music by Jimmy Fortune.
American Cowboy Music Co., 1983.
Best-selling record by The Statler Brothers in *Today* (Mercury, 84).

Elvira
Words and music by Dallas Frazier.
Mariposa Music Inc., 1965.

Best-selling record by The Oak Ridge Boys from *Fancy Free* (MCA, 81). Nominated for a Grammy Award, Country Song of the Year, 1981.

Elvis Has Just Left the Building
Words and music by Frank Zappa.
Munchkin Music, 1988.
Introduced by Frank Zappa on *Broadway the Hard Way* (Barking Pumpkin, 88). The outspoken satirist here counters the 'Elvis is alive' mania that marked 1988.

Elvis Is Everywhere
Words and music by MoJo Nixon.
Muffin Stuffin, 1987/La Rana, 1987.
Introduced by MoJo Nixon and Skid Roper on the album *Bo-Day-Shus* (Enigma, 87), this song's satirical lyrics offer inspired commentary on both Presleymania and the more recent popular passion for television star Michael J. Fox.

Emergency
Words and music by George Brown, Ronald Bell, Charles Smith, James Taylor, Robert Bell, Curtis Williams, and James Bonneford.
Delightful Music Ltd., 1984.
Best-selling record by Kool & The Gang from the album *Emergency* (De-Lite, 85).

Emotion in Motion
Words and music by Ric Ocasek.
Lido Music Inc., 1986.
Best-selling record by Ric Ocasek from the album *This Side of Paradise* (Warner Bros., 86). The author is the main singer and songwriter of The Cars.

Emotional Rescue (English)
Words and music by Mick Jagger and Keith Richards.
Colgems-EMI Music, 1980.
Best-selling record by The Rolling Stones from *Emotional Rescue* (Rolling Stones, 80).

The Empire Strikes Back
Words and music by John Williams.
Warner-Tamerlane Music, 1980/Bantha Music, 1980.
Best-selling record by Meco (RSO, 80). Introduced in the film and soundtrack album *The Empire Strikes Back* (80).

Empty Garden (Hey Hey Johnny) (English)
Music by Elton John, words by Bernie Taupin.
Intersong, USA Inc., 1982.
Best-selling record by Elton John from *Jump Up* (Geffen, 82).

Encore
Words and music by Terry Lewis and James Harris, III.
Tan Division Music Publishing, 1983/Flyte Tyme Tunes, 1983.
Best-selling record by Cheryl Lynn from *Preppies* (Columbia, 84).

The End of the Innocence
Words and music by Don Henley and Bruce Hornsby.
Cass County Music Co., 1989/Zappo Music, 1989.
Best-selling record by Don Henley from *The End of the Innocence*
(Geffen, 89). Nominated for Grammy Awards, Record of the Year,
1989, and Song of the Year, 1989.

Endless Farewell
Words and music by Dave Pirner.
LFR Music, 1988/Almo Music Corp., 1988.
Introduced by Soul Aslyum on *Hang Time* (Twin/Tone/A&M, 88).

Endless Love
Words and music by Lionel Richie, Jr.
PGP Music, 1981/Brockman Enterprises Inc., 1981.
Best-selling record by Diana Ross and Lionel Richie, Jr. (Motown, 81).
Introduced in the movie and soundtrack album *Endless Love* (81).
Nominated for an Academy Award, Best Song, 1981; Grammy Awards,
Record of the Year, 1981, and Song of the Year, 1981.

Endless Summer Nights
Words and music by Richard Marx.
Chi-Boy, 1987.
Best-selling record by Richard Marx, from *Richard Marx* (EMI-
Manhattan, 88).

Especially for You
Words and music by Pat DiNizio and Jim Babjak.
Famous Monsters Music, 1987/Colgems-EMI Music, 1987.
Best-selling record The Smithereens in *Green Thoughts* (Enigma, 88).
The song titled after an earlier Smithereens album.

Eternal Flame
Words and music by Susannah Hoffs, Billy Steinberg, and Tom Kelly.
EMI-Blackwood Music Inc., 1988/Bangophile Music, 1988/Sony Tunes,
1988/Denise Barry Music, 1988.
Best-selling record in 1989 by The Bangles, from *Everything* (Columbia,
88).

Even a Dog Can Shake Hands
Words and music by Warren Zevon, Peter Buck, Mike Mills, and Bill
Berry.
Night Garden Music, 1987/Unichappell Music Inc., 1987.

Introduced by Warren Zevon on the album *Sentimental Hygiene* (Island, 87). Zevon's co-authors are members of folk-rock group REM.

Even It Up
Words and music by Ann Wilson, Sue Ennis, and Nancy Wilson.
Strange Euphoria Music, 1980/Know Music, 1980/Sheer Music, 1980.
Best-selling record by Heart from *Bebe Le Strange* (Portrait, 80).

Even Now
Words and music by Bob Seger.
Gear Publishing, 1982.
Best-selling record by Bob Seger & The Silver Bullet Band from *Nine Tonight* (Capitol, 83).

Even the Nights Are Better
Words and music by J. L. Wallace, Ken Bell, and Terry Skinner.
Hall-Clement Publications, 1979.
Best-selling record by Air Supply from *Now and Forever* (Arista, 82).

Ever After
Words and music by Stephen Sondheim.
BMG Music, 1987.
Introduced by Tom Aldredge and company of the musical *Into the Woods* (cast album, RCA, 88).

Ever Fallen in Love (English)
Words and music by Pete Shelley.
EMI-Virgin, 1979.
Performed by Fine Young Cannibals in the film and on the soundtrack album of *Something Wild* (MCA, 86).

Ever Since the World Ended
Words and music by Mose Allison.
Audre Mae Music, 1987.
Introduced by Mose Allison on the album *Ever Since the World Ended* (Blue Note, 87), this song provides an optimistic report from one of music's mos delightfully cynical observers.

Everchanging Times
Words and music by Burt Bacharach, Carole Bayer Sager, and Bill Conti.
United Artists Music Co., Inc., 1987/EMI-April Music/New Hidden Valley Music Co./Carole Bayer Sager Music/Polygram International/EMI-Blackwood Music Inc.
Introduced by Siedah Garrett on the album *Baby Boom* (Qwest, 87).

Everlasting Love (English)
Words and music by Howard Jones.
Hojo, England, 1989.

Best-selling record by Howard Jones from *Cross That Line* (Elektra, 89).

Every Breath You Take (English)
Words and music by Sting (pseudonym for Gordon Sumner).
Reggatta Music, Ltd., 1983/Illegal Songs, Inc., 1983.
Best-selling record by The Police from *Synchronicity* (A & M, 83). Won a Grammy Award, and Song of the Year, 1983. Nominated for a Grammy Award, Record of the Year, 1983.

Every Day
Words and music by Dave Loggins and J. D. Martin.
Leeds Music Corp., 1984/Patchwork Music, 1984/Music of the World, 1984.
Best-selling record by The Oak Ridge Boys from *Greatest Hits 2* (MCA, 84).

Every Day I Write the Book (English)
Words and music by Elvis Costello.
Plangent Visions Music, Inc., London, England, 1983.
Best-selling record by Elvis Costello from *Punch the Clock* (Columbia, 83).

Every Dog Has His Day
Words and music by Mitch Easter.
Forsythia Music, 1988.
Introduced by Let's Active on *Every Dog Has His Day* (I.R.S., 88). The songwriter is better known for producing the seminal New Folk act, R.E.M.

Every Grain of Sand
Words and music by Bob Dylan.
Special Rider Music, 1981.
Introduced by Bob Dylan on *Shot of Love* (Columbia, 81).

Every Little Kiss
Words and music by Bruce Hornsby.
Zappo Music, 1986/Bob-a-Lew Music, 1986.
Best-selling record by Bruce Hornsby & The Range, from the album *The Way It Is* (RCA, 86); thi s song became a hit on its second release, after Hornsby won a Grammy Award for Best New Artist of the Year.

Every Little Step
Words and music by L. A. Reid (pseudonym for Antonio Reid) and Babyface (pseudonym for Kenny Edmunds).
Kear Music, 1988/Hip-Trip Music Co., 1988.
Best-selling record in 1989 by Bobby Brown, from *Don't Be Cruel*

(MCA, 88). Nominated for a Grammy Award, Rhythm 'n' Blues Song of the Year, 1989.

Every Little Thing She Does Is Magic (English)
Words and music by Sting (pseudonym for Gordon Sumner).
Virgin Music, 1981.
Best-selling record by The Police from *Ghost in the Machine* (A & M, 81).

Every Rose Has Its Thorn
Words and music by Bobby Dall, C. C. Deville, Brett Michaels, and Rikki Rockett.
Sweet Cyanide, 1988/Willesden Music, Inc., 1988.
Best-selling record by Poison, from *Open Up and Say Ahh* (Capitol, 88).

Every Time I Turn Around
Words and music by Jody Hart Angelo and Gary Portnoy.
Addax Music Co., Inc., 1984.
Introduced by Gary Portnoy on *Punky Brewster* (84).

Every Time You Go Away
Words and music by Daryl Hall.
Unichappell Music Inc., 1980/Hot Cha Music Co., 1980.
Best-selling record by Paul Young from the album *The Secret of Association* (Columbia, 85). Nominated for a Grammy Award, Song of the Year, 1985.

Every Woman in the World
Words and music by Dominic Bugatti and Frank Musker.
Unichappell Music Inc., 1980.
Best-selling record by Air Supply from *Lost in Love* (Arista, 80).

Everybody Dance
Words and music by Jesse Johnson and Ta Mara.
Crazy People Music/Almo Music Corp., 1985/Almo Music Corp., 1985.
Best-selling record by Ta Mara & The Seen from the album *Ta Mara & The Seen* (A & M, 85).

Everybody Have Fun Tonight (American-English)
Words and music by Wang Chung, words and music by Peter Wolf.
Chung Music Ltd., 1986/Warner-Tamerlane Music, 1986/Petwolf Music, 1986/Chappell & Co., Inc., 1986.
Best-selling record by Wang Chung from the album *Mosaic* (Geffen, 86).

Everybody Wants to Rule the World (English)
Words and music by Roland Orzabal, Ian Stanley, and Chris Hughes.
Amusements Ltd., England, 1985/EMI-Virgin, 1985.

Best-selling record by Tears for Fears from the album *Songs from the Big Chair* (Mercury, 85).

Everybody Wants You
Words and music by Billy Squier.
Songs of the Knight, 1982.
Best-selling record by Billy Squier from *Emotions in Motion* (Capitol, 82).

Everybody's Got to Learn Sometime (English)
Words and music by James Warren.
WB Music, 1980.
Best-selling record by The Korgis from *Dumb Waiters* Asylum, 80).

Everyday Clothes
Words and music by Jonathan Richman.
Rockin Leprechaun, 1989/Rounder Music.
Introduced by by Jonathan Richman on *Jonathan Richman* (Rounder, 89).

Everyday Is Like Sunday (English)
Words by Morrissey (pseudonym for Tommy Morrissey), music by Stephen Street.
Linder Ltd., 1988/Warner-Tamerlane Music, 1988/Copyright Control, 1988.
Introduced by Morrissey, the poet laureate of the depressed, in *Viva Hate* (Sire, 88).

Everyone Is Good
Words and music by Terre Roche.
Deshufflin' Inc., 1989.
Introduced by The Roches on *Speak* (Paradox, 89).

Everything
Words and music by Gardner Cole and James Newton Howard.
Sizzling Blue Music, 1989/Newton House Music.
Best-selling record by Jody Watley from *Larger Than Life* (MCA, 89).

Everything I Miss at Home
Words and music by James Harris, III and Terry Lewis.
Flyte Tyme Tunes, 1988.
Best-selling record by Cherrelle, from *Affair* (Tabu, 88).

Everything I Need (Australian)
Words and music by Colin Hay.
EMI-April Music, 1985.
Introduced by Men at Work on the album *Two Hearts* (Columbia, 85).

Everything Is Broken
Words and music by Bob Dylan.
Special Rider Music, 1989.
Introduced by by Bob Dylan on *Oh Mercy* (Columbia 89).

Everything She Wants (English)
Words and music by George Michael.
Chappell & Co., Inc., 1984.
Best-selling record by Wham! in 1985 from the album *Make It Big*
(Columbia, 84).

Everything That Glitters (Is Not Gold)
Words and music by Dan Seals and Bob McDill.
Pink Pig Music, 1986/Hall-Clement Publications, 1986.
Best-selling record by Dan Seals from the album *Won't Be Blue*
Anymore (EMI-America, 86). Dan Seals was a member of the singing
group England Dan and John Ford Coley.

Everything That Touches You
Words and music by Michael Kamen.
Mother Fortune Inc., 1980.
Introduced by by Sheryl Lee Ralph in *Reggae* (Musical, 80).

Everything Works If You Let It
Words and music by Richard Nielsen.
Screen Gems-EMI Music Inc., 1980.
Best-selling record by Cheap Trick (Epic, 80). Introduced in the film &
soundtrack album *Roadie* (80).

Everything You Got
Words and music by Mike Czekaj.
Copyright Control, 1989.
Introduced by The Fuzztones on *In Heat* (Beggar's Banquet, 89).

Everything Your Heart Desires
Words and music by Daryl Hall.
Hot Cha Music Co., 1988/Careers Music Inc., 1988.
Best-selling record by Hall and Oates, from *Ooh Yeah* (Arista, 88).

Everything's Turning to White (Australian)
Words and music by Paul Kelly.
Australian Mushroom, Australia, 1989.
Introduced by Paul Kelly & the Messengers on *So Much Water So*
Close to Home (A & M, 89). The song is based on a short story by
Raymond Carver.

Everywhere (English)
Words and music by Christine McVie.
Fleetwood Mac Music Ltd., 1987.

Best-selling record in 1988 by Fleetwood Mac, from *Tango in the Night* (Warner Bros., 87).

Everywhere You Look
Words and music by Bennett Salvay, Jesse Fredericke, and Jeff Franklin.
Introduced by Jesse Fredericke as the theme song for the television series *Full House.*

Express Yourself
Words and music by Madonna and Steve Bray.
WB Music, 1989/Bleu Disque Music, 1989/Lost in Music, 1989/Black Lion, 1989.
Best-selling record by Madonna from *Like a Prayer* (Sire, 89).

Expressway to Your Heart
Words and music by Kenny Gamble and Leon Huff.
Double Diamond Music, 1967/Columbine Music Inc., 1967/One Song Publishing, 1967.
Revived in 1987 by The Breakfast Club, from their album *The Breakfast Club* (MCA).

Eye in the Sky (English)
Words and music by Eric Woolfson and Alan Parsons.
Careers Music Inc., 1982.
Best-selling record by The Alan Parsons Project from *Eye in the Sky* (Arista, 82).

Eye of Fatima, Pt. 1
Words and music by Camper Van Beethoven.
Camper Van Beethoven Music, 1987/Bug Music, 1987.
Introduced by Camper Van Beethoven on *Our Beloved Revolutionary Sweetheart* (Virgin, 99). The psychedelic heroes of the 80's emerge with an overground sound.

Eye of the Tiger (The Theme from *Rocky III*)
Words and music by Frank Sullivan and Jim Peterik.
Holy Moley Music, 1982/Rude Music, 1982/WB Music, 1982/Easy Action Music, 1982.
Best-selling record by Survivor from *Eye of the Tiger* (Scotti Brothers, 82). Introduced in the film & soundtrack album *Rocky III* (Liberty, 82). Nominated for an Academy Award, Best Song, 1982; a Grammy Award, Song of the Year, 1982.

Eyes Without a Face (English)
Words and music by Billy Idol and Steve Stevens.
Boneidol Music, 1983/Chrysalis Music Group, 1983/WB Music, 1983/

Sitting Pretty.
Best-selling record by Billy Idol from *Rebel Yell* (Chrysalis, 84).

F

Face the Face (English)
Words and music by Pete Townshend.
Eel Pie Music, 1985.
Best-selling record by Pete Townshend from the album *White City*
(Atco, 85).

Face to Face
Words and music by Randy Owen.
Maypop Music, 1987.
Best-selling record in 1988 by Alabama, from *Just Us* (RCA, 87).

The Facts of Life
Words and music by Alan Thicke, Gloria Loring, and Al Burton.
Norbud, 1981/Bramalea Music, 1981/Thickouit Music, 1981.
Introduced on the TV series *The Facts of Life* (81).

Fade Away
Words and music by Bruce Springsteen.
Bruce Springsteen Publishing, 1980.
Best-selling record by Bruce Springsteen from *The River* (Columbia,
81).

Fairytale of New York (Irish)
Words and music by Shane MacGowan, Jem Finer, and Randy Owen.
Stiff Music America, England, 1987.
Introduced by Irish folk-rockers The Pogues on *If I Should Fall from
Grace with God* (Island, 88).

Faith (English)
Words and music by George Michael.
Morrison Leahy, England, 1987/Chappell & Co., Inc., 1987.
Best-selling record by George Michael, from the album *Faith*
(Columbia, 87).

Faith, Hope and Glory
Words and music by Kenny Vance, Philip Namanworth, and Matthew

117

Wilder.
OPC, 1989/Geffen Music, 1989/Streetwise Music, 1989/WB Music, 1989.
Introduced by Delbert McClinton and Rebecca Russell in the film and soundtrack LP *Heart of Dixie* (A & M, 89).

Faithfully
Words and music by Jonathan Cain.
Twist & Shout Music, 1982.
Best-selling record by Journey from *Frontiers* (Columbia, 83).

Faithless Love
Words and music by John David Souther.
WB Music, 1974/Golden Spread Music, 1974.
Best-selling record by Glen Campbell (Atlantic America, 84).
    Nominated for a Grammy Award, Country Song of the Year, 1984.

Fake
Words and music by Jimmy Jam (pseudonym for James Harris, III) and Terry Lewis.
Flyte Tyme Tunes, 1987/Avant Garde Music Publishing, Inc., 1987.
Best-selling record by Alexander O'Neal, from the album *Hearsay* (Tabu, 87). The songwriters are former members of the Time (which was originally called Flyte Tyme).

Faking Love
Words and music by Bobby Braddock and Matraca Berg.
Tree Publishing Co., Inc., 1982.
Best-selling record by T. G. Sheppard and Karen Brooks (Warner Brothers, 82).

Fall in Love with Me
Words and music by Maurice White, D. Vaughn, and Wayne Vaughn.
EMI-April Music, 1983/Yougoulei Music, 1983/Wenkewa Music, 1983/ Out Time Music.
Best-selling record by Earth, Wind & Fire from *Powerlight* (Columbia, 83).

Fall on Me
Words and music by Peter Buck, Bill Berry, Mike Mills, and Michael Stipe.
Night Garden Music, 1986.
Best-selling record by R.E.M. from the album *Life's Rich Pageant* (I.R.S., 86).

Fallen Angel
Words and music by Robbie Robertson and Martin Page.
Medicine Hat Music, 1987/Martin Page Music, 1987/Zomba Music, 1987.

Introduced by Robbie Robertson on his album *Robbie Robertson* (Geffen, 87), this song is dedicated to Richard Manuel, Robertson's former colleague in the Band, who had committed suicide.

Fallin' Again
Words and music by Teddy Gentry, Greg Fowler, and Randy Owen.
Maypop Music, 1988.
Best-selling record by Alabama, from *Alabama Live* (RCA, 88).

Fallin' in Love
Words and music by Randy Goodrum and Brent Maher.
EMI-April Music, 1985/Random Notes, 1985/Welbeck Music Corp., 1985/Blue Quill Music, 1985.
Best-selling record by Sylvia from the album *One Step Closer* (RCA, 85).

Falling
Words and music by Gene McFadden and Franne Golde.
Rightsong Music, 1986/Franne Golde Music Inc., 1986/Gene McFadden, 1986/Su-Ma Publishing Co., Inc., 1986.
Introduced by Melba Moore on the album *A Lot of Love* (Capitol, 86).
The song was performed on the soap opera *As the World Turns*.

Falling Again
Words and music by Bob McDill.
Hall-Clement Publications, 1980.
Best-selling record by Don Williams from *I Believe in You* (MCA, 81).

Falling for You for Years
Words and music by Troy Seals and Mike Reed.
WB Music, 1987/Two-Sons Music, 1987/BMG Songs Inc., 1987.
Best-selling record by Conway Twitty, from the album *Borderline* (MCA, 87).

Fame
Words by Dean Pitchford, music by Michael Gore.
EMI-Affiliated, 1980.
Best-selling record by Irene Cara (RSO, 80). Introduced in the film & soundtrack album *Fame* (80). Nominated for an Academy Award, Best Song, 1980; Nominated for an Academy Award, Best Song, 1980; a Grammy Award, Song of the Year, 1980.

Family Man (English)
Words and music by Mike Oldfield, Morris Pert, Tim Cross, Rick Fenn, Mike Frye, and Maggie Reilly.
Josef Weinberger, Frankfurt, Germany, 1982/Chappell & Co., Inc., 1982/EMI-April Music, 1982/EMI-Virgin.
Best-selling record by Daryl Hall and John Oates from *H2O* (RCA, 83).

Famous Blue Raincoat (Canadian)
Words and music by Leonard Cohen.
Stranger Music Inc., 1971.
Revived in 1986 by Jennifer Warnes on *Famous Blue Raincoat: The Songs of Leonard Cohen* (Cypress, 86).

Famous Last Words of a Fool
Words and music by Dean Dillon and Rex Huston.
Tree Publishing Co., Inc., 1988/Forrest Hills Music Inc., 1988.
Best-selling record by George Strait, from the album *If You Ain't Lovin' You Ain't Livin' (MCA, 88).*

Fantastic Voyage
Words and music by Fred Alexander, Otis Stokes, Norman Beavers, Mark Wood, Marvin Craig, Fred Lewis, Tie Meyer McCain, Steven Shockley, and Thomas Shelby.
Portrait/Solar Songs Inc., 1980/Circle L Publishing, 1980.
Best-selling record by Lakeside from *Fantastic Voyage* (Solar, 81).

Fantasy
Words and music by Aldo Nova.
ATV Music Corp., 1982.
Best-selling record by Aldo Nova from *Aldo Nova* (Portrait, 82).

Far Away Lands
Words and music by David Pomeranz, music by Peter Schless.
Marilor Music, 1987/Upward Spiral, 1987/Lincoln Pond Music, 1987.
Introduced by by David Pomeranz and Sasha Malinin (Cypress, 87), in an example of artistic detente between U.S. and Russian musicians.

Far Far Away from My Heart
Words and music by Sammy Llanas and Kurt Neumann.
Lla-Mann, 1989.
Introduced by by The BoDeans on *Home* (Reprise, 89).

Far from Over
Words and music by Frank Stallone and Vince DiCola.
Famous Music Corp., 1983.
Best-selling record by Frank Stallone (RSO, 83). Introduced in the film *Staying Alive* (83).

The Farm Yard Connection (English)
Words and music by Fun Boy Three.
Plangent Visions Music, Inc., London, England, 1982.
Introduced by Fun Boy Three in *Waiting* (Chrysalis, 83).

(Keep Feeling) Fascination (English)
Words and music by Phil Oakey and Jo Callis.

Virgin Music, 1983/WB Music, 1983.
Best-selling record by Human League from *Fascination* (A & M, 83).

Fast Car
Words and music by Tracy Chapman.
EMI-April Music, 1988/Purple Rabbit Music, 1988.
Introduced by Tracy Chapman on *Tracy Chapman* (Elektra, 88). With this moving tale of a thwarted escape Chapman broke through to the commercial marketplace and paved the way for other thoughtful singer-songwriters. Won a Grammy Award, and Best New Artist, 1988. Nominated for a Grammy Award, Record of the Year Song of the Year, 1988.

Fat
Words by Al Yankovic, words and music by Michael Jackson.
Mijac Music, 1987/Warner-Tamerlane Music, 1987.
A parody of the Michael Jackson hit 'Bad.' Best-selling record by Weird Al Yankovic from *Even Worse* (Rock 'N' Roll, 88).

Father Figure (English)
Words and music by George Michael.
Morrison Leahy, England, 1987/Chappell & Co., Inc., 1987.
Best-selling record in 1988 by George Michael from *Faith* (CBS, 87).

Fatherhood Blues
Words by Richard Maltby, music by David Shire.
Fiddleback, 1984/Long Pond Music, 1984/Progeny Music, 1984/ Revelation Music Publishing Corp., 1984.
Introduced by James Congdon, Martin Vidnovic and Todd Graff in *Baby* (83).

Favorite Waste of Time
Words and music by Marshall Crenshaw.
MHC Music, 1983.
Best-selling record by Bette Midler from *No Frills* (Atlantic, 83).

Feed Me
Words by Howard Ashman, music by Alan Menken.
WB Music, 1982.
Introduced by Ron Taylor as the voice of Audrey II in *Little Shop of Horrors* (82).

Feel It Again (Canadian)
Words and music by Ray Coburn.
Screen Gems-EMI Music Inc., 1986/Auto Tunes, 1986.
Introduced by Honeymoon Suite on the album *The Big Prize* (Warner Bros., 86). The song was featured on a episode of the television series *Miami Vice.*

Feelin' the Feelin'
Words and music by David Bellamy.
Bellamy Brothers Music, 1986.
Best-selling record by The Bellamy Brothers from the album *The Bellamy Brothers' Greatest Hits, MCA, 86).*

Feels So Real (Won't Let Go)
Words and music by Patrice Rushen and Fred Washington.
Baby Fingers Music, 1984/Mumbi Music, 1984.
Best-selling record by Patrice Rushen from *Now* (Elektra, 84).

Feels So Right
Words and music by Randy Owen.
Maypop Music, 1980.
Best-selling record by Alabama from *Feels So Right* (RCA, 81).

Fewer Threads Than These
Words and music by Bucky Jones, Kevin Welch, and Gary Nicholson.
Cross Keys Publishing Co., Inc., 1987.
Best-selling record by Holly Dunn, from the album *Cornerstone* (MTM, 87), this song was previously recorded by Dan Seals.

Fidelity
Words and music by Garland Jeffreys.
EMI-April Music, 1982/Garland Jeffreys Music/April Music, Inc., 1982.
Introduced by Garland Jeffreys on *Guts for Love* (Epic, 82).

Fields of Fire (Scottish)
Words and music by Big Country.
Virgin Music, 1983.
Best-selling record by Big Country from *The Crossing* (Mercury, 84).

'57 Chevy
Words and music by Tom DeLuca and Taylor Rhodes.
Gennaro, 1986/Nashlon, 1986.
Introduced by Tom DeLuca on the album *Down to the Wire* (Epic, 86). It was nominated for a prize at the World Popular Song Festival in Tokyo.

Fifty-six Reasons to Go Downtown
Words by Iris Berry, music by Gary Eaton.
City Girl Music, 1989/Burn Em Up Music, 1989.
Introduced by The Ringling Sisters in *The Radio Tokyo Tapes, Vol. 4* (Chameleon, 89).

(You Gotta) Fight for Your Right (to Party)
Words and music by Beastie Boys, words and music by Rick Rubin.
Def Jam, 1986/Brooklyn Dust Music, 1986.
Best-selling record in 1987 by The Beastie Boys, from the album

Licensed to Ill (Def Jam, 86). White rap's finest joke band produced its only anthem with this song and lived it to the fullest in 1987.

Fight the Power
Words and music by Carlton Ridenhook, Hank Shocklee, Eric Sadler, and Keith Shocklee.
Def American Songs, 1989.
Best-selling record by Public Enemy from Spike Lee's film *Do the Right Thing* and its soundtrack album (Motown, 89). Nominated for a Grammy Award, Rap Song of the Year, 1989.

The Final Countdown (Swedish)
English words and music by Joey Tempest.
Screen Gems-EMI Music Inc., 1986.
Best-selling record by Europe, from the album *The Final Countdown* (Epic, 86).

Find Another Fool
Words and music by Marv Ross.
Bonnie Bee Good Music, 1981/Geffen/Kaye Music, 1981.
Best-selling record by Quarterflash from *Quarterflash* (Geffen, 82).

Find Your Way Back
Words and music by Craig Chaquico and Thomas Borsdorf.
Lunatunes Music, 1981.
Best-selling record by Jefferson Starship from *Modern Times* (Grunt, 81).

Finder of Lost Loves
Words by Carole Bayer Sager, music by Burt Bacharach.
SVO Music, 1984/New Hidden Valley Music Co., 1984/Carole Bayer Sager Music, 1984/Spelling Venture Music, 1984.
Introduced by Dionne Warwick and Glenn Jones on *Finder of Lost Loves* (84). Featured on the LP *Finder of Lost Loves* (Arista, 85).

A Fine Fine Day (English)
Words and music by Tony Carey.
Warner-Tamerlane Music, 1984.
Best-selling record by Tony Carey from *Some Tough City* (MCA, 84).

A Fine Mess
Words by Dennis Lambert, music by Henry Mancini.
EMI Golden Torch Music, 1986/EMI-Gold Horizon Music Corp./ Tuneworks Music.
Introduced by the Temptations in the film *A Fine Mess* (86).

The Finer Things (American-English)
Words by Will Jennings, music by Steve Winwood.
F.S. Ltd., England, 1986/WB Music, 1986/Willin' David, 1986/Blue Sky

Rider Songs, 1986.
Best-selling record by Steve Winwood, from the album *Back in the High Life* (Island, 86).

The Finest
Words and music by Terry Lewis and James Harris, III.
Flyte Tyme Tunes, 1986/Avant Garde Music Publishing, Inc., 1986.
Best-selling record by The S.O.S. Band from the album *Sands of Time* (Epic, 86). The songwriting/producing duo was the hottest pair in the business of dance-oriented rock in 1986.

Finish What Ya Started
Words and music by Eddie Van Halen, Alex Van Halen, Sammy Hagar, and Michael Anthony.
Yessup Music Co., 1988.
Best-selling record by Van Halen from OU812 (Warner Bros., 88).

Finishing the Hat
Words and music by Stephen Sondheim.
WB Music, 1981.
Introduced by Mandy Patinkin in *Sunday in the Park with George* (83).

Fire
Words and music by Bruce Springsteen.
Bruce Springsteen Publishing, 1978.
Revived in 1986 by Robert Gordon on the album *Cover Me* (Rhino), a collection of songs by Bruce Springsteen performed by other artists. A rendition by 'the Boss' himself was featured on the five-record set *Bruce Springsteen & The E Street Band Live, 1975-1985* (Columbia, 86).

Fire and Ice
Words and music by Tom Kelly, Scott Sheets, and Pat Benatar.
Chrysalis Music Group, 1981/Big Tooth Music Corp., 1981/Sony Tunes, 1981.
Best-selling record by Pat Benatar from *Precious Time* (Chrysalis, 81).

Fire and Smoke
Words and music by Earl Thomas Conley.
EMI-April Music, 1981.
Best-selling record by Earl Thomas Conley (Sunbird, 81).

A Fire I Can't Put Out
Words and music by Darrell Staedtler.
Music City Music, 1982.
Best-selling record by George Strait from *Greatest Hits* (MCA, 83).

Fire Lake
Words and music by Bob Seger.

Gear Publishing, 1980.
Best-selling record by Bob Seger from *Against the Wind* (Capitol, 80).

Fire with Fire
Words and music by Chas Sandford.
Fallwater Music, 1986.
Introduced by Wild Blue in the film *Fire with Fire* (86); also used on the album *No More Jinx* (Chrysalis, 86).

The First Man You Remember (English)
Words by Don Black and Charles Hart, music by Andrew Lloyd Webber.
The Really Useful Group, 1989.
Introduced by Diana Morrison in the musical and London cast album of *Aspects of Love* (Polydor, 89).

The First Time I Loved Forever
Words by Melanie, music by Lee Holdridge.
Compelling Music, 1989.
Introduced by Lisa Angelle in the television series and soundtrack album *Beauty and the Beast* (Capitol, 89).

The First Time It Happens
Words and music by Joe Raposo.
ATV Music Corp., 1981.
Introduced in the film *The Great Muppet Caper* (81). Nominated for an Academy Award, 1981.

First We Take Manhattan (Canadian)
Words and music by Leonard Cohen.
Stranger Music Inc.
Performed by Jennifer Warnes on the album *Famous Blue Raincoat* (Cypress, 86). With this collection of Cohen's songs, Warnes became the foremost interpreter of the Canadian poet's world since Judy Collins. Revived in 1988 by Leonard Cohen on *I' m Your Man* (Columbia).

Fish Below the Ice (English)
Words and music by Dave Allen, Barry Andrews, Martin Barker, and Carl Marsh.
Point Music Ltd., England, 1985.
Introduced by Shriekback on the album *Oil and Gold* (Island, 85).

Fisherman's Daughter (Canadian)
Words and music by Daniel Lanois.
Hamstein Music, 1989/Aluda Music.
Introduced by Daniel Lanois, former producer for Robbie Robertson and Bob Dylan, on *Acadie* (Opal, 89).

Fishin' in the Dark
Words and music by Wendy Waldman and Jim Photoglo.
Screen Gems-EMI Music Inc., 1986/Moon & Stars Music, 1986/Burger Bits, 1986.
Best-selling record The Nitty Gritty Dirt Band, from the album *Hold On* (Warner Bros., 86). Singer-songwriter Waldman broke away from the Los Angeles mold to make a successful transition to Nashville Collaborator.

Fishnet
Words and music by Morris Day, James Harris, III, and Terry Lewis.
Yadsirrom Music, 1988/WB Music, 1988/Flyte Tyme Tunes, 1988.
Best-selling record by Morris Day from *Daydreaming* (Warner Bros., 88). The recording marked a collaborative reunion of Prince's proteges, The Time.

5 A.M. in Amsterdam
Words and music by Michelle Shocked.
Polygram Songs, 1988.
Introduced by Michelle Shocked on *The Texas Campfire Tapes* (Mercury, 88). Recorded at the Kerrville Folk Festival in Texas, this song was released in its rudimentary form to emphasize Shocked's folk roots.

The Flame (American-English)
Words and music by Robert Mitchell and Dick Graham.
Lorimar Music Publishing Co., 1987/Hidden Pun, 1987.
Best-selling record by Cheap Trick from the album *Lap of Luxury* (Epic, 88); a major comeback song for 70's good-time band.

Flames of Paradise
Words and music by Bruce Roberts and Andy Goldmark.
Broozertoones, Inc., 1987/Nonpariel Music, 1987.
Best-selling record by Jennifer Rush and Elton John, from the album *Heart over Mind* (Epic, 87).

Flashdance...What a Feeling (German)
English words by Keith Forsey and Irene Cara, music by Giorgio Moroder.
Intersong, USA Inc., 1983/Famous Music Corp., 1983.
Best-selling record by Irene Cara (Casablanca, 83). Introduced in the film and soundtrack album *Flashdance* (83). Won an Academy Award, and Best Song, 1983. Nominated for a Grammy Award, Record of the Year, 1983.

Flight of the Snowbirds, see Love Lights the World (Rendezvous).

Flip Ya Flip
Words and music by Nils Lofgren.

Hilmer Music Publishing Co., 1985.
Introduced by Nils Lofgren on the album *Flip* (Columbia, 85).

Flirt
Words and music by Leon F. Sylvers, III.
Jobete Music Co., 1988/R.K.S., 1988.
Best-selling record by Evelyn 'Champagne' King, from *Flirt* (EMI-Manhattan, 88).

Flirtin' with Disaster
Words and music by David Lawrence Hludeck, Danny Joe Brown, and Banner Harvey Thomas.
Mister Sunshine Music, Inc., 1979.
Best-selling record by Molly Hatchet from *Flirtin' with Disaster* (Epic, 80).

Flo's Yellow Rose
Words and music by Fred Werner and Suzie Glickman.
WB Music, 1981.
Best-selling record by Hoyt Axton (Elektra, 81). Introduced on *Flo's Yellow Rose* (81).

Flying High Again (English)
Words and music by Ozzy Osbourne, Randy Rhoads, Bob Daisley, and Lee Gary Kerslake.
Blizzard Music, London, England, 1981.
Best-selling record by Ozzy Osbourne from *Diary of a Madman* (Jet, 81).

Folies Bergeres
Words and music by Maury Yeston.
Yeston Music, Ltd., 1975.
Introduced by Lilian Montevecchi in *Nine* (Musical, 82).

Folksinger
Words and music by Phranc.
Folkswim, 1989.
Introduced by Phranc on *I Enjoy Being a Girl* (Island, 89).

Fool for Your Love
Words and music by Don Singleton.
Tree Publishing Co., Inc., 1983/Black Sheep Music Inc., 1983.
Best-selling record by Mickey Gilley (Epic, 83).

Fool Hearted Memory
Words and music by Alan R. Mevis and Byron Hill.
Welbeck Music Corp., 1982/Make Believus Music, 1982/Mevis Believus Music.
Best-selling record by George Strait from *Greatest Hits* (MCA, 82).

Fool in the Rain (English)
Words and music by John Paul Jones, Jimmy Page, and Robert Plant.
Flames of Albion Music, Inc., 1979.
Best-selling record by Led Zeppelin from *In Through the Out Door*
(Swan Song, 80).

Foolin' (English)
Words and music by Steve Clark, Robert John 'Mutt' Lange, and Joe
Elliott.
Zomba Music, 1983.
Best-selling record by Def Leppard from *Pyromania* (Mercury, 83).

Foolish Beat
Words and music by Debbie Gibson.
Creative Bloc, 1987/Possibilities Publishing, 1987.
Best-selling record in 1988 by Debbie Gibson, from *Out of the Blue*
(Atlantic, 87). Gibson was youngest person ever to write, produce,
and sing a number one hit.

Foolish Heart
Words and music by Steve Perry and Randy Goodrum.
Street Talk Tunes, 1984/EMI-April Music, 1984/Random Notes, 1984.
Best-selling record by Steve Perry in 1985 from the album *Street Talk*
(Columbia, 84).

Footloose
Words by Dean Pitchford, music by Kenny Loggins.
Famous Music Corp., 1984/Ensign Music, 1984.
Best-selling record by Kenny Loggins (Columbia, 84). Introduced in the
film and soundtrack album *Footloose* (84). Nominated for an
Academy Award, Best Song, 1984.

For a Rocker
Words and music by Jackson Browne.
Night Kitchen Music, 1983.
Best-selling record by Jackson Browne from *Lawyers in Love* (Asylum,
84).

For All the Wrong Reasons
Words and music by David Bellamy.
Famous Music Corp., 1982/Bellamy Brothers Music, 1982.
Best-selling record by The Bellamy Brothers (Elektra/Curb, 82).

(I Love You) For Sentimental Reasons
Words by Deek Watson, music by William Best.
Duchess Music Corp., 1945.
Revived in 1986 by Linda Ronstadt on the album *For Sentimental
Reasons* (Asylum, 86).

For the Sake of the Song
Words and music by Townes Van Zandt.
Silver Dollar Music, 1987.
Introduced by Townes Van Zandt on the album *At My Window* (Sugar
    Hill, 87), marking the legendary, grizzled country-folk writer's return
    to recording after a long absence.

For You
Words and music by Bruce Springsteen.
Bruce Springsteen Publishing, 1972.
Revived by Manfred Mann's Earth Band on *Chance* (Warner Brothers,
    81).

For You to Love
Words and music by Luther Vandross and Marcus Miller.
EMI-April Music, 1988/Uncle Ronnie's Music, 1988/Sunset Burgundy
    Music, Inc., 1988/MCA Music, 1988.
Best-selling record in 1989 by Luther Vandross from *Any Love* (Epic,
    88).

For Your Eyes Only
Words and music by Bill Conti and M. Leeson.
EMI Unart Catalogue, 1981.
Best-selling record by Sheena Easton (Liberty, 81). Introduced in the
    film *For Your Eyes Only* (81). Nominated for an Academy Award,
    Best Song, 1981.

Ford Econoline
Words and music by Nanci Griffith.
Wing & Wheel Music, 1987.
Introduced by Nanci Griffith on the album *Lone Star State of Mind*
    (MCA, 87).

Foreign Affairs
Words and music by Tony Joe White.
Tony Joe White Music, 1987/Screen Gems-EMI Music Inc., 1987.
Introduced by Tina Turner on *Foreign Affairs* (Capitol, 89).

Forever and Ever, Amen
Words and music by Paul Overstreet and Don Schlitz.
Writer's Group Music, 1987/Scarlet Moon Music, 1987/Don Schlitz
    Music, 1987.
Best-selling record by Randy Travis, from the album *Always and
    Forever* (Warner Bros., 87). Won a Country Music Association
    Award, and Country Song of the Year, 1987;a Grammy Award, and
    Country Song of the Year, 1987.

Forever Came Today
Words and music by Eric Ambel and Scott Kempner.

Prince of the Bronx Music, 1988/Screen Gems-EMI Music Inc., 1988/
Vibemeister, 1988/Ebbett's Field Music, 1988.
Introduced by Eric Ambel on *Roscoe's Gang* (Enigma, 88). Ambel also
appears as the leader of The Del Lords.

Forever Man (English)
Words and music by Jerry Williams.
EMI-Blackwood Music Inc., 1985/Urge Music, 1985.
Best-selling record by Eric Clapton from the album *Behind the Sun*
(Warner Bros., 85).

Forever Young (English)
Words and music by Rod Stewart, Jim Cregan, and Kevin Savigar.
Rod Stewart, 1988/Kevin Savigar, 1988/PSO Ltd., 1988/Intersong, USA
Inc., 1988.
Best-selling record by Rod Stewart from *Out of Order* (Warner Bros.,
88).

Forever Young (The Wild Ones)
Words and music by Sammy Llanas and Kurt Neumann.
Lla-Mann, 1987/Intersong, USA Inc., 1987.
Introduced by The BoDeans on *Outside Looking In* (Slash, 87).

Forever Your Girl
Words and music by Oliver Leiber.
Virgin Music, 1988/Oliver Leiber Music, 1988.
Best-selling record in 1989 by Paula Abdul, from *Forever Your Girl*
(Virgin, 88).

Forget Me Nots
Words and music by Patrice Rushen, Fred Washington, and Terry
McFadden.
Baby Fingers Music, 1981/Freddie Dee Music, 1981/Yanina Music,
1981.
Best-selling record by Patrice Rushen from *Straight from the Heart*
(Elektra, 82).

Forgiving You Was Easy
Words and music by Willie Nelson.
Willie Nelson Music Inc., 1984.
Best-selling record by Willie Nelson from the album *Me and Paul*
(Columbia, 85).

Forgotten Town (English)
Words and music by Henry Priestman.
Virgin Music, 1988.
Introduced by The Christians on *The Christians* (Island, 88). Priestman
promises to be a major new writer.

Fortress Around Your Heart (English)
Words and music by Sting (pseudonym for Gordon Sumner).
Reggatta Music, Ltd., 1985.
Best-selling record by Sting from the album *The Dream of the Blue Turtles* (A & M, 85).

40 Hour Week (for a Livin')
Words and music by Dave Loggins, Lisa Silver, and Don Schlitz.
Music of the World, 1984/MCA, Inc./Leeds Music Corp./Patchwork Music/Don Schlitz Music.
Best-selling record by Alabama from the album *40 Hour Week* (RCA, 85). Nominated for a Grammy Award, Country Song of the Year, 1985.

Four in the Morning (I Can't Take Anymore)
Words and music by Jack Blades.
Kid Bird Music, 1985.
Best-selling record by Night Ranger from the album *Seven Wishes* (MCA, 85).

Fourteen Carat Mind
Words and music by Dallas Frazier and Larry Lee.
Acuff-Rose Publications Inc., 1981.
Best-selling record by Gene Watson (MCA, 81).

Fourth of July
Words and music by Dave Alvin.
Blue Horn Toad, 1987.
Recorded by X on the album *See How We Are* (Elektra, 87). Introduced by Dave Alvin, formerly the guitarist for X, on the album *Romeo's Escape* (Epic, 87).

Fran and Janie
Words and music by Craig Carnelia.
Carnelia Music, 1982.
Introduced by Sandy Faison and Maureen Silliman in *Is There Life After High School* (82).

Frankie (English)
Words and music by Joy Denny.
Atlantic Recording Corp., England, 1985.
Best-selling record by Sister Sledge from the album *When the Boys Meet the Girls* (Atlantic, 85).

Franklin Shepard, Inc.
Words and music by Stephen Sondheim.
WB Music, 1981/Rilting Music Inc.
Introduced by Lonny Price in *Merrily We Roll Along* (81).

Freak-a-Zoid
Words and music by Vincent Calloway, Reggie Calloway, and William Simmons.
Hip-Trip Music Co., 1983/Midstar Music, Inc., 1983.
Best-selling record by Midnight Star from *No Parking on the Dance Floor* (Solar, 83).

Freakshow on the Dancefloor
Words and music by James Alexander, Michael Beard, Mark Bynum, Larry Dodson, Harvey Henderson, Lloyd Smith, Winston Stewart, Frank Thompson, and Allen A. Jones.
Warner-Tamerlane Music, 1984/Bar-Kay Music, 1984.
Best-selling record by The Bar-Kays from *Dangerous* (Mercury, 84).

Freaky Dancin'
Words and music by Larry Blackmon and Tomi Jenkins.
Better Days Music, 1981/Polygram International, 1981.
Best-selling record by Cameo from *Knights of the Sound Table* (Chocolate City, 81).

Free Bird
Words and music by Allen Collins and Ronnie Van Zant.
Duchess Music Corp., 1975/Hustlers Inc., 1975.
Revived in 1988 by Will to Power on *Will to Power* (Epic, 88) as part of medley with 'Baby I Love Your Way.'

Free Fallin' (English)
Words and music by Tom Petty and Jeff Lynne.
Gone Gator Music, 1989/EMI-April Music, 1989.
Best-selling record By Tom Petty from *Full Moon Fever* (MCA, 89),

Free Nelson Mandela (English)
Words and music by Jerry Dammers and Rhoda Dakar.
Plangent Visions Music, Inc., London, England, 1984.
Introduced by Special AKA from the album *In the Studio* (Chrysalis, 85). Re-released to capitalize on late 1985 anti-apartheid sentiments inspired by 'Sun City.' Mandela was one of South Africa's jailed Black leaders.

Freedom (English)
Words and music by George Michael.
Chappell & Co., Inc., 1984.
Best-selling record by Wham! featuring George Michael in 1985 from the album *Make It Big* (Columbia, 84).

Freedom
Words and music by Jackson Browne.
Swallow Turn Music, 1988.
Introduced by Jackson Browne at Freedomfest, an international

celebration for imprisoned South African activist Nelson Mandela's seventieth birthday.

Freedom Overspill (American-English)
Words and music by Steve Winwood, George Fleming, and Jake Hooker.
F.S. Ltd., England, 1986/EMI-April Music.
Best-selling record by Steve Winwood from the album *Back in the High Life* (Island, 86).

Freeway of Love
Words and music by Narada Michael Walden and Jeffrey Cohen.
Gratitude Sky Music, 1985/Polo Grounds Music, 1985.
Best-selling record by Aretha Franklin from the album *Who's Zoomin' Who* (Arista, 85). Won a Grammy Award, and Rhythm 'n' Blues Song of the Year, 1985.

Freeze-Frame
Words and music by Peter Wolf and Seth Justman.
Center City Music, 1981/Pal-Park Music, 1981.
Best-selling record by J. Geils Band from *Freeze-Frame* (EMI-America, 82).

Freeze Tag
Words and music by Suzanne Vega.
Waifersongs, 1985/AGF Music Ltd., 1985.
Introduced by Suzanne Vega on the album *Suzanne Vega* (A & M, 85).

Freezing
Words by Suzanne Vega, music by Philip Glass.
AGF Music Ltd., 1986.
Introduced by Linda Ronstadt on the album *Songs from Liquid Days* (CBS, 86), an experiment in songwriting, pairing the avant-garde composer Glass with some of the top lyricists of the day, including Paul Simon and Laurie Anderson.

Fresh
Words and music by James Taylor, Sandy Linzner, George Brown, Curtis Williams, Charles Smith, Ronald Bell, Robert Bell, and James Bonneford.
Delightful Music Ltd., 1984.
Best-selling record by Kool & The Gang from the album *Emergency* (De-Lite, 85).

Friction
Words and music by Pat MacDonald.
Mambadaddi, 1986/I.R.S. Music, 1986/Criterion Music Corp., 1986.
Introduced by Timbuk 3 on the album *Greetings from Timbuk 3* (I.R.S., 86).

Friday Night Blues
Words and music by Sonny Throckmorton and Rafe Van Hoy.
Tree Publishing Co., Inc., 1979/Cross Keys Publishing Co., Inc., 1980.
Best-selling record by John Conlee from *John Conlee's Greatest Hits*
   (MCA, 80).

Friends
Words and music by Johnny Slate and Dan Morrison.
Warner House of Music, 1980.
Best-selling record by Razzy Bailey from *Makin Friends* (RCA, 81).

Friends
Words and music by Andre Cymone and Jody Watley.
EMI-April Music, 1989/Ultrawave, 1989/Rightsong Music, 1989.
Best-selling record by Jody Watley with Eric B & Rakim, from *Larger
   Than Life* (MCA, 89).

Friends and Lovers (Both to Each Other)
Words and music by Paul Gordon and Jay Gruska.
WB Music, 1986/French Surf Music, 1986/Colgems-EMI Music, 1986.
Best-selling record by Gloria Loring and Carl Anderson; featured on the
   albums *Carl Anderson* (Epic, 86) and *Gloria Loring* (EMI-America,
   86). The song was introduced on the soap opera *Days of Our Lives*. It
   was also recorded by Eddie Rabbitt and Juice Newton (RCA).

Fright Night
Words and music by J. Lamont.
National League Music, 1985/EMI Golden Torch Music, 1985/Ring Inc.
Introduced by J. Geils Band in the film *Fright Night* (85).

From a Distance
Words and music by Julie Gold.
Julie Gold's Music, 1987/Wing & Wheel Music, 1987.
Introduced by Nanci Griffith on the album *Lone Star State of Mind*
   (MCA, 87), this is one of the strongest country songs of the year.

From a Jack to a King
Words and music by Ned Miller.
Jamie Music Publishing Co., 1957.
Revived by Ricky Van Shelton on *Loving Proof* (Columbia, 88).

From Small Things (Big Things One Day Come)
Words and music by Bruce Springsteen.
Bruce Springsteen Publishing, 1979.
Featured on *D.E. 7th* by Dave Edmunds (Columbia, 82).

From the Word Go
Words and music by Chris Waters and Michael Garvin.
Tree Publishing Co., Inc., 1986.

Best-selling record by Michael Martin Murphey from *River of Time* (Warner Bros., 89).

Funkin' for Jamaica (N.Y.)
Words and music by Tom Browne.
Thomas Browne Publishing, 1980/Roaring Fork Music, 1980.
Best-selling record by Tom Browne from *Lone Approach* (GRP, 80).

Funky Cold Medina
Words and music by Marvin Young, Michael Ross, and Matt Dike.
Varry White Music, 1989.
Best-selling record by Tone Loc from *Loc-ed After Dark* (Delicious Vinyl/Island, 89). Nominated for a Grammy Award, Rap Song of the Year, 1989.

Funky Town
Words and music by Steve Greenburg.
Steve Greenberg Music, 1979/Rick's Music Inc., 1979.
Best-selling record by Lipps, Inc. from *Mouth to Mouth* (Casablanca). Revived in 1987 by Pseudo Echo on the album *Love an Adventure* (RCA, 87).

Future 40's (String of Pearls)
Words and music by Syd Straw, Michael Stipe, and Jody Harris.
Straw Songs, 1989/Night Garden Music/Unichappell Music Inc./ Raybeats Music.
Introduced by Syd Straw on *Surprise Me* (Virgin, 89).

The Future's So Bright, I Gotta Wear Shades
Words and music by Pat MacDonald.
Mambadaddi, 1986/I.R.S. Music, 1986/Criterion Music Corp., 1986.
Best-selling record by Timbuk 3 from the album *Greetings from Timbuk 3* (I.R.S., 86).

G

Gail Loves Me
Words and music by Jonathan Richman.
Rockin Leprechaun, 1987.
Introduced by Jonathan Richman and The Modern Lovers on *Modern Lovers 88* (Rounder, 88) . The title of this song is also its only lyric.

The Games I Play
Words and music by William Finn.
Introduced by Stephen Bogardus in *March of the Falsettos* (81).

Games People Play (English)
Words and music by Eric Woolfson and Alan Parsons.
Irving Music Inc., 1979.
Best-selling record by The Alan Parsons Project from *The Turn of a Friendly Card* (Arista, 80).

Games Without Frontiers
English words and music by Peter Gabriel.
Hidden Music, 1980.
Introduced by Peter Gabriel on *Peter Gabriel* (Mercury, 80).

Garden of Earthly Delights (English)
Words and music by Andy Partridge.
Virgin Songs, 1989.
Introduced by by XTC on *Oranges and Lemons* (Geffen, 89).

The Garden Path to Hell
Words and music by Rupert Holmes.
Holmes Line of Music, 1985.
Introduced by Cleo Laine in the musical *The Mystery of Edwin Drood* (85), which moved to Broadway after originating at the Delacorte Theatre in New York's Central Park.

General Hospi-tale
Words and music by Harry King and L. Tedesco.
Solid Smash Music Publishing Co., Inc., 1981/American Broadcasting

Music, Inc., 1981.
Best-selling record by The Afternoon Delights (MCA, 81).

Genius of Love
Words and music by Tom Tom Club.
Metered Music, Inc., 1981.
Best-selling record by Tom Tom Club from *Tom Tom Club* (Sire, 82).

Get Closer
Words and music by Jonathan Carroll.
Cherry Lane Music Co., 1981.
Best-selling record by Linda Ronstadt from *Get Closer* (Asylum, 82).

Get Down on It
Words and music by Ronald Bell, Eumir Deodato, Robert Mickens,
    James Taylor, Charles Smith, Robert Bell, and George Brown.
Delightful Music Ltd., 1981/WB Music, 1981.
Best-selling record by Kool & The Gang from *Something Special* (De-
    Lite, 82).

Get It On (Bang a Gong) (English)
Words and music by Marc Feld.
Essex International Inc., 1971/Westminster Music, Ltd., 1971.
Revived by The Power Station on the album *The Power Station*
    (Capitol, 85).

Get It On
Words and music by Lenny Wolf and Marty Wolfe.
Blue Vision Music, 1988.
Best-selling record by Kingdom Come, from *Kingdom Come* (Polydor,
    88). This song was regarded by many as a blatant copy of several Led
    Zeppelin tunes, notably 'Kashmir.'

Get It Right
Words and music by Luther Vandross and Marcus Miller.
Uncle Ronnie's Music, 1983/EMI-April Music, 1983/Thriller Miller
    Music, 1983.
Best-selling record by Aretha Franklin from *Get It Right* (Arista, 83).

Get on Your Feet
Words and music by John DeFaria, Jorge Casas, and Clay Ostwald.
Foreign Imported, 1989.
Best-selling record by Gloria Estefan from *Cuts Both Ways* (Epic, 89).

Get outa My Dreams, Get into My Car (American-English)
Words and music by Robert John 'Mutt' Lange (pseudonym for John
    Robert Lange) and Billy Ocean.
Zomba Music, 1988.
Best-selling record by Billy Ocean from the album *Tear Down These*

Walls (Jive, 88). One of the year's worst titles, seemingly based on a line from the Ringo Starr version of 'You're Sixteen.'

Getcha Back
Words and music by Mike Love and Terry Melcher.
Careers Music Inc., 1985.
Best-selling record by The Beach Boys from the album *The Beach Boys* (CBS, 85).

Ghost Town (English)
Words and music by Jerry Dammers.
Plangent Visions Music, Inc., London, England, 1981.
Introduced by The Specials on the Ep *Ghost Town/Why?/Friday Night Saturday Morning* in 1981. Written about the 1981 riots in England.

Ghost Train
Words and music by Rickie Lee Jones.
Easy Money Music, 1989.
Introduced by Rickie Lee Jones on *Flying Cowboys* (Geffen, 89), a comeback album by the jazz/pop singer who scored with 'Chuck E's in Love.'

Ghostbusters
Words and music by Ray Parker, Jr.
EMI Golden Torch Music, 1984/Raydiola Music, 1984.
Best-selling record by Ray Parker, Jr. (Arista, 84). Introduced in the film and soundtrack album *Ghostbusters* (84). Nominated for an Academy Award, Best Song, 1984.

Ghosts upon the Road
Words and music by Eric Andersen.
AGF Music Ltd., 1988/Wind and Sand Music, 1988.
Introduced by Eric Andersen on *Ghosts upon the Road* (Gold Castle, 89). The song is an epic epistle about the early days of the 1960's, by a folksinger who experienced them.

The Gift (Canadian)
Words and music by Ian Tyson.
Slick Fork Music, 1987.
Introduced by Ian Tyson, formerly a member of the Canadian folk duo Ian and Sylvia, on the album *Cowboyography* (Sugar Hill, 87). Tyson also wrote 'Someday Soon' for Judy Collins.

The Gigolo
Words and music by O'Bryan Burnette and Don Cornelius.
Big Train Music Co., 1981.
Best-selling record by O'Bryan (Capitol, 82).

Gimme All Your Lovin'
Words and music by Billy Gibbons, Dusty Hill, and Frank Beard.
Hamstein Music, 1983.
Best-selling record by ZZ Top from *Eliminator* (Warner Brothers, 83).

Gimme Some Lovin' (English)
Words and music by Steve Winwood, Muff Winwood, and Spencer
Davis.
Island Music, 1966/Irving Music Inc., 1966.
Revived by The Blues Brothers on *The Blues Brothers* (Atlantic, 80).

Gimme Your Love
Words and music by Narada Michael Walden and Jeffrey Cohen.
Gratitude Sky Music, 1989.
Best-selling record by Aretha Franklin and James Brown, from *Gimme
Your Love* (Arista, 89).

Gingham and Yarn
Words and music by Joe Raposo.
Jonico Music Inc., 1986.
Introduced by Ivy Austin in the 1986 Broadway musical *Raggedy Ann*.

Girl Can't Help It
Words and music by Steve Perry, Jonathan Cain, and Neal Schon.
Street Talk Tunes, 1986/Rock Dog Music, 1986/Frisco Kid Music, 1986/
Colgems-EMI Music, 1986.
Best-selling record by Journey from the album *Raised on Radio*
(Columbia, 86). The title was borrowed from a 1956 Jayne Mansfield
film.

Girl, Don't Let It Get You Down
Words and music by Kenny Gamble and Leon Huff.
Mighty Three Music, 1979.
Best-selling record by The O'Jays from *The Year 2000* (TSOP, 80).

Girl I Almost Married
Words and music by Joey Harris.
Joey Harris Music, 1989/Bug Music, 1989.
Introduced by The Beat Farmers on *Poor and Famous* (MCA, 89).

Girl I Got My Eyes on You
Words and music by Gene Griffin, Wesley Adams, Larry Singletary,
and Larry McLain.
Cal-Gene Music, 1988/Virgin Music.
Best-selling record in 1989 by Today from *Today* (Motown, 88).

Girl, I'm Gonna Miss You (German)
English words and music by Frank Farian, Dietman Kawohl, and Peter
Bischof-Fallenstein.

MCA Music, 1989.
Best-selling record by Milli Vanilli from *Girl, You Know It's True*
(Arista, 89).

A Girl in Trouble (Is a Temporary Thing)
Words and music by Debora Iyall, Peter Woods, Frank Zincavage, and
David Kahne.
Talk Dirty Music, 1984/Seesquared Music, 1984.
Best-selling record by Romeo Void from *Instincts* (Columbia, 84).

The Girl Is Mine
Words and music by Michael Jackson.
Mijac Music, 1982/Warner-Tamerlane Music, 1982.
Best-selling record by Michael Jackson and Paul McCartney from
Thriller (Epic, 82).

The Girl Who Used to Be Me
Words by Alan Bergman and Marilyn Bergman, music by Marvin
Hamlisch.
Famous Music Corp., 1989/Polygram Songs, 1989/Threesome Music
Co., 1989.
Introduced by Patti Austin in the 1989 film *Shirley Valentine*.
Nominated for an Academy Award, Best Original Song, 1989.

Girl, You Know It's True (German)
English words and music by Dietman Kawohl, Frank Farian, and Peter
Bischof-Fallenstein.
FMP Songs, Berlin, Germany, 1989/Ed. Intro, Berlin, Germany, 1989/
MCA Music, 1989.
Best-selling record by Milli Vanilli from *Girl, You Know It's True*
(Arista, 89).

Girlfriend
Words and music by Larry White, Lee Peters, and Kirk Crumpler.
Kamalar, 1986/Let's Shine, 1986.
Best-selling record by Bobby Brown from the album *King of Stage*
(MCA, 86).

Girlfriend
Words and music by Babyface (pseudonym for Kenny Edmunds) and L.
A. Reid (pseudonym for Antonio Reid).
Kermy, 1987/Hip-Trip Music Co., 1987.
Best-selling record by Pebbles, from *Pebbles* (RCA, 88).

Girls
Words and music by Dwight Twilley.
Dionio Music, 1984.
Best-selling record by Dwight Twilley from *Jungle* (EMI-America, 84).

Girls, Girls, Girls
Words and music by Tommy Lee, Nikki Sixx, and Mick Mars.
Motley Crue, 1987/Mick Mars, 1987/Krell, 1987/Sikki Nixx, 1987.
Best-selling record by Motley Crue, from the album *Girls, Girls, Girls*
    (Elektra, 87).

The Girls I Never Kissed
Words and music by Jerry Leiber and Mike Stoller.
Introduced by Frank Sinatra and Paul Anka (Reprise, 87). With this
    single, the label's founding artist, Sinatra, helped celebrate its return
    to the marketplace.

Girls Just Want to Have Fun
Words and music by Robert Hazard.
Heroic Music, 1979.
Best-selling record by Cyndi Lauper from *She's So Unusual* (Portrait,
    84). Nominated for a Grammy Award, Record of the Year, 1984.

A Girls Night Out
Words and music by Jeff Hawthorne Bullock and Brent Maher.
Welbeck Music Corp., 1984/Blue Quill Music, 1984.
Best-selling record by The Judds from the album *Why Not Me* (RCA,
    85).

The Girls of Summer
Words and music by Stephen Sondheim.
WB Music, 1982.
Introduced by Craig Lucas in *Marry Me a Little* (81).

Girls on Film (English)
Words and music by Andy Taylor, John Taylor, Roger Taylor, Simon
    Le Bon, and Nick Rhodes.
BIOT Music Ltd., London, England, 1981.
Best-selling record by Duran Duran from *Carnival* (Harvest, 81).

Girls Talk (English)
Words and music by Elvis Costello.
Plangent Visions Music, Inc., London, England, 1979.
Featured in *Mad Love* (Asylum, 80) by Linda Ronstadt.

Give a Little Love
Words and music by Paul Kennerley.
Irving Music Inc., 1988.
Best-selling record by The Judds from *(The Judds) Greatest Hits* (RCA/
    Curb, 88).

Give Her a Great Big Kiss, also known as **Give Him a Great Big
    Kiss**
Words and music by George Morton.

Trio Music Co., Inc., 1964/Unart Music Corp., 1964/Tender Tunes
Music Co., Inc., 1964/Screen Gems-EMI Music Inc., 1964.
Revived in 1986 by the New York Dolls on the album *Night of the
Living Dolls* (Mercury), a compilation of previously recorded tracks.

Give It All You Got
Music by Chuck Mangione.
Gates Music Inc., 1980.
Best-selling record by Chuck Mangione from *Fun and Games* (A & M,
80).

Give It to Me Baby
English words and music by Rick James.
Jobete Music Co., 1981.
Best-selling record by Rick James from *Street Songs* (Gordy, 81).

Give It Up
Words and music by Harry Casey and Deborah Carter.
Harrick Music Inc., 1982.
Best-selling record by K. C. from *KC Ten* (Mecca/Alpha Distributors,
84).

Give Me His Last Chance
Words and music by Lionel Cartwright.
Silverline Music, Inc., 1987/Long Run Music Co., Inc., 1987.
Best-selling record by Lionel Cartwright from *Lionel Cartwright* (MCA,
89).

Give Me One More Chance
Words and music by James P. Pennington and Sonny LeMaire.
BMG Music, 1984/Tree Publishing Co., Inc., 1984.
Best-selling record by Exile (Epic, 84).

Give Me the Night (English)
Words and music by Rod Temperton.
Almo Music Corp., 1980.
Best-selling record by George Benson from *Give Me the Night* (Warner
Brothers, 80). Also on *The George Benson Collection* (WB, 81).
Nominated for a Grammy Award, Rhythm 'n' Blues Song of the
Year, 1980.

Give Me the Reason
Words and music by Luther Vandross and Nat Adderley, Jr.
EMI-April Music, 1986/Uncle Ronnie's Music, 1986/Dillard, 1986.
Best-selling record by Luther Vandross from the album *The Night I Fell
in Love* (Epic, 86). Nominated for a Grammy Award, Rhythm 'n'
Blues Song of the Year, 1986.

Give Me Wings
Words and music by Don Schlitz.
Irving Music Inc., 1986/Eaglewood Music, 1986/MCA Music, 1986/Don Schlitz Music, 1986.
Best-selling record by Michael Johnson from the album *Wings* (MCA, 86).

Giving It up for Your Love
Words and music by Jerry Williams.
EMI-Blackwood Music Inc., 1979/Urge Music, 1979.
Best-selling record by Delbert McClinton from *The Jealous Kind* (Capitol, 80).

Giving Up Easy
Words and music by Jerry Foster and Bill Rice.
EMI-April Music, 1979.
Best-selling record by Leon Everette (RCA, 81).

Giving You the Best That I Got
Words and music by Anita Baker, Skip Scarborough, and Randy Holland.
All Baker's Music, 1988/Alexscar Music, 1988/Eyedot Music, 1988.
Best-selling record by Anita Baker from *Giving You the Best That I Got* (Elektra, 88). Won a Grammy Award, and Rhythm 'n' Blues Song of the Year, 1988. Nominated for a Grammy Award, Record of the Year Song of the Year, 1988.

The Glamorous Life
Words and music by Prince Rogers Nelson.
Girlsongs, 1984.
Best-selling record by Sheila E. from *Sheila E. in the Glamourous Life* (Warner Brothers, 84). Nominated for a Grammy Award, Rhythm 'n' Blues Song of the Year, 1984.

Gloria (Italian)
English words by Trevor Veitch, Italian words and music by Giancarlo Bigazzi and Umberto Tozzi.
Sugar Song Publications, 1980/Music of the World, 1980.
Best-selling record by Laura Branigan from *Branigan* (Atlantic, 82).

Glory Days
Words and music by Bruce Springsteen.
Bruce Springsteen Publishing, 1984.
Best-selling record by Bruce Springsteen from the album *Born in the U.S.A.* (Columbia, 84).

Glory of Love (Theme from *The Karate Kid, Part 2*)
Words and music by Peter Cetera and David Foster.
BMG Songs Inc., 1986/Air Bear, 1986/Warner-Tamerlane Music, 1986.

Best-selling record by Peter Cetera from the album *Solitude/Solitare* (Warner Bros., 86). Introduced by Peter Cetera in the film *The Karate Kid, Part 2* (86). Nominated for an Academy Award, 1986.

The Glow
Words and music by Willie Hutch.
Stone Diamond Music, 1985.
Introduced by Willie Hutch in the film and soundtrack album *The Last Dragon* (Motown, 85).

Go Home
Words and music by Stevie Wonder.
Jobete Music Co., 1985/Black Bull Music, 1985.
Best-selling record by Stevie Wonder in 1986 from the album *In Square Circle* (Motown, 85).

Go Man Go
Words and music by Kirk Kelly.
Rambling, Woody, Zimmerman Publishing, 1988/Backlash Enterprises.
Revived by Kirk Kelly on *Legacy* (Windham Hill, 89), the song was introduced on *Go Man Go* (SST, 88).

Go See the Doctor
Words and music by Moe Dewese.
Willesden Music, Inc., 1987.
Introduced by Kool Moe Dee on his album *Kool Moe Dee* (Rooftop/ Jive, 87); in this song, written in the lobby of a New York City health clinic, the streetwise rapper reacts to the current climate of sexual caution.

God Bless the U.S.A.
Words and music by Lee Greenwood.
Music of the World, 1984/Sycamore Valley Music Inc., 1984.
Best-selling record by Lee Greenwood from *You've Got a Good Love Comin* (MCA, 84). Nominated for a Grammy Award, Country Song of the Year, 1984.

God Will
Words and music by Lyle Lovett.
Michael H. Goldsen, Inc., 1986/Lyle Lovett, 1986.
Best-selling record by Lyle Lovett, one of country's finest new writer-performers, from his album *Lyle Lovett* (MCA, 86).

God's Comic (English)
Words and music by Declan MacManus (pseudonym for Elvis Costello).
Plangent Visions Music, Inc., London, England, 1988, 1989.
Introduced by Elvis Costello on *Spike* (Warner Bros., 89).

(Pop Pop Pop Pop) Goes My Mind
Words and music by Gerald Levert and Marc Gordon.
Trycet, 1986/Ferncliff.
Best-selling record by Levert from the album *Bloodline* (Atlantic, 86).

Goin' Down
Words and music by Greg Guidry and D. Martin.
World Song Publishing, Inc., 1980/WB Music.
Best-selling record by Greg Guidry from *Over the Lines* (Columbia/
    Badlands, 82).

Goin' Gone
Words and music by Patrick Alger, Bill Dale, and Fred Koller.
Forerunner Music, 1986/Lucrative, 1986/Foreshadow Songs, Inc., 1986/
    Bug Music, 1986/Little Laurel Music, 1986.
This venerable country ballad was revived by Kathy Mattea in *Untasted
    Honey* (Mercury, 87).

Goin' Southbound
Words and music by Stanard Ridgway.
Mondo Spartacus Music, 1989/Illegal Songs, Inc., 1989/Criterion Music
    Corp., 1989.
Introduced by Stan Ridgway, former member of Wall of Voodoo, on
    Mosquitos (Geffen, 89).

Goin' to the Bank
Words and music by Dennis Lambert, Andy Goldmark, and Franne
    Golde.
Tuneworks Music, 1986/Franne Gee, 1986/Rightsong Music, 1986/
    Nonpariel Music, 1986/Careers Music Inc., 1986.
Best-selling record by The Commodores from the album *United*
    (Polydor, 86).

Going Back to Cali
Words and music by Rick Rubin and J. T. Smith.
Def Jam, 1987.
Best-selling record by LL Cool J from the film and soundtrack album
    Less Than Zero (Def Jam, 87). Nominated for a Grammy Award, Best
    Rap Performance, 1988.

Going, Going, Gone
Words and music by Jan Crutchfield.
Jan Crutchfield Music, 1983.
Best-selling record by Lee Greenwood from *Somebody's Gonna Love
    You* (MCA, 84).

Going in Circles
Words and music by Jerry Peters and Anita Poree.
Porpete Music, 1986.

Best-selling record by The Gap Band from the album *Gap Band VII* (RCA, 86).

Going Where the Lonely Go
Words and music by Merle Haggard and Dean Holloway.
Shade Tree Music Inc., 1982.
Best-selling record by Merle Haggard from *Going Where The Lonely Go* (Epic, 83).

Gonna Take a Lot of River
Words and music by Jon Kurhajetz and Mark Henley.
Reynsong Music, 1988/Wrensong, 1988.
Best-selling record by The Oak Ridge Boys, from *Monongahela* (MCA, 88).

Good Friends
Words and music by Joni Mitchell.
Crazy Crow Music, 1985.
Introduced by Joni Mitchell on the album *Dog Eat Dog* (Geffen, 85).

The Good Life
Words and music by Phil Davis and Doug Erikson.
Flip 'n' Dog, 1989/Music of the World.
Introduced by Firetown on *The Good Life* (Atlantic, 89).

Good Lovin'
Words and music by Rudy Clark and Arthur Resnick.
Hudson Bay Music, 1965.
This 1966 hit by the Young Rascals was revived in 1989 by Terri Minsky as the themesong for the short-lived television series *Doctor, Doctor*.

Good News
Words and music by Shirley Eikhard.
Visa Music, 1983.
Featured on *White Shoes* by Emmylou Harris (Warner Brothers, 83).

Good Ole Boys Like Me
Words and music by Bob McDill.
Hall-Clement Publications, 1979.
Best-selling record by Don Williams (MCA, 80).

Good Thing (English)
Words and music by David Steele and Roland Gift.
Walt Disney Music, 1987.
Introduced in the 1987 film *Tin Men*. Best-selling record by Fine Young Cannibals from *The Raw and the Cooked* (MCA, 89).

Good Thing Going (Going Gone)
Words and music by Stephen Sondheim.
WB Music, 1981/Rilting Music Inc.
Introduced by Lonny Price in *Merrily We Roll Along* (81).

Good Times (Australian)
Words and music by Dave Faulkner.
EMI Unart Catalogue, 1987.
Introduced by the Hoodoo Gurus on the album *Lose Your Cool* (Elektra, 87).

Good Times (Australian)
Words and music by George Young and Harry Vanda.
CBS Unart Catalog Inc., 1987.
Best-selling record by Inxs and Jimmy Barnes, from the movie *The Lost Boys* and its soundtrack album (Atlantic, 87). This songwriting team has been responsible for many hits, including 'Friday on My Mind,' by the Easybeats.

Good to Go
Words and music by James Avery, Tony Fischer, Robert Reed, and T. Reed, Jr.
Polygram International, 1986/Maxx Kidd's Music, 1986.
Introduced by Trouble Funk in the film *Good to Go* and featured on its soundtrack album (Island, 86). The movie was a belated effort to showcase the 'Go Go Music' street dance scene of Washington, DC, and starred Art Garfunkel in a role similar to John Travolta's in the disco film *Saturday Night Fever*. The later dance craze was all but played out by the time *Good to Go* was released, however.

Good Work
Words and music by Kurt Neumann and Sammy Llanas.
Lla-Mann, 1989.
Introduced by by The BoDeans on *Home* (Reprise, 89).

Goodbye
Words and music by Jeff Watson and Jack Blades.
Kid Bird Music, 1985/Rough Play, 1985.
Best-selling record by Night Ranger from the album *Seven Wishes* (MCA, 86).

Goodbye Emil
Words by Barry Harman, music by Keith Hermann.
WB Music, 1987/BHB Productions, 1987/Keith Hermann Music, 1987.
Introduced by Alison Fraser in the musical *Romance*, Romance (1988).

Goodbye My Friend
Words and music by Karla Bonoff.
Seagrape Music Inc., 1986.

Introduced by Karla Bonoff on *New World* (Gold Castle, 88). Revived in 1989 by Linda Ronstadt orn *Cry Like a Rainstorm, Howl Like the Wind* (Elektra, 89).

Goodbye Saving Grace
Words and music by Jon Butcher.
Grand Pasha, 1987.
Best-selling record by Jon Butcher, from the album *Wishes* (Capitol, 87).

Goodbye to You
Words and music by Zack Smith.
EMI-Blackwood Music Inc., 1981.
Best-selling record by Scandal from *Scandal* (Columbia, 83).

Goodnight My Love
Words and music by George Motola and John Manascalco.
Unichappell Music Inc., 1956/Freddy Bienstock Music Co., 1956/Trio Music Co., Inc., 1956.
Revived in 1989 by El DeBarge on *Rock, Rhythm, and Blues* (Warner Bros., 89), this was one of many fine interpretations of classic rhythm and blues songs by contemporary artists on the album.

Goodnight Saigon
Words and music by Billy Joel.
Joelsongs, 1981.
Best-selling record by Billy Joel from *The Nylon Curtain* (Columbia, 83).

Goody Two Shoes (English)
Words and music by Adam Ant and Marco Pirroni.
EMI Music Publishing, 1982/Colgems-EMI Music, 1982.
Best-selling record by Adam Ant from *Friend or Foe* (Epic, 82).

The Goonies 'R' Good Enough
Words and music by Cyndi Lauper, Stephen Lunt, and Arthur Stead.
Warner-Tamerlane Music, 1985.
Best-selling record by Cyndi Lauper (Portrait, 85). Introduced in the film *The Goonies* (85).

Got a Hold on Me (English)
Words and music by Christine McVie and Todd Sharp.
Alimony Music, 1984/Cement Chicken Music, 1984.
Best-selling record by Christine McVie from *Christine McVie* (Warner Brothers, 84).

Got My Heart Set on You
Words and music by Dobie Gray and Bud Reneau.
Simonton, 1984/N2D Publishing, 1984.

Best-selling record by John Conlee from the album *Harmony* (Columbia, 86).

Got My Mind Set on You
Words and music by Rudy Clark.
Carbert Music Inc.
Originally recorded in the 1960's, this best-selling revival by George Harrison was the first hit from his comeback album, *Cloud Nine* (Dark Horse, 87).

Gotta Get You Home Tonight
Words and music by McKinley Horton and Ronnie Broomfield.
Screen Gems-EMI Music Inc., 1984.
Best-selling record by Eugene Wilde from the album *Eugene Wilde* (Atlantic, 85).

Gotta Serve Somebody
Words and music by Bob Dylan.
Special Rider Music, 1979.
Revived in 1987 by Luther Ingram (Profile), in 1986 this song earned Bob Dylan his only Grammy Award.

Graceland
Words and music by Paul Simon.
Paul Simon Music, 1986.
Best-selling record by Paul Simon on *Graceland* (Warner Bros., 86). Graceland is the name of Elvis Presley's mansion, now a museum, in Tennessee. Won a Grammy Award, and Best Record of the Year, 1987. Nominated for a Grammy Award, Song of the Year, 1986.

The Grammy Song
Words and music by Loudon Wainwright.
Snowden Music, 1980.
Introduced on *Fame and Wealth* by Loudon Wainwright (Rounder, 83).

Grandma Got Run over by a Reindeer
Words and music by Randy Brooks.
Kris Publishing, 1979.
Best-selling record by Elmo 'n' Patsy from *Grandma Got Run over by a Reindeer* (Soundwaves, 84).

Grandpa (Tell Me 'Bout the Good Old Days)
Words and music by Jamie O'Hara.
Cross Keys Publishing Co., Inc., 1986.
Best-selling record by The Judds from the album *Rockin' with the Rhythm* (RCA, 86). Won a Grammy Award, and Country Song of the Year, 1986. Nominated for a Country Music Association Award, Song of the Year, 1986.

Grandpa Was a Carpenter
Words and music by John Prine.
Bruised Oranges, 1973.
Introduced by John Prine in 1974 on *Sweet Revenge,* the song was
   revived by Prine on *Will the Circle Be Unbroken, Vol. II* (Universal,
   89).

The Grass Is Always Greener
Words by Fred Ebb, music by John Kander.
Fiddleback, 1981/Kander & Ebb Inc., 1981.
Introduced by Marilyn Cooper and Lauren Bacall in *Woman of the Year*
   (81).

Gravity
Words and music by Michael Sembello.
WB Music, 1985/Gravity Raincoat Music, 1985.
Introduced by Michael Sembello in the film *Cocoon* (85).

Gravity's Angel
Words and music by Laurie Anderson.
Difficult Music, 1984.
Introduced by Laurie Anderson on *Mr. Heartbreak* (Warner Brothers,
   84).

Great Gosh a Mighty
Words and music by Richard Penniman and Billy Preston.
Paytons, 1986/WEP, 1986.
Introduced by Little Richard (the stage name of Richard Penniman) in
   the 1986 film *Down and Out in Beverly Hills.* The song appears both
   on the film's soundtrack album and on Little Richard's album
   Lifetime Friend (Warner Bros., 86). It marks the singer-songwriter's
   return to rock 'n' roll after several years in the ministry.

The Greatest Love of All
Words by Linda Creed, music by Michale Masser.
EMI Golden Torch Music, 1977/EMI-Gold Horizon Music Corp., 1977.
Revived in 1986 by Whitney Houston from her album *Whitney Houston*
   (Arista, 85). The song served as an epitaph for co-writer Linda Creed,
   who died of cancer before it completed its ascent of the pop charts.
   Originally recorded by George Benson. Nominated for a Grammy
   Award, Record of the Year, 1986.

A Groovy Kind of Love
Words and music by Toni Wine and Carole Bayer
Screen Gems-EMI Music Inc., 1966.

Revived in 1988 by Phil Collins in the film *Buster* and on its soundtrack album (Atlantic). The song was originally a hit for The Mindbenders.

Growing up in Public
Words and music by Lou Reed and Michael Fonfara.
Metal Machine Music, 1980.
Introduced by Lou Reed in *Growing up in Public* (RCA, 80).

Guilty (English)
Words and music by Barry Gibb, Robin Gibb, and Maurice Gibb.
Gibb Brothers Music, 1980.
Best-selling record by Barbra Streisand and Barry Gibb from *Guilty* (Columbia, 80).

Guilty
Words and music by Jimmy Hamilton and Maurice Hayes.
Temp Co., 1986.
Best-selling record by Yarbrough & Peoples from the album *Guilty* (RCA, 86).

Guitar Town
Words and music by Steve Earle.
Goldline Music Inc., 1986.
Best-selling record by Steve Earle from the album *Guitar Town* (MCA, 86). Nominated for a Grammy Award, Country Song of the Year, 1986.

Guitars, Cadillacs, Etc., Etc.
Words and music by Dwight Yoakam.
Coal Dust West, 1986.
Best-selling record by Dwight Yoakam from the album *Guitars, Cadillacs, Etc., Etc.* (Reprise, 86).

Gulf Coast Highway
Words and music by James Hooker, Nanci Griffith, and Danny Flowers.
Wing & Wheel Music, 1987/Rick Hall Music, 1987/Danny Flowers Music, 1987.
Introduced by Nanci Griffith on *Little Love Affairs* (MCA, 88). One of the year's best country-folk songs, this one presents the life and times of a quintessential Texas couple.

Gus the Theatre Cat (English)
Words by T. S. Eliot, words and music by Andrew Lloyd Webber.
Deco Music, 1982/Charles Koppelman Music, 1982/Jonathan Three Music Co., 1982/Martin Bandier Music, 1982.
Introduced by Stephen Hanan in *Cats* (82). Adapted from the poetry of T. S. Eliot.

Gypsy
Words and music by Suzanne Vega.
AGF Music Ltd., 1987/Waifersongs, 1987.
Introduced by Suzanne Vega on the album *Solitude Standing* (A & M).

Gypsy Love Songs (English)
Words and music by Richard Thompson.
Beeswing Music, 1988.
Introduced by Richard Thompson on *Amnesia* (Capitol, 88), a return to
    recording by the folk-rock giant.

H

Had a Dream About You, Baby
Words and music by Bob Dylan.
Special Rider Music, 1987.
Introduced by Bob Dylan in the film *Hearts of Fire* and on the album of
  the same title (Columbia, 87). Dylan portrayed a reclusive former
  rock star in his first film appearance since *Pat Garrett and Billy the
  Kid.*

Hairspray
Words and music by Rachel Sweet, Anthony Battaglea, and Willa
  Bassen.
MCA Music, 1987.
Introduced by Rachel Sweet in the film *Hairspray* and on its soundtrack
  album (MCA, 88). The song was written and performed in a style to
  evoke the movie's setting--Baltimore in 1962. Sweet has been
  compared to a young Brenda Lee, one of the stars of that era.

Hairstyles and Attitudes
Words and music by Pat MacDonald.
Mambadaddi, 1986/I.R.S. Music, 1986/Criterion Music Corp., 1986.
Introduced by Timbuk 3 on the album *Greetings from Timbuk 3* (I.R.S.,
  86).

Half Past Forever (Till I'm Blue in the Heart)
Words and music by Tom Brasfield.
Colgems-EMI Music, 1986.
Best-selling record by T. G. Sheppard from the album *It Still Rains in
  Memphis* (Columbia, 86).

Hand in Hand (American-German)
English words and music by Tom Whitlock, music by Giorgio Moroder.
Giorgio Moroder Publishing Co., 1988.
Introduced by Koreana as the official theme of the 1988 Summer
  Olympics. Featured on *Hand in Hand* (Polydor, 88).

Hand of Kindness (English)
Words and music by Richard Thompson.
Island Music, 1983.
Introduced by Richard Thompson on *Hand of Kindness* (Hannibal, 83).

Hand to Hold Onto
Words and music by John Cougar Mellencamp.
Full Keel Music, 1983.
Best-selling record by John Cougar from *American Fool* (Riva, 83).

Handle with Care
Words and music by Traveling Wilburys.
Copyright Control, 1988.
Introduced by The Traveling Wilburys, an all-star collaboration by Bob
    Dylan, George Harrison, Tom Petty, Jeff Lynne, and Roy Orbison, on
    Traveling Wilburys Volume 1 (Wilbury/Warner Bros., 88). While it
    was on the charts, Orbison died of a heart attack.

Hands Across America
Words and music by Marc Blatte, John Carnes, and Larry Gottleib.
USA for Africa, 1986/Julann Music, 1986.
Introduced by Voices of America (EMI-America, 86) as theme for
    Hands Across America Day, an attempt to raise money for charity by
    people linking hands coast to coast. The song won the Ralph S. Peer
    award for creative excellence.

Hands to Heaven (English)
Words and music by Dave Glaspar and Marcus Lillington.
Virgin Music, 1987.
Best-selling record by Breathe, from *All That Jazz* (A & M, 88).

Hang Fire (English)
Words and music by Mick Jagger and Keith Richards.
Colgems-EMI Music, 1981.
Best-selling record by The Rolling Stones from *Tattoo You* (Rolling
    Stones, 82).

Hang on St. Christopher
Words and music by Tom Waits.
Polygram International, 1987.
Performed by Tom Waits on the album *Frank's Wild Years* (Island, 87),
    which comprised songs based on Waits's earlier play of the same
    title.

Hangin' on a Limb
Words and music by Neil Young.
Silver Fiddle, 1989.
Introduced by Neil Young on *Freedom* (Reprise, 89).

Hangin' on a String (English)
Words and music by Carl McIntosh, Jane Eugene, and Steve Nichol.
Brampton Music Ltd., England/Virgin Music Ltd., 1985.
Best-selling record by Loose Ends from the album *A Little Spice* (MCA, 85).

Hangin' on to the Good Times
Words and music by Bill Payne, Paul Barrere, Fred Tackett, and Craig Fuller.
Little Music, 1988/Feat Music, 1988.
Introduced by Little Feat on the album *Let It Roll* (Warner Bros., 88).

Hangin' Tough
Words and music by Maurice Starr.
Maurice Starr Music, 1988/EMI-April Music, 1988.
Best-selling record by New Kids on the Block from *Hangin' Tough* (Columbia, 89).

Hanging on a Heartbeat
Words and music by Rob Hyman, Eric Bazilian, Glenn Goss, and Jeff Ziv.
Human Boy Music, 1982/Dub Notes, 1982.
Introduced by The Hooters on the album *Nervous Night* (Columbia, 85).

Happy (American-English)
Words and music by David Townshend, Bernard Jackson, and David Conley.
Brampton Music Ltd., England, 1987/Below the Surface Music.
Best-selling record by Surface, from the album *Surface* (Columbia, 87).

Happy Birthday Dear Heartache
Words and music by Mack David and Archie Jordan.
Collins Court Music, 1984.
Best-selling record by Barbara Mandrell (MCA, 84).

Happy, Happy Birthday Baby
Words and music by Margo Sylvia and Gilbert Loper.
Arch Music Co., Inc., 1957/Donna Music Publishing Co., 1957.
Revived in 1986 by Ronnie Milsap on the album *Greatest Hits, Vol. 2* (RCA, 86).

Happy Hour (English)
Words and music by P. D. Heaton and Stan Cullimore.
Go! Discs Ltd., England, 1986.
Introduced by by the Housemartins on the album *London 0 Hull 4* (Elektra, 86).

Happy Man
Words and music by Greg Kihn and Steven Wright.

Rye-Boy Music, 1982/Well Received Music, 1982.
Best-selling record by The Greg Kihn Band from *Kihntinued* (Beserkley, 82).

Happy Together
Words and music by Gary Bonner and Alan Gordon.
Hudson Bay Music, 1966.
Revived in 1987 by the Turtles, who had the original hit in 1967, for the film *Making Mr. Right.*

Hard Day on the Planet
Words and music by Loudon Wainwright.
Snowden Music, 1986.
Introduced by by Loudon Wainwright on the album *More Love Songs* (Rounder, 87).

Hard Habit to Break
Words and music by Stephen Kipner and John Parker.
EMI-April Music, 1984/Stephen A. Kipner Music, 1984/Parker Music, 1984.
Best-selling record by Chicago from *Chicago 17* (Full Moon, 84). Nominated for a Grammy Award, Record of the Year, 1984.

Hard Love
Words and music by Bob Franke.
Telephone Pole Music Publishing Co., 1982.
Featured in *New Goodbyes, Old Helloes* by Claudia Schmidt (Flying Fish, 83).

A Hard Rain's Gonna Fall
Words and music by Bob Dylan.
Special Rider Music, 1963.
Revived in 1989 by Edie Brickell & New Bohemians in the film and soundtrack album *Born on the Fourth of July* (MCA).

Hard Times
Words and music by James Taylor.
Country Road Music Inc., 1981.
Best-selling record by James Taylor from *Dad Loves His Work* (Columbia, 81).

Hard to Be a Diva
Words and music by Barry Keating.
Introduced by Shara McKnight in the musical *Starmites,* which had a brief run on Broadway in 1989.

Hard to Say I'm Sorry
Words and music by Peter Cetera and David Foster.
BMG Music, 1982/Foster Frees Music Inc., 1982.

Best-selling record by Chicago from *Chicago 16* (Full Moon/Warner Brothers, 82). Introduced in the film *The Summer Lovers* (82).

Harden My Heart
Words and music by Marv Ross.
Bonnie Bee Good Music, 1980/WB Music, 1980.
Best-selling record by Quarterflash from *Quarterflash* (Geffen, 81).

The Hardest Time
Words and music by David Hidalgo and Louie Perez.
Davince Music, 1987/No K. O. Music, 1987.
Introduced by Los Lobos on the album *By the Light of the Moon* (Slash/WB, 87).

Harlem Shuffle (English)
Words and music by Keith Relf and Earl Nelson.
Marc-Jean, 1963/Bug Music, 1963/Keymen Music, 1963.
Best-selling record by the Rolling Stones from the album *Dirty Work* (Columbia, 86). Introduced by Bob and Earl in 1963.

Harry's Wall
Words and music by Loudon Wainwright.
Snowden Music, 1989.
Introduced by Loudon Wainwright on *Therapy* (Silvertone, 89).

Has He Got a Friend for Me (English)
Words and music by Richard Thompson.
Beeswing Music, 1972.
Performed by Maria McKee on *Maria McKee* (Geffen, 89).

Hate to Lose Your Lovin'
Words and music by Paul Barrere and Craig Fuller.
Little Music, 1988/Feat Music, 1988.
Introduced by Little Feat on *Let It Roll* (Warner Bros., 88).

Have a Heart
Words and music by Bonnie Hayes.
Monster Music, 1989/Bob-a-Lew Music, 1989.
Introduced by Bonnie Raitt on *Nick of Time* (Capitol, 89), this song hit the charts in 1990, after Raitt won four Grammy awards, including Best Album of the Year for 1989.

Have a Little Faith in Me
Words and music by John Hiatt.
Lillybilly, 1987/Bug Music, 1987.
Introduced by John Hiatt on the album *Bring the Family* (A & M, 87).

Have Mercy
Words and music by Paul Kennerley.

Irving Music Inc., 1985.
Best-selling record by The Judds from the album *Rockin' with Rhythm*
(RCA, 85).

Have You Ever Loved Somebody
Words and music by Barry Eastmond and Terry Skinner.
Zomba Music, 1986/Willesden Music, Inc., 1986.
Best-selling record by Freddie Jackson, from the album *Just Like the
First Time* (Capitol, 86).

Have You Had Your Love Today
Words and music by Terry Stubbs and Dernick Pearson.
Trycep Publishing Co., 1989/Willesden Music, Inc., 1989.
Best-selling record by The O'Jays from *Serious* (EMI, 89).

Have Yourself a Merry Little Christmas
Words and music by Hugh Martin and Ralph Blane.
Leo Feist Inc., 1944.
Revived in 1987 by the Pretenders for the album *A Very Special
Christmas*.

The Hawk (El Gavilan)
Words and music by Kris Kristofferson.
Resaca Music Publishing Co., 1986.
Introduced by Marianne Faithfull in the film *Trouble in Mind* (86) and
on the soundtrack album (Island, 86). Perhaps Kristofferson's most
probing lyric since 'Me and Bobby McGee,' the song was enhanced
by a magnificent vocal performance and compelling arrangement.

Hazy Shade of Winter
Words and music by Paul Simon.
Paul Simon Music, 1966.
Revived in 1987 by The Bangles in the film *Less Than Zero* and on its
soundtrack album.

He Reminds Me
Words and music by Russell Stone and Mike McNaught.
Dejamus Inc., 1982.
Featured on *Windsong* by Randy Crawford (Warner Brothers, 82).

He Stopped Loving Her Today
Words and music by Bobby Braddock and Curly Putman.
Tree Publishing Co., Inc., 1978.
Nominated for a Grammy Award, Country Song of the Year, 1980.

Head over Heels
Words and music by Charlotte Caffey and Kathy Valentine.
Daddy Oh Music, 1984/Some Other Music, 1984.
Best-selling record by The Go-Go's from *Talk Show* (I.R.S., 84).

Head to Toe
Words and music by Full Force.
Forceful Music, 1987/Willesden Music, Inc.
Best-selling record by Lisa Lisa and Cult Jam, from the album *Spanish Fly* (Columbia, 87).

A Headache Tomorrow (or a Heartache Tonight)
Words and music by Chick Rains.
Blue Lake Music, 1980/Chick Rains Music, 1980.
Best-selling record by Mickey Gilley (Epic, 81).

Headed for a Heartbreak
Words and music by Kip Winger.
Verseau Music, 1989/Small Hope Music, 1989/Virgin Songs, 1989.
Best-selling record by Winger from *Winger* (Atlantic, 89).

Headlines
Words and music by Bill Simmons, Bobby Lovelace, Vincent Calloway, Belinda Lipscomb, Reggie Calloway, and Melvin Gentry.
Hip-Trip Music Co., 1986/Midstar Music, Inc., 1986.
Best-selling record by Midnight Star from the album *Headlines* (Elektra, 86).

Healing Hands (English)
Words and music by Elton John and Bernie Taupin.
Big Pig Music, 1989/Intersong, USA Inc., 1989.
Best-selling record by Elton John from *Sleeping with the Past* (MCA, 89).

The Heart
Words and music by Kris Kristofferson.
EMI Music Publishing, 1986/Resaca Music Publishing Co., 1986.
Best-selling record by Lacy J. Dalton from *Survivor* (Universal, 89).

Heart and Soul
Words and music by Mike Chapman and Nicky Chinn.
BMG Music, 1981.
Best-selling record by Huey Lewis & The News from *Sports* (Chrysalis, 83).

Heart and Soul (English)
Words and music by Carol Decker and Ronnie Rogers.
Virgin Music, 1987.
Best-selling record by T'Pau; from the album *T'Pau* (Virgin, 87).
Decker is the group's lead singer and Rogers, its former guitarist.

Heart Country
Words and music by Paul Davis and Doug Erikson.
Flip 'n' Dog, 1987.

Introduced by Firetown on the album *In the Heart of the Heart Country* (Atlantic, 87).

Heart Full of Soul
Words and music by Graham Gouldman.
Glenwood Music Corp., 1965.
Revived in 1987 by Chris Isaak on the album *Chris Isaak* (Warner Bros.).

Heart Hotels
Words and music by Dan Fogelberg.
EMI-April Music, 1979.
Best-selling record by Dan Fogelberg from *Phoenix* (Full Moon, 80).

A Heart in New York (English)
Words and music by Benny Gallagher and Graham Lyle.
Irving Music Inc., 1981.
Best-selling record by Art Garfunkel from *Scissors Cut* (Columbia, 81).

Heart of Mine
Words and music by Bob Dylan.
Special Rider Music, 1981.
Best-selling record by Bob Dylan from *Shot of Love* (Columbia, 81).

The Heart of Rock and Roll
Words and music by Johnny Colla and Huey Lewis.
Hulex Music, 1983/Chrysalis Music Group, 1983.
Best-selling record by Huey Lewis & The News from *Sports* (Chrysalis, 84). Nominated for a Grammy Award, Record of the Year, 1984.

Heart of the Country
Words and music by Wendy Waldman and Donny Lowery.
Sheddhouse Music, 1985/Screen Gems-EMI Music Inc., 1984/Moon & Stars Music, 1985.
Best-selling record by Kathy Mattea from the album *From My Heart* (Mercury, 85).

Heart to Heart
Words and music by Kenny Loggins, Michael McDonald, and David Foster.
Milk Money Music, 1982/Genevieve Music, 1982/Foster Frees Music Inc., 1982.
Best-selling record by Kenny Loggins from *High Adventure* (Columbia, 82).

Heartbeat
Words and music by Eric Kaz and Wendy Waldman.
Glasco Music, Co., 1986/Cotillion Music Inc., 1986/Moon & Stars Music, 1986.

Best-selling record by Don Johnson, star of the popular television series *Miami Vice,* from his album *Heartbeat* (Epic, 86). This first collaboration by Kaz and Waldman surpassed the success of the former's 'Love Has No Pride' and *Love Has Got Me,* Waldman's 1974 debut album for Warner Bros.

Heartbeat in the Darkness
Words and music by Dave Loggins and Russell Smith.
MCA, Inc., 1986/Patchwork Music, 1986.
Best-selling record by Don Williams from the album *New Moves* (Capitol, 86). Now a successful country writer, Loggins is most known for writing and singing the poignant pop hit 'Please Come to Boston.'

Heartbreak Beat (English)
Words and music by Richard Butler, Jon Aston, and Timothy Butler.
EMI-Blackwood Music Inc., 1987.
Best-selling record by The Psychedlic Furs, from the album *Midnight to Midnight* (Columbia, 87).

Heartbreak Hotel
Words and music by Michael Jackson.
Warner-Tamerlane Music, 1981.
Best-selling record by The Jacksons from *Triumph* (Epic, 80).

Heartbreaker (English)
Words and music by Geoff Gill and Cliff Wade.
Dick James Music Inc., 1979.
Best-selling record by Pat Benatar from *In the Heat of the Night* (Chrysalis, 80).

Heartbreaker (English)
Words and music by Barry Gibb, Robin Gibb, and Maurice Gibb.
Gibb Brothers Music, 1982.
Best-selling record by Dionne Warwick from *Heartbreaker* (Arista, 82).

Hearts
Words and music by Jeff Barish.
Mercury Shoes Music, 1980/Great Pyramid Music, 1980.
Best-selling record by Marty Balin from *Balin* (EMI-America, 81).

Hearts Aren't Made to Break (They're Made to Love)
Words and music by Roger Murrah and Steve Dean.
Tom Collins Music Corp., 1986.
Best-selling record by Lee Greenwood from the album *Streamline* (MCA, 86).

Hearts of Stone
Words and music by Bruce Springsteen.

Bruce Springsteen Publishing, 1986.
Revived in 1986 by Southside Johnny & The Asbury Jukes on *Cover Me* (Rhino, 86), a collection of tunes written by Bruce Springsteen. Southside Johnny is the quintessential Springsteen cover band, having recorded many of the writer's songs.

Hearts on Fire
Words and music by Randy Meisner and Eric Kaz.
Nebraska Music, 1980/EMI Unart Catalogue, 1980/Glasco Music, Co., 1980.
Best-selling record by Randy Meisner from *One More Song* (Epic, 81).

Hearts on Fire (Canadian)
Words and music by Bryan Adams and Jim Vallance.
Adams Communications, Inc., 1987/Calypso Toonz, 1987/Irving Music Inc., 1987.
Best-selling record by Bryan Adams, from the album *Into the Fire* (A & M, 87).

The Heat Is On
Words by Keith Forsey, music by Harold Faltermeyer.
Famous Music Corp., 1985.
Best-selling record by Glenn Frey (MCA, 85). Introduced in the film *Beverly Hills Cop* (85); featured on its soundtrack album.

Heat of the Moment (English)
Words and music by John Wetton and Geoffrey Downes.
WB Music, 1982/Polygram International, 1982.
Best-selling record by Asia from *Asia* (Geffen, 82).

Heat of the Night (Canadian)
Words and music by Bryan Adams and Jim Vallance.
Adams Communications, Inc., 1987/Calypso Toonz, 1987/Irving Music Inc., 1987.
Best-selling record by Bryan Adams, from the album *Into the Fire* (A & M, 87). This song was inspired by a scene in the film *The Third Man*.

Heaven (Canadian)
Words and music by Bryan Adams and Jim Vallance.
Irving Music Inc., 1983/Adams Communications, Inc., 1983/Calypso Toonz, 1983.
Introduced in the film *A Night in Heaven* (83). Best-selling record by Bryan Adams from *Reckless* (A&M, 85).

Heaven
Words and music by David Byrne.
Index Music, 1979/Bleu Disque Music, 1979.
Revived in 1986 by Simply Red on the album *Picture Book* (Elektra,

86). Introduced by The Talking Heads on the album *Fear of Music* (Sire, 79).

Heaven
Words and music by Jani Lane.
Virgin Songs, 1988/Dick Dragon Music, 1988/Crab Salad Music, 1988/ Likete Split Music, 1988/Rich McBitch Music, 1988/Great Lips Music, 1988.
Best-selling record in 1989 by Warrant from *Dirty Rotten Filthy Stinkin' Rich* (Columbia, 88).

Heaven Help Me (English)
Words and music by Deon Estus and George Michael.
Morrison Leahy, England, 1988/Estus Music, 1988/Rok-Mil Music, 1988/EMI-Blackwood Music Inc., 1988/Chappell & Co., Inc., 1988.
Best-selling record by Deon Estus from *Spell* (Mika/Polydor, 89).

Heaven Help My Heart (English-Swedish)
Music by Benny Andersson and Bjorn Ulvaeus, English words by Tim Rice.
Three Knights, Ltd., 1988.
Introduced by Judy Kuhn in the musical *Chess* which opened on Broadway in 1988; also on the cast album (RCA).

Heaven in Your Eyes (Canadian)
Words and music by Paul Dean, Mike Reno, Johnny Dexter, and Debra Mae Moore.
Sordid Songs, 1986/Duke Reno Music, 1986/Irving Music Inc., 1986/ Poetical License, 1986/Famous Music Corp., 1986/Ensign Music, 1986.
Introduced by Loverboy in the film *Top Gun* (86) and on the soundtrack album (Columbia, 86).

Heaven Is a Place on Earth
Words and music by Rick Nowels and Ellen Shipley.
Future Furniture, 1987/Shipwreck.
Best-selling record by Belinda Carlisle, from the album *Heaven on Earth* (MCA, 87).

Heaven on Earth
Words by Barry Harman, music by Grant Sturiale.
Chappell & Co., Inc., 1986.
Introduced by Emily Zacharias in the 1986 Off Broadway musical *Olympus on My Mind.*

Heavy Metal (Takin' a Ride)
Words and music by Don Felder.
Fingers Music, 1981.

Best-selling record by Don Felder (Full Moon/Asylum, 81). Introduced in the film and soundtrack album *Heavy Metal* (81).

Hell and High Water
Words and music by T. Graham Brown and Alex Harvey.
EMI-April Music, 1986/Ides of March Music Division, 1986/Preshus Child, 1986.
Best-selling record by T. Graham Brown from the album *I Tell It Like It Used to Be* (Capitol, 86).

Hello
Words and music by Lionel Richie, Jr.
Brockman Enterprises Inc., 1983.
Best-selling record by Lionel Richie from *Can't Slow Down* (Motown, 84). Nominated for a Grammy Award, Song of the Year, 1984.

Hello Again
Words and music by Neil Diamond and Alan Lindgren.
Stonebridge Music, 1980.
Best-selling record by Neil Diamond (Capitol, 80). Introduced in the film & soundtrack album of *The Jazz Singer* (80).

Hello Again
Words and music by Ric Ocasek.
Lido Music Inc., 1984.
Best-selling record by The Cars from *Heartbeat City* (Elektra, 84).

Hello, It's Me
Words and music by Lou Reed and John Cale.
Metal Machine Music, 1989.
Introduced by Lou Reed and John Cale as part of a 'song cycle' in tribute to the late pop artist Andy Warhol which they presented at the Brooklyn Academy of Music in 1989. The performance was the first reunion of these former members of the Velvet Underground, a 1960's group sponsored by Warhol, in twenty years.

Hello Little Girl
Words and music by Stephen Sondheim.
BMG Music, 1987.
Introduced by Danielle Ferland and Robert Westenberg in the musical *Into the Woods* also on the cast album (RCA).

Hello Mary Lou
Words and music by Gene Pitney.
Champion Music, 1961.
Revived by The Statler Brothers on the album *Pardners in Rhyme* (Mercury, 85).

Hello Stranger
Words by Doc Pomus, music by Mac Rebennack.
Skull Music, 1987/Stazybo Music, 1987.
Introduced by Marianne Faithfull on the album *Strange Weather* (Island, 87). Doc Pomus penned numerous hits in the 1950's for the Drifters and Dion and the Belmonts; Rebennack is the legendary Creole keyboard man, Dr. John.

Her Town Too
Words and music by James Taylor, John David Souther, and Waddy Wachtel.
Country Road Music Inc., 1981/Lead Sheetland Music, 1981/EMI Music Publishing, 1981.
Best-selling record by James Taylor and J. D. Souther from *Dad Loves His Work* (Columbia, 81).

Here and Now
Words and music by Terry Steele and David L. Elliott.
EMI-April Music, 1989/Ollie Brown Sugar Music, Inc., 1989/DLE Music, 1989.
Best-selling record by Luther Vandross from *The Best of Love* (Epic, 89).

Here Comes My Girl
Words and music by Tom Petty and Mike Campbell.
Skyhill Publishing Co., Inc., 1979/Almo Music Corp.
Best-selling record by Tom Petty & The Heartbreakers from *Damn the Torpedoes* (Backstreet, 80).

Here Comes the Rain Again (English)
Words and music by Annie Lennox and Dave Stewart.
BMG Songs Inc., 1983.
Best-selling record by Eurythmics from *Touch* (RCA, 84).

Here I Am
Words and music by Norman Sallitt.
Al Gallico Music Corp., 1980/Turtle Music, 1980.
Best-selling record by Air Supply from *The One That You Love* (Arista, 81).

Here I Am Again
Words and music by Shel Silverstein.
Evil Eye Music Inc., 1985.
Best-selling record by Johnny Rodriquez (Epic, 85).

Here I Go Again (English)
Words and music by David Coverdale and Bernie Marsden.
Seabreeze, 1982/CC, 1982/WB Music, 1982.
Best-selling record by Whitesnake, from the album *Whitesnake* (Geffen,

87). In a different version, this song was a hit in Britain in 1982 on an album called *Saints and Sinners* that was not released in the United States.

Here to Stay
Words and music by George Acogny, Daniel Bechet, and Julian Littman.
Charisma Music Publishing Co., Ltd., 1986.
Introduced by Sister Sledge in the film *Playing for Keeps* and on the soundtrack album (Atlantic, 86).

Here Today (English)
Words and music by Paul McCartney.
MPL Communications Inc., 1982.
Introduced by Paul McCartney in *Tug of War* (Columbia, 82). Song was dedicated to John Lennon.

Here with Me
Words and music by Kevin Cronin and R. Brown.
Fate Music, 1988/Roliram Lorimar Music, 1988.
Best-selling record by REO Speedwagon, from *The Hits* (Epic, 88).

Hero, see **Wind Beneath My Wings.**

Hero Takes a Fall
Words and music by Susanna Hoffs and Vicki Peterson.
Bangophile Music/Illegal Songs, Inc., 1984.
Introduced by The Bangles on the album *All over the Place* (Columbia, 85).

He's a Heartache (Looking for a Place to Happen)
Words and music by Jeff Silbar and Larry Henley.
WB Gold Music Corp., 1982/Warner House of Music, 1982.
Best-selling record by Janie Fricke (Columbia, 83).

He's Back
Words and music by Alice Cooper, Tom Kelly, and Kane Roberts.
Ezra Music Corp., 1986/Ensign Music, 1986/Sony Tunes, 1986/Screen Gems-EMI Music Inc., 1986.
Introduced by Alice Cooper in the film *Friday the 13th, Part 6* (86); performed on the album *Constrictor* (MCA, 86).

He's Back and I'm Blue
Words and music by Michael Woody and Robert Anderson.
Termite Music, 1987/Bughouse, 1987.
Best-selling record by The Desert Rose Band, from *The Desert Rose Band* (MCA, 87).

He's So Shy
Words by Cynthia Weil, music by Tom Snow.
Mann & Weil Songs Inc., 1980/Braintree Music, 1980/Snow Music, 1980/ATV Music Corp., 1980.
Best-selling record by The Pointer Sisters from *Special Things* (Planet, 80).

He's Sure the Man I Love, also known as **He's Sure the Boy I Love**
Words and music by Barry Mann and Cynthia Weil.
Screen Gems-EMI Music Inc., 1962.
Revived in 1988 by Darlene Love on *Paint Another Picture* (Columbia). The Crystals, a girl group for whom Love provided uncredited vocals, had the original hit with this song in 1963.

Hey Baby
Words and music by Henry Lee Summer.
Leesum Music, Inc., 1989/Virgin Songs, 1989.
Best-selling record by Henry Lee Summer from *I've Got Everything* (CBS Associated, 89).

Hey Bobby
Words and music by K. T. Oslin.
Wooden Wonder, 1988.
Best-selling record in 1989 by K. T. Oslin from *This Woman* (RCA, 88).

Hey, Jack Kerouac
Words and music by Natalie Merchant and Robert Buck.
Christian Burial, 1987.
Introduced by 10,000 Maniacs on the album *In My Tribe* (Elektra, 87). This was the first song since Aztec Two-Step's 'The Persecution and Resurrection of Dean Moriarity' to explore the Beatnik ethos espoused by Kerouac, author of the beat classic *On the Road*.

Hey Lover
Words and music by S. Moore and K. Washington.
Bush Burnin' Music, 1988.
Best-selling record by Freddie Jackson, from *Don't Let Love Slip Away* (Capitol, 88).

Hey Nineteen
Words and music by Walter Becker and Donald Fagen.
Zeitgeist Music Co., 1980/Freejunket Music, 1980.
Best-selling record by Steely Dan from *Gaucho* (MCA, 80).

Hidden Love
Words and music by Peter Case.

Trumpet Blast Music, 1989/Bug Music.
Introduced by Peter Case on *The Man with the Blue, Postmodern, Fragmented, Neo-Traditionalist Guitar* (Geffen, 89).

High Cotton
Words and music by Roger Murrah and Scott Anders.
Shobi Music, 1989.
Best-selling record by Alabama from *Southern Star* (RCA, 89).

High Horse
Words and music by James Ibbotson.
Unami Music, 1984.
Best-selling record by Nitty Gritty Dirt Band on the album *Partners, Brothers, and Friends* (Warner Bros.,85).

High on Emotion (English)
Words and music by Chris DeBurgh.
Irving Music Inc., 1984.
Best-selling record by Chris DeBurgh from *Man on the Line* (A&M, 84).

High on You
Words and music by Frankie Sullivan and Jim Peterik.
Rude Music, 1984/WB Music/Easy Action Music.
Best-selling record by Survivor in 1985 from the album *Vital Signs* (Epic, 84).

High School Nights
Words and music by Dave Edmunds, Sam Gould, and John David.
Mel-Bren Music Inc., 1985/Albion Music Ltd./WB Music.
Introduced by Dave Edmunds in the film *Porky's Revenge* (85).

Higher Love
Words by Will Jennings, music by Steve Winwood.
F.S. Ltd., England, 1986/Willin' David, 1986/Blue Sky Rider Songs, 1986.
Best-selling record by Steve Winwood from the album *Back in the High Life* (Warner Bros., 86). Won a Grammy Award, and Record of the Year, 1986. Nominated for a Grammy Award, Song of the Year, 1986.

Highway 40 Blues
Words and music by Larry Cordle.
Amanda-Lin Music, 1979/Polygram International, 1979.
Best-selling record by Ricky Skaggs from *Highway & Heartaches* (Epic, 83).

Highway Patrolman
Words and music by Bruce Springsteen.

Bruce Springsteen Publishing, 1982.
Featured on *Johnny 99* by Johnny Cash (Columbia, 83). Introduced by
Bruce Springsteen in *Nebraska* (Columbia, 82).

Highway Robbery
Words and music by Michael Garvin, Bucky Jones, and Tom Shapiro.
Cross Keys Publishing Co., Inc., 1987/Polygram International, 1987/
McBec Music, 1987/Tree Publishing Co., Inc., 1987/Terrace
Entertainment Corp., 1987.
Best-selling record in 1989 by Tanya Tucker from *Strong Enough to
Bend* (Capitol, 88).

Highwayman
Words and music by Jim Webb.
White Oak Songs, 1977.
Introduced by Waylon Jennings, Willie Nelson, Johnny Cash, and Kris
Kristofferson on the album *The Highwayman* (Columbia, 85). Won a
Grammy Award, and Country Song of the Year, 1985.

The Hills of Tomorrow
Words and music by Stephen Sondheim.
WB Music, 1981.
Introduced by Company of *Merrily We Roll Along* (81).

Him
Words and music by Rupert Holmes.
Holmes Line of Music, 1979/WB Music, 1979.
Best-selling record by Rupert Holmes from *Partners in Crime* (MCA,
80).

Hip to Be Square
Words and music by Bill Gibson, Sean Hopper, and Huey Lewis.
Hulex Music, 1986.
Best-selling record by Huey Lewis & The News from the album *Fore!*
(Chrysalis, 86).

Hippy Hippy Shake
Words and music by Chas Romero.
Jonware Music Corp., 1964.
Revived in 1988 by The Georgia Satellites for the film *Cocktail* and its
soundtrack album (Elektra), which was one of the year's most
successful. The Swingin' Blue Jeans had the original hit with this
song.

Hit and Run
Words and music by Lloyd Smith, Allen A. Jones, Michael Beard, Larry
Dudson, Sherman Guy, Mark Bynum, Harvey Henderson, Charles
Allen, Winston Stewart, Frank Thompson, and James Alexander.

Bar-Kay Music, 1982/Warner-Tamerlane Music, 1982.
Best-selling record by The Bar-Kays from *Night Cruising* (Mercury, 82).

Hit Me with Your Best Shot (Canadian)
Words and music by Eddie Schwartz.
ATV Music Corp., 1980.
Best-selling record by Pat Benatar from *Crimes of Passion* (Chrysalis, 80).

Hit the Road Jack
Words and music by Percy Mayfield.
Tangerine Music Corp., 1961.
Revived in 1989 by Buster Poindexter and his Banshees of Blue in the film and soundtrack album *The Dream Team* (RCA, 89).

Hold Me (English)
Words and music by Christine McVie and Robbie Patton.
Fleetwood Mac Music Ltd., 1982/Red Snapper, 1982.
Best-selling record by Fleetwood Mac from *Mirage* (Warner Brothers, 82).

Hold Me
Words and music by Sheila Escovedo, Connie Guzman, and E. Minnifield.
Sister Fate Music, 1987/Pretty Man, 1987/Teete, 1987.
Best-selling record by Sheila E., from the album *Sheila E.* (Paisley Park, 87).

Hold Me
Words and music by K. T. Oslin.
Wooden Wonder, 1987.
Best-selling record by K.T. Oslin, from *This Woman* (RCA, 88). Won a Grammy Award, and Country Song of the Year, 1988.

Hold Me Daddy (English)
Words and music by Andy Partridge.
Virgin Songs, 1989.
Introduced by XTC on *Oranges and Lemons* (Geffen, 89).

Hold Me Now (English)
Words and music by Tom Bailey, Alannah Currie, and Joe Leeway.
Zomba Music, 1983.
Best-selling record by The Thompson Twins from *Into The Gap* (Arista, 84).

Hold On (Canadian)
Words and music by Ian Thomas.
Mark Cain Music, 1982.
Best-selling record by Santana from *Shango* (Columbia, 82).

Hold on Tight (English)
Words and music by Jeff Lynne.
EMI-April Music, 1981.
Best-selling record by ELO from *Time* (Jet, 81).

Hold on to My Love (English)
Words and music by Robin Gibb and Blue Weaver.
Gibb Brothers Music, 1980/Pentagon Music Co., 1980.
Best-selling record by Jimmy Ruffin from *Sunrise* (RSO, 80).

Hold on to the Nights
Words and music by Richard Marx.
Chi-Boy, 1987.
Best-selling record in 1988 by Richard Marx, from *Richard Marx*
    (Chyralis, 87). This was one of four songs to reach the top five from
    Marx's debut album.

Holding Back the Years (English)
Words and music by Mick Hucknall and Neil Moss.
EMI-April Music, 1986.
Best-selling record by Simply Red from the album *Picture Book*
    (Elektra, 86).

Holding On (English)
Words and music by Steve Winwood and Will Jennings.
F.S. Ltd., England, 1988/Warner-Tamerlane Music, 1988/Willin' David,
    1988/Blue Sky Rider Songs, 1988.
Best-selling record in 1989 by Steve Winwood from *Roll with It*
    (Virgin, 88).

Holding Out for a Hero
Words and music by Jim Steinman and Dean Pitchford.
Ensign Music, 1984.
Best-selling record by Bonnie Tyler (Columbia, 84). Introduced in the
    film and soundtrack album *Footloose* (84).

Hole in My Heart (All the Way to China)
Words and music by R. Orange.
DJO Publishing Corp., 1988.
Introduced by Cyndi Lauper in the film *Vibes* and on the single (Epic,
    88).

Holier Than Thou
Words and music by Dan Goggins.
Introduced by Edwina Lewis in the 1986 off Broadway musical
    Nunsense.

Holy Mother (English)
Words and music by Eric Clapton and Stephen Bishop.

E.C. Music, England, 1986/Stephen Bishop Music Publishing Co., 1986. Introduced by Eric Clapton on the album *August.* The song is dedicated to the memory of Richard Manuel of The Band.

Home
Words and music by Charlie Smalls.
Warner-Tamerlane Music, 1974.
Introduced by Stephanie Mills in the 1975 Broadway musical *The Wiz;* revived by her on *Home* (MCA, 89).

Home Again in My Heart
Words and music by Josh Leo and Wendy Waldman.
Warner/Elektra/Asylum Music, 1985/Screen Gems-EMI Music Inc., 1985/Moon & Stars Music, 1985.
Best-selling record by Nitty Gritty Dirt Band from the album *20 Years of Dirt* (Warner Bros., 86).

Home by Another Way
Words and music by James Taylor.
Country Road Music Inc., 1988.
Introduced by James Taylor on *Never Die Young* (CBS, 88).

Home of the Brave
Words and music by Jeff Pezzati.
Introduced by Naked Raygun on the album *All Rise* (Homestead, 86).

The Homecoming Queen's Got a Gun
Words and music by Julie Brown, Terrence McNally, Charlie Coffey, and Ray Colcord.
Stymie Music, 1984.
Performed by Julie Brown on the album *Trapped in the Body of a White Girl* (Sire, 87). The song was previously featured on Brown's debut album, *Goddess in Progress.*

Homeless (American-South African)
English words and music by Paul Simon and Joseph Shabalala.
Paul Simon Music, 1986.
Introduced by Paul Simon on the album *Graceland* (Warner Bros., 86), his collaboration with one of South Africa's most influential musicians.

Honey (Open That Door)
Words and music by Mel Tillis.
Cedarwood Publishing Co., Inc., 1962.
Best-selling record by Ricky Skaggs from *Country Boy* (Epic, 84).

The Honey Thief (English)
Words and music by Bill McLeod, John McElhone, Graham Skinner, and Harry Travers.

EMI-Virgin, 1986.
Best-selling record in 1987 by Hipsway, from the album *Hipsway* (Columbia, 86).

Honky Tonk Man
Words and music by Johnny Horton, Tillman Franks, and Howard Hausey.
Cedarwood Publishing Co., Inc., 1956.
Revived in 1986 by Dwight Yoakam from the album *Guitars, Cadillacs, Etc., Etc.* (Reprise, 86); originally recorded by Johnny Horton.

Honky Tonk Moon
Words and music by Dennis O'Rourke.
Hannah Rhodes Music, 1986.
Best-selling record by Randy Travis from *Old 8 x 10* (Warner Bros., 88).

Honky Tonkin'
Words and music by Hank Williams.
Fred Rose Music, Inc., 1948.
Revived by Hank Williams, Jr. from *High Notes* (Elektra, 82).

Honor Bound
Words and music by Charlie Black, Thomas Rocco, and Austin Roberts.
Chappell & Co., Inc., 1984/Polygram International, 1984/MCA, Inc., 1984/Chriswald Music, 1984/Hopi Sound Music, 1984.
Best-selling record by Earl Thomas Conley from the album *Treadin' Water* (RCA, 85).

Hooked on Classics
Chappell & Co., Inc., 1981.
Best-selling record by The Royal Philharmonic Orchestra, conducted by Louis Clark from *Hooked on Classics* (RCA, 81). Medley of classical tunes.

Hooked on Music
Words and music by Mac Davis.
Song Painter Music, 1980.
Best-selling record by Mac Davis from *Texas in My Rear View Mirror* (Casablanca, 81).

Hopes on Hold (English)
Words and music by Lou Reed and Ruben Blades.
Metal Machine Music, 1988/Paper Boy Publishing, 1988.
Introduced by Ruben Blades in *Nothing But the Truth* (Elektra, 88), the first English-language album by the Panamanian-born artist singer.

Horses
Words and music by Walter Becker and Rickie Lee Jones.

Easy Money Music, 1989.
Introduced by Rickie Lee Jones on *Flying Cowboys* (Geffen, 89). Co-author Becker, formerly half of Steely Dan, produced Jones' album.

Hot Girls in Love (Canadian)
Words and music by Paul Dean and Bruce Fairbarn.
EMI-Blackwood Music Inc., 1983.
Best-selling record by Loverboy from *Keep It Up* (Columbia, 83).

Hot in the City (English)
Words and music by Billy Idol.
Chrysalis Music Group, 1982.
Best-selling record by Billy Idol from *Billy Idol* (Chrysalis, 82).

Hot Rod Hearts
Words and music by Bill LaBounty and Stephen Geyer.
Captain Crystal Music, 1980/EMI-Blackwood Music Inc., 1980/Darjen Music, 1980.
Best-selling record by Robbie Dupree from *Robbie Dupree* (Elektra, 80).

Hourglass (English)
Words by Chris Difford, music by Glenn Tilbrook.
Virgin Music, 1987.
Best-selling record by Squeeze, from the album *Babylon and On* (A & M), this was the first hit song for the critically acclaimed songwriting duo.

House in Algiers (French)
English words by Julian More, music by Gilbert Becaud.
Introduced by Georgia Brown in the musical *Roza,* which had a short run on Broadway in 1987.

Housequake
Words and music by Prince Rogers Nelson.
Controversy Music, 1987.
Introduced by Prince in the film *Sign 'o' the Times* and on the album of the same title (Paisley Park, 87).

How Am I Supposed to Live Without You
Words and music by Michael Bolton and Doug James.
EMI-April Music, 1983/Is Hot Music, Ltd., 1983/EMI-Blackwood Music Inc., 1983.
Best-selling record by Laura Branigan from *Branigan 2* (Atlantic, 83). Revived in 1989 by Michael Bol ton on *Soul Provider* (Colombia, 89).

How 'bout Us
Words and music by Dana Walden.

Walkin Music, 1981.
Best-selling record by Champaign from *How 'bout Us* (Columbia, 81).

How Can I Fall (English)
Words and music by Dave Glaspar and Marcus Lillington.
Virgin Music, 1988.
Best-selling record by Breathe, from *All That Jazz* (A & M, 88).

How Do I Make You
Words and music by Billy Steinberg.
Sony Tunes, 1979.
Best-selling record by Linda Ronstadt in *Mad Love* (Asylum, 80).

How Do I Survive
Words and music by Paul Bliss.
EMI-April Music, 1979.
Best-selling record by Amy Holland from *Amy Holland* (Capitol, 80).

How Do I Turn You On
Words and music by Tom Reid and Robert Byrne.
BMG Songs Inc., 1986/Colgems-EMI Music, 1986.
Best-selling record in 1987 by Ronnie Milsap, from the album *Lost in
    the Fifties Tonight* (RCA, 86).

How Do You Keep the Music Playing
Words by Marilyn Bergman and Alan Bergman, music by Michel
    Legrand.
WB Music, 1982.
Introduced in the film *Best Friends* (82). Best-selling record by Patti
    Austin and James Ingram (Qwest, 82). Nominated for an Academy
    Award, Best Song, 1982.

How Many Times Can We Say Goodbye
Words and music by Steve Goldman.
Goldrian Music, 1983.
Best-selling record by Dionne Warwick and Luther Vandross from *How
    Many Times Can We Say Goodbye* (Arista, 83).

How Old Are You
Words and music by Loudon Wainwright.
Snowden Music, 1983.
Introduced by Loudon Wainwright on the album *I'm All Right*
    (Columbia, 85).

How Shall I See You Through My Tears
Words by Lee Breuer, music by Bob Telson.
Boodle Music, 1984/Otis Lee Music.
Revived in 1988 for the Broadway production of *The Gospel at
    Colonues*, where it was performed by the J. D. Steele Singers with

soloist Javetta Stelle. Also included on the cast album (Elektra Nonesuch, 88).

How Soon Is Now (English)
Words by Morrissey, music by Johnny Marr.
Morrissey/Marr Songs Ltd., England, 1985.
Introduced by The Smiths on the album *Meat Is Murder* (Sire, 85).

How the Heart Approaches What It Yearns
Words and music by Paul Simon.
Paul Simon Music, 1978.
Introduced by Paul Simon in the album and the film *One Trick Pony* (80).

How Things Change
Words and music by Douglas Bernstein and Denis Markell.
Introduced by Donna Murphy in the 1989 revue *Showing Off.*

How Will I Know
Words and music by Gary Merrill, Shannon Rubicam, and Narada Michael Walden.
Irving Music Inc., 1985.
Best-selling record by Whitney Houston in 1986 from the album *Whitney Houston* (Arista, 85). One of the greatest debut records of all-time, this album produced three other topten songs.

Howard the Duck
Words and music by Thomas Dolby, George Clinton, and Allee Willis.
MCA, Inc., 1986/Off Backstreet Music.
Introduced by Dolby's Cube featuring Cherry Bomb in the film *Howard the Duck* (86); also released as a single.

How'm I Doin'
Words and music by Charles Strouse.
Charles Strouse Music, 1985.
Introduced by Lenny Wolpe in the off Broadway musical *Mayor* (85). The title is a favorite question from former New York Mayor Edward I. Koch, whose administration was the basis of this play.

Human
Words and music by James Harris, III and Terry Lewis.
Flyte Tyme Tunes, 1986.
Best-selling record by Human League from the album *Crash* (A & M, 86).

Human Nature
Words by John Bettis, music by Jeffrey Porcaro.
John Bettis Music, 1982/Porcara Music, 1982.
Best-selling record by Michael Jackson from *Thriller* (Epic, 83).

Human Touch (Australian)
Words and music by Rick Springfield.
Vogue Music, 1983.
Best-selling record by Rick Springfield from *Living in Oz* (RCA, 83).

Hundreds of Hats
Words and music by Jonathan Sheffer and Howard Ashman.
Introduced by Dick Latessa & Cast of *Diamonds* (84).

Hungry Heart
Words and music by Bruce Springsteen.
Bruce Springsteen Publishing, 1980.
Best-selling record by Bruce Springsteen from *The River* (Columbia, 80).

Hungry Like the Wolf (English)
Words and music by Duran Duran.
BIOT Music Ltd., London, England, 1983.
Best-selling record by Duran Duran from *Rio* (Capitol, 83).

The Hungry Wolf
Words and music by John Doe and Exene Cervenka, music by X.
Eight/Twelve Music, 1982.
Introduced by X in *More Fun in the New World* (Elektra, 82).

Hurricane
Words and music by Keith Stegall, Tom Schuyler, and Stewart Harris.
EMI-Blackwood Music Inc., 1980.
Best-selling record by Leon Everette (RCA, 81).

Hurt
Words and music by Jimmie Crane and Al Jacobs.
EMI-Miller Catalogue.
Revived in 1986 by Juice Newton on the album *Old Flame* (RCA, 86).
   Originally recorded by Timi Yuro.

Hurt So Bad
Words and music by Teddy Randazzo, Bobby Hart, and Bobby Wilding.
Vogue Music, 1965.
Revived by Linda Ronstadt in *Mad Love* (Asylum, 80).

Hurts So Good
Words and music by John Cougar Mellencamp and George Michael
   Green.
Full Keel Music, 1982.
Best-selling record by John Cougar from *American Fool* (Rival, 82).

Hymne
Music by Vangelis.

WB Music, 1987.
Performed by Joe Kenyon on the album *Hymne* (Mercury, 87); the
music was originally used for a wine commercial.

Hyperactive (English)
Words and music by Dennis Nelson, Tony Haynes, and Robert Palmer.
Island Music, 1985/Bungalow Music, N.V., 1985/Les Etoiles de la
Musique, 1985.
Best-selling record by Robert Palmer from the album *Riptide* (Atlantic,
86).

Hypnotize Me (English)
Words and music by Wang Chung.
Chong, England, 1987/Warner-Tamerlane Music.
Best-selling record by Wang Chung from the album *Mosaic* (Geffen,
87). The song was introduced in the movie *Inner Space*.

Hysteria (English)
Words and music by Steve Clark, Phil Collen, Joe Elliott, Robert John
'Mutt' Lange, and Rick Savage.
Bludgeon Riffola Music, 1987/Zomba Music, 1987.
Best-selling record in 1988 by Def Leppard, from *Hysteria* (Mercury,
87).

I

I Ain't Ever Satisfied
Words and music by Steve Earle.
Goldline Music Inc., 1981.
Introduced by Steve Earle on *Exit 0* (MCA, 87), an album on the
rocking edge of country music.

I Ain't Gonna Stand for It
Words and music by Stevie Wonder.
Jobete Music Co., 1980/Black Bull Music, 1980.
Best-selling record by Stevie Wonder from *Hotter Than July* (Tamla,
80).

I Ain't Got Nobody
Words and music by Roger Graham and Spencer Williams.
Chappell & Co., Inc./Intersong, USA Inc./Diamond Dave Music/Jerry
Vogel Music Co., Inc.
Revived by David Lee Roth as part of a medley with 'Just a Gigolo,'
from the album *Crazy from the Heat* (Warner Bros., 85).

I Ain't Living Long Like This
Words and music by Rodney Crowell.
Happy Sack Music Ltd., 1978.
Best-selling record by Waylon Jennings from *What Goes Around Comes
Around* (RCA, 80).

I Always Do
Words and music by Mark Heard.
Ideola Music, 1988.
Introduced by Phil Keaggy & Sunday's Child on *Phil Keaggy &
Sunday's Child* (Myrrh, 89).

I Always Get Lucky with You
Words and music by Tex Whitson, Freddy Powers, and Gary Church.
Shade Tree Music Inc., 1981.
Best-selling record by George Jones from *Shine On* (Epic, 83).

I Am a Patriot
Words and music by Steve Van Zandt.
Blue Midnight Music, 1984.
Revived in 1989 by Jackson Browne on *World in Motion* (Elektra).

I Am by Your Side (Canadian)
Words and music by Corey Hart.
Liesse Publishing, 1986.
Best-selling record by Corey Hart from the album *Fields of Fire* (EMI-
America, 86).

I Am Love
Words and music by Maurice White, David Foster, and Allee Willis.
Saggifire Music, 1983/Off Backstreet Music, 1983/Foster Frees Music
Inc., 1983.
Best-selling record by Jennifer Holliday from *Feel My Soul* (Geffen,
83).

I Am What I Am
Words and music by Jerry Herman.
Jerryco Music Co., 1983.
Introduced by George Hearn in *La Cage Au Folles* (83).

I and I
Words and music by Bob Dylan.
Special Rider Music, 1983.
Introduced on *Infidels* by Bob Dylan (Columbia, 83).

I Beg Your Pardon, also known as **(I Never Promised You a) Rose
Garden**
Words and music by Joe South.
Lowery Music Co., Inc., 1967.
Revived by Kon Kan on *Move to Move* (Atlantic, 88), this song made
the charts again in 1989, eighteen years after it was nominated for
two Grammys.

I Believe in You (English)
Words and music by Roger Cook and Sam Hogin.
Cookhouse Music, 1980/Roger Cook Music, 1980.
Best-selling record by Don Williams from *I Believe in You* (MCA, 80).
Nominated for a Grammy Award, Country Song of the Year, 1980.

I Blinked Once
Words and music by Steve Forbert.
Geffen Music, 1988/Rolling Tide Music, 1988.
Introduced by Steve Forbert on *Streets of This Town* (Geffen, 88).

I Can Dream About You
Words and music by Dan Hartman.

EMI-Blackwood Music Inc., 1983.
Best-selling record by Dan Hartman from *I Can Dream About You*
(MCA, 84).

I Can Have It All
Words by Garry Trudeau, music by Elizabeth Swados.
Music of the World, 1983.
Introduced by Laura Dean in *Doonesbury* (83).

I Can Hear Your Heartbeat (English)
Words and music by Chris Rea.
Magnet Music Ltd., England, 1983/Intersong, USA Inc., 1983.
Introduced on the 1983 album *Water Sign,* the song was revived by
Chris Rea on *New Light through Old Windows* (EMI, 89).

**I Can Tell by the Way You Dance (How You're Gonna Love Me
Tonight)**
Words and music by Robb Strandlund and Sandy Pinkard.
Tree Publishing Co., Inc., 1980/Jensong Music, Inc., 1980.
Best-selling record by Vern Gosdin (Compleat, 84).

I Can't Forget (Canadian)
Words and music by Leonard Cohen.
Stranger Music Inc., 1987.
Introduced by Leonard Cohen on *I'm Your Man* (CBS, 88).

I Can't Get Close Enough
Words and music by Sonny LeMaire and James P. Pennington.
Tree Publishing Co., Inc., 1987/Pacific Island Music, 1987.
Best-selling record by Exile, from the album *Shelter from the Night*
(Epic, 87).

I Can't Go for That (No Can Do)
Words and music by Daryl Hall, John Oates, and Sara Allen.
Fust Buzza Music, Inc., 1981/Hot Cha Music Co., 1981/Unichappell
Music Inc., 1981.
Best-selling record by Daryl Hall and John Oates from *Private Eyes*
(RCA, 82).

I Can't Help It (English)
Words and music by Barry Gibb.
Gibb Brothers Music, 1979.
Best-selling record by Andy Gibb and Olivia Newton-John from *After
Dark* (RSO, 80).

I Can't Hold Back
Words and music by Frank Sullivan and Jim Peterik.
Rude Music, 1984/WB Music, 1984/Easy Action Music, 1984.
Best-selling record by Survivor from *Vital Signs* (Scotti Brothers, 84).

I Can't Stand It (English)
Words and music by Eric Clapton.
Unichappell Music Inc., 1981.
Best-selling record by Eric Clapton from *Another Ticket* (RSO, 81).

I Can't Stop Loving You
Words and music by Michael Jackson.
Mijac Music, 1987/Warner-Tamerlane Music.
This best-selling record by Michael Jackson was the first hit from his
long-awaited album *Bad* (Epic, 87).

I Can't Tell You Why
Words and music by Glenn Frey, Don Henley, and Timothy B. Schmidt.
WB Music, 1979/Jeddrah Music, 1979/Red Cloud Music Co., 1979.
Best-selling record by The Eagles from *The Long Run* (Asylum, 80).

I Can't Turn Around
Words and music by Isaac Hayes.
Duchess Music Corp., 1986.
Introduced by J. M. Silk (RCA, 86). This song is the first major-label
example of 'House Music,' a Chicago-originated dance groove, in
answer to Washington, DC's 'Go Go Music.'

I Can't Wait
Words and music by Stevie Nicks, Rick Nowels, and Eric Pressly.
Welsh Witch Publishing, 1985/Future Furniture, 1985.
Best-selling record by Stevie Nicks from the album *Rock a Little*
(Atlantic, 86).

I Can't Wait (Netherlands)
English words and music by John Smith.
Poolside, 1986.
Best-selling record by Nu Shooz from the album *Poolside* (Atlantic, 86).

I Can't Win for Losin' You
Words and music by Robert Byrne and Rick Bowles.
Colgems-EMI Music, 1986.
Best-selling record by Earl Thomas Conley, from the album *Too Many
Times* (RCA, 86).

I Could Never Miss You More Than I Do (English)
Words and music by Neil Harrison.
Abesongs USA, 1978.
Best-selling record by Lulu from *Lulu* (Alfa, 81).

I Could Never Take the Place of Your Man
Words and music by Prince Rogers Nelson.
Controversy Music, 1987.

Best-selling record in 1988 by Prince, from the 1987 documentary *Sign 'o' Times* and its soundtrack album (Paisley Park, 87).

I Couldn't Leave You If I Tried
Words and music by Rodney Crowell.
Coolwell Music, 1988.
Best-selling record by Rodney Crowell, from *Diamonds and Dirt* (Columbia, 88). Nominated for a Grammy Award, Country Song of the Year, 1988.

I Didn't Mean to Turn You On
Words and music by James Harris, III and Terry Lewis.
Flyte Tyme Tunes, 1985/Avant Garde Music Publishing, Inc., 1985.
Best-selling record by Robert Palmer from the album *Riptide* (Atlantic, 86). Introduced by Cherelle in 1985.

I Do What I Do (Theme from *9 1/2 Weeks*) (American-English)
Words and music by Jonathan Elias, John Taylor, and Michael Des Barres.
Tritec Music Ltd., England, 1986/Music Design Publishing, 1986/ Famous Music Corp., 1986.
Introduced by John Taylor in the 1986 film *9 1/2 Weeks* and on soundtrack album (Capitol, 86).

I Do You
Words and music by Linda Mallah and Rich Kelly.
Meow Baby, 1987/Rick Kelly.
Best-selling record by the Jets, from the album *Magic* (MCA, 87).

I Don't Care
Words and music by Buck Owens.
Blue Book Music, 1964.
Revived by Ricky Skaggs from *Waitin' for the Sun to Shine* (Epic, 82).

I Don't Know a Thing About Love
Words and music by Harlan Howard.
Tree Publishing Co., Inc., 1983.
Best-selling record by Conway Twitty (Warner Brothers, 84).

I Don't Know for Sure
Words and music by Bob Mould.
Husker Music, 1986.
Introduced by Husker Du on the album *Candy Apple Grey* (Warner Bros., 86). On their first major-label album, this prototypical speed punk band from Minneapolis took on a mellower but no less anguished edge to their music.

I Don't Know Where to Start
Words and music by Thom Schuyler.

Briarpatch Music, 1981/Debdave Music Inc., 1981.
Best-selling record by Eddie Rabbitt from *Step By Step* (Electra, 82).

I Don't Know Why You Don't Want Me
Words and music by Rosanne Cash and Rodney Crowell.
Chelcait Music, 1985/Atlantic Music Corp., 1985/Coolwell Music, 1985/
Granite Music Corp., 1985.
Best-selling record by Rosanne Cash from the album *Rhythm and
Romance* (Columbia, 85). Nominated for a Grammy Award, Country
Song of the Year, 1985.

I Don't Like Mondays (Iranian)
English words and music by Bob Geldof.
Zomba Music, 1979.
Best-selling record by The Boomtown Rats from *The Fine Art of
Surfacing* (Columbia, 80).

I Don't Mind at All (English)
Words and music by Lyle Workman and Brent Bourgeois.
Polygram International, 1987/Lena May, 1987/Ackee Music Inc., 1987/
Bourgeoise Zee, 1987.
Best-selling record by Bourgeois Tagg, from the album *Yo Yo* (Island,
87).

I Don't Mind the Thorns (If You're the Rose)
Words and music by Jan Buckingham and Linda Young.
Warner-Tamerlane Music, 1985/Pullman Music, 1985/Duck Songs,
1985.
Best-selling record by Lee Greenwood from the album *Streamline*
(MCA, 85).

I Don't Need You (Icelandic)
English words and music by Rick Christian.
Bootchute Music, 1978.
Best-selling record by Kenny Rogers from *Share Your Love* (Liberty,
81).

I Don't Think I'm Ready for You
Words and music by Steve Dorff, Milton Brown, Burt Reynolds, and
Snuff Garrett.
Music of the World, 1985/Happy Trails, 1985.
Song by Anne Murray in the film *Stick* (85). Introduced on the album
Heart over Mind (Capitol, 84).

I Don't Think She's in Love Anymore
Words and music by Kent Robbins.
Royalhaven Music, Inc., 1981.
Best-selling record by Charley Pride (RCA, 82).

I Don't Wanna Be a Memory
Words and music by Sonny LeMaire and James P. Pennington.
Tree Publishing Co., Inc., 1983/BMG Music, 1983.
Best-selling record by Exile (Epic, 84).

I Don't Wanna Go on with You Like That (English)
Words by Bernie Taupin, music by Elton John.
Big Pig Music, 1988/Intersong, USA Inc., 1988.
Best-selling record by Elton John, from *Reg Strikes Back* (MCA, 88).

I Don't Wanna Know (English)
Words and music by John Martyn.
Warlock Music, 1978/Island Music, 1978.
Revived in 1987 by Richie Havens, on his album *Simple Things* (RBI, 87).

I Don't Wanna Live without Your Love (American-English)
Words and music by Diane Warren and Albert Hammond.
Realsongs, 1988/Albert Hammond Enterprises, 1988/WB Music, 1988.
Best-selling record by Chicago, from *Chicago XIX* (Reprise, 88).
   Keeping pace with their former lead singer, Peter Cetera, Chicago had another hit with this song.

I Don't Wanna Lose Your Love
Words and music by Joey Carbone.
Sixty Ninth Street Music, 1983.
Best-selling record by Crystal Gayle from *Cage the Songbird* (Warner Brothers, 84).

I Don't Want to Do It
Words and music by Bob Dylan.
Special Rider Music, 1985.
Introduced by George Harrison in the film *Porky's Revenge* (85).

I Don't Want to Feel What I Feel
Words and music by William Finn.
Introduced by Lilias White in the 1989 musical *Romance in Hard Times*.

I Don't Want to Live without You (English)
Words and music by Mick (Foreigner) Jones.
Heavy Pedal, 1987/Intersong, USA Inc., 1987.
Best-selling record in 1988 by Foreigner, from *Inside Information* (Atlantic, 87).

I Don't Want to Lose Your Love
Words and music by Gene McFadden, Linda Vitali, John Whitehead, and Jimmy McKinney.
Su-Ma Publishing Co., Inc., 1987/Bush Burnin' Music, 1987.

Best-selling record in 1987 by Freddie Jackson, from the album *Just Like the First Time* (Capitol, 86).

I Don't Want to Spoil the Party (English)
Words and music by John Lennon and Paul McCartney.
Northern Songs, Ltd., England, 1964/Maclen Music Inc., 1964.
Revived by Rosanne Cash on *Hits 1979-1989* (Columbia, 89).

I Don't Want Your Love (English)
Words and music by John Taylor, Nick Rhodes, and Simon Lebon.
Skintrade, 1988/Colgems-EMI Music, 1988.
Best-selling record by Duran Duran, from *Big Thing* (Capitol, 88), which marked a return to form by the New Wave idols.

I Dreamed a Dream (French-English)
English words by Herbert Kretzmer, French words by Alain Boublil and Jean Marc Natel, music by Claude-Michel Schonberg.
Alain Boublil Music Ltd., 1980, 1986.
Performed by Randy Graff in the 1987 Broadway production of *Les Miserables* and on the original cast album (Geffen, 87). Neil Diamond also recorded it on his album *Hot August Night II* (Columbia, 87).

I Drink Alone
Words and music by George Thorogood.
Del Sounds Music, 1985.
Introduced by George Thorogood on the album *Maverick* (EMI-America, 85).

I Drove All Night
Words and music by Billy Steinberg and Tom Kelly.
Sony Tunes, 1989/Denise Barry Music.
Best-selling record by Cyndi Lauper from *A Night to Remember* (Epic, 89).

I Eat Out
Words and music by Loudon Wainwright.
Snowden Music, 1986.
Introduced by Loudon Wainwright on the album *More Love Songs* (Rounder, 87), this song further details the life and times of the itinerant songwriter.

I Feel for You
Words and music by Prince Rogers Nelson.
Controversy Music, 1979.
Best-selling record by Chaka Khan from *I Feel for You* (Warner Brothers, 84). Won a Grammy Award, and Rhythm 'n' Blues Song of the Year, 1984.

I Feel Good All Over
Words and music by Gabe Hardeman and Annette Hardeman.
Gabeson, 1987/On the Move.
Best-selling record by Stephanie Mills, from the album *If I Were Your Woman* (MCA, 87).

I Feel Like Loving You Again
Words and music by Bobby Braddock and Sonny Throckmorton.
Tree Publishing Co., Inc., 1978/Cross Keys Publishing Co., Inc., 1978.
Best-selling record by T. G. Sheppard (Warner Brothers, 80).

I Fell in Love Again Last Night
Words and music by Paul Overstreet and Thomas Schuyler.
Writer's Group Music, 1985/Scarlet Moon Music, 1985.
Best-selling record by Forester Sisters from the album *Forester Sisters* (Warner Bros., 85).

I Found Someone
Words and music by Michael Bolton and Mark Mangold.
EMI-April Music, 1987/Is Hot Music, Ltd., 1987/But For Music, 1987.
Best-selling record by Cher, from the album *Cher* (Geffen, 87).

I. G. Y. (What a Beautiful World)
Words and music by Donald Fagen.
Freejunket Music, 1982.
Best-selling record by Donald Fagen from *The Nightfly* (Warner Brothers, 82). Nominated for a Grammy Award, Song of the Year, 1982.

I Get Weak
Words and music by Diane Warren.
Realsongs, 1987.
Best-selling record in 1988 by Belinda Carlisle from *Heaven on Earth* (MCA, 87).

I Go Crazy (English)
Words and music by James Mitchell, Kevin Mills, Nick Marsh, and Rocco Barker.
Nancy Hughes, 1987/Famous Music Corp., 1987.
Performed by Flesh for Lulu on the soundtrack of the film *Some Kind of Wonderful* and on its album (MCA, 87); also featured on the group's album *Long Live the New Flesh* (Capitol, 87).

I Go to Extremes
Words and music by Billy Joel.
Joel, 1989.
Introduced by Billy Joel from *Storm Front* (Columbia, 89).

I Got Dreams
Words and music by Steve Wariner and Bill LaBounty.
Steve Wariner, 1989/Screen Gems-EMI Music Inc., 1989/Irving Music
    Inc., 1989.
Best-selling record by Steve Wariner from *I Got Dreams* (MCA, 89).

I Got Lost in Her Arms
Words and music by Irving Berlin.
Irving Berlin Music Corp., 1946.
Introduced in the musical *Annie Get Your Gun,* the song was originally
    titled 'I Got Lost in His Arms.' Revived in 1986 by Tony Bennett on
    the album *The Art of Excellence.*

I Got Mexico
Words and music by Eddy Raven and Frank J. Myers.
Michael H. Goldsen, Inc., 1983/Ravensong Music, 1983.
Best-selling record by Eddy Raven (RCA, 84).

I Got You (Australian)
Words and music by Neil Finn.
Enz Music, 1980.
Featured on *True Colours* by Split Enz (A & M, 80).

I Guess It Never Hurts to Hurt Sometimes
Words and music by Randy Van Warner.
Fourth Floor Music Inc./Fiction Music, 1980/Terraform Music, 1980.
Best-selling record by The Oak Ridge Boys from *Deliver* (MCA, 84).

I Guess That's Why They Call It the Blues (English)
Words by Bernie Taupin, music by Elton John.
Intersong, USA Inc., 1983.
Best-selling record by Elton John from *Too Low for Zero* (Geffen, 83).

I Hate Myself for Loving You
Words and music by Joan Jett and Desmond Child.
Lagunatic Music, 1987/Desmobile Music Inc., 1987/EMI-April Music,
    1987/Virgin Music, 1987.
Best-selling record by Joan Jett and the Blackhearts, from *Up Your Alley*
    (CBS Associated, 88).

I Have Learned to Respect the Power of Love
Words and music by Angela Winbush and Rene Moore.
Careers Music Inc., 1986/Moore & Moore.
Best-selling record by Stephanie Mills from the album *Stephanie Mills*
    (MCA, 86).

I Have Loved You, Girl (But Not Like This Before)
Words and music by Earl Thomas Conley.

Blue Moon Music, 1975/Equestrian Music, 1975.
Best-selling record by Earl Thomas Conley (RCA, 83).

I Have Never Felt This Way Before (English)
Words by Don Black, music by Andrew Lloyd Webber.
Dick James Music Inc., 1985.
Introduced by Bernadette Peters in the musical *Song and Dance* (85).

I Heard a Rumour (English)
Words and music by Sarah Dallin, Siobhan Fahey, Keren Woodward,
    Matt Aitken, Pete Waterman, and Mike Stock.
In A Bunch Music, London, England, 1987/Warner-Tamerlane Music,
    1987/Terrace Entertainment Corp., 1987.
Introduced by Bananarama in the film *Disorderlies* and on its
    soundtrack album (Tin Pan Apple/Polygram, 87); the group also had a
    best-selling record with the song. The trio of Stock, Aitken, and
    Waterman emerged in 1987 as one of the year's top producing teams.

I Heard It Through the Grapevine
Words and music by Norman Whitfield and Barrett Strong.
Stone Agate Music, 1966.
Revived in 1987 in an award-winning commercial for California raisins,
    featuring dancing claymation raisins led by the voice of drummer
    Buddy Miles. The 'group,' the California Raisins, subsequently
    released an album under the same name. Revived by Roger from *The
    Many Facets of Roger* (Warner Bros., 82).

I Just Called to Say I Love You
Words and music by Stevie Wonder.
Jobete Music Co., 1984/Black Bull Music, 1984.
Best-selling record by Stevie Wonder (Motown, 84). Introduced in the
    film and soundtrack album *The Woman in Red* (84). Won an
    Academy Award, and Best Song, 1984;a Grammy Award, and Song
    of the Year, 1984.

I Keep Coming Back
Words and music by Johnny Slate, Jim Hurt, and Larry Keith.
WB Music, 1980.
Best-selling record by Razzy Bailey (RCA, 80).

I Keep Forgettin' (Every Time You're Near)
Words and music by Jerry Leiber and Mike Stoller.
Bienstock Publishing Co., 1962/Jerry Leiber Music, 1962/Mike Stoller
    Music, 1962.
Best-selling record by Michael McDonald from *If That's What It Takes*
    (Warner Brothers, 82).

I Knew Him So Well (English)
Words by Tim Rice, words and music by Bjorn Ulvaeus and Benny

Andersson.
Union Songs Musikfoerlag, Sweden, 1985/MCA, Inc., 1985.
Introduced by Elaine Paige on the album *Chess* (RCA, 85).

I Knew Love
Words and music by Roger Brown.
Dixie Stars, 1987.
Introduced by Nanci Griffith on *Little Love Affairs* (MCA, 88).

I Knew You Were Waiting (for Me) (English)
Words and music by Simon Climie and Dennis Morgan.
Chrysalis Music Group, 1987/Little Shop of Morgansongs, 1987.
Best-selling record in 1987 by Aretha Franklin and George Michael,
    from the album *Aretha* (Arista, 86).

I Know Him So Well (English)
Words by Tim Rice, music by Bjorn Ulvaeus and Benny Andersson.
This song from the English play *Chess,* which did not reach Broadway
    by the close of 1987, was revived by Whitney Houston in a duet with
    her mother, Cissy Houston, on her album *Whitney* (Arista).

I Know How He Feels
Words and music by Rick Bowles and William Robinson.
Maypop Music, 1988/Alabama Band Music Co., 1988.
Best-selling record by Reba McEntire, from *Reba* (MCA, 88).

I Know the Way to You by Heart
Words and music by Tony Laiola.
Blue Lake Music, 1983.
Best-selling record by Vern Gosdin from the album *Time Stood Still*
    (Compleat, 85). Introduced by Marlow Tackett.

I Know There's Something Going On (English)
Words and music by Russ Ballard.
Russell Ballard, Ltd., Middlesex, England, 1982/Island Music, 1982.
Best-selling record by Frida from *Somethings Going On* (Atlantic, 82).

I Know Things Now
Words and music by Stephen Sondheim.
BMG Music, 1987.
Introduced by Danielle Ferland in the musical *Into the Woods* and on
    the cast album (RCA, 88).

I Know What Boys Like
Words and music by Christopher Butler.
Merovingian Music, 1980.
Best-selling record by The Waitresses from *Wasn't Tomorrow*
    Wonderful? (Polydor, 82).

I Know What I Like
Words and music by Chris Hayes and Huey Lewis.
Hulex Music, 1986.
Best-selling record in 1987 by Huey Lewis & The News, from the
album *Fore!* (Chrysalis, 86).

I Know Where I'm Going
Words and music by Don Schlitz, Craig Bickhardt, and Brent Maher.
MCA Music, 1987/Don Schlitz Music/Colgems-EMI Music/EMI-April
Music/Welbeck Music/Blue Quill Music.
Best-selling record by the Judds from the album *Heart Land* (MCA, 87).

I Lie
Words and music by Thomas William Damphier.
Coal Miner's Music Inc., 1980.
Best-selling record by Loretta Lynn (MCA, 82).

I Like
Words and music by Teddy Riley, Gene Griffin, Aaron Hall, and
Timothy Gatling.
Cal-Gene Music, 1988/Virgin Music, 1988/Zomba Music, 1988.
Best-selling record in 1989 by Guy from *Guy* (Uptown, 88).

I Like 'Em Big and Stupid
Words and music by Julie Brown, Terrence McNally, Charlie Coffey,
and Ray Colcord.
Stymie Music, 1984.
Performed by Julie Brown on the album *Trapped in the Body of a White
Girl* (Sire, 87), this song was introduced on her earlier record
Goddess in Progress.

I Like It
Words and music by Dino.
Island Music, 1989/Onid Music, 1989.
Best-selling record by Dino from *24/7* (4th & Broadway, 89).

I Like My Body
Words and music by Gary Taylor.
Morning Crew, 1987.
Introduced by Chico DeBarge in the film *Police Academy 4* and on the
soundtrack album (Sire, 87).

I Live for Your Love
Words and music by Pam Reswick, Steve Werfel, and Alan Rich.
O'Lyric Music, 1987/Tuneworks Music, 1987/Vandorf Songs Co., 1987/
Reswick-Werfel, 1987/Besame West Music, 1987/BMG Songs Inc.,
1987/Careers Music Inc., 1987/Nelana Music, 1987.
Best-selling record in 1988 by Natalie Cole, from *Everlasting* (EMI-
Manhattan, 87).

I Lobster But Never Flounder
Words and music by Bobby Braddock and Sparky Braddock
(pseudonym for Wilma Sue Lawrence).
Tree Publishing Co., Inc., 1979.
Featured on *Writers in Disguise* by Pinkard and Bowen (Warner
Brothers, 84).

I Looked in the Mirror
Words and music by Mose Allison.
Audre Mae Music, 1987.
Introduced by Mose Allison, on the album *Ever Since the World Ended*
(Blue Note, 87).

I Love a Rainy Night
Words and music by Eddie Rabbitt, Even Stevens, and David Malloy.
Debdave Music Inc., 1980/Briarpatch Music, 1980.
Best-selling record by Eddie Rabbitt from *Horizon* (Elektra, 80).

I Love L.A.
Words and music by Randy Newman.
Six Pictures Music, 1983.
Introduced by Randy Newman in *Trouble in Paradise* (Warner Brothers,
83).

I Love My Mom
Words and music by Suzzy Roche.
Deshufflin' Inc., 1987.
Introduced by The Roches in the play *Mama Drama* at the Ensemble
Studio Theater in New York City in 1987. In addition to this
previously unrecorded song written for the author's baby daughter, the
production used three other songs by the Roche sisters. Revived in
1989 by The Roches on *Speak* (Ponder, 1989)].

I Love Rock and Roll
Words and music by Jake Hooker and Alan Merrill.
Finchley Music Corp., 1975.
Best-selling record by Joan Jett & The Blackhearts from *I Love Rock
and Roll* (Boardwalk, 82).

I Love to Dance
Words by Alan Bergman and Marilyn Bergman, music by Billy
Goldenberg.
Izzylumoe Music, 1978/Threesome Music Co., 1978.
Introduced by Dorothy Loudon and Vincent Gardenia in *Ballroom*
(Musical, 78). Performed by Sandy Duncan in *Five, Six, Seven,
Eight... Dance* (Revue, 83).

I Love to See You Smile
Words and music by Randy Newman.

Twice As Nice Music, 1989/MCA Music, 1989.
Introduced by Randy Newman on the soundtrack of the film
Parenthood; album released by Reprise, 1989. Nominated for an
Academy Award, Best Original Song, 1989.

I Love You (English)
Words and music by Derek Holt.
CBB Music, Torquay Devon, British Virgin Islands, 1980.
Best-selling record by The Climax Blues Band from *Flying the Flag*
(Warner Brothers, 81).

I Love You in the Strangest Way
Words and music by Pat MacDonald.
Mambadaddi, 1986/I.R.S. Music/Criterion Music Corp.
Introduced by Timbuk 3 on the album *Greetings from Timbuk 3* (I.R.S.,
86).

I Loved 'Em Every One
Words and music by Phil Sampson.
Tree Publishing Co., Inc., 1980.
Best-selling record by T. G. Sheppard from *I Love 'Em All* (Warner/
Curb, 81).

I Loved You Yesterday
Words and music by Lyle Lovett.
Michael H. Goldsen, Inc., 1987/Lyle Lovett, 1987.
Introduced by Lyle Lovett on *Pontiac* (MCA/Curb, 87).

I Made It Through the Rain
Words and music by Gerald Kenny, Drey Shepperd, Bruce Sussman,
Jack Feldman, and Barry Manilow.
Unichappell Music Inc., 1979.
Best-selling record by Barry Manilow from *Barry* (Arista, 80).

I Married Her Just Because She Looks Like You
Words and music by Lyle Lovett.
Michael H. Goldsen, Inc., 1988/Lyle Lovett, 1988.
Best-selling record by Lyle Lovett & His Large Band from *Lyle Lovett
& His Large Band* (MCA, 89).

I Miss You
Words and music by Lynn Malsby.
Spectrum VII, 1985.
Best-selling record by Klymaxx from the album *Meeting in the Ladies
Room* (Constellation, 85).

I Missed (English)
Words and music by David Conley, Bernard Jackson, and Everett
Collins.

Colgems-EMI Music, 1988/Deep Faith Music, 1988.
Best-selling record by Surface, from *Second Wave* (Columbia, 88).

I Must Be Dreaming
Words and music by Willy DeVille.
Sanpan Music Inc., 1985.
Introduced by Willy DeVille on the album *Sportin' Life* (Atlantic, 86).
   Best-selling record by Giuffria from the album *Silk and Steel* (Camel/
   MCA, 86).

I Need a Good Woman Bad
Words and music by Earl Thomas Conley.
EMI-April Music, 1987.
Introduced by Earl Thomas Conley on the album *Too Many Times*
   (RCA, 87).

I Need Love
Words and music by J. Smith, B. Erving, Darrell Pierce, Dwayne
   Simon, and S. Etts.
Def Jam, 1987.
Best-selling record by LL Cool J, from the album *Bigger and Deffer*
   (Def Jam, 87).

I Need More of You
Words and music by David Bellamy.
Bellamy Brothers Music, 1985/Famous Music Corp., 1985.
Best-selling record by The Bellamy Brothers from the album *Howard
   and David* (MCA, 85).

I Never Wanted to Love You
Words and music by William Finn.
Introduced by company of *March of the Falsettos* (81).

I Pledge My Love
Words and music by Dino Fekaris and Freddy Perren.
Perren Vibes Music, Inc., 1979.
Best-selling record by Peaches and Herb from *Twice the Fire* (Polydor,
   80).

I Prefer the Moonlight
Words and music by G. Chapman and Mark Wright.
Riverstone Music, Inc., 1987/EMI-Blackwood Music Inc., 1987/Land of
   Music Publishing, 1987.
Best-selling record by Kenny Rogers, from the album *I Prefer the
   Moonlight* (RCA, 87).

I Ran (English)
Words and music by Ali Score, Paul Reynolds, Mike Score, and Frank
   Maudley.

Zomba Music, 1982.
Best-selling record by A Flock of Seagulls from *A Flock of Seagulls* (Jive, 82).

I Really Don't Need No Light
Words and music by Jeffrey Osborne and David Wolinski.
Almo Music Corp., 1982/March 9 Music, 1982/WB Music, 1982/ Overdue Music, 1982.
Best-selling record by Jeffrey Osborne from *Jeffrey Osbourne* (A & M, 82).

I Remember Holding You
Words and music by Joe Pasquale.
Joe Pasquale Music, 1988.
Best-selling record by Boys Club, from *Boys Club* (MCA, 88).

I Sang Dixie
Words and music by Dwight Yoakam.
Coal Dust West, 1988.
Best-selling record in 1989 by Dwight Yoakam from *Buenas Noches from a Lonely Room* (Reprise, 88).

I Saw a Stranger with Your Hair
Words and music by John Gorka.
Red House Music, 1987/Lost Lake Arts Music, 1987.
Introduced on *I Know* (Red House, 87). Revived in 1989 by John Gorka on *Legacy* (Windham Hill, 89).

I Saw Her Standing There, see **I Saw Him Standing There.**

I Saw Him Standing There, also known as **I Saw Her Standing There** (English)
Words and music by John Lennon and Paul McCartney.
Gil Music Corp., 1963/Northern Music Corp., 1963.
Tiffany revived the Beatle's classic, with slight modification, on her album *Tiffany* (MCA, 87) and her rendition was a hit in 1988.

I Saw It on TV
Words and music by John Fogerty.
Wenaha Music Co., 1984.
Introduced by John Fogerty on the album *Centerfield* (Warner Bros., 85).

I Should Be So Lucky (English)
Words and music by Mike Stock, Matt Aitken, and Pete Waterman.
All Boys USA Music, 1987.
Best-selling record by Kylie Minogue from *Kylie* (Geffen, 88). The famous hit-making producers scored an international smash with this song, which topped the charts in eleven countries.

I Should Be with You
Words and music by Steve Wariner.
Steve Wariner, 1988.
Best-selling record by Steve Wariner from *I Should Be with You* (MCA, 88).

I Stand Alone
Words and music by Maury Yeston.
Yeston Music, Ltd., 1988/Screen Gems-EMI Music Inc., 1988.
Introduced by Placido Domingo in *Goya, a Life in Song* (Columbia, 89), an album of superstar performances released prior to the show's projected Broadway opening.

I Still Believe (Irish)
Words and music by Antonio Armato and Bepee Cantarelli.
Anta, 1988/Chrysalis Music Group, 1988/Colgems-EMI Music, 1988.
Best-selling record by Brenda K. Starr from *Brenda K. Starr* (MCA, 88).

I Still Believe in Waltzes
Words and music by Michael Hughes, Johnny MacRae, and Bob Morrison.
Southern Nights Music Co., 1980.
Best-selling record by Conway Twitty and Loretta Lynn (MCA, 81).

I Still Believe in You
Words and music by Chris Hillman and Steve Hill.
Bar-None Music, 1987/Bug Music, 1987.
Best-selling record in 1989 by The Desert Rose Band from *Running* (MCA/Curb, 88).

I Still Can't Get over Loving You
Words and music by Ray Parker, Jr.
Raydiola Music, 1983.
Best-selling record by Ray Parker, Jr. from *Woman out of Control* (Arista, 84).

I Still Dream (English)
Words and music by Richard Thompson.
Beeswing Music, 1988.
Introduced by Richard Thompson on *Amnesia* (Capitol, 88).

I Still Haven't Found What I'm Looking For (Irish)
Words and music by U2.
Polygram International, 1987.
Best-selling record by U2, this was the first hit from one of the year's most significant albums, *The Joshua Tree* (Island, 87). Nominated for a Grammy Award, Song of the Year, 1987.

I Still Look for You
Words and music by Michael Noble and Carl Struck.
WB Music, 1986/Bob Montgomery Music Inc./Warner-Tamerlane Music/Writers House Music Inc.
Introduced by Southern Pacific on the album *Killbilly Hill* (Warner Bros., 86).

I Sweat (Going Through the Motions)
Words and music by Nona Hendryx.
Eat Your Heart Out Music, 1984.
Introduced by Nona Hendryx in the film and soundtrack album *Perfect* (Arista, 85).

I Think I Can Beat Mike Tyson
Words and music by Will Smith, Pete Q. Harris, and Jeff Townes.
Zomba Music, 1989.
Introduced by D.J. Jazzy Jeff and the Fresh Prince on *And in This Corner* (Jive, 89). Nominated for a Grammy Award, Rap Song of the Year, 1989.

I Think I'll Just Stay Here and Drink
Words and music by Merle Haggard.
Shade Tree Music Inc., 1981.
Best-selling record by Merle Haggard from *The Way I Am* (MCA, 81).

I Think It's Gonna Rain Today
Words and music by Randy Newman.
Unichappell Music Inc., 1966.
Revived in 1988 by Bette Midler in the film and soundtrack album of *Beaches* (Atlantic, 88). This song was originally recorded by Judy Collins.

I Think It's Love
Words and music by Jermaine Jackson, Michael Omartian, and Stevie Wonder.
Black Stallion County Publishing, 1986/All Nations Music/Black Bull Music/Jobete Music Co.
Best-selling record by Jermaine Jackson from the album *Precious Moments* (Arista, 86).

I Think We're Alone Now
Words and music by Ritchie Cordell (pseudonym for Ritchie Rosenblatt) and Bo Gentry (pseudonym for Robert Ackoff).
Big Seven Music Corp., 1967.
Revived in 1987 by Tiffany, on the album *Tiffany* (MCA); this was the first of two songs by Ritchie Cordell to make the charts in 1987, twenty years after this tune was a hit for Tommy James and the Shondells.

I Thought He Was Mr. Right But He Left
Words and music by Kacey Jones and Barbara Cloyd.
Zama Lama Music, 1988/Glaser Holmes Publications, 1988/Red
Snapper, 1988/William Thomas, 1988.
Introduced by Ethel and the Shameless Hussies on *Born to Burn* (MCA,
88).

I Told a Lie to My Heart
Words and music by Hank Williams, Jr.
Acuff-Rose Publications Inc., 1984.
Introduced by Willie Nelson on the album *Half Nelson* (Columbia, 85).
This is a previously unreleased demo.

I Told You So
Words by Fred Ebb, music by John Kander.
Kander & Ebb Inc., 1981/Fiddleback, 1981.
Introduced by Roderick Cook and Grace Keagy in *Woman of the Year*
(81).

I Told You So
Words and music by Randy Travis.
Three Story, 1988.
Best-selling record in 1988 by Randy Travis from *Always and Forever*
(Warner Bros., 87). Won an American Music Award for Best Country
Song, 1988.

I Wanna Be a Cowboy
Words and music by Brian Chatton, Nico Ramsden, Nick Richards, and
Jeff Jeopardi.
Protoons Inc., 1986/Terrace Entertainment Corp.
Best-selling record by The Cure from the album *Boys Don't Cry*
(Profile, 86).

I Wanna Be Your Lover
Words and music by Prince Rogers Nelson.
Controversy Music, 1979.
Best-selling record by Prince from *Prince* (Warner Brothers, 80).

I Wanna Dance with Somebody (Who Loves Me)
Words and music by Gary Merrill and Shannon Rubicam.
Irving Music Inc., 1986/Boy Meets Girl.
Best-selling record by Whitney Houston, from the album *Whitney*
(Arista, 87). The artist turned again to the authors of 'How Will I
Know,' one of the hits from her debut album, for the first big single
from her long-awaited follow-up album.

I Wanna Dance with You
Words and music by Eddie Rabbitt and B. J. Walker, Jr.
Eddie Rabbitt Music Publishing, 1988/Fishin' Fool Music, 1988.

Best-selling record by Eddie Rabbitt, from *I Wanna Dance with You* (RCA, 88).

I Wanna Go Back
Words and music by Danny Chauncey, Morty Byron, and Ira Walker.
Danny Tunes, 1987/Warner-Tamerlane Music, 1987/Buy Rum, 1987/ Raski, 1987/WB Music, 1987.
Best-selling record in 1987 by Eddie Money, from the album *Can't Hold Back* (Columbia, 86).

I Wanna Have Some Fun
Words and music by Full Force.
Forceful Music, 1988/Willesden Music, Inc., 1988.
Best-selling record in 1989 by Samantha Fox from *I Wanna Have Some Fun* (Jive, 88).

I Want a New Drug
Words and music by Chris Hayes and Huey Lewis.
Hulex Music, 1983/Chrysalis Music Group, 1983.
Best-selling record by Huey Lewis & The News from *Sports* (Chrysalis, 84).

I Want Candy
Words and music by Rob Feldman, Jerry Goldstein, Richard Gottehrer, and Bert Berns.
Grand Canyon Music, Inc., 1965/Web 4 Music Inc., 1965.
Revived by Bow Wow Wow from *The Last of the Mohicans* (RCA, 82).

I Want Her
Words and music by Keith Sweat and Teddy Riley.
Vintertainment, 1987/Keith Sweat Publishing, 1987/Zomba Music, 1987.
Best-selling record in 1988 by Keith Sweat, from *Make It Last Forever* (Vintertainment, 87).

I Want It All
Words by Richard Maltby, music by David Shire.
Fiddleback, 1984/Progeny Music, 1984/Revelation Music Publishing Corp., 1984/Long Pond Music, 1984.
Introduced by Beth Fowler, Catherine Cox and Liz Callaway in *Baby* (83).

I Want That Man (English)
Words and music by Alannah Currie and Tom Bailey.
Point Music Ltd., 1989.
Introduced by Blondie on *Def, Dumb, and Blonde* (Sire, 89).

I Want to Be Your Man
Words and music by Larry Troutman.

Troutman's Music, 1987/Saja Music Co., 1987.
Best-selling record by Roger, from the album *Unlimited* (Reprise, 87).

I Want to Hold Your Hand (English)
Words and music by John Lennon and Paul McCartney.
Northern Songs, Ltd., England, 1963/Duchess Music Corp., 1963.
Revived by Lakeside from *Your Wish Is My Command* (Solar, 82).

I Want to Know What Love Is (English)
Words and music by Mick (Foreigner) Jones.
Somerset Songs Publishing, Inc., 1984/Little Doggies Productions Inc., 1984.
Best-selling record by Foreigner from the album *Agent Provocateur* (Atlantic, 85). Nominated for a Grammy Award, Song of the Year, 1985.

I Want to Know You Before We Make Love
Words and music by Candy Parton and Becky Hobbs.
Irving Music Inc., 1987/Beckaroo, 1987.
Best-selling record by Conway Twitty, from the album *Borderline* (MCA, 87).

I Want to Make the World Turn Around
Words and music by Steve Miller.
Sailor Music, 1986.
Best-selling record by Steve Miller from the album *Living in the 20th Century* (Capitol, 86).

I Want You Bad
Words and music by Terry Adams.
Tomata du Plenti, 1987/High Varieties, 1987.
Introduced by The Long Ryders on their album *Two Fisted Tales* (Island, 87). The author plays keyboards in NRBQ, a highly regarded 'bar band,' who have also recorded this song on their album *At Yankee Stadium*.

I Want You to Hurt Like I Do
Words and music by Randy Newman.
Twice As Nice Music, 1988.
Introduced by Randy Newman on *Land of Dreams* (Reprise, 88).

I Want Your Sex (English)
Words and music by George Michael.
Morrison Leahy, England, 1987/Chappell & Co., Inc., 1987.
Best-selling record by George Michael, from the album *Faith;* introduced on the soundtrack of the film *Beverly Hills Cop II* and on its soundtrack album (MCA, 87). The explicit title of this song sparked much controversy; its video was re-edited to rebuke claims that it promoted promiscuity.

I Was Country When Country Wasn't Cool
Words and music by Kye Fleming and Dennis Morgan.
Pi-Gem Music Publishing Co., Inc., 1981.
Best-selling record by Barbara Mandrell from *Barbara Mandrell Live*
(MCA, 81). Nominated for a Grammy Award, Country Song of the
Year, 1981.

I Will Be There
Words and music by Tom Snow and Jennifer Kimball.
Snow Music, 1987/Michael H. Goldsen, Inc./Sweet Angel Music.
Best-selling record by Dan Seals, from the album *On the Front Line*
(EMI-America, 87).

I Will Follow (Irish)
Words and music by Larry Mullen, The Edge (pseudonym for Dave
Evans), Adam Clayton, and Bono (pseudonym for Paul Hewson).
Polygram International, 1980.
Featured in *Boy* by U2 (Island, 82).

I Will Follow
Words and music by James Taylor.
Country Road Music Inc., 1981.
Introduced by James Taylor in *Dad Loves His Work* (Columbia, 81).

I Will Survive
Words and music by Dino Fekaris and Freddy Perven.
Perren Vibes Music, Inc., 1978.
Revived in 1989 by Safire in the film *She Devil*.

I Wish He Didn't Trust Me So Much
Words and music by P. LuBoff, Harold Payne, and J. Eubanks.
Pea Pod Music, 1985/Pass It On Music, 1985/Legs Music, Inc., 1985.
Best-selling record by Bobby Womack from the album *So Many Rivers*
(MCA, 85).

I Wish I Had a Girl
Words and music by Henry Lee Summer.
Leesum Music, Inc., 1986.
Best-selling record by Henry Lee Summer, from the album *Henry Lee
Summer* (CBS-Associated, 88).

I Wish I Was Eighteen Again
Words and music by Sonny Throckmorton.
Tree Publishing Co., Inc., 1978.
Best-selling record by George Burns from *I Wish I Was Eighteen Again*
(Mercury, 80).

I Wish It So
Words and music by Marc Blitzstein.

Chappell & Co., Inc., 1959.
Introduced in the 1959 musical *Juno,* this song was revived by Emily
Loesser in the revue *Together Again (for the First Time),* which she
staged with her mother, Jo Sullivan, in 1989.

I Wish That I Could Hurt That Way Again
Words and music by Rafe Vanhoy, Curly Putman, and Roger Cook.
Tree Publishing Co., Inc., 1986/Cross Keys Publishing Co., Inc.
Best-selling record by T. Graham Brown from the album *I Tell It Like It
Used to Be* (Capitol, 86).

I Wonder Do You Think of Me
Words and music by Sanger D. Shafer.
Acuff-Rose Publications Inc., 1986.
Best-selling record by Keith Whitley from *I Wonder Do You Think of
Me* (RCA, 89); the song became a poignant epitaph for the country
singer, who died in 1989.

I Wonder If I Take You Home
Words and music by Full Force.
My My Music, 1985/Mokajumbi, 1985/Personal Music, 1985.
Best-selling record by Lisa Lisa and Cult Jam with Full Force from the
album *Lisa Lisa and Cult with Full Force* (Columbia, 85).

I Wonder Who She's Seeing Now
Words and music by Jimmy George and Lou Pardini.
Geffen Music, 1987/Lucky Break, 1987/Pardini, 1987.
Best-selling record by The Temptations, from the album *Together Again*
(Motown, 87).

I Wonder Who's out Tonight
Words and music by Marie Burns and Ron Riddle.
Cak Songs, 1986/Songs of Jennifer/Thunderkat/Marie Burns.
Introduced by The Burns Sisters on the television documentary *After the
Sexual Revolution: Women in the Eighties* and on their LP *The Burns
Sisters Band.* Co-author is the group's drummer-orchestrator.

I Won't Back Down (English)
Words and music by Tom Petty and Jeff Lynne.
Gone Gator Music, 1989/EMI-April Music, 1989.
Best-selling record by Tom Petty from *Full Moon Fever* (MCA, 89).

I Won't Be Home Tonight (English)
Words and music by Tony Carey.
WB Music, 1982.
Best-selling record by Tony Carey from *Toney Carey (I Won't Be Home
Tonight)* (Rocshire, 83).

I Won't Forget You
Words and music by Bobby Dall, C. C. Deville, Brett Michaels, and Rikki Rockett.
Sweet Cyanide, 1987/Willesden Music, Inc., 1987.
Best-selling record by Poison, from the album *Look What the Cat Dragged In* (Enigma, 87).

I Won't Hold You Back
Words and music by Steve Lukather.
BMG Songs Inc., 1982.
Best-selling record by Toto from *Toto IV* (Columbia, 83).

I Won't Need You Anymore (Always and Forever)
Words and music by Troy Seals and Max D. Barnes.
Warner-Tamerlane Music, 1987/Face the Music, 1987/Blue Lake Music, 1987.
Best-selling record by Randy Travis, from the album *Always and Forever* (Warner Bros., 87).

I Won't Take Less Than Your Love
Words and music by Paul Overstreet and Paul Schlitz.
MCA Music, 1987/Don Schlitz Music, 1987/Writer's Group Music, 1987/Scarlet Moon Music, 1987.
Best-selling record in 1988 by Tanya Tucker with Paul Davis and Paul Overstreet, from *Love Me Like You Used To* (Capitol, 87).

I Would Die 4 U
Words and music by Prince Rogers Nelson.
Controversy Music, 1984/WB Music, 1984.
Best-selling record by Prince & The Revolution from the film and soundtrack album *Purple Rain* (Warner Brothers, 84).

I Wouldn't Change You If I Could
Words and music by Arthur Q. Smith and Paul H. Jones.
Peer International Corp., 1952.
Best-selling record by Ricky Skaggs from *Highways & Heartaches* (Epic, 83).

I Wouldn't Have Missed It for the World
Words and music by Kye Fleming, Dennis Morgan, and Charles Quillen.
Hall-Clement Publications, 1981.
Best-selling record by Ronnie Milsap from *Theirs No Gettin' over Me* (RCA, 82).

I Write Your Name
Words and music by Jim Carroll and Wayne Woods.
Dr. Benway Music, 1983.
Introduced by Jim Carroll in *I Write Your Name* (Atlantic, 83).

Ice Cream for Crow
Words and music by Don Van Vliet.
Singing Ink Music, 1982.
Introduced on *Ice Cream for Crow* by Captain Beefheart (Virgin/Epic, 82).

Icy Blue Heart
Words and music by John Hiatt.
Lillybilly, 1988/Bug Music, 1988.
Introduced by Emmylou Harris on *Bluebird* (Reprise, 89).

I'd Love to Lay You Down
Words and music by Johnny MacRae.
Tree Publishing Co., Inc., 1978.
Best-selling record in 1980 by Conway Twitty (MCA).

I'd Rather Have Nothin' All of the Time Than Something for a Little While
Words and music by Bert Williams.
Revived by Ben Harney in *Williams and Walker*, a play about the legendary black vaudevillian Bert Williams, who also created the 1903 Broadway musical *Dahomey*. It was the first major Broadway production written and performed by black artists.

I'd Still Say Yes
Words and music by Babyface (pseudonym for Kenny Edmunds), Gary Scelsa, and Joyce Fenderella Irby.
Now & Future, 1987/PSO Ltd., 1987/Klymaxx, 1987/Hip-Trip Music Co., 1987/Hip Chic, 1987.
Best-selling record by Klymaxx, from the album *Klymaxx* (MCA, 87).

Ideal World (English)
Words and music by Henry Priestman and Mark Herman.
Virgin Music, 1988/Copyright Control, 1988.
Introduced by The Christians on *The Christians* (Island, 88).

If Anyone Falls
Words and music by Sandy Stewart and Stephanie Nicks.
Welsh Witch Publishing, 1982/Sweet Talk Music Co., 1982.
Best-selling record by Stevie Nicks from *The Wild Heart* (Modern, 83).

If Ever You're in My Arms Again
Words by Cynthia Weil, words and music by Michael Masser, music by Tom Snow.
Almo Music Corp., 1984/Prince Street Music, 1984/Snow Music, 1984/ Dyad Music, Ltd., 1984.
Best-selling record by Peabo Bryson from *Straight from the Heart* (Elektra, 84).

If Hollywood Don't Need You Honey I Still Do
Words and music by Bob McDill.
Hall-Clement Publications, 1982.
Best-selling record by Don Williams from *Listen to the Radio* (MCA, 82).

If I Could Turn Back Time
Words and music by Diane Warren.
Realsongs, 1989.
Best-selling record by Cher from *Heart of Stone* (Geffen, 89).

If I Had a Boat
Words and music by Lyle Lovett.
Michael H. Goldsen, Inc., 1987/Lyle Lovett, 1987.
Introduced by Lyle Lovett on *Pontiac* (MCA/Curb, 87).

If I Had a Rocket Launcher (Canadian)
Words and music by Bruce Cockburn.
Golden Mountain Music Inc., 1984.
Best-selling record by Bruce Cockburn in 1985 from the album *Stealing Fire* (Gold Mountain, 84).

If I Had You
Words and music by Kerry Chater and Danny Mayo.
Acuff-Rose Publications Inc., 1988/Tioaga Street Music, 1988/Hear No Evil, 1988.
Best-selling record by Alabama from *Southern Star* (RCA, 89).

If I Had You
Words and music by Steve Dorff, Gary Harju, and Larry Herbstritt.
Careers Music Inc., 1980.
Originally recorded in 1980 for a solo project that was cancelled because of Karen Carpenter's death in 1983, the song was first released on The Carpenters' album *Love Lines* (A & M, 89).

If I Loved You
Words by Oscar II Hammerstein, music by Richard Rodgers.
Williamson Music, 1945.
Revived by Barbra Streisand on *The Broadway Album* (Columbia, 85).

If I Only Had a Brain
Words by E.Y. 'Yip' Harburg, music by Harold Arlen.
Leo Feist Inc., 1939.
This tune from the classic film *The Wizard of Oz* was revived by Michael Feinstein on *The MGM Album* (Elektra, 89).

If I Sing
Words by Richard Maltby, music by David Shire.
Progeny Music, 1989/Revelation Music Publishing Corp., 1989/Long

Pond Music, 1989/Fiddleback, 1989.
Introduced by Richard Muenz in *Closer Than Ever*, a concert setting of songs by Maltby and Shire, who earlier wrote the Broadway Musical *Baby*.

If I'd Been the One
Words and music by Don Barnes, Jeff Carlisi, Donnie Van Zant, and Larry Steele.
Rocknocker Music Co., 1983.
Best-selling record by 38 Special from *Tour De Force* (A & M, 83).

If I'm Not Your Lover
Words and music by Al B. Sure, Timothy Gatling, and Terry Riley.
EMI-April Music, 1988/Across 110th Street Music, 1988/Zomba Music, 1988/Donril Music, 1988/Cal-Gene Music, 1988.
Best-selling record in 1989 by Al B. Sure from *In Effect Mode* (Warner Bros., 88).

If It Ain't One Thing It's Another
Words and music by Richard 'Dimples' Fields and Belinda Wilson.
On the Boardwalk Music, 1982/Dat Richfield Kat Music, 1982/Songs Can Sing, 1982.
Best-selling record by Richard 'Dimples' Fields from *Mr. Look So Good* (Boardwalk, 82).

If It Don't Come Easy
Words and music by Dave Gibson and Craig Karp.
Silverline Music, Inc., 1988/Songmedia, 1988.
Best-selling record in 1988 by Tanya Tucker, from *Love Me Like You Used To* (Capitol, 87).

If It Isn't Love
Words and music by James III Harris and Terry Lewis.
Avant Garde Music Publishing, Inc., 1988/Flyte Tyme Tunes, 1988.
Best-selling record by New Edition, from *Heart Break* (MCA, 88).

If Love Was a Train
Words and music by Michelle Shocked.
Polygram Songs, 1988.
Introduced by Michelle Shocked on *Short Sharp Shocked* (Mercury, 88), this was one of the most requested songs from the radical folksinger.

If Love Were All (English)
Words and music by Noel Coward.
Warner Brothers, Inc., 1929.
Revived by Barbara Cook on *It's Better with a Band* (Moss Music Group, 81).

If Only You Knew
Words and music by Kenny Gamble, Dexter Wansel, and Cynthia
  Biggs.
Assorted Music, 1981.
Best-selling record by Patti LaBelle from *I'm in Love Again*
  (Philadelphia International, 84).

If She Knew What She Wants
Words and music by Jules Shear.
Funzalo Music, 1986/Juters Publishing Co.
Best-selling record by The Bangles from the album *Different Light*
  (Columbia, 86). Also released on *Demo-itis* by Jules Shear (Enigma,
  86).

If She Would Have Been Faithful
Words and music by Randy Goodrum and Stephen Kipner.
EMI-April Music, 1987/Stephen A. Kipner Music, 1987/California
  Phase Music, 1987.
Best-selling record by Chicago, from the album *18* (Warner Bros., 87).

If This Is It
Words and music by John Colla and Huey Lewis.
Hulex Music, 1983/Chrysalis Music Group, 1983.
Best-selling record by Huey Lewis & The News from *Sports* (Chrysalis,
  84).

If This World Were Mine
Words and music by Marvin Gaye.
Jobete Music Co., 1967.
Featured on *Instant Love* by Cheryl Lynn (Columbia, 82).

If Tomorrow Never Comes
Words and music by Kent Blazy and Garth Brooks.
Evanlee, 1989/Major Bob Music, 1989.
Best-selling record by Garth Brooks from *Garth Brooks* (Capitol, 89).

If We Hold on Together
Words by Will Jennings, music by James Horner.
MCA Music, 1988.
Introduced by Diana Ross for the animated film *The Land Before Time*;
  also on its soundtrack album (MCA, 88).

If We Were in Love
Words by Alan Bergman and Marilyn Bergman, music by John
  Williams.
EMI Variety Catalogue, 1981/Threesome Music Co., 1981.
Introduced by Placido Domingo in *Yes Giorgio* (81). Nominated for an
  Academy Award, Best Song of the Year, 1982.

If Wishes Were Changes
Words and music by Nanci Griffith and James Hooker.
Irving Music Inc., 1989/Ponder Heart Music, 1989.
Introduced by by Nanci Griffith on *Storms* (MCA, 89).

If You Ain't Lovin' (You Ain't Livin')
Words and music by Tom Collins.
Beechwood Music, 1954.
Best-selling record by Ricky Van Shelton, from *Loving Proof*
   (Columbia, 88).

If You Can Do It: I Can Too
Words and music by Paul Laurence.
Bush Burnin' Music, 1987.
Best-selling record in 1988 by Meli'sa Morgan from *Good Love*
   (Capitol, 87).

If You Change Your Mind
Words and music by Rosanne Cash and Hank Devito.
Chelcait Music, 1987/Almo Music Corp., 1987/Bug Music, 1987/Little
   Nemo, 1987.
Best-selling record in 1988 by Rosanne Cash, from *King's Record Shop*
   (Columbia, 87).

If You Don't Know Me by Now
Words and music by Leon Huff and Kenny Gamble.
Assorted Music, 1972.
Won a Grammy Award, and Rhythm 'n' Blues Song of the Year, 1989.

If You Ever Change Your Mind
Words and music by Parker McGee and Bob Gundry.
Dawnbreaker Music Co., 1980/Silver Nightingale Music, 1980.
Best-selling record by Crystal Gayle from *These Days* (Columbia, 80).

If You Leave (English)
Words and music by Orchestral Manoeuvres in the Dark.
Virgin Music, 1986/Famous Music Corp.
Best-selling record by Orchestral Manoeuvres in the Dark from the 1986
   film *Pretty in Pink* and subsequent soundtrack album (A & M, 86).

If You Love Somebody Set Them Free (English)
Words and music by Sting (pseudonym for Gordon Sumner).
Reggatta Music, Ltd., 1985.
Best-selling record by Sting from the album *The Dream of the Blue
   Turtles* (A & M, 85).

If You Think You're Lonely Now
Words and music by Bobby Womack, Patrick Moten, and Richard
   Griffin.

Ashtray Music, 1981/Moriel, 1981/ABKCO Music Inc., 1981.
Best-selling record by Bobby Womack from *The Poet* (Beverly Glen, 82).

If You're Gonna Play in Texas (You Gotta Have a Fiddle in the Band)
Words and music by Dan Mitchell and Murry Kellum.
Baray Music Inc., 1984/Dale Morris Music, 1984.
Best-selling record by Alabama from *Roll On* (RCA, 84).

If You're Thinking You Want a Stranger (There's One Coming Home)
Words and music by Blake Mevis and David Willis.
Polygram International, 1981.
Best-selling record by George Strait from *Greatest Hits* (MCA, 82).

Iko-Iko
Words and music by Marylin Jones, Sharon Jones, Joe Jones, and Jessie Thomas.
Arc Music, 1964/Melder Publishing Co., Inc., 1964.
Revived in 1983 by the Belle Stars on their album, *The Belle Stars.*
Their rendition was used on the soundtrack of the 1989 hit movie *Rain Man* and released on the album of the film (Capitol, 89).

I'll Always Come Back
Words and music by K. T. Oslin.
Wooden Wonder, 1987.
Best-selling record in 1988 by K.T. Oslin, from *80's Ladies* (MCA, 87).

I'll Always Love You
Words and music by Jimmy George.
Auspitz Music, 1987/Lucky Break, 1987.
Best-selling record by Taylor Dayne from *Tell It To My Heart* (MCA, 88). Nominated for a Grammy Award, Rhythm 'n' Blues Song of the Year, 1988.

I'll Be Alright without You
Words and music by Steve Perry, Jonathan Cain, and Neal Schon.
Colgems-EMI Music, 1986.
Best-selling record in 1987 by Journey, from the album *Raised on Radio* (Columbia, 86).

I'll Be Loving You (Forever)
Words and music by Maurice Starr.
EMI-April Music, 1988/Maurice Starr Music, 1988.
Best-selling record by New Kids on the Block from *Hangin' Tough* (Columbia, 88).

I'll Be over You
Words and music by Steve Lukather and Randy Goodrum.
BMG Songs Inc., 1986/California Phase Music.
Best-selling record by Toto from the album *Farenheit* (Columbia, 86).

I'll Be There for You
Words and music by Nick Ashford and Valerie Simpson.
Nick-O-Val Music, 1989.
Best-selling record by Ashford and Simpson from *Love or Physical* (Capitol, 89).

I'll Be There for You
Words and music by Jon Bon Jovi and Richie Sambora.
Bon Jovi Publishing, 1988/New Jersey Underground, 1988/Polygram Songs, 1988.
Best-selling record in 1989 by Bon Jovi from *New Jersey* (Mercury/Polygram, 88).

I'll Be You
Words and music by Paul Westerberg.
NAH Music, 1989.
Introduced by The Replacements on *Don't Tell a Soul* (Sire, 89).

I'll Be Your Baby Tonight
Words and music by Bob Dylan.
Special Rider Music, 1969.
Revived in 1987 by Judy Rodman on the album *A Place Called Love* (MTM, 87).

I'll Come Back as Another Woman
Words and music by Bob Carpenter and Kent Robbins.
Let There Be Music Inc., 1985/Irving Music Inc., 1985.
Best-selling record in 1987 by Tanya Tucker, from the album *Girls Like Me* (Capitol, 86).

I'll Keep It with Mine
Words and music by Bob Dylan.
Special Rider Music, 1965.
Rhythm 'n' Blues Bob Dylan on the five-record retrospective *Biograph* (Columbia, 85). Previously recorded by Nico with the Velvet Underground and by others.

I'll Leave This World Loving You
Words and music by Wayne Kemp.
Tree Publishing Co., Inc., 1974.
Best-selling record by Ricky Van Shelton, from *Loving Proof* (Columbia, 88).

I'll Never Stop Loving You
Words and music by Dave Loggins and J. D. Martin.
Music of the World, 1985/Leeds Music Corp., 1985/Patchwork Music, 1985.
Best-selling record by Gary Morris from the album *Anything Goes* (Warner Bros., 85).

(No Matter How High I Get) I'll Still Be Lookin' up to You
Words and music by Bobby Womack and P. Kisch.
ABKCO Music Inc., 1985/Ashtray Music, 1985.
Best-selling record by Wilton Felder featuring Bobby Womack, from the album *Secrets* (MCA, 85).

I'll Still Be Loving You
Words and music by Mary Ann Kennedy, Pat Bunch, Pam Rose, and Todd Cerney.
Warner-Tamerlane Music, 1986/Heart Wheel, 1986/Chriswald Music, 1986/Hopi Sound Music, 1986/Chappell & Co., Inc., 1986.
Best-selling record in 1987 by Restless Heart, from the album *Wheels* (RCA, 86). Nominated for a Grammy Award, Country Song of the Year, 1987.

I'll Tumble 4 Ya (English)
Words and music by Roy Hay, Jon Moss, Michael Craig, and George O'Dowd.
Virgin Music, 1982.
Best-selling record by Culture Club from *Kissing to be Clever* (Virgin/ Epic, 83).

I'll Wait
Words and music by Eddie Van Halen, Alex Van Halen, Michael Anthony, David Lee Roth, and Michael H. McDonald.
Van Halen Music, 1983/Genevieve Music, 1983/Diamond Dave Music, 1983.
Best-selling record by Van Halen from *1984* (Warner Brothers, 84).

Illusions
Words and music by Will Holt.
Lemon Tree Music, Inc., 1981.
Introduced by Jane White in *Ah, Men* (81).

I'm Alive
Words and music by Clint Ballard, Jr.
Camelback Mountain Music Corp., 1982.
Best-selling record by ELO from the film and sountrack album *Xanadu* (MCA, 80).

I'm Alright (Theme from *Caddyshack*)
Words and music by Kenny Loggins.

Milk Money Music, 1980.
Best-selling record by Kenny Loggins (Columbia, 80). Introduced in the film & soundtrack album *Caddyshack* (80).

I'm Coming Out
Words and music by Bernard Edwards and Nile Rodgers.
Chic Music Inc., 1980.
Best-selling record by Diana Ross from *Diana* (Motown, 80).

I'm for Love
Words and music by Hank Williams, Jr.
Bocephus Music Inc., 1985.
Best-selling record by Hank Williams, Jr. from the album *Five-O* (Warner Bros., 85).

I'm for Real
Words and music by Howard Hewett and Stanley Clark.
Warner Brothers, Inc., 1986/E/A Music/Make It Big/Clarkee.
Best-selling record by Howard Hewett from the album *I Commit to Love* (Elktra, 86).

I'm Glad You Didn't Know Me
Words and music by Craig Carnelia.
Carnelia Music, 1982.
Introduced by Philip Hoffman and Cynthia Carle in *Is There Life After High School* (82).

I'm Goin' Down
Words and music by Bruce Springsteen.
Bruce Springsteen Publishing, 1984.
Best-selling record by Bruce Springsteen in 1985 from the album *Born in the U.S.A.* (Columbia, 84).

I'm Gonna Get You
Words and music by Dennis Linde.
Dennis Linde Music, 1988.
Best-selling record by Eddy Raven from *Best of Eddy Raven* (RCA, 88).

I'm Gonna Hire a Wino to Decorate Our Home
Words and music by DeWayne Blackwell.
Peso Music, 1982/Wallet Music, 1982.
Best-selling record by David Frizzell (Warner/Viva, 82). Nominated for a Grammy Award, Country Song of the Year, 1982.

I'm Gonna Lose You (English)
Words and music by Mick Hucknall.
SBK Songs Ltd., England/WB Music, 1987.
Introduced by Simply Red in the film and on the soundtrack album *Frantic* (Elektra, 88).

I'm Gonna Love Her for the Both of Us
Words and music by Jim Steinman.
E. B. Marks Music Corp., 1981/Peg Music Co., 1981.
Best-selling record by Meat Loaf from *Dead Ringer* (Cleveland
International, 81).

I'm Gonna Miss You Girl (Canadian)
Words and music by Jesse Winchester.
Fourth Floor Music Inc./Fiction Music, 1988/Hot Kitchen Music, 1988.
Best-selling record by Michael Martin Murphey, from *River of Time*
(RCA, 88).

I'm Gonna Tear Your Playhouse Down
Words and music by Earl Randall.
Jec Publishing Corp., 1972.
Best-selling record by Paul Young from the album *The Secret of
Association* (Columbia, 85).

I'm in Love
Words and music by Kashif (pseudonym for Michael Jones).
Music of the World, 1981.
Best-selling record by Evelyn King from *I'm in Love* (RCA, 81).

I'm in Love
Words and music by Paul Laurence and Timmy Allen.
Bush Burnin' Music, 1987/Willesden Music, Inc., 1987.
Best-selling record by Lillo Thomas, from the album *Lillo* (Capitol, 87).

I'm into Something Good
Words by Gerry Goffin, music by Carole King.
Screen Gems-EMI Music Inc., 1964.
Revived in 1989 by Peter Noone in the film and soundtrack album *The
Naked Gun* (Cypress, 89).

I'm No Angel
Words and music by Tony Colton and P. Palmer.
EMI-April Music, 1987/ATV Music Corp., 1987/Unichappell Music
Inc., 1987.
Best-selling record by The Gregg Allman Band, from the album *I'm No
Angel* (Epic, 87).

I'm No Stranger to the Rain
Words and music by Sonny Curtis and Ron Hellard.
Tree Publishing Co., Inc., 1986.
Best-selling record in 1989 by Keith Whitley from *Don't Close Your
Eyes* (RCA, 88).

I'm Not Ashamed to Cry
Words and music by Jack Elliott.
Underdog, 1987.
Introduced by Ramblin' Jack Elliott (Bear Creek, 1987); the singer-songwriter, whose folksinging inspired Bob Dylan and Arlo Guthrie in the 1960's, had gone many years without issuing a record.

I'm Not from Here
Words and music by James McMurtry.
Short Trip Music, 1989.
Introduced by James McMurtry, son of novelist Larry McMurtry, on *Too Long in the Wasteland* (Columbia, 89).

I'm on Fire
Words and music by Bruce Springsteen.
Bruce Springsteen Publishing, 1984.
Best-selling record by Bruce Springsteen in 1985 from the album *Born in the U.S.A.* (Columbia, 84).

I'm Real
Words and music by Full Force, words and music by James Brown.
Forceful Music, 1988/Willesden Music, Inc., 1988.
Best-selling record by James Brown, from *I'm Real* (Scotti Brothers, 88).

I'm So Excited
Words and music by Anita Pointer, June Pointer, Trevor Lawrence, and Ruth Pointer.
Braintree Music, 1982/Ruth Pointer Publishing, 1982/EMI-Blackwood Music Inc., 1982/Anita Pointer Publishing, 1982/Leggs Four Publishing, 1982.
Best-selling record by The Pointer Sisters from *So Excited* (Planet, 82).

I'm So Glad I'm Standing Here Today
Words and music by Joe Sample and Will Jennings.
Irving Music Inc., 1981/Blue Sky Rider Songs, 1981/Four Knights Music Co., 1981.
Best-selling record by The Crusaders from *Standing Tall* (MCA, 81).

I'm Still Crazy
Words and music by Vern Gosdin, Steve Gosdin, and Buddy Cannon.
Hookem Music, 1989/Buddy Cannon Music, 1989/Polygram International, 1989.
Best-selling record by Vern Gosdin from *Alone* (Columbia, 89).

I'm Still Standing (English)
Words by Bernie Taupin, music by Elton John.

Intersong, USA Inc., 1983.
Best-selling record by Elton John from *Elton John's Greatest Hits, Volume III, 1979-1987* (Geffen, 83).

I'm Supposed to Have Sex with You
Words and music by Tonio K. (pseudonym for Steve Krikorian).
Famous Music Corp., 1987/Polygram International, 1987/Evie Music Inc., 1987.
Introduced by Tonio K. on the soundtrack of the film *Summer School* and on its album.

I'm That Type of Guy
Words and music by James T. Smith and Dwayne Simon.
Def Jam, 1989/L.L. Cool J Music, 1989/D & D Music, 1989/Virgin Music, 1989.
Best-selling record by LL Cool J from *Walking with a Panther* (Def Jam, 89).

I'm Your Man (English)
Words and music by George Michael.
Chappell & Co., Inc., 1985.
Best-selling record by Wham! featuring George Michael from the album *Music from the Edge of Heaven* (Columbia, 85).

I'm Your Man (Canadian)
Words and music by Leonard Cohen.
Stranger Music Inc., 1987.
Introduced by Leonard Cohen on *I'm Your Man* (Columbia, 88).

Immortal for a While
Words and music by Terry Adams.
Dollar Clef Music, 1989.
Introduced by NRBQ, on *Wild Weekend* (Virgin, 89).

Impossible
Words and music by Peabo Bryson.
Peabo Bryson Enterprises, Inc., 1984/WB Music, 1984.
Introduced by Peabo Bryson in *I Am Love* (Capitol, 82).

Impossible Dreamer
Words and music by Joni Mitchell.
Crazy Crow Music, 1985.
Introduced by Joni Mitchell on the album *Dog Eat Dog* (Geffen, 85).

In a Big Country (Scottish)
Words and music by Big Country.
Virgin Music, 1983.
Best-selling record by Big Country from *The Crossing* (Mercury, 83).

In-A-Gadda-Da-Vida
Words and music by Doug Ingle.
Cotillion Music Inc., 1968/Ten-East Music, 1968/Itasca Music, 1968.
Revived in 1987 by Slayer for the film and soundtrack album *Less than Zero* (Def Jam, 87).

In a Letter to You
Words and music by Dennis Linde.
EMI-Blackwood Music Inc., 1989/Dennis Linde Music, 1989.
Best-selling record by Eddy Raven from *Temporary Sanity* (Universal, 89).

In a New York Minute
Words and music by Michael Garvin, Chris Waters, and Tom Shapiro.
Tree Publishing Co., Inc., 1985/O'Lyric Music, 1985.
Best-selling record by Ronnie McDowell from the album *In a New York Minute* (Epic, 85).

In America
Words and music by Charles Hayward, James Marshall, Joel DiGregorio, Charlie Daniels, Tom Crain, and Fred Edwards.
Hat Band Music, 1980.
Best-selling record by The Charlie Daniels Band from *Full Moon* (Epic, 80).

In Buddy's Eyes
Words and music by Stephen Sondheim.
Herald Square Music Co., 1971.
Revived by Barbara Cook on the album *Follies* (RCA, 85). This concert album featured the original cast of the 1971 musical.

In Cars
Words and music by Jimmy Webb.
White Oak Songs, 1981.
Introduced by Jim Webb in *Angel Heart* (Columbia/Lorimar, 82).

In God's Country (Irish)
Words and music by U2.
Polygram International, 1987.
Best-selling record U2, from the album *The Joshua Tree* (Island, 87).

In Love
Words and music by Mike Reid and Sam Dees.
BMG Songs Inc., 1986/Milsap.
Best-selling record by Ronnie Milsap from the album *Lost in the Fifties Tonight* (MCA, 86).

In Love with the Flame (English)
Words and music by Linda Thompson and Betsy Cook.

Firesign Music Ltd., England, 1985/Chappell & Co., Inc., 1985.
Introduced by Linda Thompson on the album *One Clear Moment* (Warner Bros., 85).

In My Darkest Hour
Words and music by Dave Mustaine and Dave Ellefson.
Mustaine Music, 1987/Theory Music, 1988/E.L.F., 1988.
Introduced by Megadeth in the film and on the soundtrack album *The Decline and Fall of Western Civilization, Part II, The Metal Years* (Capitol, 88).

In My Dreams
Words and music by Kevin Cronin and Tom Kelly.
Fate Music, 1987/Denise Barry Music, 1987.
Best-selling record by REO Speedwagon, from the album *Life as We Know It* (Epic, 87).

In My Eyes
Words and music by Barbara Wyrick.
Intersong, USA Inc., 1983.
Best-selling record by John Conlee (MCA, 84).

In My House
Words and music by Rick James.
Stone City Music, 1985.
Best-selling record by The Mary Jane Girls from the album *Only Four You* (Gordy, 85).

In the Air Tonight (English)
Words and music by Phil Collins.
Hit & Run Music, 1981.
Best-selling record by Phil Collins from *Face Value* (Atlantic, 81).
    Featured on *Miami Vice* (84).

In the Cards
Words by David Zippel, music by Alan Menken.
Menken Music, 1984/Trunksong Music, 1984.
Introduced by Wade Raley in *Diamonds* (84).

In the Dark
Words and music by Billy Squier.
Songs of the Knight, 1981.
Best-selling record by Billy Squier from *Don't Say No* (Capitol, 81).

In the Garden (English)
Words and music by Van Morrison.
Screen Gems-EMI Music Inc., 1986.
Introduced by Van Morrison on the album *No Guru, No Method, No Teacher* (Polygram, 86).

In the Middle of the Land (Australian)
Words and music by Dave Faulkner.
Copyright Control, 1987.
Introduced by the Hoodoo Gurus on the album *Blow Your Cool* (Elektra, 87).

(Pride) In the Name of Love (Irish)
Words and music by Bono (pseudonym for Paul Hewson), The Edge
   (pseudonym for Dave Evans), Adam Clayton, and Larry Mullen.
Island Music, 1984.
Best-selling record by U2 from *The Unforgettable Fine* (Island, 84).

In the Shape of a Heart
Words and music by Jackson Browne.
Swallow Turn Music, 1986.
Best-selling record by Jackson Browne from the album *Lives in the Balance* (Elektra, 86).

In This Love (English)
Words and music by David Coverdale and John Sykes.
Whitesnake, 1987/WB Music, 1987.
Best-selling record by Whitesnake, from the album *Whitesnake* (Geffen, 87).

In Too Deep (English)
Words and music by Tony Banks, Phil Collins, and Mike Rutherford.
Hit & Run Music, 1986.
Best-selling record by Genesis, from the album *Invisible Touch*
   (Atlantic, 86); this was the fifth single from this album to reach the
   top five.

In Your Eyes (Theme from *Say Anything*)
Words and music by Peter Gabriel.
Cliofine, 1987/Hidden Pun, 1987.
Introduced by Peter Gabriel on his 1987 album, *So,* the song became a
   best-seller after its use in the 1989 film *Say Anything* and was
   featured on the soundtrack album (WTG).

In Your Letter
Words and music by Gary Richrath.
Slam Dunk Music, 1980.
Best-selling record by REO Speedwagon from *Hi Infidelity* (Epic, 81).

In Your Room
Words and music by Susannah Hoffs, Billy Steinberg, and Tom Kelly.
EMI-Blackwood Music Inc., 1988/Bangophile Music, 1988/Sony Tunes,
   1988/Denise Barry Music, 1988.
Best-selling record by The Bangles from *Everything* (Columbia, 88). A
   collaboration between the hitmaking duo behind 1987's 'So

Emotional,' for Whitney Houston, and 'Alone,' for Heart, and the lead singer of the Bangles.

Incident on 57th Street
Words and music by Bruce Springsteen.
Bruce Springsteen Publishing, 1987.
Performed by Bruce Springsteen & The E Street Band. A live version, released as the B-side of 'Fire' has a playing time of ten minutes and three seconds, making it the longest B-side in history. The original studio version is on *The Wild, the Innocent, and the E Street Shuffle*.

Independence Day
Words and music by Bruce Springsteen.
Bruce Springsteen Publishing, 1979.
Introduced by Bruce Springsteen in *The River* (Columbia, 80).

Independence Day
Words and music by David Byrne.
Index Music, 1989.
Introduced by David Byrne on *Rei Momo* (Luaka Boys/Sire, 89).

Infatuation (English)
Words and music by Rod Stewart, Duane Hitchings, and Michael Omartian.
Rod Stewart, 1984/Full Keel Music, 1984/Roland Robinson Music, 1984.
Best-selling record by Rod Stewart from *Camouflage* (Warner Brothers, 84).

An Innocent Man
Words and music by Billy Joel.
Joelsongs, 1983.
Best-selling record by Billy Joel from *An Innocent Man* (Columbia, 84).

Insanity Street
Words and music by Lillie Palmer.
Maizery Music, 1989/Lost Lake Arts Music, 1989.
Introduced by Lillie Palmer on *Legacy* (Windham Hill, 89). This anti-war lament is based on a poem by Eunice Anttalainen.

Inside Love (So Personal)
Words and music by Kashif (pseudonym for Michael Jones).
Music of the World, 1983.
Best-selling record by George Benson from *In Your Eyes* (Warner Brothers, 83).

Interesting Drug (English)
Words by Morrissey (pseudonym for Tommy Morrissey), music by Stephen Street.

221

Bona Relations Music, 1989/Warner-Tamerlane Music, 1989/Copyright
    Control, 1989.
Introduced by Morrissey on *Morrissey* (Sire, 89).

Into the Heart (Irish)
Words and music by Bono (pseudonym for Paul Hewson), Larry
    Mullen, Adam Clayton, and The Edge (pseudonym for Dave Evans).
Polygram International, 1980.
Introduced by U2 in *Boy* (Island, 80).

Into the Night
Words and music by Benny Mardones and Robert Tepper.
Conus Music, 1980.
Best-selling record by Benny Mardones from *Never Run, Never Hide*
    (Polydor, 80). Song, and album became hits again in 1988. (Polydor,
    80).

Invincible (Theme from *The Legend of Billie Jean*)
Words and music by Holly Knight and Simon Climie.
Makiki Publishing Co., Ltd., 1985/BMG Songs Inc., 1985/Chrysalis
    Music Group, 1985.
Best-selling record by Pat Benatar (Chrysalis, 85). Introduced in the film
    and soundtrack album *The Legend of Billie Jean* 85.

Invisible Touch (English)
Words and music by Phil Collins and Mike Rutherford.
Hit & Run Music, 1986.
Best-selling record by Genesis from the album *Invisible Touch* (Atlantic,
    86).

I.O.U.
Words and music by Kerry Chater and Austin Roberts.
Vogue Music, 1983/MCA, Inc., 1983.
Best-selling record by Lee Greenwood from *Somebody's Gonna Love
    You* (MCA, 83). Nominated for a Grammy Award, Country Song of
    the Year, 1983.

Ireland (English)
Words and music by Marianne Faithfull and Barry Reynolds.
Island Music, 1983.
Introduced by Marianne Faithfull on *A Child's Adventure* (Island, 83).

Iris
Words and music by Mike Craver.
Introduced by Mike Craver in the 1987 show *Oil City Symphony* and on
    the original cast album (DEG, 88). The show was the winner of 1988
    Critics' Cirle Award for Best Off-Broadway Musical.

Is It Love (English)
Words and music by Richard Page, Steven George, Robert John 'Mutt' Lange, and Pat Mastellotto.
Warner-Tamerlane Music, 1986/Entente Music/Poppy-Due.
Best-selling record by Mr. Mister in 1986 from the album *Welcome to the Real World* (RCA, 85).

Is It Still Over
Words and music by Ken Bell and Larry Henley.
Ensign Music, 1988.
Best-selling record in 1989 by Randy Travis from *Old 8 X 10* (Warner Bros., 88).

Is It You
Words and music by Lee Ritenour, Eric Tagg, and Bill Champlin.
Rit of Habeas, 1981.
Best-selling record by Lee Ritenour from *'Rit'* (Elektra, 81).

Is That All There Is
Words and music by Jerry Leiber and Mike Stoller.
Jerry Stoller, 1966/Mike Stoller Music, 1966.
Revived in 1989 by Peggy Lee with the re-release of her album *Mirrors* (A & M, 75).

Is There Something I Should Know (English)
Words and music by Duran Duran.
BIOT Music Ltd., London, England, 1983.
Best-selling record by Duran Duran from *Arena* (Capitol, 83).

Is This Love
Words and music by Jim Peterik and Frankie Sullivan.
Easy Action Music, 1986/WB Music/Rude Music/Warner-Tamerlane Music.
Best-selling record by Survivor from the album *When Seconds Count* (Scotti Bros./CBS Associated, 86).

Islands in the Stream (English)
Words and music by Barry Gibb, Robin Gibb, and Maurice Gibb.
Gibb Brothers Music, 1983.
Best-selling record by Kenny Rogers and Dolly Parton from *Eyes That See in the Dark* (RCA, 83).

It Ain't Cool to Be Crazy About You
Words and music by Dean Dillon and Robbie Porter.
Larry Butler Music Co., 1986/EMI-Blackwood Music Inc./Southwind Music, Inc.
Best-selling record by George Strait from the album *#7* (MCA, 86).

It Ain't Enough (Canadian)
Words and music by Corey Hart.
Liesse Publishing, 1982.
Best-selling record by Corey Hart from *First Offense* (EMI-America, 84).

It Didn't Take Long
Words and music by Holly Knight.
Jiru Music, 1980/BMG Music, 1980.
Best-selling record by Spider from *Between the Lines* (Dreamland, 81).

It Don't Hurt Me Half as Bad
Words and music by Joe Allen, Deoin Lay, and Bucky Lindsey.
EMI Music Publishing, 1977.
Best-selling record by Ray Price (Dimension, 81).

It Isn't, It Wasn't, It Ain't Never Gonna Be
Words and music by Diane Warren and Albert Hammond.
Albert Hammond Enterprises, 1989/WB Music/Realsongs.
Best-selling record by Whitney Houston and Aretha Franklin (Arista, 89); featured on Aretha's album *Through the Storm* (Arista, 89).

It Might Be You
Words by Alan Bergman and Marilyn Bergman, music by Dave Grusin.
EMI-Gold Horizon Music Corp., 1982/Threesome Music Co., 1982/EMI Golden Torch Music, 1982.
Best-selling record by Stephen Bishop (Warner Brothers, 83). Introduced in the film and soundtrack album *Tootsie* (83). Nominated for an Academy Award, Best Song, 1982.

It Must Be Good for Me
Words by Jack Wohl and Jim Haimes, music by Mitch Leigh.
Andrew Scott Inc., 1966.
Revived in 1988 by Emily Zacharias in *Chu Chem*, a show that closed in its out-of-town tryout in Philadelphia, in 1966, when Moly Picon withdrew.

It Takes a Little Rain
Words and music by Roger Murrah and Steve Dean.
Tom Collins Music Corp., 1987.
Best-selling record by The Oak Ridge Boys, from the album *Where the Fast Lane Ends* (MCA, 87).

It Would Take a Strong Strong Man (English)
Words and music by Mike Stock, Matt Aitken, and Pete Waterman.
All Boys USA Music, 1987.
Best-selling record by Rick Astley from *Whenever You Need Somebody* (RCA, 88).

Itchin' for a Scratch
Words and music by Robin Halpin, Steve Stein, Doug Wimbish, and
Keith LeBlanc, words and music by Force M.D.'s.
Atlantic Recording Corp., England, 1985/Tee Girl Music, 1985/T-Boy
Music, 1985.
Introduced by Force M.D.'s (T-Boy, 85). Featured in the film *Rappin'*
(85).

It'll Be Me
Words and music by Sonny LeMaire and James P. Pennington.
Tree Publishing Co., Inc., 1986/Pacific Island Music.
Best-selling record by Exile from the album *Greatest Hits* (Epic, 86).

It's a Love Thing
Words and music by William Shelby and Dana Griffey.
Portrait/Solar Songs Inc., 1980.
Best-selling record by The Whispers from *Imagination* (Solar, 81).

It's a Lovely, Lovely World
Words and music by Boudleaux Bryant.
Acuff-Rose Publications Inc., 1952.
Best-selling record by Gail Davies (Warner Brothers, 81).

It's a Miracle (English)
Words and music by George O'Dowd, Jon Moss, Roy Hay, Mickey
Craig, and Phil Pickett.
Virgin Music, 1983/Warner-Tamerlane Music, 1983.
Best-selling record by Culture Club from *Colour by Numbers* (Epic, 84).

It's a Mistake (Australian)
Words and music by Colin Hay.
EMI-April Music, 1983.
Best-selling record by Men at Work from *Cargo* (Columbia, 83).

It's a Sin (English)
Words and music by Neil Tennant and Chris Lowe.
Virgin Music, 1987.
Best-selling record by the Pet Shop Boys, from the album *Actually*
(EMI-America, 87).

It's All Over Now Baby Blue
Words and music by Bob Dylan.
M. Witmark & Sons, 1965.
The Byrds' 1987 revival of this song on their album *Never Before*
caught on in 1988. The album was a collection of previously
unrealesed tracks.

It's Better with a Band
Words by David Zippel, music by Wally Harper.

Notable Music Co., Inc., 1981.
Performed by Sandy Duncan in *Five-Six-Seven-Eight...Dance* (83).

It's Getting Harder to Love You
Words and music by Michael Rupert and Jerry Colker.
Introduced by Mara Getz in the 1987 Los Angeles production of the
    musical *Mail*.

It's Gonna Be a Beautiful Night
Words and music by Prince Rogers Nelson.
Dramatis Music Corp., 1987.
Introduced by Prince in the film and soundtrack album *Sign 'o' the
    Times* (Paisley Park, 87).

It's Gonna Take a Miracle
Words and music by Teddy Randarro, Bobby Weinstein, and Lou
    Stallman.
Vogue Music, 1965.
Revived by Deniece Williams from *Niecy* (Arc, 82). Nominated for a
    Grammy Award, Rhythm 'n' Blues Song of the Year, 1982.

It's in the Way You Use It (English-Canadian)
Words and music by Eric Clapton and Robbie Robertson.
E.C. Music, England, 1986.
Introduced in the 1986 film *The Color of Money* (soundtrack album,
    MCA). Co-writer Robertson, formerly of The Band, previously served
    as musical director of *The King of Comedy* and its soundtrack album.
    Martin Scorcese directed both films. Best-selling record by Eric
    Clapton from the album *August* (MCA, 86).

It's Just a Matter of Time
Words and music by Brook Benton, Hendricks Belford, and Clyde Otis.
Eden Music, Inc., 1958/Times Square Music Publications Co., 1958.
Revived in 1989 by Randy Travis on *No Holding Back* (Warner Bros.,
    89) and *Rock and Rhythm and Blues* (Warner Bros., 89).

It's Like We Never Said Goodbye (English)
Words and music by Roger Greenaway and Geoff Stephens.
Dejamus Inc., 1978.
Best-selling record by Crystal Gayle from *Miss the Mississippi*
    (Columbia, 80).

It's Money That Matters
Words and music by Randy Newman.
Twice As Nice Music, 1988.
Best-selling record by Husband and Wife Randy Newman from *Land of
    Dreams* (Reprise, 88).

It's My Turn
Words by Carole Bayer Sager, music by Michael Masser.
Colgems-EMI Music, 1980/Unichappell Music Inc., 1980/Begonia
  Melodies, Inc., 1980.
Best-selling record by Diana Ross (Motown, 80). Introduced in the film
  & soundtrack album to *It's My Turn* (80).

It's No Crime
Words and music by L. A. Reid (pseudonym for Antonio Reid),
  Babyface (pseudonym for Kenny Edmunds), and Daryl Simmons.
Sony Tunes, 1989/Kear Music/Green Skirt Music.
Best-selling record by Babyface from *Tender Lover* (Solar, 89).

It's Not Enough
Words and music by Martin Page and Tommy Funderburk.
Martin Page Music, 1988/Zomba Music/Emotional Rex Music/DJO
  Music.
Best-selling record by Starship from *Love Among the Cannibals* (RCA,
  89).

It's Not Over ('Til It's Over)
Words and music by Robbie Nevil, John Van Torgeron, and Phil
  Galdston.
MCA Music, 1987/Tongerland, 1987/Kazoom, 1987.
Best-selling record by Starship, from the album *No Protection* (Grunt,
  87).

It's Now or Never
Words and music by Aaron Schroeder and Wally Gold.
Gladys Music, 1960.
Revived by John Schneider from *Now or Never* (Scotti Brothers, 81).

It's Only Love (Canadian)
Words and music by Bryan Adams and Jim Valance.
Adams Communications, Inc., 1985/Calypso Toonz, 1985/Irving Music
  Inc., 1985.
Best-selling record by Bryan Adams and Tina Turner from the album
  Reckless (A & M, 85).

It's Raining Again (English)
Words and music by Rick Davies and Roger Hodgson.
Delicate Music, 1982.
Best-selling record by Supertramp from ... *famous last words* (A & M,
  82).

It's Raining Men
Words and music by Paul Jabara and Paul Shaffer.
Songs of Manhattan Island Music Co., 1981/Olga Music, 1981/Postvalda

Music, 1981.
Best-selling record by The Weather Girls (Columbia, 83).

It's Still Rock and Roll to Me
Words and music by Billy Joel.
Impulsive Music, 1980/EMI-April Music, 1980.
Best-selling record by Billy Joel from *Glass Houses* (Columbia, 80).

It's Such a Small World
Words and music by Rodney Crowell.
Granite Music Corp., 1988/Coolwell Music, 1988.
Best-selling record by husband and wife Rodney Crowell and Rosanne
  Cash, from *Diamonds and Dirt* (Columbia, 88).

It's the End of the World as We Know It (and I Feel Fine)
Words and music by Bill Berry, Peter Buck, Mike Mills, and Michael
  Stipe.
Night Garden Music, 1987/Unichappell Music Inc., 1987.
Introduced by R.E.M. on the album *Document* (IRS, 87), a national
  breakthrough for this favorite band of college audiences.

It's the Real Thing
Words and music by Angela Winbush.
Angel Notes Music, 1989/WB Music.
Best-selling record by Angela Winbush from *The Real Thing* (Mercury,
  89).

I've Been Around Enough to Know
Words and music by Bob McDill and Dickey Lee.
Hall-Clement Publications, 1975.
Best-selling record by John Schneider from *Too Good to Stop Now*
  (MCA, 84).

I've Been in Love Before (English)
Words and music by Nick Eede.
EMI-Virgin, 1987.
Best-selling record by Cutting Crew, from the album *Broadcast* (Virgin,
  87).

I've Been Lookin'
Words and music by James Ibbotson and Jeff Hanna.
Jeff Who Music, 1988/Bughouse, 1988.
Best-selling record by Nitty Gritty Dirt Band, from *Workin Band*
  (Warner Bros., 88).

I've Got a Rock and Roll Heart
Words and music by Troy Seals, Eddie Setser, and Steve Diamond.
WB Music, 1981/Warner-Tamerlane Music, 1981/Diamond Mine Music,
  1981/Face the Music, 1981.

Best-selling record by Eric Clapton from *Money & Cigarettes* (Duck, 83).

I've Never Been to Me
Words and music by Ron Miller and Ken Hirsh.
Stone Diamond Music, 1976.
Revived by Charlene on *I've Never Been To Me* Motown, 82).

I've Noticed a Change
Words and music by Douglas J. Cohen.
Introduced by June Gable, Liz Callahan, and Stephen Bogardus in *No Way to Treat a Lady*. The author received a Richard Rodgers development grant prior to the show's Broadway production.

I've Still Got My Bite
Words and music by Micki Grant.
Introduced by Mabel King in *It's So Nice to Be Civilized* (80).

Ivory Tower (English)
Words and music by Van Morrison.
Essential Music, 1986.
Introduced by Van Morrison on the album *No Guru, No Method, No Teacher* (Polygram, 86).

J

Jack and Diane
Words and music by John Cougar Mellencamp.
Full Keel Music, 1982.
Best-selling record by John Cougar from *American Fool* (Riva/Mercury, 82).

Jack Gets Up
Words and music by Leo Kottke.
Round Wound Sound, 1989/Bug Music.
Introduced by Leo Kottke on *My Father's Face* (Private Music, 89).

Jacob's Ladder
Words and music by Bruce Hornsby and John Hornsby.
Zappo Music, 1986/Basically Gasp Music/Bob-a-Lew Music.
Introduced by Huey Lewis & The News on the album *Fore* (Chrysalis, 86).

Jam on It
Words and music by Maurice Cenac.
Wicked Stepmother Music Publishing Corp., 1984/Wedot Music, 1984.
Best-selling record by Newcleus from *Jam on Revenge* (Sunnyview, 84).

Jam Tonight
Words and music by Freddie Jackson and Paul Laurence.
Wavemaker Music Group Inc., 1987.
Best-selling record in 1987 by Freddie Jackson, perhaps the most popular black ballad singer of the era, from the album *Just Like the First Time* (Capitol, 86). Jackson started out in a band called LJE with co-author Paul Laurence.

James
Words and music by Vicki Peterson.
Illegal Songs, Inc., 1984/Bangophile Music, 1984.
Introduced by The Bangles on *All over the Place* (Columbia, 84).

Jamie
Words and music by Ray Parker, Jr.
Raydiola Music, 1984.
Best-selling record by Ray Parker, Jr. from *Chartbusters* (Arista, 84).

Jammin' Me
Words and music by Tom Petty, Mike Campbell, and Bob Dylan.
Gone Gator Music, 1987/Wild Gator Music, 1987/Special Rider Music, 1987.
Best-selling record by Tom Petty, from the album *Let Me Up I've Had Enough* (MCA, 87). This song was the product of a spontaneous writing session by Dylan and Petty; Campbell, whose credits include 'The Boys of Summer,' was called in later to polish the effort.

Jane
Words and music by David Friedberg, Jim McPherson, Craig Chaquico, and Paul Kantner.
Pods Publishing, 1979/Lunatunes Music, 1979/Little Dragon Music, 1979/Kosher Dill Music, 1979.
Best-selling record by The Jefferson Starship from *Freedom at Point Zero* (Grunt, 80).

Jeanny (German)
Words and music by Falco (pseudonym for Hans Hoelzl).
Bolland, Germany, 1985/Nada, Germany/Manuskript, Germany.
Introduced by Falco on the album *Falco 3* (A & M, 86). The song went to number one on the West German charts despite the indignant reaction of women's groups to its video, which depicted the rape and murder of a young girl.

Jeopardy
Words and music by Greg Kihn and Steven Wright.
Rye-Boy Music, 1983/Well Received Music, 1983.
Best-selling record by The Greg Kihn Band from *With the Naked Eye* (Beserkley, 83).

Jersey Girl
Words and music by Tom Waits.
Fifth Floor Music Inc., 1980.
Introduced by Tom Waits on *Heartattack and Vine* (Asylum, 80).
Recorded by Bruce Springsteen on *Bruce Springsteen & The E Street Band Live, 1975-1985* (Columbia, 84).

Jerusalem (English)
Words by William Blake, words and music by C. Hubert and H. Parry.
Robertson Publishing, 1978/Theodore Presser Co., 1978.
Performed by Judy Collins on her album *Trust Your Heart* (Gold Castle,

87); the song, based on a poem by Blake, was originally from the 1981 film *Chariots of Fire.*

Jesse
Words and music by Carly Simon and Mike Mainieri.
Quackenbush Music, Ltd., 1980/Redeye Music Publishing Co., 1980.
Best-selling record by Carly Simon from *Lounge Upstairs* (Warner Brothers, 80).

Jesse (English)
Words and music by China Burton.
Virgin Music Ltd., 1984.
Introduced by Julian Lennon on the album *Valotte* (Atlantic, 84).

Jessie's Girl (Australian)
Words and music by Rick Springfield.
Songs of Polygram, 1981.
Best-selling record by Rick Springfield from *Working Class Dog* (RCA, 81).

Jimmy Lee
Words and music by Jeffrey Cohen, Preston Glass, and Narada Michael Walden.
Gratitude Sky Music, 1986/Bellboy Music, 1986.
Best-selling record in 1987 by Aretha Franklin, from the album *Aretha* (Arista, 86).

Joan Crawford
Words and music by Albert Bouchard, David R. Ruter, and John Lennert Rigg.
B. O'Cult Songs, Inc., 1981.
Introduced by Blue Oyster Cult on *Fire of Unknown Origin* (Columbia, 81).

Joanna
Words and music by Charles Smith, James Taylor, James Bonneford, Ronald Bell, Curtis Williams, Robert Bell, George Brown, and Clifford Adams.
Delightful Music Ltd., 1983.
Best-selling record by Kool & The Gang from *In the Heart* (De-Lite, 83).

Joe Knows How to Live
Words and music by Graham Lyle, Troy Seals, and Max D. Barnes.
Good Single Ltd., England, 1986/Irving Music Inc., 1988/WB Music, 1988/Two-Sons Music, 1988/Tree Publishing Co., Inc., 1988.
Best-selling record by Eddy Raven, from *Best of Eddy Raven* (RCA, 88).

Joe Stalin's Cadillac
Words and music by David Lowery.
Camper Van Beethoven Music, 1986.
Introduced by Camper Van Beethoven on the album *Camper Van Beethoven* (Pitch-A-Tent, 86). Author Lowery is the vocalist for this group, who were the underground favorites of the year.

Johannesburg
Words and music by Gil Scott-Heron.
Brouhaha Music, 1975/Cayman Music, 1975.
Revived by Gil Scott-Heron on *The Best of Gil Scott-Heron* (Arista, 84).

Johnny B. Goode
Words and music by Chuck Berry.
Arc Music, 1958.
Revived in 1988 by Judas Priest on *Ram It Down* (Columbia). Their rendition, which turns the archetypal rocker of Chuck Berry's original into a heavy metal maniac, was introduced in the film *Johnny B. Goode* and is included in its soundtrack album (Atlantic, 88).

Johnny 99
Words and music by Bruce Springsteen.
Bruce Springsteen Publishing, 1982.
Featured on *Johnny 99* by Johnny Cash (Columbia, 83). Introduced by Bruce Springsteen on *Nebraska* (Columbia, 82).

JoJo
Words and music by David Foster and Boz Scaggs.
BMG Music, 1980/Foster Frees Music Inc., 1980/Almo Music Corp., 1980/Irving Music Inc., 1980.
Best-selling record by Boz Scaggs from *Middle Man* (Columbia, 80).

Jokerman
Words and music by Bob Dylan.
Special Rider Music, 1983.
Introduced by Bob Dylan on *Infidels* (Columbia, 83).

Jose Cuervo
Words and music by Cathy Jordan.
Easy Listening Music Corp., 1981/Galleon Music, Inc., 1981.
Best-selling record by Shelly West (Warner/Viva, 83).

Joshua Noveck
Words and music by Douglas Bernstein and Denis Markell.
Introduced by Beanne Cox in the 1989 revue production *Showing Off.*

Joy
Words and music by Reggie Calloway, Joel Davis, and Vincent Calloway.

Calloco, 1988/Hip-Trip Music Co., 1988.
Best-selling record by Teddy Pendergrass, from *Joy* (Elektra, 88).

Joy and Pain
Words and music by Frankie Beverly.
Amazement Music, 1988.
Best-selling record in 1989 by Donna Allen from *Heaven on Earth* (Oceana, 88).

Joystick
Words and music by Bobby Harris and Eric Fearman.
Jobete Music Co., 1983.
Best-selling record by The Dazz Band from *Joystick* (Motown, 84).

Judas Kiss
Words and music by Scott Kempner.
Prince of the Bronx Music, 1987.
Introduced by The Del Lords *Based on a True Story* (Enigma, 88).

Juicy Fruit
Words and music by James Mtume.
Mtume Music Publishing, 1983.
Best-selling record by Mtume from *Juicy Fruit* (Epic, 83).

Juke Box Hero (English)
Words and music by Lou Gramm and Mick (Foreigner) Jones.
Somerset Songs Publishing, Inc., 1981/ESP Management Inc., 1981.
Best-selling record by Foreigner from *4* (Atlantic, 82).

Julia
Words and music by John Jarvis and Don Cook.
Tree Publishing Co., Inc., 1987/Cross Keys Publishing Co., Inc., 1987.
Best-selling record Conway Twitty, from the album *Borderline* (MCA, 87).

Jump
Words and music by Eddie Van Halen, Alex Van Halen, Michael Anthony, and David Lee Roth.
Van Halen Music, 1983/Diamond Dave Music, 1983.
Best-selling record by Van Halen from *1984* (Warner Brothers, 84). Revived in 1986 by Big Daddy on th e album *Meanwhile...Back in the States* (Rhino). A deft parody of the previous Van Halen hit, as done by devoted musical descendants of rockabilly great Eddi e Cochran.

Jump (for My Love)
Words and music by Marti Sharron, Steve Mitchell, and Gary Skardina.
Welbeck Music, 1983/Stephen Mitchell Music, 1983/Anidraks Music,

1983.
Best-selling record by The Pointer Sisters from *Break Out* (Planet, 84).

Jump Start
Words and music by Reggie Calloway and Vincent Calloway.
Colloco, 1987.
Best-selling record by Natalie Cole, from the album *Everlasting* (Manhattan, 87).

Jump to It
Words and music by Luther Vandross and Marcus Miller.
EMI-April Music, 1982/Uncle Ronnie's Music, 1982/Sunset Burgundy Music, Inc., 1982.
Best-selling record by Aretha Franklin from *Jump to It* (Arista, 82).

Jumpin' Jack Flash
Words and music by Mick Jagger and Keith Richards.
Mirage Music, Ltd., London, England, 1968/ABKCO Music Inc., 1968.
Revived in 1986 by Aretha Franklin in the film *Jumpin' Jack Flash*. The original by the Rolling Stones is on the soundtrack album (Mercury, 86).

Jungle Fever
Words by Michael Colby, music by Paul Katz.
Introduced by Elizabeth Austin in the musical *Tales of Tinseltown* (85).

Jungle Love
Words and music by Jesse Johnson, Morris Day, and Prince Rogers Nelson.
Tionna Music, 1984/WB Music, 1984.
Best-selling record by The Time from the album *Ice Cream Castle* (Warner Bros., 85). Performed by Morris Day and The Time in the film and soundtrack album *Purple Rain*.

Junior's Bar
Words and music by Joe Grushecky, Gil Snyder, and Eddie Britt.
Cleveland International, 1980/Brick Alley, 1980.
Introduced by by The Iron City House Rockers on *Have a Good Time (But Get out Alive)* (MCA, 80).

Just a Gigolo
Words by Irving Caesar, music by Leonello Casucci.
Wiener Boheme Verlag, Vienna, Austria, 1930/Chappell & Co., Inc., 1930/Irving Caesar Music Corp., 1930.
Revived by David Lee Roth in a medley with 'I Ain't Got Nobody' from the album *Crazy from the Heat* (Warner Bros., 85).

Just Another Love
Words and music by Paul Davis.

Web 4 Music Inc., 1986.
Best-selling record by Tanya Tucker from the album *Girls Like Me*
(Capitol, 86).

Just Another Movie
Words and music by Pat MacDonald.
Mambadaddi, 1986/I.R.S. Music/Criterion Music Corp.
Introduced by Timbuk 3 on the album *Greetings from Timbuk 3* (I.R.S.).

Just Another Night (English)
Words and music by Mick Jagger.
Promopub B. V., CH-1017 Amsterdam, Netherlands, 1985.
Best-selling record by Mick Jagger from the album *She's the Boss*
(Columbia, 85).

Just Another Woman in Love
Words and music by Patti Ryan and Wanda Mallette.
Southern Nights Music Co., 1982.
Best-selling record by Anne Murray from *A Little Good News* (Capitol,
84).

Just As I Am
Words and music by Dick Wagner and Robert Hegel.
Don Kirshner Music Inc., 1982/Rightsong Music/Mystery Man Music.
Best-selling record by Air Supply from the album *Air Supply* (Arista,
85).

Just Be Good to Me
Words and music by Terry Lewis and James Harris, III.
Flyte Tyme Tunes, 1983/Avant Garde Music Publishing, Inc., 1983.
Best-selling record by The S.O.S. Band from *On the Rise* (Tabu, 83).

Just Be Yourself
Words and music by Charles Singleton, Larry Blackmon, and Tomi
Jenkins.
All Seeing Eye Music, 1981/Cameo Five Music.
Best-selling record by Cameo from *Alligator Woman* (Chocolate City,
82).

Just Because
Words and music by Michael O'Hara, Sami McKinney, and Alex
Brown.
O'Hara Music, 1988/Texas City/Lil Mama Music/Music of the World/
Avid One Music.
Best-selling record in 1989 by Anita Baker from *Giving You the Best
That I Got* (Elektra, 88).

Just Between You and Me
Words and music by Lou Gramm.

Colgems-EMI Music, 1989/Knighty Knight.
Best-selling record by Lou Gramm from *Long Hard Look* (Atlantic, 89).

Just Coolin'
Words and music by Gerald Levert and Marc Gordon.
Trycep Publishing Co., 1988/Ferncliff/Willesden Music, Inc.
Best-selling record in 1989 by Levert, featuring Heavy D, from *Just Coolin'* (Atlantic, 88).

Just Got Paid
Words and music by Johnny Kemp and Gene Griffin.
Mochrie Music, 1988/Cal-Gene Music, 1988/Virgin Music Ltd., 1988/ Zomba Music, 1988.
Best-selling record by Johnny Kemp, from *Secrets of Flying* (Columbia, 88). Nominated for a Grammy Award, Country Song of the Year, 1988.

Just in Case
Words and music by James P. Pennington and Sonny LeMaire.
Pacific Island Music, 1986/Tree Publishing Co., Inc.
Best-selling record by the Forester Sisters from the album *Perfume, Ribbons, and Pearls* (Warner Bros., 86).

Just Like Fire Would (English)
Words and music by Chris Bailey.
Introduced by The Saints on the album *All Fool's Day* (TVT, 87).

Just Like Honey (English)
Words and music by Jim Reid.
Introduced by Jesus and Mary Chain on the album *Psychocandy* (Reprise, 86). Winner of College Media Journal Award for Song of the Year .

Just Like Jesse James
Words and music by Desmond Child and Diane Warren.
Realsongs, 1989/EMI-April Music/Desmobile Music Inc.
Best-selling record by Cher from *Heart of Stone* (Geffen, 89).

Just Like Paradise
Words and music by David Lee Roth and Brent Tuggle.
Diamondback Music Co., 1987/Tuggle Tunes Music, 1987.
Best-selling record by David Lee Roth from *Skyscraper* (Warner Bros., 88).

Just My Daydream
Words and music by William Robinson.
Jobete Music Co., 1982.
Featured on *Jump to It* by Aretha Franklin (Arista, 82).

Just Once
Words and music by Barry Mann and Cynthia Weil.
ATV Music Corp./Mann & Weil Songs Inc./MCA, Inc.
Best-selling record by Quincy Jones featuring James Ingram from the
album *The Dude* (A&M, 81).

Just One of the Guys
Words and music by Marc Tanner and Jon Reede.
EMI-Golden Torch Music Corp., 1985/JonoSongs, 1985/Otherwise
Publishing.
Introduced by Shalamar in the film *Just One of the Guys* (85).

(Do You Love Me) Just Say Yes
Words and music by Bob DiPiero, John Scott Sherrill, and Dennis
Robbins.
Little Big Town Music, 1988/American Made Music, 1988/Old Wolf
Music, 1988/Corey Rock, 1988/Wee B Music, 1988.
Best-selling record by Highway 101, from *101 2* (Warner Bros., 88).

Just the Facts
Words and music by Jimmy Jam (pseudonym for James Harris, III) and
Terry Lewis.
MCA Music, 1987/Flyte Tyme Tunes, 1987.
Introduced by Patti La Belle on the soundtrack of the film *Dragnet* and
on its album (MCA, 87).

Just the Motion (English)
Words and music by Linda Thompson.
Island Music, 1982.
Introduced by Richard and Linda Thompson on *Shoot out the Lights*
(Hannbal, 82).

Just the Two of Us
Words and music by Bill Withers, William Salter, and Ralph
MacDonald.
Antisia Music Inc., 1981/Bleunig Music, 1981.
Best-selling record by Grover Washington, Jr. and Bill Withers from
Winelight (Elektra, 81). Won a Grammy Award, and Rhythm 'n'
Blues Song of the Year, 1981. Nominated for Grammy Awards,
Record of the Year, 1981, and Song of the Year, 1981.

Just the Way You Like It
Words and music by Terry Lewis and James Harris, III.
Flyte Tyme Tunes, 1984/Avant Garde Music Publishing, Inc., 1984.
Best-selling record by The S.O.S. Band from *Just the Way You Like It*
(Tabu, 84).

Just to Satisfy You
Words and music by Don Bowman and Waylon Jennings.

Irving Music Inc., 1964/Parody Publishing, 1964.
Best-selling record by Waylon and Willie from *Black on Black* (RCA, 82).

Just to See Her
Words and music by Jimmy George and Lou Pardini.
Unicity Music, Inc., 1987/Lucky Break, 1987/Lars, 1987.
Best-selling record by Smokey Robinson, from the album *One Heartbeat* (Motown, 87). Nominated for a Grammy Award, Rhythm 'n' Blues Song of the Year, 1987.

K

Karma Chameleon (English)
Words and music by George O'Dowd, Jon Moss, Roy Hay, Mickey
  Craig, and Phil Pickett.
Virgin Music, 1983/Warner-Tamerlane Music, 1983.
Best-selling record by Culture Club from *Colour by Numbers* (Epic, 83).

Kayleigh (English)
Words and music by Fish (pseudonym for Derek William Dick).
Charisma Music Publishing Co., Ltd., 1985/Chappell & Co., Inc., 1985.
Best-selling record by Marillion from the album *Misplaced Childhood*
  (Capitol, 85).

Keep It Confidential
Words and music by Ellie Greenwich, Jeffrey Kent, and Ellen Foley.
Jent Music Inc., 1985/My Own Music/Urban Noise Music.
Introduced by Gina Taylor in the Broadway musical and cast album
  Leader of the Pack (Elecktra/Asylum, 85).

Keep on Loving You
Words and music by Kevin Cronin.
Fate Music, 1980.
Best-selling record by REO Speedwagon from *Hi Infidelity* (Epic, 80).

Keep on Movin' (English)
Words and music by Romeo.
Virgin Music, 1989.
Best-selling record by Soul II Soul from *Keep on Movin'* (Virgin, 89).

Keep the Fire Burnin'
Words and music by Kevin Cronin.
Fate Music, 1982.
Best-selling record by REO Speedwagon from *Good Trouble* (Epic, 82).

Keep Your Hands to Yourself
Words and music by Don Baird.
No Surrender, 1986/Warner-Tamerlane Music/Eleksylum Music.

Best-selling record by Georgia Satellites from the album *Georgia Satellites* (Elektra, 86). Introduced on the English extended-play (EP) record *Keep the Faith.*

Keeping the Faith
Words and music by Billy Joel.
Joelsongs, 1983.
Best-selling record by Billy Joel in 1985 from the album *An Innocent Man* (Columbia, 84).

Key Largo
Words and music by Sonny Limbo and Bertie Higgins.
Jen-Lee Music Co., 1981/Chappell & Co., Inc., 1981/Lowery Music Co., Inc., 1981/Brother Bill's Music, 1981.
Best-selling record by Bertie Higgins from *Just Another Day in Paradise* (Kat Family, 82).

Kid (English)
Words and music by Chrissie Hynde.
MCA, Inc., 1980.
Introduced by The Pretenders in *The Pretenders* (Sire, 80).

The Kid Herself
Words by Fred Ebb, music by John Kander.
Fiddleback, 1987/Kander & Ebb Inc., 1987.
Introduced in the 1987 revival of *Flora, The Red Menace*. The song was written for the original production, but never used. Other numbers written for the new production are 'Mister Just Give Me a Job,' 'The Joke,' 'I'm Keeping It Hot,' and 'Where Did Everybody Go.'

Kids in America (English)
Words and music by Ricky Wilde and Marty Wilde.
Finchley Music Corp., 1981.
Best-selling record by Kim Wilde from *Kim Wilde* (EMI-America, 82).

Kids of the Baby Boom
Words and music by David Bellamy.
Bellamy Brothers Music, 1987.
Best-selling record by The Bellamy Brothers, from the album *Country Rap* (MCA/Curb, 87).

Killin' Time
Words and music by Clint Black and Hayden Nicholas.
Howlin' Hits Music, 1989.
Best-selling record by Clint Black from *Killin' Time* (RCA, 89).

King for a Day (English)
Words and music by Tom Bailey, Alannah Currie, and Joe Leeway.
Bennie Benjamin Music, Inc., 1986.

Best-selling record by The Thompson Twins in 1986 from the album *Here's to Future Days* (Arista, 85).

King for a Day (English)
Words and music by Colin Moulding.
Virgin Songs, 1989.
Introduced by XTC on *Oranges and Lemons* (Geffen, 89).

King of Pain (English)
Words and music by Sting (pseudonym for Gordon Sumner).
Illegal Songs, Inc., 1983/Reggatta Music, Ltd., 1983.
Best-selling record by The Police from *Synchonicity* (A & M, 83).

King of the New York Street
Words and music by Dion DiMucci, words by Bill Tuohy.
County Line, 1988/Skinny Zach Music Inc.
Introduced by Dion on *Yo Frankie* (Arista, 89). Former leader of the Belmonts, Dion was inducted into the Rock and Roll Hall of Fame in 1989.

King's Call (Iranian)
English words and music by Phil Lynott.
Chappell & Co., Inc., 1980.
Introduced by Phil Lynott on *Solo in Soho* (Warner Brothers, 80).

Kiss
Words and music by Prince Rogers Nelson.
Controversy Music, 1986.
Best-selling record by Prince & the Revolution from the album *Parade* (Warner Bros., 86). Featured in the film *Under the Cherry Moon* (86). Nominated for a Grammy Award, Rhythm 'n' Blues Song of the Year, 1986.

Kiss Him Goodbye, also known as **Na Na Hey Hey (Kiss Him Goodbye)**
Words and music by Gary DeCarlo, Dale Frashver, and Paul Leka.
MRC Music Corp., 1969.
Revived in 1987 by the Nylons, from the album *Happy Together* (Open Air/Windham Hill). The song was originally recorded by Steam.

Kiss Me Deadly
Words and music by Mick Smiley.
Makiki Publishing Co., Ltd., 1988/BMG Songs Inc., 1988.
Best-selling record by Lita Ford from *Lita* (RCA, 88). Joan Jett's former partner in the Runaways here achieved solo success after a long struggle.

Kiss Me, Son of God
Words and music by They Might Be Giants.

They Might Be Giants Music, 1988.
Introduced by They Might Be Giants on *Lincoln* (Restless, 88).

Kiss of the Spider Woman
Words by Fred Ebb, music by John Kander.
Kander & Ebb Inc., 1989/Fiddleback.
Introduced by Brent Barret in *And the World Goes Round with Kander and Ebb,* a revue staged at the Whole Theater in Montclair, New Jersey, in 1989. The performance featured this debut of the title tune for the songwriters' musical slated for a future Broadway opening.

Kiss on My List
Words and music by Janna Allen and Daryl Hall.
Hot Cha Music Co., 1980/Unichappell Music Inc., 1980/Fust Buzza Music, Inc., 1980.
Best-selling record by Daryl Hall and John Oates from *Voices* (RCA, 81).

Kiss the Bride (English)
Words by Bernie Taupin, music by Elton John.
Intersong, USA Inc., 1983.
Best-selling record by Elton John from *Too Low for Zero* (Geffen, 83).

Kiss the Girl
Words by Howard Ashman, music by Alan Menken.
Walt Disney Music, 1989.
Introduced by the animal chorus in the animated musical feature *The Little Mermaid* and its soundtrack album (Disney, 89), the song was the work of the team who earlier provided the songs for *Little Shop of Horrors*. Nominated for an Academy Award, Best Original Song, 1989.

Kisses on the Wind (English)
Words and music by Neneh Cherry and Cameron McVey.
Virgin Music, 1989.
Best-selling record by Neneh Cherry from *Raw Like Sushi* (Virgin, 89).

Kissing a Fool (English)
Words and music by George Michael.
Morrison Leahy, England, 1988/Chappell-Warner Brothers, 1987.
Best-selling record by George Michael from *Faith* (Columbia, 88); this was the fifth song from the album to reach number one.

Knight Moves
Words and music by Suzanne Vega.
Waifersongs, 1985/AGF Music Ltd., 1985.
Introduced by Suzanne Vega on the album *Suzanne Vega* (A & M, 85).

Knocking at Your Back Door
Words and music by Ritchie Blackmore, Roger Glover, and Ian Gillan.
Blackmore Music Ltd., 1985/Rugged Music Ltd., 1985/Pussy Music Ltd., 1985.
Best-selling record by Deep Purple in 1985 from the album *Perfect Stranger* (Mercury, 84).

Kokoku
Words and music by Laurie Anderson.
Difficult Music, 1984.
Introduced by Laurie Anderson on *Mr. Heartbreak* (Warner Brothers, 84).

Kokomo
Words and music by Mike Love, Terry Melcher, John Phillips, and Scott Mackenzie.
Walt Disney Music, 1988/Honest John Music, 1988/Clair Audient, 1988/Daywin Music, 1988.
Best-selling record by The Beach Boys, from the film and soundtrack album of *Cocktail* (Elektra, 88). The group's first number one song since 1966's 'Good Vibrations' was written by four members of the California rock scene of the 1960's. Nominated for a Grammy Award, Best Song for a Movie or TV, 1988.

Kyrie (English)
Words and music by Richard Page, Steven George, and Robert John 'Mutt' Lange.
Warner-Tamerlane Music, 1985/Entente Music.
Best-selling record by Mr. Mister in 1986 from the album *Welcome to the Real World* (RCA, 85). The song is based on the Latin phrase meaning 'Lord, Have Mercy,' previously used in songs by several popular groups, including The Association ('Requiem').

L

La Bamba
Words and music by William Clauson.
Kemo Music Co., 1958/Warner-Tamerlane Music, 1958.
Revived in 1987 by Los Lobos as the title song for the biographical film about 1950's star Ritchie Valens; the Mexican-American band performs the song in the film and on the soundtrack album (Slash/ Warner Bros., 87). 'La Bamba' was originally the flipside of Valens' big hit 'Oh Donna'; its use in the film sparked reviewed interest in Los Lobos, whose rendition of the song went to the top of the charts. Nominated for Grammy Awards, Best Record of the Year, 1987, and Best Song of the Year, 1987.

L.A. County
Words and music by Lyle Lovett.
Michael H. Goldsen, Inc., 1987/Lyle Lovett, 1987.
Introduced by Lyle Lovett in *Pontiac* (MCA/Curb, 87) and popularized in 1988.

La Isla Bonita
Words and music by Madonna, Patrick Leonard, and Bruce Gaitsch.
WB Music, 1919, 1986/Bleu Disque Music/Lost in Music/Johnny Yuma/ Edge of Fluke.
Best-selling record in 1987 by Madonna, from the album *True Blue* (Warner Brothers, 86).

Labeled with Love (English)
Words by Chris Difford, music by Glenn Tilbrook.
Illegal Songs, Inc., 1980.
Introduced by Squeeze on *Argybargy* (A & M, 80).

Ladder of Success (English)
Words and music by Ray Davies.
Davray Music, Ltd., London, England, 1985.
Introduced by Ray Davies in the film and soundtrack album *Return to Waterloo* (85), which he wrote and starred in.

The Ladies Who Lunch
Words and music by Stephen Sondheim.
Herald Square Music Co., 1970.
Revived by Barbra Streisand on *The Broadway Album* (Columbia, 85).
 Introduced by Elaine Stritch in *Company* (1970).

Lady
Words and music by Lionel Richie, Jr.
Brockman Enterprises Inc., 1980.
Best-selling record by Kenny Rogers from *Kenny Rogers' Greatest Hits*
 (Liberty, 80). Nominated for Grammy Awards, Record of the Year,
 1980, and Song of the Year, 1980.

Lady (You Bring Me Up) (Icelandic)
English words and music by William King, Howard Hudson, and S.
 King.
Jobete Music Co., 1981/Hanna Music, 1981/Commodores Entertainment
 Publishing Corp, 1981.
Best-selling record by The Commodores from *In the Pocket* (Motown,
 81). Nominated for a Grammy Award, Rhythm 'n' Blues Song of the
 Year, 1981.

Lady Down on Love
Words and music by Randy Owen.
Maypop Music, 1981/Buzzherb Music, 1981.
Best-selling record by Alabama from *The Closer You Get* (RCA, 83).
 Nominated for a Grammy Award, Country Song of the Year, 1983.

The Lady in Red (English)
Words and music by Chris DeBurgh.
Almo Music Corp., 1919, 1986.
Best-selling record in 1987 by Chris DeBurgh, from the album *Into the
 Night* (A & M, 86). The song went to number one in England, then
 became a hit in the United States upon its re-release here.

A Lady Like You
Words and music by Jim Weatherly and Keith Stegall.
EMI-Blackwood Music Inc., 1984/Bright Sky Music, 1984/Charlie
 Monk Music, 1984.
Best-selling record by Glen Campbell from the album *Letter to Home*
 (Atlantic, 85).

Lady Soul
Words and music by Mark Holden.
Dream Dealers Music, 1986/Buchu Music/BMG Songs Inc.
Best-selling record by the Temptations from the album *To Be Continued*
 (Gordy, 86). Featured on the television series *227*.

The Lady Takes the Cowboy Every Time
Words and music by Larry Gatlin.
Larry Gatlin Music, 1984.
Best-selling record by Larry Gatlin and the Gatlin Brothers Band
(Columbia, 84).

Lady You Are
Words and music by Kevin McCord, Dave Roberson, and Albert
Hudson.
Duchess Music Corp., 1984/Park's Music, 1984.
Best-selling record by One Way from *Lady* (MCA, 84).

Lakota
Words and music by Joni Mitchell and Larry Klein.
Crazy Crow Music, 1985.
Introduced by Joni Mitchell on *Chalk Mark in a Rainstorm* (Geffen, 88).

The Lambeth Walk (English)
Words and music by Noel Gay (pseudonym for Reginald B. Armitage)
and Douglas Forber.
Polygram International, 1937.
Revived in 1986 by Robert Lindsay, Emma Thompson, and Ensemble in
the Broadway revival of the English musical *Me and My Girl.*
Featured on the cast album (Manhattan, 86).

Land of Confusion (English)
Words and music by Tony Banks, Phil Collins, and Mike Rutherford.
Hit & Run Music, 1986.
Best-selling record by Genesis from the album *Invisible Touch* (Atlantic,
86).

Land of 1000 Dances
Words and music by Chris Kenner.
Thursday Music Corp., 1963.
Revived by Wrestlers on *The Wrestling Album* (Epic, 85). Epitomizing
rock *n' wrestling mania, which probably began with Freddie Blassie
and 'Hey, Ya Pencil-Neck Geek' from the late seventies, this remake
featured a brigade of professional wrestlers of the eighties, including
Roddy Piper, Junkyard Dog, Mean Gene Okerlund, and Captain Lou
Albano.*

Landlord
Words and music by Nick Ashford and Valerie Simpson.
Nick-O-Val Music, 1980.
Best-selling record by Gladys Knight & The Pips from *About Love*
(Columbia, 80).

The Language of Love
Words and music by Dan Fogelberg.

Hickory Grove Music, 1984/EMI-April Music, 1984.
Best-selling record by Dan Fogelberg from *Windows and Walls* (Full
  Moon/Epic, 84).

Lasso the Moon
Words and music by Steve Dorff and Milton Brown.
Ensign Music, 1985.
Introduced by Gary Morris in the film *Rustler's Rhapsody* (85).

Last Date, see (Lost His Love) On Our Last Date.

The Last Dragon
Words and music by Norman Whitfield and B. Miller.
Stone Diamond Music, 1985/EMI Golden Torch Music, 1985.
Introduced by Dwight David in the film and soundtrack album *The Last
  Dragon* (Motown, 85).

The Last One to Know
Words and music by Matraca Berg and Jane Mariash.
Tapadero Music, 1987/Dixie Stars, 1987.
Best-selling record by Reba McEntire, from the album *The Last One to
  Know* (MCA, 87).

The Late Great Johnny Ace
Words and music by Paul Simon.
Paul Simon Music, 1981.
Introduced by Simon and Garfunkel on *The Concert in Central Park*
  (Warner Brothers, 82).

Late in the Evening
Words and music by Paul Simon.
Paul Simon Music, 1978.
Best-selling record by Paul Simon (Warner Brothers, 80). Introduced in
  the film & soundtrack album *One Trick Pony* (80).

Late Night
Music by Paul Shaffer.
Postvalda Music, 1989.
This themesong for *The David Letterman Show,* for which Paul Shaffer
  is musical director, was nominated for a Grammy as Best Pop
  Instrumental Performance when the writer-artist recorded it on his
  album *Coast to Coast* (Capitol, 89).

Late Nite Comic
Words and music by Brian Gari.
Tenacity Music, 1977/Foxborough Music, 1988.
Introduced by Melinda Tanner in the revue *You Won't Find That Here*
  (1977). Revived in 1988 by Robert LuPone in the musical *Late Nite*

Comic. Sung by Brian Gari on the album *Late Nite Comic* (Original Cast, 88).

(I Was Born in a) Laundromat
Words and music by Victor Krummenacher, Greg Lisher, David Lowery, and Chris Pedersen.
Camper Van Beethoven Music, 1989.
Introduced by Camper Van Beethoven in *Key Lime Pie* (Virgin, 89).

Lawyers in Love
Words and music by Jackson Browne.
Night Kitchen Music, 1983.
Best-selling record by Jackson Browne from *Lawyers in Love* (Asylum, 83).

Lay Down Your Weary Tune
Words and music by Bob Dylan.
Special Rider Music, 1964.
A Bob Dylan classic recorded in 1963 and re-released by Dylan on the five-record retrospective *Biograph* (Columbia, 85).

Lay Your Hands on Me (English)
Words and music by Tom Bailey, Alannah Currie, and Joe Leeway.
Zomba Music, 1985.
Best-selling record by Thompson Twins from the album *Here's to Future Days* (Arista, 85). Introduced in the film and soundtrack album *Perfect* (85).

Lay Your Hands on Me
Words and music by Jon Bon Jovi and Richie Sambora.
Bon Jovi Publishing, 1988.
Best-selling record in 1989 by Bon Jovi from *New Jersey* (Mercury, 88).

Leader of the Band
Words and music by Dan Fogelberg.
Hickory Grove Music, 1981/EMI-April Music, 1981.
Best-selling record by Dan Fogelberg from *The Innocent Age* (Full Moon/Epic, 81).

Lean on Me
Words and music by Bill Withers.
Interior Music, 1972.
Revived in 1987 by Club Nouveau on the album *Life, Love, and Pain* (Tommy Boy/Warner Bros., 86) Revived in 1989 by Thelma Houston and The Winans in the album *Lean on Me* onits Soundtrack album (WB, 89). Nominated for a Grammy Award, Rhythm 'n' Blues Song of the Year, 1987.

Leaning on the Lamp Post (English)
Words and music by Noel Gay (pseudonym for Reginald B. Armitage).
Polygram International, 1937.
Revived in 1986 by Robert Lindsay in the Broadway revival of the
English musical *Me and My Girl*. Featured on the cast album
(Manhattan, 86).

Learn How to Live
Words and music by Billy Squier.
Songs of the Knight, 1982.
Introduced by Billy Squier on *Emotions in Motion* (Capitol, 82).

Learning How to Love You
Words and music by John Hiatt.
Lillybilly, 1987.
Introduced by John Hiatt on the album *Bring the Family* (A & M, 87),
of which it forms the centerpiece.

Learning to Fly (English)
Words and music by David Gilmour, Anthony Moore, Bob Ezrin, and
Jon Carin.
Pink Floyd, London, England, 1987.
Best-selling record by Pink Floyd, from the album *A Momentary Lapse
of Reason* (Columbia, 87).

Leather and Lace
Words and music by Stephanie Nicks.
Welsh Witch Publishing, 1975.
Best-selling record by Stevie Nicks with Don Henley from *Bella Donna*
(Modern, 81).

Leave a Light On
Words and music by Rick Nowels and Ellen Shipley.
Future Furniture, 1989/Shipwreck/Virgin Songs.
Best-selling record by Belinda Carlisle from *Runaway Horses* (MCA,
89).

Leave It All to Me
Words and music by Paul Anka, Alan Bergman, and Marilyn Bergman.
Paulanne Music Inc./Threesome Music Co.
Introduced by Frank Sinatra and Paul Anka (Reprise, 87). Anka teamed
with the Oscar-winning husband-and-wife lyricists to create this song
for Sinatra's return to the label he founded.

Leave Me Lonely
Words and music by Gary Morris.
Gary Morris Music, 1986.
Best-selling record in 1987 by Gary Morris, from the album *Plain
Brown Wrapper* (Warner Bros., 86).

Left in the Dark
Words and music by Jim Steinman.
Lost Boys Music, 1980/Charles Family Music, 1980/Alibee Music, 1980/Dela Music, 1980.
Best-selling record by Barbra Streisand from *Emotion* (Columbia, 84).

Left of Center
Words and music by Suzanne Vega and Steve Addabbo.
AGF Music Ltd., 1986/Waifersongs/Famous Music Corp.
Introduced by Suzanne Vega, with Joe Jackson on keyboards, on the soundtrack of the 1986 film *Pretty in Pink* and on its album (A & M, 86).

Legacy
Words and music by Pierce Pettis.
Let's Have Lunch Music, 1989/Lost Lake Arts Music.
Introduced by Pierce Pettis on *Legacy* (Windham Hill, 89); also released on *While the Serpent Lies Sleeping* (Windham Hill, 89).

Legalize It
Words and music by Mojo Nixon.
Muffin Stuffin, 1989/La Rana.
Introduced by Mojo Nixon and Skid Roper on *Root Hog or Die* (Enigma, 89).

Legendary Hearts
Words and music by Lou Reed.
Metal Machine Music, 1982.
Introduced on *Legendary Hearts* by Lou Reed (RCA, 83).

Legs
Words and music by Billy Gibbons, Dusty Hill, and Frank Beard.
Hamstein Music, 1983.
Best-selling record by ZZ Top from *Eliminator* (Warner Brothers, 84).

Leningrad
Words and music by Billy Joel.
Joel, 1989.
Introduced by Billy Joel on *Storm Front* (Columbia, 89).

Lenny Bruce
Words and music by Bob Dylan.
Special Rider Music, 1981.
Introduced by Bob Dylan *Shot of Love* (Columbia, 82).

A Lesson in Leavin'
Words and music by Randy Goodrum and Brent Maher.
Chappell & Co., Inc., 1979/Sailmaker Music, 1979/Welbeck Music,

1979/Blue Quill Music, 1979.
Best-selling record by Dottie West (United Artists, 80).

Lessons in Love (English)
Words and music by Mark King, Wally Badarou, and Phil Gould.
Level 42 Songs, 1987/Chappell & Co., Inc., 1987/Island Visual Arts, 1987.
Best-selling record by Level 42, from the album *Running in the Family* (Polygram, 87).

Let Freedom Ring
Words and music by Bruce Sussman, Jack Feldman, and Barry Manilow.
Townsway Music, 1987/Appogiatura Music Inc./Camp Songs Music.
Introduced by Barry Manilow as the finale of the CBS television special *We the People 200*, celebrating the two hundredth anniversary of the Constitution.

Let Go
Words and music by Daryl Duncan.
Almo Music Corp., 1989.
Best-selling record by Sharon Bryant from *Here I Am* (Wing, 89).

Let Him Go
Words and music by William Wadhams.
Famous Music Corp., 1984/Big Wad/Famous Music Corp., 1984.
Best-selling record by Animotion from the album *Animotion* (Mercury, 85).

Let It Be (English)
Words and music by John Lennon and Paul McCartney.
Maclen Music Inc., 1970.
Revived in 1987 by Ferry Aid, an ad hoc group including Paul McCartney, Mark Knopfler, Kate Bush, and Boy George, among others. Proceeds from the Profile-label record went to benefit the survivors of a ferry boat disaster in Zeebrugge, Belgium.

Let It Whip
Words and music by Reginald Andrews and Leon Chancler.
Ujima Music, 1981/Mac Vac Alac Music Co., 1981.
Best-selling record by The Dazz Band from *Keep It Live* (Mowtown, 82). Nominated for a Grammy Award, Rhythm 'n' Blues Song of the Year, 1982.

Let Me Be the Clock
Words and music by William Robinson.
Bertam Music Co., 1980.
Best-selling record by Smokey Robinson from *Warm Thoughts* (Tamla, 80).

Let Me Be the One (Canadian)
Words and music by David Foster.
Brampton Music Ltd., England, 1986.
Best-selling record by Five Star from the album *Luxury of Life* (RCA, 86).

Let Me Be the One
Words and music by Lewis Martinee.
Panchin, 1987.
Best-selling record by Expose, from the album *Exposure* (Arista, 87).

Let Me Be Your Angel
Words and music by Narada Michael Walden and Bunny Hill.
Walden Music, Inc., 1980/Cotillion Music Inc., 1980/Brassheart Music, 1980.
Best-selling record by Stacy Lattisaw from *Stacy Lattisaw* (Cotillion, 80).

Let Me Dance for You
Words by Edward Kleban, music by Marvin Hamlisch.
Wren Music Co., Inc., 1985/American Compass Music Corp., 1985.
Introduced in the film version and soundtrack album of the hit musical *A Chorus Line* (85).

Let Me Down Easy (Canadian)
Words and music by Bryan Adams and Jim Vallance.
Irving Music Inc., 1985/Adams Communications, Inc., 1985/Calypso Toonz, 1985.
Introduced by Roger Daltrey on the album *Under a Raging Moon* (Atlantic, 85).

Let Me Go
Words and music by Ray Parker, Jr.
Raydiola Music, 1982.
Best-selling record by Ray Parker, Jr. from *The Other Woman* (Arista, 82).

Let Me Love You Tonight
Words and music by Jeff Wilson, Dan Greer, and Steve Woodard.
Kentucky Wonder Music, 1980/Pure Prairie League Music, 1980.
BS by Pure Prairie League from *Firin' Up* (Casablanca, 80).

Let Me Tell You About Love
Words and music by Paul Kennerley and Brent Maher.
Brick Hithouse Music, 1989/Irving Music Inc./EMI-April Music/ Welbeck Music Corp./Blue Quill Music.
Best-selling record by The Judds from *River of Time* (Curb/RCA, 89).

Let Me Tickle Your Fancy
Words and music by Jermaine Jackson, Paul M. Jackson, Jr., Pamela
Sawyer, and Marilyn McLeod.
Fat Jack the Second Music Publishing Co., 1982/Jobete Music Co.,
1982/Stone Diamond Music, 1982.
Best-selling record by Jermaine Jackson from *Let Me Tickle Your Fancy*
(Motown, 82).

Let Me up I've Had Enough
Words and music by Tom Petty and Mike Campbell.
Gone Gator Music, 1987/Wild Gator Music, 1987.
Introduced by Tom Petty and the Heartbreakers on the album *Let Me
Up I've Had Enough* (MCA, 87).

Let My Love Open the Door (English)
Words and music by Pete Townshend.
Towser Tunes Inc., 1980.
Best-selling record by Pete Townshend from *Empty Glass* (Atco, 80).

Let My People Go Go
Words and music by Bob Walkenhorst.
Screen Gems-EMI Music Inc., 1986.
Introduced by the Rainmakers on the album *The Rainmakers* (Mercury,
86).

Let the Feeling Flow
Words and music by Peabo Bryson.
WB Music, 1981/Peabo Bryson Enterprises, Inc., 1981.
Best-selling record by Peabo Bryson from *I Am Love* (Capitol, 82).

Let the Music Play
Words and music by Chris Barbosa and Ed Chisolm.
Shapiro, Bernstein & Co., Inc., 1983/Emergency Music Inc., 1983.
Best-selling record by Shannon from *Let the Music Play* (Mirage, 84).

Let the River Run, also known as **Theme from Working Girl**
Words and music by Carly Simon.
TCF, 1988/C'est Music, 1988.
Introduced by Carly Simon on the soundtrack of the film *Working Girl*;
also on the soundtrack album (Arista, 88). Won an Academy Award,
and Best Song, 1988.

Let Us Begin, see **What Are We Making Weapons For.**

Lethal Weapon
Words and music by Michael Kamen.
Warner-Tamerlane Music, 1987.
Introduced by Honeymoon Suite on the soundtrack of the movie *Lethal
Weapon* and on its album (Warner Bros., 87).

Let's Dance (English)
Words and music by David Bowie.
Jones Music Co., 1983.
Best-selling record by David Bowie from *Let's Dance* (RCA, 83).

Let's Fall to Pieces Together
Words and music by Dickey Lee, Tommy Rocco, and Johnny Russell.
Hall-Clement Publications, 1983/Sunflower County Songs, 1983.
Best-selling record by George Strait from *Right or Wrong* (MCA, 84).

Let's Get Serious
Words and music by Stevie Wonder and Lee Garrett.
Black Bull Music, 1980/Jobete Music Co., 1980/Broadcast Music Inc., 1980.
Best-selling record by Jermaine Jackson from *Let's Get Serious* (Motown, 80). Nominated for a Grammy Award, Rhythm 'n' Blues, 1980.

Let's Go (English)
Words and music by Wang Chung.
Chong, England, 1987/Warner-Tamerlane Music, 1987.
Best-selling record by Wang Chung, from the album *Mosaic* (Warner Bros., 87).

Let's Go All the Way
Words and music by Gary Cooper.
Lifo, 1986.
Best-selling record by Sly Fox from the album *Let's Go All the Way* (Capitol, 86).

Let's Go Crazy
Words and music by Prince Rogers Nelson.
Controversy Music, 1984/WB Music, 1984.
Best-selling record by Prince & the Revolution (Warner Brothers, 84). Introduced in the film and soundtrack album *Purple Rain* (84).

Let's Go to Heaven in My Car
Words and music by Brian Wilson, Eugene Landy, and Gary Usher.
Beach Bum Music, 1987/Fire Mist, 1987/Beachhead Music, 1987.
Performed by Beach Boy Brian Wilson in a rare solo effort for the soundtrack of the film *Police Academy 4* and its album (Sire, 87). Wilson shares credit for the song with his therapist.

Let's Groove
Words and music by Maurice White, Wayne Vaughn, and Wanda Vaughn.
Saggifire Music, 1981/Yougoulei Music, 1981.
Best-selling record by Earth, Wind & Fire from *Raise!* (Arc/Columbia, 81).

Let's Hear It for the Boy
Words by Dean Pitchford, music by Tom Snow.
Ensign Music, 1984.
Best-selling record by Deniece Williams (Columbia, 84). Introduced in
the film and soundtrack album *Footloose* (84). Nominated for an
Academy Award, Best Song, 1984.

Let's Stay Together
Words and music by Al Green, Willie Mitchell, and Al Jackson.
One For Three, 1971/Al Green Music Inc, 1971.
Revived by Tina Turner from *Private Dancer* (Capitol, 84).

Let's Stop Talkin' About It
Words and music by Rory Bourke, Rafe Van Hoy, and Deborah Allen.
Unichappell Music Inc., 1983/Van Hoy Music, 1983/Chappell & Co.,
Inc., 1982/Duchess Music Corp., 1983.
Best-selling record by Janie Fricke (Columbia, 84).

Let's Talk Dirty in Hawaiian
Words and music by John Prine and Fred Koller.
Spoondevil, 1987/Grandma Annie Music, 1987/Lucrative, 1987.
Introduced by John Prine, one of the premier singer-songwriters of the
1970's, on a record on the Oh Boy label. This novelty song ridicules
censorship problems in the music business.

Let's Wait Awhile
Words and music by James Harris, III, Terry Lewis, Janet Jackson, and
Reginald Andrews.
Flyte Tyme Tunes, 1986/Crush Club, 1986.
Best-selling record in 1987 by Janet Jackson, from her album *Control*
(A & M, 86). When this single reached number one, Jackson became
the first female artist to achieve five number one singles in a row.

Let's Work (English)
Words and music by Mick Jagger and Dave Stewart.
Promopub B. V., CH-1017 Amsterdam, Netherlands, 1987/BMG Songs
Inc., 1987.
Introduced by Mick Jagger in the album *Primitive Cool* (Columbia, 87),
this song proved to be a big hit among devotees of aerobics.

The Letter, see **Vanna, Pick Me a Letter.**

Letter in the Mail
Words and music by James Taylor.
Country Road Music Inc., 1988.
Introduced by James Taylor on *Never Die Young* (CBS, 89), this is one
of Taylor's most moving story-songs.

Liar, Liar
Words and music by James Donna.
Celann Music Co., 1965.
Originally a 1965 garage band classic by the Castaways, the song was revived by Debbie Harry for the 1988 film *Married to the Mob* and its soundtrack album (Reprise).

Lick It Up
Words and music by Paul Stanley and Vinnie Vincent.
Kiss, 1983/Kissway Music, Inc., 1983.
Best-selling record by Kiss from *Lick it Up* (Mercury, 83).

Lie to You for Your Love
Words and music by Frankie Miller, David Bellamy, Howard Bellamy, and Jeff Barry.
Chrysalis Music Group, 1985/Bellamy Brothers Music, 1985/Steeple Chase Music, 1985.
Best-selling record by The Bellamy Brothers from the album *Howard and David* (MCA, 85).

Life Gets Better (English)
Words and music by Graham Parker.
Participation Music, Inc., 1983.
Introduced on The Real Macaw by Graham Parker (Arista, 83).

Life Goes On
Words by John Bettis, music by George Tipton.
Introduced by Billy Vera and the Beaters as the theme for the TV sitcom *Empty Nest*.

Life in a Looking Glass (American-English)
Words by Leslie Bricusse, music by Henry Mancini.
EMI Golden Torch Music, 1986/EMI-Gold Horizon Music Corp., 1986.
Introduced by Tony Bennett in the movie *That's Life*. Nominated for an Academy Award, Best Song, 1986.

Life in a Northern Town (English)
Words and music by Nick Laird-Clowes and Gilbert Gabriel.
Cleverite, England, 1985/Farrowise, England.
Best-selling record in 1986 by The Dream Academy from the album *The Dream Academy* (Warner Bros., 85).

Life in One Day (English)
Words and music by Howard Jones.
Warner-Tamerlane Music, 1985.
Best-selling record by Howard Jones from the album *Life in One Day* (Elektra, 85).

Life in the Slaw Lane
Words and music by Kip Addotta, Kim Bullard, and Biff Maynard.
The song was registered for copyright on behalf of the writers.
  Introduced by Kip Addotta on the album *Life in the Slaw Lane*
  (Rhino, 86).

Life Is Hard
Words and music by Pat MacDonald.
Mambadaddi, 1986/I.R.S. Music/Criterion Music Corp.
Introduced by Timbuk 3 on the album *Greetings from Timbuk 3* (I.R.S.,
  86).

Life Story
Words by Richard Maltby, music by David Shire.
Fiddleback/Long Pond Music/Progeny Music/Revelation Music
  Publishing Corp.
Introduced by Lynne Wintersteller in the revue *Closer Than Ever* (89).

Life Turned Her That Way
Words and music by Harlan Howard.
Tree Publishing Co., Inc., 1964.
Best-selling record in 1988 by Ricky Van Shelton, from *Wild Eyed
  Dream* (Columbia, 87).

Life's Highway
Words and music by Richard Leigh and Roger Murrah.
EMI-April Music, 1986/Lion Hearted Music/EMI-Blackwood Music Inc.
Best-selling record by Steve Wariner from the album *Life's Highway*
  (MCA, 86).

Lift Me Up (Like a Dove)
Words by Lee Breuer, music by Bob Telson.
Boodle Music, 1984/Otis Lee Music, 1988.
Revived in 1988 by Clarence Fourta and The Five Blind Boys in the
  musical and on the album *The Gospel at Colonus* (Elektra Nonesuch,
  88).

Light at the End of the Tunnel (English)
Music by Andrew Lloyd Webber, words by Richard Stilgoe.
Really Useful Music, 1987.
Introduced by the company of the musical *Starlight Express,* which
  opened on Broadway in 1987. Performed by Ritchie Havens on the
  album *Music and Songs from 'Starlight Express'* (MCA, 87).

Light of Day
Words and music by Bruce Springsteen.
Bruce Springsteen Publishing.
Introduced in the film *Light of Day* by the Barbusters, the group created

for the movie's storyline and fronted by its stars, Joan Jett and Michael J. Fox.

Lightning in a Bottle
Words and music by Jimmy Webb.
White Oak Songs, 1988.
Introduced by Glen Campbell on *Light Years* (MCA, 88). The album reunites singer Campbell and songwriter Webb, but does not rival the work the two did in their heyday--'Galveston,' 'Wichita Lineman' and 'By the Time I Get to Phoenix.'

Lights of Downtown
Words and music by Stephen McCarthy.
Huevos Rancheros Music, 1985.
Introduced by The Long Ryders on the album *State of Our Union* (Island, 85).

Lights Out
Words and music by Peter Wolf and Don Covay.
Pal-Park Music, 1984/Ze'ev Music, 1984.
Best-selling record by Peter Wolf from *Lights Out* (EMI-America, 84).

Like a Prayer
Words and music by Madonna and Patrick Leonard.
WB Music, 1989/Johnny Yuma/Lost in Music.
Best-selling record by Madonna from *Like a Prayer* (Sire, 89). The makers of Pepsi withdrew a high-priced commercial featuring a portion of the video for this song in response to outrage in some quarters over the religous symbols it used. The notoriety of this action spurred further interest in the song.

Like a Rock
Words and music by Bob Seger.
Gear Publishing, 1986.
Best-selling record by Bob Seger & The Silver Bullet Band from the album *Like a Rock* (Capitol, 86).

Like a Virgin
Words and music by Billy Steinberg and Tom Kelly.
Sony Tunes, 1984/Denise Barry Music, 1984.
Best-selling record by Madonna from *Like a Virgin* (Warner Brothers, 84).

Like an Inca
Words and music by Neil Young.
Silver Fiddle, 1982.
Featured in *Trans* by Neil Young (Reprise, 83).

Like No Other Night (Canadian)
Words and music by Don Barnes, John Bettis, Jim Vallance, and Jeff
  Carlisi.
Rocknocker Music Co., 1986/John Bettis Music.
Best-selling record by 38 Special from the album *Strength in Numbers*
  (A & M, 86). Co-writer Jim Vallance frequently collaborates with
  Bryan Adams.

Limelight (Canadian)
Words by Neil Peart, music by Alex Lifeson and Geddy Lee.
Core Music Publishing, 1981.
Best-selling record by Rush from *Moving Pictures* (Mercury, 81).

Listen Like Thieves (Australian)
Words and music by Inxs.
MCA, Inc., 1986.
Best-selling record by Inxs from the album *Listen Like Thieves*
  (Atlantic, 86).

Listen to Your Heart (Swedish)
English words and music by Per Gessle, words and music by Person.
Screen Gems-EMI Music Inc., 1989.
Best-selling record by Roxette from *Look Sharp!* (EMI, 89).

Little April Shower
Words by Larry Morey, music by Frank Churchill.
Wonderland Music, 1942.
Performed by Michael Stipe, Natalie Merchant, and The Roches on *Stay
  Awake* (A & M, 88). The tune is from *Bambi*.

A Little Bit in Love
Words and music by Steve Earle.
Goldline Music Inc., 1984.
Best-selling record by Patty Loveless from *If My Heart Had Windows*
  (MCA, 88).

A Little Bit More
Words and music by Gene McFadden, Linda Vitali, and Jimmy
  McKinney.
Bush Burnin' Music, 1986/Gene McFadden, 1986/Su-Ma Publishing
  Co., Inc., 1986/Careers Music Inc., 1986.
Best-selling record by Melba Moore and Freddie Jackson from the
  album *A Lot of Love* (Capitol, 86).

A Little Bit of Love (Is All It Takes)
Words and music by Ric Wyatt, Jr. and Chris Perren.
House of Champions Music, 1985.
Best-selling record by New Edition from the album *All for Love* (MCA,
  86).

Little Darlin'
Words and music by Maurice Williams.
Excellorec Music Co., Inc., 1957.
Revived in 1987 by Dustin Hoffman and Warren Beatty as Chuck and Lyle in the film *Ishtar*. The release of this number as a single (on Capitol) marked the stars' recording debut, although Hoffman had previously played a songwriter in the film *Who Is Harry Kellerman ... and Why Is He Saying Those Terrible Things about Me?'* in which he sang tunes by Shel Silverstein.

The Little Drummer Boy
Words and music by Katherine Davis, Henry Drenato, and Aemy Simeone.
Mills Music Inc./International Korwin Corp.
Revived in 1987 by Bob Seger, for the album *A Very Special Christmas* (A & M), which became the most successful holiday album ever.

A Little Good News
Words and music by Charlie Black, Rory Bourke, and Thomas Rocco.
Chappell & Co., Inc., 1983/Polygram International, 1983.
Best-selling record by Anne Murray from *A Little Good News* (Capitol, 83). Nominated for a Grammy Award, Country Song of the Year, 1983.

Little H and Little G
Words and music by Ronald Melrose.
Rabbit Rabbit Music Co., 1982.
Introduced by Ensemble of *Upstairs at O'Neals* (82).

A Little in Love (English)
Words and music by Alan Tarney.
ATV Music Corp., 1980.
Best-selling record by Cliff Richard from *I'm No Hero* (EMI-America, 80).

A Little Is Enough (English)
Words and music by Pete Townshend.
Towser Tunes Inc., 1980.
Best-selling record by Pete Townshend from *Empty Glass* (Atco, 80).

Little Jackie Wants to Be a Star
Words and music by Full Force.
Forceful Music, 1989/Willesden Music, Inc./My My Music.
Best-selling record by Lisa Lisa and Cult Jam from *Straight to the Sky* (Columbia, 89).

Little Jeannie (English)
Words by Gary Osborne, music by Elton John.

Intersong, USA Inc., 1980.
Best-selling record by Elton John from *21 at 33* (MCA, 80).

Little Liar
Words and music by Joan Jett and Desmond Child.
Lagunatic Music, 1988/Desmobile Music Inc./EMI-April Music/Virgin
    Songs.
Best-selling record in 1989 by Joan Jett and the Blackhearts, from *Up
    Your Alley* (CBS Assoc., 88).

Little Lies (English)
Words and music by Christine McVie and Eddy Quintela.
Fleetwood Mac Music Ltd., 1987.
Best-selling record by Fleetwood Mac, from the album *Tango in the
    Night* (Warner Bros., 87).

Little Love Affairs
Words by Nanci Griffith, music by James Hooker.
Wing & Wheel Music, 1987/Colgems-EMI Music, 1988.
Introduced by Nanci Griffith on *Little Love Affairs* (MCA, 88).

Little Miss S (English)
Words by Edie Brickell, music by Edie Brickell & New Bohemians.
Geffen Music, 1986/Withrow Publishing, 1988/Edie Brickell Songs,
    1988/Strange Mind Productions, 1988.
A portrait of Warhol-era glamour girl Edie Sedgewick. Introduced by
    Edie Brickell & New Bohemians on *Shooting Rubberbands at the
    Stars* (Geffen, 88).

Little Red Corvette
Words and music by Prince Rogers Nelson.
Controversy Music, 1982.
Best-selling record by Prince from *1999* (Warner Brothers, 83).

A Little Respect (English)
Words and music by Vince Clarke and Andy Bell.
Sonet Publishing Ltd., London, England, 1988/Emile Music.
Best-selling record in 1989 by Erasure from *The Innocents* (Sire, 88).

Little Rock
Words and music by Pat McManus, Bob DiPiero, and Gerry House.
Combine Music Corp., 1986/Music City Music.
Best-selling record Reba McEntire from the album *Whoever's in New
    England* (MCA, 86).

Little Rock 'n' Roller
Words and music by Steve Earle.
Goldline Music Inc., 1986.
Introduced by Steve Earle on the album *Guitar Town* (MCA, 86).

Little Things, see **Baby, It's the Little Things.**

Little Too Late
Words and music by Alex Call.
Unichappell Music Inc., 1981/Roseynotes Music, 1981.
Best-selling record by Pat Benatar from *Get Nervous* (Chrysalis, 83).

Little Walter
Words and music by Denzil Foster and Thom McElroy.
Polygram Songs, 1988/Two Tuff-Enuff Music, 1988.
Best-selling record by Tony! Toni! Tone'! from *Who?* (Polygram, 88).

Little Wild One (No. 5)
Words and music by Marshall Crenshaw.
Colgems-EMI Music, 1985/House of Greed Music, 1985.
Introduced by Marshall Crenshaw on the album *Downtown* (Warner
    Bros., 85).

Live
Words and music by Emmit Rhodes.
La Brea Music, 1984/Thirty-Four Music, 1984.
Featured on *All over the Place* by The Bangles (Columbia, 84).

Live My Life
Words and music by Allee Willis and Danny Sembello.
Streamline Moderne, 1986/Texas City, 1986/No Pain, No Gain, 1986/
    Unicity Music, Inc., 1986.
Introduced by Boy George in the film and soundtrack album *Hiding Out*
    (Virgin, 87).

Live to Tell
Words and music by Madonna and Patrick Leonard.
WB Music, 1986/Bleu Disque Music, 1986/Lost in Music, 1986/Johnny
    Yuma, 1986.
Best-selling record by Madonna from the album *True Blue* (Warner
    Bros., 86). The song was the theme of the film *At Close Range* (86).

Lives in the Balance
Words and music by Jackson Browne.
Swallow Turn Music, 1986.
Introduced by Jackson Browne on the album *Lives in the Balance*
    (Asylum, 86). With topical references to on-going efforts to
    overthrow the Nicaraguan government, this song was showcased on
    the television series *Miami Vice* and used on the soundtrack album
    Miami Vice II.

Livin' on a Prayer
Words and music by Jon Bon Jovi, Richie Sambora, and Desmond
    Child.
Bon Jovi Publishing, 1986/Polygram Music Publishing Inc., 1986/EMI-
    April Music, 1986/Desmobile Music Inc., 1986.

Despite nearly being left off the album *Slippery When Wet* (Polygram, 86), this song went on to be a best-seller for Bon Jovi, 1987.

Living a Lie
Words and music by Chris Stamey and Peter Holsapple.
Misery Loves Co., 1982.
Introduced on *Repercussion* by The dBs (Albion, 82).

The Living Daylights (English)
Words by Pal Waaktaar, music by John Barry.
ATV Music Corp., 1987/United Lion Music Inc., 1987.
Introduced by a-ha in the film and on the soundtrack album *The Living Daylights* (Warner Bros., 87). Waaktaar is a member of a-ha.

Living in a Box (English)
Words and music by Marcus Vere and Steve Piggot.
Brampton Music Ltd., England, 1987/WB Music, 1987.
Best-selling record by Living in a Box, from the album by the same title (Chrysalis, 87).

Living in America
Words and music by Dan Hartman and Charlie Midnight.
EMI-April Music, 1985/Second Nature Music Inc./EMI-Blackwood Music Inc./Janiceps.
Introduced by James Brown in the 1985 film *Rocky IV* and used on the movie soundtrack album. Best-selling record by James Brown from the album *Gravity* (Scotti Bros., 86). Nominated for a Grammy Award, Rhythm 'n' Blues Song of the Year, 1986.

Living in Sin
Words and music by Jon Bon Jovi.
Bon Jovi Publishing, 1988.
Best-selling record in 1989 by Bon Jovi from *New Jersey* (Mercury, 88).

Living in the Promiseland
Words and music by Bucky Jones.
Blue Water, 1986/Bluebear Waltzes/Skunk DeVille.
Best-selling record by Willie Nelson from the album *The Promiseland* (Columbia, 86). Revived in 1987 by David Lynn Jones on the album *Hard Time on Easy Street* (Mercury, 87).

Living Inside Myself
Words and music by Gino Vannelli.
Black Keys, 1981.
Best-selling record by Gino Vannelli from *Night Walker* (Arista, 81).

Living It Up
Words and music by Rickie Lee Jones.

Easy Money Music, 1981.
Introduced by Rickie Lee Jones on *Pirates* (Warner Brothers, 82).

Living Proof
Words and music by Johnny MacRae and Suzanna Clark.
Intersong, USA Inc., 1988/Hide a Bone Music.
Best-selling record in 1989 by Ricky Van Shelton from *Living Proof* (Columbia, 88).

Living Through Another Cuba (English)
Words and music by Andy Partridge.
EMI-Virgin, 1980.
Performed by XTC in *Life in the European Theatre* (Sire, 82).

The Living Years (English)
Words and music by Mike Rutherford and Brian Robertson.
Kongride, England/Michael Rutherford Music, 1988/Warner-Tamerlane Music/Hit & Run Music.
Best-selling record in 1989 by Mike and the Mechanics from *Living Years* (Atlantic, 88). Nominated for Grammy Awards, Record of the Year, 1989, and Song of the Year, 1989.

Loco de Amor (Crazy for Love)
Words and music by David Byrne.
Index Music, 1986.
Introduced by David Byrne and Celia Cruz in the film and on the soundtrack album of *Something Wild* (MCA, 86). Byrne is the leader of the Talking Heads, while Celia Cruz is known among Latin music fans as the 'Queen of Salsa.'

The Loco-Motion
Words by Gerry Goffin, music by Carole King.
Screen Gems-EMI Music Inc., 1962.
Revived in 1988 by Kylie Minogue on *Kylie* (Geffen, 88).

Lone Star State of Mind
Words and music by Patrick Alger, Gene Levine, and Fred Koller.
Lucrative, 1987/Bait and Beer, 1987.
Introduced by Nanci Griffith on her album *Lone Star State of Mind* (MCA, 87).

Lonely Alone
Words and music by J. D. Martin and John Jarrard.
MCA, Inc., 1986/Alabama Band Music Co.
Best-selling record by the Forester Sisters from the album *Perfume, Ribbons, and Pearls* (Warner Bros., 86).

Lonely Boy
Words and music by George Gershwin.

New World Music Corp. (NY), 1987.
Introduced by Cynthia Haymon and Ruby Hinds on the special television tribute to George Gershwin, *'S Wonderful*. The song was originally written for Ann Brown to sing *Porgy and Bess,* but she rejected it in favor of 'Summertime.'

Lonely Nights
Words and music by Harris Stewart and Keith Stegall.
EMI-Blackwood Music Inc., 1981.
Best-selling record by Mickey Gilley from *You Don't Know Me* (Epic, 81).

Lonely Ol' Night
Words and music by John Cougar Mellencamp.
Full Keel Music, 1985.
Best-selling record by John Cougar Mellencamp from the album *Scarecrow* (Mercury, 85).

Lonely Town
Words and music by Stanard Ridgway (pseudonym for Stanard Funston).
Mondo Spartacus Music, 1989/Illegal Songs, Inc./Criterion Music Corp.
Introduced by Stan Ridgway on *Mosquitos* (Geffen, 89).

Long Gone Dead
Words and music by Chip Kinman and Tony Kinman.
Black Impala Music, 1984.
Introduced by Rank and File on *Long Gone Dead* (Slash, 84).

Long Hard Road (the Sharecropper's Dream)
Words and music by Rodney Crowell.
Coolwell Music, 1984/Granite Music Corp., 1984.
Best-selling record by The Nitty Gritty Dirt Band (Warner Brothers, 84).

A Long Line of Love
Words and music by Paul Overstreet and Thom Schuyler.
Bethlehem Music, 1986.
Best-selling record by Michael Martin Murphey from the album *Americana* (Warner Bros., 87).

A Long Night
Music by Alec Wilder, words by Loonis Reeves McGlohon.
Ludlow Music Inc., 1981/Saloon Songs, Inc., 1981.
Introduced by Frank Sinatra on *She Shot Me Down* (Reprise, 81).

Long Slide (for an Out)
Words and music by Dan Zanes.
Of the Fire Music, 1987/Big Thrilling Music.

Introduced by The Del Fuegos on the album *Stand Up* (Slash/Warner Bros., 87).

Long White Cadillac
Words and music by Dave Alvin.
Twin Duck Music, 1989.
Best-selling record by Dwight Yoakam from *Just Lookin' for a Hit* (Reprise, 89).

The Longest Summer
Words and music by Wendy Waldman.
Moon & Stars Music, 1987/Screen Gems-EMI Music Inc., 1987.
Introduced by Wendy Waldman on the album *Letters Home* (Cypress, 87).

The Longest Time
Words and music by Billy Joel.
Joelsongs, 1983/EMI-Blackwood Music Inc., 1983.
Best-selling record by Billy Joel from *An Innocent Man* (Columbia, 84).

Longings for a Simpler Time
Words and music by Jerry Leiber and Mike Stoller.
WB Music, 1974/Jerry Leiber Music/Mike Stoller Music.
Introduced by Peggy Lee on *Mirrors* (A & M, 75), an album successfully reissued in 1989.

Longshot
Words and music by Alan Scott and Gary Pickus.
Stone Diamond Music, 1986.
Introduced by Stacy Lattisaw on the album *Take Me All the Way* (Motown, 86). Grand Prize winner at the Seventeenth Annual Yamaha World Pop Festival.

The Look (Swedish)
English words and music by Per Gessle.
Jimmie Fun, 1989.
Best-selling record by Roxette from *Look Sharp!* (EMI, 89).

Look Away
Words and music by Diane Warren.
Realsongs, 1988.
Best-selling record by Chicago, from *Chicago XIX* (Reprise, 88).

The Look of Love (English)
Words and music by Martin Fry, Mark Lickley, Stephen Singleton, and David Palmer.
Virgin Music, 1982.
Best-selling record by ABC from *The Lexicon of Love* (Mercury, 82).

Look out Any Window
Words and music by Bruce Hornsby and John Hornsby.
Zappo Music, 1988/Basically Gasp Music, 1988.
Best-selling record by Bruce Hornsby & The Range from *Scenes from the Southside* (RCA, 88). Southern Gothic pop-rock.

Look over There
Words and music by Jerry Herman.
Jerryco Music Co., 1983.
Introduced by Gene Barry in *La Cage Au Folles* (83).

Look What You Done to Me
Words and music by Boz Scaggs and David Foster.
BMG Music, 1980/Foster Frees Music Inc., 1980/Irving Music Inc., 1980.
Best-selling record by Boz Scaggs (Columbia, 80). Featured in the film & soundtrack album *Urban Cowboy* (80).

Lookin' for Love
Words and music by Wanda Mallette, Patti Ryan, and Bob Morrison.
Southern Nights Music Co., 1979.
Best-selling record by Johnny Lee from *Lookin' for Love* (Asylum, 80). Nominated for a Grammy Award, Country Song of the Year, 1980.

Looking at You (across the Breakfast Table)
Words and music by Irving Berlin.
Irving Berlin Music Corp., 1929.
Revived in 1987 by Michael Feinstein on the album *Michael Feinstein Sings Irving Berlin* (Columbia).

Looking for a New Love
Words and music by Andre Cymone and Jody Watley.
EMI-April Music, 1987/Intersong, USA Inc., 1987/Ultrawave, 1987.
Best-selling record by Jody Watley, from the album *Jody Watley* (MCA, 87), her first solo effort since leaving Shalamar. Watley received a Grammy as Best New Artist of the Year.

Looking for the Next Best Thing
Words and music by Kenny Edwards, Leroy P. Marinell, and Warren Zevon.
Tiny Tunes, 1982/Valgovino Music, 1982/Zevon Music Inc., 1982.
Introduced by Warren Zevon in *The Envoy* (Asylum, 82).

Loosey's Rap
Words and music by Rick James.
Stone City Music, 1988/National League Music, 1988.
Best-selling record by Rick James featuring Roxanne Shante, from *Wonderful* (Reprise, 88).

Lord, I Hope This Day Is Good
Words and music by Dave Hanner.
Sabal Music, Inc., 1981.
Best-selling record by Don Williams from *Especially for You* (MCA, 82).

Losing My Mind
Words and music by Stephen Sondheim.
Herald Square Music Co., 1971/Rilting Music Inc., 1971/Burthen Music Co., Inc., 1971.
Revived in 1989 by Liza Minnelli on *Results* (Epic, 89), this number from the musical *Follies* was a big hit in England and launched Minnelli's pop comeback.

Lost in Emotion
Words and music by Full Force.
Forceful Music, 1987/Willesden Music, Inc., 1987/My My Music, 1987/Careers Music Inc., 1987.
Best-selling record by Lisa Lisa and Cult Jam, from the album *Spanish Fly* (Columbia, 87).

Lost in Love (Australian)
Words and music by Graham Russell.
BMG Music, 1980.
Best-selling record by Air Supply from *Lost in Love* (Arista, 80).

Lost in the Fifties Tonight (In the Still of the Night)
Words and music by Mike Reid, Troy Seals, and Freddy Parris.
BMG Songs Inc., 1985/WB Music, 1956/Llee Music, 1956.
Best-selling record by Ronnie Milsap from *Greatest Hits, Vol. 2* (RCA, 85). The central musical theme is from one of rock 'n' roll's greatest 'do-wop' classics. Nominated for a Grammy Award, Country Song of the Year, 1985.

Lost in You (English)
Words and music by Rod Stewart and Andy Taylor.
Intersong, USA Inc., 1988/EMI-April Music, 1988/Poetlord Music, 1988/Rod Stewart, 1988.
Best-selling record by Rod Stewart from *Out of Order* (Warner Bros., 88).

Lost in Your Eyes
Words and music by Deborah Gibson.
EMI-April Music, 1988/Possibilities Publishing.
Best-selling record by Debbie Gibson from *Electric Youth* (Atlantic, 89).

Lotta Love
Words and music by Neil Young.
Silver Fiddle.

Revived in 1989 by Dinosaur Jr. on *The Bridge: A Tribute to Neil Young* (Caroline, 89), an album on which Young's works undergo some radical interpretations.

Louisiana 1927
Words and music by Randy Newman.
Warner-Tamerlane Music, 1974.
Revived in the 1986 Dallas Theater Center production of the play *All the King's Men*. Music from Randy Newman's album *Good Ol' Boys* was used throughout the play. This tune, written in 1974, is about Huey Long, who was also the inspiration of the Robert Penn Warren novel.

Lovable (English)
Words and music by Elvis Costello (pseudonym for Declan MacManus) and Cait O'Riordan.
Plangent Visions Music, Inc., London, England, 1986.
Introduced by Elvis Costello on the album *King of America* (Columbia, 86). Co-writer O'Riordan is a former member of The Pogues. DeClan McManus is Costello's real name.

Love Affair with Everyday Livin' (English)
Words and music by Rolo McGinty.
Introduced by the Woodentops on the album *Giant* (Columbia, 86). The author registered the song for copyright in 1985.

Love and Affection (English)
Words and music by Joan Armatrading.
Irving Music Inc., 1986.
Performed by Sly Stone and Martha Davis in the 1986 film *Soul Man* and on the soundtrack album (A & M, 86).

Love and Anger (English)
Words and music by Kate Bush.
Kate Bush Music, Ltd., London, England, 1989/Screen Gems-EMI Music Inc.
Introduced by Kate Bush on *The Sensual World* (Columbia, 89).

Love and Mercy
Words and music by Brian Wilson and Eugene Landy.
Beach Bum Music, 1988/Beachhead Music, 1988.
Introduced by Brian Wilson, founder and voice of the Beach Boys, on his long awaited solo album *Brian Wilson* (Reprise, 88). Co-writer Landy is Wilson's psychotherapist.

Love at the Five and Dime
Words and music by Nanci Griffith.
Wing It, 1986.
Best-selling record by Kathy Mattea from the album *Walk the Way the*

Wind Blows (Mercury, 86). Introduced by Nanci Griffith on the album *Daddy Said* (Rounder, 86).

Love Bites (English)
Words and music by Steve Clark, Phil Collen, Joe Elliott, Robert John 'Mutt' Lange, and Rick Savage.
Bludgeon Riffola Music, 1987/Zomba Music, 1987.
Best-selling record in 1988 by Def Leppard, from *Hysteria* (Mercury, 87).

A Love Bizarre
Words and music by Sheila Escovedo and Prince Rogers Nelson.
Sister Fate Music, 1985.
Best-selling record by Sheila E. in 1986 from the album *Romance 1600* (Warner Bros., 85). Introduced by Sheila E. in the film and on the soundtrack album of *Krush Groove* (85).

Love Can't Happen
Words and music by Maury Yeston.
Yeston Music, Ltd., 1989.
Introduced by David Carroll in *Grand Hotel.* This lavish, 1989 Broadway musical included a number of thirty-year-old songs by Robert Wright and George Forrest, authors of *Kismet* and *Song of Norway*, among others, in addition to new tunes penned by Yeston, such as this.

Love Changes
Words and music by Skip Scarborough.
Alexscar Music, 1987.
Best-selling record in 1988 by Kashif and Meli'sa Morgan from *Love Changes* (Arista, 87).

Love Come Down
Words and music by Kashif (pseudonym for Michael Jones).
MCA, Inc., 1982/Kashif Music, 1982.
Best-selling record by Evelyn King from *Get Loose* (RCA, 82).

Love Don't Care (Whose Heart It Breaks)
Words and music by Earl Thomas Conley and Randy Scruggs.
Labor of Love Music, 1984/EMI-April Music, 1984/EMI-Blackwood Music Inc., 1984.
Best-selling record by Earl Thomas Conley from the album *Treadin' Water* (RCA, 85).

Love Has Finally Come at Last
Words and music by Bobby Womack.
ABKCO Music Inc., 1983/Ashtray Music, 1983/Spaced Hands Music, 1983/Beverly Glen Publishing, 1983.

Best-selling record by Bobby Womack and Patti La Belle from *The Poet II (Beverly Glen, 84)*.

Love Helps Those
Words and music by Paul Overstreet.
Scarlet Moon Music, 1988.
Best-selling record by Paul Overstreet (MTM, 88).

Love in an Elevator
Words and music by Steven Tyler and Joe Perry.
Swag Song Music, 1989.
Best-selling record by Aerosmith from *Pump* (Geffen, 89).

Love in the First Degree
Words and music by Jim Hurt and James Dubois.
Warner House of Music, 1980.
Best-selling record by Alabama from *Feels So Right* (RCA, 82).

Love Is a Battlefield
Words and music by Mike Chapman and Holly Knight.
Mike Chapman Publishing Enterprises, 1983/BMG Songs Inc., 1983.
Best-selling record by Pat Benatar from *Live from Earth* (Chrysalis, 83).

Love Is a House
Words and music by Martin Lascelles, Geoff Gurd, and G. Foster.
Tee Girl Music, 1987.
Introduced by The Force M.D.'s on the album *Touch and Go* (Tommy Boy, 87).

Love Is a Stranger (English)
Words and music by Annie Lennox and Dave Stewart.
Red Network Music, 1982/Carbert Music Inc., 1982.
Best-selling record by Eurythmics from *Sweet Dreams (Are Made of This)* (RCA, 83).

Love Is Alive
Words and music by Kent Robbins.
Irving Music Inc., 1984.
Best-selling record by The Judds from the album *Why Not Me* (RCA, 85). Nominated for a Grammy Award, Country Song of the Year, 1985.

Love Is Alright Tonite (Australian)
Words and music by Rick Springfield.
Portal Music, 1981/Muscleman Music, 1981.
Best-selling record by Rick Springfield from *Working Class Dog* (RCA, 82).

Love Is Being Loved
Words and music by Mickey Rooney.
Timic, 1987.
Introduced by Jan Rooney on the Silver Star label. The author and
singer are husband and wife.

Love Is for Lovers
Words and music by Peter Holsapple and Darby Hall.
Misery Loves Co., 1984.
Introduced by The dBs on *Like This* (Bearsville, 84).

Love Is Forever
Words and music by Barry Eastmond and Billy Ocean.
Zomba Music, 1986.
Best-selling record by Billy Ocean from the album *Love Zone* (Sire, 86).

Love Is Gonna Bring Us Back Alive
Words and music by Rickie Lee Jones and Pascal Neber Meyer.
Easy Money Music, 1989.
Introduced by Rickie Lee Jones on *Flying Cowboys* (Geffen, 89).

Love Is in Control (Finger on the Trigger) (American-English)
Words and music by Quincy Jones, Merria Ross, and Rod Temperton.
Yellow Brick Road Music, 1982/Almo Music Corp., 1982/Grager
  Music, 1982.
Best-selling record by Donna Summer from *Donna Summer* (Geffen,
  82).

Love Is My Decision (Theme from *Arthur 2 On the Rocks*)
Words and music by Burt Bacharach, Carole Bayer Sager, and Chris
  DeBurgh.
WB Music, 1988/New Hidden Valley Music Co., 1988/Almo Music
  Corp., 1988/Warner-Tamerlane Music, 1988/Carole Bayer Sager
  Music, 1988.
Introduced by Chris DeBurgh in the film and soundtrack album *Arthur 2
  On the Rocks* (A & M, 88).

Love Is on a Roll (American-English)
Words and music by Roger Cook and John Prine.
Roger Cook Music, 1983/Big Ears Music Inc., 1983/Bruised Oranges,
  1983.
Best-selling record by Don Williams (MCA, 83).

Love Is the Seventh Wave (English)
Words and music by Sting (pseudonym for Gordon Sumner).
Magnetic Music Publishing Co., 1985/Reggatta Music, Ltd., 1985/Illegal
  Songs, Inc., 1985.
Best-selling record by Sting from the album *The Dream of the Blue
  Turtles* (A & M, 85).

Love Light in Flight
Words and music by Stevie Wonder.
Jobete Music Co., 1984/Black Bull Music, 1984.
Best-selling record by Stevie Wonder from the soundtrack album *The Woman in Red* (Motown, 85). Introduced in the film *The Woman in Red* (85).

Love Lights the World (Rendezvous), also known as Flight of the Snowbirds
Words by Jeremy Lubbock and Linda Thompson Jenner, music by David Foster.
Air Bear, 1987/Nero Publishing, 1987/Hollysongs, 1987.
Performed by David Foster and the Red Army chorus at Rendezvous '87 Peace Festival in Quebec City, Canada (Atlantic, 87). This song originated on Foster's solo album as an instrumental called 'Flight of the Snowbirds,' before the Red Army Choir transformed it, with the help of the lyricists, into a song about world peace.

Love Like We Do
Words and music by Edie Brickell.
Geffen Music, 1987/Edie Brickell Songs, 1987/Withrow Publishing, 1987/Strange Mind Productions, 1987.
Introduced by Edie Brickell & New Bohemians on *Shooting Rubberbands at the Stars* (Geffe n, 88).

Love Lives On
Words by Cynthia Weil and Will Jennings, music by Barry Mann and Bruce Broughton.
MCA Music, 1987/Music of the World, 1987.
Introduced by Joe Cocker on the soundtrack of the film *Harry and the Hendersons* and on its album (MCA, 87).

Love Makes Such Fools of Us All
Words by Michael Stewart, music by Cy Coleman.
Notable Music Co., Inc., 1980.
Introduced by Marianne Tatum in *Barnum* (80).

(If You) Love Me Just a Little
Words and music by La La (pseudonym for LaForrest Cope) and Full Force.
Little Tanya, 1987/MCA Music, 1987/Forceful Music, 1987/Willesden Music, Inc., 1987.
Best-selling record by La La, from the album *La La* (Arista, 86). La La previously penned the Whitney Houston smash 'You Give Good Love.'

Love Me Like You Used To
Words and music by Paul Davis and Bobby Emmons.

Web 4 Music Inc., 1987/Paul & Jonathan, 1987/Rightsong Music, 1987/ Attadoo, 1987.
Best-selling record by Tanya Tucker, from the album *Love Me Like You Used To* (Capitol, 87).

Love Me Tomorrow
Words and music by Peter Cetera and David Foster.
BMG Music, 1982/Foster Frees Music Inc., 1982/Irving Music Inc., 1982.
Best-selling record by Chicago from *Chicago 16* (Full Moon/Warner Brothers, 82).

Love My Way (English)
Words and music by John Ashton, Timothy Butler, Richard Butler, and Vincent Ely.
EMI-Blackwood Music Inc., 1982.
Best-selling record by The Psychedelic Furs from *Forever Now* (Columbia, 83).

Love Never Goes Away
Words and music by Al Kasha and Joel Hirschhorn.
Morning Pictures Music, 1978/Fire and Water Songs.
Introduced by Debby Boone in *Seven Brides for Seven Brothers* (82).

Love on a Two Way Street
Words and music by Sylvia Robinson and Bert Keyes.
Gambi Music Inc., 1968.
Revived by Stacy Lattisaw from *With You* (Atlantic, 81).

Love on the Rocks (American-French)
English words and music by Neil Diamond, English words and music by Gilbert Becaud.
Artistique Editions Music, France, 1980/Stonebridge Music, 1980.
Best-selling record by Neil Diamond (Capitol, 81). Introduced in the film & soundtrack album *The Jazz Singer* (80).

Love on Your Side (English)
Words and music by Tom Bailey, Alannah Currie, and Joe Leeway.
Zomba Music, 1982.
Best-selling record by The Thompson Twins from *Side Kicks* (Arista, 83).

Love out Loud
Words and music by Tom Schuyler.
Screen Gems-EMI Music Inc., 1988/Bethlehem Music.
Best-selling record in 1989 by Earl Thomas Conley from *Heart of It All* (RCA, 88).

Love Over and Over Again
Words and music by Bobby DeBarge and Bunny DeBarge (pseudonym for Etterlene Jordan).
Jobete Music Co., 1980.
Best-selling record by Switch from *This Is My Dream* (Gordy, 80).

Love Overboard
Words and music by Reggie Calloway.
Calloco, 1987/Hip-Trip Music Co., 1987.
Best-selling record in 1988 by Gladys Knight & The Pips from *All Our Love* (MCA, 87).

Love Plus One (English)
Words and music by Nick Heyward.
Bryan Morrison Music, Inc., 1982.
Best-selling record by Haircut One Hundred from *Pelican West* (Arista, 82).

Love Power
Words by Carole Bayer Sager, music by Burt Bacharach.
New Hidden Valley Music Co., 1987/Carole Bayer Sager Music, 1987.
Best-selling record by Dionne Warwick, from the album *Reservations for Two* (Arista, 87). This song marked a return by Bacharach to writing for Warwick, as he had done with his previous partner, Hal David, throughout the 1960's.

Love Radiates Around
Words and music by Mark Johnson.
Cold Weather Music, 1980/New Media Music.
Introduced by The Roches on the album *Another World* (Warner Bros., 85).

Love Saw It
Words and music by L. A. Reid (pseudonym for Antonio Reid), Babyface (pseudonym for Kenny Edmunds), and Daryl Simmons.
Kear Music, 1988/Green Skirt Music/Hip-Trip Music Co.
Best-selling record in 1989 by Karyn White from *Karyn White* (Warner Bros., 88).

Love Shack
Words and music by B-52s.
Man Woman Together Now Music, 1989/Irving Music Inc.
Best-selling record by The B-52's from *Cosmic Thing* (Reprise, 89).

Love Somebody (Australian)
Words and music by Rick Springfield.
Vogue Music, 1984.
Best-selling record by Rick Springfield from the film and soundtrack to *Hard to Hold* (RCA, 84).

Love Someone Like Me
Words and music by Holly Dunn and Radney Foster.
Lawyer's Daughter, 1987/Uncle Artie, 1987.
Best-selling record by Holly Dunn, from the album *Cornerstone* (MTM, 87).

Love Song (English)
Words and music by Robert Smith, Simon Gallup, Boris Williams, Porl Thompson, Roger O'Donnell, and Laurence Tolhurst.
Fiction Music Inc., 1989.
Best-selling record by The Cure from *Disintegration* (Elektra, 89).

Love Song
Words and music by Frank Hannon and Jeff Keith.
City Kidd Music, 1989.
Best-selling record by Tesla from *The Great Radio Controversy* (Geffen, 89).

Love Stinks
Words and music by Peter Wolf and Seth Justman.
Center City Music, 1979/Pal-Park Music, 1979.
Best-selling record by The J. Geils Band from *Love Stinks* (EMI-America, 80).

A Love Supreme
Words by Phil Downing and D. Cole, music by John Coltrane.
Jowcol, 1964.
Revived in 1988 by Phil Downing, (Island). This jazz standard, written by tenor sax legend John Coltrane, became a hit in England when given a disco treatment.

Love Survives
Words and music by Al Kasha, Joel Hirschhorn, and Michael Lloyd.
Mike Curb Productions, 1989/Goldcrest-Sullivan-Bluth Music.
Introduced by Irene Cara on the soundtrack of the animated feature *All Dogs Go to Heaven* (album, MCA, 89).

Love the World Away
Words and music by Bob Morrison and Johnny Wilson.
Southern Nights Music Co., 1980.
Best-selling record by Kenny Rogers from *Kenny Rogers' Greatest Hits* (United Artists, 80).

Love Theme from *St. Elmo's Fire* (Instrumental)
Words and music by David Foster.
EMI-Gold Horizon Music Corp., 1985/Foster Frees Music Inc., 1985.
Best-selling record by David Foster (Atlantic, 85). Introduced in the film and soundtrack album *St. Elmo's Fire* (85).

Love Theme from *Shogun* (Mariko's Theme)
Music by Maurice Jarre.
Addax Music Co., Inc., 1980.
Best-selling record by Meco (RSO, 80). Introduced on the TV mini-series *Shogun*.

Love T.K.O.
Words and music by Cecil Womack and Gib Nobel.
Assorted Music, 1980.
Best-selling record by Teddy Pendergrass from *TP* (Philadelphia International, 80).

Love to See You
Words and music by Suzzy Roche.
Deshufflin' Inc., 1985.
Introduced by The Roches on the album *Another World* (Warner Bros., 85).

Love Touch (Theme from *Legal Eagles*)
Words and music by Mike Chapman, Holly Knight, and Gene Black.
Makiki Publishing Co., Ltd., 1986/BMG Songs Inc./Mike Chapman Publishing Enterprises.
Best-selling record by Rod Stewart from the album *Rod Stewart* (Warner Bros., 86). Introduced by Rod Stewart in the 1986 film *Legal Eagles*.

Love Walks In
Words and music by Eddie Van Halen, Michael Anthony, Sammy Hagar, and Alex Van Halen.
Yessup Music Co., 1986.
Best-selling record by Van Halen from the album *5150* (Warner Bros., 86).

Love Will Conquer All
Words and music by Lionel Richie, Jr., Cynthia Weil, and Greg Phillinganes.
Brockman Music, 1986/Dyad Music, Ltd./Poppy's Music.
Best-selling record by Lionel Richie from the album *Dancing on the Ceiling* (Motown, 86).

Love Will Find Its Way to You
Words and music by Dave Loggins and J. D. Martin.
MCA Music, 1987/Patchwork Music, 1987.
Best-selling record in 1988 by Reba McEntire from *The Last One to Know* (MCA, 87).

Love Will Save the Day
Words and music by C. Toni.
House of Fun Music, 1985.

Best-selling record in 1988 by Whitney Houston from *Whitney* (Arista, 87).

Love Will Tear Us Apart (English)
Words and music by Ian Curtis, words and music by Joy Division.
Fractured Music, England, 1980/Zomba Music.
Revived in 1988 by the Swans (Caroline, 88). This underground anthem has had many lives.

Love Will Turn You Around
Words and music by Kenny Rogers, Even Stevens, Thom Schuyler, and David Malloy.
Lionsmate Music, 1982/Debdave Music Inc., 1982/Briarpatch Music, 1982/Lionscub Music, 1982.
Best-selling record by Kenny Rogers from *Love Will Turn You Around* (Liberty, 82).

Love Wore a Halo (Back Before the War)
Words and music by Nanci Griffith.
Wing & Wheel Music, 1987.
Introduced by Nanci Griffith on *Little Love Affairs*, (MCA, 88). Song forms the basis of the country singer's novel-in-progress, about a unique post-war couple.

Love, You Ain't Seen the Last of Me
Words and music by Kendall Franceschi.
W.B.M. Music, 1987.
Best-selling record by John Schneider, from his *Greatest Hits* album (MCA, 87).

Love You Down
Words and music by Melvin Riley.
Music of the World, 1986/Off Backstreet Music, 1986/Ready for the World Music, 1986/Trixie Lou Music, 1986.
Best-selling record in 1987 by Ready for the World, from the album *Long Time Coming* (MCA, 86).

Love Zone
Words and music by Barry Eastmond, Wayne Braithwaite, and Billy Ocean.
Zomba Music, 1986.
Best-selling record by Billy Ocean from the album *Love Zone* (Jive, 86).

Lovelight
Words and music by O'Bryan Burnette and Don Cornelius.
Big Train Music Co., 1984.
Best-selling record by O'Bryan from *Be My Lover* (Capitol, 84).

Lovely One
Words and music by Michael Jackson and Randy Jackson.
Renjack Music, 1980/Mijac Music, 1980.
Best-selling record by The Jacksons from *Triumph* (Epic, 80).

Lover Boy
Words and music by Keith Diamond, Billy Ocean, Robert John 'Mutt'
  Lange, Billy Alessi, and Bobby Alessi.
Zomba Music, 1984/Willesden Music, Inc., 1984/Alessi Music, 1979.
Best-selling record by Billy Ocean in 1985 from the album *Suddenly*
  (Arista, 84).

The Lover in Me
Words and music by Babyface (pseudonym for Kenny Edmunds), L. A.
  Reid (pseudonym for Antonio Reid), and Daryl Simmons.
Kear Music, 1988/Hip-Trip Music Co./Green Skirt Music.
Best-selling record in 1989 by Sheena Easton from *The Lover in Me*
  (MCA, 88).

Lovergirl
Words and music by Teena Marie (pseudonym for Teena Marie
  Brockert).
CBS Inc., 1984/Midnight Magnet, 1985.
Best-selling record by Teena Marie from the album *Starchild* (Epic, 85).

Love's Been a Little Bit Hard on Me
Words and music by Gary Burr.
WB Gold Music Corp., 1982.
Best-selling record by Juice Newton from *Quiet Lies* (Capitol, 82).

Love's Calling
Words and music by Sam Cooke.
ABKCO Music Inc., 1984.
Introduced by Womack and Womack on the album *Radio M.U.S.C. Man*
  (Elektra, 85). This song is one of twenty Sam Cooke had been
  working on at the time of his death.

Love's Got a Line on You
Words and music by Zack Smith and Kathe Green.
KJG Music, 1981/EMI-Blackwood Music Inc., 1981.
Best-selling record by Scandal from *Scandal* (Columbia, 83).

Love's on the Line
Words and music by Bruce Springsteen.
Bruce Springsteen Publishing, 1982.
Featured in *On the Line* by Gary U.S. Bonds (EMI-America, 82).

Lovin' Her Was Easier
Words and music by Kris Kristofferson.
EMI Music Publishing, 1970.

Lovin' on Next to Nothin'
Words and music by Alan Rich, Jeffrey Pescetto, and Howie Rice.
Nelana Music, 1987/Rashida Music, 1987/Limited Funds Music, 1987/ Texas City, 1987.
Best-selling record by Gladys Knight & The Pips, from *All Our Love* (MCA, 87).

Lovin' Only Me
Words and music by Even Stevens and Hilary Kanter.
ESP Management Inc., 1988.
Best-selling record in 1989 by Ricky Skaggs from *Comin' Home to Stay* (Epic, 88).

Lovin' You
Words and music by Kenny Gamble and Leon Huff.
Downstairs Music, Inc., 1987/Piano, 1987/Mighty Three Music.
Best-selling record by the O'Jays, from the album *Let Me Touch You* (P.I.R., 87).

Loving the Sinner, Hating the Sin
Words and music by Steve Wynn.
Poison Brisket Music, 1988.
Introduced by Dream Syndicate on *Ghost Stories* (Enigma, 88).

Loving up a Storm
Words and music by Dan Morrison and Johnny Slate.
Warner House of Music, 1979.
Best-selling record by Razzy Bailey (RCA, 80).

Luck in My Eyes (Canadian)
Words and music by k.d. lang (pseudonym for Kathy Dawn Lang) and Ben Mink.
Bumstead (SOCAN)/Zavion (SOCAN).
Best-selling record by k. d. lang and The Reclines from *Absolute Torch and Twang* (Sire, 89). Nominated for a Grammy Award, Country Song of the Year, 1989.

Lucky Charm
Words and music by Babyface (pseudonym for Kenny Edmunds), Greg Scelsa, and Daryl Simmons.
Kear Music, 1988/Gregorian Chance Music/PSO Music/Hip-Trip Music Co.
Best-selling record in 1989 by The Boys from *Messages from the Boys* (Motown, 88).

Lucky Girl
Words and music by Joni Mitchell.
Crazy Crow Music, 1985.
Introduced by Joni Mitchell on the album *Dog Eat Dog* (Geffen, 85).

Lucky Star
Words and music by Madonna Ciccone.
WB Music, 1983/Bleu Disque Music, 1983/Webo Girl, 1983.
Best-selling record by Madonna from *Madonna* (Sire, 84).

Luka
Words and music by Suzanne Vega.
Waifersongs, 1987/Warner Brothers-Seven Arts Music, 1987.
Best-selling record by Suzanne Vega, from the album *Solitude Standing* (A & M, 87). This song about child abuse touched a nerve in a year when children in jeopardy generated major news stories throughout the country. Nominated for Grammy Awards, Best Record of the Year, 1987, and Best Song of the Year, 1987.

Lullabye (English)
Words and music by Robert Smith, Simon Gallup, Boris Williams, Porl Thompson, Roger O'Donnell, and Laurence Tolhurst.
Fiction Music Inc., 1989.
Best-selling record by The Cure from *Disintegration* (Elektra, 89).

Lyin' in a Bed of Fire
Words and music by Steve Van Zandt.
Blue Midnight Music, 1982.
Introduced by Little Steven & The Disciples of Soul on *Men Without Women* (EMI, 82).

Lynda
Words and music by Bill LaBounty and Pat McLaughlin.
Screen Gems-EMI Music Inc., 1987.
Best-selling record by Steve Wariner, from his *Greatest Hits* album. (MCA, 87).

M

Mad About You
Words and music by Paula Brown, James Whelan, and Mitchell Young Evans.
Alpine One, 1986/Careers Music Inc./This Is Art/BMG Songs Inc.
Best-selling record by Belinda Carlisle from the album *Belinda Carlisle* (MCA, 86).

Madison Avenue Soul
Words and music by Lamar Alford.
Revived in 1988 by the Students on *Martin*, a musical written in 1981 about the life of Martin Luther King, Jr.

Madonna of the Wasps (English)
Words and music by Robyn Hitchcock.
Two Crabs, England, 1989.
Introduced by Robyn Hitchcock and the Egyptians on *Queen Elvis* (A & M, 89).

Magic
Words and music by John Farrar.
John Farrar Music, 1980.
Best-selling record by Olivia Newton-John from the film and soundtrack to *Xanadu* (MCA, 80).

Magic
Words and music by Ric Ocasek.
Lido Music Inc., 1984.
Best-selling record by The Cars from *Heartbeat City* (Elektra, 84).

Magic Man
Words and music by Herb Alpert, Michael Stokes, and Melvin Ragin.
Almo Music Corp., 1981/Irving Music Inc., 1981.
Best-selling record by Herb Alpert from *Magic Man* (A & M, 81).

The Magic Train
Words by P. G. Wodehouse and Guy Bolton, music by Jerome Kern.

Polygram International, 1924.

Revived in 1989 by Davis Gaines and Paige O'Hara in a production of *Sitting Pretty* made possible by the discovery of the previously unpublished score from the 1924 musical in a warehouse in New Jersey in 1982. This song foreshadows Kern's more famous 'Make Believe,' from *Showboat.*

Major Tom (Coming Home) (German)
English words and music by Peter Shilling and David Lodge.
Southern Music Publishing Co., Inc., 1982.
Best-selling record by Peter Shilling (Elektra, 83).

Make a Move on Me
Words and music by John Farrar and Tom Snow.
John Farrar Music, 1981/Snow Music, 1981.
Best-selling record by Olivia Newton-John from *Physical* (MCA, 82).

Make It Last Forever
Words and music by Keith Sweat and Teddy Riley.
WB Music, 1987/Zomba Music, 1987/E/A Music, 1987/Keith Sweat Publishing, 1987/Vintertainment, 1987/Donril, 1987.
Best-selling record in 1988 by Keith Sweat (in a duet with Jacci McGhee), from *Make It Last Forever* (Vintertainment, 87).

Make It Real
Words and music by Linda Mallah, Rich Kelly, and Dan Powell.
Meow Baby, 1987/Rick Kelly, 1987/Demerie Music, 1987.
Best-selling record record in 1988 by the Jets, from *Magic* (MCA, 88).

Make Love Stay
Words and music by Dan Fogelberg.
Hickory Grove Music, 1982/EMI-April Music, 1982.
Best-selling record by Dan Fogelberg from *Dan Fogelberg/Greatest Hits* (Full Moon/Epic, 83).

Make Me Lose Control
Words and music by Eric Carmen and Dean Pitchford.
Eric Carmen, 1988/Island Music, 1988/Pitchford, 1988.
Best-selling record by Eric Carmen, former lead singer for the Raspberries, from his album *Best Of* (Arista, 88).

Make My Day
Words and music by Dewayne Blackwell.
Peso Music, 1984/Wallet Music, 1984.
Best-selling record by T. G. Sheppard with Clint Eastwood (Warner/ Curb, 84).

Make My Life with You
Words and music by Gary Burr.

Garwin Music Inc., 1984/Sweet Karol Music, 1984.
Best-selling record by The Oak Ridge Boys from the album *Step on Out* (MCA, 85).

Make No Mistake, He's Mine, see **Make No Mistake, She's Mine.**

Make No Mistake, She's Mine, also known as **Make No Mistake, He's Mine**
Words and music by Kim Carnes.
Moonwindow Music, 1985.
Revived in 1987 by Ronnie Milsap and Kenny Rogers on the album *Heart and Soul* (RCA, 87). Originally released as a single by the writer in a duet with Barbra Streisand, under the title 'Make No Mistake, He's Mine.'

Make That Move
Words and music by William Shelby, Ricky Smith, and Kevin Spencer.
Portrait/Solar Songs Inc., 1980.
Best-selling record by Shalamar from *Three for Love* (Solar, 81).

Make up Your Mind
Words and music by George Curtis Jones, Starleana Young, and Stephen Washington.
Lucky Three Music Publishing Co., 1982/Red Aurra Publishing, 1982.
Best-selling record by Aurra from *A little Love* (Salsoul, 82).

Makin' Thunderbirds
Words and music by Bob Seger.
Gear Publishing, 1983.
Introduced by Bob Seger on *The Distance* (Capitol, 83).

Makin' up for Lost Time
Words and music by Gary Morris and Dave Loggins.
WB Music, 1986/Gary Morris Music/Leeds Music Corp./Patchwork Music.
Best-selling record by Crystal Gayle and Gary Morris.

Makin' Whoopee
Words by Gus Kahn, music by Walter Donaldson.
Chappell & Co., Inc., 1928/Donaldson Publishing Co., 1928/Gilbert Keyes Music Co., 1928/Tobago Music Co., 1928.
Revived in 1989 by Michelle Pfeiffer, portraying a nightclub singer in the film *The Fabulous Baker Boys* (soundtrack album, GRP, 89). Also recorded by Dr. John with Rickie Lee Jones on his album *In a Sentimental Mood* (Warner Bros., 89).

Making Love
Words and music by Carole Bayer Sager, Burt Bacharach, and Bruce Roberts.

Twentieth Century Music Corp., 1982/New Hidden Valley Music Co.,
   1982/Carole Bayer Sager Music, 1982/Fox Fanfare Music Inc., 1982.
Best-selling record by Roberta Flack from *I'm the One* (Atlanta, 82).
   Introduced in the film *Making Love* (82).

Making Love Out of Nothing at All
Words and music by Jim Steinman.
E. B. Marks Music Corp., 1983/Lost Boys Music, 1983.
Best-selling record by Air Supply from *Greatest Hits* (Arista, 83).

Making Plans
Words and music by Dolly Parton.
Velvet Apple Music, 1980.
Best-selling record by Dolly Parton with Porter Wagoner (RCA, 80).

Mama Don't Cry
Words by Michael Champagne, music by Elliot Weiss.
Bittersuite Co., 1987.
Introduced by Claudine Casson-Jellison in the musical *Bittersuite* ('87).

Mama He's Crazy
Words and music by Kenny O'Dell.
Kenny O'Dell Music, 1983.
Best-selling record by The Judds from *Why Not Me* (RCA, 84).
   Nominated for a Grammy Award, Country Song of the Year, 1983.

Mama Used to Say
Words and music by Junior Gisombe and Bob Carter.
Colgems-EMI Music, 1981/Junior Music, Ltd., 1981.
Best-selling record by Junior from *'Ji'* (Mercury, 82).

Mamacita
Words and music by Gerald Levert and Marc Gordon.
Trycep Publishing Co., 1988/Willesden Music, Inc., 1988.
Best-selling record by Troop, from *Troop* (Atlantic, 88).

Maman
Words and music by Jim Wann.
Shapiro, Bernstein & Co., Inc., 1981.
Introduced by Jim Wann in *Pump Boys and Dinettes* (81).

Mama's Got a Lover
Words and music by Lou Reed.
Metal Machine Music, 1986.
Introduced by Lou Reed on the album *Mistral* (RCA, 86).

Mama's Never Seen Those Eyes
Words and music by J. L. Wallace and Terry Skinner.
Hall-Clement Publications, 1986.

Best-selling record by the Forester Sisters from the album *The Forester Sisters* (Warner Bros., 86).

Man at the Top
Words and music by Bruce Springsteen.
Bruce Springsteen Publishing, 1986.
Performed by Nils Lofgren at the Bridge benefit in Mountain View, California, in 1986.

A Man in Need (English)
Words and music by Richard Thompson.
Island Music, 1981.
Introduced by Richard Thompson in *Shoot out the Lights* (Hannibal, 82).

Man in the Long Black Coat
Words and music by Bob Dylan.
Special Rider Music, 1989.
Introduced by Bob Dylan in *Oh Mercy* (Columbia, 89).

Man in the Mirror
Words and music by Siedah Garrett and Greg Ballard.
Yellow Brick Road Music, 1987/MCA Music, 1987/Aerostation Corp., 1987.
Best-selling record in 1988 by Michael Jackson, from *Bad* (Epic, 87).
  Nominated for a Grammy Award, Record of the Year, 1988.

Man on the Corner (English)
Words and music by Phil Collins.
Hit & Run Music, 1981.
Best-selling record by Genesis from *Abacab* (Atlantic, 82).

Man on Your Mind (Australian)
Words and music by Glenn Shorrock and Kerryn Tolhurst.
Little River Band Music, Victoria, Australia, 1981.
Best-selling record by Little River Band from *Time Exposure* (Capitol, 82).

Man Size Love
Words and music by Rod Temperton.
Rodsongs, 1986/EMI-April Music/MGM/UA Music Inc.
Introduced by Klymaxx in the film *Running Scared* (86) and on the soundtrack album (MCA, 86).

Mandinka (Irish)
Words and music by Sinead O'Connor.
Dizzy Heights Music Publishing, Ltd., 1987/Chrysalis Music Group, 1987.
Introduced by Sinead O'Connor on *The Lion and the Cobra* (Chrysalis,

87) and popularized in 1988. The shaven-headed singer virtually defined the year's alternative music style.

Mandolin Rain
Words and music by Bruce Hornsby and John Hornsby.
Zappo Music, 1986/Basically Gasp Music.
Introduced by Bruce Hornsby & The Range on the album *The Way It Is* (RCA, 86).

Maneater
Words and music by Daryl Hall, John Oates, and Sara Allen.
Fust Buzza Music, Inc., 1982/Hot Cha Music Co., 1982/Unichappell Music Inc., 1982.
Best-selling record by Hall and Oates from *H2O* (RCA, 82).

Maniac
Words and music by Michael Sembello and Dennis Matkosky.
Intersong, USA Inc., 1983/Famous Music Corp., 1983.
Best-selling record by Michael Sembello (Casablanca, 83). Introduced in the film and soundtrack album *Flashdance* (83). Nominated for an Academy Award, Best Song, 1983; Nominated for an Academy Award, Best Song, 1983; Grammy Awards, Record of the Year, 1983, and Song of the Year, 1983.

Manic Monday
Words and music by Prince (pseudonym for Prince Rogers Nelson).
Controversy Music, 1986.
Best-selling record by The Bangles from the album *Different Light* (Columbia, 86). Prince wrote the song for the all-girl quartet after a backstage visit with them.

March of the Yuppies
Words and music by Charles Strouse.
Charles Strouse Music, 1985.
Introduced by Nancy Giles in the Off Broadway musical *Mayor* (85).

Marilyn Monroe
Words and music by David Frishberg.
Swiftwater Music, 1981.
Introduced by David Frishberg in *The David Frishberg Songbook* (Omnisound, 83).

Marlene on the Wall
Words and music by Suzanne Vega.
Waifersongs, 1985/AGF Music Ltd., 1985.
Introduced by Suzanne Vega on the album *Suzanne Vega* (A & M, 85).
This song is dedicated to Marlene Dietrich.

Marty Feldman Eyes
Words and music by Bruce Baum and Dick Bright.
Hollywood Boulevard Music, 1981.
Best-selling record by Bruce 'Baby Man' Baum (Horn 11, 81).

Mary's Prayer (English)
Words and music by Gary Clark.
Copyright Control, 1987.
Best-selling record by Danny Wilson (a group), from the album *Meet Danny Wilson* (Virgin, 87). Songwriter Clark is the vocalist of the group.

Master Blaster (Jammin')
Words and music by Stevie Wonder.
Jobete Music Co., 1980/Black Bull Music.
Best-selling record by Stevie Wonder from *Hotter Than July* (Tamla, 80).

Material Girl
Words and music by Peter Brown and Robert Rans.
Minong Music, 1984.
Best-selling record by Madonna in 1985 from the album *Like a Virgin* (Warner Bros., 84).

A Matter of Trust
Words and music by Billy Joel.
Joelsongs, 1986.
Best-selling record by Billy Joel from the album *The Bridge* (Columbia, 86).

Maureen, Maureen
Words and music by John Prine.
Big Ears Music Inc., 1985/Bruised Oranges, 1985.
Introduced by John Prine on the album *Aimless Love* (Oh Boy, 85).

Maybe We Went Too Far
Words and music by Zack Smith, Patty Smyth, and Keith Mack.
EMI-Blackwood Music Inc., 1984.
Introduced by Scandal on *Warrior* (Columbia, 84).

Maybe Your Baby's Got the Blues
Words and music by Troy Seals and Graham Lyle.
WB Music, 1986/Two-Sons Music, 1986/Irving Music Inc., 1986.
Best-selling record in 1987 by the Judds, from the album *Heart Land* (RCA/Curb, 86).

Mayor of Simpleton (English)
Words and music by Andy Partridge.

Virgin Music, 1989.
Introduced by XTC on *Oranges and Lemons* (Geffen, 89).

Me and All the Other Mothers
Words and music by Loudon Wainwright.
Snowden Music, 1989.
Introduced by Loudon Wainwright on *Therapy* (Silvertone, 89).

Me Myself and I
Words and music by Kevin Mercer, Dave Jolicoeur, Vincent Mason,
   Paul Huston, and George Clinton.
Tee Girl Music, 1979/Bridgeport Music Inc.
Best-selling record by De La Soul from *Three Feet High and Rising*
   (Tommy Boy, 89). Here De La Soul raps over a rhythm track from
   the Funkadelic classic '(Not Just) Knee Deep' from the album *Uncle
   Jam Wants You*. Nominated for a Grammy Award, Rap Song of the
   Year, 1989.

Mean Green Monster from Outer Space
Words by Howard Ashman, music by Alan Menken.
Warner-Tamerlane Music, 1986/Safespace Music/Menken Music/
   Trunksong Music/WB Music/Geffen Music/Shop Talk.
Introduced by the voice of Levi Stubbs in the 1986 film *Little Shop of
   Horrors* and on its soundtrack album. The movie was based on a
   long-running Off Broadway show, itself inspired by a 1960 low-
   budget horror film. Stubbs, a member of the legendary Motown group
   The Four Tops, was the voice of Audrey II, a man-eating plant, in the
   more recent film. Nominated for an Academy Award, Song of the
   Year, 1986.

Meat Is Murder (English)
Words by Morrissey, music by Johnny Marr.
Morrissey/Marr Songs Ltd., England, 1985.
Introduced by The Smiths on the album *Meat Is Murder* (Sire, 85).

The Meek Shall Inherit
Words by Howard Ashman, music by Alan Menken.
WB Music, 1982/Geffen Music/Trunksong Music.
Revived in 1986 by Rick Moranis, Michelle Weeks, Tichina Arnold, and
   Tisha Campbell in the film and on the soundtrack album of *Little
   Shop of Horrors* (86).

Meet Me Half Way
Words by Tom Whitlock, music by Giorgio Moroder.
GMPC, 1987/Go Glow, 1987.
Best-selling record by Kenny Loggins. Introduced in the movie and on
   the soundtrack album *Over the Top* (Columbia, 87).

Meet Me in Montana
Words and music by Paul Davis.
Web 4 Music Inc., 1984.
Best-selling record by Marie Osmond with Dan Seals from the album
There's No Stopping Your Heart (Capitol, 85).

Meet Me in My Dreams Tonight
Words and music by Brian Wilson.
Beach Bum Music, 1988/Beachhead Music, 1988.
Introduced by Brian Wilson on *Brian Wilson* (Reprise, 88).

Meet on the Ledge (English)
Words and music by Richard Thompson.
Island Music.
Revived in 1987 by Fairport Convention on the album *In Real Time
(Live '87)* This was a live remake of the group's traditional closing
tune.

Memories Can't Wait
Words and music by David Byrne and Jerry Harrison.
Bleu Disque Music, 1979/Index Music, 1979.
Rhythm 'n' Blues Living Colour on *Vivid* (Columbia, 88). Introduced by
Talking Heads on *Fear of Music* in 1979.

Memory (English)
Words by Trevor Nunn and T. S. Eliot, music by Andrew Lloyd
Webber.
Deco Music, 1982/Charles Koppelman Music, 1982/Jonathan Three
Music Co., 1982/Martin Bandier Music, 1982.
Introduced by Betty Buckley in the musical *Cats* (82). Best-selling
records by Barbra Streisand from *Memories* (Columbia) and Barry
Manilow from *Here Comes the Night* (Arista, 82). Adapted from T. S.
Eliot's poetry, primarily 'Rhapsody on a Windy Night,' written in
1917.

The Men All Pause
Words and music by Bernadette Cooper, Joyce Simmons, and D.
McDaniels.
Spectrum VII, 1984.
Best-selling record by Klymaxx from the album *Meeting in the Ladies
Room* (MCA, 85). Featured in the film *The Slugger's Wife* (85).

Men and Women
Words and music by Andrew Ratshin.
Liv Tunes, 1989/Lost Lake Arts Music.
Introduced by Uncle Bonsai on *Legacy* (Windham Hill, 89).

Men Without Shame
Words and music by Slim Jim Phantom (pseudonym for James

McDonnell), Lee Rocker, and Earl Slick (pseudonym for Frank Madeloni).
Pressed Ham Hits, 1985/Willesden Music, Inc., 1985/Oil Slick Music, 1985.
Best-selling record by Phantom, Rocker & Slick from the album *Phantom, Rocker & Slick* (EMI-America, 85).

Menemsha
Words and music by Carly Simon, music by Peter Wood.
C'est Music, 1983/Hythefield Music, 1983.
Introduced by Carly Simon on *Hello Big Man* (Warner Brothers, 83).

Mercedes Boy
Words and music by Pebbles.
MCA Music, 1987/Unicity Music, Inc., 1987/Jenn-a-Bug Music, 1987.
Best-selling record by Pebbles, from *Pebbles* (MCA, 88).

The Message
Words and music by Melvin Glover, Sylvia Robinson, E. Fletcher, and Clifton Chase.
Sugar Hill Music Publishing, Ltd., 1982.
Best-selling record by Grand Master Flash & The Furious Five from *The Message* (Sugarhill, 82).

Metal Beach
Words and music by Brian Wilson.
Beach Bum Music, 1988/Postvalda Music.
Introduced by Paul Shaffer on *Coast to Coast* (Capitol, 89).

Method of Modern Love
Words and music by Daryl Hall and Janna Allen.
Hot Cha Music Co., 1984/Unichappell Music Inc., 1984/Fust Buzza Music, Inc., 1984.
Best-selling record by Daryl Hall and John Oates in 1985 from the album *Big Bam Boom* (RCA, 84).

The Metro
Words and music by John Crawford.
Safespace Music, 1982.
Best-selling record by Berlin from *Pleasure Victim* (Geffen, 83).

Mexican Radio
Words and music by Stanard Funsten, Charles Gray, Oliver Nanini, and Marc Moreland.
Big Talk Music, 1982.
Best-selling record by Wall of Voodoo from *Call of the West* (I.R.S., 83).

Miami Vice Theme
Words and music by Jan Hammer.
MCA, Inc., 1985.
Best-selling record by Jan Hammer (MCA, 85). Introduced on the
television series *Miami Vice* (84).

Mickey
Words and music by Nicky Chinn and Mike Chapman.
Mike Chapman Publishing Enterprises, 1979/BMG Music, 1979.
Best-selling record by Toni Basil from *Word of Mouth* (Chrysalis, 82).

Middle of the Road
Words and music by Chrissie Hynde.
MCA, Inc., 1984.
Best-selling record by The Pretenders from *Learning to Crawl* (Warner
Brothers, 84).

Midnight Blue
Words and music by Lou Gramm and Bruce Turgon.
Colgems-EMI Music, 1987/Acara, 1987.
Best-selling record by Lou Gramm, from the album *Ready or Not*
(Atlantic, 87).

Midnight Flight (Canadian)
Words and music by Kate McGarrigle.
Garden Court Music Co., 1983.
Introduced by Kate and Anna McGarrigle in *Love Over and Over*
(Polydor, 83).

Midnight Hauler
Words and music by James DuBois and Wood Newton.
Warner House of Music, 1981.
Best-selling record by Razzy Bailey from *Makin' Friends* (RCA, 81).

Miles Away
Words and music by Phil Davis and Doug Erikson.
Flip 'n' Dog, 1989/Music of the World.
Introduced by Firetown on *The Good Life* (Atlantic, 89).

(How to Be a) Millionaire (English)
Words and music by Martin Fry and Mark White.
Neutron Music, England, 1986/10 Music Ltd., England, 1986/Nymph
Music, 1986.
Best-selling record by ABC from the album *How to Be a Zillionaire*
(Polygram, 86).

Mind Your Own Business
Words and music by Hank Williams.
Acuff Rose Music, 1949/Rightsong Music, 1949/Hiram, 1949.

Revived by Hank Williams, Jr. on the album *Montana Cafe* (Warner/Curb, 86).

Minimum Love
Words and music by Mac McAnnally and Gerry Wexler.
I've Got the Music Co., 1982/Song Tailors Music Co., 1982.
Best-selling record by Mac McAnnally (Warner Brothers, 83).

Miracle Mile
Words and music by Dan Stuart and Steve Wynn.
Poison Brisket Music, 1985/Hang Dog Music, 1985.
Introduced by Danny and Dusty on the album *The Lost Weekend* (A & M, 85).

Mirror Mirror
Words and music by Michael Sembello and Dennis Natkosky.
Koppelman Family Music, 1981/Bandier Family Music, 1981/Foghorn Music, 1981/Rosstown Music, 1981/R. L. August Music Co., 1981.
Best-selling record by Diana Ross from *Why Do Fools Fall in Love* (RCA, 82).

Misled
Words and music by Ronald Bell, James Taylor, Charles Smith, George Brown, Robert Bell, Curtis Williams, and James Bonneford.
Delightful Music Ltd., 1984.
Best-selling record by Kool & The Gang from the album *Emergency* (De-Lite, 85).

Miss Celie's Blues (Sisters) (American-English)
Words and music by Quincy Jones and Rod Temperton, words by Lionel Richie, Jr.
WB Music, 1985/Rodsongs, 1985/Brockman Music, 1985.
Introduced by Tata Vega in the film *The Color Purple* (85). Nominated for an Academy Award, Song of the Year, 1985.

Miss Me Blind (English)
Words and music by George O'Dowd, Jon Moss, Roy Hay, and Michael Craig.
Virgin Music, 1983.
Best-selling record by Culture Club from *Colour by Numbers* (Epic, 84).

Miss Sun
Words and music by David Paich and Boz Scaggs.
Hudmar Publishing Co., Inc., 1980.
Best-selling record by Boz Scaggs from *Hits* (Columbia, 80).

Miss You Like Crazy
Words and music by Michael Masser, Gerry Goffin, and Preston Glass.
Prince Street Music, 1989/Lauren Wesley Music/Screen Gems-EMI

Music Inc./Irving Music Inc./Gemia Music.
Best-selling record by Natalie Cole from *Good to Be Back* (EMI, 89).

Miss You Much
Words and music by Terry Lewis and James Harris, III.
Flyte Tyme Tunes, 1989.
Best-selling record by Janet Jackson from *Rhythm Nation 1814* (A & M, 89). Nominated for a Grammy Award, Rhythm 'n' Blues Song of the Year, 1989.

Missed Opportunity
Words and music by Daryl Hall, John Oates, and Sara Allen.
Hot Cha Music Co., 1988/Careers Music Inc., 1988.
Best-selling record by Hall and Oates, from *Ooh Yeah* (Arista, 88).

Missing You
Words and music by Dan Fogelberg.
Hickory Grove Music, 1982/EMI-April Music, 1982.
Best-selling record by Dan Fogelberg from *Dan Fogelberg/Greatest Hits* (Full Moon/Epic, 82).

Missing You
Words and music by John Waite, Chas Sanford, and Mark Leonard.
Hudson Bay Music, 1984/Paperwaite Music, 1984/Fallwater Music, 1984/Markmeem Music, 1984.
Best-selling record by John Waite from *No Brakes* (EMI-America, 84).

Missing You
Words and music by Lionel Richie, Jr.
Brockman Enterprises Inc., 1984.
Best-selling record by Diana Ross in 1985 from the album *Swept Away* (RCA, 84). This song is dedicated to Marvin Gaye, who was killed in 1984.

A Mission in Life
Words and music by Stanard Ridgway.
Mondo Spartacus Music, 1989/Illegal Songs, Inc./Criterion Music Corp.
Introduced by Stan Ridgway on *Mosquitos* (Geffen, 89).

Missionary Man (English)
Words and music by Dave Stewart and Annie Lennox.
RCA Music Ltd., London, England, 1986/Red Network Music.
Best-selling record by Eurythmics from the album *Revenge* (MCA, 86).

Mr. D.J.
Words and music by Dallas Austin, Fenderella, and Doug E. Fresh.
Diva 1 Music, 1989/Sony Tunes.
Introduced by Joyce Fenderella Irby in *Maximum Thrust* (Motown, 89).

Mr. Me
Words and music by They Might Be Giants.
They Might Be Giants Music, 1988.
They Might Be Giants introduced this ersetz sea-chantey on *Lincoln* (Restless, 88).

Mr. Roboto
Words and music by Dennis De Young.
Stygian Songs, 1983.
Best-selling record by Styx from *Kilroy was Here* (A & M, 83).

Mister Sandman
Words and music by Pat Ballard.
Edwin H. Morris, 1954.
Revived by Emmylou Harris with Linda Ronstadt and Dolly Parton on *Trio* (Warner Brothers, 81).

Mr. Telephone Man
Words and music by Ray Parker, Jr.
Raydiola Music, 1983.
Best-selling record by New Edition in 1985 from the album *New Edition* (MCA, 84).

Misunderstanding (English)
Words and music by Phil Collins.
Hit & Run Music, 1980.
Best-selling record by Genesis from *Duke* (Atlantic, 80).

Mixed Emotions (English)
Words and music by Mick Jagger and Keith Richards.
Promopub B. V., CH-1017 Amsterdam, Netherlands, 1989.
Best-selling record by the Rolling Stones from *Steel Wheels* (Rolling Stones Records/Columbia, 89). The Stones returned to classic form with this autobiographical account of their ambivalence about reuniting.

Modern Day Romance
Words and music by Kix Brooks (pseudonym for Leon Brooks) and Daniel Tyler.
Golden Bridge Music, 1985/Mota Music, 1985/Oil Slick Music, 1985.
Best-selling record by Nitty Gritty Dirt Band from the album *Partners, Brothers, and Friends* (Warner Bros., 85).

Modern Girl
Words and music by Dominic Bugatti and Frank Musker.
Unichappell Music Inc., 1980.
Best-selling record by Sheena Easton from *Sheena Easton* (EMI, 81).

Modern Love (English)
Words and music by David Bowie.
Jones Music Co., 1983.
Best-selling record by David Bowie from *Let's Dance* (EMI-America, 83).

Modern Woman (from *Ruthless People*)
Words and music by Billy Joel.
Joelsongs, 1986.
Best-selling record by Billy Joel from the album *The Bridge* (Epic, 86). Introduced by Billy Joel in the 1986 film *Ruthless People* and on the soundtrack album.

Moments Like This
Words by Frank Loesser, music by Burton Lane.
Famous Music Corp., 1938.
Revived in 1986 by Tony Bennett on the album *The Art of Excellence* (Columbia, 86). Introduced in the film *College Swing*.

Mommy Daddy You and I
Words and music by David Byrne, music by Chris Frantz, Jerry Harrison, and Tina Weymouth.
Index Music, 1988.
Introduced by Talking Heads on *Naked* (Sire, 88).

Mona Lisa's Lost Her Smile
Words and music by Johnny Cunningham.
Rocksmith Music, 1984/Lockhill-Selma Music, 1984.
Best-selling record by David Allan Coe (Columbia, 84).

Money Changes Everything
Words and music by Thomas Gray.
ATV Music Corp., 1978.
Introduced by The Brains on *The Brains* (Mercury, 80). Rhythm 'n' Blues Cyndi Lauper *She's So Unusual* (Portrait, 83).

Money for Nothing (English)
Words and music by Mark Knopfler and Sting (pseudonym for Gordon Sumner).
Chariscourt Ltd., 1985/Almo Music Corp., 1985/Virgin Music Ltd., 1985.
Best-selling record by Dire Straits from the album *Brothers in Arms* (Warner Bros., 85). Nominated for Grammy Awards, Record of the Year, 1985, and Song of the Year, 1985.

Monkey (English)
Words and music by George Michael.
Morrison Leahy, England, 1987/Chappell & Co., Inc., 1987.

Best-selling record in 1988 by George Michael, from *Faith* (Columbia, 87).

Mony Mony
Words and music by Bobby Bloom, Tommy James, Ritchie Cordell, and Bo Gentry.
Big Seven Music Corp., 1968.
Revived in 1987 by Billy Idol on the album *Vital Idol* (Chrysalis, 87).
The second Ritchie Cordell-Tommy James song revived this year, this one was inspired by the Mutal of New York (MONY) building visible from James's apartment window.

Moon at the Window
Words and music by Joni Mitchell.
Crazy Crow Music, 1982.
Introduced by Joni Mitchell in *Wild Things Run Fast* (Asylum, 82).

The Moon Is a Harsh Mistress
Words and music by Jim Webb.
White Oak Songs, 1974.
Revived by Linda Ronstadt in *Get Closer* (Asylum, 82).

The Moon Is Still over Her Shoulder
Words and music by Hugh Prestwood.
Lawyer's Daughter, 1984.
Best-selling record in 1987 by Michael Johnson, from the album *Wings* (RCA, 86).

Moonfall
Words and music by Rupert Holmes.
Holmes Line of Music, 1986.
Released by Judy Collins (Polygram, 86). Introduced by Patti Cohenour and Howard McGillin in the 1985 Broadway musical *The Mystery of Edwin Drood* and on the cast album (Polygram, 86).

Moonlighting
Words by Al Jarreau, music by Lee Holdridge.
ABC Circle, 1985/American Broadcasting Music, Inc.
Introduced by Al Jarreau as the theme of the television series *Moonlighting*.

Moonlighting (Theme)
Best-selling record by Al Jarreau, from the album *Moonlighting* (RCA, 87). This television theme was first released as a single in England, where its success prompted the U.S. release. Nominated for a Grammy Award, Best Song for TV/Movies, 1987.

More Bounce to the Ounce - Part 1
Words and music by Roger Troutman.

Rubber Band Music, Inc., 1980.
Best-selling record by Zapp from *Zapp* (Warner Brothers, 80).

More Love
Words and music by William Robinson.
Jobete Music Co., 1980.
Best-selling record by Kim Carnes from *Romance Dance* (EMI-America, 80).

More Than I Can Say
Words and music by Sonny Curtis and Jerry Allison.
Warner-Tamerlane Music, 1960.
Best-selling record by Leo Sayer from *Living in a Fantasy* (Warner Brothers, 80).

More Than Just the Two of Us
Words and music by Michael Carey Schneider and Mitch Crane.
Shel Sounds Music, 1980/Sneaker Songs, 1980.
Best-selling record by Sneaker from *Sneaker* (Handshake, 81).

More Than You Know
Words and music by Martika, Michael Jay, and Marvin Morrow.
Famous Music Corp., 1989/Marvin Morrow Music/Tika Tunes/Ensign Music.
Best-selling record by Martika from *Martika* (Columbia, 89).

More Than You'll Ever Know
Words and music by Michael Ruff.
Polygram Songs, 1988/Oman Kahalil, 1988/Ruff Mix Music, 1988.
Introduced by Carl Anderson (Polydor, 88). Featured on the soap opera *Days of Our Lives*.

Mornin'
Words and music by Al Jarreau, Jay Graydon, and David Foster.
Al Jarreau Music, 1983/Garden Rake Music, Inc., 1983/Foster Frees Music Inc., 1983.
Best-selling record by Al Jarreau from *Jarreau* (Warner Brothers, 83).

Mornin' Ride
Words and music by Steve Bogard and Jeff Tweel.
Chappell & Co., Inc., 1987/Unichappell Music Inc., 1987.
Best-selling record in 1987 by Lee Greenwood, from the album *Love Will Find Its Way to You* (MCA, 86).

Morning Desire
Words and music by Dave Loggins.
Leeds Music Corp., 1985/Patchwork Music, 1985.
Best-selling record in 1986 by Kenny Rogers from the album *The Heart of the Matter* (RCA, 85)..

Morning Train
Words and music by Florrie Palmer.
Unichappell Music Inc., 1981.
Best-selling record by Sheena Easton from *Sheena Easton* (EMI America, 81).

Motel Matches (English)
Words and music by Elvis Costello.
Plangent Visions Music, Inc., London, England, 1980.
Introduced by Elvis Costello on *Get Happy* (Columbia, 80).

Mountain Music
Words and music by Randy Owen.
Maypop Music, 1980.
Best-selling record by Alabama from *Mountain Music* (RCA, 82).

Mountain of Love
Words and music by Harold Dorman.
Morris Music, Inc., 1959/Canadiana-Morris, 1959.
Revived by Charley Pride (RCA, 82).

Mountains O' Things
Words and music by Tracy Chapman.
EMI-April Music, 1987/Purple Rabbit Music, 1987.
Introduced by Tracy Chapman on *Tracy Chapman* (Elektra, 88).

Move Away (English)
Words and music by Culture Club, words and music by Phil Pickett.
Virgin Music, 1986/Warner-Tamerlane Music.
Best-selling record by Culture Club from the album *From Luxury to Heartache* (Epic, 86).

Move On
Words and music by Stephen Sondheim.
WB Music, 1981.
Introduced by Mandy Patinkin and Bernadette Peters in *Sunday in the Park with George* (83).

Move with Me Sister
Words and music by Dan Zanes and Tom Lloyd.
Copyright Control, 1989.
Introduced by The Del Fuegos in *Smoking in the Fields* (RCA, 89).

Mrs. Green
Words and music by Michael Quercio.
Latin Songs, 1985.

Introduced by The Three O'Clock on the album *Arrive Without Travelling* (I.R.S., 85).

Muddy Water
Words and music by Roger Miller.
Roger Miller Music, 1985/Tree Publishing Co., Inc., 1985.
Introduced by Daniel Jenkins and Ron Richardson in the musical *Big River* (85).

Murphy's Law (Canadian)
Words and music by Geraldine Hunt and Daniel Joseph.
Hygroton, 1981/Lo Pressor, 1981.
Best-selling record by Cheri (Venture, 82).

Murphy's Romance
Words and music by Carole King.
Elorac Music, 1985.
Introduced by Carole King in the film *Murphy's Romance* (85).

Muscles
Words and music by Michael Jackson.
Mijac Music, 1982.
Best-selling record by Diana Ross from *Silk Electric* (RCA, 82).

The Music of Goodbye
Words by Alan Bergman and Marilyn Bergman, music by John Barry.
MCA, Inc., 1986/Music of the World.
Introduced by Melissa Manchester and Al Jarreau on the soundtrack of the film *Out of Africa* (85).

The Music of the Night (English)
Words by Charles Hart and Richard Stilgoe, music by Andrew Lloyd Webber.
Really Useful Music, 1987/Polygram International, 1987.
Performed by Michael Crawford on the cast album of the musical *The Phantom of the Opera* (87). The show and song were hits in Britain before the Broadway opening in 1988.

The Music Went Out of My Life
Words and music by Peter Allen.
Irving Music Inc., 1988.
Introduced by veteran cabaret singer Julie Wilson in her Broadway debut in the musical *Legs Diamond* (88).

My Attorney, Bernie
Words and music by David Frishberg.
Swiftwater Music, 1982.
Introduced by David Frishberg in *The Dave Frishberg Songbook, Volume Two* (Omnisound, 83).

My Baby (English)
Words and music by Chrissie Hynde.
MCA, Inc., 1986.
Introduced by the Pretenders on the album *Get Close* (Sire, 86).

My Baby Worships Me
Words and music by Steve Earle.
Goldline Music Inc., 1982, 1986.
Performed by Tom Principato on the album *Smokin'* (Powerhouse, 86).

My Baby's Got Good Timing
Words and music by Dan Seals and Bob McDill.
Pink Pig Music, 1984/Hall-Clement Publications, 1984.
Best-selling record by Dan Seals from the album *San Antone* (EMI-
America, 85).

My Brain Is Hanging Upside Down (Bonzo Goes to Bitburg)
Words and music by Dee Dee Ramone, Joey Ramone, and Jean
Beauvoir.
Taco Tunes Inc., 1986.
Introduced by the Ramones on the album *Animal Boy* (Sire, 86). This
unique pop song was written about President Reagan's controversial
trip to the World War II military cemetery in Bitburg, West Germany.

My City Was Gone (English)
Words and music by Chrissie Hynde.
MCA Music, 1982.
Introduced by The Pretenders as the A-Side of 'Back on the Chain
Gang' (Sire, 82). Featured on *Learning to Crawl* (Sire, 83).

My Edge of the Razor
Words and music by John Hiatt.
Lillybilly, 1982.
Introduced on *All of a Sudden* by John Hiatt (Geffen, 82).

My Elusive Dreams
Words and music by Claude Putman and Billy Sherrill.
Tree Publishing Co., Inc., 1967.
Revived by David Allan Coe on the album *Darlin' Darlin'* (Columbia,
85).

My Ever Changing Moods (English)
Words and music by Paul Weller.
Colgems-EMI Music, 1984.
Best-selling record by The Style Council from *My Ever Changing
Moods* (Geffen, 84).

My Fantasy
Words and music by Gene Griffin and William Aquart.

Cal-Gene Music, 1989/Virgin Music.
Introduced by Teddy Riley featuring Guy in the film and on the
soundtrack LP *Do the Right Thing* (Motown, 89).

My Father's House
Words and music by Bruce Springsteen.
Bruce Springsteen Publishing, 1982.
Revived in 1986 by Emmylou Harris on the album *Thirteen* (Warner
Bros., 86).

My Father's Shoes
Words and music by Cliff Eberhardt.
Aixoise Music, 1989.
Introduced by Cliff Eberhardt on *Legacy* (Windham Hill, 89).

My Favorite Year
Words and music by Michelle Broutman and Karen Gottlieb.
Words & Wings Songs, 1982.
Performed by Michael Feinstein on *Isn't It Romantic* (Elektra, 88), the
song had been written for but not used in the film of the same name.

My First Love
Words and music by David Lewis and Wayne Lewis.
Jodaway Music, 1989.
Best-selling record by Atlantic Starr from *We're Movin' Up* (Warner
Bros., 89).

My Forever Love
Words and music by Gerald Levert and Marc Gordon.
Ferncliff, 1987.
Best-selling record by Gerald Levert, from the album *The Big
Throwdown* (Atlantic, 87).

My Girl (Canadian)
Words and music by Bill Henderson and Brian MacLeod.
ATV Music Corp., 1980.
Best-selling record by Chilliwack from *Wanna Be A Star* (Millennium,
81).

My Girl
Words and music by William Robinson and Ronald White.
Jobete Music Co., 1964.
Revived by Daryl Hall and John Oates (RCA, 85) as part of a medley
with 'The Way You Do the Things You Do.'

My Girl
Words and music by William Robinson and Ronald White.
Jobete Music Co., 1964.

Revived in 1988 by Suave on the album *I'm Your Playmate* (Capitol, 88).

My Heart
Words and music by Don Pfrimmer and Charles Quillen.
Hall-Clement Publications, 1979/Polygram International, 1979.
Best-selling record by Ronnie Milsap from *Milsap Magic* (RCA, 80).

My Heart Can't Tell You No (English)
Words and music by Simon Climie and Dennis Morgan.
Chrysalis Music Group, 1988/Little Shop of Morgansongs.
Best-selling record in 1989 by Rod Stewart from *Out of Order* (Warner Bros., 88).

My Heroes Have Always Been Cowboys
Words and music by unknown composer/lyricist .
Polygram International, 1976.
Best-selling record by Willie Nelson from the film and soundtrack album *The Electric Horseman* (Columbia, 80).

My Home Town
Introduced by Bruce Springsteen on the album *Born in the U.S.A.* (Columbia, 84), this song was inspired by the closing of a New Jersey factory. It was the seventh single from the album to make the top ten, thus equalling Michael Jackson's record.

My House
Words and music by Lou Reed.
Metal Machine Music, 1981.
Introduced by Lou Reed on *The Blue Mask* (RCA, 82).

My Life Is Good
Words and music by Randy Newman.
Six Pictures Music, 1983.
Introduced by Randy Newman in *Trouble in Paradise* (Warner Brothers, 83).

My Little Buttercup
Words and music by Randy Newman.
OPC, 1986.
Introduced by Randy Newman in the film *Three Amigos* and its soundtrack album (Warner Bros., 86).

My Love
Words and music by Lionel Richie, Jr.
Brockman Enterprises Inc., 1982.
Best-selling record by Lionel Richie from *Lionel Richie* (Motown, 83).

My Mind Is on You
Words and music by Dave Loggins and Don Schlitz.
Leeds Music Corp., 1985/MCA, Inc., 1985/Patchwork Music, 1985/Don Schlitz Music, 1985.
Introduced by Gus Hardin on the album *Wall of Tears* (RCA, 85).

My Name Joe
Words and music by David Massengill.
David Massengill Music, 1989.
Introduced by David Massengill on *Legacy* (Windham Hill, 89).

My, Oh My
Words and music by Noddy Holder and Jim Lea.
Whild John, London, England, 1984/Barn Music, London, England, 1984.
Best-selling record by Slade from *Keep Your Hands off My Power Supply* (CBS Associated, 84).

My Old Yellow Car
Words and music by Thom Schuyler.
Briarpatch Music, 1983/Debdave Music Inc., 1983.
Featured on *Dream Baby* by Lacy J. Dalton (Columbia, 83).

My Only Love
Words and music by Jimmy Fortune.
Statler Brothers Music, 1984.
Best-selling record by The Statler Brothers from the album *Pardners in Rhyme* (Mercury, 85).

My Prerogative
Words and music by Gene Griffin and Bobby Brown.
Cal-Gene Music, 1988/Virgin Music, 1988.
Best-selling record by Bobby Brown from *Don't Be Cruel* (MCA, 88).

My Secret Place
Words and music by Joni Mitchell.
Crazy Crow Music, 1987.
Introduced by Joni Mitchell in *Chalk Mark in a Rainstorm* (Geffen, 88), in a duet with Peter Gabriel.

My Toot Toot, also known as **My Tu Tu**
Words and music by Sidney Simien.
Sid Sim Publishing, 1984/Flat Town Music.
Introduced by Rockin' Sidney on the album *My Zydeco Shoes Got the Zydeco Blues* (Maison de Soul). Best-selling record by Jean Knight from *My Toot Toot* (Mirage, 85) and Denise La Salle (Malaco, 85).

My Tu Tu, see **My Toot Toot.**

Mystery (English)
Words and music by Rod Temperton.
Rodsongs, 1986.
Introduced by Anita Baker on the album *Rapture* (Elektra, 86).

Mystery Achievement (English)
Words and music by Chrissie Hynde.
MCA, Inc., 1979.
Introduced by The Pretenders on *The Pretenders* (Sire, 80).

Mystery Lady
Words and music by Keith Diamond, Billy Ocean, and James Woodley.
Zomba Music, 1984/Willesden Music, Inc.
Introduced by Billy Ocean on the album *Suddenly* (Arista, 84).

N

Na Na Hey Hey (Kiss Him Goodbye), see **Kiss Him Goodbye.**

Name of the Game
Words and music by Dan Hartman and Charlie Midnight.
EMI-Blackwood Music Inc., 1985.
Introduced by Dan Hartman in the film and soundtrack album *Fletch*
    (MCA, 85).

Nasty
Words and music by James Harris, III, Terry Lewis, and Janet Jackson.
Flyte Tyme Tunes, 1986.
Best-selling record by Janet Jackson from the album *Control* (A & M,
    86). The younger sister of Michael Jackson.

Natasha (English)
Words by Dick Vosberg, music by Frank Lazarus.
Regent Music, 1978.
Introduced by David Garrison in *A Day in Hollywood/A Night in the
    Ukraine* (Musical, 80).

The Natural
Music by Randy Newman.
TSP Music, Inc., 1984/Randy Newman Music, 1984.
Introduced by Randy Newman in the film and soundtrack album *The
    Natural* (84).

Natural High
Words and music by Freddy Powers.
Mount Shasta Music Inc., 1984.
Best-selling record by Merle Haggard from the album *Kern River* (Epic,
    85).

Naughty Girls Need Love Too
Words and music by Full Force.
Forceful Music, 1987/Willesden Music, Inc., 1987.

Best-selling record in 1988 Samantha Fox from her album *Samantha Fox* (Jive, 87).

Navajo Rug (Canadian)
Words and music by Ian Tyson and Tom Russell.
Slick Fork Music, 1987/End of the Trail.
Best-selling record by Ian Tyson, from the album *Cowboyography* (Sugar Hill, 87).

Neal Cassady
Words and music by Bruce Jay Paskow.
Hargus McSneakerbottom Pub., 1988.
Introduced by the Washington Squares on *Fair and Square* (Gold Castle, 89).

Nearly in Love (English)
Words and music by Richard Thompson.
Island Music, 1986.
Introduced by Richard Thompson on the album *Daring Adventures* (Polygram, 86).

Need You Tonight (Australian)
Words and music by Andrew Farriss and Michael Hutchence.
MCA Music, 1987.
Best-selling record by Inxs, from the album *Kick* (Atlantic, 87).

Nelson
Words and music by Jerry Herman.
Jerryco Music Co., 1979.
Introduced by by Peggy Hewett in *A Day in Hollywood/A Night in the Ukraine* (Musical, 80).

Neutron Dance
Words and music by Allee Willis and David Sembello.
Off Backstreet Music, 1985/Unicity Music, Inc., 1985.
Best-selling record by the Pointer Sisters in 1985 from the album *Break Out* (Planet, 84). Introduced in the film *Beverly Hills Cop* (85); included on the soundtrack album of the film.

Never
Words and music by Holly Knight, Walter Bloch, and Ann Wilson.
Makiki Publishing Co., Ltd., 1985/BMG Songs Inc., 1985/Strange Euphoria Music, 1985/Know Music, 1985.
Best-selling record by Heart from the album *Heart* (Capitol, 85).

Never as Good as the First Time (English)
Words and music by Sade (pseudonym for Helen Folasade Adu) and Stuart Matthewman.

Sony Tunes, 1986.
Best-selling record by Sade from the album *Promise* (Epic, 86).

Never Be the Same
Words and music by Christopher Geppert.
BMG Music, 1979.
Best-selling record by Christopher Cross from *Christopher Cross* (Warner Brothers, 80).

Never Be You
Words and music by Tom Petty and Benmont Tench.
Gone Gator Music, 1986.
Best-selling record by Rosanne Cash from the album *Rhythm and Romance* (Columbia, 86).

Never Before
Words and music by Gene Clark.
Tickson Music, 1987.
Discovered on a 1966 Byrds' tape, this song was titled and released on their 1987 album *Never Before* (CBS) and popularized in 1988.

Never Die Young
Words and music by James Taylor.
Country Road Music Inc., 1988.
Introduced by James Taylor on *Never Die Young* (CBS, 88).

Never Ending Story
Words and music by Giorgio Moroder and Keith Forsey.
Budde Music, 1984/Colgems-EMI Music, 1984.
Best-selling record by Limahl from the album *Don't Suppose* (EMI-America, 85). Introduced in the film *Never Ending Story* (85).

Never Gonna Give You Up (English)
Words and music by Mike Stock, Matt Aitken, and Pete Waterman.
Terrace Entertainment Corp., 1987.
Best-selling record in 1988 by Rick Astley, from *Whenever You Need Somebody* (RCA, 87).

Never Gonna Let You Go
Words by Cynthia Weil, music by Barry Mann.
ATV Music Corp., 1981/Mann & Weil Songs Inc., 1981.
Best-selling record by Sergio Mendes from *Sergio Mendes* (A & M, 83).

Never Had It So Good
Words and music by Mary Chapin Carpenter.
Getarealjob Music, 1989/EMI-April Music.
Introduced by Mary Chapin Carpenter on *State of the Heart* (Columbia, 89).

Never Knew Love Like This
Words and music by James III Harris and Terry Lewis.
Flyte Tyme Tunes, 1987/Avant Garde Music Publishing, Inc., 1987.
Best-selling record in 1988 by Alexander O'Neal featuring Cherrelle,
    from *Hearsay* (Tabu, 87).

Never Knew Love Like This Before
Words and music by James Mtume and Reginald Lucas.
Frozen Butterfly Music Publishing, 1979.
Best-selling record by Stephanie Mills from *Sweet Sensation* (20th
    Century, 80). Won a Grammy Award, and Rhythm 'n' Blues Song of
    the Year, 1980.

Never Mind
Words and music by Harlan Howard.
Tree Publishing Co., Inc., 1986.
Introduced by Nanci Griffith on *Little Love Affairs* (MCA, 88).

Never Surrender (Canadian)
Words and music by Corey Hart.
Liesse Publishing, 1985.
Best-selling record by Corey Hart from the album *Boy in the Box* (EMI-
    America, 85).

Never Tear Us Apart (Australian)
Words and music by Andrew Farriss and Michael Hutchence.
Tol, 1987/MCA Music, 1987.
Best-selling record in 1988 by Inxs, from *Kick* (Atlantic, 87).

Never the Luck
Words and music by Rupert Holmes.
Holmes Line of Music, 1986.
Performed by Judy Collins (Polygram, 86). Introduced by Joe Grifasi in
    the Broadway musical *The Mystery of Edwin Drood* (85) and on the
    cast album (Polygram, 86).

New Age
Words and music by Lou Reed.
Oakfield Avenue Music Ltd., 1980/Unichappell Music Inc., 1980.
Featured on *Protect the Innocent* by Rachel Sweet (Columbia, 80).

New Attitude
Words and music by Sharon Robinson, Jonathan Gilutin, and Bunny
    Hull.
Unicity Music, Inc., 1985/Off Backstreet Music, 1985/Rockomatic
    Music, 1985/Brassheart Music, 1985/Robin Hill Music, 1985.
Best-selling record by Patti LaBelle from the album *Patti* (MCA, 85).
    Nominated for a Grammy Award, Song of the Year, 1985.

A New England (English)
Words and music by Billy Bragg.
Chappell & Co., Inc., 1983.
Introduced by Billy Bragg; collected on the album *Back to Basics*
(Elektra, 87). This New Wave English folksinger exhibits a simple
guitar-vocal style reminiscent of such 1960's protest singers as Phil
Ochs. Kirsty MacColl had a hit in England with this song.

New Fool at an Old Game
Words and music by Steve Bogard, Rich Giles, and Sheila Stephen.
Chappell & Co., Inc., 1988/EEG Music.
Best-selling record in 1989 by Reba McEntire from *Reba* (MCA, 88).

New Looks
Words and music by Charles Fox.
WB Music, 1985.
Introduced by Dr. John in the film *European Vacation* (85).

New Moon on Monday (English)
Words and music by Duran Duran.
BIOT Music Ltd., London, England, 1983.
Best-selling record by Duran Duran from *Seven and the Ragged Tiger*
(Capitol, 84).

New Orleans Ladies
Words and music by H. Garrick and L. Medici.
Break of Dawn Music Inc., 1976.
Revived in 1987 by Gabriel on the NSO label.

New Orleans Wins the War
Words and music by Randy Newman.
Twice As Nice Music, 1988.
Introduced by Randy Newman in *Land of Dreams* (Reprise, 88).

New Sensation (Australian)
Words and music by Andrew Farriss and Michael Hutchence.
MCA Music, 1987.
Best-selling record in 1988 by Inxs, from *Kick* (Atlantic, 87).

New Shade of Blue
Words and music by John McFee and Andre Pessis.
Long Tooth Music, 1988/Endless Frogs Music, 1988.
Best-selling record by Southern Pacific from *Zuma* (Warner Bros., 88).

The New World
Words and music by John Doe and Exene Cervenka, music by X.
Eight/Twelve Music, 1983.
Introduced by X on *More Fun in the New World* (Electra, 83).

New World Man (Canadian)
Words by Neil Peart, music by Alex Lifeson and Geddy Lee.
Core Music Publishing, 1982.
Best-selling record by Rush from *Signals* (Mercury, 82).

New Year's Day (Irish)
Words and music by Bono (pseudonym for Paul Hewson), Larry
    Mullen, Adam Clayton, and The Edge (pseudonym for Dave Evans).
Island Music, 1983.
Best-selling record by U2 from *War* (Island, 83).

New York, New York
Words and music by Melvin Glover, Sylvia Robinson, Edward Fletcher,
    and Reginald Griffin.
Sugar Hill Music Publishing, Ltd., 1983.
Best-selling record by Grand Master Flash & The Furious Five (Sugar
    Hill, 83).

News from Nowhere
Words and music by Dan Zanes.
Of the Fire Music, 1987/Big Thrilling Music.
Best-selling record by The Del Fuegos, from the album *Stand Up*
    (Slash/Warner Bros., 87).

Newspapers
Words and music by Stanard Ridgway.
Mondo Spartacus Music, 1989/Illegal Songs, Inc./Criterion Music Corp.
Introduced by Stan Ridgway on *Mosquitos* (Geffen, 89).

The Next Generation (English)
Words and music by Neneh Cherry and Booga Bear.
Virgin Music, 1989/Copyright Control.
Introduced by Neneh Cherry from *Raw Like Sushi* (Virgin, 89).

The Next Time I Fall
Words and music by Robert Caldwell and Paul Gordon.
Sin Drome, 1986/EMI-Blackwood Music Inc./Chappell & Co., Inc./
    French Surf Music.
Best-selling record by Peter Cetera with Amy Grant from the album
    Solitude/Solitaire (Warner Bros., 86).

Nice 'N' Slow
Words and music by Barry Eastmond and Jolyon Skinner.
Zomba House, 1988.
Best-selling record by Freddie Jackson from *Don't Let Love Slip Away*
    (Capitol, 88). Won an American Music Award for Best Soul Song.

Nick of Time
Words and music by Bonnie Raitt.

Kokomo Music, 1989.
Best-selling record by Bonnie Raitt from *Nick of Time* (Capitol, 89),
marking the commercial breakthrough for the veteran blues/rocker.

Night (Feel Like Getting Down)
Words and music by Billy Ocean and Nigel Martinez.
EMI-Blackwood Music Inc., 1981/World Song Publishing, Inc., 1981.
Best-selling record by Billy Ocean from *Nights (Feel Like Getting
Down)* (Epic, 81).

Night After Night
Words and music by Bob Dylan.
Special Rider Music, 1987.
Introduced by Bob Dylan in the film *Hearts of Fire* and on its album
(Columbia, 87).

The Night Dolly Parton Was Almost Mine
Words and music by Jim Wann.
Shapiro, Bernstein & Co., Inc., 1981.
Introduced by Mark Hardwick in *Pump Boys and Dinettes* (81).

A Night in Tunisia
Music by John Brooks 'Dizzy' Gillespie, words by Frank Paparelli.
MCA Music, 1944.
Revived by Chaka Khan on *What Cha Gonna Do for Me* (Warner
Brothers, 81).

The Night Owls (Australian)
Words and music by Graham Goble.
Colgems-EMI Music, 1981.
Best-selling record by Little River Band from *Time Exposure* (Capitol,
81).

The Night Spanish Eddie Cashed It In, also known as **Spanish Eddie**
Words and music by David Palmer and Chuck Cochran.
Tyrell-Mann Music Corp., 1985/Glory Music Co., 1985.
Best-selling record by Laura Branigan from the album *Hold Me*
(Atlantic, 85).

A Nightmare on My Street
Words and music by Will Smith, Jeff Townes, and Pete Q. Harris.
Zomba Music, 1988.
Best-selling record by D.J. Jazzy Jeff and the Fresh Prince, from *He's
the D.J., I'm the Rapper* (Jive, 88). This is a rap song about drug
abuse.

Nightshift
Words and music by Walter Orange, Dennis Lambert, and Frannie
Golde.

Rightsong Music, 1984/Franne Golde Music Inc., 1984/Tuneworks
  Music, 1984/Walter Orange Music, 1984.
Best-selling record by The Commodores from the album *Nightshift*
  (Motown, 85). This song is a tribute to Jackie Wilson and Marvin
  Gaye, who died in 1984. Nominated for a Grammy Award, Song of
  the Year, 1985.

Nikita (English)
Words and music by Elton John and Bernie Taupin.
Intersong, USA Inc., 1986.
Best-selling record by Elton John from the album *Ice on Fire* (Warner
  Bros., 86). The song refers to past Russian leader Nikita Khrushchev.

Nine Months Later
Words and music by Rudi Protrudi.
Copyright Control, 1989.
Introduced by The Fuzztones on *In Heat* (Beggar's Banquet, 89).

9 to 5
Words and music by Dolly Parton.
Velvet Apple Music, 1980/Warner-Tamerlane Music, 1980.
Best-selling record by Dolly Parton (RCA, 81). Introduced in the film &
  soundtrack album *9 to 5* (81). Won an Academy Award, and Best
  Song, 1980;a Grammy Award, and Country Song, 1981. Nominated
  for a Grammy Award, Song of the Year, 1981.

19 (English)
Words and music by Paul Hardcastle, W. Coutourie, and J. McCord.
Crysallis Records Inc., England, 1985/Virgin Music, 1985/Oval Music
  Co., 1985.
Best-selling record by Paul Hardcastle from the album *Rain Forest*
  (Chrysallis, 85). This is a musical soundtrack to a spoken vocal from
  the television docudrama *Vietnam Requiem* (85).

Nineteen Eighty-Two
Words and music by James Blackmon and Carl Vipperman.
Grand Alliance, 1985/Grand Coalition.
Best-selling record by Randy Travis from the album *Storms of Life*
  (Warner Bros., 86). Before it was updated, this song was entitled
  '1962.' Won a Country Music Association Award, 1986.

Nite and Day
Words and music by Al B. Sure and Kyle West.
Al B. Sure, 1988/Key West Inc., 1988/Across 110th Street Music, 1988/
  EMI-April Music, 1988.
Best-selling record by Al B. Sure from *In Effect Mode* (Warner Bros.,
  88).

No Condom, No Sex
Words and music by Stewart Pfalzer.
Rando Music, 1988.
Introduced by Cruise Control (Sire, 88), this exemplifies the pop
    community's effort to promote a 'Safe Sex' message.

No Gettin' over Me
Words and music by Tom Brasfield and Walt Aldridge.
Colgems-EMI Music, 1981.
Best-selling record by Ronnie Milsap from *There's No Gettin' over Me*
    (RCA, 81).

No Money Down
Words and music by Lou Reed.
Metal Machine Music, 1986.
Introduced by Lou Reed on the album *Mistrial* (RCA, 86).

No More Lonely Nights (English)
Words and music by Paul McCartney.
MPL Communications Inc., 1984.
Best-selling record by Paul McCartney (Columbia, 84). Introduced in
    the film and soundtrack album *Give My Regards to Broad Street* (84).

No More Rhyme
Words and music by Deborah Gibson.
EMI-April Music, 1989/Possibilities Publishing.
Best-selling record by Debbie Gibson from *Electric Youth* (Atlantic, 89).

No Night So Long
Words by Will Jennings, music by Richard Kerr.
Irving Music Inc., 1980.
Best-selling record by Dionne Warwick from *No Night So Long* (Arista,
    80).

No One Is Alone
Words and music by Stephen Sondheim.
BMG Songs Inc., 1987.
Introduced by Kim Crosby, Chip Zien, Ben Wright, and Danielle
    Ferland in the musical *Into the Woods,* which opened on Broadway in
    1987; original cast album is on RCA/Red Seal label.

No One Is to Blame (English)
Words and music by Howard Jones.
Howard Jones, England, 1985.
Best-selling record by Howard Jones from the album *Action Replay*
    (Elektra, 86). Introduced on *Dream into Action* in a significantly
    different form.

No Place Like Home
Words and music by Paul Overstreet.
Writer's Group Music, 1986/Scarlet Moon Music, 1986.
Best-selling record in 1987 by Randy Travis, from the album *Storms of Life* (Warner Bros., 86).

No Regrets
Words and music by Tom Rush.
Tubbs Hill Music, 1967.
Emmylou Harris revived this folk standard on *Bluebird* (Reprise, 89).

No Reply at All (English)
Words and music by Tony Banks, Phil Collins, and Mike Rutherford.
Hit & Run Music, 1981.
Best-selling record by Genesis from *Abacab* (Atlantic, 81).

No Reservations
Words and music by Bob Mould.
Husker Music, 1986.
Introduced by Husker Du on the album *Warehouse Songs and Stories* (Warner Bros., 87).

No Surrender
Words and music by Bruce Springsteen.
Bruce Springsteen Publishing, 1984.
Introduced by Bruce Springsteen in *Born in the U.S.A.* (Columbia, 84).

No Way Out
Words and music by Peter Wolf and Ina Wolf.
Petwolf Music, 1984/Jobete Music Co., 1984/Stone Diamond Music, 1984/Kikiko Music Corp., 1984.
Best-selling record by The Jefferson Starship from *Nuclear Furniture* (Grunt, 84).

No Way Out
Words and music by Paul Anka and Michael McDonald.
Paulanne Music Inc., 1987/Genevieve Music, 1987.
Introduced by Julia Migenes and Paul Anka as the title song for the 1987 Columbia Pictures film *No Way Out*.

No Way to Treat a Lady (Canadian)
Words and music by Bryan Adams and Jim Vallance.
Irving Music Inc., 1982/Adams Communications, Inc./Calypso Toonz.
Best-selling record by Bonnie Raitt from the album *Nine Lives* (Warner Bros., 86).

Nobody
Words and music by Kye Fleming and Dennis Morgan.
Tom Collins Music Corp., 1982.

Best-selling record by Sylvia from *Just Sylvia* (RCA, 82). Nominated for a Grammy Award, Country Song of the Year, 1982.

Nobody
Words and music by Bert Williams.
Revived by Ben Harney in *Williams and Walker*, a 1986 show about Bert Williams and George Walker, the first black entertainers to headline an integrated Broadway show.

Nobody Falls Like a Fool
Words and music by Peter McCann and Mark Wright.
EMI-April Music, 1985/New & Used Music, 1985/EMI-Blackwood Music Inc., 1985/Land of Music Publishing, 1985.
Best-selling record by Earl Thomas Conley from *Greatest Hits* (RCA, 85).

Nobody in His Right Mind Would Have Left Her
Words and music by Dean Dillon.
Hall-Clement Publications, 1986.
Best-selling record by George Strait from the album *#7* (MCA, 86).

Nobody Said It Was Easy
Words and music by Tony Haseldon.
Screen Gems-EMI Music Inc., 1982.
Best-selling record by Le Roux from *Keep the Fire Burnin'* (RCA, 82).

Nobody There But Me
Words and music by Bruce Hornsby.
Zappo Music, 1987/Bob-a-Lew Music, 1987.
Introduced by Willie Nelson on the album *Island in the Sea* (Columbia, 87).

Nobody Wants to Be Alone
Words and music by Michael Masser and Rhonda Fleming.
Almo Music Corp., 1985/Prince Street Music, 1985/Irving Music Inc., 1985/Eaglewood Music, 1985.
Best-selling record by Crystal Gayle from the album *Nobody Wants to Be Alone* (Warner Bros., 85).

Nobody's Fool
Words and music by Tom Keifer.
Chappell & Co., Inc., 1986/Evesongs Inc., 1986.
Best-selling record in 1987 by Cinderella, from the album *Night Songs* (Mercury, 86).

Nobody's Fool (Theme from *Caddyshack II*)
Words and music by Kenny Loggins and Michael Towers.

Milk Money Music, 1988/WB Music, 1988/Tiger Bay Music, 1988/
Warner-Tamerlane Music, 1988.
Introduced by Kenny Loggins in the film and on the soundtrack album
Caddyshack II (Columbia, 88). Featured on *Back to Avalon*
(Columbia, 88).

Not a Day Goes By
Words and music by Stephen Sondheim.
WB Music, 1981.
Introduced by Jim Walton in *Merrily We Roll Along* (81).

Not Alone Anymore
Words and music by Traveling Wilburys.
Copyright Control, 1988.
Introduced by the Traveling Wilburys on *Traveling Wilburys Volume I*
(Wilbury, 88). Twenty years earlier, member Roy Orbison released
'Only the Lonely,' which this song answers.

Not Enough Love in the World
Words and music by Don Henley, Danny Kortchmar, and Benmont
Tench.
Cass County Music Co., 1984/Kortchmar Music, 1984.
Best-selling record by Don Henley from the album *Building the Perfect
Beast* (Geffen, 85).

Not Like You
Words and music by Debbi Peterson, Susanna Hoffs, and David Kahne.
EMI-Blackwood Music Inc., 1985/Bangophile Music/Seesquared Music.
Introduced by The Bangles on the album *Different Light* (Columbia, 86).

Nothin' at All
Words and music by Mark Mueller.
Music of the World, 1986.
Best-selling record by Heart in 1986 from the album *Heart* (Capitol,
85).

Nothin' But a Good Time
Words and music by Bobby Dall, C. C. Deville, Brett Michaels, and
Rikki Rockett.
Sweet Cyanide, 1988.
Best-selling record by Poison, from *Open Up and Say Ahh* (Capitol, 88).

Nothing But Flowers
Words and music by David Byrne, music by Chris Frantz, Jerry
Harrison, and Tina Weymouth.
Index Music, 1988.
Best-selling record by Talking Heads, from *Naked* (Sire, 88).

Nothing Can Come Between Us (English)
Words and music by Sade (pseudonym for Helen Folesade Adu),
   Andrew Hale, and Stewart Matthewman.
Angel Music Ltd., 1988/Sony Tunes, 1988/Famous Music Corp., 1988.
Best-selling record by Sade, from *Stronger Than Pride* (Epic, 88).

Nothing Has Been Proved (English)
Words and music by Chris Lowe and Neil Tennant.
Virgin Music, 1989.
Introduced by Dusty Springfield in the film and soundtrack LP *Scandal*
   (Capitol-EMI, 89).

Nothing I Can Do About It Now
Words and music by Beth Neilsen Chapman.
WB Music, 1989/Refuge Music, Inc./Macy Place Music.
Best-selling record by Willie Nelson from *A Horse Called Music*
   (Columbia, 89).

Nothing in Common (English)
Words and music by Tom Bailey and Alannah Currie.
Zomba Music, 1986.
Introduced by the Thompson Twins in the 1986 film *Nothing in
Common* and on the soundtrack album (Arista).

Nothing Really Happened
Words and music by Craig Carnelia.
Carnelia Music, 1982.
Introduced by Alma Cuervo in *Is There Life After High School* (82).

Nothing's Gonna Change My Love for You
Words and music by Michael Masser.
Prince Street Music, 1985/Almo Music Corp., 1985/Screen Gems-EMI
   Music Inc., 1985.
Introduced by George Benson on his album *20/20* in 1985. Revived in
   1987 by Glenn Medeiros on the album *Glenn Medeiros* (Amherst,
   87).

Nothing's Gonna Stop Us Now
Words and music by Diane Warren and Albert Hammond.
Realsongs, 1987/Albert Hammond Enterprises, 1987.
Best-selling record by Starship (Grant, 87); introduced in the 1987 film
   Mannequin. Nominated for an Academy Award, Best Original Song,
   1987; Nominated for an Academy Award, Best Original Song, 1987;
   a Grammy Award, Best song for TV/Movies, 1987.

Nothing's Gonna Stop Us Now
Words by Jesse Fredericke, music by Bennett Salvay.
Introduced by David Pomeranz as the theme for the television series
   Perfect Strangers.

Notorious (English)
Words and music by John Taylor, Nick Rhodes, and Simon LeBon.
Copyright Control, 1986.
Best-selling record by Duran Duran from the album *Notorious* (Capitol, 86).

Now
Words by David Rogers, music by Charles Strouse.
Four Kids Music, 1978.
Introduced by P. J. Benjamin and Sandy Falson in *Charlie and Algernon* (musical, 80).

Now and Forever (You & Me) (Canadian)
Words and music by David Foster, Jim Vallance, and Randy Goodrum.
Air Bear, 1986/Irving Music Inc./Calypso Toonz/California Phase Music.
Best-selling record by Anne Murray from the album *Something to Talk About* (Capitol, 86).

Now Let the Weeping Cease
Words by Lee Breuer, music by Bob Telson.
Boodle Music, 1988/Otis Lee Music, 1988.
Revived in 1988 by The Soul Stirrers with soloist Willie Rogers in the musical album *The Gospel at Colonus* (Elektra-Nonesuch, 88).

Nowhere Road
Words and music by Steve Earle and Reno Kling.
Goldline Music Inc., 1987.
Best-selling record by Steve Earle, from the album *Exit O* (MCA, 87).

Number One
Words and music by Joni Mitchell.
Crazy Crow Music, 1986.
Introduced by Joni Mitchell at the Amnesty International Conspiracy of Hope Concert at the Meadowlands in New Jersey on June 15th, 1986.

Number One in America
Words and music by David Massengill.
David Massengill Music, 1987.
Introduced by David Massengill on *Fast Folk Sixth Anniversary Issue* (Fast Folk, 88).

O

O Superman
Words and music by Laurie Anderson.
Difficult Music, 1981.
Introduced by Laurie Anderson on *Big Science* (Warner Brothers, 82).

The Oak Tree
Words and music by Morris Day.
Yadsirrom Music, 1985.
Best-selling record by Morris Day from the album *The Color of Success* (Warner Bros., 85).

Oasis
Words and music by Marcus Miller and Mark Stevens.
Sunset Burgundy Music, Inc., 1988/MCA Music, 1988.
Best-selling record by Roberta Flack, from *Oasis* (Atlantic, 88).

Ob-La-Di, Ob-La-Da
Words and music by John Lennon and Paul McCartney.
Northern Songs, Ltd., England, 1968/Maclen Music Inc., 1968.
Revived as the themesong for the television series *Life Goes On*.

Obsession
Words and music by Holly Knight and Michael Desbarres.
Pacific Island Music, 1983/BMG Music, 1983/Mike Chapman Publishing Enterprises, 1983/BMG Songs Inc., 1983.
Best-selling record by Animotion from the album *Animotion* (Mercury, 85).

Ocean Front Property
Words and music by Dean Dillon, Chuck Cochran, and Royce Porter.
Tree Publishing Co., Inc., 1987/Larry Butler Music Co., 1987/ Southwing, 1987/EMI-Blackwood Music Inc., 1987.
Best-selling record by George Strait, from the album *Ocean Front Property* (MCA, 87).

Off On Your Own (Girl)
Words and music by Al B. Sure and Kyle West.
EMI-April Music, 1988/Across 110th Street Music, 1988.
Best-selling record by Al B. Sure, from *In Effect Mode* (Warner Bros., 88).

Off the Wall (English)
Words and music by Rod Temperton.
Rodsongs, 1979.
Best-selling record by Michael Jackson from *Off the Wall* (Epic, 80).

Oh No
Words and music by Lionel Richie, Jr.
Jobete Music Co., 1981/Brockman Enterprises Inc., 1981.
Best-selling record by The Commodores from *In the Pocket* (Motown, 81).

Oh, Sheila (English)
Words and music by Melvin Riley, Gordon Strozier, and Gerald Valentine.
Ready for the World Music, 1985/Excalibur Lace Music, 1985/Trixie Lou Music, 1985/MCA, Inc., 1985/Off Backstreet Music, 1985/Walk on Moon Music, 1985.
Best-selling record by Ready for the World from the album *Ready for the World* (MCA, 85).

Oh, Sherrie
Words and music by Steve Perry, Randy Goodrum, Bill Cuomo, and Craig Krampf.
Street Talk Tunes, 1984/EMI-April Music, 1984/Pants Down Music, 1984/Random Notes, 1984/Phosphene Music, 1984.
Best-selling record by Steve Perry from *Street Talk* (Columbia, 84).

Oh Yeah (German)
Words and music by Boris Blank and Dieter Meier.
WB Music, 1985.
Performed by Yello in the films *The Secret of My Success* ('87) and *Ferris Beuller's Day Off* ('86). Originally appeared on a 1985 album.

Oh Yes I Can
Words and music by David Crosby.
Stay Straight Music, 1989.
Introduced by David Crosby from *Oh Yes I Can* (A & M, 89), the song charts the singer-songwriter's recovery from drug abuse, as does his book of the same title.

Oh, You Crazy Moon
Words by Johnny Burke, music by James Van Heusen.
WB Music, 1939/Music Sales Corp., 1939.

The posthumous release of *Let's Get Lost,* a film biography of trumpeter
   Chet Baker, inspired the re-release of his 1977 album *The Best Thing
   for You* (A & M, 88).

Ohio Afternoon
Words and music by Mark Hardwick, Mike Craver, and Debbie Monk.
Introduced by Mark Hardwick, Mike Craver, Debbie Monk, and Mary
   Murfitt in the 1987 Off-Broadway production *Oil City Symphony.*

Oklahoma Nights
Words and music by Jimmy Webb.
White Oak Songs, 1981.
Introduced by Arlo Guthrie in *Power of Love* (Warner Brothers, 81).

Old-Fashion Love
Words and music by Milan Williams.
Jobete Music Co., 1980/Old Fashion Music, 1980.
Best-selling record by The Commodores from *Heroes* (Motown, 80).

An Old Fashioned Song
Words and music by Douglas Bernstein and Denis Markell.
Revived by the cast of the musical revue *Showing Off* in 1989, this song
   was introduced by the ensemble of television's 1979 special *ABC
   Comedy Zone.*

Old Flame (Icelandic)
English words and music by Donny Lowery and Mac McAnnally.
New Envoy Music, 1981.
Best-selling record by Alabama from *Feels So Right* (RCA, 81).

Old Flames Can't Hold a Candle to You
Words and music by Hugh Moffatt and Pebe Sebert.
Rightsong Music, 1978.
Best-selling record by Dolly Parton from *Dolly Dolly Dolly* (RCA, 80).

Old Folks
Words and music by Mike Reid.
BMG Songs Inc., 1987.
Best-selling record by Mike Reid and Ronnie Milsap from *Signatures*
   (RCA, 88), an album comprising the work of five of Nashville's best
   songwriters performing their own songs. Reid is a former lineman for
   the Cincinnati Bengals football team who has written other songs for
   Milsap.

Old Friends
Words and music by Stephen Sondheim.
WB Music, 1981.
Introduced by Ann Morrison in *Merrily We Roll Along* (81).

Old Hippie
Words and music by David Bellamy.
Bellamy Brothers Music, 1985.
Best-selling record by The Bellamy Brothers from the album *Howard and David* (MCA, 85).

The Old Man Down the Road
Words and music by John Fogerty.
Wenaha Music Co., 1984.
Best-selling record by John Fogerty from the album *Centerfield* (Warner Bros., 85).

Old Men Sleeping on the Bowery
Words and music by Willie Nile.
Lake Victoria Music, 1979.
Introduced by Willie Nile on *Willie Nile* (Arista, 80).

The Old Songs
Words and music by David Pomeranz and Buddy Kaye.
WB Music, 1979/Upward Spiral Music, 1979.
Best-selling record by Barry Manilow from *If I Should Love Again* (Arista, 81). Introduced by David Pomeranz on *The Truth of Us* (Pacific Records, 80).

Old Time Rock and Roll
Words and music by George Jackson and Tom Jones, III.
Muscle Shoals Sound Publishing Co., Inc., 1977.
Best-selling record by Bob Seger and The Silver Bullet Band (Capitol, 83). Featured in the film *Risky Business* (83). Introduced in *Stranger in Town* (Capitol, 78)

Older Women
Words and music by James O'Hara.
Tree Publishing Co., Inc., 1981.
Best-selling record by Ronnie McDowell (Epic, 81).

On My Own
Words and music by Burt Bacharach and Carole Bayer Sager.
New Hidden Valley Music Co., 1986/Carole Bayer Sager Music.
Best-selling record by Patti LaBelle and Michael McDonald from the album *Winner in You* (MCA, 86).

On My Own (French-English)
French words by Alain Boublil and Jean Marc Natel, English words by Herbert Kretzmer, music by Alain Boublil and Claude-Michel Schonberg.
Editions Musicales, Paris, France, 1980, 1986/Alain Boublil Music Ltd., 1980, 1986.
Introduced by Frances Ruffelle in the London Production of *Les*

Miserables and recreated on Broadway in 1987 where the performer won a Tony Award. Recorded on the Broadway cast album. Also sung by Elaine Paige on the album *Stages* (Atlantic, 87).

(Lost His Love) On Our Last Date, also known as **Last Date**
Words and music by Floyd Cramer.
Acuff-Rose Publications Inc., 1964.
Revived by Emmylou Harris on *Last Date* (Warner Brothers, 82).

On Our Own (From *Ghostbusters II*)
Words and music by L. A. Reid (pseudonym for Antonio Reid),
    Babyface (pseudonym for Kenny Edmunds), and Daryl Simmons.
Kear Music, 1989/Hip-Trip Music Co./Green Skirt Music.
Best-selling record by Bobby Brown from the film and soundtrack
    album *Ghostbusters II* (Warner Bros., 89).

On the Dark Side
Words and music by John Cafferty.
Warner-Tamerlane Music, 1982/John Cafferty Music, 1982.
Best-selling record by John Cafferty & The Beaver Brown Band (Scotti
    Brothers, 84). Introduced in the film and sountrack album *Eddie and
    the Cruisers* (82).

On the Nickel
Words and music by Tom Waits.
Fifth Floor Music Inc., 1980.
Featured in *Heartattack and Vine* by Tom Waits (Asylum, 80). Used in
    the film *On the Nickel* (80).

On the Other Hand
Words and music by Paul Overstreet and Don Schlitz.
Writer's Group Music, 1986/Scarlet Moon Music/MCA, Inc./Don
    Schlitz Music.
Best-selling record by Randy Travis from the album *Storms of Life*
    (Warner Bros., 86). Won a Country Music Association Award, and
    Song of the Year, 1986.

On the Radio (American-German)
Music by Giorgio Moroder, English words by Donna Summer.
Revelation Music Publishing Corp., 1979/Rick's Music Inc., 1979/Sweet
    Summer Night Music, 1979.
Best-selling record by Donna Summer from *On the Radio - Greatest
    Hits, Vol I & II* (Casablanca, 80).

On the Road Again
Words and music by Willie Nelson.
Willie Nelson Music Inc., 1979.
Best-selling record by Willie Nelson (Columbia, 80). Introduced in the
    film & soundtrack album *Honeysuckle Rose* (80). Won a Grammy

Award, and Country Song of the Year, 1980. Nominated for an Academy Award, 1980.

On the Western Skyline
Words and music by Bruce Hornsby and John Hornsby.
Zappo Music, 1986/Basically Gasp Music.
Best-selling record by Bruce Hornsby & The Range from the album *The Way It Is* (RCA, 86).

On the Wings of a Nightingale (English)
Words and music by Paul McCartney.
MPL Communications Inc., 1984.
Best-selling record by Everly Brothers from *EB84* (Mercury, 84).

On the Wings of Love
Words and music by Peter Schless and Jeffrey Osborne.
Lincoln Pond Music, 1982/Almo Music Corp., 1982/March 9 Music, 1982.
Best-selling record by Jeffrey Osborne from *Jeffrey Osborne* (A & M, 82).

On Third Street
Words and music by David Lasley.
Almo Music Corp., 1981.
Introduced by David Lasley on *Missin' Twenty Grand* (EMI, 82).

On Your Shore (Irish)
Words by Roma Ryan, music by Enya.
EMI-Blackwood Music Inc., 1988.
Introduced by Enya in *Watermark* (Geffen, 88). The singer was previously a member of the Irish folk group Clannad.

Once Bitten
Words and music by Billy Steinberg, Tom Kelly, Michael Greeley, David Currier, and Linda Chase.
Billy Steinberg Music, 1985/Denise Barry Music, 1985/Polifer Music, 1985/Brigitte Baby Publishing, 1985.
Introduced by 3 Speed in the film *Once Bitten* (85).

Once Bitten Twice Shy
Words and music by Ian Hunter.
EMI-April Music, 1975/Ian Hunter Music.
Best-selling record by Great White from *Twice Shy* (Capitol, 89).

Once in a Blue Moon
Words and music by Tom Brasfield and Robert Byrne.
Colgems-EMI Music, 1986.
Best-selling record by Earl Thomas Conley from the album *Earl Thomas Conley's Greatest Hits* (RCA, 86).

Once in a Lifetime (American-English)
Words and music by David Byrne, Chris Franz, Jerry Harrison, Tina
    Weymouth, and Brian Eno.
Bleu Disque Music, 1980/E.G. Music, 1980.
Best-selling record by Talking Heads from *Remain in Light* (Sire, 81).
    Rereleased in the film and soundtrack album *Stop Making Sense*
    (1984).

Once We Might Have Known
Words and music by Peter Kingsbery.
Edwin Ellis Music, 1985/Nurk Twins Music.
This was the fourth single release by Cock Robin from the album *Cock
    Robin* (Columbia, 85). First three singles, 'When Your Heart Is
    Weak,' 'Thought You Were on My Side,' and 'The Promise You
    Made,' were major international hits, reaching the top ten in France,
    Germany, Spain, Norway, Holland, and Italy.

One
Words and music by James Hetfield and Lars Ulrich.
Creeping Death Music, 1988.
Best-selling record in 1989 by Metallica from *...And Justice for All*
    (Elektra, 88). This anti-war song was based on the Dalton Trumbo
    novel *Johnny Got His Gun*. Nominated for a Grammy Award, Heavy
    Metal Song of the Year, 1989.

One (English)
Words and music by Barry Gibb, Robin Gibb, and Maurice Gibb.
Gibb Brothers Music, 1989/Careers Music Inc.
Best-selling record by The Bee Gees from *One* (Warner Bros., 89).

One Clear Moment
Words and music by Linda Thompson and Betsy Cook.
Firesign Music Ltd., England, 1984/Chappell & Co., Inc., 1984.
Introduced by Linda Thompson on the album *One Clear Moment*
    (Warner Bros., 85).

One Day at a Time
Words and music by Marijohn Wilkin and Kris Kristofferson.
Buckhorn Music Publishing Co., Inc., 1973.
Best-selling record by Cristy Lane (United Artists, 80).

One Fine Day
Words by Gerry Goffin, music by Carole King.
Screen Gems-EMI Music Inc., 1963.
Revived by Carole King in *Pearls* (Capitol, 80).

One for the Money
Words and music by B. Moore and M. Williams.
Tapadero Music, 1987/Dixie Stars, 1987.

Best-selling record by T. G. Sheppard, from the album *One for the Money* (Columbia, 87).

One Friend
Words and music by Dan Seals.
Pink Pig Music, 1987.
Best-selling record in 1988 by Dan Seals from *The Best* (Capitol, 87).

One Good Woman
Words and music by Peter Cetera and Patrick Leonard.
Fall Line Orange Music, 1988/Johnny Yuma, 1988.
Best-selling record by Peter Cetera from *One More Story* (Full Moon, 88).

One Heartbeat
Words by S. Legassick, music by B. Ray.
Chubu, 1987.
Best-selling record by Smokey Robinson, from the album *One Hearbeat* (Motown, 87).

One Hello
Words by Carole Bayer Sager, music by Marvin Hamlisch.
Chappell & Co., Inc., 1982/Red Bullet Music, 1982/Twentieth Century-Fox Music Corp., 1982/Carole Bayer Sager Music, 1982/Fox Fanfare Music Inc., 1982.
Introduced in the film *I Oughta Be in Pictures* (82) by Dinah Manoff.

One Hundred Percent Chance of Rain
Words and music by Charlie Black and Austin Roberts.
Chappell & Co., Inc., 1986/Chriswald Music/Hopi Sound Music/MCA, Inc.
Best-selling record by Gary Morris from the album *Anything Goes* (Warner Bros., 86).

One Hundred Ways
Words and music by Kathy Wakefield, Benjamin Wright, and Tony Coleman.
State of the Arts Music, 1981/Kidada Music Inc., 1981.
Best-selling record by Quincy Jones featuring James Ingram from *The Dude* (A & M, 82).

The One I Love
Words and music by Bill Berry, Peter Buck, Mike Mills, and Michael Stipe.
Night Garden Music, 1987/Unichappell Music Inc., 1987.
Best-selling record by R.E.M. from the album *Document* (I.R.S., 87); this was the breakthrough single for the former underground band.

The One I Loved Back Then, also known as **The Corvette Song**
Words and music by Gary Gentry.
Algee Music Corp., 1986.
Best-selling record by George Jones from the album *Wine Colored Roses* (Epic, 86).

One in a Million (English)
Words and music by Henry Priestman.
Virgin Music, 1988.
Introduced by The Christians on *The Christians* (Island, 88).

One in a Million You
Words and music by Sam Dees.
Irving Music Inc., 1980.
Best-selling records in 1980 by Larry Graham from *One in a Million You* (Warner Brothers) and by Johnny Lee from *Lookin' for Love* (Asylum).

One Lonely Night
Words and music by Neal Doughty.
Jonisongs, 1984.
Best-selling record by REO Speedwagon from the album *Wheels Are Turning* (Epic, 85).

One Love at a Time
Words and music by Paul Davis and Paul Overstreet.
Web 4 Music Inc., 1986/Writer's Group Music/Scarlet Moon Music.
Best-selling record by Tanya Tucker from the album *Girls Like Me* (Capitol, 86).

One Moment in Time (English)
Words and music by Albert Hammond and John Bettis.
Albert Hammond Enterprises, 1987/John Bettis Music, 1987/W.B.M. Music, 1987.
Best-selling record by Whitney Houston from *One Moment in Time*; *Music of the XXIII Olympiad* (Arista, 88). Nominated for a Grammy Award, Best Song for a Film or TV, 1988.

One More Hour
Words and music by Randy Newman.
Wide Music, 1981.
Introduced by Jennifer Warnes in the film and soundtrack album *Ragtime* (81). Nominated for an Academy Award, Best Song, 1981.

One More Night (English)
Words and music by Phil Collins.
Hit & Run Music, 1984.
Best-selling record by Phil Collins from the album *No Jacket Required* (Atlantic, 85).

One More Try (English)
Words and music by George Michael.
Morrison Leahy, England, 1987/Chappell & Co., Inc., 1987.
Best-selling record in 1988 by George Michael from the album *Faith*
(Columbia, 87).

One Night in Bangkok (English-Swedish)
English words and music by Benny Andersson, Tim Rice, and Bjorn
Ulvaeus.
Union Songs Musikfoerlag, Sweden, 1984/MCA, Inc., 1984.
Best-selling record by Murray Head from the album *Chess* (RCA, 85).
As he did with 'Jesus Christ Superstar,' Murray Head introduced a
song from a play before its opening, in this case *Chess* scheduled for
1986 in England.

One Night Love Affair (Canadian)
Words and music by Bryan Adams and Jim Vallance.
Adams Communications, Inc., 1984/Calypso Toonz, 1984/Irving Music
Inc., 1984.
Best-selling record by Bryan Adams from the album *Reckless* (A & M,
85).

One Night Only
Words by Tom Eyen, music by Henry Krieger.
Dreamgirls Music, 1981/Dreamette's Music, 1981/August Dream Music
Ltd., 1981.
Introduced by Jennifer Holliday and Vondee Curtis Hall in *Dreamgirls*
(81). Featured in *Call Me* by Sylvester (Megatone, 83).

One Nite Stan
Words and music by Kacey Jones and Jon Iger.
Zama Lama Music, 1988/Glaser Holmes Publications, 1988/Tigertrax,
1988/Blue Drops, 1988.
Introduced by Ethel and the Shameless Hussies on *Born to Burn* (MCA,
88).

One of the Boys
Words by Fred Ebb, music by John Kander.
Fiddleback, 1981/Kander & Ebb Inc., 1981.
Introduced by Lauren Bacall in *Woman of the Year* (81).

One of the Living
Words and music by Holly Knight.
Makiki Publishing Co., Ltd., 1985/BMG Songs Inc., 1985.
Introduced by Tina Turner in the film and soundtrack album *Mad Max
Beyond Thunderdome* (Capitol, 85). Best-selling record by Tina
Turner (Capitol, 85).

One of These Days
Words and music by Camper Van Beethoven.
Camper Van Beethoven Music, 1987/Bug Music, 1987.
Introduced by Camper Van Beethoven on *Our Beloved Revolutionary Sweetheart* (Virgin, 88).

One on One
Words and music by Daryl Hall.
Hot Cha Music Co., 1982/Unichappell Music Inc., 1982.
Best-selling record by Daryl Hall and John Oates from *H2O* (RCA, 83).

One Owner Heart
Words and music by Walt Aldridge, Tom Brasfield, and Mac McAnnally.
Colgems-EMI Music, 1984/Beginner Music, 1984/Tom Brasfield Music, 1984.
Best-selling record by T. G. Sheppard from the album *Livin' on the Edge* (Warner Bros., 85).

One Promise Too Late
Words and music by Dave Loggins, Lisa Silver, and Don Schlitz.
MCA Music, 1987/Patchwork Music, 1987/Don Schlitz Music, 1987/ Music of the World, 1987.
Best-selling record by Reba McEntire, from her *Greatest Hits* album (MCA, 87).

One Silk Sheet
Words by Marc Elliott, music by Larry Hochman.
Ba-Ba-Do Music, 1985.
Introduced by James Lecesne in the musical *One Man Band* (85).

One Simple Thing (English)
Words and music by Dave Christenson and Rich Nevens.
Still Life, 1986/Warner-Tamerlane Music.
Best-selling record by The Stabilizers from the album *Tyranny* (Columbia, 86).

One Step Forward
Words and music by Chris Hillman and Bill Wildes.
Bar-None Music, 1987/Bug Music, 1987.
Best-selling record in 1988 by The Desert Rose Band, from *The Desert Rose Band* (MCA/Curb, 87).

One Step over the Line
Words and music by John Hiatt.
Lillybilly, 1989/Bug Music.
Introduced by John Hiatt on *Will the Circle Be Unbroken, Vol. II* (Universal, 89).

One Step Up
Words and music by Bruce Springsteen.
Bruce Springsteen Publishing, 1987.
Introduced by Bruce Springsteen on the album *Tunnel of Love*
   (Columbia, 87).

One Sunny Day
Words and music by Bill Wolfer and Dean Pitchford.
Wolftoons Music, 1986/Pitchford.
Introduced by Ray Parker, Jr. and Helen Terry on the soundtrack of the
   movie *Quicksilver* (86).

The One That You Love (Australian)
Words and music by Graham Russell.
Careers Music Inc., 1981/Nottsongs, 1981.
Best-selling record by Air Supply from *The One That You Love* (Arista,
   81).

One Thing Leads to Another (English)
Words and music by Cy Curnin, Adam Woods, Jamie West-Oram,
   Rupert Greenall, and Alfred Agius.
Colgems-EMI Music, 1982.
Best-selling record by The Fixx from *Reach the Beach* (MCA, 83).

1999
Words and music by Prince Rogers Nelson.
Controversy Music, 1982.
Best-selling record by Prince from *1999* (Warner Brothers, 83).

1969
Words and music by Iggy Pop.
Paradox Music, 1969.
Revived in 1988 by the Pretenders on the b-side of 'Windows of the
   World' (Polydor). The orginal version was by the Stooges on *The
   Stooges*.

One Time for Old Times (Canadian)
Words and music by Gary O'Connor.
EMI-April Music, 1983.
Introduced by 38 Special on *Tour de Force* (A & M, 83).

One Time One Night
Words and music by David Hidalgo and Louie Perez.
Davince Music, 1987/No K. O. Music, 1987.
Introduced by Los Lobos on the album *By the Light of the Moon* (Slash/
   Warner Bros., 87).

One Trick Pony
Words and music by Paul Simon.

Paul Simon Music, 1979.
Best-selling record by Paul Simon (Warner Brothers, 80). Introduced in the film & soundtrack album *One Trick Pony* (80).

1-2-3
Words and music by Gloria Estefan and Enrique Garcia.
Foreign Imported, 1987.
Best-selling record in 1988 by Gloria Estefan & Miami Sound Machine (Epic, 87).

1-2-3 Go (This Town's a Fairground)
Words and music by Joe Jackson.
Almo Music Corp., 1983.
Introduced in *Mike's Murder* by Joe Jackson (A & M, 83).

One Vision (English)
Words by Queen.
Queen Music Ltd., 1985/Beechwood Music, 1985.
Introduced by Queen in the film and soundtrack album *Iron Eagle* (Capitol, 85).

One Way Love (Better Off Dead)
Words and music by Steve Goldstein, Duane Hitchings, Craig Krampf, and Eric Nelson.
Irving Music Inc., 1985/EMI-Blackwood Music Inc., 1985/Almo Music Corp., 1985/EMI-April Music, 1985.
Introduced by E. G. Daily in the film *Better Off Dead* (85).

The One You Love
Words and music by Glenn Frey and Jack Tempchin.
Red Cloud Music Co., 1982/Night River Publishing, 1982.
Best-selling record by Glenn Frey from *No Fun Aloud* (Asylum, 82).

Only a Fool
Words and music by Karla Bonoff.
Seagrape Music Inc., 1979.
Rhythm 'n' Blues Maura O'Connell on *Helpless Heart* (Warner Bros., 89).

Only a Lonely Heart Knows
Words and music by Dennis W. Morgan and Steve Davis.
Tom Collins Music Corp., 1983/Dick James Music Inc., 1983.
Best-selling record by Barbara Mandrell (MCA, 83).

Only Darkness Has the Power (English)
Words and music by The Mekons.
Low Noise America Music, 1989.
Introduced by The Mekons on *The Mekons Rock n' Roll* (Twintone, 89).

The Only Flame in Town (English)
Words and music by Elvis Costello.
Plangent Visions Music, Inc., London, England, 1984.
Introduced by Elvis Costello in *Goodbye Cruel World* (Columbia, 84).

Only in My Dreams
Words and music by Debbie Gibson.
Creative Bloc, 1987.
Best-selling record by Debbie Gibson, from the album *Out of the Blue*
    (Atlantic, 87). This was the sixteen-year-old pop music prodigy's first
    hit.

Only One
Words and music by James Taylor.
Country Road Music Inc., 1985.
Introduced by James Taylor on the album *That's Why I'm Here*
    (Columbia, 86).

The Only One (English)
Words and music by Jimmy Page and Robert Plant.
Succubus Music, 1988/Talk Time Music, Inc., 1988.
Introduced by Jimmy Page on *Outrider* (Geffen, 88), this song is a
    collaboration between the two most famous principals in the
    legendary rock group Led Zeppelin.

Only One You
Words and music by Michael Garvin and Bucky Jones.
Tree Publishing Co., Inc., 1981/Cross Keys Publishing Co., Inc., 1981.
Best-selling record by T. G. Sheppard from *Finally!* (Warner/Curb, 82).

Only the Lonely
Words and music by Martha Davis.
Clean Sheets Music, 1981.
Best-selling record by The Motels from *All For One* (Capitol, 82).

Only the Young
Words and music by Steve Perry, Neal Schon, and Jonathan Cain.
Twist & Shout Music, 1983/Weed High Nightmare Music, 1983/
    Colgems-EMI Music, 1983.
Best-selling record by Journey (Warner Bros., 85). Featured in the film
    Vision Quest (83) and its soundtrack album. Introduced by Patty
    Smyth and Scandal in 1985 on the LP *The Warrior* (Columbia, 84).

Only Time Will Tell (English)
Words and music by John Wetton and Geoffrey Downes.
WB Music, 1982/Polygram International, 1982.
Best-selling record by Asia from *Asia* (Geffen, 82).

Only with You
Words and music by Maury Yeston.
Yeston Music, Ltd., 1975.
Introduced by Raul Julia in *Nine* (Musical, 82).

Only You (English)
Words by Richard Stilgoe, music by Andrew Lloyd Webber.
Really Useful Music, 1987.
Introduced by Greg Mowry and Riva Rice in the 1987 Broadway
    production of *Starlight Express,* a show that made its debut in
    London. The song was also recorded by Peter Hewlett and Josie
    Aiello on the album *Music and Songs from 'Starlight Express'* (MCA,
    87).

Ooo La La La
Words and music by Teena Marie and Allen McGrier.
EMI-April Music, 1988/McNella Music, 1988/Oh-Ber, 1988/Midnight
    Magnet, 1988.
Best-selling record by Teena Marie, from the album *Naked to the World*
    (Epic, 88).

Open Arms
Words and music by Steve Perry and Jonathan Cain.
Weed High Nightmare Music, 1981.
Best-selling record by Journey from *Escape* (Columbia, 82).

Open Letter (to a Landlord)
Words by T. Morris and Vernon Reid.
Dare to Dream Music, 1988.
Introduced by Living Colour on *Vivid* (Columbia, 88).

Open Your Heart
Words and music by Madonna, Gardner Cole, and Peter Rafelson.
WB Music, 1986/Bleu Disque Music, 1986/Lost in Music, 1986/
    Rafelson Music, 1986/Bertus, 1986.
Best-selling record by Madonna from the album *True Blue* (Sire/Warner
    Bros., 86).

Operator
Words and music by Boaz Watson, Vincent Calloway, Belinda
    Lipscomb, and Reggie Calloway.
Hip-Trip Music Co., 1984/Midstar Music, Inc.
Best-selling record by Midnight Star from the album *Planetary Invasion*
    (Elektra, 85).

Opportunities (Let's Make Lots of Money) (English)
Words and music by Nick Tennant and Chris Lowe.
Cage Music Ltd., England, 1986/10 Music Ltd., England/Virgin Music.

Best-selling record by Pet Shop Boys from the album *Please* (EMI-American, 86).

Opportunity to Cry
Words and music by Willie Nelson.
Tree Publishing Co., Inc., 1982.
Featured in *Poncho and Lefty* (Epic, 83) by Willie Nelson and Waylon Jennings.

Orinoco Flow (Irish-Australian)
Words by Roma Ryan, music by Enya.
EMI Music Publishing, 1988.
Introduced by Eyna on *Watermark* (Geffen, 88).

The Other Guy (Australian)
Words and music by Graham Goble.
Screen Gems-EMI Music Inc., 1983.
Best-selling record by Little River Band from *Greatest Hits* (Capitol, 83).

The Other Woman
Words and music by Ray Parker, Jr.
Raydiola Music, 1982.
Best-selling record by Ray Parker, Jr. from *The Other Woman* (Arista, 82).

Our Favorite Restaurant
Words by Michael Champagne, music by Elliot Weiss.
Bittersuite Co., 1987.
Introduced by Joseph Neil, John Jellison, Claudine Casson-Jellison, and Joy Franz in the musical *Bittersuite* (87).

Our House (English)
Words and music by Charles Smyth and Christopher Foreman.
WB Music, 1982.
Best-selling record by Madness from *Madness* (Warner Brothers, 83).

Our Lips Are Sealed
Words and music by Jane Weidlin and Terry Hall.
Plangent Visions Music, Inc., London, England, 1981/Lipsync Music, 1981.
Best-selling record by The Go-Go's from *Beauty and the Beat* (I.R.S., 81).

Our Love (Theme from *No Mercy*)
Words and music by Michael McDonald and David Pack.
Genevieve Music, 1985/Art Street Music.
Introduced by Michael McDonald on the album *No Looking Back*

(Warner Bros., 85). Performed by Michael McDonald in the film *No Mercy* (86).

Our Love Is on the Fault Line (English)
Words and music by Reece Kirk.
Irving Music Inc., 1981.
Best-selling record by Crystal Gayle from *True Love* (Warner Brothers, 83).

Our Night
Words and music by Gary Portnoy and Judy Hart Angelo.
Koppelman Family Music, 1983/R. L. August Music Co., 1983/Bandier Family Music, 1983/Yontrop Music, 1983/Judy Hart Angelo Music, 1983.
Introduced by Bob Walton and Kathleen Rowe McAllen in *Preppies* (83).

Our Time
Words and music by Stephen Sondheim.
WB Music, 1981.
Introduced by Jim Walton, Lonny Price, and Ann Morrison in *Merrily We Roll Along* (81).

Out Here on My Own
Words and music by Michael Gore and Leslie Gore.
MGM Affiliated Music, Inc., 1979/EMI Variety Catalogue.
Best-selling record by Irene Cara (RSO, 80). Introduced in the film & soundtrack album *Fame* (80). Nominated for an Academy Award, 1980.

Out of Love
Words and music by John Prine and Bill Caswell.
Big Ears Music Inc., 1987/Bruised Oranges/Black Sheep Music Inc.
Introduced by John Prine on the album *German Afternoons* (Oh Boy, 87).

Out of the Blue
Words and music by Debbie Gibson.
Creative Bloc, 1987/Possibilities Publishing.
Best-selling record in 1988 by Debbie Gibson, from *Out of the Blue* (Atlantic, 87).

Out of Touch
Words and music by Daryl Hall and John Oates.
Hot Cha Music Co., 1984/Unichappell Music Inc., 1984.
Best-selling record by Daryl Hall and John Oates from *Big Bam Boom* (RCA, 84).

Out of Work
Words and music by Bruce Springsteen.
Bruce Springsteen Publishing, 1982.
Best-selling record by Gary U.S. Bonds from *On the Line* (EMI-America, 82).

Out of Your Shoes
Words and music by Jill Wood, Patti Ryan, and Sharon Spivey.
Ha-Deb Music, 1989/Mickey James Music.
Best-selling record by Lorrie Morgan from *Leave the Light On* (RCA, 89).

Out That Door (Australian)
Words and music by Dave Faulkner.
Copyright Control, 1987.
Introduced by the Hoodoo Gurus on the album *Blow Your Cool* (Electra, 87).

Outta the World
Words and music by Nick Ashford and Valerie Simpson.
Nick-O-Val Music, 1984.
Best-selling record by Ashford and Simpson in 1985 from the album *Solid* (Capitol, 84).

Over You
Words and music by Austin Roberts and Bobby Hart.
Colgems-EMI Music, 1981/Father Music, 1981.
Introduced in the film *Tender Mercies* (81). Best-selling record by Lane Brody (Liberty, 81). Nominated for an Academy Award, Best Song, 1983.

Overkill (Australian)
Words and music by Colin Hay.
EMI-April Music, 1983.
Best-selling record by Men at Work from *Cargo* (Columbia, 83).

Owner of a Lonely Heart (English)
Words and music by Trevor Rabin, Jon Anderson, Chris Squire, and Trevor Horn.
WB Music, 1983/Unforgettable Songs, 1983.
Best-selling record by Yes from *90125* (Atco, 83).

P

P. Y. T. (Pretty Young Thing)
Words and music by James Ingram and Quincy Jones.
Eiseman Music Co., Inc., 1982/Hen-Al Publishing Co., 1982/Kings
  Road Music, 1982/Yellow Brick Road Music, 1982.
Best-selling record by Michael Jackson from *Thriller* (Epic, 83).
  Nominated for a Grammy Award, Rhythm 'n' Blues Song of the
  Year, 1983.

Pac-Man Fever
Words and music by Jerry Buckner and Gary Garcia.
BGO Music, 1981.
Best-selling record by Buckner and Garcia from *Pac-Man Fever*
  (Columbia, 82).

Pads, Paws, and Claws (English)
Words and music by Declan MacManus and Paul McCartney.
Plangent Visions Music, Inc., London, England, 1988, 1989.
Introduced by Elvis Costello on *Spike* (Warner Bros., 89); Costello,
  under his real name, teams with Paul McCartney as a songwriter.

Panama
Words and music by Eddie Van Halen, Alex Van Halen, Michael
  Anthony, and David Lee Roth.
Van Halen Music, 1983/Diamond Dave Music, 1983.
Best-selling record by Van Halen from *1984* (Warner Brothers, 84).

Papa Can You Hear Me
Words by Alan Bergman and Marilyn Bergman, music by Michel
  Legrand.
Emanuel Music, 1983/Threesome Music Co., 1983/Ennes Productions,
  Ltd., 1983/F Sharp Productions, 1983.
Introduced by Barbra Streisand in the film and soundtrack album *Yentl*
  (83). Nominated for an Academy Award, Best Song, 1983.

Papa Don't Preach
Words and music by Brian Elliot and Madonna.
Elliot Music Co., Inc., 1986/Jacobsen.
Best-selling record by Madonna from the album *True Blue* (Sire/Warner Bros., 86). This plea for parental understanding from an unwed, pregnant teenager aroused much controversy.

Paper in Fire
Words and music by John Mellencamp.
Full Keel Music, 1987.
Best-selling record by John Cougar Mellencamp, from the album *The Lonesome Jubilee* (Mercury, 87).

Paradise (Italian)
Music by David Romani and Mauro Malavasi, English words by Tanyayette Willoughby.
WB Music, 1981.
Best-selling record by Change from *Miracles* (Atlantic, 81).

Paradise (English)
Words and music by Sade (pseudonym for Helen Folesade Adu), Andrew Hale, Stuart Matthewman, and Paul Denman.
Angel Music Ltd., 1988/Sony Tunes, 1988/Famous Music Corp., 1988.
Best-selling record by Sade, from *Stronger Than Pride* (Epic, 88).

Paradise City
Words and music by Guns N' Roses.
Guns N' Roses, 1987.
Best-selling record in 1989 by Guns N' Roses from *Appetite for Destruction* (Geffen, 87).

Paradise Tonight
Words and music by Mark Wright and Bill Kenner.
Receive Music, 1982/EMI Unart Catalogue, 1982.
Best-selling record by Charly McClain and Mickey Gilley (Epic, 83).

Parallel Lines
Words and music by Todd Rundgren.
Todd Rundgren, 1987/Fiction Music Inc.
Introduced by Todd Rundgren on *Nearly Human* (Warner Bros., 89). Rundgren wrote the song for use in *Up against It,* a musical version of a previously unproduced screenplay written by the late Joe Orton for the Beatles. New York Shakespeare Festival producer Joseph Papp bought the rights to the play and had it rewritten as a musical, with Rundgren's songs. Philip Casanov and Alison Frasier performed this number in the 1989 Off Broadway production.

Parents Just Don't Understand
Words and music by Will Smith, Jeff Townes, and Pete Q. Harris.

Zomba Music, 1988.

Best-selling record by D.J. Jazzy Jeff and the Fresh Prince from *He's the D.J., I'm the Rapper* (Jive, 88). Nominated for a Grammy Award, Best Rap Performance, 1988.

Part-Time Lover

Words and music by Stevie Wonder.

Jobete Music Co., 1985/Black Bull Music, 1985.

Best-selling record by Stevie Wonder from the album *In Square Circle* (Motown, 85).

Partners After All

Words and music by Chips Moman and Bobby Emmons.

Rightsong Music, 1987/Chips Moman Music, 1987/Attadoo, 1987.

Introduced by Willie Nelson, from the album *Partners* (Columbia, 87).

Party All the Time

Words and music by Rick James.

Stone City Music, 1985/National League Music, 1985.

Best-selling record by Eddie Murphy from the album *How Could It Be* (Columbia, 85), which marked the comedian's debut as a singer.

Party Time

Words and music by Bruce Channel.

Tree Publishing Co., Inc., 1980.

Best-selling record by T. G. Sheppard from *I Love 'Em All* (Warner/ Curb, 81).

Party Train

Words and music by Lonnie Simmons, Ronnie Wilson, Charles Wilson, and Rudy Taylor.

Temp Co., 1983.

Best-selling record by The Gap Band from *The Gap Band V - Jammin'* (Total Experience, 83).

Partyman

Words and music by Prince (pseudonym for Prince Rogers Nelson).

Controversy Music/WB Music.

Best-selling record by Prince from the film and soundtrack album *Batman* (Warner Bros., 89).

Partyup

Words and music by Prince Rogers Nelson.

Controversy Music, 1980.

Introduced by Prince in *Dirty Mind* (Warner Brothers, 80).

Pass the Dutchie

Words and music by Jackie Mitoo, Lloyd Ferguson, and Fitzroy Simpson.

Music Sales Corp., 1981.

Best-selling record by Musical Youth from *The Youth of Today* (MCA, 83).

Passion (English)

Words and music by Rod Stewart, Phil Chen, Jim Cregan, Gary Grainger, and Kevin Stuart Savigar.

Full Keel Music, 1980/WB Music, 1980/Rod Stewart, 1980.

Best-selling record by Rod Stewart from *Foolish Behaviour* (Warner Brothers, 80).

Paths That Cross

Words and music by Patti Smith and Fred Smith.

Druse Music Inc., 1988/Stratium Music Inc., 1988.

Introduced by Patti Smith on *Dream of Life* (Arista, 88). Former poet Patti and her husband Fred 'Sonic' came out of domestic retirement to offer this moody lament.

Patience

Words and music by Guns N' Roses.

Guns N' Roses, 1987.

Best-selling record in 1989 by Guns N' Roses, from *G N' R Lies* (Geffen, 87).

Peace in Our Time (English)

Words and music by Elvis Costello.

Plangent Visions Music, Inc., London, England, 1983.

Introduced by Elvis Costello on *Goodbye Cruel World* (Columbia, 83).

Peeping Tom

Words and music by Rockwell, Janet Cole, and Antoine Greene.

Jobete Music Co., 1985.

Introduced by Rockwell in the film and soundtrack album *The Last Dragon* (Motown, 85).

Peg and Pete and Me

Words and music by Stanard Ridgway.

Mondo Spartacus Music, 1989/Illegal Songs, Inc./Criterion Music Corp.

Introduced by Stan Ridgway on *Mosquitos* (Geffen, 89).

Penny Lover

Words and music by Lionel Richie, Jr. and Brenda Harvey-Richie.

Brockman Enterprises Inc., 1983.

Best-selling record by Lionel Richie from *Can't Slow Down* (Motown, 84).

People Alone

Words by Will Jennings, music by Lalo Shifrin.

EMI-Gold Horizon Music Corp., 1980/Irving Music Inc., 1980.

Introduced in the film *The Competition* (80). Nominated for an
Academy Award, 1980.

People Are People (English)
Words and music by Martin Gore.
Warner-Tamerlane Music, 1985.
Best-selling record by Depeche Mode from the album *People Are
People* (Warner Bros., 85).

People Get Ready
Words and music by Curtis Mayfield.
Warner-Chappell Music, 1964.
Revived by Jeff Beck and Rod Stewart on the album *Flash* (Epic, 85).

People Have the Power
Words and music by Patti Smith and Fred Smith.
Druse Music Inc., 1988/Stratium Music Inc., 1988.
Introduced by Patti Smith on *Dream of Life* (Arista, 88). A return to
sentiments of the early 1970's.

People Like Us
Words and music by Gary Portnoy and Judy Hart Angelo.
Koppelman Family Music, 1983/R. L. August Music Co., 1983/Bandier
Family Music, 1983/Yontrop Music, 1983/Judy Hart Angelo Music,
1983.
Introduced by Company of *Preppies* (83).

People Who Died
Words and music by Jim Carroll.
Earl McGrath Music, 1980.
Introduced by Jim Carroll in *Catholic Boy* (Atco, 80).

Percy's Song
Words and music by Bob Dylan.
Special Rider Music, 1963.
Released by Bob Dylan for the first time on the five-record retrospective
Biograph (Columbia, 85).

Perfect Strangers
Words and music by Rupert Holmes.
Holmes Line of Music, 1986.
Introduced by Betty Buckley and Patti Cohenour in the 1985 Broadway
musical *The Mystery of Edwin Drood* and on the cast album
(Polygram, 86). A recording by Rupert Holmes and Rita Coolidge
(Polygram) was released in 1986.

Perfect Way (English)
Words and music by Green Strohmeyer-Gartside and David Gamson.
Jouissance, 1985/WB Music, 1985/David Gamson, 1985.

Best-selling record by Scritti Politti from the album *Cupid and Psyche 85* (Warner Bros., 85).

Perfect World
Words and music by Tonio K. (pseudonym for Steve Krikorian) and Glen Burtnick.
BMG Songs Inc., 1986/Polygram International.
Introduced by Tonio K. on the album *Romeo Unchained* (What/A & M, 86). Christian-oriented songwriter Tonio's previous best work was contained on an album *Life in the Food Chain*. This song was also released by Glen Burtnick on the album *Glen Burtnick* (A & M).

Perfect World
Words and music by Alex Call.
Lew-Bob Songs, 1988.
Best-selling record by Huey Lewis & The News from *Perfect World* (Chryaslis, 88).

Perhaps Love
Words and music by John Denver.
Cherry Lane Music Co., 1980.
Best-selling record by Placido Domingo and John Denver from *Seasons of the Heart* (RCA, 82). Featured on Domingo's *Perhaps Love* (CBS, 82) and Denver's *Seasons of the Heart*.

Personally
Words and music by Paul Kelly.
Tree Publishing Co., Inc., 1978/Five of a Kind, Inc.
Best-selling record by Karla Bonoff from *Wild Heard of the Young* (Columbia, 82).

Peter Gunn Theme, also known as **Style**
Music by Henry Mancini.
Northridge Music, Inc., 1958.
Best-selling record by Grand Master Flash from the album *The Source* (Elektra, 86). Also recorded by Art of Noise with Duane Eddy (Chrysalis).

Peter Pan
Words and music by Chris Williamson.
Bird Ankles Music, 1980.
Introduced by Chris Williamson on *Blue Rider* (Olivia, 80).

The Phantom of the Opera (English)
Words by Charles Hart, words and music by Andrew Lloyd Webber, Rod Stilgoe, and Mike Batt.
The Really Useful Group, 1987.
Recorded by Steve Harley and Sarah Brightman on the London cast

album of the musical *The Phantom of the Opera* (Polydor, 87), which was a hit before the show opened on Broadway in 1988.

Photograph (English)
Words and music by Steve Clark, John Savage, Robert John 'Mutt' Lange, Pete Willis, and Joe Elliott.
Zomba Music, 1983.
Best-selling record by Def Leppard from *Pyromania* (Mercury, 83).

Physical
Words and music by Stephen Kipner and Terry Shaddick.
Stephen A. Kipner Music, 1981/EMI-April Music, 1981/Terry Shaddick Music, 1981.
Best-selling record by Olivia Newton-John from *Physical* (MCA, 81).

Piano in the Dark
Words and music by Brenda Russell, Jeff Hull, and Scott Cutler.
Rutland Road, 1988/Colgems-EMI Music, 1988/WB Music, 1988.
Best-selling record by Brenda Russell, from *Get Here* (A & M, 88). Nominated for a Grammy Award, Rhythm 'n' Blues Song of the Year, 1988.

Pickin' up Strangers
Words and music by Byron Hill.
Welbeck Music Corp., 1980.
Best-selling record by Johnny Lee (Full Moon/Asylum, 81).

A Picture of Lisa
Words and music by N. S. Leibowitz and George Feltenstein.
Introduced by Matthew McClanahan in the musical *Attack of the Killer Revue* (85).

Pictures of Matchstick Men (English)
Words and music by Francis Michael Rossi.
Northern Music Co., 1968/Valley Music Ltd.
Revived in 1989 by Camper Van Beethoven on *Key Lime Pie* (Virgin, 89), where they updated this 1960's hit for Status Quo.

Pilot of the Airwaves (English)
Words and music by Charmain Dore.
Polygram International, 1978.
Best-selling record by Charlie Dore from *Where to Now?* (Island, 80).

Pink Bedroom
Words and music by John Hiatt.
Lillybilly, 1980.
Performed by Lou Ann Barton on *Forbidden Tones* (Spindletop, 86).

Pink Cadillac
Words and music by Bruce Springsteen.
Bruce Springsteen Publishing, 1983.
Introduced by Bruce Springsteen on the flipside of the single 'Dancing in the Dark' (Columbia, 83).   Revived by Natalie Cole on *Everlasting* (EMI-Manhattan, 87).

Pink Houses
Words and music by John Cougar Mellencamp.
Full Keel Music, 1983.
Best-selling record by John Cougar Mellencamp from *Uh-Huh* (Warner Brothers, 83).

A Place to Fall Apart
Words and music by Merle Haggard, Willie Nelson, and Freddy Powers.
Mount Shasta Music Inc., 1984.
Best-selling record by Merle Haggard from the album *Merle Haggard's Epic Hits* (Epic, 85).

Planet Rock
Words by Ellis Williams, words and music by Arthur Henry Baker, John Miller, Bhambatta Aasim, and Robert Allen, music by John Robie.
Shakin Baker Music, Inc., 1982.
Best-selling record by Afrika Bambaataa & The Soul Sonic Force (Tommy Boy, 82) from *PlanetRock - The Album* (Tommy Boy, 86).

Play the Game Tonight
Words and music by Kerry Livgren, Phil Ehart, Richard Williams, Robert Frazier, and Danny Flowers.
Don Kirshner Music Inc., 1982/EMI-Blackwood Music Inc., 1982/Fifty Grand Music, Inc., 1982.
Best-selling record by Kansas from *Vinyl Confessions* (Kirshner, 82).

Please Don't Go
Words and music by Harry Casey and Richard Finch.
Harrick Music Inc., 1979/Sherlyn Publishing Co., Inc., 1979.
Best-selling record by Teri DeSario with K.C. from *Do You Wanna Go Party* (Casablanca, 80).

Please Don't Go Girl
Words and music by Maurice Starr.
Maurice Starr, 1988.
Best-selling record by New Kids on the Block, from *Hangin' Tough* (Columbia, 88).

The Pleasure Principle
Words and music by Monte Moir.
Flyte Tyme Tunes, 1986.

Best-selling record by Janet Jackson, from the album *Control* (A & M, 86). This was the first single from Janet Jackson not to reach the top ten; it was also the first not penned in part by her.

Poem of the River
Words and music by Scott Kempner.
Prince of the Bronx Music, 1987.
Introduced by The Del Lords on *Based on a True Story* (Enigma, 88).

Point of No Return
Words and music by Lewis Martinee.
Panchin, 1985.
Best-selling record by Expose, from the album *Exposure* (Atlantic, 87). This song became a hit two years after its initial success in the dance halls.

Poison
Words and music by Alice Cooper, Desmond Child, and John McCurry.
Ezra, 1989/Kat and Mouse Music/EMI-April Music/Desmobile Music Inc.
Best-selling record by Alice Cooper from *Trash* (Epic, 89), marking a return to the charts of the inventor of 'shock rock.'

Poison in the Well
Words and music by Natalie Merchant and Dennis Drew.
Christian Burial Music, 1989.
Introduced by 10,000 Maniacs on *Blind Man's Zoo* (Elektra, 89).

Poison Years
Words and music by Bob Mould.
Granary Music, 1989.
Introduced by Bob Mould on *Workbook* (Virgin, 89), the song details the breakup of Mould's former band, Husker Du.

Poncho and Lefty
Words and music by Townes Van Zandt.
EMI Unart Catalogue, 1972/EMI-April Music, 1972.
Best-selling record by Willie Nelson and Merle Haggard from *Poncho and Lefty* (Epic, 83).

Poor Old Tom
Words and music by Peter Case.
Trumpet Blast Music, 1989/Bug Music.
Introduced by Peter Case on *The Man with the Blue, Postmodern, Fragmented, Neo-Traditionalist Guitar* (Geffen, 89).

Pop Goes the World (Australian)
Words and music by Men Without Hats.
Polygram Songs, 1987.
Best-selling record in 1988 by Men Without Hats, from *Pop Goes the World* (Mercury, 88).

Pop Life
Words and music by Prince Rogers Nelson.
Controversy Music, 1985.
Best-selling record by Prince & The Revolution from the album *Around the World in a Day* (Warner Bros., 85).

Pop Singer
Words and music by John Mellencamp (pseudonym for John Cougar Mellencamp).
Full Keel Music, 1989.
Best-selling record by John Cougar Mellencamp from *Big Daddy* (Mercury, 89). The pop rocker here offers a disenchanted view of his trade, but in the same year redeemed it as producer of the new folk standout James McMurtry.

Porn Wars
Words and music by Frank Zappa.
Munchkin Music, 1985.
Introduced by Frank Zappa on the album *Frank Zappa Meets the Mothers of Prevention* (Barking Pumpkin, 85).

Pour Some Sugar on Me (English)
Words and music by Steve Clark, Phil Collen, Joe Elliott, Robert John 'Mutt' Lange, and Rick Savage.
Bludgeon Riffola Music, 1987/Zomba Music, 1987.
Best-selling record in 1988 by Def Leppard from *Hysteria* (Mercury, 87).

Power of Love
Words and music by T-Bone Burnette.
Black Tent Music, 1983.
Featured on *Power of Love* by Arlo Guthrie (Warner Brothers, 81).

The Power of Love
Words and music by Chris Hayes, Huey Lewis, and Johnny Colla.
Hulex Music, 1985/Chrysalis Music Group, 1985.
Best-selling record by Huey Lewis & The News (Chrysalis, 85). Introduced in the film and soundtrack album *Back to the Future* (MCA, 85). Nominated for an Academy Award, Song of the Year, 1985; Grammy Award, Record of the Year, 1985.

The Power of Love (You Are My Lady) (German)
English words and music by Candy Derouse, Gunther Mende, Jennifer
 Rush, and Mary Applegate.
EMI-April Music, 1986.
Introduced by Jennifer Rush as a single in Germany. Eventually became
 a number one hit in England. Song is included on the album *Jennifer
 Rush* (Epic, 86). Also recorded by Air Supply.

Powerful Stuff
Words and music by Michael Henderson, Robert Field, and Wally
 Wilson.
Walt Disney Music, 1988/Cross Keys Publishing Co., Inc., 1988/Cross
 Under, 1988/Colgems-EMI Music, 1988.
Introduced by The Fabulous Thunderbirds in the film and on the
 soundtrack album *Cocktail* (Elektra, 88).

Precious (English)
Words and music by Chrissie Hynde.
MCA, Inc., 1980.
Introduced by The Pretenders in *The Pretenders* (Sire, 80).

Pressure
Words and music by Billy Joel.
Joelsongs, 1981.
Best-selling record by Billy Joel from *The Nylon Curtain* (Columbia,
 82).

Pretty Boy Floyd
Words and music by Woody Guthrie.
Fall River Music Inc., 1961.
The folk highlight of 1988, a year filled with folk music. It was revived
 by Bob Dylan on *Folkways: A Vision Shared: A Tribute to Woody
 Guthrie and Leadbelly* (Columbia, 88) and Guthrie's own rendition
 was released on *Dust Bowl Ballads* (Rounder, 88).

Pretty in Pink (English)
Words and music by Richard Butler, Timothy Butler, Vincent Ely,
 Duncan Kilburn, John Ashton, and Roger Morris.
EMI-Blackwood Music Inc., 1981.
Introduced by The Psychedelic Furs on *Talk, Talk, Talk* (Columbia, 81).
 Revived in 1986 by Psychadelic Furs of the film and soundtrack
 album *Pretty in Pink* (A & M, 86).

(Oh) Pretty Woman
Words and music by Roy Orbison and Bill Dees.
Acuff-Rose Publications Inc., 1964.

The Pride Is Back
Words and music by Marc Blatte, Larry Gottleib, and Alan Monde.

Kool Koala, 1986.

Performed by Kenny Rogers and Nickie Ryder (RCA, 86). The song originated as a Bruce Springsteen-inspired patriotic commercial message for the Chrysler Corporation. It was the first such transition to make the pop charts since the Seekers did 'I'd Like to Teach the World to Sing,' which started out as a Coca-Cola commercial.

Pride of Man

Words and music by Hamilton Camp.

WB Music, 1963.

Revived in 1989 by the Washington Squares on *Fair and Square* (Gold Castle, 89), this folk anthem was originally popularized by Shawn Phillips.

Princess of Little Italy

Words and music by Steve Van Zandt.

Blue Midnight Music, 1982.

Introduced by Little Steven & The Disciples of Soul on *Men Without Women* (EMI-America, 82).

Prison Blues (English)

Words and music by Jimmy Page and Chris Farlow.

Succubus Music, 1988.

Introduced by Jimmy Page on *Outrider* (Geffen, 88). This was first solo effort from former lead guitarist of Led Zeppelin.

Prisoner of Hope

Words and music by Sterling Whipple and Gerald Metcalf.

Elektra/Asylum Music Inc., 1981.

Best-selling record by Johnny Lee from *Lookin' for Love* (Asylum, 81).

Privacy

Words and music by Craig Carnelia.

Carnelia Music, 1978.

Introduced off-Broadway in *The No-Frills Revue* (87).

Private Dancer (English)

Words and music by Mark Knopfler.

Almo Music Corp., 1984.

Best-selling record by Tina Turner in 1985 from the album *Private Dancer* (Capitol, 84).

Private Eyes

Words and music by Warren Pash, Sara Allen, Janna Allen, and Daryl Hall.

Fust Buzza Music, Inc., 1981/Hot Cha Music Co., 1981/Almo Music Corp., 1981/Unichappell Music Inc., 1981.

Best-selling record by Daryl Hall and John Oates from *Private Eyes* (RCA, 81).

Private Idaho
Words and music by Frederick Schneider, J. Keith Strickland, Ricky Wilson, Cynthia Wilson, and Kate Pierson.
Island Music, 1980.
Best-selling record by The B-52's from *Wild Planet* (Warner Brothers, 80).

The Promise (English)
Words and music by Clyde Farrington, Mike Floreale, and Andrew Mann.
Virgin Music, 1988.
Best-selling record by When in Rome from *When in Rome* (Virgin, 88).

The Promise You Made
Words and music by Peter Kingsbery.
Edwin Ellis Music, 1984/Nurk Twins Music.
Introduced by Cock Robin on the album *Cock Robin* (Columbia, 85). Single went to number one in Holland.

Promises, Promises (Australian)
Words and music by Pete Byrne and Rob Fisher.
Almo Music Corp., 1983.
Best-selling record by Naked Eyes on *Naked Eyes* (EMI-America, 83).

Protect Yourself/My Nuts
Words and music by Damon Wimbley, Darren Robinson, Mark Morales, Jimmy Glenn, and Steve Linsley.
Missing Ball, 1987/Fat Boys, 1987.
Introduced by the Fat Boys on the popular sex therapy television show *Ask Dr. Ruth*. This rap describes the increasing sexual caution among even the most macho element.

Proud to Fall (English)
Words and music by Ian McCullough.
Chappell & Co., Ltd., London, England, 1989/Zoo Music, England/WB Music.
Introduced by Ian McCullough, former leader of Echo & The Bunnymen, on *Candleland* (Sire/Reprise, 89).

Prove Your Love
Words and music by Seth Swirsky and Arnie Roman.
November Nights, 1987/Chappell & Co., Inc., 1987/Jobete Music Co., 1987.
Best-selling record in 1988 by Taylor Dayne, from *Tell It to My Heart* (Arista, 87).

Pull Over
Words and music by Gerald Levert and Marc Gordon.

Trycep Publishing Co./Ferncliff/Willesden Music, Inc.
Best-selling record in 1989 by Levert from *Just Coolin'* (Atlantic, 88).

Pulling Mussels (from the Shell)
Words by Chris Difford, music by Glenn Tilbrook.
Illegal Songs, Inc., 1980.
Introduced by Squeeze on *Argybargy* (A & M, 80).

Pump up the Jam (English)
Words and music by Manuella Kamosi and Thomas De Quincey.
BMC, UK, England/Colgems-EMI Music, 1989.
Best-selling record by Technotronic featuring Felly from *Pump up the Jam* (Arista, 89).

Pump Up the Volume (English)
Words and music by Steve Young and Andrew Biggs.
MNS, England, 1987/WB Music, 1987.
Best-selling record in 1988 by M.A.R.R.S. (4th & Broadway, 87).

Punk Rock Girl
Words and music by Dead Milkmen.
Golf Pro Music, 1988/Bug Music.
Introduced by Dead Milkmen on *Beezlebubba* (Enigma, 89).

Purple Rain
Words and music by Prince Rogers Nelson.
Controversy Music, 1984/WB Music, 1984.
Best-selling record by Prince (Warner Brothers, 84). Introduced in the film and soundtrack album *Purple Rain* (84).

Purple Toupee
Words and music by They Might Be Giants.
They Might Be Giants Music, 1988.
Introduced by They Might Be Giants on *Lincoln* (Restless, 88), the song satirizes the entire Sixties in less than two minutes.

Push It
Words and music by Herb Azor.
Next Plateau Entertainment, 1987/Turnout Brothers Publishing Co., 1987.
Best-selling record in 1988 by Salt-N-Pepa, from *Hot, Cool, and Vicious* (Next Plateau, 87). Nominated for a Grammy Award, Best Rap Performance, 1988.

Put a Little Love in Your Heart
Words and music by Jimmie Holiday, Randy Myers, and Jackie DeShannon (pseudonym for Sharon Lee Dawn).
Unart Music Corp., 1969.

Revived in 1988 by Annie Lennox and Al Green in the movie and on the soundtrack album of *Scrooged* (A & M, 88). .

Put Your Hands on the Screen
Words and music by Martin Briley.
Miserable Melodies, 1983/Chrysalis Music Group, 1983.
Featured on *One Night with a Stranger* by Martin Briley (Mercury, 83)

Put Your Mouth on Me
Words and music by Eddie Murphy, Narada Michael Walden, and Jeffrey Cohen.
Eddie Murphy Music, 1989/Gratitude Sky Music/Penzafire Music/Virgin Music.
Best-selling record by Eddie Murphy from *So Happy* (Columbia, 89).

Puttin' on the Ritz
Words and music by Irving Berlin.
Irving Berlin Music Corp., 1929, 1946.
Revived by Taco in *After Eight* (RCA, 83).

Putting It Together
Words and music by Stephen Sondheim.
WB Music, 1984.
Revived by Barbra Streisand on *The Broadway Album* (Columbia, 85). Song was introduced in 1984 in the musical *Sunday in the Park With George* and extensively rewritten for Streisand to perform.

Putting up with Me
Words and music by Mose Allison.
Audre Mae Music, 1987.
Introduced by Mose Allison on the album *Ever Since the World Ended* (Blue Note, 87).

Q

? (Modern Industry)
Words and music by David Kahne and Kendall Jones.
Seesquared Music, 1985/Bouillabaisse Music, 1985.
Introduced by Fishbone on the album *Fishbone* (Columbia, 85).

Queen of Hearts
Words and music by Hank DeVito.
Drunk Monkey Music, 1979.
Best-selling record by Juice Newton from *Juice* (Capitol, 81).

R

Radio Free Europe
Words and music by William Berry, Peter Buck, Mike Mills, and
   Michael Stipe.
Night Garden Music, 1981.
Best-selling record by R.E.M. from *Murmur* (I.R.S., 83).

Radio Ga-Ga (English)
Words and music by Roger Taylor.
Beechwood Music, 1983.
Best-selling record by Queen from *The Works* (Capitol, 84).

Radio Heart
Words and music by Steve Davis and Dennis Morgan.
Tapadero Music, 1984/Tom Collins Music Corp., 1984.
Best-selling record by Charly McClain from the album *Radio Heart*
   (Epic, 85).

Radio Waves (English)
Words and music by Roger Waters.
Pink Floyd, London, England, 1987.
Best-selling record by Roger Waters, from the album *Radio K.A.O.S.*
   (Columbia, 87).

Rag Doll
Words and music by Steven Tyler, Joe Perry, Jim Vallance, and Holly
   Knight.
Aero Dynamic Music, 1987/Irving Music Inc., 1987/Calypso Toonz,
   1987/Makiki Publishing Co., Ltd., 1987/Knighty Knight, 1987/BMG
   Songs Inc., 1987.
Best-selling record in 1988 by Aerosmith, from *Permanent Vacation*
   (Geffen, 87). Vallance and Knight, two of the pop's craftiest
   hitmakers, here aided the rock duo's return to the charts.

The Rain
Words and music by Vince Bell.

Def Jam, 1986.
Best-selling record by Oran 'Juice' Jones from the album *Juice*
(Columbia, 86).

Rain Forest (English)
Words and music by Paul Hardcastle.
Oval Music Co., 1985/Virgin Music, 1985.
Best-selling record by Paul Hardcastle from the album *Rain Forest*
(Chrysalis, 85).

Rain on You
Words and music by Phil Davis, Doug Erikson, and Butch Vig.
Flip 'n' Dog, 1987.
Introduced by Firetown on the album *In the Heart of the Heart Country*
(Atlantic, 87). Co-author Butch Vig also owned the Madison,
Wisconsin recording studio where the band recorded this album; he
eventually became a member of the group as well.

Rappin' Rodney
Words and music by Rodney Dangerfield, Dennis Blair, Scott Henry,
Douglas Hoyt, J. B. Moore, and R. Ford, Jr.
Best-selling record by Rodney Dangerfield from *Rappin' Rodney* (RCA,
83).

Rapture
Words by Debbie Harry, music by Chris Stein.
Chrysalis Music Group, 1980.
Best-selling record by Blondie from *Autoamerican* (Chrysalis, 81).

Raspberry Beret
Words and music by Prince Rogers Nelson.
Controversy Music, 1985.
Best-selling record by Prince & The Revolution from the album *Around
the World in a Day* (Warner Bros., 85).

Rave On
Words and music by Sonny West, Norman Petty, and Bill Tilghman.
Wren Music Co., Inc., 1958.
Revived in 1988 by John Cougar Mellencamp in the film and on the
soundtrack album *Cocktail* (Elektra, 88). Buddy Holly first made it a
hit thirty years earlier.

Read 'em and Weep
Words and music by Jim Steinman.
E. B. Marks Music Corp., 1981/Peg Music Co., 1981.
Best-selling records by Meat Loaf from *Dead Ringer* (Cleveland
International, 81) and Barry Manilow from *Barry Manilow's Greatest
Hits, Vol. II* (Arista, 83).

Readin,' Rightin,' Route 23
Words and music by Dwight Yoakam.
Coal Dust West, 1987.
Introduced by Dwight Yoakam on the album *Hillbilly Deluxe* (Reprise, 87). The title comes from a phrase from the author's childhood that made fun of hillbillies.

Ready to Begin Again (Manya's Song)
Words and music by Jerry Leiber and Mike Stoller.
Jerry Leiber Music, 1975/Mike Stoller Music/WB Music.
Revived in 1989 by Peggy Lee on *Mirrors* (A & M, reissued 89), this song was first introduced in the musical *The Madwoman of Chaillot*.

The Real End
Words and music by Rickie Lee Jones.
Easy Money Music, 1984.
Best-selling record by Rickie Lee Jones from *The Magazine* (Warner Brothers, 84).

Real Love
Words and music by Michael McDonald and Patrick Henderson.
Tauripin Tunes, 1980/Monosteri Music, 1980/EMI-April Music, 1980.
Best-selling record by The Doobie Brothers from *One Step Closer* (Warner Brothers, 80).

Real Love
Words and music by Andre Cymone and Jody Watley.
EMI-April Music, 1989/Ultrawave/Rightsong Music.
Best-selling record by Jody Watley from *Larger Than Life* (MCA, 89).

Real Men (English)
Words and music by Joe Jackson.
Almo Music Corp., 1982.
Introduced by Joe Jackson on *Night and Day* (A & M, 82).

The Real One
Words and music by John Hiatt.
Lillybilly, 1988/Bug Music, 1988.
Introduced by Marti Jones on *Used Guitars* (A & M, 88).

Realities
Words and music by Christine Lavin.
CL-2, 1988/Rounder Music.
Christine Lavin revived this astute commentary on relationships in 1989 on *Fast Folk Sixth Anniversary Issue*. It was introduced on *Good Thing He Can't Read My Mind* (Philo, 88).

Reality Row (English)
Words and music by Andy White.

Chappell & Co., Ltd., London, England, 1986.
Introduced by Andy White on the album *Rave On* (MCA, 86).

Rebel Yell (American-English)
Words and music by Billy Idol and Steve Stevens.
Boneidol Music, 1983/WB Music, 1983/Chrysalis Music Group, 1983/
Sitting Pretty, 1983.
Best-selling record by Billy Idol from *Rebel Yell* (Chrysalis, 84).

Reckless
Words and music by Gretchen Cryer.
Gretchen Cryer, 1988.
Introduced by Gretchen Cryer in her 1989 cabaret show, *Back in My
Life*.

Red Neckin' Love Makin' Night
Words and music by Max D. Barnes and Troy Seals.
Blue Lake Music, 1981/Warner-Tamerlane Music, 1981.
Best-selling record by Conway Twitty (MCA, 81).

Red Rain (English)
Words and music by Peter Gabriel.
Cliofine, 1986/Hidden Pun.
Introduced by Peter Gabriel on the album *So* (Geffen, 86).

Red, Red Wine
Words and music by Neil Diamond.
Tallyrand Music, 1968.
Neil Diamond fist released this song in 1968. UB40 used it on *Labour
of Love* (A & M, 83) and the album and single were revived in 1988.
Their rendition was the first reggae single ever to reach number one
on the charts.

Red Roses (Won't Work Now)
Words and music by Jimbeau Hinson and David Murphy.
Goldrian Music, 1984/N2D Publishing, 1984.
Introduced by Reba McEntire on the album *Have I Got a Deal for You*
(MCA, 85).

The Reflex
Words and music by Duran Duran.
BIOT Music Ltd., London, England, 1983.
Best-selling record by Duran Duran from *Seven and the Ragged Tiger*
(Capitol, 84).

Refugee
Words and music by Tom Petty and Mike Campbell.

Skyhill Publishing Co., Inc., 1979/Tarka Music Co.
Best-selling record by Tom Petty & The Heartbreakers from *Damn the Torpedoes* (Backstreet, 80).

Relax (English)
Words and music by Peter Gill, William Johnson, and Mark O'Toole.
Island Music, 1984.
Best-selling record by Frankie Goes to Hollywood from *Welcome to the Pleasure Dome* (Island, 84). Introduced in the film *Body Double* (84).

Remember (The First Time)
Words and music by Lamont Coward.
Lamont Coward, 1989/Bright Light Music.
Introduced by Eric Gable on *Caught in the Act* (Orpheus, 89).

Remo's Theme: What If?
Words and music by Tommy Shaw and Richie Cannata.
Tranquility Base Songs, 1985.
Best-selling record by Tommy Shaw from the album *What If* (A & M, 85). Introduced in the film *Remo Williams: The Adventure Begins* (85).

Rene and Georgette Magritte with Their Dog After the War
Words and music by Paul Simon.
Paul Simon Music, 1982.
Introduced by Paul Simon on *Hearts and Bones* (Warner Brothers, 83).

Reptile (Australian)
Words by Steve Kilbey, music by The Church.
Funzalo Music, 1988/Bug Music, 1988/MCA Music, 1988.
Introduced by The Church on *Starfish* (Arista, 88).

Rescue Me
Words and music by Al B. Sure and Kyle West.
EMI-April Music, 1988/Across 110th Street Music, 1988/Willarie Publishing Co., 1988.
Best-selling record by Al B. Sure, from *In Effect Mode* (Warner Bros., 88).

Respect Yourself
Words and music by Mack Rice and Luther Ingram.
East/Memphis Music Corp., 1971/Klondike Enterprises Ltd., 1971.
Revived in 1986 by Bruce Willis, star of the popular television series *Moonlighting* (Motown).

Rest Your Love on Me (English)
Words and music by Barry Gibb.
Unichappell Music Inc., 1976.
Best-selling record by Conway Twitty (MCA, 81).

Restless
Words by Vicki Peterson, music by Susanna Hoffs.
Bangophile Music, 1984/Illegal Songs, Inc., 1984.
Introduced by The Bangles on *All over the Place* (Columbia, 84).

Restless Heart
Words and music by John Waite.
Alley Music, 1984.
Best-selling record by John Waite in 1985 from the album *No Brakes*
(EMI-America, 84).

The Revolution Will Not Be Televised
Words and music by Gil Scott-Heron.
Bob Thiele Music, Ltd., 1974.
        Revived by Gil Scott-Heron on *The Best of Gil Scott-Heron*
(Arista, 84).

Rhythm Is Gonna Get You
Words and music by Gloria Estefan and Enrique Garcia.
Foreign Imported, 1987.
Best-selling record by Gloria Estefan & The Miami Sound Machine,
from the album *Let It Loose* (Epic, 87).

Rhythm Nation
Words and music by Janet Jackson, James Harris, III, and Terry Lewis.
Black Ice Music, 1989/Flyte Tyme Tunes.
Best-selling record by Janet Jackson from *Rhythm Nation 1814* (A & M,
89).

Rhythm of Love (German)
English words and music by Rudolf Schenker and Klaus Meine.
Breeze, 1988/WB Music, 1988.
Best-selling record by Scorpions, from *Savage Amusement* (Mercury,
88).

Rhythm of the Night
Words and music by Diane Warren.
Edition Sunset Publishing Inc., 1984/BMG Songs Inc., 1984.
Best-selling record by DeBarge from the album *Rhythm of the Night*
(Motown, 85). Introduced in the film and soundtrack album *The Last
Dragon* (85).

Ricky
Words and music by Nicky Chinn, Mike Chapman, Al Yankovic,
Harold Adamson, and Eliot Daniel.
BMG Music, 1981/Mike Chapman Publishing Enterprises, 1981.
Best-selling record by Weird Al Yankovic from *Dare to be Stupid*
(Rock 'n' Roll, 83), Parody of 'Mickey' and 'I Love Lucy Theme
Song.'

The Riddle (English)
Words and music by Nik Kershaw.
Irving Music Inc., 1984.
Introduced by Nik Kershaw on the album *The Riddle* (MCA, 85).

Ride Across the River
Words and music by Mark Knopfler.
Chariscourt Ltd., 1985/Almo Music Corp.
Introduced by Dire Straits on the album *Brothers in Arms* (Warner
    Bros., 85).

Ride Like the Wind
Words and music by Christopher Geppart.
BMG Music, 1979.
Best-selling record by Christopher Cross from *Christopher Cross*
    (Warner Brothers, 80).

Riding with the King
Words and music by John Haitt.
Lillybilly, 1983.
Introduced on *Riding with the King* by John Hiatt (84).

Right from the Heart
Words and music by Earl Rose and Kathleen Wakefield.
American Broadcasting Music, Inc., 1985/Amadeus Music Co., 1985/
    EMI-April Music, 1985/Lady of the Lakes Music, 1985.
Introduced by Johnny Mathis on the soap opera *Ryan's Hope* (85).
    Performed by Johnny Mathis on the album *Right from the Heart*
    (Columbia, 85).

Right Hand Man
Words and music by Gary Scruggs.
Earthly Delights, 1987.
Introduced by Eddy Raven on the album *Right Hand Man* (RCA, 87).

Right Here Waiting
Words and music by Richard Marx.
Chi-Boy, 1989.
Best-selling record by Richard Marx from *Repeat Offender* (EMI, 89).

Right Next Door (Because of Me)
Words and music by Dennis Walker.
Calhoun Street, 1987.
Best-selling record by Robert Cray, from the album *Strong Persuader*
    (Hightone/Mercury, 87).

Right on Track
Words and music by Steve Bray and Steve Gilroy.
MCA Music, 1987/Unicity Music, Inc., 1987/Short Order, 1987.

Best-selling record by The Breakfast Club, from the album *The Breakfast Club* (MCA, 87). Bray, who has written many hits for Madonna, was originally a member of this band.

Right or Wrong
Words and music by Arthur Sizemore and Paul Biese.
Edwin H. Morris, 1921.
Best-selling record by George Strait from *Right or Wrong* (MCA, 84).

Ring on Her Finger, Time on Her Hands
Words and music by Don Goodman, Mary Ann Kennedy, and Pam Rose.
Tree Publishing Co., Inc., 1981/Love Wheel Music, 1981/Southern Soul Music, 1981.
Best-selling record by Lee Greenwood from *Greatest Hits* (MCA, 82). Nominated for a Grammy Award, Country Song of the Year, 1982.

Rio (English)
Words and music by Duran Duran.
BIOT Music Ltd., London, England, 1982.
Best-selling record by Duran Duran from *Rio* (Capitol, 83).

Rio Grande
Words and music by Brian Wilson and Andy Paley.
Beach Bum Music, 1988/Beachhead Music, 1988.
Introduced by Brian Wilson on *Brian Wilson* (Reprise, 88). 'California Saga' revisited.

Rise and Stand Again
Words by Peter Udell, music by Garry Sherman.
Music Theatre International, 1983.
Introduced by Rhetta Hughes in *Amen Corner* (83).

The River
Words and music by Bruce Springsteen.
Bruce Springsteen Publishing, 1980.
Introduced by Bruce Springsteen on *The River* (Columbia, 80).

River Deep, Mountain High
Words and music by Jeff Barry, Ellie Greenwich, and Phil Spector.
Mother Bertha Music, Inc., 1966.
Performed by Darlene Love in the Broadway musical *Leader of the Pack* (85), which was based on the life of songwriter Ellie Greenwich and included many of her songs from the 1960's. Love was the lead singer on many of legendary producer Phil Spector's finest recordings of that era.

River in the Rain
Words and music by Roger Miller.

Roger Miller Music, 1985/Tree Publishing Co., Inc., 1985.
Introduced by Daniel Jenkins and Ron Richardson in the musical *Big River* (85).

River of Fools
Words and music by David Hidalgo and Louie Perez.
Davince Music, 1987/No K. O. Music, 1987.
Introduced by Los Lobos on the album *By the Light of the Moon* (Slash/Warner Bros., 87).

Road to Nowhere
Words by David Byrne, music by Chris Frantz, Tina Weymouth, and Jerry Harrison.
Index Music, 1985/Bleu Disque Music, 1985.
Best-selling record by The Talking Heads from the album *Little Creatures* (Sire, 85).

Roadrunner
Words and music by Jonathan Richman.
Modern Love Songs, 1975.
Revived in 1986 by Joan Jett & The Blackhearts on the album *Good Music* (CBS Associated/Blackheart Records, 86). Introduced by Jonathan Richman & The Modern Lovers on *The Modern Lovers* (Beserkley). Although the song was originally written about Boston and its environs, Jett's version changes the setting of the Stop and Shop food chain to her native New York.

Rock and a Hard Place (English)
Words and music by Mick Jagger and Keith Richards.
Promopub B. V., CH-1017 Amsterdam, Netherlands, 1989.
Best-selling record by The Rolling Stones from *Steel Wheels* (Rolling Stones Records/Columbia, 89).

Rock and Roll Girls
Words and music by John Fogerty.
Wenaha Music Co., 1984.
Best-selling record by John Fogerty from the album *Centerfield* (Warner Bros., 85).

Rock in the U.S.A. (A Salute to 60's Rock)
Words and music by John Cougar Mellencamp.
Full Keel Music, 1986.
Best-selling record by John Cougar Mellencamp from the album *Scarecrow* (Polygram, 86). The invocation of the name of sixties star Mitch Ryder, who had one album produced by Mellencamp, is noteworthy in this song.

Rock Lobster
Words and music by Fred Schneider and Ricky Wilson.

Boo-Fant Tunes, Inc., 1978.
Best-selling record by The B-52's from *The B-52's* (Warner Brothers, 80).

Rock Me Amadeus (German)
English words and music by Rob Bolland, Ferdi Bolland, and Falco (pseudonym for Hans Hoelzl).
Colgems-EMI Music, 1986.
Best-selling record by Falco from the album *Falco 3* (A & M, 86).
Perhaps the first classical rap song, this one was inspired by Mozart.

Rock Me Tonight (for Old Times Sake)
Words and music by Paul Laurence (pseudonym for Paul Laurence Jones).
Paul Laurence Jones, III, 1985/Bush Burnin' Music, 1985.
Best-selling record by Freddie Jackson from the album *Rock Me Tonight* (Capitol, 85).

Rock Me Tonite
Words and music by Billy Squier.
Songs of the Knight, 1984.
Best-selling record by Billy Squier from *Signs of Life* (Capitol, 84).

Rock 'n' Roll Is King (English)
Words and music by Jeff Lynne.
EMI-April Music, 1983.
Best-selling record by ELO from *Secret Messages* (A & M, 83).

Rock of Ages (English)
Words and music by Steve Clark, Robert John 'Mutt' Lange, and Joe Elliott.
Zomba Music, 1983.
Best-selling record by Def Leppard from *Pyromania* (Mercury, 83).

Rock of Rages
Words and music by Ellie Greenwich and Jeffrey Kent.
My Own Music, 1985/Jent Music Inc., 1985.
Introduced by Dinah Manoff in the musical and it's original cast album *Leader of the Pack* (Elektra/Asylum, 85).

Rock On (From *Dream a Little Dream*) (English)
Words and music by David Essex.
EMI-April Music, 1974.
Revived by Michael Damian in the film and soundtrack album *Dream a Little Dream* (Cypress/A & M, 89).

Rock Steady
Words and music by Babyface (pseudonym for Kenny Edmunds), D. Ladd, and Boaz Watson.

Hip-Trip Music Co., 1987/Hip Chic/Midstar Music, Inc./Hitwell.
Best-selling record by The Whispers, from the album *Just Gets Better with Time* (Solar, 87).

Rock the Casbah (English)
Words and music by Paul Simonon, Topper Headon, Joe Strummer (pseudonym for John Mellor), and Mick (The Clash) Jones.
Nineden, Ltd., London, England, 1982.
Best-selling record by The Clash from *Combat Rock* (Epic, 82).

Rock This Town
Words and music by Brian Setzer.
Zomba Music, 1981.
Best-selling record by The Stray Cats from *Built for Speed* (EMI-America, 82).

Rock Wit'cha
Words and music by Babyface (pseudonym for Kenny Edmunds) and Daryl Simmons.
Kear Music, 1988/Sony Tunes/Green Skirt Music.
Best-selling record in 1989 by Bobby Brown from *Don't Be Cruel* (MCA, 88).

Rock You Like a Hurricane (German)
English words and music by Rudolf Schenker, Klaus Meine, and Herman Rarebell.
WB Music, 1984.
Best-selling record by The Scorpions from *Love at first Sting* (Mercury, 84).

Rocket (English)
Words and music by Steve Clark, Phil Collen, Joe Elliott, Robert John 'Mutt' Lange, and Rick Savage.
Bludgeon Riffola Music, 1987/Zomba Music.
Best-selling record in 1989 by Def Leppard from *Hysteria* (Mercury/Polygram, 87).

Rocket 2U
Words and music by Robert Nunn.
Groupie Music, 1987.
Best-selling record in 1988 by The Jets, from *Magic* (MCA, 87).

Rockin' in the Free World
Words and music by Neil Young.
Silver Fiddle, 1989.
Introduced by Neil Young on *Freedom* (Reprise, 89).

Rockin' with the Rhythm of the Rain
Words and music by Don Schlitz and Brent Maher.

MCA, Inc., 1986/Don Schlitz Music/Welbeck Music/Blue Quill Music.
Best-selling record by the Judds from the album *Rockin' with the Rhythm* (RCA, 86).

Rockit
Words and music by Herbie Hancock, Bill Laswell, and Michael Beinhorn.
Hancock Music Co., 1983/Dad Music, 1983/More Cut Music, 1983.
Best-selling record by Herbie Hancock from *Future Shock* (Columbia, 83).

Roll with It (English)
Words by Will Jennings, music by Steve Winwood.
F.S. Ltd., England, 1988/Warner-Tamerlane Music, 1988/Willin' David, 1988/Blue Sky Rider Songs, 1988.
Best-selling record by Steve Winwood from *Roll with It* (Virgin, 88).
Nominated for a Grammy Award, Record of the Year, 1988.

Romance
Words and music by Bill Berry, Peter Buck, Mike Mills, and Michael Stipe.
Night Garden Music, 1987/Unichappell Music Inc., 1987.
Introduced by R.E.M. in the film and album *Made in Heaven* (Elektra, 87).

Romance (Love Theme from *Sing*)
Words and music by Patrick Leonard and Dean Pitchford.
TSP Music, Inc., 1989/Triple Star Music.
Introduced by Paul Carrack and Terri Nunn in the film and soundtrack album *Sing* (Columbia, 89).

Romancing the Stone (English)
Words and music by Eddy Grant.
Greenheart Music, Ltd., London, England, 1984.
Best-selling record by Eddy Grant from *Going for Broke* (Portrait, 84).

Romeo and Juliet (English)
Words and music by Mark Knopfler.
Almo Music Corp., 1980.
Introduced by Dire Straits on *Making Movies* (Warner Brothers, 80).

Romeo's Tune
Words and music by Steve Forbert.
Rolling Tide Music, 1976/Colgems-EMI Music, 1976.
Best-selling record by Steve Forbert from *Jackrabbit Slim* (Nemperor, 80).

Roni
Words and music by Babyface (pseudonym for Kenny Edmunds).

Kear Music, 1988/Hip-Trip Music Co.
Best-selling record in 1989 by Bobby Brown from *Don't Be Cruel*
(MCA, 88).

Room Full of Mirrors
Words and music by Jimi Hendrix.
Bella Godiva Music, 1970.
Revived in 1986 by the Pretenders on *Get Close* (Sires, 86). Song was
originally recorded by Jimi Hendrix on the Rainbow Bridge
soundtrack album.

Room to Move (English)
Words and music by Simon Climie, Roger Fisher, and Dennis Morgan.
Chrysalis Music Group, 1989/Almo Music Corp./Little Shop of
Morgansongs.
Best-selling record by Animotion from *Animotion* (Polydor, 89).

Rooms on Fire
Words and music by Rick Nowels.
Welsh Witch Publishing, 1989/Warner-Tamerlane Music/Future
Furniture/Colgems-EMI Music.
Best-selling record by Stevie Nicks from *The Other Side of the Mirror*
(Modern, 89).

Rosanna
Words and music by David Paich.
Hudmar Publishing Co., Inc., 1982.
Best-selling record by Toto from *Toto* (Columbia, 82). The song is
dedicated to the actress Rosanna Arquette. Won a Grammy Award,
and Record of the Year, 1982. Nominated for a Grammy Award,
Song of the Year, 1982.

The Rose
Words and music by Amanda McBroom.
Warner-Tamerlane Music, 1979.
Best-selling record by Bette Midler from the film & soundtrack album
of *The Rose* (Atlantic, 80). Nominated for Grammy Awards, Record
of the Year, 1980, and Song of the Year, 1980.

(I Never Promised You a) Rose Garden, see **I Beg Your Pardon**.

Rose in Paradise
Words and music by Stewart Harris and Jim McBride.
EMI-Blackwood Music Inc., 1987/EMI-April Music, 1987.
Introduced by Waylon Jennings on the album *Hangin' Tough* (MCA,
87).

Rosemary
Words and music by Lenny Kravitz, words by Lisa Bonet.

Miss Bessie Music, 1989.
Introduced by Lenny Kravitz on *Let Love Rule* (Virgin, 89).

Roses Are Red
Words and music by Babyface (pseudonym for Kenny Edmunds).
Kermy, 1988/Hip-Trip Music Co., 1988.
Best-selling record by The Mac Band featuring The McCampbell
   Brothers, from *The Mac Band* (MCA, 88).

Rough Boys (English)
Words and music by Pete Townshend.
Towser Tunes Inc., 1980.
Introduced by Pete Townshend on *Empty Glass* (Atco, 80).

Round and Round
Words and music by Warren DeMartini, Stephen Pearcy, and Robbin
   Crosby.
Time Coast Music, 1984/Rightsong Music, 1984/Ratt Music, 1984.
Best-selling record by Ratt from *Out of the Cellar* (Elektra, 84).

'Round Midnight
Words by Bernie Hanigan, music by Cootie Williams, words and music
   by Thelonious Monk.
Advanced Music Corp., 1944.
Revived in 1986 by Linda Ronstadt on the album *For Sentimental
   Reasons* (Asylum, 86).

Roxanne, Roxanne
Words and music by Curtis Bedeau, Frederick Reeves, Lucien George,
   Brian George, Paul George, Hugh Clarke, Jeffrey Campbell, Gerard
   Charles, and Shaun Fequiere.
Kadoc Music, 1984/Mokajumbi, 1984/Adra Music, 1984.
Best-selling record by UTFO (Select, 85). Originally a B-side, this song
   was discovered in the discos of New York City and inspired a
   number of response records including 'Roxanne's Revenge,'
   'Roxanne's Doctor - The Real Man,' 'Queen of Rox (Shante-Rox
   On),' 'Sparky's Turn (Roxanne You're Thru),' 'Roxanne's a Man
   (The Untold Story),' and 'The Real Roxanne.'

Rumors
Words and music by Marcus Thompson, Michael Marshall, and Alex
   Hill.
J. King IV, 1986.
Best-selling record by Timex Social Club from the album *Vicious
   Rumors* (Danya, 86). This was the highest charted independent single
   of the year. After the song was turned down by Con Funk Shun, its
   authors, who got their group's name from a high school club,
   performed it.

Run for the Roses
Words and music by Dan Fogelberg.
Hickory Grove Music, 1980/EMI-April Music, 1980.
Best-selling record by Dan Fogelberg from *The Innocent Age* (Full
   Moon/Epic, 82). Used as theme for the Kentucky Derby.

Run, Runaway (English)
Words and music by Noddy Holder and Jim Lea.
Whild John, London, England, 1984/Barn Music, London, England,
   1984.
Best-selling record by Slade from *Keep Your Hands off My Power
   Supply* (CBS Associated, 84).

Run Sister Run
Words and music by Jack Herrick and Tommy Thompson.
On the Trail Music, 1986/Southern Melody Music.
Introduced by The Red Clay Ramblers as accompaniment to the play *A
   Lie of the Mind,* produced in New York in 1985. The song was used
   on the subsequent album (Sugar Hill, 86).

Run to You (Canadian)
Words and music by Bryan Adams and Jim Vallance.
Adams Communications, Inc., 1984/Calypso Toonz, 1984/Irving Music
   Inc., 1984.
Best-selling record by Bryan Adams from *Reckless* (A & M, 84).

Runaway
Words and music by Jon Bon Jovi and George Karak.
Famous Music Corp., 1983/George Karaoglou Publishing, 1983/Simile
   Music, Inc., 1983.
Best-selling record by Bon Jovi from *Bon Jovi* (Mercury, 84).

Runaway
Words and music by Del Shannon (pseudonym for Charles Westover),
   music by Max Crook.
Unichappell Music Inc., 1961/Mole Hole Music, 1961.
Revived in 1986 by Del Shannon as the opening theme of the television
   series *Crime Story,* with updated lyrics; also released by Luis
   Cardenas (Capitol) and featured on his album *Animal Instinct* (Allied
   Artists).

Runaway, Go Home
Words and music by Larry Gatlin.
Larry Gatlin Music, 1985.
Best-selling record by Larry Gatlin & The Gatlin Brothers Band from
   the album *Smile* (Columbia, 85).

Runaway Train
Words and music by John Stewart.

Bugle Publishing, 1987/Bug Music, 1987.
Best-selling record in 1988 by Rosanne Cash from *King's Record Shop* (Columbia, 87).

The Runner (Canadian)
Words and music by Ian Thomas.
Intersong, USA Inc., 1981.
Best-selling record by Manfred Mann's Earth Band from *Somewhere in Afrika* (Arista, 84).

Runnin' down a Dream (English)
Words and music by Tom Petty, Jeff Lynne, and Mike Campbell.
Gone Gator Music, 1989/EMI-April Music/Wild Gator Music/WB Music.
Best-selling record by Tom Petty from *Full Moon Fever* (MCA, 89).

Running Away
Words and music by Frankie Beverly.
Amazement Music, 1981.
Best-selling record by Maze featuring Frankie Beverly from *Live in New Orleans* (Capitol, 81).

Running in the Family (English)
Words and music by Mark King, Wally Badarou, and Phil Gould.
Level 42 Songs, 1987/Chappell & Co., Inc., 1987/Island Visual Arts, 1987.
Best-selling record by Level 42, from the album *Running in the Family* (Polydor, 87).

Running up That Hill (English)
Words and music by Kate Bush.
Colgems-EMI Music, 1985.
Best-selling record by Kate Bush from the album *Hounds of Love* (EMI-America, 85).

Running With the Night
Music by Lionel Richie, Jr., words by Cynthia Weil.
Brockman Enterprises Inc., 1983/Dyad Music, Ltd., 1983.
Best-selling record by Lionel Richie from *Can't Slow Down* (Motown, 83).

Rush Hour
Words and music by Jane Wiedlin and Peter Rafelson.
I Before E Music Co., 1988/Rafelson Music, 1988.
Best-selling record by Jane Wiedlin a former member of the Go-Gos gone solo, from *Fur* (EMI-Manhattan, 88).

Rush of Speed
Words and music by Elizabeth Swados.

Introduced in the musical *The Red Sneaks,* a 1989 show that featured another socially-relevant score from the composer of *Runaways.*

Russians (English)
Words and music by Sting (pseudonym for Gordon Sumner).
Magnetic Music Publishing Co., 1986/Reggatta Music, Ltd./Illegal Songs, Inc./Atlantic Music Corp.
Best-selling record by Sting in 1986 from the album *The Dream of the Blue Turtles* (A & M, 85) .

S

Sacred Emotion
Words and music by Carl Sturken and Evan Rogers.
Music of the World, 1988/Bayjun Beat.
Best-selling record by Donny Osmond from *Donny Osmond* (Capitol, 89).

Sad and Lonely Child
Words and music by Elizabeth Swados.
Introduced in the 1989 musical *The Red Sneaks*.

Sad Sad Sad (English)
Words and music by Mick Jagger and Keith Richards.
Promopub B. V., CH-1017 Amsterdam, Netherlands, 1989.
Introduced by The Rolling Stones on *Steel Wheels* (Rolling Stones Records/Columbia, 89).

Sad Songs (Say So Much) (English)
Words by Bernie Taupin, music by Elton John.
Intersong, USA Inc., 1984.
Best-selling record by Elton John from *Breaking Hearts* (Geffen, 84).

The Safety Dance (Canadian)
Words and music by Ivan Doroschuk.
Off Backstreet Music, 1981.
Best-selling record by Men Without Hats from *Rhythm of Youth* (Backstreet, 83).

St. Elmo's Fire (Man in Motion) (English)
Words and music by David Foster and John Parr.
EMI-Gold Horizon Music Corp., 1985/Foster Frees Music Inc., 1985/ Carbert Music Inc., 1985/EMI Golden Torch Music, 1985.
Best-selling record by John Parr (Atlantic, 85). Introduced in the film *St. Elmo's Fire*; performed on its soundtrack album.

Sally (English)
Words and music by Sade (pseudonym for Helen Folesade Adu), music by Stuart Matthewman.
Silver Angel Music, 1985/Sony Tunes, 1985.
Introduced by Sade on the album *Diamond Life* (Epic, 85).

The Salt in My Tears
Words and music by Martin Briley.
Chrysalis Music Group, 1982/Miserable Melodies, 1982.
Best-selling record by Martin Briley from *One Night with a Stranger* (Mercury, 83).

Same Old Lang Syne
Words and music by Dan Fogelberg.
Hickory Grove Music, 1979/EMI-April Music.
Best-selling record by Dan Fogelberg from *The Innocent Age* (Full Moon, 80).

Same Ole Me
Words and music by Paul Overstreet.
Silverline Music, Inc., 1981.
Best-selling record by George Jones from *Still the Same Old Me* (Epic, 82).

Sample the Dog
Words and music by Pat MacDonald.
Mambadaddi, 1987/Atlantic Music Corp., 1987/I.R.S. Music, 1987.
This paean to the virtues of the home-studio was Introduced by Timbuk 3 in *Eden Alley* (I.R.S., 88).

San Diego Serenade
Words and music by Tom Waits.
Fifth Floor Music Inc., 1979.
Featured on *Take Heart* by Juice Newton (Capitol, 80).

Sanctified Lady
Words and music by Marvin Gaye and Gordon Banko.
EMI-April Music, 1985/Connie's Bank of Music, 1985.
Best-selling record by Marvin Gaye from the album *Dream of a Lifetime* (Columbia).

Sanctify Yourself (English)
Words and music by Simple Minds.
Colgems-EMI Music, 1986.
Best-selling record by Simple Minds from the album *Once upon a Time* (A & M, 86).

Sanctuary
Words and music by Rod MacDonald.

Blue Flute Music, 1988.
Introduced by Rod MacDonald on *White Buffalo* (Mountain Railroad, 88).

Sand Castles
Words and music by Rod MacDonald.
Blue Flute Music, 1988.
Introduced by Rod Macdonald on *White Buffalo* (Mountain Railroad, 88).

Santa Baby
Words and music by Joan Jarvis, Phil Springer, and Tony Springer.
Hudson Bay Music, 1953/Tamir Music, 1953.
Revived in 1987 by Madonna on the album *A Very Special Christmas* (A & M).

Santa Claus Is Back in Town
Words and music by Jerry Leiber and Mike Stoller.
Elvis Presley Music, 1957, 1985/Rightsong Music, 1957, 1985.
Performed by Dwight Yoakam (Reprise, 87).

Santa Claus Is Coming to Town
Words and music by J. Fred Coots and Haven Gillespie.
Leo Feist Inc., 1934.
Revived by Bruce Springsteen on the B-Side of 'My Hometown' (Columbia, 85).

Santa Claus Is Watching You
Words and music by Ray Stevens.
Lowery Music Co., Inc., 1985.
Introduced by Ray Stevens on the album *I Have Returned* (MCA, 85).

Sara
Words and music by Ina Wolf and Peter Wolf.
Kikiko Music Corp., 1986/Petwolf Music.
Best-selling record by Starship in 1986 from the album *Knee Deep in the Hoopla* (RCA, 85), which marked a major return to form for the scaled down Jefferson Starship.

Sarafina
Words and music by Hugh Masekela.
Warner-Tamerlane Music, 1987.
Introduced by the cast of *Sarafina*, which opened in New York in 1987. Performed on a television special about the show in 1988, and on the cast album (RCA, 88).

Sat in Your Lap (English)
Words and music by Kate Bush.

Kate Bush Music, Ltd., London, England, 1981.
Introduced by Kate Bush in *The Dreaming* (EMI-America, 82).

Satellite
Words and music by Rob Hyman, Eric Bazilian, and Rick Chertoff.
Dub Notes, 1987/Human Boy Music, 1987/Hobbler Music, 1987.
Introduced by The Hooters on the album *One Way Home* (Columbia,
    87). A lyric against television religion in the year of the downfall of
    Jim and Tammy Bakker.

Satellite (English)
Words and music by Declan MacManus.
Plangent Visions Music, Inc., London, England, 1988.
Introduced by Elvis Costello on *Spike* (Warner Bros., 89).

Satisfied
Words and music by Richard Marx.
Chi-Boy, 1989.
Best-selling record by Richard Marx from *Repeat Offender* (EMI, 89).

Saturday Love
Words and music by James Harris, III and Terry Lewis.
Flyte Tyme Tunes, 1986/Avant Garde Music Publishing, Inc.
Best-selling record by Cherrelle with Alexander O'Neal from the album
    High Priority (Epic, 86).

Sausalito Summernight (Netherlands)
Dutch words and music by Marc Boon Lucian and Robert Vundernik.
Southern Music Publishing Co., Inc., 1980/Holland Music, 1980.
Best-selling record by Diesel from *Watts in a Tank* (Regency, 81).

Save a Prayer (English)
Words and music by Duran Duran.
Tritec Music Ltd., England, 1982.
Best-selling record by Duran Duran in 1985 from the album *Rio*
    (Capitol, 83). A live concert version of this song is included on the
    group's album *Arena* (Capitol, 84).

Save Me
Words and music by Peter Cetera and David Foster.
Fall Line Orange Music, 1989/Air Bear.
Introduced by Peter Cetera as the theme for the television series
    Baywatch.

Save the Overtime for Me
Words by Bubba Knight, Gladys Knight, and Sam Dees, music by
    Ricky Smith and Joey Gallo.
Richer Music, 1983/Chappell & Co., Inc., 1983/Bubba Knight
    Enterprises Ltd., 1983/Irving Music Inc., 1983/Shakeji, 1983/Lijesrika

Music Pub., 1983.
Best-selling record by Gladys Knight & The Pips from *Visions* (Columbia, 83).

Save Your Love (for Number 1)
Words and music by Rene Moore and Angela Winbush.
A La Mode Music, 1985.
Best-selling record by Rene and Angela from the album *Street Called Desire* (Mercury, 85).

Savin' My Love for You
Words and music by Mike Clark.
Warner-Tamerlane Music, 1986/Flying Dutchman.
Best-selling record by Pake McEntire from the album *Too Old to Grow Up* (RCA, 86).

Saving All My Love for You
Words and music by Michael Masser and Gerry Goffin.
Prince Street Music, 1978/Screen Gems-EMI Music Inc., 1978.
Best-selling record by Whitney Houston from the album *Whitney Houston* (Arista, 85).

Say Goodbye to Hollywood
Words and music by Billy Joel.
EMI-Blackwood Music Inc.
Revived by Billy Joel from *Songs in the Attic* (Columbia, 81).
  Introduced on *Turnstiles*.

Say Hello
Words by Sammy Cahn, music by Richard Evan Behrke.
Sergeant Music Co., 1981/Elliot Music Co., Inc., 1981.
Best-selling record by Frank Sinatra (Reprise, 81).

Say It Again
Words and music by Bunny Sigler and Carol Davis.
EMI-Blackwood Music Inc., 1987/Henry SueMay Music, 1987.
Best-selling record in 1988 by Jermaine Stewart from *Say It Again* (Arista, 87).

Say It Isn't So
Words and music by Daryl Hall.
Hot Cha Music Co., 1983/Unichappell Music Inc., 1983.
Best-selling record by Daryl Hall and John Oates from *Rock 'N Soul, Part 1* (RCA, 83).

Say It Isn't True
Words and music by Jackson Browne.
Night Kitchen Music, 1983.
Introduced by Jackson Browne in *Lawyers in Love* (Asylum, 83).

Say Say Say (English)
Words and music by Paul McCartney and Michael Jackson.
MPL Communications Inc., 1983/Mijac Music, 1983.
Best-selling record by Paul McCartney and Michael Jackson from *Pipes of Peace* (Columbia, 83).

Say You, Say Me (Title Song from *White Nights*)
Words and music by Lionel Richie, Jr.
Brockman Enterprises Inc., 1985.
Best-selling record by Lionel Richie from the album *Dancing on the Ceiling* (Motown, 85). Introduced in the film *White Nights* (85). Won an Academy Award, and Song of the Year, 1985.

Say You Will
Words and music by Mick (Foreigner) Jones and Lou Gramm.
Heavy Pedal, 1987/Colgems-EMI Music, 1987/Intersong, USA Inc., 1987.
Best-selling record in 1988 by Foreigner, from *Inside Information* (Atlantic, 87).

Say You'll Be Mine
Words and music by Christopher Cross.
BMG Music, 1979.
Best-selling record by Christopher Cross from *Christopher Cross* (Warner Brothers, 81).

Scandalous
Words and music by Prince (pseudonym for Prince Rogers Nelson) and John Nelson.
Controversy Music, 1989/WB Music.
Best-selling record by Prince from the film and soundtrack LP *Batman* (Warner Bros., 89). Co-writer John Nelson is Prince's father.

Scatterlings of Africa (South African)
Afrikaans words and music by Johnny Clegg.
WB Music, 1982.
Introduced by Juluka on *Scatterlings of Africa* (Warner Brothers, 82).

Scissor Cut
Words and music by Jimmy Webb.
White Oak Songs, 1981.
Introduced by Jim Webb in *Angel Heart* (Columbia/Lorimar, 82).

Scott and Jamie
Words and music by Fred Small.

Pine Barrens Music, 1988.
Introduced by Fred Small on *I Will Stand Fast* (Flying Fish, 88).

Scratch My Back (and Whisper in My Ear)
Words and music by Marcell Strong, Raymond Moore, and Earl Cage, Jr.
Fame Publishing Co., Inc., 1970.
Best-selling record by Razzy Bailey (RCA, 82).

Se La
Words and music by Lionel Richie, Jr. and Greg Phillinganes.
Brockman Music, 1986.
Introduced by Lionel Richie on the album *Dancing on the Ceiling* (Motown, 86), bringing a Caribbean flavor to the singer's repertoire.

Sea of Love
Words and music by George Khoury and Phi Battiste.
Fort Knox Music Co., 1959.
Revived by The Honeydrippers on *Volume One* (Esparanza, 84).

The Search Is Over
Words and music by Frankie Sullivan and Jim Peterik.
Rude Music, 1984/Easy Action Music, 1984.
Best-selling record by Survivor in 1985 from the album *Vital Signs* (Epic, 84).

Search Your Heart
Words and music by Steve Forbert.
Geffen Music, 1988/Rolling Tide Music, 1988.
Introduced by Steve Forbert on *Streets of the Town* (Geffen, 88).

Seasons Change
Words and music by Lewis Martinee.
Panchin, 1987/Screen Gems-EMI Music Inc., 1987.
Best-selling record by Expose, from the album *Exposure* (Arista, 87).

Second Chance
Words and music by Jeff Carlisi, Max Carl, and Cal Curtis.
Rocknocker Music Co., 1988/EMI-Blackwood Music Inc./Cal Curtis Music/Too Tall Music.
Best-selling record in 1989 by .38 Special from *Rock and Roll Strategy* (A & M, 88).

Second Thoughts
Words and music by Craig Carnelia.
Carnelia Music, 1982.
Introduced by Company of *Is There Life After High School* (82).

Secret Lovers
Words and music by David Lewis and Wayne Lewis.
Almo Music Corp., 1986/Jodaway Music.
Best-selling record by Atlantic Starr from the album *As the Band Turns*
(A & M, 86).

The Secret of My Success
Words and music by Jack Blades, David Foster, Tom Keane, and Mike
Landau.
Music of the World, 1987/MCA Music, 1987/Five Storks, 1987/Warner-
Tamerlane Music, 1987/Air Bear, 1987.
Introduced by Night Ranger as the title song for the film and soundtrack
album of the same name (MCA, 87). Also included on the album *Big
Life* by Night Ranger (MCA, 87). Nominated for a Golden Globe
Award as Best Song from a Movie, 1987.

Secret Rendezvous
Words and music by L. A. Reid (pseudonym for Antonio Reid),
Babyface (pseudonym for Kenny Edmunds), and Daryl Simmons.
Kear Music, 1988/Green Skirt Music/Hip-Trip Music Co.
Best-selling record in 1989 by Karyn White from *Karyn White* (Warner
Bros., 88).

Secret Separation (English)
Words by Jeanette Obstoj, music by Cy Curnin, Jamie West-Oram,
Rupert Greenall, and Danny Brown.
Rats Said the Tyrant, England/Colgems-EMI Music, 1986/Copyright
Control.
Best-selling record by The Fixx from the album *Walkabout* (MCA, 86).

The Seduction (Love Theme from *American Gigolo*) (German)
German words and music by Giorgio Moroder.
Ensign Music, 1980.
Best-selling record by The James Last Band from *Seduction* (Polydor,
80). Introduced in the film *American Gigolo* (80).

See a Little Light
Words and music by Bob Mould.
Granary Music, 1989.
Introduced by Bob Mould on *Workbook* (Virgin, 89).

Seeds
Words and music by Bruce Springsteen.
Bruce Springsteen Publishing, 1985.
Introduced by Bruce Springsteen on his 1984-85 tour, dedicated to
displaced oil workers of Houston, Texas.

Seeing's Believing
Words and music by Rodney Crowell.

Jolly Cheeks Music, 1980.
Featured in *Right or Wrong* by Rosanne Cash (Columbia, 80).

Self Control (English-Italian)
English words by Steve Piccolo, Italian words and music by Raffaele
Riefoli and Giancarlo Bigazzi.
Edition Sunrise Publishing, Inc., 1984.
Best-selling record by Laura Branigan from *Self Control* (Atlantic, 84).

Self Destruction
Zomba Music, 1989/Willesden Music, Inc.
Introduced by Stop the Violence Movement (Jive, 89). Top rappers like
Heavy D., Doug E. Fresh, MC. Lyte, Kool Moe Dee, Chuck D, and
Flavor Flav contributed to this message song which was the rap
record of the year. Proceeds were donated to the National Urban
League.

Send Her My Love
Words and music by Steve Perry and Jonathan Cain.
Twist & Shout Music, 1982.
Best-selling record by Journey from *Frontiers* (Columbia, 83).

Sentimental Street
Words and music by Jack Blades and Francis Fitzgerald.
Kid Bird Music, 1985.
Best-selling record by Night Ranger from the album *Seven Wishes*
(MCA, 85).

Separate But Equal
Words and music by Lamar Alford.
Revived in 1988 at the Martin Luther King, Jr. Internatiional Chapel at
Morehouse College for a production of *Martin*, about the life and
writings of a great civil rights leader, by the King Players.

Separate Lives (Love Theme from *White Nights*)
Words and music by Stephen Bishop.
Stephen Bishop Music Publishing Co., 1985/EMI-Gold Horizon Music
Corp., 1985.
Best-selling record Phil Collins and Marilyn Martin (Atlantic, 85).
Introduced in the film and soundtrack album *White Nights* (Atlantic,
85). Nominated for an Academy Award, Song of the Year, 1985.

Separate Ways (World's Apart)
Words and music by Steve Perry and Jonathan Cain.
Twist & Shout Music, 1982.
Best-selling record by Journey from *Frontiers* (Columbia, 83).

September Girls
Words and music by Alex Chilton.

Almo Music Corp., 1974/Koala Music Inc.

Revived in 1986 by The Bangles on *Different Light* (Columbia, 86).
Introduced by Big Star in the seventies. Chilton was the lead singer of
the Boxtops, who sang on such hits as 'The Letter.'

September Song
Words by Maxwell Anderson, music by Kurt Weill.

DeSylva, Brown & Henderson, Inc., 1938/Hampshire House Publishing
Corp., 1938.

Revived by Lou Reed on the album *Lost in the Stars: The Music of
Kurt Weill* (A & M, 85).

Sequel
Words and music by Harry Chapin.

Chapin Music, 1980.

Best-selling record by Harry Chapin from *Sequel* (Boardwalk, 80).

Serenade
Words and music by Tom Waits.

Fifth Floor Music Inc., 1974.

Performed by Dion on *Yo Frankie* (Arista, 89).

Set 'Em up Joe
Words and music by Hank Cochran, Vern Gosdin, Dean Dillon, and
Buddy Cannon.

Tree Publishing Co., Inc., 1987/Sabal Music, Inc., 1987/Larry Butler
Music Co., 1987/EMI-Blackwood Music Inc., 1987/Hookem Music,
1987.

Best-selling record by Vern Gosdin from *Chiseled in Stone* (Columbia,
88). A tribute to Ernest Tubb, who recorded 'Two Glassees, Joe' in
1954.

Set Me Free
Words and music by Todd Rundgren, Roger Powell, Kasim Sultan, and
John Wilcox.

Unearthly Music Inc., 1979/Fiction Music Inc., 1979.

Best-selling record by Utopia from *Adventures in Utopia* (Bearsville,
80).

Set Me Free (Rosa Lee)
Words and music by Cesar Rosas.

Ceros, 1986.

Introduced by Los Lobos on the album *By the Light of the Moon* (Slash/
Warner Bros., 87).

Set the House Ablaze (English)
Words and music by Paul Weller.

Colgems-EMI Music, 1981.

Introduced by Paul Weller on *Sound Affects* (Polydor, 81).

Seven Spanish Angels
Words and music by Troy Seals and Eddie Setser.
Warner-Tamerlane Music, 1984/WB Music, 1984/Two-Sons Music, 1984.
Best-selling record by Ray Charles with Willie Nelson from the album *Friendship* (Columbia, 85).

Seven Summers
Words and music by Tito Larriva.
Placa Music, 1985.
Introduced by Cruzados on the album *Cruzados* (Arista, 85).

Seven Wonders
Words and music by Sandy Stewart and Stevie Nicks.
Welsh Witch Publishing, 1987.
Best-selling record by Fleetwood Mac, from the album *Tango in the Night* (Warner Bros., 87).

Seven Year Ache
Words and music by Rosanne Cash.
Hotwire Music, 1979/Atlantic Music Corp., 1979.
Best-selling record by Rosanne Cash from *Seven Years Ache* (Columbia, 81).

17
Words and music by Rick James.
Stone City Music, 1984.
Best-selling record by Rick James from *Reflections* (Gordy, 84).

Sex (I'm A)
Words and music by John Crawford, David Diamond, and Terri Nunn.
Safespace Music, 1982.
Best-selling record by Berlin from *Pleasure Victim* (Warner Brothers, 83).

Sexual Healing
Words and music by Marvin Gaye, Odell Brown, and David Ritz.
EMI-April Music, 1982/EMI-Blackwood Music Inc., 1982.
Best-selling record by Marvin Gaye from *Midnight Love* (Columbia, 82). Nominated for a Grammy Award, Rhythm 'n' Blues Song of the Year, 1982.

(She's) Sexy & 17
Words and music by Brian Setzer.
Willesden Music, Inc., 1983.
Best-selling record by The Stray Cats from *Rant n' Rave with the Stray Cats* (EMI-America, 83).

Sexy Eyes
Words and music by Christopher Dunn, Robert Mather, and Keith
   Stegall.
EMI-April Music, 1980.
Best-selling record by Dr. Hook from *Sometimes You Win* (Capitol, 80).

Sexy Girl
Words and music by Jack Tempchin and Glenn Frey.
Night River Publishing, 1984/Red Cloud Music Co., 1984.
Best-selling record by Glenn Frey from *The All-nighter* (MCA, 84).

Shackles
Words and music by Ralph Rice.
Arrival Music, 1983/Alva Music, 1983.
Best-selling record by R.J.'s Latest Arrival (Golden Boy/Quality, 84).

Shaddup Your Face
Words and music by Joe Dolce.
EMI-April Music, 1980.
Best-selling record by Joe Dolce from *Shaddup Your Face* (MCA, 81).

Shadows of the Night
Words and music by David Leigh Byron.
Inner Sanctum, 1980.
Best-selling record by Pat Benatar (Chrysalis, 82).

Shake It Up
Words and music by Ric Ocasek.
Lido Music Inc., 1981.
Best-selling record by The Cars from *Shake It Up* (Elektra, 82).

Shake It up Tonight
Words and music by Michael Sutton and Brenda Sutton.
EMI-April Music, 1981.
Best-selling record by Cheryl Lynn from *In the Night* (Columbia, 81).

Shake You Down
Words and music by Gregory Abbott.
Charles Family Music, 1986/Alibee Music/Grabbitt Music.
Best-selling record by Gregory Abbott from the album *Shake You Down*
   (Columbia, 86).

Shake Your Love
Words and music by Debbie Gibson.
EMI April Canada, 1987/Possibilities Publishing, 1987.
Best-selling record by Debbie Gibson, from the album *Out of the Blue*
   (Atlantic, 87).

Shakedown
Words and music by Harold Faltermeyer, Keith Forsey, and Bob Seger.
Famous Music Corp., 1987/Gear Publishing/Kilauea Music.
Introduced by Bob Seger in the film and on the soundtrack album
  Beverly Hills Cop II (MCA, 87). Best-selling record by Bob Seger.
  Nominated for a Golden Globe Award as Best Song from a Movie,
  1987. Nominated for an Academy Award, Best Original Song, 1987.

Shame on the Moon
Words and music by Rodney Crowell.
Coolwell Music, 1981/Granite Music Corp., 1981.
Best-selling record by Bob Seger & The Silver Bullet Band from *The
  Distance* (Capitol, 82).

Shanghai Breezes
Words and music by John Denver.
Cherry Lane Music Co., 1981.
Best-selling record by John Denver from *Seasons of the Heart* (RCA,
  82).

Share Your Love with Me
Words and music by Al Bragg and Deadric Malone.
Duchess Music Corp., 1963.
Best-selling record by Kenny Rogers from *Share Your Love* (Liberty,
  81).

Sharkey's Day
Words and music by Laurie Anderson.
Difficult Music, 1984.
Introduced by Laurie Anderson in *Mr. Heartbreak* (Warner Brothers,
  84).

Sharkey's Night
Words and music by Laurie Anderson.
Difficult Music, 1984.
Introduced by Laurie Anderson in *Mr. Heartbreak* (Warner Brothers,
  84).

Sharp Dressed Man
Words and music by Billy Gibbons, Dusty Hill, and Frank Beard.
Hamstein Music, 1983.
Best-selling record by ZZ Top from *Eliminator* (Warner Brothers, 83).

Shattered Dreams (English)
Words and music by Clark Datchler.
Copyright Control, 1987.
Best-selling record in 1988 by Johnny Hates Jazz, from *Turn Back the
  Clock* (Virgin, 87).

She and I
Words and music by Dave Loggins.
MCA, Inc., 1986/Patchwork Music.
Best-selling record by Alabama from the album *Alabama's Greatest Hits* (RCA, 86).

She Blinded Me with Science (English)
Words and music by Thomas Dolby and Joe Kerr.
Zomba House, 1982/WB Music, 1982.
Best-selling record Thomas Dolby from *Blinded by Science* (Capitol, 83).

She Bop
Words and music by Cyndi Lauper, Stephen Lunt, Gary Corbett, and Richard Chertoff.
Rella Music Corp., 1983/Noyb Music, 1983/Perfect Pinch Music, 1983/ Hobbler Music, 1983/Wall to Wall Music, 1983.
Best-selling record by Cyndi Lauper from *She's So Unusual* (Portrait, 84).

She Can't Say That Anymore
Words and music by John Conlee.
WB Gold Music Corp., 1980.
Best-selling record by John Conlee from *John Conlee's Greatest Hits* (MCA, 83).

She Don't Love Nobody
Words and music by John Hiatt.
Lillybilly, 1984/Bug Music.
Introduced by The Desert Rose Band on *Running* (MCA/Curb, 88).
    Nominated for a Grammy Award, Country Song of the Year, 1989.

She Drives Me Crazy (English)
Words and music by David Steele and Roland Gift.
Virgin Music, 1989.
Best-selling record by Fine Young Cannibals from *The Raw and the Cooked* (A & M, 89).

She Got the Goldmine (I Got the Shaft)
Words and music by Tim DuBois.
Warner House of Music, 1981.
Best-selling record by Jerry Reed (MCA, 82).

She Hates to Go Home
Words and music by Marshall Crenshaw and Leroy Preston.
MHC Music, 1989/Whiskey Drinkin' Music/Bug Music.
Introduced by Marshall Crenshaw on *Good Evening* (Warner Bros., 89).

She Keeps the Home Fires Burning
Words and music by Dennis Morgan, Don Pfrimmer, and Mike Reid.
Tom Collins Music Corp., 1985/Collins Court Music, 1985/BMG Songs
    Inc., 1985.
Best-selling record by Ronnie Milsap from the album *Greatest Hits, Vol.
    2* (RCA, 85) .

She Left Love All over Me
Words and music by Chester Lester.
Warner House of Music, 1981.
Best-selling record by Razzy Bailey from *Feelin' Right* (RCA, 82).

She Loves the Jerk
Words and music by John Hiatt.
Lillybilly, 1983.
Introduced by Rodney Crowell on *Street Language* (Columbia, 86).

She Moves, Eyes Follow
Words and music by Jimmy Webb.
White Oak Songs, 1985.
Introduced by Kenny Rankin on *Hiding in Myself* (Cypress, 88).

She Reminds Me of You
Words and music by Phil Davis and Doug Ericksen.
Flip 'n' Dog, 1989/Music of the World.
Introduced by Firetown on *The Good Life* (Atlantic, 89).

She Said the Same Things to Me
Words and music by John Hiatt.
Lillybilly, 1985.
Introduced by John Hiatt on the album *Warming up to the Ice Age*
    (Geffen, 85).

She Sure Got Away with My Heart
Words and music by James Aldridge and Howard Brasfield.
Colgems-EMI Music, 1982.
Best-selling record by John Anderson (Warner Brothers, 84).

She Twists the Knife Again (English)
Words and music by Richard Thompson.
Island Music, 1985.
Introduced by Richard Thompson on the album *Across a Crowded
    Room* (Mercury, 85).

She Used to Be Somebody's Baby
Words and music by Larry Gatlin.
Larry Gatlin Music, 1986.
Best-selling record by The Gatlin Brothers--Larry, Steve, and Rudy--
    from the album *Partners* (Columbia, 86).

She Wants to Dance with Me (English)
Words and music by Rick Astley.
All Boys USA Music, 1989.
Best-selling record by Rick Astley from *Hold Me in Your Arms* (RCA, 89).

She Was Hot (English)
Words and music by Mick Jagger and Keith Richards.
Colgems-EMI Music, 1983.
Best-selling record by The Rolling Stones from *Undercover* (Rolling Stones, 84).

She Was K.C. at Seven
Words and music by Craig Carnelia.
Carnelia Music, 1987.
Introduced by Craig Carnelia in the Off-Broadway musical *Three Postcards* (87).

She Won't Talk to Me
Words and music by Luther Vandross and Hubert Eaves, III.
EMI-April Music, 1988/Uncle Ronnie's Music/EMI-Blackwood Music Inc./Heumar Music.
Best-selling record in 1989 by Luther Vandross from *Any Love* (Epic, 88).

She Works Hard for the Money
Words and music by Donna Summer and Michael Omartian.
Sweet Summer Night Music, 1983/All Nations Music, 1983.
Best-selling record by Donna Summer from *She Works Hard for the Money* (Mercury, 83).

She's a Bad Mama Jama
Words and music by Leon Haywood.
Jim-Edd Music, 1981.
Best-selling record by Carl Carlton from *Carl Carlton* (20th Century-Fox, 81). Nominated for a Grammy Award, Rhythm 'n' Blues Song of the Year, 1981.

She's a Beauty
Words and music by Steve Lukather, David Foster, and Fee Waybill.
Foster Frees Music Inc., 1983/BMG Songs Inc., 1983/Screen Gems-EMI Music Inc., 1983/Boone's Tunes, 1983.
Best-selling record by The Tubes from *Outside Inside* (Capitol, 83).

She's a Miracle
Words and music by James P. Pennington and Sonny LeMaire.
Tree Publishing Co., Inc., 1984/Careers Music Inc., 1984.
Best-selling record by Exile from the album *Hang onto Your Heart* (Epic, 85).

She's Crazy for Leaving
Words and music by Rodney Crowell and Guy Clark.
Granite Music Corp., 1988/Coolwell Music/Chappell & Co., Inc.
Best-selling record in 1989 by Rodney Crowell from *Diamonds and Dirt*
   (Columbia, 88).

She's Got a Single Thing in Mind
Words and music by Walt Aldridge.
Colgems-EMI Music, 1989.
Best-selling record by Conway Twitty from *House on Old Lonesome
   Road* (MCA, 89).

She's Got a Way
Words and music by Billy Joel.
EMI-April Music, 1971/Impulsive Music, 1971.
Best-selling record by Billy Joel from *Songs in the Attic* (Columbia, 81).

She's Got Her Ticket
Words and music by Tracy Chapman.
EMI-April Music, 1986/Purple Rabbit Music, 1986.
Introduced by Tracy Chapman in *Tracy Chapman* (Elektra, 88).

She's Having a Baby (English)
Words and music by Dave Wakeling and Ian Ritchie.
Famous Music Corp., 1987/Nancy Hughes, 1987/MCA Music, 1987.
Introduced by Dave Wakeling from the film and soundtrack album of
   She's Having a Baby (I.R.S., 88).

She's King (French)
English words and music by Marty Wilson-Piper.
Funzalo Music, 1988.
Introduced by Marty Wilson-Piper a member of The Church, in a solo
   album, *Art Attack* (Ryko, 88).

She's Like the Wind
Words and music by Patrick Swayze and Stacey Widelitz.
Troph, 1987.
Best-selling record by Patrick Swayze, with Wendy Fraser, from the
   soundtrack album *Dirty Dancing* (RCA, 87). Co-author Swayze was
   also one of the film's stars.

She's No Lady
Words and music by Lyle Lovett.
Fast Fade Music, 1987/Lyle Lovett, 1987.
Introduced by Lyle Lovett in *Pontiac* (MCA, 88). Nominated for a
   Grammy Award, Country Song of the Year, 1988.

She's Not Really Cheatin' (She's Just Gettin' Even)
Words and music by Randy Shaffer.

Baray Music Inc., 1982/Wood Hall Publishing Co., 1982.
Best-selling record by Moe Bandy (Columbia, 82).

She's on the Left
Words and music by Robert Brookins, Jeffery Osborne, Tony Haymes,
and Clinton Blanson.
Sac-Boy, 1988/Chances R Publishing, 1988/March 9 Music, 1988/Almo
Music Corp., 1988/Haynestorm Music, 1988.
Best-selling record by Jeffrey Osborne, from *One Love-One Dream* (A
& M, 88).

She's out of My Life
Words and music by Tom Bahler.
Tom Bahler, 1978/Senor Music, 1978/Yellow Brick Road Music, 1978.
Best-selling record by Michael Jackson from *Off the Wall* (Epic, 80).

She's Single Again
Words and music by Charlie Craig and Peter McCann.
EMI-Blackwood Music Inc., 1985/EMI-April Music, 1985/New & Used
Music, 1985.
Best-selling record by Janie Fricke from the album *Somebody Else's
Fire* (Columbia, 85).

She's So Cold (English)
Words and music by Mick Jagger and Keith Richards.
Colgems-EMI Music, 1980.
Best-selling record by The Rolling Stones from *Emotional Rescue*
(Rolling Stones, 80).

She's Strange
Words and music by Larry Blackmon, Charlie Singleton, Nathan
Leftenant, and Tomi Jenkins.
All Seeing Eye Music, 1984/Cameo Five Music, 1984.
Best-selling record by Cameo from *She's Strange* (Atlanta Artists, 84).

She's Too Good to Be True
Words and music by Sonny LeMaire and James P. Pennington.
Tree Publishing Co., Inc., 1985/Pacific Island Music, 1985.
Best-selling record in 1987 by Exile, from their *Greatest Hits* album
(Epic, 86).

Shine, Shine, Shine
Words and music by Bud McGuire and Ken Bell.
EMI-April Music, 1987/Butler's Bandits, 1987/Next o Ken, 1987/Ensign
Music, 1987.
Best-selling record by Eddy Raven, from the album *Right Hand Man*
(RCA, 87).

Shining Star
Words and music by Leo Graham, Jr. and Paul Richmond.
Content Music, Inc., 1980.
Best-selling record by The Manhattans from *After Midnight* (Columbia, 80). Nominated for a Grammy Award, Rhythm 'n' Blues Song of the Year, 1980.

Ship of Fools (Save Me from Tomorrow) (English)
Words and music by Karl Wallinger.
Polygram International, 1986.
Best-selling record in 1987 by World Party, from the album *Private Revolution* (Chrysalis, 86).

Ship of Fools (English)
Words and music by Robert Plant and Phil Johnstone.
Virgin Music, 1987.
Best-selling record by Robert Plant from *Now and Zen* (Esparanza, 88).

Shipbuilding (English)
Words and music by Elvis Costello and Clive Langer.
Plangent Visions Music, Inc., London, England, 1982/Warner Brothers, Inc., 1982.
Introduced by Elvis Costello in *Punch the Clock* (Columbia, 83).

Shock the Monkey (English)
Words and music by Peter Gabriel.
Hidden Music, 1982.
Best-selling record by Peter Gabriel from *Peter Gabriel (Security)* (Geffen, 82).

Shoo-Rah Shoo-Rah
Words and music by Allen Toussaint.
Marsaint Music Inc., 1981/Warner-Tamerlane Music, 1981.
Featured on *Rock Away* by Phoebe Snow (Mirage, 81).

Shotgun down the Avalanche
Words and music by Shawn Colvin and John Leventhal.
AGF Music Ltd., 1988/Scred Songs.
Introduced on the album *Fast Folk Sixth Anniversary Issue* (Fast Folk, 88), this song was also performed by Shawn Colvin on *Steady On* (Columbia, 89).

Should I Do It
Words and music by Layng Martine, Jr.
Unichappell Music Inc., 1981/Watch Hill Music, 1981.
Best-selling record by The Pointer Sisters from *Black & White* (Planet, 82).

Should I Say Yes (Netherlands)
English words and music by John Smith and Valerie Day.
Poolside, 1988.
Best-selling record by Nu Shooz from *Told U So* (Atlantic, 88).

Should've Known Better
Words and music by Richard Marx.
Chi-Boy, 1987.
Best-selling record by Richard Marx, from the album *Richard Marx*
(EMI-Manhattan, 87).

Should've Never Let You Go
Words and music by Neil Sedaka and Phil Cody.
Kirshner/April Music Publishing, 1978/Kiddio Music Co., 1978.
Neil and Dara Sedaka from *In The Pocket* (Elektra, 80).

Shout (English)
Words and music by Roland Orzabal and Ian Stanley.
Exaskeletal, 1985.
Best-selling record by Tears for Fears from the album *Songs from the
Big Chair* (Mercury, 85).

(Come on) Shout
Words and music by Marti Sharron and Gary Skardina.
Welbeck Music Corp., 1985/Anidraks Music/Girl Productions.
Introduced by Alex Brown in the film *Girls Just Want to Have Fun*
(85); which was inspired by Cyndi Lauper's song of the same title.

The Show
Words and music by Douglas David and Ricky Walters.
Mark of Aries, 1985/Keejue.
Released by Doug E. Fresh and The Get Fresh Crew. Featured on *Rap's
Greatest Hits* (Reality/Danga). Won the First Annual Indie Award as
Best 12-Inch Single of the Year.

Show and Tell
Words and music by Jerry Fuller.
EMI-Blackwood Music Inc., 1989/Fullness Music Co.
Best-selling record by Peabo Bryson from *All My Love* (Capitol, 89).

Show Her
Words and music by Mike Reid.
BMG Music, 1982.
Best-selling record by Ronnie Milsap from *Keyed Up* (RCA, 84).

Show Me (English)
Words and music by Chrissie Hynde.
MCA, Inc., 1984.

Best-selling record by The Pretenders from *Learning to Crawl* (Sire, 84).

Show Me the Way
Words and music by Junior Potts, Joey Gallo, and Angela Winbush.
Almo Music Corp., 1987/Don't You Know, 1987.
Best-selling record by Regina Belle, from the album *All by Myself* (Columbia, 87).

Shower Me with Your Love (English)
Words and music by Bernard Jackson.
Colgems-EMI Music, 1989.
Best-selling record by Surface from *Second Wave* (Columbia, 89).

The Side I'll Never Show
Words and music by Steve Wynn.
Poison Brisket Music, 1988.
Introduced by Dream Syndicate in *Ghost Stories* (Enigma, 88).

Sidewalk Talk
Words and music by Madonna.
House of Fun Music, 1986/Lost in Music.
Best-selling record by Jellybean (EMI-America, 86).

Sign 'o' the Times
Words and music by Prince Rogers Nelson.
Controversy Music, 1987.
Best-selling record by Prince (Paisley Park, 87). Featured in the film and album of the same name.

Sign Your Name (English)
Words and music by Terence Trent D'Arby.
Young Terrence, 1987/Virgin Nymph, 1987.
Best-selling record in 1988 by Terence Trent D'Arby from *Wishing Well* (Columbia, 87).

Silent Night (Australian)
Words by Joseph Mohr, music by Franz Gruber.
Revived in 1987 by Stevie Nicks on the album *A Very Special Christmas* (A & M). This holiday classic was written by an Austrian priest and a church organist in 1818.

Silent Running (English)
Words and music by Mike Rutherford and Brian Robertson.
Hit & Run Music, 1985/WB Music, 1985.
Best-selling record by Mike & The Mechanics from the album *Mike & The Mechanics* (Atlantic, 85).

Silent Treatment
Words and music by Earl Thomas Conley.
EMI-April Music, 1983.
Best-selling record by Earl Thomas Conley (Sunbird, 81).

Silhouette
Words and music by Kenny Gurewitz.
EMI-Blackwood Music Inc., 1988/Brenee, 1988/Kuzu Music, 1988.
Best-selling record by Kenny G from *Silhouette* (Arista, 88), this was
    the lone instrumental best-seller of 1988.

Silly People
Words and music by Stephen Sondheim.
WB Music, 1982.
Introduced by Suzanne Henry and Craig Lucas in *Marry Me a Little*
    (82).

Silvio
Words and music by Bob Dylan and Robert Hunter.
Special Rider Music, 1988/Ice Nine Publishing Co., Inc., 1988.
Introduced by Bob Dylan in *Down in the Groove* (Columbia, 88). A
    unique collaboration between Dylan and the lyricist for the Grateful
    Dead.

Simple
Words and music by Maury Yeston.
Yeston Music, Ltd., 1975.
Introduced by Anita Morris in *Nine* (Musical, 82).

Simple Song
Words and music by Lyle Lovett.
Michael H. Goldsen, Inc., 1987/Lyle Lovett, 1987.
Introduced by Lyle Lovett in *Pontiac* (MCA/Curb, 87) and popularized
    in 1988.

Simple Things
Words and music by Jim Tullio and Allen Rubens.
Tools, 1985.
Introduced by by Richie Havens on the album *Simple Things* (RBI, 87).

Simply Irresistible (English)
Words and music by Robert Palmer.
Heavy Nova Music, 1988/Polygram International, 1988.
Best-selling record by Robert Palmer from *Irresistible* (Island, 88).

Simply Meant to Be
Words by George Merrill and Shannon Rubicam, music by Henry
    Mancini.
TSP Music, Inc., 1987/Triple Star Music, 1987/Boy Meets Girl, 1987.

Introduced by Jennifer Warnes and Gary Morris on the soundtrack of the film *Blind Date* and on its album (Rhino, 87).

Since I Don't Have You
Words by James Beaumont, Janet Vogel, Joseph Verscharen, Walter Lester, and John Taylor, music by Joseph Rock and Lennie Martin.
Bonnyview Music Corp., 1959/Southern Music Publishing Co., Inc., 1959.
Revived by Don McLean from *Chain Lighting* (Millennium, 81).

Since You're Gone
Words and music by Ric Ocasek.
Lido Music Inc., 1981.
Best-selling record by The Cars from *Shake It Up* (Elektra, 82).

Sincerely Yours
Words and music by Ricardo Pagan and Joseph Malloy.
Shaman Drum Music, 1989.
Best-selling record by Sweet Sensation (with Romeo J.D.) from *Take It While It's Hot* (ATCO, 89).

Sing
Words and music by Jonathan Cain, Martin Page, and Dean Pitchford.
TSP Music, Inc., 1989/Triple Star Music.
Introduced by Mickey Thomas in the film and on the soundtrack album *Sing* (Columbia, 89).

Singin' a Song
Words by Marc Elliott, music by Larry Hochman.
Ba-Ba-Do Music, 1985.
Introduced by Kay Cole, Judy Gibson, and Vanessa Williams in the musical *One Man Band* (85).

Single Life
Words and music by Larry Blackmon and Tomi Jenkins.
All Seeing Eye Music, 1985/Larry Junior Music, 1985.
Best-selling record by Cameo from the album *Single Life* (Polygram, 85).

Sister Christian
Words and music by Kelly Keagy.
Kid Bird Music, 1983.
Best-selling record by Night Ranger from *Midnight Madness* (Camel/ MCA, 84).

Sister Kate (Theme from the television show *Sister Kate*)
Words and music by Brian Rawlings and Mason Cooper.
Introduced by Amy Grant in 1989 as the theme for the television series *Sister Kate*.

Sister Rosa
Words and music by Cyril Neville, Darrell Johnson, Liryca Charmaine
  Neville, and Jason Neville.
Screen Gems-EMI Music Inc., 1989/William Claffey & Associates/
  Johnson Music.
Introduced by The Neville Brothers on *Yellow Moon* (A & M, 89). This
  song concerns civil rights activist Rosa Parks and the story of the
  movement she symbolized.

Sisters (English)
Words and music by Richard Thompson.
Island Music, 1980.
Introduced on *Sunnyvista* by Richard Thompson (Hannibal, 83).

Sisters
Words and music by Jim Wann.
Shapiro, Bernstein & Co., Inc., 1981.
Introduced by Cass Morgan and Debra Monk in *Pump Boys and
  Dinettes* (81).

Sisters Are Doin' It for Themselves (English)
Words and music by Annie Lennox and Dave Stewart.
RCA Music Ltd., London, England, 1985/Blue Network Music Inc.,
  1985.
Best-selling record by Eurythmics and Aretha Franklin from the albums
  Be Yourself Tonight (RCA, 85) and *Who's Zoomin' Who* (Arista, 85).

Sitting on a Fence (English)
Words and music by P. D. Heaton and Stan Cullimore.
Go! Discs Ltd., England, 1986.
Best-selling record by The Housemartins, from the album *London O
  Hull 4* (Elektra, 86). Melodic protest music from England.

'65 Love Affair
Words and music by Paul Davis.
Web 4 Music Inc., 1981.
Best-selling record by Paul Davis from *Love Night* (Arista, 82).

Skateaway (English)
Words and music by Mark Knopfler.
Almo Music Corp., 1980.
Best-selling record by Dire Straits from *Making Movies* (Warner
  Brothers, 81).

Skeletons
Words and music by Stevie Wonder.
Jobete Music Co., 1987/Black Bull Music, 1987.
Best-selling record by Stevie Wonder, from the album *Characters*

(Motown, 87). Nominated for a Grammy Award, Rhythm 'n' Blues Song of the Year, 1987.

Sledgehammer (English)
Words and music by Peter Gabriel.
Cliofine, 1986/Hidden Pun.
Best-selling record by Peter Gabriel from the album *So* (Warner Bros., 86). Gabriel was formerly a member of Genesis. Nominated for Grammy Awards, Record of the Year, 1986, and Song of the Year, 1986.

Sleep Talk (English)
Words and music by Alvin Moody, Vince Bell, and Russell Simmons.
Def Jam, 1989/Slam City/Rush Groove Music.
Best-selling record by Alyson Williams from *Raw* (Def Jam/Columbia, 89).

Sleeping Bag
Words and music by Billy Gibbons, Dusty Hill, and Frank Beard.
Hamstein Music, 1985.
Best-selling record by ZZ Top from the album *Afterburner* (Warner Bros., 85).

Slow Burn
Words and music by Tommy Rocco and Charlie Black.
Chappell & Co., Inc., 1983/Polygram International, 1983.
Best-selling record by T.G. Sheppard (Warner/Curb, 84).

Slow Down (English)
Words and music by Carl McIntosh, Steve Nichol   and Jane Eugene.
Brampton Music Ltd., England, 1986/MCA Music, 1986/Virgin Music, 1986.
Best-selling record in 1987 by Loose Ends, from the album *The Zagora* (MCA, 86).

Slow Hand
Music by Michael Clark, words by John Bettis.
Warner-Tamerlane Music, 1980/Flying Dutchman, 1980/WB Music, 1980.
Best-selling record by The Pointer Sisters from *Black & White* (Planet, 81).

Small Blue Thing
Words and music by Suzanne Vega.
Waifersongs, 1985.
Introduced by Suzanne Vega on the album *Suzanne Vega* (A & M, 85).

Small Craft Warnings
Words by Barry Harman, music by Keith Hermann.

WB Music, 1987/BHB Productions, 1987/Keith Hermann Music, 1987.
Introduced by Deborah Graham and Robert Hoshour in the 1988
  musical *Romance, Romance.*

Small Paradise
Words and music by John Cougar Mellencamp.
HG Music, Inc., 1979.
Best-selling record by John Cougar from *John Cougar* (Riva, 80).

Small Town
Words and music by John Cougar Mellencamp.
Full Keel Music, 1985.
Best-selling record in 1986 by John Cougar Mellencamp from the album
  Scarecrow (Riva, 85).

Small Town Boy (English)
Words and music by Jimmy Somerville, Larry Steinbachek, and Steve
  Bronski.
Bronski Music Ltd., England, 1984/William A. Bong Ltd., England,
  1984.
Best-selling record by Bronski Beat from the album *The Age of Consent*
  (MCA, 85).

Small Town Girl
Words and music by John Jarvis and Don Cook.
Tree Publishing Co., Inc., 1987/Cross Keys Publishing Co., Inc., 1987.
Best-selling record by Steve Wariner, from the album *It's a Crazy
  World* (MCA, 87).

Small Towns (Are Smaller for Girls)
Words and music by Mark Sanders, Alice Randall, and Verna
  Thompson.
Midsummer Music, 1987/AMR, 1987/EMI-April Music, 1987/Ides of
  March Music Division, 1987.
Introduced by Holly Dunn on the album *Cornerstone* (MTM, 87).

Smokey Mountain Rain
Words and music by Kye Fleming and Dennis Morgan.
Hall-Clement Publications, 1980.
Best-selling record by Ronnie Milsap from *Greatest Hits* (RCA, 80).

Smokin' in the Boy's Room
Words and music by Michael 'Cub' Koda and Michael Lutz.
Big Tree Enterprises Ltd., 1973.
Revived by Motley Crue on the album *Theatre of Pain* (Elektra, 85).

Smoking Gun
Words and music by D. Amy (pseudonym for Bruce Bromberg), Robert
  Cray, and Richard Cousins.

Calhoun Street, 1987/Bug Music, 1987/Robert Cray, 1987.
Best-selling record by Robert Cray, from the album *Strong Persuader* (Hightone/Mercury, 87); this was easily the bluesiest cut to enter the 1987 top forty.

Smooth Criminal
Words and music by Michael Jackson.
Mijac Music, 1987/Warner-Tamerlane Music, 1987.
Best-selling record in 1988 by Michael Jackson from *Bad* (Epic, 87).

Smooth Operator (English)
Words and music by Sade (pseudonym for Helen Folasade Adu) and St. John.
Sony Tunes, 1984.
Best-selling record by Sade from the album *Diamond Life* (Epic, 85).

Smooth Sailin' Tonight
Words and music by Angela Winbush.
Angel Notes Music, 1987/USA Exotica, 1987.
Best-selling record by The Isley Brothers, from the album *Smooth Sailin'* (Warner Bros., 87).

Smuggler's Blues
Words and music by Glenn Frey and Jack Tempchin.
Red Cloud Music Co., 1984/Night River Publishing, 1984.
Best-selling record by Glenn Frey from the album *The Allnighter* (MCA, 85). Featured on the television series *Miami Vice* in an episode inspired by and featuring Glenn Frey and his songs; also used on the album of music from the series.

Snap Your Fingers
Words and music by Grady Martin and Alex Zenetis.
Fred Rose Music, Inc., 1962.
Revived in 1987 by Ronnie Milsap on the album *Heart and Soul* (RCA, 87).

Sneaker Prison
Words and music by Shaun Benjamin.
Introduced in the 1989 musical *The Red Sneaks*.

So Alive (English)
Words by Daniel Ash, words and music by Love and Rockets.
Warner-Tamerlane Music, 1989.
Best-selling record by Love and Rockets from *Love and Rockets* (RCA, 89).

So Alone
Words and music by Lou Reed and Michael Fontara.

Metal Machine Music, 1980.
Introduced by Lou Reed in *Growing up in Public* (RCA, 80).

So Bad (English)
Words and music by Paul McCartney.
MPL Communications Inc., 1983.
Best-selling record by Paul McCartney from *Pipes of Peace* (Columbia, 84).

So Different Now
Words and music by Felix Cavaliere and Michael Mugrage.
Largo Music, Inc., 1987.
Introduced by Felix Cavaliere on the soundtrack of the film *Hiding Out* and its album (Virgin, 87). Cavaliere was the lead vocalist of the popular 1960's group the Rascals.

So Emotional
Words and music by Billy Steinberg and Tom Kelly.
Sony Tunes, 1987/Denise Barry Music.
Best-selling record by Whitney Houston, from her album *Whitney* (Arista, 87). One of 1987's hotter songwriting teams provided Houston with her sixth straight number-one song, equaling the record shared by the Beatles and the Bee Gees.

So Far So Good
Words and music by Tom Snow and Cynthia Weil.
Snow Music, 1986/Dyad Music, Ltd.
Introduced by Sheena Easton in the 1986 film *About Last Night* and on the subsequent soundtrack album (EMI-America, 86).

So Fine
Words and music by Johnny Otis.
Eldorado Music Co., 1955.
Revived by Howard Johnson from *Keepin' Love New* (A & M, 82).

So Good
Words and music by Peter Vale, Steven Waters, and Sue Shifrin.
Chappell & Co., Inc., 1988/Abacus Music/Intersong, USA Inc./Palancar Music.
Best-selling record in 1989 by Al Jarreau from *Heart's Horizon* (Reprise, 88).

So in Love (English)
Words and music by OMD, words and music by Steve Hague.
Virgin Music Ltd., 1985/Charisma Music Publishing Co., Ltd., 1985/ Unforgettable Songs, 1985/Unichappell Music Inc., 1985.

Introduced by Orchestral Manoeuvres in the Dark from the album *Crush* (A & M, 85).

So Long Ago
Words and music by Nanci Griffith.
Wing & Wheel Music, 1987.
Introduced by Nanci Griffith on *Little Love Affairs* (MCA, 88).

Sold Me Down the River (Irish)
Words and music by Eddie Macdonald and Mike Peters.
Illegal Songs, Inc., 1989.
Introduced by The Alarm on *Change* (IRS, 89).

Soldier of Love
Words and music by Cal Sturken and Evan Rogers.
Bayjun Beat, 1988/Music of the World.
Best-selling record by Donny Osmond from *Donny Osmond* (Capitol, 89).

Solid
Words and music by Nicholas Ashford and Valerie Simpson.
Nick-O-Val Music, 1984.
Best-selling record by Ashford and Simpson from *Solid* (Capitol, 84).

Solitaire (French-English)
English words by Diane Warren, French words and music by Martine Clemenceau.
BMG Songs Inc., 1982.
Best-selling record by Laura Branigan from *Branigan 2* (Atlantic, 83).

Solsbury Hill (German)
English words and music by Peter Gabriel.
Hit & Run Music, 1977.
Rhythm 'n' Blues Peter Gabriel on *Peter Gabriel/Plays Live* (Geffen, 83).

Some Fools Never Learn
Words and music by John Sherrill.
Sweet Baby Music, 1982.
Best-selling record by Steve Wariner from the album *One Good Night Deserves Another* (MCA, 85).

Some Guys Have All the Luck
Words and music by Jeff Fortgang.
Kirshner/April Music Publishing, 1973.
Best-selling record by Rod Stewart from *Camouflage* (Warner Brothers, 84).

Some Kind of Friend
Words by Adrienne Anderson, music by Barry Manilow.
Townsway Music, 1982/Angela Music, 1982.
Best-selling record by Barry Manilow from *Oh Julie!* (Arista, 83).

Some Kind of Lover
Words and music by Andre Cymone and Jody Watley.
Ultrawave, 1987/EMI-April Music, 1987/Intersong, USA Inc., 1987.
Best-selling record in 1988 by Jody Watley winner of a Grammy for
    Best New Artist, 1987, from *Jody Watley* (MCA, 87). Won a
    Grammy Award, and Best New Artist, 1988.

Some Like It Hot (English)
Words and music by Robert Palmer, Andy Taylor, and John Taylor.
BIOT Music Ltd., London, England, 1985/Tritec Music Ltd., England,
    1985/Bungalow Music, N.V., 1985/Ackee Music Inc., 1985.
Best-selling record by The Power Station from the album *The Power
    Station* (Capitol, 85).

Some Things Are Better Left Unsaid
Words and music by Daryl Hall.
Hot Cha Music Co., 1984/Unichappell Music Inc., 1984.
Best-selling record by Daryl Hall and John Oates in 1985 from the
    album *Big Bam Boom* (RCA, 84).

Somebody (Canadian)
Words and music by Bryan Adams and Jim Vallance.
Adams Communications, Inc., 1985/Calypso Toonz, 1985/Irving Music
    Inc., 1985.
Best-selling record by Bryan Adams from the album *Reckless* (A & M,
    85).

Somebody Else's Guy
Words and music by Jocelyn Brown and Annette Brown.
Jocelyn Brown's Music, 1980.
Best-selling record by Jocelyn Brown (Vinyl Dreams, 84).

Somebody Lied
Words and music by J. Chambers and L. Jenkins.
Galleon Music, Inc., 1987.
Best-selling record by Ricky Van Shelton, from the album *Wild Eyed
    Dream* (Columbia, 87).

Somebody Loves You
Words and music by Phil Keaggy.
Sebastian Music, 1988/Word Music.
Introduced by Phil Keaggy and Sunday's Child on *Phil Keaggy and
    Sunday's Child* (Myrrh, 88).

Somebody Should Leave
Words and music by Harlan Howard and Chick Rains.
Tree Publishing Co., Inc., 1984/Choskee Bottom Music, 1984/Cross
   Keys Publishing Co., Inc., 1984.
Best-selling record by Reba McEntire from the album *Have I Got a
   Deal for You* (MCA, 85).

Somebody's Baby
Words and music by Jackson Browne and Danny Kortchmar.
WB Music, 1982/WB Gold Music Corp., 1982/Night Kitchen Music,
   1982.
Best-selling record by Jackson Browne (Asylum, 82). Introduced in the
   film & soundtrack album *Fast Times at Ridgemont High* (82).

Somebody's Gonna Love You
Words and music by Don Cook and Rafe Van Hoy.
Cross Keys Publishing Co., Inc., 1982/Unichappell Music Inc., 1982/
   Van Hoy Music, 1982.
Best-selling record by Lee Greenwood from *Somebody's Gonna Love
   You* (MCA, 83).

Somebody's Knockin'
Words and music by Ed Penny and Jerry Gillespie.
Chiplin Music Co., 1980/Tri-Chappell Music Inc., 1980.
Best-selling record by Terri Gibbs from *Somebody's Knockin'* (MCA,
   81). Nominated for a Grammy Award, Country Song of the Year,
   1981.

Somebody's Needin' Somebody
Words and music by Len Chera.
Intersong, USA Inc., 1984/Ja-Len Music Co/Intersong USA, Inc., 1984.
Best-selling record by Conway Twitty (Warner Brothers, 84).

Somebody's Watching Me
Words and music by Rockwell.
Jobete Music Co., 1983.
Best-selling record by Rockwell from *Somebody's Watching Me*
   (Motown, 84).

Someday (Canadian)
Words and music by Glass Tiger, words and music by Jim Vallance.
Colgems-EMI Music, 1986/Tiger Shards/Irving Music Inc./Calypso
   Toonz.
Best-selling record by Glass Tiger from the album *Thin Red Line*
   (Manhattan, 86).

Someday
Words and music by Sammy Llanas and Kurt Neumann.
Lla-Mann, 1987/Intersong, USA Inc., 1987.

Introduced by The BoDeans on *Outside Looking In* (Slash, 87);
popularized in 1988.

Someday, Someway
Words and music by Marshall Crenshaw.
Belwin-Mills Publishing Corp., 1980/MHC Music, 1980.
Best-selling record by Robert Gordon from *Are You Gonna Be the One*
(RCA, 81).

Someday When Things Are Good
Words and music by Merle Haggard and Leona Williams.
Shade Tree Music Inc., 1984.
Best-selling record by Merle Haggard from *His Epic Hits - The First
Eleven - To be continued* (Epic, 84).

Someone Could Lose a Heart Tonight
Words and music by David Malloy, Eddie Rabbitt, and Even Stevens.
Briarpatch Music, 1981/Debdave Music Inc., 1981.
Best-selling record by Eddie Rabbitt from *Step by Step* (Elektra, 82).

Someplace Better Than This
Words and music by Steve Wynn.
Poison Brisket Music, 1988.
Introduced by Dream Syndicate on *Ghost Stories* (Enigma, 88).

Someplace Else
Words and music by George Harrison.
Ganga Publishing Co., 1986/Zero Productions, 1986.
Revived in 1987 by George Harrison on the album *Cloud Nine* (Dark
Horse, 87). Originally used in the Madonna film *Shanghai Surprise,*
which Harrison produced.

Someplace Where Love Can't Find Me
Words and music by John Hiatt.
Lillybilly, 1989/Bug Music.
Introduced by Marshall Crenshaw on *Good Evening* (Warner Bros., 89).

Something About You (English)
Words and music by Mark Lindup, Phil Gould, Boon Gould, Mark
King, and Wally Badarou.
Chappell & Co., Inc., 1986/Island Music.
Best-selling record in 1986 by Level 42 from the album *World Machine*
(Polygram, 85).

Something Happened
Words and music by Lou Reed.
Metal Machine Music, 1988.

Introduced by Lou Reed in the film and on the soundtrack album
Permanent Record (Epic, 88).

Something in My Heart
Words and music by Wayland Patton.
Polygram International, 1984.
Best-selling record by Ricky Skaggs from the album *Country Boy* (Epic,
85).

Something in the Way (You Make Me Feel)
Words and music by Angela Winbush.
Angel Notes Music, 1989/WB Music.
Best-selling record by Stephanie Mills from *Home* (MCA, 89).

Something in Your Eyes
Words and music by Richard Carpenter and Pamela Phillips Oland.
Almo Music Corp., 1987/Hammer & Nails Music, 1987/Irving Music
Inc., 1987/Pamalybo, 1987.
Introduced by Richard Carpenter and Dusty Springfield on the album
Time (A & M, 87). The album marked Carpenter's first work since
the death of his sister Karen, and provided one of two comeback
showcases for classic British singer Springfield.

Something Just Ain't Right
Words and music by Keith Sweat and Teddy Riley.
WB Music, 1987/E/A Music, 1987/Vintertainment, 1987/Donril, 1987/
Zomba Music, 1987.
Best-selling record in 1988 by Keith Sweat, from *Make It Last Forever*
(Vintertainment, 88).

Something New
Words and music by Pat DiNizio.
Famous Monsters Music, 1987/Colgems-EMI Music, 1987.
Introduced by The Smithereens on *Green Thoughts* (Enigma, 88). The
title is taken from a Beatles album.

Something of a Dreamer
Words and music by Mary Chapin Carpenter.
Getarealjob Music, 1988/EMI-April Music, 1988.
Introduced by Mary Chapin Carpenter on *State of the Heart* (Columbia,
89).

Something Real
Words and music by Phoebe Snow.
EMI-April Music, 1988/Phoebe Snow Music.
Introduced by Phoebe Snow on *Something Real* (Elektra, 89).

Something So Strong (Australian)
Words and music by Neil Finn and Mitchell Froom.

Roundhead, 1986/Wyoming Flesh, 1986.
Best-selling record in 1987 by Crowded House, from the album *Crowded House* (Chrysalis, 86).

Something to Grab For
Words and music by Ric Ocasek.
Lido Music Inc., 1982.
Best-selling record by Ric Ocasek from *Beatitude* (Warner Brothers, 83).

Something's on Your Mind
Words and music by Hubert Eaves, III and James Williams.
Trumar Music, 1983/Huemar Music, 1983/Diesel Music, 1983.
Best-selling record by D Train featured on *The Best of 'D' Train* (Prelude, 86) (Prelude, 84).

Sometime Other Than Now
Words and music by John Hiatt.
Lillybilly, 1988/Bug Music, 1988.
Introduced by John Hiatt on *Slow Turning* (A & M, 88).

Sometimes a Lady
Words and music by Eddy Raven and Frank Myers.
Ravensong Music, 1986/Michael H. Goldsen, Inc./Collins Court Music.
Best-selling record by Eddy Raven from the album *Love and Other Hard Times* (RCA, 86).

Somewhere down the Crazy River
Words and music by Robbie Robertson.
Medicine Hat Music, 1987.
Introduced by Robbie Robertson on the album *Robbie Robertson* (Geffen, 87). In this dramatic scenerio, complete with monologue, the former member of the Band distills the essence of that group.

Somewhere Down the Line
Words and music by Lewis Anderson and Casey Kelly.
Old Friends Music, 1983/Golden Bridge Music, 1983.
Best-selling record by T.G. Sheppard (Warner/Curb, 84).

Somewhere down the Road
Words and music by Cynthia Weil, music by Tom Snow.
ATV Music Corp., 1981/Mann & Weil Songs Inc., 1981/Snow Music, 1981.
Best-selling record by Barry Manilow from *If I Should Love Again* (Arista, 81).

Somewhere I Belong
Words by Dean Pitchford, music by Marvin Hamlisch.

Famous Music Corp., 1985/Ensign Music, 1985.
Introduced by Teddy Pendergrass in the film *Daryl* (85).

Somewhere in the Night
Words and music by Bill Chinnock.
Fountain Square Music Publishing Co. Inc, 1986.
Introduced by Bill Chinnock on the television soap opera *Search for Tomorrow* in 1986. The show won a daytime Emmy for outstanding music direction and composition. Featured on the album *Learning to Survive the Modern Age* (CBS Associated).

Somewhere Out There
Words and music by James Horner, Barry Mann, and Cynthia Weil.
MCA, Inc., 1986/Music of the World.
Best-selling record by Linda Ronstadt and James Ingram. Versions by these two pop stars and by Phillip Glasser and Betsy Cathcart were both featured on the soundtrack of the 1986 animated film *An American Tail* and on its subsequent album. Nominated for an Academy Award, Song of the Year, 1986.

Somewhere That's Green
Words by Howard Ashman, music by Alan Menken.
WB Music, 1982/Geffen Music/Trunksong Music.
Revived in 1986 by Ellen Greene in the film and on the soundtrack album of the musical *Little Shop of Horrors* (86). Green reprised her role as the female lead from the original Off Broadway production of the show.

Somewhere Tonight
Words and music by Harlan Howard and Rodney Crowell.
Tree Publishing Co., Inc., 1987/Granite Music Corp./Coolwell Music.
Best-selling record by Highway 101, from the album *Highway 101* (Warner Bros., 87).

Song for a Future Generation
Words and music by Frederick Schneider, Cynthia Wilson, Ricky Wilson, Catherine Pierson, and Julie Strickland.
Island Music, 1983.
Introduced on *Whammy* by The B-52's (Warner Brothers, 83).

Song for the Dreamers
Words and music by Dan Stuart and Steve Wynn.
Poison Brisket Music, 1985/Hang Dog Music, 1985.
Introduced by Danny and Dusty on the album *The Lost Weekend* (A & M, 85).

Song of the South
Words and music by Bob McDill.
Polygram International, 1989.
Best-selling record by Alabama from *Southern Star* (RCA, 89).

Song on the Sand
Words and music by Jerry Herman.
Jerryco Music Co., 1983.
Introduced by Gene Barry in *La Cage Au Folles* (83).

Songbird
Music by Kenny Gorlich.
Brenee, 1987.
Best-selling record by Kenny G., from the album *Duotones* (Arista, 87).
  This was the year's top instrumental.

Sorry Naomi
Words and music by Dan Stuart, Chris Cavacas, and Jack Waterson.
Dick James Music Inc., 1987.
Introduced by Green on Red on the album *The Killer Inside* (Mercury,
  87). This song answers Naomi Judd of the country group the Judds,
  who made the song request 'Grandpa (Tell Me About the Good Old
  Days).'

Sorry Somehow
Words and music by Grant Hart.
Husker Music, 1986.
Introduced by Husker Du on the album *Candy Apple Grey* (Warner
  Bros., 86).

Soul Corruption (English)
Words and music by Graham Parker.
Geep Music Ltd., England.
Performed by Graham Parker on *Live Alive in America* (RCA, 89).

Soul Kiss
Words and music by Mark Goldenberg.
Music of the World, 1985.
Best-selling record by Olivia Newton-John from the album *Soul Kiss*
  (MCA, 85).

Soul Man
Words and music by Isaac Hayes and David Porter.
Almo/Irving Music, 1967/Walden Music, Inc., 1967.
Revived in 1986 by Sam Moore and Lou Reed in the film *Soul Man*
  and on the soundtrack album (A & M).

Soul Provider
Words and music by Michael Bolton and Andy Goldmark.

Mr. Bolton's Music, 1989/Nonpariel Music.
Best-selling record by Michael Bolton from *Soul Provider* (Columbia, 89).

Souls (Australian)
Words and music by Rick Springfield.
Vogue Music, 1983.
Best-selling record by Rick Springfield from *Living in Oz* (RCA, 83).

The Sound of Goodbye
Words and music by Hugh Prestwood.
Parquet Music, 1983/Lawyer's Daughter, 1983.
Best-selling record by Crystal Gayle from *Cage the Songbird* (Warner Brothers, 84).

Soup for One
Words and music by Bernard Edwards and Nile Rodgers.
Warner-Tamerlane Music, 1982.
Best-selling record by Chic (Mirage, 82). Introduced in the film *Soup for One* (82).

South Central Rain (I'm Sorry)
Words and music by Mike Mills, Bill Berry, Peter Buck, and Michael Stipe.
Unichappell Music Inc., 1984.
Best-selling record by R.E.M. from *Reckoning* (I.R.S., 84).

South to a Warmer Place
Words by Loonis Reeves McGlohon, music by Alec Wilder.
Ludlow Music Inc., 1980/Saloon Songs, Inc., 1980.
Introduced by by Frank Sinatra on *She Shot Me Down* (Reprise, 81).

Southern Cross
Words and music by Stephen Stills, Richard Curtis, and Michael Curtis.
Kenwon Music, 1974/Catpatch Music/Gold Hill Music, Inc.
Best-selling record by Crosby, Stills and Nash from *Daylight Again* (Atlantic, 82).

Southern Rains
Words and music by Roger Murrah.
Magic Castle Music, Inc., 1980/EMI-Blackwood Music Inc., 1980.
Best-selling record by Mel Tillis (Elektra, 81).

Sowing the Seeds of Love (English)
Words and music by Roland Orzabal and Curt Smith.
Virgin Music, 1989.
Best-selling record by Tears for Fears from *The Seeds of Love* (Fontana, 89).

Spaceballs
Words and music by Jeffrey Pescetto, Clyde Lieberman, and Mel
    Brooks.
Colgems-EMI Music, 1987/United Lion Music Inc.
Introduced by The Spinners on the soundtrack of the film *Spaceballs*
    and its album (Atlantic, 87).

Spanish Eddie, see The Night Spanish Eddie Cashed It In.

Spanish Johnny
Words and music by Paul Siebel.
Sweet Jelly Roll Music, Inc., 1978.
Featured on *Evangeline* by Emmylou Harris (Warner Brothers, 81).

Spare Parts
Words and music by Bruce Springsteen.
Bruce Springsteen Publishing, 1987.
Introduced by Bruce Springsteen on the album *Tunnel of Love*
    (Columbia, 87).

Special Lady
Dark Cloud Music, 1979.
Best-selling record by Ray, Goodman, & Brown from *Ray, Goodman &
    Brown* (Polydor, 80).

Speed of the Sound of Loneliness
Words and music by John Prine.
Big Ears Music Inc., 1986/Bruised Oranges, 1986.
Introduced by Kim Carnes, on the album *View from the House* (MCA,
    88).

Spend the Night (Ce Soir)
Words and music by Angela Winbush.
Angel Notes Music, 1989/WB Music.
Best-selling record by The Isley Brothers from *Spend the Night* (Warner
    Bros., 89).

Spies Like Us
Words and music by Paul McCartney.
MPL Communications Inc., 1986.
Best-selling record Paul McCartney on the soundtrack of the 1986 film
    of the same title. Also used on the soundtrack album (Capitol, 86),
    the song was a best-seller for McCartney, marking twenty years--out
    of twenty-three--in which the songwriter hit the Top Ten. He missed
    in 1972, 1981, and 1985.

The Spirit of Radio (Canadian)
Words by Neil Peart, music by Geddy Lee and Alex Lifeson.

Core Music Publishing, 1980.
Best-selling record by Rush from *Permanent Waves* (Mercury, 80).

Spirit of the Forest
Words and music by Kenny Young.
E.L.F., 1989.
Introduced by Mark Knopfler, Bruce Cockburn, Tina Turner, Bonnie
   Raitt, and Pink Floyd to promote Operation Greenpeace, an
   organization devoted to preserving the world's forests.

Spirits in the Material World (English)
Words and music by Sting (pseudonym for Gordon Sumner).
Virgin Music, 1981.
Best-selling record by The Police from *Ghost in the Machine* (A & M,
   82).

Spy in the House of Love
Words and music by Don Was (pseudonym for Donald Fagenson) and
   Dave Was (pseudonym for David Weiss).
MCA Music, 1988/Semper Fi Music, 1988/Monkeys, Dogs, Cattle, Ltd.,
   1988.
Best-selling record by Was (Not Was), from *What Up, Dog?* (Chyrsalis,
   88). The title is taken from a novel by Anais Nin.

Square Biz
Words and music by Teena Marie (pseudonym for Teena Marie
   Brockert) and Allen McGrier.
Jobete Music Co., 1981/McNella Music, 1981.
Best-selling record Teena Marie from *It Must Be Magic* (Gordy, 81).

Square Pegs
Words and music by Christopher Butler, Daniel Klayman, Marc
   Williams, Tracy Wormworth, Patty Donahue, and William Ficca.
Belfast Music, 1982.
Featured in *I Could Rule the World If I Could Only Get the Parts* by
   The Waitresses (Polydor, 83). Introduced on the TV series *Square
   Pegs* (83).

Stainsby Girls (English)
Words and music by Chris Rea.
Magnet Music Ltd., England, 1988/Intersong, USA Inc.
Introduced by Chris Rea on *New Light through Old Windows* (EMI, 89).

Stand
Words and music by Bill Berry, Peter Buck, Mike Mills, and Michael
   Stipe.
Night Garden Music, 1988/Unichappell Music Inc.
Best-selling record in 1989 by R.E.M. from *Green* (Warner Bros., 88).

Stand Back
Words and music by Stephanie Nicks and Prince Rogers Nelson.
Welsh Witch Publishing, 1983/Controversy Music, 1983.
Best-selling record by Stevie Nicks from *The Wild Heart* (Modern, 83).

Stand by Me
Words and music by Jerry Leiber, Mike Stoller, and Ben E. King.
Unichappell Music Inc., 1961/A.D.T. Enterprises, Inc., 1961/Trio Music
   Co., Inc.
Revived by Mickey Gilley (Full Moon, 80).   **Revived by** Ben E.
   King in the film and soundtrack of *Stand by Me* (Atlantic, 86). Best-
   selling record by Ben E. King from *The Best of Ben E. King
   (Atlantic, 86)*.

Stand or Fall (English)
Words and music by Peter Greenall, Adam Woods, Cy Curnin, Charles
   Barrett, and Jamie West-Oram.
Colgems-EMI Music, 1981.
Best-selling record by The Fixx from *Shuttered Rooms* (MCA, 82).

Standing on the Top
Words and music by Rick James.
Stone City Music, 1982.
Best-selling record by The Temptations Featuring Rick James from
   Reunion (Gordy, 82).

A Star Is Born
Words by Barry Harmon, music by Grant Sturiale.
Chappell & Co., Inc., 1986.
Performed in the Off Broadway musical *Olympus on My Mind*, 1986.

Starlight Express (English)
Music by Andrew Lloyd Webber, words by Richard Stilgoe.
Really Useful Music, 1987.
Introduced by Greg Mowry in the 1987 Broadway production of
   Starlight Express, but was included in the earlier production in
   England. Also performed by El DeBarge on the album *Music and
   Songs from 'Starlight Express'* (MCA, 87).

Stars
Words and music by Ronnie Dio, Vivian Campbell, and Jimmy Bain.
Niji Music, 1985.
Introduced by Hear 'n' Aid from the album *Hear 'n' Aid* (Mercury, 86).
   The heavy metal contribution to the famine relief effort, this album
   featured an extended guitar break by a host of the genre's stars.

Stars on 45
Best-selling record by Stars on 45 (Radio Records, 81). Record is a
   medley of 'Venus,' 'Sugar Sugar,' 'No Reply,' 'I'll Be Back,' 'Drive

My Car,' 'Do You Want to Know a Secret,' 'We Can Work It Out,'
'I Should Have Known Better,' 'Nowhere Man,' and 'You're Gonna
Lose That Girl.'

Start Me Up (English)
Words and music by Mick Jagger and Keith Richards.
Screen Gems-EMI Music Inc., 1981.
Best-selling record by The Rolling Stones from *Tattoo You*
   (Rolling Stones, 81).

Start of a Romance
Words and music by Tommy McConnell and Joe Williams.
Alligator Music, 1989.
Best-selling record by Skyy from *Start of a Romance* (Atlantic, 89).

(Just Like) Starting Over
Words and music by John Lennon.
Lenono Music, 1980.
Best-selling record by John Lennon from *Double Fantasy* (Geffen, 80).

Starting over Again
Words and music by Donna Summer and Bruce Sudano.
Rick's Music Inc., 1979/Earbourne Music, 1979/Sweet Summer Night
   Music, 1979.
Best-selling record by Dolly Parton from *Dolly Dolly Dolly* (RCA, 80).

State of Shock
Words and music by Michael Jackson and Randy Hansen.
Mijac Music, 1984/Warner-Tamerlane Music, 1984.
Best-selling record by Michael Jackson and Mick Jagger from The
   Jacksons' *Victory* (Epic, 84).

Stay the Night
Words and music by Peter Cetera and David Foster.
BMG Songs Inc., 1984/Foster Frees Music Inc., 1984.
Best-selling record by Chicago from *Chicago 17* (Full Moon, 84).

Stay with Me Tonight
Words and music by Raymond Jones.
Zubaida Music, 1983/BMG Music, 1983.
Best-selling record by Jeffrey Osborne from *Stay with Me Tonight* (A &
   M, 83).

Stay Young (English)
Words and music by Benny Gallagher and Graham Lyle.
Irving Music Inc., 1976.
Best-selling record by Don Williams (MCA, 84).

Steady
Words and music by Jules Shear and Cyndi Lauper.
Funzalo Music/Rella Music Corp., 1983.
Introduced by by Jules Shear on the album *The Eternal Return* (EMI-America, 85).

Steal Away
Words by Robbie Dupuis, music by Rick Chudacoff.
Big Ears Music Inc., 1979/Chrome Willie Music, 1979/Gouda Music, 1979/Grandma Annie Music, 1979.
Best-selling record by Robbie Dupree from *Robbie Dupree* (Elektra, 80).

Steel River (English)
Words and music by Chris Rea.
Magnet Music Ltd., England, 1988/Intersong, USA Inc.
Introduced by Chris Rea on *New Light through Old Windows* (EMI, 89).

Step by Step
Words and music by Eddie Rabbitt, Even Stevens, and David Malloy.
Briarpatch Music, 1981/Debdave Music Inc., 1981.
Best-selling record by Eddie Rabbitt from *Step by Step* (Elektra, 81).

Step That Step
Words and music by Mark Miller.
G.I.D. Music, 1983.
Best-selling record by Sawyer Brown from the album *Sawyer Brown* (Capitol, 85).

Steppin' Out (English)
Words and music by Joe Jackson.
Almo Music Corp., 1982.
Best-selling record by Joe Jackson from *Night and Day* (A & M, 82). Nominated for a Grammy Award, Record of the Year, 1982.

Sticky Wicked
Words and music by Prince Rogers Nelson.
Controversy Music, 1988.
Introduced by Chaka Khan on *C.K.* (Warner Bros., 88). This rap song features a solo by the famous jazz trumpeter Miles Davis.

Still a Thrill
Words and music by Andre Cymone and Jody Watley.
Ultrawave, 1987/EMI-April Music, 1987/Rightsong Music, 1987.
Best-selling record by Jody Watley, from the album *Jody Watley* (MCA, 87).

Still in Saigon
Words and music by Dan Daley.
Dreena Music, 1981/Dan Daley Music, 1981.

Best-selling record by The Charlie Daniels Band from *Windows* (Epic, 82).

Still Losing You
Words and music by Mike Reid.
BMG Songs Inc., 1984.
Best-selling record by Ronnie Milsap from *One More Try for Love* (RCA, 84).

Still of the Night (English)
Words and music by David Coverdale and John Sykes.
WB Music, 1987.
Best-selling record by Whitesnake, from the album *Whitesnake* (Geffen, 87), this number recalls the heyday of Led Zeppelin.

Still Such a Thing
Words and music by Nick Ashford and Valerie Simpson.
Nick-O-Val Music, 1980.
Introduced on *High-Rise* by Ashford and Simpson (Capitol, 83).

Still Taking Chances
Words and music by Michael Murphy.
Timberwolf Music, 1982.
Best-selling record by Michael Murphy from *Michael Martin Murphey* (Liberty, 83).

Still They Ride
Words and music by Steve Perry, Neal Schon, and Jonathan Cain.
Weed High Nightmare Music, 1981.
Best-selling record by Journey from *Escape* (Columbia, 82).

Still Waiting
Words and music by Prince Rogers Nelson.
Controversy Music, 1987.
Introduced by Rainy Davis on the album *Sweetheart* (Columbia, 87).

Still within the Sound of My Voice
Words and music by Jimmy Webb.
White Oak Songs, 1986.
Performed by Linda Ronstadt on *Cry Like a Rainstorm, Howl Like the Wind* (Elektra, 89).

Stir It Up
Words and music by Allee Willis and Michael Sembello.
Unicity Music, Inc., 1984/Off Backstreet Music, 1984.
Introduced by Patti LaBelle in the film *Beverly Hills Cop* (85); used on its soundtrack album.

Stomp (American-English)
Words and music by Louis Johnson, George Johnson, Valerie Johnson, and Rod Temperton.
State of the Arts Music, 1980/Brojay Music, 1980/Kidada Music Inc., 1980.
Best-selling record by The Brothers Johnson from *Light up the Night* (A & M, 80).

Stone Cold (English)
Words and music by Ritchie Blackmore, Roger Glover, and Joe Lynn Turner.
Thames Talent Publishing, Ltd., 1981/Lyon Farm Music Ltd., 1981.
Best-selling record by Rainbow from *Straight Between the Eyes* (Mercury, 82).

Stone Love
Words and music by Charles Smith and James Taylor, words and music by Kool and the Gang.
Delightful Music Ltd., 1986.
Best-selling record in 1987 by Kool and the Gang, from the album *Forever* (Mercury, 86).

Stood Up
Words and music by John Hiatt.
Lillybilly, 1987.
Introduced by John Hiatt on the album *Bring the Family* (A & M, 87).

Stop Doggin' Me Around, also known as **Doggin' Around**
Words and music by Lena Agree.
Lena Music, Inc., 1960.
Revived by Klique on *Try It Out* (MCA, 83). Originally a hit for Jackie Wilson.

Stop Draggin' My Heart Around
Words and music by Tom Petty and Mike Campbell.
Gone Gator Music, 1981/Wild Gator Music, 1981.
Best-selling record by Stevie Nicks with Tom Petty & The Heartbreakers from *Bella Donna* (Modern, 81).

Stop the Violence
Words and music by Lawrence Parker.
Zomba Music, 1988.
Introduced by Boggie Down Productions, from *By All Means Necessary* (Jive, 88). This rap song addressed the growing violence at concerts for such music, and paved the way for efforts to curb it.

Stop to Love
Words and music by Luther Vandross and Nat Adderly, Jr.
EMI-April Music, 1987/Uncle Ronnie's Music, 1987/Dillard, 1987.

Best-selling record in 1987 by Luther Vandross from the album *Give Me the Reason* (Epic, 86).

Stop Your Sobbing (English)
Words and music by Ray Davies.
Jay-Boy Music Corp., 1964.
Best-selling record by The Pretenders from *The Pretenders* (Sire, 80).

The Story Goes On
Words by Richard Maltby, music by David Shire.
Fiddleback, 1984/Long Pond Music, 1984/Progeny Music, 1984/
    Revelation Music Publishing Corp., 1984.
Introduced by Liz Callaway in *Baby* (83).

Storybook Love
Words and music by Willy DeVille.
Crosstown, 1987.
Introduced by Willy DeVille on the soundtrack of the film *The Princess Bride* and on its album (Warner Bros., 87). Nominated for an Academy Award, Best Original Song, 1987.

Straight from the Heart (Canadian)
Words and music by Bryan Adams and Eric Kagna.
Irving Music Inc., 1980/Adams Communications, Inc., 1980.
Best-selling record by Bryan Adams from *Cuts Like a Knife* (A & M, 83).

Straight to the Heart (English)
Words and music by Graham Lyle and Terry Britten.
Irving Music Inc., 1986/Chappell & Co., Inc., 1986.
Best-selling record in 1987 by Crystal Gayle, from the album *Straight to the Heart* (Warner Bros., 86).

Straight Up
Words and music by Elliott Wolf.
Virgin Music, 1988/Elliott Wolff Music.
Best-selling record in 1989 by Paula Abdul from *Forever Your Girl* (Virgin, 88).

Strange Weather
Words and music by Tom Waits and Kathleen Brennan.
Jalma Music, 1987.
Introduced by Marianne Faithfull on the album *Strange Weather* (Island, 87). This cut offered one of 1987's more perfect marriages of writer and song, with Waits and Faithfull a couple of rare birds of the same ruffled feather.

Stranger in My House
Words and music by Mike Reid.

BMG Songs Inc., 1983.
Best-selling record by Ronnie Milsap from *Keyed Up* (RCA, 83). Won a
Grammy Award, and Country Song of the Year, 1983.

Stranger in the House (English)
Words and music by Elvis Costello.
Plangent Visions Music, Inc., London, England, 1980.
Introduced by Elvis Costello in *Get Happy* (Columbia, 80).

Stray Cat Strut
Words and music by Brian Setzer.
Zomba Music, 1981.
Best-selling record The Stray Cats from *Built for Speed* (EMI-America,
83).

Street Corner
Words and music by Nick Ashford and Valerie Simpson.
Nick-O-Val Music, 1982.
Best-selling record by Ashford and Simpson from *Street Opera* (Capitol,
82).

Street Rock
Words and music by Kurtis Blow, Bill Black, and Tashim.
Kuwa Music, 1986.
Introduced by Kurtis Blow and Bob Dylan on the album *Kingdom Blow*
(Polygram, 86). The performance was noteworthy in pairing Dylan,
who had perfected 'talking blues' in the sixties, with the king of rap
music, the eighties' version of that genre.

Streets of Bakersfield
Words and music by Homer Joy.
Sony Tree Publishing, 1988.
Old and new country traditions united in the duet by Dwight Yoakman
and Buck Owens, from *Buenas Noches from a Lonely Room* (Warner
Bros., 88).

The Stroke
Words and music by Billy Squier.
Songs of the Knight, 1981.
Best-selling record by Billy Squier from *Don't Say No* (Capital, 81).

Stroker's Theme
Words and music by Charlie Daniels.
Music of the World, 1983.
Best-selling record by The Charlie Daniels Band (Epic, 83). Introduced
in the film *Stroker Ace* (83).

Strong Enough to Bend
Words and music by Beth Neilsen-Chapman and Don Schlitz.

Uncle Artie, 1988/Don Schlitz Music, 1988.
Best-selling record by Tanya Tucker, from *Strong Enough to Bend*
  (Capitol, 88).

Strong Heart
Words and music by Tommy Rocco, Charlie Black, and Austin Roberts.
Chappell & Co., Inc., 1986/MCA, Inc./Chriswald Music/Hopi Sound
  Music/Bibo Music Publishers.
Best-selling record by T. G. Sheppard from the album *It Still Rains in
  Memphis* (Columbia, 86).

Strung Out
Words and music by Paul Laurence.
Bush Burnin' Music, 1986.
Introduced by Paul Laurence (Capitol, 86). The lyrics deal with the evils
  of free-basing cocaine.

Strut (English)
Words and music by Charlene Dore and Julian Littman.
Polygram International, 1983.
Best-selling record by Sheena Easton from *A Private Heaven* (EMI-
  America, 84).

Stuck on You
Words and music by Lionel Richie, Jr.
Brockman Enterprises Inc., 1983.
Best-selling record by Lionel Richie from *Can't Slow Down* (Motown,
  84).

Stuck with You
Words and music by Chris Hayes and Huey Lewis.
Hulex Music, 1986.
Best-selling record by Huey Lewis & The News from the album *Fore!*
  (Chrysalis, 86).

The Stuff That Dreams Are Made Of
Words and music by Carly Simon.
C'est Music, 1987.
Introduced by Carly Simon on the album *Coming Around Again* (Arista,
  86).

Style, see Peter Gunn Theme.

Subcity
Words and music by Tracy Chapman.
Purple Rabbit Music, 1989/EMI-April Music.
Introduced by Tracy Chapman on *Crossroads* (Elektra, 89).

423

Suddenly
Words and music by John Farrar.
John Farrar Music, 1980.
Best-selling record by Olivia Newton-John from the film and soundtrack
    album *Xanadu* (MCA, 80).

Suddenly
Words and music by Keith Diamond and Billy Ocean.
Zomba Music, 1984/Willesden Music, Inc., 1984.
Best-selling record by Billy Ocean in 1985 from the album *Suddenly*
    (Arista, 84).

Suddenly Last Summer
Words and music by Martha Davis.
Clean Sheets Music, 1983.
Best-selling record by The Motels from *Little Robbers* (Capitol, 83).

Suddenly Seymour
Words by Howard Ashman, music by Alan Menken.
WB Music, 1982.
Introduced by Ellen Greene and Lee Wilkof in *Little Shop of Horrors*
    (82).

Sue Lee
Words and music by Willie Nile and Rick Chertoff.
River House, 1986/Hobbler Music, 1986.
Introduced by Patty Smyth on the album *Never Enough* (Columbia, 87).

Suedehead (English)
Words and music by Morrissey, words and music by Stephen Street.
Linder Ltd., 1988/Warner-Tamerlane Music, 1988/Copyright Control,
    1988.
Introduced by Morrissey on *Viva Hate* (Sire, 88).

Sugar Daddy
Words and music by David Bellamy.
Famous Music Corp., 1980/Bellamy Brothers Music, 1980.
Best-selling record by The Bellamy Brothers (Warner Brothers, 80).

Sugar Walls
Words and music by Alexander Nevermind (pseudonym for Prince).
Tionna Music, 1984.
Best-selling record by Sheena Easton in 1985 from the album *A Private
    Heaven* (EMI-America, 84).

Sukiyaki
Words and music by Tom Leslie, Buzz Cason, and Hachidai Nakamura.
Toshiba Music Publishing Co., Ltd., Tokyo, Japan, 1963/Beechwood

Music, 1963.
Revived by A Taste of Honey from *Twice as Sweet* (Capitol, 81).

Summer of Love
Words and music by Marty Balin.
Great Pyramid Music, 1989.
Introduced by Jefferson Airplane on *Jefferson Airplane* (Epic, 89), a
   celebration of their heyday by the reunited group.

Summer of '69 (Canadian)
Words and music by Bryan Adams and Jim Vallance.
Adams Communications, Inc., 1984/Calypso Toonz, 1984/Irving Music
   Inc., 1984.
Best-selling record by Bryan Adams from the album *Reckless* (A & M,
   85).

Summer Wages (Canadian)
Words and music by Ian Tyson.
WB Music, 1987.
Introduced by Ian Tyson on the album *Cowboyography* (Sugar Hill, 87).

Summer Wind
Words and music by Chris Hillman and Steve Hill.
Bar-None Music, 1987/Bug Music, 1987.
Best-selling record by The Desert Rose Band from *Running* (MCA/
   Curb, 88).

Summerfly
Words and music by Cheryl Wheeler.
Cheryl Wheeler Music, 1987/Blue Gate Music/Bug Music.
Introduced by Maura O'Connell on *Helpless Heart* (Warner Bros., 89).

Summer's Cauldron (English)
Words and music by Andy Partridge.
EMI-Virgin, 1986/Virgin Music Ltd., 1986.
Introduced by XTC on the album *Skylarking* (Geffen, 87).

The Sun Always Shines on T.V. (Norwegian)
English words and music by Pal Waaktaar.
ATV Music Corp., 1985.
Best-selling record by A-Ha in 1986 from the album *Hunting High and
   Low* (Warner Bros., 85).

Sun City
Words and music by Steve Van Zandt.
Solidarity, 1985.
Best-selling record by Artists United Against Apartheid from the album
   Sun City (Capitol, 85) which featured an all-star group of urban, rap,
   street, and pop musicians, and jazz great Miles Davis. This song calls

upon musicians of all types to avoid performing in Sun City, a resort community frequented by whites from South Africa, in order to protest that country's policy of racial separation.

Sunday
Words and music by Stephen Sondheim.
WB Music, 1981.
Introduced by Company of *Sunday in the Park with George* (84).

Sunday in the South
Words and music by Jay Booker.
Screen Gems-EMI Music Inc., 1986.
Best-selling record by Shenandoah from *The Road Not Taken* (Columbia, 89).

Sunglasses at Night (Canadian)
Words and music by Corey Hart.
Liesse Publishing, 1983.
Best-selling record by Corey Hart from *First Offense* (EMI-America, 84).

Sunset Grill
Words and music by Don Henley, Dan Kortchmar, and Benmont Tench.
Cass County Music Co., 1984/Woody Creek Music, 1984.
Introduced by Don Henley on the album *Building the Perfect Beast* (Geffen, 85).

Super Bowl Shuffle
Words and music by Bobby Daniels, Lloyd Barry, Richard Meyer, and Melvin Owens.
Red Label, 1985.
Best-selling record by the Chicago Bears Shufflin Crew (Red Label, 86), exploiting their victory in Super Bowl XX.

Superbad
Words and music by Christopher Jasper.
Jasper Stone, 1988.
Best-selling record by Chris Jasper from *Superbad* (CBS-Associated, 88).

Superhero Girl
Words and music by Barry Keating.
Introduced by Liz Larsen in the musical fantasy *Starmites*, which ran briefly on Broadway in 1989.

Superman
Words and music by Gary Zekley and Mitch Bottler.
Teenie Bopper Music Publishers, 1968.

Best-selling record by R.E.M. from the album *Life's Rich Pageant*
(I.R.S., 86). Introduced by The Clique in 1968.

Superwoman
Words and music by L. A. Reid (pseudonym for Antonio Reid),
   Babyface (pseudonym for Kenny Edmunds), and Daryl Simmons.
Green Skirt Music, 1988/Kear Music/Hip-Trip Music Co.
Best-selling record in 1989 by Karyn White from *Karyn White* (Warner
   Bros., 88), this song became the number one rhythm and blues record
   of the year. Nominated for a Grammy Award, Rhythm 'n' Blues Song
   of the Year, 1989.

Surfin' Bird
Words and music by Al Frazier, Carl White, John Earl Harris, and
   Turner Wilson.
Beechwood Music, 1964.
Revived in 1987 by Pee Wee Herman in the movie and on the
   soundtrack album *Back to the Beach* (Columbia, 87).

Surprise Surprise
Words by Edward Kleban, music by Marvin Hamlisch.
Wren Music Co., Inc., 1985/American Compass Music Corp., 1985.
Introduced by Greg Burge in the film and soundtrack album *A Chorus
   Line* (Casablanca, 85). This song was added to the score of the film
   version of the hit Broadway play. Nominated for an Academy Award,
   Song of the Year, 1985.

Surrender to Me
Words and music by Ross Vannelli and Richard Marx.
Rockwood Music, 1988/Security Hogg Music/United Artists Music Co.,
   Inc./EMI-April Music/United Lion Music Inc./EMI-Blackwood Music
   Inc.
Best-selling record by Ann Wilson and Robin Zander from the film
   Tequila Sunrise (soundtrack album, Capitol, 89).

Surround Me with Love
Words and music by Wayland Hollyfield and Norris Wilson.
Polygram International, 1981/EMI Music Publishing, 1981.
Best-selling record by Charly McClain (Epic, 81).

Sussudio (English)
Words and music by Phil Collins.
Hit & Run Music, 1985.
Best-selling record by Phil Collins from the album *No Jacket Required*
   (Atlantic, 85).

Suzanne
Words and music by Steve Perry and Jonathan Cain.
Street Talk Tunes, 1986/Frisco Kid Music/Colgems-EMI Music.

Best-selling record by Journey from the album *Raised on Radio*
(Columbia, 86).

Sweet Baby
Words and music by George Duke.
Mycenae Music Publishing Co., 1981.
Best-selling record by Stanley Clarke and George Duke from *The
Clarke/Duke Project* (Epic, 81).

Sweet Child O' Mine
Words and music by Guns N' Roses.
Guns N' Roses Music, 1987.
Best-selling record in 1988 by Guns N' Roses, from *Appetite for
Destruction* (Geffen, 87).

Sweet Dreams (Australian)
Words and music by Graham Russell.
Careers Music Inc., 1981/Nottsongs, 1981.
Best-selling record by Air Supply from *The One That You Love* (Arista,
82).

Sweet Dreams (Are Made of This) (English)
Words and music by Annie Lennox and Dave Stewart.
BMG Songs Inc., 1983.
Best-selling record by Eurythmics from *Sweet Dreams (Are Made of
This)* (RCA, 83).

Sweet Dreams
Words and music by Don Gibson.
Acuff-Rose Publications Inc., 1955.
Revived by Patsy Cline as the title track of the 1985 film and
soundtrack album *Sweet Dreams,* based on her life story.

Sweet Fire of Love (Canadian-Irish)
Words and music by Robbie Robertson, words and music by U2.
Medicine Hat Music, 1987/Polygram International, 1987.
Introduced by Robbie Robertson on the album *Robbie Robertson*
(Geffen, 87).

Sweet Freedom (Theme from *Running Scared*)
Words and music by Rod Temperton.
Rodsongs, 1986/EMI-April Music/MGM/UA Music Inc./Almo Music
Corp.
Introduced by Michael McDonald in the film and the soundtrack album
of *Running Scared* (86).

Sweet Jane
Words and music by Lou Reed.
Oakfield Avenue Music Ltd., 1970/Unichappell Music Inc., 1970.

Songwriter Lou Reed reportedly considered the Cowboy Junkies' revival of his much recorded song on *Trinity Sessions* (RCA, 88) the definitive version.

Sweet Kentucky Ham
Words and music by David Frishberg.
Swiftwater Music, 1987.
Performed by David Fishberg on the album *Can't Take You Nowhere* (Fantasy, 87). Fishberg follows in the Mose Allison tradition of supper club blues singing.

Sweet Lies (English)
Words and music by Robert Palmer, Frank Blair, and Dony Wynn.
Bungalow Music, N.V., 1988/Polygram International, 1988.
Introduced by Robert Palmer in the film and soundtrack album *Sweet Lies* (Island, 88).

Sweet Love
Words and music by Anita Baker, Louis Johnson, and Gary Bias.
Old Brompton Road Pub., 1986/Jobete Music Co.
Best-selling record by Anita Baker from the album *Rapture* (Elektra, 86). This song established Baker as a soul singer of the first rank. Won a Grammy Award, and Rhythm 'n' Blues Song of the Year, 1986.

Sweet Sensation
Words and music by James Mtume and Reggie Lucas.
Frozen Butterfly Music Publishing, 1979.
Best-selling record by Stephanie Mills from *Sweet Sensation* (20th Century, 80).

Sweet Sixteen
Words and music by Billy Idol.
Boneidol Music, 1986/Chrysalis Music Group, 1986.
Best-selling record in 1987 by Billy Idol, from the album *Whiplash Smile* (Chrysalis, 86).

Sweet, Sweet Baby (I'm Falling)
Words and music by Maria McKee, Steve Van Zandt, and Benmont Tench.
Blue Midnight Music, 1985/Little Diva Music, 1985/Blue Gator Music, 1985.
Introduced by Lone Justice on the album *Lone Justice* (Geffer, 85).

The Sweetest Taboo
Words and music by Sade (pseudonym for Helen Folasade Adu) and Martin Ditcham.
Sony Tunes, 1986.
Best-selling record by Sade from the album *Promise* (Epic, 86).

The Sweetest Thing (I've Ever Known)
Words and music by Otha Young.
Sterling Music Co., 1976/Addison Street Music, 1976.
Best-selling record by Juice Newton from *Juice* (Capitol, 81).

Sweetheart
Words and music by Frankie Previte and William Elworthy.
Knockout Music Co., 1981/EMI Music Publishing, 1981.
Best-selling record by Franke & The Knockouts from *Franke & The Knockouts* (Millennium, 81).

Sweetheart Like You
Words and music by Bob Dylan.
Special Rider Music, 1983.
Introduced by Bob Dylan on *Infidels* (Columbia, 83).

Swept Away
Words and music by Daryl Hall and Sara Allen.
Fust Buzza Music, Inc., 1984/Unichappell Music Inc., 1984.
Best-selling record by Diana Ross from *Swept Away* (RCA, 84).

Swept Away
Words and music by Steve Dorff, John Bettis, and Christopher Cross.
Warner/Elektra/Asylum Music, 1988/Dorff Songs, 1988/WB Music, 1988/John Bettis Music, 1988/BMG Songs Inc., 1988.
Introduced by Christoper Cross on the television series *Growing Pains*. Released as a single (Warner Bros., 88).

Swing the Mood (English)
Best-selling record by Jive Bunny and the Masterminds from *Jive Bunny: The Album* (Music Factory, 89). This medley of popular music history from 'In the Mood' to the early days of rock and roll reached number one in five countries. The record was produced by John Pickles and his son Andy.

Swingin'
Words and music by John D. Anderson and Lionel Delmore.
John Anderson Music Co. Inc., 1982/Hall-Clement Publications, 1982.
Best-selling record by John Anderson from *Wild & Blue* (Warner Brothers, 83).

Swingin' Party
Words and music by Paul Westerberg.
NAH Music, 1985.
Introduced by The Replacements on the album *Tim* (Sire, 85).

Synchronicity II (English)
Words and music by Sting (pseudonym for Gordon Sumner).

Reggatta Music, Ltd., 1983/Illegal Songs, Inc., 1983.
Best-selling record by The Police from *Synchronicity* (A & M, 83).

System of Survival
Words and music by Skylark.
Sputnick Adventure, 1987/EMI April Canada, 1987.
Best-selling record by Earth, Wind, & Fire, from the album *Touch the World* (Columbia, 87).

T

Tainted Love (English)
Words and music by Ed Cobb.
Equinox Music, 1976.
Best-selling record by Soft Cell from *Non-Stop Erotic Cabaret* (Sire, 82).

Take a Little Rhythm (Canadian)
Words and music by Ali Thompson.
Almo Music Corp., 1980.
Best-selling record by Ali Thompson (A & M, 80).

Take It Away (English)
Words and music by Paul McCartney.
MPL Communications Inc., 1982.
Best-selling record by Paul McCartney from *Tug of War* (Columbia, 82).

Take It Easy (English)
Words and music by Andy Taylor and Steve Jones.
Poetlord Music, 1986/Marilor Music.
Introduced by by Andy Taylor in the film and on the soundtrack of *American Anthem* (Atlantic, 86).

Take It Easy on Me (Australian)
Words and music by Graham Goble.
Little River Band Music, Victoria, Australia, 1981.
Best-selling record by Little River Band from *Time Exposure* (Capitol, 82).

Take It on the Run
Words and music by Gary Richrath.
Slam Dunk Music, 1980.
Best-selling record by REO Speedwagon from *Hi Infidelity* (Epic, 81).

Take It So Hard (English)
Words and music by Keith Richards and Steve Jordan.

Promopub BV, 1988.
Best-selling record by Keith Richards from *Talk Is Cheap* (Virgin, 88).
A solo effort from the Rolling Stones' guitarist.

Take Me Down
Words and music by Mark Gray and James P. Pennington.
Irving Music Inc., 1980/BMG Songs Inc., 1980.
Best-selling record by Alabama from *Mountain Music* (RCA, 82).

Take Me Home (English)
Words and music by Phil Collins.
Hit & Run Music, 1986/WB Music.
Best-selling record by Phil Collins in 1986 from the album *No Jacket Required* (Atlantic, 85).

Take Me Home Tonight
Words and music by Mike Leeson, Peter Vale, Ellie Greenwich, Jeff Barry, and Phil Spector.
C & D, 1986/Arlon/Chappell & Co., Inc./Mother Bertha Music, Inc./ Trio Music Co., Inc.
Best-selling record by Eddie Money in a duet with Ronnie Spector who repeats her classic refrain from 'Be My Baby.' From the album *Can't Hold Back* (Columbia, 86).

Take Me to Heart
Words and music by Marv Ross.
Narrow Dude Music, 1983/Bonnie Bee Good Music, 1983/WB Music, 1983.
Best-selling record by Quarterflash from *Take Another Picture* (Geffen, 83).

Take My Breath Away (Love Theme from *Top Gun*)
Words and music by Giorgio Moroder and Tom Whitlock.
GMPC, 1986/Famous Music Corp.
Introduced by Berlin on the soundtrack of the 1986 film *Top Gun*. Best-selling record by Berlin from the soundtrack album (Columbia, 86), even though the group was selected to record the song only when no other Columbia artist could be found. Won an Academy Award, and Song of the Year, 1986.

Take My Heart
Words and music by Charles Smith, James Taylor, George Brown, and Eumir Deodato.
WB Music, 1981.
Best-selling record by Kool & The Gang from *Something Special* (De-Lite, 81).

Take Off (Canadian)
Words and music by Kerry Crawford, Jonathan Goldsmith, Mark

Giacommelli, Rick Moranis, and Dave Thomas.
McKenzie Brothers, 1981.
Best-selling record by Bob & Doug McKenzie from *Great White North*
(Mercury, 82).

Take on Me (Norwegian)
English words and music by Pal Weaktaar, Mags Furuholem, and
Marten Harket.
ATV Music Corp., 1985.
Best-selling record by A-Ha from the album *Hunting High and Low*
(Warner Bros, 85).

Take the Skinheads Bowling
Words and music by Camper Van Beethoven.
Campbell-Connelly, Inc., 1985.
Introduced by Camper Van Beethoven on the album *Telephone Free
Landslide Victory* (Independent Project Records, 85).

Take Your Time
Words and music by Danny Sembello and Donnell Spencer, Jr.
No Pain, No Gain, 1987/Honey-Look Music, 1987/Unicity Music, Inc.,
1987.
Best-selling record by Pebbles, from *Pebbles* (MCA, 88).

Take Your Time (Do It Right) Part 1
Words and music by Harold Clayton and Sigidi.
Avant Garde Music Publishing, Inc., 1980/Interior Music, 1980.
Best-selling record by S.O.S. Band from *S.O.S.* (Tabu, 80).

Taken In (English)
Words and music by Mike Rutherford and Christopher Neil.
Hit & Run Music, 1985/G3/Arlon/Chappell & Co., Inc.
Best-selling record by Mike & The Mechanics in 1986 from the album
Mike & The Mechanics (Atlantic, 85).

Takin' It Easy
Words and music by Lacy Dalton, Mark Sherrill, and Billy Sherrill.
Algee Music Corp., 1981.
Best-selling record by Lacy J. Dalton (Columbia, 81).

Talent Show
Words and music by Paul Westerberg.
NAH Music, 1989.
Introduced by The Replacements from *Don't Tell a Soul* (Sire, 89).

Talk Dirty to Me
Words and music by Bobby Dall, C. C. Deville, Brett Michaels, and
Rikki Rockett.
Sweet Cyanide, 1986.

Best-selling record in 1987 by Poison, from the album *Look What the Cat Dragged In* (Enigma, 86).

Talk of the Town (English)
Words and music by Chrissie Hynde.
MCA, Inc., 1980.
Introduced by The Pretenders on *Pretenders II* (Sire, 82)

Talk Talk
Words and music by Edwin Hollis and Mark Hollis.
Lexicon Music Inc., 1982.
Best-selling record by Talk Talk from *The Party's Over* (EMI-America, 82).

Talk to Me
Words and music by Chas Sandford.
Fallwater Music, 1985.
Best-selling record by Stevie Nicks from the album *Rock a Little* (Modern, 85).

Talk to Me of Mendocino
Words and music by Kate McGarrigle.
Garden Court Music Co., 1975.
Revived by Linda Ronstadt on *Get Closer* (Asylum, 82).

Talk to Ya Later
Words and music by David Foster and Steve Lukather, music by Tubes.
Pseudo Songs, 1981/Irving Music Inc., 1981/Foster Frees Music Inc., 1981/BMG Songs Inc., 1981.
Best-selling record by The Tubes from *The Completion Backwards Principle* (Capitol, 81).

Talkin' 'bout a Revolution
Words and music by Tracy Chapman.
EMI-April Music, 1982/Purple Rabbit Music, 1982.
Introduced by Tracy Chapman on *Tracy Chapman* (Elektra, 88).

Talking in the Dark (English)
Words and music by Elvis Costello.
Plangent Visions Music, Inc., London, England, 1979.
Featured in *Mad Love* by Linda Ronstadt (Asylum, 80).

Talking in Your Sleep
Words and music by Jimmy Marinos, Wally Palmar, Mike Skill, Coz Canler, and Pete Solley.
Foreverendeavor Music, Inc., 1983.
Best-selling record by The Romantics from *In Heat* (Nemperor, 83).

Tall Cool One (English)
Words and music by Robert Plant and Phil Johnstone.
Virgin Music, 1987.
Introduced by Robert Plant on *Now and Zen* (Esperanza, 88).

Tangled in Your Web
Words and music by Richard Barone.
Miniature Music, 1987.
Introduced by Richard Barone in *Cool Blue Halo* (Passport, 87) and
  popularized in 1988.

Tarzan Boy (Irish)
Words and music by Naimy Hackett and Maurizio Bassi.
Screen Gems-EMI Music Inc., 1986.
Best-selling record by Baltimora from the album *Living in the
  Background* (Capitol, 86).

Tasty Love
Words and music by Paul Laurence and Freddie Jackson.
Bush Burnin' Music, 1986.
Best-selling record by Freddie Jackson from the album *Just Like the
  First Time* (Capitol, 86).

Taxi
Words and music by Homer Banks and Charles Brooks.
Backlog Music, 1983.
Best-selling record by J. Blackfoot (Soundtown, 84).

The Taxi Ride (Canadian)
Words and music by Jane Siberry.
Red Sky, 1985/Wing It.
Introduced by Jane Siberry on the album *One More Colour* (Open Air,
  86).

The Tea Leaf Prophecy (Lay down Your Arms)
Words and music by Joni Mitchell, music by Larry Klein.
Crazy Crow Music, 1988.
Introduced by Joni Mitchell in *Chalk Mark in a Rainstorm* (Geffen, 88).

Teacher Teacher (Canadian)
Words and music by Bryan Adams and Jim Vallance.
Irving Music Inc., 1984/Adams Communications, Inc., 1984/Calypso
  Toonz, 1984.
Best-selling record by 38 Special from the film and soundtrack album
  Teachers (Capitol, 84). Revived on *Flashback* (A&M, 87)

Tear Stained Letter (English)
Words and music by Richard Thompson.
Island Music, 1980.

Revived in 1988 by Jo-el Sonnier on *Come On Joe*, the song was first recorded by the writer on *Hand of Kindness* in 1983.

Tearing Us Apart (English)
Words and music by Eric Clapton and Greg Phillinganes.
E.C. Music, England, 1986/Poopys, 1986.
Best-selling record in 1987 by Eric Clapton, from the album *August* (Duck/Warner Bros., 86).

Tears of the Lonely
Words and music by Wayland Holyfield.
Polygram International, 1978.
Best-selling record by Mickey Gilley from *You Don't Know Me* (Epic, 82).

Telefone (Long Distance Love Affair)
Words and music by Gregory Mathieson and Trevor Veitch.
Mighty Mathieson Music, 1983/Slapshot Music, 1983.
Best-selling record by Sheena Easton from *Best Kept Secret* (EMI-America, 83).

Telepathy
Words and music by J. Coco (pseudonym for Prince).
Controversy Music, 1987.
Introduced by Deborah Allen on the album *Telepathy* (RCA, 87).

Tell Her About It
Words and music by Billy Joel.
Joelsongs, 1983.
Best-selling record by Billy Joel from *An Innocent Man* (Columbia, 83).

Tell It Like It Is
Words and music by George Davis and Lee Diamond.
Olrap Publishing Co., Inc., 1966/Conrad Music.
Revived by Heart in *Greatest Hits Live*. Rhythm 'n' Blues Billy Joe Royal on *The Royal Treatment* (Atlantic, 88) (Epic, 80).

Tell It to My Heart
Words and music by Seth Swirsky and Ernie Gold.
Chappell & Co., Inc., 1987/November Nights, 1987/Goldpoint, 1987.
Best-selling record by Taylor Dayne, from the album *Tell It to My Heart* (Arista, 87).

Tell Me a Lie
Words and music by Barbara Wyrick and Mickey Buckins.
Colgems-EMI Music, 1973/Fame Publishing Co., Inc., 1973.
Best-selling record by Janie Fricke (Columbia, 83).

Tell Me on a Sunday (English)
Words by Don Black, music by Andrew Lloyd Webber.
Dick James Music Inc., 1980.
Introduced by Marti Webb in the British musical *Tell Me on a Sunday*.
Performed by Bernadette Peters in the Broadway musical *Song and Dance* (85).

Tell Me Tomorrow
Words and music by Gary Goetzman and Mike Piccirillo.
Chardax Music, 1981.
Best-selling record by Smokey Robinson from *Yes It's You Lady* (Tamla, 82).

Tell That Girl to Shut Up
Words and music by Christopher Butler.
Island Music, 1980.
Featured in *The Right to Be Italian* by Holly & The Italians (Virgin, 81).

Telling Me Lies (English)
Words and music by Linda Thompson and Betsy Cook.
Firesign Music Ltd., England, 1985/Chappell & Co., Inc., 1985.
Revived in 1986 by Dolly Parton, Emmylou Harris, and Linda Ronstadt on the album *Trio* (Warner Bros.). Linda Thompson had introduced the song on her earlier Warner Bros. album, *Can't Stop the Girl*. Nominated for a Grammy Award, Country Song of the Year, 1987.

Temporary Beauty (English)
Words and music by Graham Parker.
Participation Music, Inc., 1982.
Introduced by Graham Parker on *Another Grey Area* (Arista, 82).

Temporary Insanity
Words and music by L. White, M. Rochelle, and S. Berry.
National League Music, 1985/Gedzerillo Music, 1985/Bullwhip Productions, 1985/WB Music, 1985.
Introduced by Townsends in the film *Police Academy II* (85).

Temptation (English)
Words and music by Glenn Gregory, Ian Craig Marsh, and Martyn Ware.
WB Music, 1982/Virgin Music, 1982.
Introduced by Heaven 17 on *The Luxury Gap* (Sire, 82).

Tempted (English)
Words and music by Chris Difford and Glenn Tilbrook.
Illegal Songs, Inc., 1981.
Best-selling record by Squeeze from *East Side Story* (A & M, 81).

The Ten Commandments of Love
Words and music by Marshall Paul.
Arc Music, 1958.
This cornerstone of rock history, originated by Harvey Fuqua and the Moonglows, was revived by Howard Hewitt on *Rock, Rhythm, and Blues* (Warner Bros., 89).

Tender Comrade (English)
Words and music by Billy Bragg.
Chappell & Co., Inc., 1988.
Introduced by Billy Bragg on *Workers Playtime* (Elektra, 88).

Tender Is the Night
Words and music by Russ Kunkel, Danny Kortchmar, and Jackson Browne.
Night Kitchen Music, 1983.
Best-selling record by Jackson Browne from *Lawyers in Love* (Asylum, 83).

A Tender Lie
Words and music by Randy Sharp.
With Any Luck Music, 1988.
Best-selling record by Restless Heart, from *Big Dreams in a Small Town* (RCA, 88).

Tender Love
Words and music by James Harris, III and Terry Lewis.
Flyte Tyme Tunes, 1986.
Introduced by Force M.D.'s in the 1985 film *Krush Groove*. Best-selling record by the same group from their album *Chillin'* (Warner Bros., 86).

Tender Lover
Words and music by Babyface (pseudonym for Kenny Edmunds), L. A. Reid (pseudonym for Antonio Reid), and Pete Q. Smith.
Hip-Trip Music Co., 1989/Kear Music/Pebbitone Music.
Best-selling record by Babyface from *Tender Lover* (Solar, 89).

Tennessee Courage
Words and music by Vern Gosdin, Rex Gosdin, and James Broun.
Bethel Music, 1989/Hookem Music.
Introduced by Keith Whitley on *I Wonder Do You Think of Me* (RCA, 89).

Tennessee Flat Top Box
Words and music by Johnny Cash.
Song of Cash Inc., 1961/WB Music.
Revived in in 1988 by Rosanne Cash on *King's Record Shop* (Columbia, 87), in a sentimental tribute by a daughter to her father.

Tennessee Homesick Blues
Words and music by Dolly Parton.
Velvet Apple Music, 1984/Warner-Tamerlane Music, 1984.
Best-selling record by Dolly Parton from the film and soundtrack album
  Rhinestone (RCA, 84).

Tennessee Plates
Words and music by John Hiatt and Mike Porter.
Lillybilly, 1988/Bug Music, 1988.
Introduced by John Hiatt in *Slow Turning* (A & M, 88).

Tennessee River
Words and music by Randy Owen.
Buzzherb Music, 1980.
Best-selling record by Alabama from *My Home's in Alabama* (RCA,
  80).

Thank God for the Radio
Words and music by Max D. Barnes and Robert John Jones.
Blue Lake Music, 1982.
Best-selling record by The Kendalls (Mercury, 84).

Thanks for My Child
Words and music by Full Force.
Forceful Music, 1988/Willesden Music, Inc., 1988.
Best-selling record by Cheryl 'Pepsi' Riley, from *Me, Myself and I*
  (Columbia, 88). In performance, this song became an anthem for
  single-motherhood.

Thanks for the Information (English)
Words and music by Van Morrison.
Essential Music, 1986.
Introduced by Van Morrison on the album *No Guru, No Method, No
  Teacher* (Polygram, 86).

That Ain't Love
Words and music by Kevin Cronin.
Fate Music, 1987.
Best-selling record by Reo Speedwagon on the album *Life As We Know
  It* (Epic, 87).

That Demon Baby of Mine
Words and music by Michael John La Chiusa.
Introduced by Ethyl Eichelberger in the 1989 Off-Off Broadway
  production *Buzzsaw Berkeley.*

That Girl
Words and music by Stevie Wonder.
Jobete Music Co., 1981/Black Bull Music, 1981.

Best-selling record by Stevie Wonder from *Stevie Wonder's Original Musicquarium* (Tamla, 82). Nominated for a Grammy Award, Rhythm 'n' Blues Song of the Year, 1982.

That Girl Could Sing
Words and music by Jackson Browne.
Swallow Turn Music, 1980.
Best-selling record by Jackson Browne from *Hold Out* (Asylum, 80).

That Rock Won't Roll
Words and music by John Scott Sherrill and Bob DiPiero.
Combine Music Corp., 1986.
Best-selling record in 1986 by Restless Heart.

That Was a Close One
Words and music by Robert Byrne.
Colgems-EMI Music, 1987.
Introduced by Earl Thomas Conley on the album *Too Many Times* (RCA, 87).

That Was Then, This Is Now
Words and music by Vance Brescia and Ed Davis.
Mosquitos, 1986.
Introduced by the Monkees on the album *Monkees' Greatest Hits* (Arista, 86). Penned by members of the cult band the Mosquitos, the song marks the Monkees' return to the pop charts after an absence of twenty years.

That Was Yesterday (English)
Words and music by Mick (Foreigner) Jones and Lou Gramm.
Somerset Songs Publishing, Inc., 1984/Little Doggies Productions Inc., 1984/Colgems-EMI Music, 1984.
Best-selling record by Foreigner from the album *Agent Provocateur* (Atlantic, 85).

That's All (English)
Words and music by Tony Banks, Phil Collins, and Mike Rutherford.
Hit & Run Music, 1983.
Best-selling record by Genesis from *Genesis* (Atlantic, 83).

That's All That Matters
Words and music by Hank Cochran.
Tree Publishing Co., Inc., 1963.
Best-selling record by Mickey Gilley from *That's All That Matters to Me* (Epic, 80).

That's the Thing About Love
Words and music by Gary Nicholson and Richard Leigh.
Cross Keys Publishing Co., Inc., 1983/EMI-April Music, 1983/White

Cottage Music, 1983/Four Sons Music, 1983.
Best-selling record by Don Williams (MCA, 84).

That's the Way Love Goes
Words and music by Lefty Frizell and Whitey Shafer.
Acuff-Rose Publications Inc., 1973.
Revived in 1984 by Merle Haggard from *His Epic Hits - The First Eleven - To be Continued* (Epic, 84).

That's What Friends Are For
Words by Carole Bayer Sager, music by Burt Bacharach.
WB Music, 1982/New Hidden Valley Music Co., 1982/Warner-Tamerlane Music, 1982/Carole Bayer Sager Music, 1982.
Best-selling record by Dionne Warwick with Elton John, Gladys Knight, and Stevie Wonder from the album *Friends* (Arista, 85). Proceeds donated to the American Foundation for AIDS Research. Introduced by Rod Stewart in the film *Nightshift* in 1982. Won a Grammy Award, and Song of the Year, 1986. Nominated for a Grammy Award, Record of the Year, 1986.

That's What Love Is All About
Words and music by Michael Bolton and Eric Kaz.
Emboe, 1987/Kaz Music Co., 1987/EMI-April Music, 1987.
Best-selling record by Michael Bolton, from the album *The Hunger* (Columbia, 87). This was the breakthrough song for the journeyman singer-songwriter.

(Sittin' On) The Dock of the Bay
Words and music by Otis Redding and Steve Cropper.
Irving Music Inc., 1968.
Michael Bolton's revival on *The Hunger* (Columbia, 87) became popular in 1988.

(I've Had) The Time of My Life
Words and music by Franke Provott, John DeNicola, and Donald Markowitz.
Knockout Music Co., 1987/Damusic, 1987/Donald Jay, 1987/R.U. Cerious, 1987/EMI-April Music, 1987.
Best-selling record Bill Medley and Jennifer Warnes, from the hit film and soundtrack album *Dirty Dancing* (RCA, 87). This big ballad from the year's most successful soundtrack album won a Golden Globe Award as Best Song from a Movie. Nominated for an Academy Award, Best Original Song, 1987; a Grammy Award, Song for a Movie/TV, 1987.

(You've Got) The Touch
Words and music by Will Robinson, John Jarrard, and Lisa Palas.

Alabama Band Music Co.
Best-selling record in 1987 by Alabama, from the album *The Touch* (RCA, 86).

(It's Just) The Way That You Love Me
Words and music by Oliver Leiber.
Virgin Music, 1988/Oliver Leiber Music.
Best-selling record in 1989 by Paula Abdul, former choreographer for Janet Jackson and others, from *Forever Your Girl* (Virgin, 88).

Theme from *Continental Divide* (Never Say Goodbye)
Music by Michael Small, words by Carole Bayer Sager.
Duchess Music Corp., 1981.
Best-selling record by Helen Reddy (MCA, 81). Introduced in the film *Continental Divide* (81).

Theme from *Doctor Detroit*
Words and music by Gerald Casale and Mark Mothersbaugh.
Devo Music, 1983.
Best-selling record by Devo (Backstreet, 83). Introduced in the film *Dr. Detroit* (83).

Theme from *Dynasty*
Words and music by Bill Conti.
Glamour Music, 1981.
Best-selling record by Bill Conti (Arista, 82).

Theme from *E.T.*
Music by John T. Williams.
Music of the World, 1982.
Best-selling record by The Walter Murphy Band from the film and soundtrack to *E.T.* (MCA, 82).

The Theme from *Hill Street Blues*
Music by Mike Post.
MTM Enterprises Inc., 1980.
Best-selling record by Mike Post from *Televison Theme Songs* (Elektra, 81). Introduced on the TV series *Hill Street Blues* (80).

Theme from *Magnum P.I.*
Music by Mike Post and Pete Carpenter.
Leeds Music Corp., 1981.
Best-selling record by Mike Post from *Television Theme Songs* (Elektra, 82). Introduced on the TV series *Magnum P. I.* (82).

Theme from *Mr. Belvedere*
Words and music by Gary Portnoy and Judy Hart Angelo.
Addax Music Co., Inc., 1985.

Introduced by Leon Redbone on the television series *Mr. Belvedere* (85).

Theme from *New York, New York*
Words and music by John Kander and Fred Ebb.
EMI Unart Catalogue, 1977.
Revived by Frank Sinatra in *Trilogy: Past, Present, Future* (Reprise, 80). Chosen as the official song of New York City. Nominated for Grammy Awards, Record of the Year, 1980, and Song of the Year, 1980.

Theme from *Raging Bull*
Words and music by Harold Wheeler and Joel Diamond.
EMI U Catalogue, 1981.
Best-selling record by Joel Diamond (Motown, 81). Introduced in the film *Raging Bull* (81).

Theme from *The Black Hole*
Words and music by William Collins, George Clinton, and J. S. Theracon, music by Jim Vitti.
Rick's Music Inc., 1980/Malbiz Publishing, 1980/Rubber Band Music, Inc., 1980.
Best-selling record by Parliament (Casablanca, 80). Introduced in the film & soundtrack album *The Black Hole* (80).

Theme from *The Dukes of Hazzard* (Good Ol' Boys)
Words and music by Waylon Jennings.
Warner-Tamerlane Music, 1979/Rich Way Music, Inc.
Best-selling record by Waylon Jennings from *Music Man* (RCA, 80). Introduced on the TV series *The Dukes of Hazzard* (79).

The Theme from *The Greatest American Hero*, also known as Believe It or Not
Words by Stephen Geyer, music by Mike Post.
EMI-April Music, 1981/EMI-Blackwood Music Inc., 1981/Mike Post Productions, Inc., 1981/Darjen Music, 1981/S J C Music, 1981.
Best-selling record by Joey Scarbury from *America's Greatest Hero* (Elektra, 81). Introduced on the TV series *The Greatest American Hero* (81).

Theme from Working Girl, see Let the River Run.

Then Came You
Words by Madeline Sunshine, music by Steve Nelson.
Addax Music Co., Inc., 1983.
Introduced on the TV Show *Webster* (83).

Then It's Love
Words and music by Dennis Linde.

Dennis Linde Music, 1987.
Best-selling record by Don Williams (Capital, 87).

There
Words by Richard Maltby, music by David Shire.
Fiddleback/Progeny Music/Revelation Music Publishing Corp./Long
    Pond Music.
Introduced by Sally Hayes and Patrick Scott Brady in *Closer Than Ever,*
    the 1989 revue based on Maltby-Shire numbers.

There Isn't Only One Girl
Words by P. G. Wodehouse and Guy Bolton, music by Jerome Kern.
Polygram International, 1924.
Revived in 1989 by Davis Gaines in *Sitting Pretty,* the 1924 musical
    brought back for several performances.

There'll Be Sad Songs (to Make You Cry)
Words and music by Wayne Braithwaite, Barry Eastmond, and Billy
    Ocean.
Zomba Music, 1986.
Best-selling record by Billy Ocean from the album *Love Zone* (Arista,
    86).

There's a Light beyond These Woods (Mary Margaret)
Words and music by Nanci Griffith.
Wing & Wheel Music, 1978, 1982, 1986.
Revived in 1986 by Nanci Griffith on the album *Lone Star State of
    Mind* (MCA). Griffith originally recorded the song on her 1978 album
    that was named after it. (Philo).

There's a Tear in My Beer
Words and music by Hank Williams.
Acuff-Rose Publications Inc., 1952, 1980.
Hank Williams Jr. redubbed a previously unissued track of this song by
    his father and the new version was used on the soundtrack of the
    1989 film *Pink Cadillac.* The younger Williams also used it on his
    Greatest Hits III album (Warner/Curb Records, 89). Nominated for a
    Grammy Award, Country Song of the Year, 1989.

There's a Winner in You
Words and music by Nicholas Ashford and Valerie Simpson.
Nick-O-Val Music, 1985.
Introduced by Patti LaBelle on the album *Winner in You* (MCA, 86).

There's No Stopping Your Heart
Words and music by Michael Brook and Ronald Karp.
Mother Tongue Music, 1985/Flying Cloud Music Inc.
Best-selling record by Marie Osmond from the album *I Only Wanted
    You* (Capitol/Curb, 86).

There's No Way
Words and music by Lisa Palas, Will Robinson, and John Jarrard.
Alabama Band Music Co., 1984.
Best-selling record by Alabama from the album *40 Hour Week* (RCA, 85).

There's Nothing Better Than Love
Words and music by Luther Vandross and J. Skip Anderson.
EMI-April Music, 1987/Uncle Ronnie's Music, 1987/JVA Publishing Co., 1987.
Best-selling record by Luther Vandross and Gregory Hines, from the album *Give Me the Reason* (Epic, 87).

There's the Girl
Words and music by Holly Knight and Nancy Wilson.
Makiki Publishing Co., Ltd., 1987/Knighty Knight, 1987/Know Music, 1987/BMG Songs Inc., 1987.
Best-selling record by Heart, from the album *Bad Animals* (Capitol, 87).

These Days
Words and music by Peter Buck, Bill Berry, Mike Mills, and Michael Stipe.
Night Garden Music, 1986.
Introduced by R.E.M. on the album *Life's Rich Pageant* (I.R.S., 86).

These Dreams
Words and music by Bernie Taupin and Martin Page.
Little Mole Music, 1986/Intersong, USA Inc./Zomba Music.
Best-selling record by Heart in 1986 from the album *Heart* (Capitol, 85).

They Dance Alone (English)
Words and music by Sting (pseudonym for Gordon Sumner).
Magnetic Music Publishing Co., 1987/Reggatta Music, Ltd., 1987/Illegal Songs, Inc., 1987.
Introduced by Sting on the album *Nothing Like the Sun* (A & M).

They Don't Know (English)
Words and music by Kirsty MacColl.
MCA, Inc., 1983.
Best-selling record by Tracey Ullman from *You Broke My Heart in 17 Places* (MCA, 84).

They Don't Make Them Like They Used To
Words and music by Burt Bacharach and Carole Bayer Sager.
New Hidden Valley Music Co., 1986/Walt Disney Music/CBS Inc./Wonderland Music.
Introduced by Kenny Rogers in the 1986 film *Tough Guys*.

They Say
Words and music by Skip Scarborough and Terry McFadden.
Unichappell Music Inc., 1983/Little Birdie Music, 1983.
Introduced on *I'm So Proud* by Deniece Williams (Columbia, 83).

They Want Money
Words and music by Moe Deweese and Teddy Riley.
Zomba Music, 1989/Willesden Music, Inc.
Introduced by Kool Moe Dee on *Knowledge Is King* (Jive, 89).

Thighs High I Wanna (Grip Your Hips and Move)
Words by Dave Grusin, Sekou Bunch, and Thomasina Smith, music by
    Thomas Browne.
Roaring Fork Music, 1980/Thomas Browne Publishing, 1980.
Best-selling record by Tom Browne from *Magic* (GRP, 81).

Thin Line Between Love and Hate
Words and music by Richard Poindexter, Robert Poindexter, and Jackie
    Members.
Cotillion Music Inc., 1971/Win or Lose Publishing, 1971.
Revived by The Pretenders on *Learning to Crawl* (Sire, 84).

A Thing About You
Words and music by Tom Petty.
Gone Gator Music, 1981.
Introduced by Tom Petty on *Hard Promises* (Backstreet, 81).

Thing Called Love
Words and music by John Hiatt.
Careers-BMG, 1988.
Introduced by Bonnie Raitt on *Nick of Time* (Capitol, 89).

Things Can Only Get Better (English)
Words and music by Howard Jones.
Warner-Tamerlane Music, 1985.
Best-selling record by Howard Jones from the album *Dream into Action*
    (Elektra, 85).

Think About Love (Think About Me)
Words and music by Richard Brannon and Tom Campbell.
Malvern Music Co., 1986/Cottonpatch Music/Polygram International.
Best-selling record by Dolly Parton from the album *Real Love* (RCA,
    86).

Think About Me (English)
Words and music by Christine McVie.
Fleetwood Mac Music Ltd., 1979.
Best-selling record by Fleetwood Mac from *Tusk* (Warner Brothers, 80).

Think I'm in Love
Words and music by Eddie Money and Randy Oda.
Soft Music, 1982.
Best-selling record by Eddie Money from *No Control* (Columbia, 82).

Thinking About Your Love
Words and music by Rodney Skipworth and Phil Turner.
Larry Spier, Inc., 1985.
Introduced by Skipworth and Turner in the film *Pumping Iron II: The Women* (85).

Thinking of You (English)
Words and music by Russell DeSalvo, Wilma Cosme, and Bob Steele.
Cutting Music, 1989.
Best-selling record in 1989 by Safire from *Safire* (Cutting/Mercury/ Polygram, 88).

Thinking of You
Words and music by Maurice White, Wayne Vaughn, and Wanda Vaughn.
EMI-April Music, 1988/Yougoulei Music, 1988/Wenkewa Music, 1988.
Best-selling record in 1988 by Earth, Wind & Fire, from *Touch the World* (Columbia, 87).

This Could Be the Night (Canadian)
Words and music by Paul Dean, Jonathan Cain, Mike Reno, and Bill Wray.
Frisco Kid Music, 1986/EMI-April Music/Duke Reno Music/Mel Dav/ EMI-Blackwood Music Inc./Dean of Music.
Best-selling record by Loverboy from the album *Lovin' Every Minute of It* (Columbia, 86).

This Crazy Love
Words and music by Roger Murrah and J. Hicks.
Tom Collins Music Corp., 1987.
Best-selling record by The Oak Ridge Boys, from the album *Where the Fast Lane Ends* (RCA, 87).

This Day
Words and music by Edwin Hawkins.
Edwin R. Hawkins Music Co., 1983.
Introduced on *Feel My Soul* by Jennifer Holliday (Geffen, 83).

This Girl's Back in Town
Words and music by Paul Jabara and Bob Esty.
Poperetta, 1987/Warner-Tamerlane Music, 1987/Fave Rave, 1987.
Introduced by Raquel Welch on her home video exercise tape *A Week with Raquel/7-Day Wake Up and Shape Up* (Total Video, 87). Also

released as a twelve-inch single for the dance and aerobics market (Columbia, 87).

This Is My Song
Words and music by Gary William Friedman and Will Holt.
Bussy Music, 1983/Devon Music, 1983/Hampshire House Publishing Corp., 1983/Lemon Tree Music, Inc., 1983.
Introduced by Company in *Taking My Turn* (83).

This Is Not America
Words and music by Pat Metheny and Lyle Mays.
Buttermilk Sky Music, 1985/OPC, 1985.
Best-selling record by David Bowie and Pat Metheny (EMI-America, 85). Introduced in the film *The Falcon and the Snowman* (85).

This Is the Time
Words and music by Billy Joel.
Joelsongs, 1986.
Best-selling record by Billy Joel from the album *The Bridge* (Columbia, 86).

This Little Girl
Words and music by Bruce Springsteen.
Bruce Springsteen Publishing, 1980.
Best-selling record by Gary U.S. Bonds from *Dedication* (EMI-America, 81).

This Missin' You Heart of Mine
Words and music by Woody Mullis and Mike Geiger.
Acuff-Rose Publications Inc., 1987/Milene Music Inc., 1987.
Best-selling record in 1988 by Sawyer Brown, from *Somewhere in the Night* (Capitol, 87).

This One's for the Children
Words and music by Maurice Starr.
Maurice Starr Music, 1989/EMI-April Music.
Best-selling record by New Kids on the Block from *Merry, Merry Christmas* (Columbia, 89).

This Property Is Condemned
Words and music by Maria McKee, music by Patrick Sugg, Gregg Sutton, and Bruce Brody.
Geffen Again Music, 1989/Little Diva Music/Warner-Tamerlane Music/ Planet Dallas Music/Doolittle Music/Let's See Music.
Introduced by Maria McKee on *Maria McKee* (Geffen, 89).

This Shirt
Words and music by Mary Chapin Carpenter.
Getarealjob Music, 1987/EMI-April Music, 1987.

Introduced by Mary Chapin Carpenter on *State of the Heart* (Columbia, 89).

This Time (Canadian)
Words and music by Bryan Adams and Jim Vallance.
Irving Music Inc., 1983/Adams Communications, Inc., 1983.
Best-selling record by Bryan Adams from *Cuts Like a Knife* (A & M, 83).

This Time
Words and music by Charlie Singleton.
Almo Music Corp., 1988/Won Ton Music.
Best-selling record in 1989 by Kiara (duet with Shanice Wilson) from *To Change and/or Make a Difference* (Arista, 88).

This Time I Know It's for Real (English)
Words and music by Mike Stock, Matt Aitken, Pete Waterman, and Donna Summer.
All Boys USA Music, 1989/Sweet Summer Night Music.
Best-selling record by Donna Summer from *Another Place and Time* (Atlantic, 89).

This Town (English)
Words and music by Declan MacManus.
Plangent Visions Music, Inc., London, England, 1988, 1989.
Introduced by Elvis Costello on *Spike* (Warner Bros., 89).

This Woman (English)
Words and music by Barry Gibb and Albhy Galuten.
Gibb Brothers Music, 1983.
Best-selling record by Kenny Rogers from *Eyes That See in the Dark* (RCA, 84).

This Woman's Work (English)
Words and music by Kate Bush.
Kate Bush Music, Ltd., London, England, 1988.
Introduced by Kate Bush in the film and on the soundtrack album *She's Having a Baby* (I.R.S., 88). Rhythm 'n' Blues Kate Bush on the album *The Sensual World* (Columbia, 89).

Three Flights Up
Words and music by Frank Christian.
Frank Christian Music, 1988.
Introduced by Frank Christian on *Fast Folk Sixth Anniversary Issue* (Fast Folk, 88).

Three-Legged Man
Words and music by Shel Silverstein.

TRO-Hollis Music, Inc., 1987.
Introduced by Ray Stevens on the album *Cracking Up* (MCA, 87).

Three Time Loser
Words and music by Dan Seals.
Pink Pig Music, 1986.
Best-selling record in 1987 by Dan Seals, from the album *On the Front Line* (EMI-America, 86).

Three Times in Love
Words and music by Tommy James and Rick Serota.
Big Tooth Music Corp., 1979/Tommy James Music Inc., 1979.
Best-selling record by Tommy James from *The Time in Love* (Millennium, 80).

Thriller (English)
Words and music by Rod Temperton.
Almo Music Corp., 1982.
Best-selling record by Michael Jackson from *Thriller* (Epic, 84).

Through the Fire
Words and music by David Foster, Tom Keane, and Cynthia Weil.
Foster Frees Music Inc., 1984/Dyad Music, Ltd., 1984/TomJon Music, 1984/Nero Publishing, 1984.
Best-selling record by Chaka Khan from the album *I Feel for You* (Warner Bros., 85). Nominated for a Grammy Award, Rhythm 'n' Blues Song of the Year, 1985.

Through the Storm (American-English)
Words and music by Albert Hammond and Diane Warren.
Albert Hammond Enterprises, 1989/WB Music/Realsongs.
Best-selling record by Aretha Franklin and Elton John from Aretha's *Through the Storm* (Arista, 89).

Through the Years
Words and music by Steve Dorff and Marty Panzer.
Peso Music, 1980/Swanee Bravo Music, 1980.
Best-selling record by Kenny Rogers from *Share Your Love* (Liberty, 82).

Throwing It All Away (English)
Words and music by Tony Banks, Phil Collins, and Mike Rutherford.
Hit & Run Music, 1986.
Best-selling record by Genesis from the album *Invisible Touch* (Atlantic, 86).

Thunder and Lighting
Words and music by Monica Lynch, Ronnie Halpin, and Douglas Wimbish.

T-Boy Music, 1986/Fly Girl Music.
Introduced by Miss Thang (Tommy Boy, 86), an answer song to 'The
Rain,' which did not inspire nearly as many replies as 1985's
'Roxanne' did.

Thunder Road
Words and music by Bruce Springsteen.
Bruce Springsteen Publishing, 1975.
Revived in 1986 by Bruce Springsteen on the album *Bruce Springsteen
& The E Street Band Live, 1975-1985* (Columbia, 86).

The Tide Is High (English)
Words and music by John Holt.
Gemrod Music, Inc., 1968.
Best-selling record by Blondie from *Autoamerican* (Chrysalis, 80).

Tight Connection to My Heart (Has Anybody Seen My Love)
Words and music by Bob Dylan.
Special Rider Music, 1985.
Best-selling record by Bob Dylan from the album *Empire Burlesque*
(Columbia, 85).

Tight Fittin' Jeans
Words and music by Mike Huggman.
Prater Music, Inc., 1980.
Best-selling record by Conway Twitty (MCA, 81).

A Tight Knit Family
Words and music by William Finn.
Introduced by Michael Rupert in *March of the Falsettos* (81).

'Til I Gain Control Again
Words and music by Rodney Crowell.
Jolly Cheeks Music, 1976.
Best-selling record by Crystal Gayle from *True Love* (Elektra, 82).

'Til My Baby Comes Home
Words and music by Luther Vandross and Marcus Miller.
EMI-April Music, 1985/Uncle Ronnie's Music, 1985/Thriller Miller
Music, 1985/MCA, Inc., 1985.
Best-selling record by Luther Vandross from the album *The Night I Fell
in Love* (Epic, 85).

Till I Loved You
Words and music by Maury Yeston.
Yeston Music, Ltd., 1987.
Best-selling record by Barbra Streisand and Don Johnson from *Till I
Loved You* (Columbia, 88). This song emanates from Yeston's
theatrical production *Goya*.

Till You're Gone
Words and music by James Aldridge and Tom Brasfield.
Colgems-EMI Music, 1982.
Best-selling record by Barbara Mandrell from *In Black & White* (MCA, 82).

Timber I'm Falling in Love with You
Words and music by Kostas Lazaridus.
Songs of Polygram, 1988.
Best-selling record by Patty Loveless from *Honky Tonk Angel* (MCA, 89).

Time (English)
Words and music by Eric Woolfson and Alan Parsons.
EMI Unart Catalogue, 1980.
Best-selling record by The Alan Parsons Project from *The Turn of a Friendly Card* (Arista, 81).

Time (English)
Words and music by Roy Hay, Jon Moss, and Michael Craig.
Virgin Music, 1982.
Best-selling record by Culture Club from *Kissing to Be Clever* (Virgin/Epic, 83).

Time After Time
Words and music by Cyndi Lauper and Rob Hyman.
Rella Music Corp., 1983/Dub Notes, 1983.
Best-selling record by Cyndi Lauper from *She's So Unusual* (Portrait, 84). Nominated for a Grammy Award, Best Song of the Year, 1984.

Time Don't Run out on Me
Words by Gerry Goffin, music by Carole King.
Screen Gems-EMI Music Inc., 1983/Elorac Music, 1983/Colgems-EMI Music, 1983.
Best-selling record by Anne Murray from the album *Heart over Mind* (Capitol, 85).

A Time for Heroes (Canadian)
Words and music by Jon Lyons, M. Scott Sotebeer, and Rik Emmett.
Little Horn Music.
Introduced by Meat Loaf, with Brian May of Queen on guitar (Orpheum, 87); the song was also recorded by the instrumental group Tangerine Dream. Legal complications prevented this from being used as a theme for the International Special Olympics, as originally was intended.

Time Is Time
Words and music by Andy Gibb and Barry Gibb.
Stigwood Music Inc., 1980/Joy U.S.A. Music Co., 1980/Hugh &

Barbara Gibb Music, 1980/Andy Gibb Music, 1980/Gibb Brothers Music, 1980.
Best-selling record by Andy Gibb from *Andy Gibb's Greatest Hits* (RSO, 80).

Time Like Your Wire Wheels
Words and music by Wendy Waldman.
Cotillion Music Inc., 1980.
Introduced by Wendy Waldman on *Which Way to Main Street* (Epic, 82).

Time out for the Burglar
Words and music by Pamela Phillips Oland, Randy Jackson, Jackie Jackson, Bernard Edwards, Robert Hart, Tony Thompson, Eddie Martinez, and Jeff Bova.
Irving Music Inc., 1987/Yonder/Yiggy/Ransaca.
Introduced by The Jacksons on the soundtrack of the film *Burglar* and its album (MCA, 87).

Time the Avenger (English)
Words and music by Chrissie Hynde.
MCA, Inc., 1984.
Introduced by The Pretenders on *Learning to Crawl* (Sire, 84).

Time Will Reveal
Words and music by Bunny DeBarge and Eldra DeBarge.
Jobete Music Co., 1983.
Best-selling record by DeBarge from *In a Special Way* (Gordy, 83).

Time Will Teach Us All (English)
Words and music by Hans Poulson and John Christie.
Spurs, England, 1986.
Best-selling record by Julian Lennon with Stevie Wonder from the English musical *Time* and on the album produced by Dave Clark, formerly of the Dave Clark Five (Capitol, 86).

Tired of Toein' the Line
Words and music by Rocky Burnette and Ron Coleman.
Cheshire Music Inc., 1979.
Best-selling record by Rocky Burnette from *The Son of Rock and Roll* (EMI-America, 80).

To All the Girls I've Loved Before (American-English)
Words by Hal David, music by Albert Hammond.
EMI-April Music, 1975/Casa David, 1975.
Best-selling record by Julio Iglesias and Willie Nelson from *1100 Bel Air Place* (Columbia, 84).

To Be a Lover
Words and music by William Bell and Booker T. Jones.
East/Memphis Music Corp., 1962/Irving Music Inc.
Best-selling record by Billy Idol from the album *Whiplash Smile*
    (Chrysalis, 86). Originally recorded by Gene Chandler in 1962.

To Know Her Is to Love Her, also known as **To Know Him Is to
    Love Him**
Revived in 1986 by John Lennon on *Menlove Avenue* (Capitol, 86).

To Know Her Is to Love Her, see **To Know Him Is to Love Him.**

To Know Him Is to Love Him, see **To Know Her Is to Love Her.**

To Know Him Is to Love Him, also known as **To Know Her Is to
    Love Her**
Words and music by Phil Spector.
Vogue Music, 1958.
Phil Spector wrote the song in 1958 as an epitaph for his father and it
    has been revived several times over the years, including by John
    Lennon on *Menlove Avenue* (Capital, 86), entitled 'To Know Her Is
    to Love Her.'

To Live and Die in L.A. (English)
Words and music by Wang Chung.
Chung Music Ltd., 1985.
Introduced by Wang Chung in the film *To Live and Die in L.A.* (85).

To Me
Words and music by Mack David and Mike Reid.
Collins Court Music, 1983/BMG Songs Inc., 1983.
Best-selling record by Barbara Mandrell and Lee Greenwood from
    Meant for Each Other (MCA, 84).

To Prove My Love
Words and music by Denzil Foster, Jay King, and Thom McElroy.
Jay King, IV, 1988.
Best-selling record by Michael Cooper from *Love Is Such a Funny
    Game* (Warner Bros., 88).

Together
Words and music by Bob DeSylva, Lew Brown, and Ray Henderson.
Chappell & Co., Inc., 1928.
Best-selling record by Tierra from *City Nights* (Boardwalk, 80).

Together
Words and music by Rob Wirth and Rik Howard.
Embassy TV, 1982.
Introduced on the TV series *Silver Spoons* (82).

Together Forever (English)
Words and music by Mike Stock, Matt Aitken, and Pete Waterman.
Terrace Entertainment Corp., 1988.
Best-selling record by Rick Astley, from *Whenever You Need Somebody* (RCA, 88).

Together Through the Years
Words and music by Charles Fox.
Performed by Roberta Flack as the title song for the television series *Valerie*.

Tom Sawyer (Canadian)
Words by Neil Peart and Pye Dubois, music by Geddy Lee and Alex Lifeson.
Core Music Publishing, 1981.
Best-selling record by Rush from *Moving Pictures* (Mercury, 81).

Tomb of the Unknown Love
Words and music by Michael Smotherman.
Seventh Son Music, 1986/If Eyes Inc., 1986/Garbo Music Division, 1986/Koppelman Family Music, 1986/Bandier Family Music, 1986/R. L. August Music Co., 1986.
Best-selling record by Kenny Rogers from the album *The Heart of the Matter* (RCA, 86).

Tombstone (Irish)
Words and music by Jem Finer.
Stiff Music America, England, 1989.
Introduced by The Pogues on *Peace and Love* (Island, 89).

Tonight
Words and music by James Taylor, Curtis Williams, Ronald Bell, George Brown, Robert Bell, Michael Ray, Clifford Adams, Charles Smith, and James Bonnefond.
Delightful Music Ltd., 1983.
Best-selling record by Kool & The Gang from *In the Heart* (De-Lite, 84).

Tonight I Celebrate My Love
Music by Michael Masser, words by Gerry Goffin.
Almo Music Corp., 1983/Prince Street Music, 1983/Screen Gems-EMI Music Inc., 1983.
Best-selling record by Peabo Bryson and Roberta Flack from *Born to Love* (Capitol, 83).

Tonight I'm Yours (Don't Hurt Me)
Words by Rod Stewart, music by Jim Cregan and Kevin Savigar.
Full Keel Music, 1981/WB Music, 1981/Rod Stewart, 1981.

Best-selling record by Rod Stewart from *Tonight I'm Yours* (Warner Brothers, 82).

Tonight Is What It Means to Be Young
Words and music by Jim Steinman.
Lost Boys Music, 1984/Off Backstreet Music, 1984.
Best-selling record by Fire Inc. (MCA, 84). Introduced in the film and soundtrack album *Streets of Fire* (84).

Tonight She Comes
Words and music by Ric Ocasek.
Lido Music Inc., 1985.
Best-selling record by The Cars from the album *Greatest Hits* (Elektra, 85).

Tonight, Tonight, Tonight (English)
Words and music by Tony Banks, Phil Collins, and Mike Rutherford.
Hit & Run Music, 1987.
Best-selling record in 1987 by Genesis, from the album *Invisible Touch* (Atlantic, 86). Television exposure as theme music in a Michelob beer commercial helped make this a hit.

Too Far Down
Words and music by Bob Mould.
Husker Music, 1986.
Introduced by Husker Du on the album *Candy Apple Grey* (Warner Bros., 86).

Too Gone Too Long
Words and music by Gene Pistilli.
EMI-April Music, 1988/High Falutin, 1988.
Best-selling record in 1988 by Randy Travis, from *Always and Forever* (Warner Bros., 87).

Too Hot
Words and music by George Brown.
Delicate Music, 1979/Gang Music Ltd., 1979.
Best-selling record by Kool & The Gang from *Ladies Night* (De-Lite, 80).

Too Late for Goodbyes (English)
Words and music by Julian Lennon.
Chappell & Co., Inc., 1984.
Best-selling record by Julian Lennon in 1985 from the album *Valotte* (Atlantic, 84). Author is the son of the late John Lennon.

Too Long in the Wasteland
Words and music by James McMurtry.
Short Trip Music, 1989.

Introduced by James McMurtry on *Too Long in the Wasteland* (Columbia, 89).

Too Many Lovers
Words and music by Mark True, Ted Lindsay, and Sam Hogin.
Cookhouse Music, 1980/Mother Tongue Music, 1980.
Best-selling record by Crystal Gayle from *These Days* (Columbia, 81).

Too Many Times
Words and music by Michael Smotherman, Scott Page, and Tony McShear.
Rowdy Boy Music, 1986/P.B.T.W. Music, 1986/Tunaday Songs, 1986.
Best-selling record by Earl Thomas Conley and Anita Pointer from the album *Too Many Times* (RCA, 86).

Too Much Is Not Enough
Words and music by David Bellamy and Ron Taylor.
Bellamy Brothers Music, 1986.
Best-selling record by The Bellamy Brothers and the Forester Sisters.

Too Much on My Heart
Words and music by Lester Fortune.
Statler Brothers Music, 1985.
Best-selling record by The Statler Brothers from the album *Pardners in Rhyme* (Mercury, 85).

Too Much Time on My Hands
Words and music by Tommy Shaw.
Stygian Songs, 1981/Almo Music Corp., 1981.
Best-selling record by Styx from *Paradise Theater* (A & M, 81).

Too Shy (English)
Words and music by Limahl and Nick Beggs.
Chappell & Co., Inc., 1983.
Best-selling record by Kajagoogoo from *White Feathers* (Capitol, 83).

Too Tight
Words and music by Michael Cooper.
Val-ie Joe Music, 1980.
Best-selling record by Con Funk Shun from *Touch* (Mercury, 81).

Total Eclipse of the Heart
Words and music by Jim Steinman.
E. B. Marks Music Corp., 1982.
Best-selling record by Bonnie Tyler from *Faster Than the Speed of Night* (Columbia, 83).

Touch a Four Leaf Clover
Words and music by David Lewis and Wayne Lewis.

Almo Music Corp., 1983/Jodaway Music, 1983.
Best-selling record by Atlantic Starr from *Yours Forever* (A & M, 83).

Touch a Hand, Make a Friend
Words and music by Homer Banks, Raymond Jackson, and Carl
    Hampton.
Irving Music Inc., 1985.
Best-selling record by The Oak Ridge Boys from the album *Step on Out*
    (MCA, 85).

Touch Me (I Want Your Body) (English)
Words and music by Michael Shreeve, J. Astrop, and Pete Q. Harris.
Zomba Music, 1987.
Best-selling record in 1987 by Samantha Fox, from the album *Touch Me*
    (Jive, 86).

Touch Me When We're Dancing
Words and music by Terry Skinner, J. L. Wallace, and Ken Bell.
Polygram International, 1979.
Best-selling record by The Carpenters from *Made in America* (A & M,
    81).

Touch of Grey
Words by Robert Hunter, music by Jerry Garcia.
Ice Nine Publishing Co., Inc., 1987.
Best-selling record by The Grateful Dead, from the album *In the Dark*
    (Arista, 87). This hit marked a major comeback for the ageless San
    Francisco band.

Tower of Song (Canadian)
Words and music by Leonard Cohen.
Stranger Music Inc., 1987.
Introduced by Leonard Cohen on *I'm Your Man* (Columbia, 88).

A Town Called Paradise (English)
Words and music by Van Morrison.
Essential Music, 1986.
Introduced by Van Morrison on the album *No Guru, No Method, No
    Teacher* (Polygram, 86).

Toy Soldiers
Words and music by Martika and Michael Jay.
Famous Music Corp., 1989/Tika Tunes/Ensign Music.
Best-selling record by Martika from *Martika* (Columbia, 89).

Trail of Broken Treaties
Words and music by Steve Van Zandt.
Little Steven Music, 1986.
Introduced by Little Steven on the album *Freedom--No Compromise*

(Manhattan, 86); another expression of political rock from the former Bruce Springsteen sideman.

Train in Vain (Stand by Me) (English)
Words and music by Michael Jones and Joe Strummer (pseudonym for John Mellor).
WB Music, 1979.
Best-selling record by The Clash from *London Calling* (Epic, 80).

Trapped
Words and music by Jimmy Cliff.
Island Music, 1972.
Recorded by Bruce Springsteen on the album *We Are the World* (Columbia, 85). Proceeds donated to the U.S.A. for Africa fund.

Travellin' Light
Words and music by Peter Case and Bobby Neuwirth.
Trumpet Blast Music, 1989/Bug Music/Dry Clam.
Introduced by Peter Case on *The Man with the Blue, Postmodern, Fragmented, Neo-Traditionalist Guitar* (Geffen, 89), with which Neuwirth, the famed travelling companion of Bob Dylan, emerged from bohemian obscurity.

Treat Me Right
Words and music by Doug Lubahn.
EMI-Blackwood Music Inc., 1980.
Best-selling record by Pat Benatar from *Crimes of Passion* (Chrysalis, 81).

Triad
Words and music by David Crosby.
Guerrilla Music, 1967.
Revived by The Byrds on *Never Before* (CBS, 87).

Trouble
Words and music by Lindsay Buckingham.
Now Sounds Music, 1981.
Best-selling record by Lindsay Buckingham from *Law and Order* (Asylum, 82).

Trouble in the Fields
Words and music by Nanci Griffith and Rick West.
Wing & Wheel Music, 1986.
Introduced by Nanci Griffith on the album *Lone Star State of Mind* (MCA, 86); here the singer-songwriter addresses the concerns of farmers. Revived in 1989 by Maura O'Connell on *Helpless Heart* (Warner Bros., 89).

461

Trouble Me
Words and music by Natalie Merchant and Dennis Drew.
Christian Burial Music, 1989.
Best-selling record by 10,000 Maniacs from *Blind Man's Zoo* (Elektra, 89).

True (English)
Words and music by Gary Kemp.
Reformation Publishing USA, 1983.
Best-selling record by Spandau Ballet from *True* (Chrysalis, 83).

True Blue
Words and music by Madonna and Steve Bray.
WB Music, 1986/Bleu Disque Music, 1986/Polygram International, 1986/Lost in Music, 1986.
Best-selling record by Madonna from the album *True Blue* (Warner Bros., 86).

True Colors
Words and music by Tom Kelly and Billy Steinberg.
Denise Barry Music, 1986/Sony Tunes, 1986.
Best-selling record by Cyndi Lauper from the album *True Colors* (Portrait, 86).

True Love
Words and music by Glenn Frey and Jack Tempchin.
Red Cloud Music Co., 1988/Night River Publishing, 1988.
Best-selling record by Glenn Frey from *Soul Searching* (MCA, 88).

True Love Ways
Words and music by Norman Petty and Buddy Holly.
Wrensong, 1958/MPL Communications Inc., 1958.
Revived by Mickey Gilley from *That's All That Matters to Me* (Epic, 80).

Truly
Words and music by Lionel Richie, Jr.
Brockman Enterprises Inc., 1982.
Best-selling record by Lionel Richie from *Lionel Richie* (Motown, 82).

Try Again
Words and music by Dana Walden, Michael Day, and Rocky Maffit.
Walkin Music, 1983.
Best-selling record by Champaign from *Modern Heart* (Columbia, 83).

Trying to Live My Life Without You
Words and music by Eugene Williams.
Happy Hooker Music Inc., 1977.

Best-selling record by Bob Seger from *Nine Tonight* (Capitol, 81).
Introduced by The J. Geils Band on the Flipside of 'I Do.'

Trying to Love Two Women
Words and music by Johhny Throckmorton.
Cross Keys Publishing Co., Inc., 1979.
Best-selling record by The Oak Ridge Boys from *Toghether* (MCA, 80).

Tuff Enuff
Words and music by Kim Wilson.
Fab Bird, 1986/Bug Music, 1986.
Best-selling record by The Fabulous Thunderbirds from the album *Tuff Enuff* (Epic, 86). Featured in the 1986 films *Tough Guys* and *Gung Ho*.

Tumblin' Down (Jamaican)
Words and music by Ziggy Marley and Tyrone Downe.
Ziggy, 1988/Colgems-EMI Music, 1988.
Best-selling record by Ziggy Marley and the Melody Makers from *Conscious Party* (Virgin, 88).

Tunnel of Love (English)
Words and music by Mark Knopfler.
Almo Music Corp., 1980.
Introduced by Dire Straits on *Making Movies* (Warner Brothers, 80).

Tunnel of Love
Words and music by Bruce Springsteen.
Bruce Springsteen Publishing, 1987.
Best-selling record by Bruce Springsteen, from the album *Tunnel of Love* (Columbia, 87).

Turn It Loose
Words and music by Don Schlitz, Craig Bickhardt, and Brent Maher.
Blue Quill Music, 1986/Colgems-EMI Music, 1986/Don Schlitz Music, 1986/MCA Music, 1986/Welbeck Music Corp., 1986.
Best-selling record in 1988 by The Judds, from *Heartland* (RCA, 87).

Turn Your Love Around
Words and music by Jay Graydon, Steve Lukather, and Bill Champlin.
Garden Rake Music, Inc., 1981/BMG Music, 1981/J S H Music, 1981.
Best-selling record by George Benson from *The George Benson Collection* (Warner Brothers, 81). Won a Grammy Award, and Rhythm 'n' Blues Song of the Year, 1982.

Turned Away
Words and music by Chuckie Booker and Donnell Spencer, Jr.
Selessongs, 1989/Honey Look.
Best-selling record by Chuckie Booker from *Chuck II* (Atlantic, 89).

Turning Away
Words and music by Tim Krekel.
EMI Music Publishing, 1983.
Best-selling record by Crystal Gayle from *Cage the Songbird* (Warner Brothers, 84).

Turning Japanese (English)
Words and music by David Fenton.
Glenwood Music Corp., 1979.
Best-selling record by The Vapors from *New Clear Days* (United Artists, 81).

Tweeter and the Monkey Man
Words and music by Traveling Wilburys.
Copyright Control, 1988.
Introduced by The Traveling Wilburys on *Traveling Wilburys Volume I* (Wilbury, 88).

Twelve Rough Years
Words and music by Elizabeth Swados.
EMI-Blackwood Music Inc., 1987.
Introduced by Ashanti Isabell in the 1987 musical *Swing*.

21 Jump Street
Words and music by Liam Sternberg.
Stephen Cannell Music, 1988.
Introduced by Holly Robinson (I.R.S., 88). Theme from the popular television show *21 Jump Street*.

Twenty Years Ago
Words and music by Michael Spriggs, Wood Newton, Dan Tyler, and Michael Noble.
Warner House of Music, 1987/WB Gold Music Corp.
Best-selling record by Kenny Rogers, from the album *They Don't Make Them Like They Used To* (RCA).

Twilight Zone (Netherlands)
English words and music by George Kooymans.
Fever Music, Inc., 1982.
Best-selling record by Golden Earring from *Cut* (21 Records, 83).

Twinkle, Twinkle Lucky Star
Words and music by Merle Haggard.
Inorbit Music, Inc., 1988.
Best-selling record in 1988 by Merle Haggard, from *Chill Factor* (Epic, 87).

Twins
Words and music by Skip Scarborough and Smokey Bates.

Music Corp. of America, 1988/Alexscar Music, 1988/Paper Boy
Publishing, 1988.
Introduced by Philip Bailey and Little Richard in the film and on the
soundtrack album *Twins* (CBS, 88).

The Twist
Words and music by Hank Ballard.
Lois Publishing Co., 1959.
Revived in 1988 by The Fat Boys on *Coming Back Hard Again* (Tin
Pan Apple), accompained by Chubby Checker, the song's popularizer,
on vocals.

Twist and Shout
Words and music by Bert Russell and Phil Medley.
Unforgettable Songs, 1960/Screen Gems-EMI Music Inc., 1960.
Revived in 1986 by comedian Rodney Dangerfield in the film *Back to
School.* In another 1986 film, *Ferris Bueller's Day Off,* actor Matthew
Broderick lip-synched The Beatles' original version, which was re-
released by Capitol that year.

Twist in My Sobriety (English)
Words and music by Tanita Tikaram.
Brogue Music, 1988.
Introduced by Tanita Tikaram on *Ancient Heart* (Reprise, 89). Also
recorded by Liza Minnelli on *Results* (Epic, 89).

Twist of Fate
Words and music by Stephen Kipner and Peter Beckett.
Stephen A. Kipner Music, 1983/EMI-April Music, 1983/Big Stick
Music, 1983/Careers Music Inc., 1983.
Best-selling record by Olivia Newton-John (MCA, 83). Introduced in the
film and soundtrack album *Two of a Kind* (83).

2 A.M.
Words and music by James S. Carter, Kevin Askins, and Maurice
Hammett.
Ted-On Music, 1988/James Car Publishing, Inc., 1988.
Best-selling record by Teddy Pendergrass, from *Joy* (Elektra, 88).

Two Dozen Roses
Words and music by Robert Byrne and Mac McAnnally.
Colgems-EMI Music, 1989/Beginner Music.
Best-selling record by Shenandoah from *The Road Not Taken*
(Columbia, 89).

Two Hearts (English)
Words and music by Phil Collins and Lamont Dozier.
Phil Collins, 1988/Hidden Pun, 1988/Beau Di O Do Music, 1988/
Warner-Tamerlane Music, 1988.

Best-selling record by Phil Collins, from the film and soundtrack album *Buster* (Atlantic, 88). Collins' co-writer is the linchpin of Motown's Holland-Dozier-Holland songwiting team. Won a Grammy Award, and Best Song for a Film or TV, 1988. Nominated for an Academy Award, Song of the Year, 1988.

Two Hearts Beat as One (Irish)
Words and music by Bono (pseudonym for Paul Hewson), Larry Mullen, Adam Clayton, and The Edge (pseudonym for Dave Evans).
Island Music, 1983.
Introduced on *War* by U2 (Island, 83).

Two Occasions
Words and music by Babyface (pseudonym for Kenny Edmunds), Darnell Johnson, and L. A. Reid (pseudonym for Antonio Reid).
Hip Hill Music Publishing Co., 1987/Hip Chic, 1987/Long Tooth Music, 1987/Peer-Southern Organization, 1987/Tammi Music Ltd., 1987.
Best-selling record by The Deele, from *Eyes of a Stranger* (Solar, 88).

Two of Hearts
Words and music by John Mitchell, Sue Gatlin, and Tim Greene.
On the Note, 1985/Bug Music, 1985/Tim Green, 1985/Four Buddies, 1985.
Best-selling record by Stacey Q (real name, Stacey Swain) from the album *Better Than Heaven* (Atlantic, 86). The song was originally a club scene hit on an independent label.

Two Story House
Words and music by Glen Tubb, David Lindsey, and Tammy Wynette.
ATV Music Corp., 1980/First Lady Songs, Inc., 1980.
Best-selling record by George Jones with Tammy Wynette (Epic, 80).

2000 Miles (English)
Words and music by Chrissie Hynde.
Virgin Music, 1983.
Introduced by The Pretenders in *Learning to Crawl* (Sire, 84).

Two to Make It Right
Words and music by David Cole.
Red Instructional Music, 1989.
Best-selling record by Seduction from *Nothing Matters without Love* (Vendetta, 89).

Two Tribes (English)
Words and music by Peter Gill, William Johnson, and Mark O'Toole.
Island Music, 1984.
Best-selling record Frankie Goes to Hollywood from *Welcome to the Pleasure Dome* (Island, 84).

Two Wrongs (Don't Make It Right)
Words and music by Ralph Hawkins and David Jones.
Venus Three Music, 1989/Pushy Publishing/Perfect Ten Music.
Best-selling record by David Peaston from *Introducing...David Peaston*
(Geffen, 89).

Typical Male (English)
Words and music by Terry Britten and Graham Lyle.
Myake, England, 1986/Almo Music Corp., 1986/WB Music, 1986.
Best-selling record by Tina Turner from the album *Break Every Rule*
(Capitol, 86).

U

U Got the Look
Words and music by Prince Rogers Nelson.
Controversy Music, 1987.
Best-selling record by Prince, from the album and movie soundtrack
Sign 'o' the Times (Paisley Park, 87). Nominated for a Grammy
Award, Rhythm 'n' Blues Song of the Year, 1987.

UHF
Words and music by Al Yankovic.
Holy Moley Music, 1989.
Introduced by Weird Al Yankovic in the film and on the soundtrack
album of *UHF* (Rock *N' Roll, 89).*

Uncle Pen
Words and music by Bill Monroe.
Kentucky Music, Inc., 1951.
Best-selling record by Ricky Skaggs (Sugar Hill/Epic, 84).

Under a Raging Moon (English)
Words and music by John Parr and Julia Downes.
Carbert Music Inc., 1985.
Best-selling record by Roger Daltrey from the album *Under a Raging
Moon* (Atlantic, 85). This song is dedicated to the late Keith Moon,
drummer of the rock group The Who, for which Daltrey was lead
singer.

Under One Banner
Words and music by Billy Nicholls.
HG Music, Inc., 1981.
Featured on *Modern Dreams* by Carolyn Mas (Mercury, 81).

Under Pressure (English)
Words and music by David Bowie, music by Queen.
Queen Music Ltd., 1981/Jones Music Co., 1981.

Best-selling record by Queen and David Bowie from *Queen's Greatest Hits* (Elektra, 82).

Under the Big Black Sun
Words and music by John Doe and Exene Cervenka, music by X.
Eight/Twelve Music, 1982.
Introduced by X on *Under the Big Black Sun* (Elektra, 82).

Under the Boardwalk
Words and music by Arthur Resnick and Kenny Young.
Hudson Bay Music, 1964.
Revived in 1986 by Bruce Willis on the album *The Return of Bruno* (Motown), which featured the star of television's *Moonlighting* as a mythical rock 'n' roller.

Under the Covers
Words and music by Janis Ian.
Mine Music, Ltd., 1981.
Best-selling record by Janis Ian from *Restless Eyes* (Columbia, 81).

Under the Milky Way (Australian)
Words and music by Steve Kilbey and Karin Jansson.
Funzalo Music, 1988/Bug Music, 1988/MCA Music, 1988.
Best-selling record by The Church in *Starfish* (Arista, 88). A breakthrough hit for this longstanding album group.

Under the Sea
Words by Howard Ashman, music by Alan Menken.
Walt Disney Music, 1989.
Introduced by Sam Wright, the voice of Sebastian the Crab, in the animated film and soundtrack album of *The Little Mermaid* (Walt Disney, 89). Won an Academy Award, and Best Original Song, 1989.

Under Your Spell
Words and music by Bob Dylan and Carole Bayer Sager.
Special Rider Music, 1986/Carole Bayer Sager Music, 1986.
Introduced by Bob Dylan on the album *Knocked Out Loaded* (Columbia, 86). This title is the product of an unusual collaboration by the rough-edged former folksinger and the stylish pop lyricist wife of Burt Bacharach.

Undercover of the Night (English)
Words and music by Mick Jagger and Keith Richards.
Colgems-EMI Music, 1983.
Best-selling record by The Rolling Stones from *Undercover* (Rolling Stones, 83).

Underground (English)
Words and music by David Bowie.

Brookwood, England, 1986/Jones Music Co., 1986.
Introduced by David Bowie in the film *Labyrinth* and on the soundtrack album (EMI-America, 86).

Understanding
Words and music by Bob Seger.
Gear Publishing, 1984.
Best-selling record by Bob Seger & The Silver Bullet Band (Capitol, 84). Introduced in the film and soundtrack album *Teachers* (84).

Unexpected Song (English)
Words by Don Black, music by Andrew Lloyd Webber.
Dick James Music Inc., 1982.
Performed by Bernadette Peters in the musical *Song and Dance* (85). Introduced in England in 1982.

Union of the Snake (English)
Words and music by Duran Duran.
Chappell & Co., Inc., 1983.
Best-selling record by Duran Duran from *Seven and the Ragged Tiger* (Capitol, 83).

United Together
Words and music by Chuck Jackson and Phil Perry.
Jay's Enterprises, Inc., 1980/Baby Love Music, Inc., 1980/Chappell & Co., Inc., 1980/Phivin International Enterprises, 1980.
Best-selling record by Aretha Franklin from *Aretha* (Arista, 80).

Until I Met You
Words and music by Hank Riddle.
King Coal Music Inc., 1980.
Best-selling record by Judy Rodman from the album *Judy* (Capitol, 86).

Until the Good Is Gone
Words and music by Steve Van Zandt.
Blue Midnight Music, 1982.
Introduced by Little Steven & The Disciples of Soul on *Men without Women* (EMI, 82).

Unwed Fathers
Words and music by John Prine and Bobby Braddock.
Tree Publishing Co., Inc., 1987/Bruised Oranges, 1987/Big Ears Music Inc., 1987.
Introduced by Tim and Mollie O'Brien on *Take Me Back* (Sugar Hill, 88).

Up the Ladder to the Roof
Words and music by Vincent Dimirco and Frank Wilson.
Stone Agate Music, 1970.

Revived in 1987 by John Kydd (Nightwave, 87), whose back-up singers
  included former Supremes Cindy Birdsong, Lynda Lawrence, and
  Scherrie Payne. The Supremes had a hit with this song in 1970.

Up Where We Belong
Words and music by Jack Nitzsche, Will Jennings, and Buffy Sainte-
  Marie.
Famous Music Corp., 1982/Ensign Music, 1982.
Best-selling record by Joe Cocker and Jennifer Warnes (Island, 82).
  Introduced in the film and soundtrack album *An Officer and a
  Gentleman* (82). Won an Academy Award, and Best Song, 1982.

Upside Down
Words and music by Bernard Edwards and Nile Rodgers.
Chic Music Inc., 1980.
Best-selling record by Diana Ross from *Diana* (Motown, 80).

Uptown Girl
Words and music by Billy Joel.
Joelsongs, 1983.
Best-selling record by Billy Joel from *An Innocent Man* (Columbia, 83).

Urgent (English)
Words and music by Mick (Foreigner) Jones.
Somerset Songs Publishing, Inc., 1981/E S P Management, Inc., 1981.
Best-selling record by Foreigner from *4* (Atlantic, 81).

Used to Blue
Words and music by Fred Knobloch and Bill LaBounty.
Montage Music Inc., 1985/Captain Crystal Music, 1985/A Little More
  Music Inc., 1985.
Best-selling record by Sawyer Brown from the album *Sawyer Brown*
  (Capitol, 85).

Useless Waltz
Words by David Frishberg, music by Bob Brookmeyer.
Swiftwater Music, 1979.
Performed by David Frishberg on *The David Frishberg Songbook, Vol.
  Two* (Omnisound), 83).

V

Vacation
Words and music by Kathy Valentine, words by Charlotte Caffey and
  Jane Wiedlin.
Some Other Music, 1980/Daddy Oh Music, 1980/Lipsync Music, 1980.
Best-selling record by The Go-Go's from *Vacation* (I.R.S., 82).

Valentine's Day
Words and music by Bruce Springsteen.
Bruce Springsteen Publishing, 1987.
Introduced by Bruce Springsteen on the album *Tunnel of Love*
  (Columbia, 87).

Valentine's Day
Words and music by James Taylor.
Country Road Music Inc., 1988.
Introduced by James Taylor on *Never Die Young* (CBS, 88).

Valeri (English)
Words and music by Richard Thompson.
Island Music, 1986.
Introduced by Richard Thompson on the album *Daring Adventures*
  (Polygram, 86).

Valerie (American-English)
Words by Will Jennings, music by Steve Winwood.
Island Music, 1982/Blue Sky Rider Songs/Willin' David.
Revived in 1987 by Steve Winwood on the album *Chronicle* (Island);
  Winwood originally used the song on the album *Talking Back to the
  Night*.

Valley Girl
Words and music by Frank Zappa and Moon Zappa.
Munchkin Music, 1982.
Best-selling record by Frank and Moon Unit Zappa from *Ship arriving
  too late to save a drowning watch* (Barking Pumpkin, 82).

The Valley Road
Words and music by Bruce Hornsby and John Hornsby.
Zappo Music, 1988/Basically Gasp Music, 1988.
Best-selling record by Bruce Hornsby and The Range, from *Scenes from the Southside* (RCA, 88).

Valotte (English)
Words and music by Julian Lennon, Justin Clayton, and Carlton Morales.
Chappell & Co., Inc., 1984.
Best-selling record by Julian Lennon from *Valotte* (Atlantic, 84).

Vamp
Words and music by Jonathan Elias and Grace Jones.
Introduced by Grace Jones in the film *Vamp* (86).

Vanna, Pick Me a Letter, also known as **The Letter**
Introduced by Dr. Dave on the album *Dr. Dave* (TSR, 87). This tribute to Vanna White, the hostess on the television game show *Wheel of Fortune*, is set to the music for the Box Tops' 1967 hit, *'The Letter.'* The new lyrics by Dave Kolin and Wayne Carson Thompson were registered for copyright in 1986.

Vanz Can't Dance, see **Zanz Can't Dance**.

Venus (Netherlands)
English words and music by R.V. Leeuwen.
Fat Zach Music, Inc., 1969.
Revived in 1986 by Bananarama from the album *True Confessions* (Polygram, 86). Introduced by Shocking Blue in 1970. This was only the fourth single ever to reach number one by two different groups (the others being 'Locomotion,' 'Please Mr. Postman,' and the legendary 'Go Away Little Girl').

Verdi Cries
Words and music by Natalie Merchant.
Christian Burial, 1987.
Introduced by 10,000 Maniacs on the album *In My Tribe* (Elektra, 87).

Veronica (English)
Words and music by Declan MacManus and Paul McCartney.
Plangent Visions Music, Inc., London, England, 1988/MPL Communications Inc., 1988.
Introduced by Elvis Costello on *Spike* (Warner Bros., 89).

Very Special
Words and music by William Jeffery and Lisa Peters.
At Home Music, 1981/Jeffix Music Co., 1981.
Best-selling record by Debra Laws from *Very Special* (Elektra, 81).

Victory
Words and music by Ronald Bell and James Taylor.
Delightful Music Ltd., 1986.
Best-selling record by Kool & The Gang from the album *Forever* (Mercury, 86).

Vienna Calling (German)
English words and music by Rob Bolland, Ferdi Bolland, and Falco (pseudonym for Hans Hoelzl).
Nada, Germany, 1986/Manuskript, Germany, 1986/Almo Music Corp., 1986.
Best-selling record by Falco from the album *Falco 3* (A & M, 86).

A View to a Kill (English)
Words by Duran Duran, music by Duran Duran, music by John Barry.
Danjag, S.A., England, 1985/Tritec Music Ltd., England, 1985.
Best-selling record by Duran Duran (Capitol, 85). Introduced in the James Bond film and soundtrack album *A View to a Kill* (Capitol, 85), which featured this group's first film soundtrack.

The Voice (English)
Words and music by Justin Hayward.
WB Music, 1981.
Best-selling record by The Moody Blues from *Long Distance Voyager* (Threshold, 81).

Voice of America's Sons
Words and music by John Cafferty.
John Cafferty Music, 1986.
Introduced by John Cafferty & the Beaver Brown Band in the 1986 film *Cobra* and on the soundtrack album (Scotti Bros., 86).

Voices Carry
Words and music by Aimee Mann, Michael Hausman, Robert Holmes, and Joseph Pesce.
Intersong, USA Inc., 1985/'Til Tunes Associates, 1985.
Best-selling record by 'Til Tuesday from the album *Voices Carry* (Epic, 85).

Voices on the Wind
Words and music by Bill Payne, Fred Tackett, Craig Fuller, and Paul Barrere.
Little Music, 1988/Feat Music, 1988.
Introduced by Little Feat on *Let It Roll* (Warner Bros., 88).

W

Wait
Words and music by Vito Bratta and Mike Tramp.
Vavoom, 1986.
Best-selling record in 1988 by White Lion, from *Pride* (Atlantic, 87).

Wait for Me
Words and music by Daryl Hall.
Hot Cha Music Co., 1979/Six Continents Music, 1979.
Best-selling record by Hall and Oates from *X-Static* (RCA, 80).

The Waiting
Words and music by Tom Petty.
Gone Gator Music, 1981.
Best-selling record by Tom Petty & The Heartbreakers from *Hard Promises* (Backstreet, 81).

Waiting for a Girl Like You (English)
Words and music by Mick (Foreigner) Jones and Lou Gramm.
Somerset Songs Publishing, Inc., 1981/E S P Management, Inc., 1981.
Best-selling record by Foreigner from *4* (Atlantic, 81).

Waiting for a Star to Fall
Words and music by Gary Merrill and Shannon Rubicam.
Irving Music Inc., 1987/Boy Meets Girl, 1987.
Best-selling record by Boy Meets Girl from *Reel Life* (RCA, 88). The group is composed of the two songwriters.

Waiting for the Weekend (English)
Words and music by David Fenton.
EMI Music Publishing, 1980.
Introduced by The Vapors in *New Clear Days* (Liberty, 80).

Waiting on a Friend (English)
Words and music by Mick Jagger and Keith Richards.
Colgems-EMI Music, 1981.

Best-selling record by The Rolling Stones from *Tattoo You* (Rolling Stones, 81).

Waiting on Love
Words and music by Sammy Llanas and Kurt Neumann.
Lla-Mann, 1987.
Introduced by The BoDeans in the film and on the soundtrack album *Permanent Record* (Epic, 88).

Wake Me Up Before You Go-Go (English)
Words and music by George Michael.
Chappell & Co., Inc., 1984.
Best-selling record by Wham from *Make it Big* (Columbia, 84).

Wake Up (Next to You) (English)
Words and music by Graham Parker.
Ellisclar, England, 1985.
Best-selling record by Graham Parker from the album *Steady Nerves* (Elektra, 85).

Wake up and Live (Jamaican)
Words and music by Bob Marley and Horace Anthony Davis.
Bob Marley Music, Ltd., Nassau, Bahamas, 1979.
Featured on *Uprising* by Bob Marley (Island, 80).

Walk Like a Man
Words and music by Bruce Springsteen.
Bruce Springsteen Publishing, 1987.
Introduced by Bruce Springsteen on the album *Tunnel of Love* (Columbia, 87).

Walk Like an Egyptian
Words and music by Liam Sternberg.
Peer International Corp., 1985.
Best-selling record by The Bangles from the album *Different Light* (Columbia, 86). The songwriter produced Rachel Sweet's first album.

Walk of Life (English)
Words and music by Mark Knopfler.
Almo Music Corp., 1985.
Best-selling record by Dire Straits from the album *Brothers in Arms* (Warner Bros., 85).

Walk on Water
Words and music by Jesse Harms.
Geffen Music, 1987/Thornwall, 1987.
Best-selling record by Eddie Money, from *Nothing to Lose* (Columbia, 88).

Walk the Dinosaur
Words and music by Don Was (pseudonym for Donald Fagenson),
   David Was (pseudonym for David Weiss), and Randall Jacobs.
MCA Music, 1988/Semper Fi Music.
Best-selling record in 1989 by Was (Not Was) from *What Up, Dog*
   (Chrysalis, 88).

Walk This Way
Words and music by Steven Tyler and Joe Perry.
Daksel Music Corp., 1975.
Revived in 1986 by Run D.M.C. on the album *Raising Hell* (Profile,
   86), with backup singing and playing provided by members of
   Aerosmith, the band that recorded the original in 1977.

Walk with an Erection
Words by Liam Sternberg and Johnny Angel, music by Liam Sternberg.
Peer International Corp.
Performed by The Swinging Erudites (Airwave, 87); this lewd parody of
   the 1986 Bangles' hit, 'Walk like an Egyptian,' was denied license by
   copyright holders, but it became an underground hit nonetheless.

Walkin' a Broken Heart
Words and music by Alan Rush and Dennis Linde.
Combine Music Corp., 1983/Dennis Linde Music, 1983.
Best-selling record by Don Williams from *Greatest Hits IV* (MCA, 85).

Walking Away
Words and music by Paul Robb.
T-Boy Music, 1988/Insoc Music.
Best-selling record in 1989 by Information Society from *Information
   Society* (Tommy Boy, 88).

Walking down Your Street
Words and music by Susanna Hoffs, music by Louis Gutierrez and
   David Kahne.
EMI-Blackwood Music Inc., 1986/Bangophile Music, 1986/Spinning
   Avenue Music, 1986/Seesquared Music, 1986.
Introduced by The Bangles on the album *Different Light* (Columbia, 86).

Walking on a Thin Line
Words and music by Andre Pessis and Kevin Wells.
Endless Frogs Music, 1983/Bug/Slimey Limey Music, 1983/McNoodle
   Music, 1983.
Best-selling record by Huey Lewis & The News from *Sports* (Chrysalis,
   84).

Walking on Sunshine
Words and music by Kimberly Rew.
Screen Gems-EMI Music Inc., 1985.

Best-selling record by Katrina and the Waves from the album *Katrina and the Waves* (Capitol, 85).

Walking on Thin Ice
Words and music by Yoko Ono.
Lenono Music, 1981/Warner-Tamerlane Music, 1981.
Best-selling record by Yoko One (Geffen, 81).

Walking Through Midnight
Words and music by Johnny Lyon and Bruce Springsteen.
Bruce Springsteen Publishing, 1988.
Introduced by Southside Johnny and The Asbury Jukes, from *Slow Dance* (Cypress, 88). Southside Johnny teamed with his former boss to write this song.

Wall of Death (English)
Words and music by Richard Thompson.
Island Music, 1982.
Introduced by Richard and Linda Thompson on *Shoot out the Lights* (Hannibal, 82).

Wall of Denial
Words and music by Stevie Ray Vaughan and Doyle Bramhall.
Stevie Ray Songs, 1988/Bramhall Publishing/Bug Music.
Introduced by Stevie Ray Vaughan on *In Step* (Epic, 89), this song details the singer's battles with drug abuse.

The Wanderer (American-German)
English words by Donna Summer, music by Giorgio Moroder.
Giorgio Moroder Publishing Co., 1980/Sweet Summer Night Music, 1980.
Best-selling record by Donna Summer from *The Wanderer* (Geffen, 80).

The Wanderer
Words and music by Ernest Maresca.
Schwartz Music Co., Inc., 1960/Rust Enterprises, Inc., 1960.
Revived in 1988 by Eddie Rabbitt in *I Wanna Dance with You* (MCA, 88).

Wango Tango
Words and music by Ted Nugent.
Magicland Music, 1980.
Best-selling record by Ted Nugent from *Scream Dream* (Epic, 80).

Wanna Be Startin' Something
Words and music by Michael Jackson.
Mijac Music, 1982/Warner-Tamerlane Music, 1982.
Best-selling record by Michael Jackson from *Thriller* (Epic, 83).

Nominated for a Grammy Award, Rhythm 'n' Blues Song of the Year, 1983.

Wanted Dead or Alive
Words and music by Jon Bon Jovi and Richie Sambora.
Bon Jovi Publishing, 1986/Polygram Music Publishing Inc., 1986.
Best-selling record in 1987, from the album *Slippery When Wet*
  (Polygram, 86).

War
Words and music by Norman Whitfield and Barrett Strong.
Stone Agate Music, 1976.
Revived in 1986 by Bruce Springsteen on the album *Bruce Springsteen
  & The E Street Band Live, 1975-1985* (Columbia, 86). The original
  version by Edwin Starr has also been reissued, with 'Stop the War
  Now' by the same writers on the flipside (Motown, 86).

War Is Hell (on the Homefront Too)
Words and music by Curly Putman, Dan Wilson, and Bucky Jones.
Tree Publishing Co., Inc., 1982/Cross Keys Publishing Co., Inc., 1982.
Best-selling record by T. G. Sheppard from *T.G. Sheppard's Greatest
  Hits* (Warner/Curb, 83).

Warning Sign
Words and music by Eddie Rabbitt and Even Stevens.
Debdave Music Inc., 1984/Briarpatch Music.
Best-selling record by Eddie Rabbitt from the album *The Best Year of
  My Life* (Warner Bros., 85).

The Warrior (English)
Words and music by Holly Knight and Nick Gilder.
Mike Chapman Publishing Enterprises, 1984/BMG Songs Inc., 1984/
  Chrysalis Music Group, 1984.
Best-selling record by Scandal from *The Warrior* (Columbia, 84).

Wasted on the Way
Words and music by Graham Nash.
Putzy-Putzy Music, 1982.
Best-selling record by Crosby, Stills and Nash from *Daylight Again*
  (Atlantic, 82).

Watch Baby Fall
Words and music by David Bromberg.
Sweet Jelly Roll Music, Inc., 1989.
Introduced by David Bromberg on *Sideman's Serenade* (Rounder, 89).

Watching the Wheels
Words and music by John Lennon.

Lenono Music, 1980.
Best-selling record by John Lennon from *Double Fantasy* (Geffen, 81).

Watching You
Words and music by Mark Adams, Raye Turner, Daniel Webster, Stephen Washington, and Steve Arrington.
Cotillion Music Inc., 1980.
Best-selling record by Slave from *Stone Jam* (Warner Brothers, 81).

Watching You (English)
Words and music by Carl McIntosh, Jane Eugene, and Steve Nichol.
Brampton Music Ltd., England, 1988/Virgin Music, 1988/MCA Music, 1988.
Best-selling record by Loose Ends, from *The Real Chuckeeboo* (MCA, 88).

Waves of Grain
Words and music by Pat MacDonald.
Mambadaddi, 1989/I.R.S. Music.
Introduced by Timbuk 3 on *Edge of Allegiance* (IRS, 89).

The Way He Makes Me Feel
Words by Alan Bergman and Marilyn Bergman, music by Michel Legrand.
Ennes Productions, Ltd., 1983/Emanuel Music, 1983/Threesome Music Co., 1983.
Best-selling record by Barbra Streisand (Columbia, 83). Introduced in the film and soundtrack album *Yentl* (83). Nominated for an Academy Award, Best Song, 1983.

The Way I Am
Words and music by Sonny Throckmorton.
Cross Keys Publishing Co., Inc., 1979.
Best-selling record by Merle Haggard from *The Way I Am* (MCA, 80).

The Way It Is
Words and music by Bruce Hornsby.
Zappo Music, 1986/Bob-a-Lew Music, 1986.
Best-selling record by Bruce Hornsby and The Range from the album *The Way It Is* (RCA, 86).

Way of the Heart
Words and music by Karla Bonoff.
Seagrape Music Inc., 1988.
Introduced by Karla Bonoff in *New World* (Gold Castle, 88).

The Way We Make a Broken Heart
Words and music by John Hiatt.
Bug Music, 1980/Bilt, 1980.

Best-selling record by Rosanne Cash, from the album *King's Record Shop* (Columbia, 87). Introduced by Ry Cooder on the album *Borderline* (Warner Bros., 80).

The Way You Do the Things You Do
Words and music by William Robinson and Bobby Rogers.
Jobete Music Co., 1964.
Revived by Daryl Hall and John Oates as part of a medley with 'My Girl' on the album *Hall and Oates Live at the Apollo* (RCA, 85).

The Way You Love Me
Words and music by Babyface (pseudonym for Kenny Edmunds), L. A. Reid (pseudonym for Antonio Reid), and Daryl Simmons.
Kear Music, 1988/Hip-Trip Music Co./Green Skirt Music.
Best-selling record in 1989 by Karyn White from *Karyn White* (Warner Bros., 88).

The Way You Make Me Feel
Words and music by Michael Jackson.
Mijac Music, 1987/Warner-Tamerlane Music, 1987.
Best-selling record by Michael Jackson, from the album *Bad* (Epic, 87).

Ways to Be Wicked
Words and music by Mike Campbell and Tom Petty.
Gone Gator Music, 1985/Wild Gator Music, 1985.
Best-selling record by Lone Justice from the album *Lone Justice* (Geffen, 85).

We All Sleep Alone
Words and music by Jon Bon Jovi, Richie Sambora, and Desmond Child.
EMI-April Music, 1988/Desmobile Music Inc., 1988/Bon Jovi Publishing, 1988/Polygram Songs, 1988.
Best-selling record by Cher from *Cher* (Geffen, 88).

We Are Here to Change the World
Words and music by Michael Jackson.
Mijac Music, 1986.
Introduced by Michael Jackson at the Disneyland premier of *Captain Eo,* a thirty-minute video special. This was Jackson's first new song since *Thriller* sold thiry-seven million units internationally in 1983.

We Are the World
Words and music by Michael Jackson and Lionel Richie, Jr.
Mijac Music, 1985/Brockman Enterprises Inc.
Best-selling record by U.S.A. for Africa from the album *We Are the World* (Columbia, 85). The most famous of the Ethiopian-aid songs, performed by a virtual hall of fame of the American pop music

community, including Bob Dylan, Ray Charles, Bruce Springsteen, and Harry Belafonte. Won Grammy Awards.

We Believe in Happy Endings
Words and music by Bob McDill.
Irving Music Inc., 1977.
Best-selling record by Earl Thomas Conley with Emmylou Harris from *The Heart of It All* (RCA, 88).

We Belong
Words and music by David Lowen and Daniel Navarro.
Screen Gems-EMI Music Inc., 1984.
Best-selling record by Pat Benatar from *Tropico* (Chrysalis, 84).

We Belong Together
Words and music by Rickie Lee Jones.
Easy Money Music, 1980.
Introduced by Rickie Lee Jones in *Pirates* (Warner Brothers, 81).

We Built This City
Words by Bernie Taupin, words and music by Martin Page, Dennis Lambert, and Peter Wolf.
Intersong, USA Inc., 1985/Little Mole Music, 1985/Zomba Music, 1985/Petwolf Music, 1985/Tuneworks Music, 1985.
Best-selling record by Starship from the album *Knee Deep in the Hoopla* (RCA, 85).

We Can Make It
Words by John Ebb, music by Fred Kander.
Fiddleback, 1983/Kander & Ebb Inc., 1983.
Introduced by Chita Rivera in *The Rink* (84).

We Didn't Start the Fire
Words and music by Billy Joel.
Joel, 1989.
Best-selling record by Billy Joel from *Storm Front* (Columbia, 89); this song encapsulates forty years of recent history. Nominated for Grammy Awards, Record of the Year, 1989, and Song of the Year, 1989.

We Don't Have to Take Our Clothes Off
Words and music by Preston Glass and Narada Michael Walden.
Bellboy Music, 1986/Chappell & Co., Inc., 1986.
Best-selling record by Jermaine Stewart from the album *Frantic Romantic* (Arista, 86).

We Don't Need Another Hero (Thunderdome) (English)
Words and music by Terry Britten and Graham Lyle.
Myax Music Ltd., England, 1985/Good Single Ltd., England, 1985.

Best-selling record by Tina Turner (Capitol, 85). Introduced in the film and soundtrack album *Mad Max: Beyond Thunderdome* (85).

We Don't Talk Anymore (English)
Words and music by Al Tarney.
ATV Music Corp., 1979.
Best-selling record by Cliff Richard from *We Don't Talk Anymore* (EMI-American, 80).

We Go a Long Way Back
Words and music by Charles Love.
EMI-Blackwood Music Inc., 1980.
Best-selling record by Bloodstone from *We Go a Long Way Back* (T-Neck, 82).

We Got the Beat
Words and music by Charlotte Caffey.
Daddy Oh Music, 1981.
Best-selling record by The Go-Go's from *Beauty and the Beat* (I. R. S., 82).

We Live So Fast (English)
Words and music by Glenn Gregory, Ian Craig Marsh, and Martyn Ware.
Virgin Music, 1982/WB Music, 1982.
Introduced by Heaven 17 in *The Luxury Gap* (Sire, 82).

We Want Some Pussy
Words and music by Luther Campbell.
Introduced by 2 Live Crew on the album *2 Live Crew Is What We Are* (Luke Skywalker Records, 87). This song and album led to the arrest of a salesgirl in Florida for distributing lewd material to minors. Charges were later dropped.

We Will Not Be Lovers (Irish)
Words and music by Mike Scott.
Dizzy Heights Music Publishing, Ltd., 1988/Chrysalis Music Group, 1988.
Introduced by The Waterboys on *Fisherman's Blues* (Chrsalis, 88). Scott was cited as 'rock's poet laureate' by Rolling Stone Magazine in 1985.

The Weekend
Words and music by Bill La Bounty and Brent Maher.
Screen Gems-EMI Music Inc., 1987.
Best-selling record by Steve Wariner, from the album *It's a Crazy World* (MCA, 87).

Weird Science
Words and music by Danny Elfman.
Music of the World, 1985.
Introduced by Oingo Boingo in the film and soundtrack album *Weird Science* (MCA, 85).

Welcome to the Boomtown
Words and music by David Baerwald and David Ricketts.
Zen of Iniquity, 1986/48/11 Music, 1986/Almo Music Corp., 1986.
Best-selling record by David and David from the album *Boomtown* (A & M, 86).

Welcome to the Human Race
Words and music by Pat MacDonald.
Mambadaddi, 1987/I.R.S. Music, 1987/Atlantic Music Corp., 1987.
Introduced by Timbuk 3 in *Eden Alley* (I.R.S., 88).

Welcome to the Jungle
Words and music by Guns N' Roses.
Guns N' Roses, 1987.
Featured in the film *The Dead Pool* and on its soundtrack album. A failure in its initial release, once Guns N' Roses achieved success as a group, this cut from their album *Appetite for Destruction* (Geffen, 87) became a best-seller.

Welcome to the Pleasure Dome (English)
Words and music by William Johnson, Mark O'Toole, Peter Gill, and Brian Nash.
Island Music, 1984.
Best-selling record in 1985 by Frankie Goes to Hollywood from the album *Welcome to the Pleasure Dome* (Island, 84).

We'll Be Together (English)
Words and music by Sting (pseudonym for Gordon Sumner).
Magnetic Music Publishing Co., 1987/Reggatta Music, Ltd., 1987/Illegal Songs, Inc., 1987/Atlantic Music Corp., 1987.
Best-selling record by Sting, from the album *Nothing Like the Sun* (A & M, 87).

We're Going All the Way
Words by Cynthia Weil, music by Barry Mann.
Dyad Music, Ltd., 1983.
Best-selling record by Jeffrey Osborne from *Stay With Me Tonight* (A & M, 84).

We're Gonna Make It (After All)
Words and music by Ellie Greenwich.
My Own Music, 1983.

Introduced by Ellie Greenwich in the musical and cast album *Leader of the Pack* (Elektra/Asylum, 85), which was based on her life story.

We're in This Love Together
Words and music by Roger Murrah and Keith Stegall.
EMI-Blackwood Music Inc., 1980/Magic Castle Music, Inc., 1980.
Best-selling record by Al Jarreau from *Breakin' Away* (Warner Brothers, 81).

We're Ready
Words and music by Tom Scholz.
Hideaway Hits, 1987.
Best-selling record in 1987 by Boston, from the album *Third Stage* (MCA, 86). This song's title seems ironic considering the seven years Scholz spent producing the group's third album.

Werewolves of London
Words and music by Warren Zevon, Leroy P. Marinell, and Robert Wachtel.
Polite Music, 1978/Zevon Music Inc., 1978.
Revived in 1986 by Warren Zevon in the film and on the soundtrack album of *The Color of Money* (Warner Bros., 86). Also on the album *A Quiet, Normal Life: The Best of Warren Zevon* (Asylum, 86).

West End Girls (English)
Words and music by Nick Tennant and Chris Lowe.
Cage Music Ltd., England, 1982/Virgin Music, 1982.
Best-selling record by Pet Shop Boys from the album *Please* (EMI-America, 86). Originally released on the Bobcat label, where it became a nightclub hit in 1982.

West LA Fadeaway
Words and music by Jerry Garcia and Robert Hunter.
Ice Nine Publishing Co., Inc., 1984.
Introduced by The Grateful Dead on the album *In the Dark* (Arista, 87).

We've Got a Good Fire Goin'
Words and music by Dave Loggins.
MCA, Inc., 1986/Patchwork Music, 1986.
Best-selling record by Don Williams from the album *New Moves* (Capitol, 86).

We've Got Each Other
Words and music by Gary Portnoy and Judy Hart Angelo.
Koppelman Family Music, 1983/Bandier Family Music, 1983/R. L. August Music Co., 1983/Yontrop Music, 1983/Judy Hart Angelo Music, 1983.
Introduced by Michael Ingram and Beth Fowler in *Preppies* (83).

We've Got the Love
Words and music by Joel Krauss and Robert Bandiera.
Virgin Music, 1986.
Introduced by Jersey Artists for Mankind at Jam '86 in Asbury Park, featuring Nils Lofgren, Clarence Clemons, Southside Johnny Lyon, and Bruce Springsteen. This charity single (Arista, 86) benefitted New Jersey's under-privileged.

We've Got Tonight
Words and music by Bob Seger.
Hideout Records/Distributing Co., 1976.
Revived by Kenny Rogers and Dolly Parton on *We've Got Tonight* (Liberty, 83).

We've Never Danced
Words and music by Neil Young.
Silver Fiddle/Marilor Music.
Introduced by Martha Davis on the soundtrack of the film *Made in Heaven* and its album (Elektra, 87).

We've Only Just Begun (The Romance Is Not Over)
Words and music by Timmy Allen and Glenn Jones.
Willesden Music, Inc., 1987/Lu Ella, 1987.
Best-selling record by Glenn Jones, from the album *Glenn Jones* (Jive, 87).

What a Thrill
Words and music by Cyndi Lauper and John Turi.
Warner-Tamerlane Music, 1985.
Introduced by Cyndi Lauper on the B-Side of the single 'Goonies *R' Good Enough' (Portrait, 85). Co-author John Turi was a partner in Lauper's first group, Blue Angel.*

What a Wonderful World
Words and music by George David Weiss and George Douglas.
Quartet Music, Inc., 1967/Range Road Music.
Louis Armstrong's rendition was revived in the film *Good Morning Vietnam* and used on its soundtrack album (A & M, 88), making it a hit twenty years after its orginal release, when it made the charts only in England.

What About Love? (Canadian)
Words and music by Sheron Alton, Brian Allen, and Jim Vallance.
Welbeck Music Corp., 1983/Irving Music Inc., 1983/Calypso Toonz, 1983.
Best-selling record by Heart from the album *Heart* (Capitol, 85).

What About Me (Australian)
Words and music by Gary Frost and Francis Frost.

Australian Tumbleweed, Australia, 1983.
Revived in 1989 by Moving Pictures on *Network* (Geffen), this 1983 tune became a surprise hit for the Australian group.

What Am I Gonna Do About You
Words and music by Doug Gilmore, Bob Simon, and Jim Allison.
Tapadero Music, 1985/Jim's Allisongs, 1985.
Best-selling record by Reba McEntire from the album *What Am I Gonna Do About You* (MCA, 86).

What Are We Making Weapons For, also known as **Let Us Begin**
Words and music by John Denver.
Cherry Mountain, 1986.
Introduced by John Denver and Soviet singer Alexandre Gradsky in a recording for release in the United Stated by RCA and in the Soviet Union by Melodiya. The song, which protests the arms race, is on Denver's album *One World* (RCA, 86).

What Cha Gonna Do for Me
Words and music by James Stuart and Ned Doheny.
Average Music, 1981/Longdog Music, 1981.
Best-selling record by Chaka Khan from *What Cha Gonna' Do for Me* (Warner Brothers, 81).

What Does It Take (Canadian)
Words and music by Derry Grehan.
Screen Gems-EMI Music Inc., 1984/Auto Tunes, 1984.
Introduced by Honeymoon Suite in the film *One Crazy Summer* and on the album *The Big Prize* (Warner Bros., 86). Nominated for Best Song at the Tokyo Song Festival.

What Have I Done to Deserve This (English)
Words and music by Neil Tennant, Chris Lowe, and Allee Willis.
Cage Music Ltd., England, 1987/10 Music Ltd., England, 1987/Texas City, 1987/Streamline Moderne, 1987.
Best-selling record by The Pet Shop Boys and Dusty Springfield, from the album *Actually* (EMI, 87). The veteran English soul singer joined younger colleagues for the second time in 1987 with this record.

What Have You Done for Me Lately
Words and music by James Harris, III and Terry Lewis.
Flyte Tyme Tunes, 1986.
Best-selling record by Janet Jackson from her breakthrough album *Control* (A & M, 86). Nominated for a Grammy Award, Rhythm 'n' Blues Song of the Year, 1986.

What I Am
Words and music by Edie Brickell, words by Kenny Withrow.
Geffen Music, 1986/Edie Brickell Songs, 1986/Withrow Publishing,
    1986/Enlightened Kitty, 1986/Strange Mind Productions, 1986.
Best-selling record by Edie Brickell & New Bohemians from *Shooting
    Rubberbands at the Stars* (Geffen, 88).

What I Didn't Do
Words and music by Wood Newton and Michael Noble.
Warner House of Music, 1985/Bobby Goldsboro Music, 1985.
Best-selling record by Steve Wariner from the album *One Good Night
    Deserves Another* (MCA, 85).

What I'd Say
Words and music by Robert Byrne and Will Robinson.
Alabama Band Music Co., 1988/Colgems-EMI Music, 1988.
Best-selling record in 1989 by Earl Thomas Conley from *The Heart of
    It All* (RCA, 88).

What It Feels Like
Words and music by Sammy Llanas and Kurt Neumann.
Lla-Mann, 1987/Intersong, USA Inc., 1987.
Introduced by The BoDeans on *Outside Looking In* (Slash, 87);
    popularized in 1988.

What Kind of Fool (English)
Words and music by Barry Gibb and Albhy Galuten.
Gibb Brothers Music, 1980/Unichappell Music Inc., 1980.
Best-selling record by Barbra Streisand and Barry Gibb from *Guilty*
    (Columbia, 81).

What She Is (Is a Woman in Love)
Words and music by Bob McDill and Paul Harrison.
Polygram International, 1988/Ranger Bob Music, 1988/Unichappell
    Music Inc., 1988.
Best-selling record by Earl Thomas Conley, from *The Heart of It All*
    (RCA, 88).

What Would I Do Without You (English)
Words and music by Van Morrison.
Essential Music, 1985.
Introduced by Van Morrison on the album *A Sense of Wonder* (Mercury,
    85).

What You Don't Know
Words and music by Lewis Martinee.
EMI Music Publishing, 1989/Panchin.
Best-selling record by Expose from *What You Don't Know* (Arista, 89).

What You Get Is What You See (English)
Words and music by Terry Britten and Graham Lyle.
Myake, England, 1986/WB Music, 1986/Almo Music Corp., 1986.
Best-selling record in 1987 by Tina Turner, from the album *Break Every Rule* (Capitol, 86).

What You Need (Australian)
Words and music by Andrew Farriss and Michael Hutchence.
MCA, Inc., 1986.
Best-selling record by Inxs from the album *Listen Like Thieves* (Atlantic, 86).

What You See Is What You Get
Words and music by Charles Strouse.
Charles Strouse Music, 1985.
Introduced by Lenny Wolpe in the Off Broadway musical *Mayor* (85).

What You'd Call a Dream
Words and music by Craig Carnelia.
Introduced by Scott Holmes in *Diamonds* (84).

Whatever Happened to Old Fashioned Love
Words and music by Lewis Anderson.
Old Friends Music, 1983.
Best-selling record by B.J. Thomas from *New Looks* (Cleveland International, 83).

What's a Memory Like You (Doing in a Love Like This)
Words and music by Charles Quillen and John Jarrard.
Dejamus Inc., 1984/Quillsong Music, 1984/Alabama Band Music Co., 1984.
Best-selling record by John Schneider from the album *A Memory Like You* (MCA, 86).

What's Forever For
Words and music by Rafe Van Hoy.
Tree Publishing Co., Inc., 1978.
Best-selling record by Michael Murphey from *Michael Martin Murphey* (Liberty, 82).

What's Going On
Words and music by Al Cleveland, Marvin Gaye, and Renauldo Benson.
Stone Agate Music, 1970/Jobete Music Co., 1970.
Revived in 1986 by Cyndi Lauper on the album *True Colors* (Portrait).

What's Going on in Your World
Words and music by David Chamberlain and Royce Porter.
Milene Music, 1989/Ha-Deb Music.
Best-selling record by George Strait from *Beyond the Blue* (MCA, 89).

What's Love Got to Do with It (English)
Words and music by Terry Britten and Graham Lyle.
Myax Music Ltd., England, 1984/Good Single Ltd., England, 1988/
  Irving Kahal Music, Inc., 1984/WM Music.
Best-selling record by Tina Turner from *Private Dancer* (Capitol, 84).
  Won a Grammy Award, and Best Record of the Year, 1984.
  Nominated for a Grammy Award, Best Song of the Year, 1984.

What's My Scene (Australian)
Words and music by Dave Faulkner.
Copyright Control, 1987.
Introduced by The Hoodoo Gurus on the album *Blow Your Cool*
  (Elektra, 87).

What's New
Words by Johnny Burke, music by Bob Haggart.
Limerick Music Corp., 1939/Marke Music Publishing Co., Inc., 1939/
  Reganesque Music Co., 1939/My Dad's Songs, 1939/M. Witmark &
  Sons, 1939.
Revived by Linda Ronstadt on *What's New* (Asylum, 83).

What's on Your Mind (Pure Energy)
Words and music by Paul Robb and Kurt Valaquen.
T-Boy Music, 1988/Insoc Music, 1988.
Best-selling record by Information Society, from *Information Society*
  (Tommy Boy/Reprise, 88).

Wheel of Fortune
Words and music by Pat MacDonald.
Mambadaddi, 1989/I.R.S. Music.
Introduced by Timbuk 3 from *Edge of Allegiance* (IRS, 89).

Wheels
Words and music by Dave Loggins.
MCA Music, 1986/Patchwork Music, 1986.
Best-selling record in 1988 by Restless Heart, from *Wheels* (MCA, 86).

When a Man Loves a Woman
Words and music by Calvin Lewis and Andrew Wright.
Cotillion Music Inc., 1980/Quinvy Music Publishing Co., 1980.
Revived by Bette Midler in the film and soundtrack album *The Rose*
  (79). Best-selling record by Bette Midler (Atlantic, 80). Rhythm 'n'
  Blues Joe Cocker on *One Night of Sin* (Capitol, 89). Nominated for a
  Grammy Award, Rhythm 'n' Blues Song of the Year, 1989.

When Doves Cry
Words and music by Prince Rogers Nelson.
Controversy Music, 1984/WB Music, 1984.

Best-selling record by Prince (Warner Brothers, 84). Introduced in the film and soundtrack album *Purple Rain* (84).

When Harpo Played His Harp
Words and music by Jonathan Richman.
Rockin Leprechaun, 1987.
Introduced by Jonathan Richman and The Modern Lovers on *Modern Lovers 88* (Rounder, 88), this song was dedicated to Harpo Marx.

When I See You Smile
Words and music by Diane Warren.
Realsongs, 1989.
Best-selling record by Bad English from *Bad English* (Epic, 89).

When I Think of You
Words and music by James Harris, III, Terry Lewis, and Janet Jackson.
Flyte Tyme Tunes, 1986.
Best-selling record by Janet Jackson from the album *Control* (A & M, 86).

When I Wanted You
Words and music by Gino Cunico.
Home Grown Music Inc., 1976.
Best-selling record by Barry Manilow from *One Voice* (Arista, 1980).

When I Win the Lottery
Words and music by Victor Krummenacher, Greg Lisher, David Lowery, and Chris Pedersen.
Camper Van Beethoven Music, 1989.
Introduced by Camper Van Beethoven on *Key Lime Pie* (Virgin, 89).

When I'm Away from You
Words and music by Frankie Miller.
Rare Blue Music, Inc., 1979.
Best-selling record by The Bellamy Brothers (Elektra, 83).

When I'm with You (Canadian)
Words and music by Arnold Lanni.
Victunes, 1985.
This song from a 1985 album was revived by Sheriff on *Sheriff* (Capitol, 1989) and became a hit after the group had disbanded.

When It's Love
Words and music by Eddie Van Halen, Alex Van Halen, Sammy Hagar, and Michael Anthony.
Yessup Music Co., 1988.
Best-selling record by Van Halen, from *OU812* (Warner Bros., 88).

When Love Breaks Down (Irish)
Words and music by Paddy McAloon.
EMI-Blackwood Music Inc., 1985.
Introduced by Prefab Sprout on the album *Two Wheels Good* (Epic, 85).

When Love Calls
Music by David Lewis, words by Wayne Lewis.
Almo Music Corp., 1980.
Best-selling record by Atlantic Starr from *Radiant* (A & M, 81).

When She Was My Girl
Words and music by Marc Blatte and Larry Gottleib.
MCA, Inc., 1980.
Best-selling record by The Four Tops from *Tonight* (Casablanca, 81).
  Nominated for a Grammy Award, Rhythm 'n' Blues Song of the
  Year, 1981.

When Smokey Sings (English)
Words and music by Martin Fry and Mark White.
EMI-Virgin, 1987.
Best-selling record by ABC, from the album *ABC in Alphabet City*
  (Mercury, 87). This song occupied the same top ten as Smokey
  Robinson's own comeback single.

When the Children Cry
Words and music by Vito Bratta and Mike Tramp.
Vavoom Music, 1986.
Best-selling record in 1989 by White Lion from *Pride* (Atlantic, 87).

When the Going Gets Tough (*Jewel of the Nile* Theme)
Best-selling record by Billy Ocean from the album *Love Zone* (Arista,
  85).

When the Going Gets Tough the Tough Get Going
Words and music by Wayne Braithwaite, Barry Eastmond, Robert John
  'Mutt' Lange, and Billy Ocean.
Zomba Music, 1985.
Best-selling record by Billy Ocean (Arista, 85). Introduced in the film
  and soundtrack album *Jewel of the Nile* (Jive, 85).

When the Hammer Came Down
Words and music by Bryon Harvey and Johnny Hott.
Gravel Bag Music, 1989/Bug Music.
Introduced by House of Freaks on *Tantilla* (Rhino, 89).

When the Heart Rules the Mind (English)
Words and music by Steve Hackett and Steve Howe.
Kid Glove, England, 1986/Steve Hackett, England, 1986/Basedown,
  1986/WB Music, 1986.

Best-selling record by GTR from the album *GTR* (Arista, 86). Arista record company president Clive Davis hosted an exclusive 'listening party' to premier the pairing, as GTR, of the guitar superstars who wrote this song.

When the Hoodoo Comes (English)
Words and music by John Butler.
Zoo Music, England, 1989/Warner-Chappell Music/WB Music.
Introduced by Deisel Park West on *Shakespeare, Alabama* (EMI, 89).

When the Love Is Good
Words and music by Kurt Neumann and Sammy Llanas.
Lla-Mann, 1989.
Introduced by The BoDeans from *Home* (Reprise, 89).

When the Night Comes (Canadian)
Words and music by Bryan Adams, Jim Vallance, and Diane Warren.
Irving Music Inc., 1989/Adams Communications, Inc./Calypso Toonz/ Realsongs.
Best-selling record by Joe Cocker from *One Night of Sin* (Capitol, 89).

When the Night Falls
Words and music by T-Bone Burnette.
Black Tent Music, 1983.
Introduced by T-Bone Burnette on *Proof Through the Night* (Warner Brothers, 83).

When the Radio Is On
Words and music by Matt Goble and Kevin Calhoun.
No Cal Music, 1989/Chrysalis Music Group, 1989.
Introduced by Paul Shaffer on *Coast to Coast* (Capitol, 89).

When the Spell Is Broken (English)
Words and music by Richard Thompson.
Island Music, 1985.
Introduced by Richard Thompson on the album *Across a Crowded Room* (Mercury, 85).

When We Make Love
Words and music by Troy Seals and Mentor Williams.
Two-Sons Music, 1983/WB Music, 1983/Welbeck Music Corp., 1983/ Dixie Stars Music, 1983.
Best-selling record by Alabama from *Roll On* (RCA, 84).

When We Ran
Words and music by John Hiatt.
Lillybilly, 1985.
Introduced by John Hiatt on the album *Warming up to the Ice Age* (Geffen, 85).

When We Was Fab (English)
Words and music by George Harrison and Jeff Lynne.
Ganga Publishing Co., 1987/Zero Productions, 1987.
Best-selling record in 1988 by George Harrison, from *Cloud Nine* (Dark Horse, 87).

When You Close Your Eyes
Words and music by Jack Blades, Alan Fitzgerald, and Brad Gillis.
Kid Bird Music, 1983.
Best-selling record by Night Ranger from *Midnight Madness* (Camel/MCA, 84).

When You Say Nothing at All
Words and music by Paul Overstreet and Don Schlitz.
Screen Gems-EMI Music Inc., 1988/Scarlet Moon Music, 1988/MCA Music, 1988/Don Schlitz Music, 1988.
Best-selling record by Keith Whitley, from *Don't Close Your Eyes* (RCA, 88).

When You Were Mine
Words and music by Prince Rogers Nelson.
Controversy Music, 1980.
Introduced by Prince on *Dirty Mind* (Warner Brothers, 80). Featured on *She's So Unusual* by Cyndi Lauper (Portrait, 83).

When You Wish upon a Star
Words and music by Ned Washington and Leigh Harline.
The Bourne Co., 1940.
Revived in 1988 by Ringo Starr on *Stay Awake* (A & M, 88), an album of new renditions of standards from Disney movies.

When Your Heart Is Weak
Words and music by Peter Kingsbery.
Nurk Twins Music, 1984/Edwin Ellis Music, 1984.
Introduced by Cock Robin on the album *Cock Robin* (Columbia, 85).

Whenever You're on My Mind
Words and music by Marshall Crenshaw and Bill Teeley.
MHC Music, 1982.
Introduced by Marshall Crenshaw in *Field Day* (Warner Brothers, 83).

Where Are You Now?
Words and music by Jimmy Harnen and R. Congdon.
Harnen/Congdon/Empire Music/Jakota Music.
Revived in 1989 by Jimmy Harnen with Synch from *Don't Fight the Midnight* (WTG).

Where Did I Go Wrong
Words and music by Joe Raposo.
Jonico Music Inc., 1987.
Introduced in the Connecticut production of the musical *The Little Rascals*.

Where Did I Go Wrong
Words and music by Steve Wariner.
Steve Wariner, 1989/Irving Music Inc.
Best-selling record by Steve Wariner from *I Got Dreams* (MCA, 89).

Where Did Your Heart Go
Words and music by David Was (pseudonym for David Weiss) and Don Was (pseudonym for Donald Fagenson).
Island Music, 1986/Polygram International, 1986.
Best-selling record by Wham! from the album *Music from the Edge of Heaven* (Columbia, 86).

Where Do Broken Hearts Go
Words and music by Frank Wildhorn and Chuck Jackson.
Scaramanga Music, 1985/Chrysalis Music Group, 1985/Baby Love Music, Inc., 1985.
Best-selling record in 1988 by Whitney Houston from the album *Whitney* (Arista, 87).

Where Do Nights Go
Words and music by Mike Reid and Rory Bourke.
BMG Songs Inc., 1987/WB Music, 1987.
Best-selling record in 1988 by Ronnie Milsap, from *Heart and Soul* (RCA, 87).

Where Do the Children Go
Words and music by Rob Hyman and Eric Bazilian.
Dub Notes, 1986/Human Boy Music.
Introduced by The Hooters on the album *Nervous Night* (Columbia, 85). The group was given a contract for the album not long after co-author Hyman collaborated with rock star Cyndi Lauper on 'Time After Time,' which became a number one song.

Where Do They Go
Words and music by Jerry Raney.
Cricket Pie Music, 1985.
Introduced by The Beat Farmers on the album *Tales of the New West* (Rhino, 85).

Where Duty Calls
Words and music by Patti Smith and Fred Smith.
Druse Music Inc., 1988/Stratium Music Inc., 1988.

Introduced by Patti Smith on *Dream of Life* (Arista, 88), this song concerns life in war-torn Beirut.

Where Everybody Knows Your Name
Words and music by Gary Portnoy and Judy Hart Angelo.
Addax Music Co., Inc., 1982.
Best-selling record by Gary Portnoy (Applause, 83). Introduced on TV series *Cheers* (82).

Where the Streets Have No Name (Irish)
Words and music by U2.
Polygram International, 1987.
Best-selling record by U2, from the album *The Joshua Tree* (Island, 87).

Which Way to America
Words and music by Vernon Reid.
Dare to Dream Music, 1988.
Introduced by Living Colour on *Vivid* (Columbia, 88).

While You See a Chance
Words by Will Jennings, music by Steve Winwood.
Island Music, 1980/Irving Music Inc., 1980/Blue Sky Rider Songs, 1980.
Best-selling record by Steve Winwood from *Arc of a Diver* (Island, 81).

Whip It
Words and music by Mark Mothersbaugh and Gerald Casale.
Devo Music, 1980/EMI-Virgin, 1980.
Best-selling record by Devo from *Freedom of Choice* (Warner Brothers, 80).

Whiskey, If You Were a Woman
Words and music by Mary Francis, Johnny MacRae, and Bob Morrison.
Southern Nights Music Co., 1987.
Best-selling record by Highway 101, from the album *Highway 101* (Warner Bros., 87).

White Buffalo
Words and music by Rod MacDonald.
Blue Flute Music, 1988.
Introduced by Rod MacDonald on *White Buffalo* (Mountain Railroad, 88).

White Horse (Danish)
English words and music by Tim Stahl and John Goldberg.
Sing a Song Publishing Co., 1984/Bleu Disque Music, 1984.
Best-selling record by Laid Back from *...Keep Smiling* (Sire, 84).

White Hot
Words and music by Henry Rollins and Greg Ginn.
Introduced by Black Flag on the album *In My Head* (SST, 86).

White Rabbit
Words and music by Grace Slick.
Irving Music Inc., 1967.
Revived in 1986 by the Jefferson Starship on the soundtrack of the film
  Platoon and on its album (Atlantic, 86). It was also used on the
  Jefferson Airplane retrospective collection *2400 Fulton Street* (RCA,
  87).

White Shoes
Words and music by Jack Tempchin.
Night River Publishing, 1980.
Featured on *White Shoes* by Emmylou Harris (Warner Brothers, 83).

The White Tent the Raft (Canadian)
Words and music by Jane Siberry.
Wing It, 1987/Red Sky, 1987.
Introduced by Jane Siberry in *The Walking* (Reprise, 88).

White Wedding
Words and music by Billy Idol.
Chrysalis Music Group, 1982.
Best-selling record by Billy Idol from *Billy Idol* (Chrysalis, 83).

Who Can It Be Now (Australian)
Words and music by Colin Hay.
EMI-Blackwood Music Inc., 1982.
Best-selling record by Men at Work from *Business as Usual* (Columbia,
  82).

Who Do You Give Your Love To
Words and music by Michael Morales.
Boom Tat Music, 1989/Polygram International.
Best-selling record by Michael Morales from *Michael Morales* (Wing,
  89).

Who Do You Love
Words and music by Ellas McDaniels.
Arc Music, 1956, 1963.
This Bo Diddley blues classic was revived in 1989 by the Jesus and
  Mary Chain for the offbeat musical film *Earth Girls Are Easy*.

Who Found Who
Words and music by Paul Gurvitz.
Chrysalis Music Group, 1987.
Best-selling record by Elisa Fiorello and Jellybean Benitez, from the

album *Who Found Who* (Chrysalis). Benitez, previously a DJ at the New York City disco Studio 54, discovered singer Fiorello on the television contest *Star Search*.

Who Made Who (Australian)
Words and music by Malcolm Young, Angus Young, and Brian Johnson.
J. Albert & Sons Music, 1986.
Introduced by AC/DC in the 1986 film *Overdrive* and on the album *Who Made Who* (Atlantic, 86).

Who Wears These Shoes (English)
Words by Bernie Taupin, music by Elton John.
Intersong, USA Inc., 1984.
Best-selling record by Elton John from *Breaking Hearts* (Geffen, 84).

Who Will You Run To
Words and music by Diane Warren.
Realsongs, 1987.
Best-selling record by Heart, from the album *Bad Animals* (Capitol, 87).

Who You Gonna Blame It on This Time
Words and music by Hank Cochran and Vern Gosdin.
Tree Publishing Co., Inc., 1987/Hookem Music.
Best-selling record in 1989 by Vern Gosdin from *Chiseled in Stone* (Columbia, 88).

Whoever's in New England
Words and music by Kendall Franceschi and Quentin Powers.
Silverline Music, Inc., 1986/W.B.M. Music, 1986.
Best-selling record by Reba McEntire from the album *Whoever's in New England* (MCA, 86). Nominated for a Grammy Award, Country Song of the Year, 1986.

Who's Cheating Who
Words and music by Jerry Hayes.
Partner, 1980/Algee Music Corp., 1980/Vogue Music, 1980.
Best-selling record by Charlie McClain (Epic, 81).

Who's Crying Now
Words and music by Steve Perry and Jonathan Cain.
Weed High Nightmare Music, 1981.
Best-selling record by Journey from *Escape* (Columbia, 81).

Who's Gonna Fill Their Shoes
Words and music by Troy Seals and Max D. Barnes.
WB Music, 1985/Two-Sons Music, 1985/Tree Publishing Co., Inc., 1985.

Best-selling record by George Jones from the album *Who's Gonna Fill Their Shoes* (Epic, 85).

Who's Holding Donna Now
Words and music by David Foster, Jay Graydon, and Randy Goodrum.
Foster Frees Music Inc., 1985/Garden Rake Music, Inc., 1985/EMI-April Music, 1985/Random Notes, 1985.
Best-selling record by DeBarge from the album *Rhythm of the Night* (Motown, 85).

Who's Johnny (*Short Circuit* Theme)
Words and music by Peter Wolf and Ina Wolf.
Petwolf Music, 1986/Chappell & Co., Inc., 1986/Kikiko Music Corp., 1986/Unichappell Music Inc., 1986.
Introduced by El DeBarge in the 1986 film *Short Circuit*. Best-selling record by El DeBarge from the album *El DeBarge* (Motown, 86).

Who's Lonely Now
Words and music by Kix Brooks and Don Cook.
Cross Keys Publishing Co., Inc., 1989.
Best-selling record by Highway 101 from *Paint the Town* (Warner Bros., 89).

Who's That Girl (English)
Words and music by Annie Lennox and Dave Stewart.
Blue Network Music Inc., 1983.
Best-selling record by Eurythmics from *Touch* (RCA, 84).

Who's That Girl
Words and music by Madonna and Patrick Leonard.
WB Music, 1987/Bleu Disque Music, 1987/Lost in Music, 1987/Johnny Yuma, 1987.
Introduced by Madonna in the film and on the soundtrack album *Who's That Girl* (Sire, 87). When this song reached the top five, Madonna's twelfth single in a row to do so, she needed just three more such hits to overtake the Beatles or twelve more to tie Elvis Presley for the longest string of chart-toppers. Nominated for a Grammy Award, Song for TV/Movie, 1987.

Who's Zoomin' Who
Words and music by Narada Michael Walden, Preston Glass, and Aretha Franklin.
Gratitude Sky Music, 1985/Bellboy Music, 1985/Springtime Music Inc., 1985.
Best-selling record by Aretha Franklin from the album *Who's Zoomin' Who* (Arista, 85).

Why Can't This Be Love
Words and music by Michael Anthony, Sammy Hagar, Alex Van Halen,

and Eddie Van Halen.
Yessup Music Co., 1986.
Best-selling record by Van Halen from the album *5150* (Warner Bros., 86). 5150 is the Los Angeles Police Department code for the criminally insane.

Why Do Fools Fall in Love
Words and music by Frankie Lymon and George Goldner.
Patricia Music Publishing Corp., 1956.
Revived by Diana Ross from *Why Do Fools Fall in Love* (RCA, 82).

Why Do You (Do What You Do), see **Do What You Do.**

Why Does It Have to Be (Wrong or Right)
Words and music by Randy Sharp and Donny Lowery.
Warner-Tamerlane Music, 1987/Rumble Seat, 1987/Sheddhouse Music, 1987.
Best-selling record Restless Heart, from the album *Wheels* (RCA, 87).

Why Don't You Spend the Night
Words and music by Bob McDill.
Hall-Clement Publications, 1979.
Best-selling record by Ronnie Milsap from *Milsap Magic* (RCA, 80).

Why Lady Why
Words and music by Randy Owen.
Maypop Music, 1980.
Best-selling record by Alabama from *My Home's in Alabama* (RCA, 80).

Why Me? (English)
Words and music by Tony Carey.
Safespace Music, 1983.
Best-selling record by Irene Cara from *What a Feeling* (Geffen, 83).

Why Not Me
Words and music by Fred Knobloch and Carson Whitsett.
EMI Unart Catalogue, 1980/Flowering Stone Music, 1980/Whitsett Churchill Music, 1980/Holy Moley Music, 1980.
Best-selling record by Fred Knoblock from *Why Not Me* (Scotti Brothers, 80).

Why Worry
Words and music by Mark Knopfler.
Chariscourt Ltd., 1985/Almo Music Corp., 1985/Viva Music, Inc., 1985.
Revived in 1986 by the Everly Brothers on *Born Yesterday* (Mercury, 86). Introduced by Dire Str aits and introduced on the album *Brothers in Arms* (Warner Bros., 85).

Why You Treat Me So Bad
Words and music by Jay King and Thom McElroy.
Jay King, IV, 1987.
Best-selling record by Club Nouveau, from the album *Life, Love, and Pain* (Tommy Boy, 87).

Why'd You Come in Here Lookin' Like That
Words and music by Bob Carlisle and Randy Thomas.
Benny Hester Music, 1989.
Best-selling record by Dolly Parton from *White Limozeen* (Columbia, 89).

The Wild Boys (English)
Words and music by Duran Duran.
Chappell & Co., Inc., 1984.
Best-selling record by Duran Duran from *Arena* (Capitol, 84).

Wild Thing
Words and music by Chip Taylor.
EMI-Blackwood Music Inc., 1965.
Revived in 1986 by Sister Carol in the film and soundtrack album *Something Wild* (MCA, 86), in 1988 by Sam Kinison on *Have You Seen Me Lately?* (Warner Bros., 88), and in 1989 for the film and sountrack album *Major League* (CRB).

Wild Thing
Words and music by Marvin Young, Tony Smith, Matt Dike, and Michael Ross.
Varry White Music, 1988.
Best-selling record by Tone Loc from *Loc-ed After Dark* (Delicious Vinyl/Island, 89). Only 'We Are the World' had greater success as a single than this song.

Wild, Wild West (English)
Words and music by The Escape Club.
EMI Music Publishing, 1988.
Best-selling record by The Escape Club, from *Wild, Wild West* (Atlantic, 88).

Wildflowers
Words and music by Dolly Parton.
Velvet Apple Music, 1986.
Best-selling record in 1988 by Dolly Parton, Linda Ronstadt, and Emmylou Harris, from *Trio* (Warner Bros., 86).

Will the Wolf Survive
Words and music by David Hidalgo and Louie Perez.
Davince Music, 1984/No K. O. Music, 1984.
Best-selling record by Los Lobos from the album *Will the Wolf Survive*

(Slash, 85). Revived in 1986 by Waylon Jennins on the album *Will the Wolf Survive* (MCA, 86).

Will the Wolf Survive
Revived in 1986 by Waylon Jennings on the album *Will the Wolf Survive* (MCA, 86).

Will You Still Love Me
Words and music by David Foster, Tom Keane, and Richard Baskin.
Air Bear, 1986/Warner-Tamerlane Music, 1986/Music of the World, 1986/Young Millionaires Club, 1986/Warm Springs, 1986.
Best-selling record in 1987 by Chicago, from the album *Chicago 18* (Warner Bros., 86).

Willie and the Hand Jive
Words and music by Johnny Otis.
Eldorado Music Co., 1958.
Revived by George Thorogood & The Destroyers on the album *Maverick* (EMI-America, 85).

Wind Beneath My Wings, also known as **Hero**
Words and music by Jeff Silbar and Larry Henley.
Warner House of Music, 1981/WB Gold Music Corp., 1981.
Best-selling records by Lou Rawls from *When the Night Comes* (Epic, 83), Gary Morris from *Why Lady Why* (Warner Brothers, 83), and Gladys Knight & The Pips from *Visions* (Columbia, 83).   Revived by Bette Midler in the film and soundtrack to *Beaches*.

The Wind Blows through My Window
Words and music by Frank Loesser.
Frank Music Co., 1955.
The song was discovered after Frank Loesser's death by his widow, Jo Sullivan. Introduced by Sullivan and her daughter, Emily Loesser, in *Together Again (for the First Time)*, their two-woman show.

Windows of the World
Words and music by Hal David and Burt Bacharach.
Casa David, 1967/New Hidden Valley Music Co., 1967.
Revived in 1988 by the Pretenders on the soundtrack album and in the film *1969* (Polydor, 88).

Wine, Women and Song
Words and music by William Robinson.
Bertam Music Co., 1980.
Introduced by Smokey Robinson on *Being with You* (Tamla, 80).

Winner Takes All (American-German)
English words and music by Giorgio Moroder and Tom Whitlock.
GMPC, 1987/Go Glow, 1987.

Introduced by Sammy Hagar in the film and on the soundtrack album
Over the Top (Columbia, 87). Best-selling record by Hagar.

The Winner Takes It All (Swedish)
English words and music by Benny Andersson and Bjorn Ulvaeus.
Artwork Music Co., Inc., 1980.
Best-selling record by Abba from *Super Trooper* (Atlantic, 80).

Winning
Words and music by Russ Ballard.
Island Music, 1977.
Best-selling record by Santana from *Zebop* (Columbia, 81).

Winter Games
Words and music by David Foster.
Air Bear, 1988.
Introduced by David Foster on *The Symphony Sessions* (Atlantic, 88).
    Written for the Winter Olympics.

Winter Wonderland
Words by Richard B. Smith, music by Felix Bernard.
Bregman, Vocco & Conn, Inc., 1934.
Revived in 1987 by The Eurythmics on the album *A Very Special
    Christmas* (A & M).

Wipe Out
Words and music by Robert Berryhill, Patrick Connelly, James Fuller,
    and Ron Wilson.
Miraleste Music, 1963/Robin Hood Music Co., 1963.
Revived in 1987 by The Fat Boys and the Beach Boys in the film and
    soundtrack album *Disorderlies* (Tin Pan Apple/Polygram, 87).

Wishing Well (English)
Words and music by Terence Trent D'Arby and Sean Oliver.
EMI-Virgin, 1987/Young Terrence, 1987/Chrysalis Music Group, 1987.
Best-selling record in 1988 Terence Trent D'Arby from *The Hardline
    According to Terence Trent D'Arby* (Columbia, 87).

With a Little Help from My Friends
Words and music by John Lennon and Paul McCartney.
Northern Songs, Ltd., England, 1967/Maclen Music Inc., 1967.
Revived by Joe Cocker as the theme for the television series *The
    Wonder Years*, the song was also featured on the album derived from
    the show (Atlantic, 89).

With Every Beat of My Heart
Words and music by Tommy Faragher, Lotti Golden, and Arthur Baker.
MCA Music, 1989/My Gig Music/Matak Music/Shakin Baker Music,

Inc.
Best-selling record by Taylor Dayne on *Can't Fight Fate* (Arista, 89).

With Every Breath I Take
Words by David Zippel, music by Cy Coleman.
Notable Music Co., Inc., 1989.
Introduced by Kay McClelland in the 1989 Broadway musical *City of Angels*.

With or without You (Irish)
Words and music by U2.
Chappell & Co., Inc., 1987/U2 Music, 1987.
Best-selling record in 1987 by U2, from the album *The Joshua Tree* (Island, 87). This was the first hit single from the album band of the year.

With You on My Arm
Words and music by Jerry Herman.
Jerryco Music Co., 1983.
Introduced by Gene Barry and George Hearn in *La Cage Au Folles* (83).

Without Us
Words by Jeff Barry, music by Tom Scott.
Bruin Music Co., 1982.
Introduced by Johnny Mathis and Deniece Williams on *Family Ties* (82).

Without Your Love
Words and music by Billy Nicholls.
HG Music, Inc., 1977.
Best-selling record by Roger Daltrey from the film and soundtrack album *McVicar* (Polydor, 80).

WKRP in Cincinnati
Words and music by James Thomas Wells and Hugh Wilson.
Fast Fade Music, 1978/MTM Enterprises Inc., 1978.
Best-selling record by Steve Carlisle (MCA/Sweet City, 81). Introduced on the TV show *WKRP in Cincinnati* (78).

Woke up in Love
Words and music by James P. Pennington.
Careers Music Inc., 1983.
Best-selling record by Exile (Epic, 84).

Woman
Words and music by John Lennon.
Lenono Music, 1981.
Best-selling record by John Lennon from *Double Fantasy* (Geffen, 81).

Woman in Love (English)
Words and music by Barry Gibb and Robin Gibb.
Gibb Brothers Music, 1980.
Best-selling record by Barbra Streisand from *Guilty* (Columbia, 80).
Nominated for Grammy Awards, Record of the Year, 1980, and Song of the Year, 1980.

A Woman in Love
Words and music by David Millet and Curtis Wright.
Willin' David, 1989/Front Burner Music.
Best-selling record by Ronnie Milsap from *Stranger Things Have Happened* (RCA, 89).

The Woman in You (English)
Words and music by Barry Gibb, Robin Gibb, and Maurice Gibb.
Gibb Brothers Music, 1982.
Best-selling record by The Bee Gees from *E-S-P* (RSO, 83).

A Woman Needs Love
Words and music by Ray Parker, Jr.
Raydiola Music, 1981.
Best-selling record by Ray Parker Jr. & Raydio from *A Woman Needs Love* (Arista, 81).

Woman's World (English)
Words by Chris Difford, music by Glenn Tilbrook.
Illegal Songs, Inc., 1981.
Introduced by Squeeze on *East Side Story* (A & M, 81).

Women Across the River
Words and music by David Olney.
Hard Ball Music, 1988.
Introduced by David Olney on *Deeper Well* (Philo, 88).

Women I've Never Had
Words and music by Hank Williams, Jr.
Bocephus Music Inc., 1979.
Best-selling record by Hank Williams from *Hank Williams Jr.'s Greatest Hits* (Elektra, 80).

Wondering Where the Lions Are (Canadian)
Words and music by Bruce Cockburn.
Golden Mountain Music Inc., 1979.
Best-selling record by Bruce Cockburn from *Dancing in the Dragon's Jaw* (Millennium, 80).

A Word in Spanish (English)
Words by Bernie Taupin, music by Elton John.
Big Pig Music, 1988/Intersong, USA Inc., 1988.

Best-selling record by Elton John from *Reg Strikes Back* (MCA, 88). This was also recorded in Spanish.

Word Up
Words and music by Larry Blackmon and Tomi Jenkins.
T-Man, 1986/Larry Junior Music, 1986/All Seeing Eye Music, 1986.
Best-selling record by Cameo from the album *Word Up* (Atlantic, 86).

Words Get in the Way
Words and music by Gloria Estefan.
Foreign Imported, 1985.
Best-selling record by Miami Sound Machine in 1986 from the album *Primitive Love* (Epic, 85). The writer is the vocalist on the track.

Words He Doesn't Say
Words by Barry Harman, music by Keith Hermann.
WB Music, 1988/BHB Productions, 1988/Keith Hermann Music, 1988.
Introduced by Scott Bakula in the 1988 Broadway musical *Romance, Romance.*

Workin' on It (English)
Words and music by Chris Rea.
Magnet Music Ltd., England, 1988/Intersong, USA Inc.
Introduced by Chris Rea on *New Light through Old Windows* (EMI, 89).

Workin' Overtime
Words and music by Nile Rodgers and Christopher Max.
Tommy Jymi, Inc., 1989/Warner-Tamerlane Music/Mike Chapman Publishing Enterprises/All Nations Music.
Best-selling record by Diana Ross from *Workin' Overtime* (Motown, 89).

Working for the Weekend (Canadian)
Words and music by Paul Dean, Mike Reno, and Matthew Frenette.
EMI-Blackwood Music Inc., 1981/EMI-April Music, 1981.
Best-selling record by Loverboy from *Get Lucky* (Columbia, 82).

Working in the Coal Mine
Words and music by Allen Toussaint.
Marsaint Music Inc., 1966.
Revived by Devo (Elektra, 81). Featured in the film & soundtrack album *Heavy Metal* (81).

World Party (Irish)
Words and music by Mike Scott, Trevor Hutchinson, and Karl Wallinger.
Dizzy Heights Music Publishing, Ltd., 1988/Chrysalis Music Group, 1988/Copyright Control, 1988/Polygram International, 1988.
Introduced by The Waterboys on *Fisherman's Blues* (Chyrsalis, 88).

When Wallinger left the Waterboys, he called his new group World Party.

World Where You Live (Australian)
Words and music by Neil Finn.
Roundhead, 1986.
Introduced by Crowded House on the album *Crowded House* (Chrysalis, 86).

A World Without Heroes
Words and music by Paul Stanley, Bob Ezrin, Lou Reed, and Gene Simmons.
Kiss, 1981/Under Cut Music Publishing Co., Inc., 1981/Metal Machine Music, 1981.
Best-selling record by Kiss from *Music from the Elder* (Casablanca, 82).

Wot's It to Ya
Words and music by Robbie Nevil and Brock Walsh.
MCA Music, 1986.
Best-selling record by Robbie Nevil, from the album *Robbie Nevil* (Manhattan, 86).

Would I Lie to You? (English)
Words and music by Annie Lennox and Dave Stewart.
Blue Network Music Inc., 1985.
Best-selling record by Eurythmics from the album *Be Yourself Tonight* (RCA, 85).

Would Jesus Wear a Rolex
Words and music by Chet Atkins and Margaret Archer.
Leona, 1987.
Introduced by Ray Stevens on the album *Crackin' Up* (MCA, 87).
    Although the song was written previously, it was ready to capitalize on this year's contretemps in the realms of television evangelism.

Would You Catch a Falling Star
Words and music by Bobby Braddock.
Tree Publishing Co., Inc., 1981.
Best-selling record by John Anderson (Warner Brothers, 82).

Wrap Her Up (English)
Words and music by Davey Johnstone, Bernie Taupin, and Elton John.
Intersong, USA Inc., 1985.
Best-selling record by Elton John from the album *Ice on Fire* (Geffen, 85).

Wrap It Up
Words and music by Isaac Hayes and David Porter.
East/Memphis Music Corp., 1970/Irving Music Inc., 1970/Pronto Music,

Inc., 1970.

Rhythm 'n' Blues The Fabulous Thunderbirds on the album *Tuff Enuff* (Epic, 86). Introduced by Archie Bell & The Drells, in 1970.

Wrapped Around Your Finger (English)
Words and music by Sting (pseudonym for Gordon Sumner).
Reggatta Music, Ltd., 1983/Illegal Songs, Inc., 1983.
Best-selling record by The Police from *Synchronicity* (A & M, 84).

Wrong 'Em Boyo (English)
Words and music by Joe Strummer (pseudonym for Joe Mellors) and Mick (The Clash) Jones.
WB Music, 1979.
Introduced by The Clash on *London Calling* (Epic, 80).

X

Xanadu (English)
Words and music by Jeff Lynne.
EMI-Blackwood Music Inc., 1980.
Best-selling record by ELO with Olivia Newton-John (MCA, 80).
   Introduced in the film and soundtrack album *Xanadu* (80).

Y

Yah Mo B There (English)
Words and music by James Ingram, Michael McDonald, Rod
Temperton, and Quincy Jones.
Eiseman Music Co., Inc., 1983/Yellow Brick Road Music, 1983/Almo
Music Corp., 1983/Genevieve Music, 1983.
Best-selling record by James Ingram with Michael McDonald from *It's
Your Night* (Quest, 83). Nominated for a Grammy Award, Best
Rhythm 'n' Blues Song of the Year, 1984.

A Year from Today
Words by P. G. Wodehouse and Guy Bolton, music by Jerome Kern.
Polygram International, 1924.
Revived in 1989 by Davis Gaines and Paige O'Hara in the musical
Sitting Pretty.

Yearning for Your Love
Words and music by Ronnie Wilson and Oliver Scott.
Temp Co., 1980/Total X Publishing Co., 1980.
Best-selling record by Gap Band from *The Gap Band III* (Mercury, 81).

The Yellow Rose
Words and music by John Wilder.
WB Music, 1984.
Best-selling record by Johnny Lee with Lane Brody (Warner Brothers,
84).

Yellow Roses
Words and music by Dolly Parton.
Velvet Apple Music, 1989.
Introduced by Dolly Parton on *White Limozeen* (Columbia, 89).

Yes, I'm Ready
Words and music by Barbara Mason.
Dandelion, 1965/Jamie Music Publishing Co., 1965.
Best-selling record by Teri DeSario with K.C. from *Moonlight Madness* (TK, 80).

Yesterday's Songs
Words and music by Neil Diamond.
Stonebridge Music, 1981.
Best-selling record by Neil Diamond from *On the Way to the Sky* (Columbia, 81).

You Again
Words and music by Don Schlitz and Paul Overstreet.
MCA Music, 1987/Don Schlitz Music, 1987/Writer's Group Music, 1987/Scarlet Moon Music, 1987.
Best-selling record by The Forester Sisters, from the album *You Again* (Warner Bros., 87).

You Ain't Goin' Nowhere
Words and music by Bob Dylan.
Dwarf Music Co., Inc., 1967.
Revived in 1989 by Chris Hillman and Roger McGuinn, former members of the Byrds, for *Will the Circle Be Unbroken, Vol. II* (Universal, 89).

You and I
Words and music by Frank Myers.
Cottonpatch Music, 1980/Mallven Music, 1980.
Best-selling record by Eddie Rabbitt and Crystal Gayle from *Radio Romance* (Elektra, 82).

You and Me Tonight
Words and music by Eban Kelly, Jimi Randolph, and K. Moore.
Virgin Nymph, 1987/EMI-Virgin, 1987.
Best-selling record by Deja, from the album *Serious* (Virgin, 87).

You Are
Words and music by Lionel Richie, Jr. and Brenda Richie.
Brockman Enterprises Inc., 1982.
Best-selling record by Lionel Richie from *Lionel Richie* (Motown, 83).

You Are My Lady
Words and music by Barry Eastmond.
Zomba Music, 1985/Barry Eastmond Music, 1985.
Best-selling record by Freddie Jackson from the album *Rock Me Tonight* (Capitol, 85).

You Are the Girl
Words and music by Ric Ocasek.
Lido Music Inc., 1987.
Best-selling record by The Cars, from the album *Door to Door* (Elektra, 87).

You Belong to the City
Words and music by Glenn Frey.
Red Cloud Music Co., 1985/Night River Publishing, 1985.
Best-selling record by Glenn Frey (MCA, 85). Featured on the season premier episode of the television series *Miami Vice* (85) and on the show's soundtrack album.

You Better Watch Your Step
Words and music by Anita Baker.
Bakers Tune, 1986.
Introduced by Anita Baker on the album *Rapture* (Elektra, 86).

You Better You Bet (English)
Words and music by Pete Townshend.
Towser Tunes Inc., 1981.
Best-selling record by The Who from *Face Dances* (Warner Brothers, 81).

You Bring Me Joy
Words and music by David Lasley.
Almo Music Corp., 1986.
Introduced by Anita Baker on the album *Rapture* (Elektra, 86).

You Came (English)
Words and music by Ricky Wilde and Kim Wilde.
Unicity Music, Inc., 1988/Rickim, 1988.
Best-selling record by Kim Wilde, from *Close* (MCA, 88).

You Can Always Count on Me
Words by David Zippel, music by Cy Coleman.
Notable Music Co., Inc., 1989.
Introduced by Randy Graff in *City of Angels,* one of the more successful American musicals to open on Broadway in years.

You Can Call Me Al
Words and music by Paul Simon.
Paul Simon Music, 1986.
Best-selling record by Paul Simon from the album *Graceland* (Warner Bros., 86). Simon drew on his exploration of South African musical forms and rhythms to portray the experiences of a typical contemporary young urban neurotic.

515

You Can Do Magic (Canadian)
Words and music by Russ Ballard.
Russell Ballard, Ltd., Middlesex, England, 1982/EMI-April Music, 1982.
Best-selling record by America from *View from the Ground* (Capitol, 82).

You Can Dream of Me
Words and music by Steve Wariner and John Hall.
Steve Wariner, 1985/Siren Songs, 1985.
Best-selling record by Steve Wariner from the album *Life's Highway* (MCA, 86).

You Can Kill Love
Words by Gretchen Cryer, music by Nancy Ford.
Valando Group, 1975.
Originally recorded on *Cryer and Ford* (RCA, 75), this song was revived by Gretchen Cryer in her 1989 revue, *Back in My Life*.

You Can Leave Your Hat On
Words and music by Randy Newman.
Randy Newman Music, 1970.
Revived in 1986 by Joe Cocker on the soundtrack of the film *9 1/2 Weeks* (Capitol, 86), and on his solo album *Cocker* (A & M, 86).

You Can't Get What You Want (Till You Know What You Want) (English)
Words and music by Joe Jackson.
Pokazuka, 1984/Almo Music Corp., 1984.
Best-selling record by Joe Jackson from *Body and Soul* (A & M, 84).

You Can't Hurry Love
Words and music by Eddie Holland, Lamont Dozier, and Brian Holland.
Stone Agate Music, 1965.
Revived by Phil Collins from *Hello, I Must Be Going* (Atlantic, 83).

You Could Have Been with Me
Words and music by Lea Maalfried.
ATV Music Corp., 1981.
Best-selling record by Sheena Easton from *You Could Have Been with Me* (EMI-America, 81).

You Done Me Wrong
Words and music by Pat McLaughlin.
Screen Gems-EMI Music Inc., 1988.
Introduced by Pat McLaughlin in the film and soundtrack album *Bull Durham* (EMI, 88).

You Don't Get Much (Without Giving)
Words and music by Kurt Neumann and Sammy Llanas.

Lla-Mann, 1989.
Introduced by The BoDeans on *Home* (Reprise, 89).

You Don't Have to Cry
Words and music by Rene Moore and Angela Winbush.
A La Mode Music, 1986/WB Music, 1986.
Best-selling record by Rene & Angela from the album *Street Called Desire* (Polygram, 86).

You Don't Know
Words and music by Robin Hild.
Virgin Music, 1987/Bittersuite Co., 1987.
Best-selling record by Scarlett and Black from *Scarlett and Black* (Virgin, 88).

You Don't Know Me
Words and music by Cindy Walker and Eddy Arnold.
Unichappell Music Inc., 1955.
Revived by Mickey Gilley on *You Don't Know Me* (Epic, 81).

You Don't Own Me
Words and music by John Madara and David White.
Merjoda Music, Inc., 1963.
Revived in 1987 by the Blow Monkeys, on the soundtrack of the film *Dirty Dancing* and its album (RCA, 87). This version transmogrified the Lesley Gore classic.

You Don't Say (English)
Words and music by Richard Thompson.
Island Music, 1985.
Introduced by Richard Thompson on the album *Across a Crowded Room* (Mercury, 85).

You Don't Want Me Anymore
Words and music by Kenneth Goorabian.
Toneman Music Inc., 1982/Wood Street Music, Inc., 1982/Al Gallico Music Corp., 1982.
Best-selling record by Steel Breeze from *Steel Breeze* (RCA, 82).

You Dream Flat Tires
Words and music by Joni Mitchell.
Crazy Crow Music, 1982.
Introduced by Joni Mitchell on *Wild Things Run Fast* (Geffen, 82).

You Get the Best from Me
Words and music by Kevin McCord and Albert Hudson.
Duchess Music Corp., 1984.
Best-selling record by Alicia Myers from *I Appreciate* (MCA, 84).

You Give Good Love
Words and music by La La (pseudonym for LaForrest Cope).
MCA, Inc., 1985/New Music Group, 1985.
Best-selling record by Whitney Houston from the album *Whitney Houston* (Arista, 85). Nominated for a Grammy Award, Rhythm 'n' Blues Song of the Year, 1985.

You Give Love a Bad Name
Words and music by Jon Bon Jovi, Richie Sambora, and Desmond Child.
Bon Jovi Publishing, 1986/PolyGram Records Inc., 1986/EMI-April Music, 1986/Desmobile Music Inc., 1986.
Best-selling record by Bon Jovi from the album *Slippery When Wet* (Polygram, 86).

You Got It (English)
Words and music by Jeff Lynne, Roy Orbison, and Tom Petty.
EMI-April Music, 1989/Orbisongs/Gone Gator Music.
Best-selling record by Roy Orbison from *Mystery Girl* (Virgin, 89).

You Got It (The Right Stuff)
Words and music by Maurice Starr.
Maurice Starr Music, 1988/EMI-April Music.
Best-selling record in 1989 by New Kids on the Block from *Hangin' Tough* (Columbia, 88).

You Got It All
Words and music by Rupert Holmes.
Holmes Line of Music, 1986.
Best-selling record in 1987 by The Jets, from the album *The Jets* (MCA, 86). With this release, songwriter Holmes moved back to the charts from Broadway, where his *Mystery of Edwin Drood* was a big success.

You Got Lucky
Words and music by Tom Petty and Mike Campbell.
Gone Gator Music, 1982/Wild Gator Music, 1982.
Best-selling record by Tom Petty & The Heartbreakers from *Long After Dark* (Backstreet, 83).

You Got Me Floating
Words and music by Jimi Hendrix.
Bella Godiva Music, 1967.
Revived in 1987 by Joan Jett and the Blackhearts on the album *Good Music* (Blackheart/CBS, 86).

You Keep Me Hanging On
Words and music by Eddie Holland, Lamont Dozier, and Brian Holland.
Stone Agate Music, 1966.

Revived in 1987 by Kim Wilde on the album *Another Step* (MCA). This was the third time the song reached the top ten, the Supremes and Vanilla Fudge having previously taken it there.

You Know I Love You Don't You (English)
Words and music by Howard Jones.
Howard Jones, England, 1986/Warner-Tamerlane Music, 1986.
Best-selling record by Howard Jones from the album *One to One* (Elektra, 86).

You Look Marvelous
Words by Billy Crystal, music by Paul Shaffer.
Billy Crystal & Paul #Shaffer, 1985/New Music Group, 1985/Postvalda Music, 1985.
Best-selling record by comedian Billy Crystal from the album *You Look Marvelous* (A & M, 85). The record is based on one of Crystal's featured characterizations on the television show *Saturday Night Live*.

You Look So Good in Love
Words and music by Kerry Chater, Rory Bourke, and Glen Ballard.
Vogue Music, 1983/Chappell & Co., Inc., 1983/MCA, Inc., 1983.
Best-selling record by George Strait from *Right or Wrong* (MCA, 84).

You Made Me Want to Sing
Words and music by Michael John La Chiusa.
Introduced by Shauna Hicks in the 1989 musical parody *Buzzsaw Berkeley*.

You Made This Love a Teardrop
Words and music by Nanci Griffith.
Irving Music Inc., 1989/Ponder Heart Music.
Introduced by Nanci Griffith on *Storms* (MCA, 89).

You Make Me Want to Love Again
Words and music by Leon Ware and Billy Valentine.
Polygram International, 1987/William V, 1987.
Introduced by Vesta Williams on the album *Vesta* (A & M, 87).

You Make Me Want to Make You Mine
Words and music by Dave Loggins.
Leeds Music Corp., 1985/Patchwork Music.
Best-selling record by Juice Newton from the album *Old Flame* (RCA, 85).

You Make My Dreams
Words and music by Daryl Hall, words by John Oates and Sara Allen.
Hot Cha Music Co., 1980/Unichappell Music Inc., 1980/Fust Buzza Music, Inc., 1980.

Best-selling record by Daryl Hall and John Oates from *Voices* (RCA, 81).

You May Be Right
Words and music by Billy Joel.
EMI April Canada, 1979/Impulsive Music, 1979.
Best-selling record by Billy Joel from *Glass Houses* (Columbia, 80).

You, Me and He
Words and music by James Mtume.
Mtume Music Publishing, 1984.
Best-selling record by Mtume from *You, Me and He* (Epic, 84).

You Might Think
Words and music by Ric Ocasek.
Lido Music Inc., 1984.
Best-selling record by The Cars from *Heartbreak City* (Elektra, 84).

You Never Gave up on Me
Words and music by Leslie Pearl.
Michael O'Connor Music, 1980.
Best-selling record by Crystal Gayle from *Hollywood Tennessee* (Columbia, 82).

You Never Looked That Good When You Were Mine
Words and music by Bob Morison and Johnny MacRae.
Southern Nights Music Co., 1986.
Introduced by George Jones and fortres crooner Patti Page on the album *Wine Colored Roses* (Epic, 86).

You Shook Me All Night Long (English)
Words and music by Angus Young, Malcolm Young, and Brian Johnson.
E. B. Marks Music Corp., 1980.
Best-selling record by AC/DC from *Back in Black* (Atlanta, 80).

You Should Be Mine (The Woo Woo Song)
Words and music by Andy Goldmark and Bruce Roberts.
Nonpariel Music, 1986/Broozertoones, Inc., 1986.
Best-selling record by Jeffrey Osborne from the album *Emotional* (A & M, 86).

You Should Have Been Gone by Now
Words and music by Eddy Raven, Frank Myers, and Don Pfrimmer.
Ravensong Music, 1986/Michael H. Goldsen, Inc., 1986/Collins Court Music, 1986.
Best-selling record by Eddy Raven from the album *Love and Other Hard Times* (RCA, 86).

You Should Hear How She Talks About You
Words and music by Tom Snow and Dean Pitchford.
Snow Music, 1981/Warner-Tamerlane Music, 1981.
Best-selling record by Melissa Manchester from *Hey Rickey* (Arista, 82).

You Shoulda Been There
Words and music by Marshall Crenshaw and Leroy Preston.
MHC, 1989/Whiskey Drinkin' Music/Bug Music.
Introduced by Marshall Crenshaw on *Good Evening* (Warner Bros., 89).

You Spin Me Round (Like a Record) (English)
Words and music by Peter Burns, Steven Coy, Timothy Lever, and
    Michael Percy.
Chappell & Co., Inc., 1985.
Best-selling record by Dead or Alive from the album *Youthquake* (Epic,
    85).

You Still Move Me
Words and music by Dan Seals.
Pink Pig Music, 1986.
Best-selling record in 1987 by Dan Seals, from the album *On the Front
    Line* (EMI-America, 86).

You Take Me for Granted
Words and music by Leona Williams.
Shade Tree Music Inc., 1981.
Best-selling record by Merle Haggard from *Poncho and Lefty* (Epic, 83).

You Understand Me
Words and music by Frank Loesser.
Frank Music Co., 1955.
Revived in 1989 by Jo Sullivan and Emily Loesser, the songwriter's
    wife and daughter, for their revue *Together Again (for the First
    Time)*. Loesser wrote the song for his last musical, *Senor Discretion
    Himself,* which was not produced until 1987.

You Wear It Well
Words and music by Chico DeBarge and Eldra DeBarge.
Jobete Music Co., 1985.
Best-selling record by El DeBarge with DeBarge from the album
    Rhythm of the Night (Motown, 85).

You Will Know
Words and music by Stevie Wonder.
Jobete Music Co., 1987/Black Bull Music, 1987.
Best-selling record in 1988 by Stevie Wonder from *Characters*
    (Motown, 87).

You Win Again
Words and music by Hank Williams.
Fred Rose Music, Inc., 1952.
Revived by Charley Pride (RCA, 80).

You Win Again (English)
Words and music by Barry Gibb, Robin Gibb, and Maurice Gibb.
Gibb Brothers Music, 1987/Unichappell Music Inc., 1987.
Introduced by The Bee Gees on the album *E.S.P.* (Warner Bros., 87).

You'll Accompany Me
Words and music by Bob Seger.
Gear Publishing, 1979.
Best-selling record by Bob Seger from *Against the Wind* (Capitol, 80).

You'll Be Back Every Night in My Dreams
Words and music by Johnny Russell and Wayland Holyfield.
Sunflower County Songs, 1978/Polygram International, 1978.
Best-selling record by The Statler Brothers from *Years Ago* (Mercury, 82).

Young Country
Words and music by Hank Williams, Jr.
Bocephus Music Inc., 1988.
Best-selling record by Hank Williams, Jr., from *Born to Boogie* (Warner/Curb, 88).

Young Love
Words and music by Paul Kennerley and Kent Robbins.
Irving Music Inc., 1988/Colter Bay Music.
Best-selling record in 1989 by The Judds from their *Greatest Hits* (RCA/Curb, 88).

Young Turks (English)
Words by Rod Stewart, music by Carmine Appice, Kevin Stuart Savigar, and Duane Hitchings.
Full Keel Music, 1981/Rod Stewart, 1981.
Best-selling record by Rod Stewart from *Tonight I'm Yours* (Warner Brothers, 81).

Your Dad Did
Words and music by John Hiatt.
Lillybilly, 1987.
Introduced by John Hiatt, from the album *Bring the Family* (A & M, 87).

Your Love (English)
Words and music by John Spinks.
Warning Tracks Inc., 1986.

Best-selling record by the Outfield from the album *Play Deep* (Columbia, 86). Spinks's record company brought him to the United States from England to learn how to write American hits. This album yielded several chart makers.

Your Love Is Driving Me Crazy
Words and music by Sammy Hagar.
WB Music, 1983.
Best-selling record by Sammy Hagar from *Three-Lock Box* (Geffen, 83).

Your Love's on the Line
Words and music by Earl Thomas Conley and Randy Scruggs.
EMI-Blackwood Music Inc., 1983/EMI-April Music, 1983/Full Armor Publishing Co., 1983.
Best-selling record by Earl Thomas Conley (RCA, 83).

Your Mama Don't Dance
Words and music by Kenny Loggins and Jim Messina.
MCA Music, 1972/Jasperilla Music Co., 1972.
Revived by Poison on *Open Up and Say Ahh* (Enigma, 88).

Your Smile
Words and music by Rene Moore and Angela Winbush.
A La Mode Music, 1986/WB Music, 1986.
Best-selling record by Rene & Angela from the album *Street Called Desire* (Polygram, 86).

Your Wildest Dreams (English)
Words and music by Justin Hayward.
Bright, England, 1986/WB Music, 1986.
Best-selling record by the Moody Blues from the album *The Other Side of Life* (Polygram, 86), which marked a comeback by this progressive band from the 1960's.

You're a Friend of Mine
Words and music by Narada Michael Walden and Jeffrey Cohen.
Gratitude Sky Music, 1986/Polo Grounds Music, 1986.
Best-selling record by Clarence Clemons and Jackson Browne in 1986 from the album *Hero* (Columbia, 85). The album was Clemons's first major effort apart from Bruce Springsteen's E Street Band, where his saxophone playing was frequently featured.

You're Gettin' to Me Again
Words and music by Pat McManus and Woody Bomar.
Music City Music, 1983.
Best-selling record by Jim Glaser (Noble Vision, 84).

You're Gonna Change
Words and music by Hank Williams.

Acuff Rose Music, 1949, 1981.
Rhythm 'n' Blues Screaming Blue Messiahs from the album *Gunshy* (Elektra, 86).

You're My Favorite Waste of Time
Words and music by Marshall Crenshaw.
MHC Music, 1982.
Introduced by Marshall Crenshaw & the Handsome, Ruthless and Stupid Band (Warner Brothers, 82).

You're My First Lady
Words and music by Mac McAnnally.
Beginner Music, 1987.
Best-selling record by T. G. Sheppard, from the album *It Still Rains in Memphis* (Columbia, 87).

You're My Latest, My Greatest Inspiration
Words and music by Kenny Gamble and Leon Huff.
Assorted Music, 1981.
Best-selling record by Teddy Pendergrass from *It's Time for Love* (Philadelphia International, 82).

You're Never Too Old for Young Love
Words and music by Rick Giles and Frank Myers.
Colgems-EMI Music, 1987.
Best-selling record by Eddy Raven, from the album *Right Hand Man* (RCA, 87).

You're Not Alone
Words and music by Jim Scott.
Virgin Music, 1988/Trinifold Music.
Best-selling record in 1989 by Chicago from *19* (Reprise, 88).

You're Not My Kind of Girl
Words and music by James Harris, III and Terry Lewis.
Flyte Tyme Tunes, 1988.
Best-selling record by New Edition, from *Heart Break* (MCA, 88).

You're Nothing without Me
Words by David Zippel, music by Cy Coleman.
Notable Music Co., Inc., 1989.
Introduced by Gregg Edelman and James Naughton in the musical *City of Angels* (89).

You're Still New to Me
Words and music by Paul Overstreet and Paul Davis.
Writer's Group Music, 1986/Scarlet Moon Music, 1986/Web 4 Music Inc., 1986.

Best-selling record by Marie Osmond with Paul Davis from the album *I Only Wanted You* (Capitol, 86).

You're the Best Break This Old Heart Ever Had
Words and music by Robert Hatch and Wayland Hollyfield.
Vogue Music, 1980/Polygram International, 1980.
Best-selling record by Ed Bruce (MCA, 82).

You're the First Time I've Thought About Leaving
Words and music by Dickey Betts and Kerry Chater.
Maplehill Music, 1982/Hall-Clement Publications, 1982.
Best-selling record by Reba McEntire from *The Best of Reba McEntire* (Mercury, 83).

You're the Inspiration
Words and music by Peter Cetera and David Foster.
BMG Songs Inc., 1984/Foster Frees Music Inc., 1984.
Best-selling record by Chicago from the album *Chicago XVII* (Warner Bros., 85).

You're the Last Thing I Needed Tonight
Words and music by Allee Willis and Don Pfrimmer.
Polygram International, 1986.
Best-selling record by John Schneider from the album *A Memory Like You* (MCA, 86).

You're the Only Woman (You and I)
Words and music by David Pack.
Rubicon Music, 1980.
Best-selling record by Ambrosia from *One-Eighty* (Warner Brothers, 80).

You're the Reason God Made Oklahoma
Words and music by Larry Collins and Sandy Pinkard.
House of Bryant Publications, 1980.
Best-selling record by David Frizzell and Shelly West (Warner Brothers, 80). Introduced in the film *Any Which Way You Can* (80). Nominated for a Grammy Award, Country Song of the Year, 1981.

You've Got Another Thing Comin'
Words and music by Rob Halford, Kenneth Downing, and Glenn Tipton.
EMI-April Music, 1981.
Best-selling record by Judas Priest from *Screaming for Vengeance* (Columbia, 81).

You've Lost That Lovin' Feeling
Words and music by Barry Mann, Cynthia Weil, and Phil Spector.
Screen Gems-EMI Music Inc., 1964.
Revived by Daryl Hall and John Oates from *Voices* (RCA, 80).

You've Still Got a Place in My Heart
Words and music by Leon Payne.
Fred Rose Music, Inc., 1978.
Best-selling record by George Jones from *You're Still Got a Place in My Heart* (Epic, 84).

Z

Zanz Can't Dance, also known as **Vanz Can't Dance**
Words and music by John Fogerty.
Wenaha Music Co., 1984.
Introduced by John Fogerty on the album *Centerfield* (Warner Bros.,
85). Fogerty was sued for libel over this song by his former boss, Sol
Zaentz, president of Fantasy Records, who claimed that the dancing
pig in the lyric who was also a pickpocket, was a slanderous
portrayal. The song was later retitled 'Vanz Can't Dance.'

Zaz Turns Blue
Words by David Was (pseudonym for David Weiss), music by Don Was
(pseudonym for Donald Fagenson).
Los Was Cosmipolitanos, 1983/State of the Artless, 1983/Polygram
International, 1983.
Introduced by Was Not Was In *Born to Laugh at Tornadoes* (Warner
Brothers, 83).

Lyricists & Composers Index

Bailey, Thomas
  Doctor! Doctor!
Bailey, Tom
  Hold Me Now
  I Want That Man
  King for a Day
  Lay Your Hands on Me
  Love on Your Side
  Nothing in Common
Bain, Jimmy
  Stars
Baird, Don
  Keep Your Hands to Yourself
Baker, Anita
  Giving You the Best That I Got
  Sweet Love
  You Better Watch Your Step
Baker, Arthur
  With Every Beat of My Heart
Baker, Arthur Henry
  Planet Rock
Bakker, Tammy Faye
  The Ballad of Jim and Tammy
Balin, Marty
  Summer of Love
Ballard, Clint, Jr.
  I'm Alive
Ballard, Glen
  All I Need
  You Look So Good in Love
Ballard, Greg
  Man in the Mirror
Ballard, Hank
  The Twist
Ballard, Pat
  Mister Sandman
Ballard, Russ
  The Border
  I Know There's Something Going On
  Winning
  You Can Do Magic
Bandiera, Robert
  We've Got the Love
Banko, Gordon
  Sanctified Lady
Banks, Homer
  Taxi
  Touch a Hand, Make a Friend

Banks, Tony
  In Too Deep
  Land of Confusion
  No Reply at All
  That's All
  Throwing It All Away
  Tonight, Tonight, Tonight
Barber, Bill
  Baby, It's the Little Things
Barbosa, Chris
  Let the Music Play
Barish, Jeff
  Hearts
Barker, Aaron
  Baby Blue
Barker, Martin
  Fish Below the Ice
Barker, Rocco
  I Go Crazy
Barnes, Don
  If I'd Been the One
  Like No Other Night
Barnes, Max D.
  Chiseled in Stone
  Drinkin' and Dreamin'
  I Won't Need You Anymore (Always
    and Forever)
  Joe Knows How to Live
  Red Neckin' Love Makin' Night
  Thank God for the Radio
  Who's Gonna Fill Their Shoes
Barnes, Richard
  Caught up in You
Barnett, Brenda
  The Clown
Barone, Richard
  Tangled in Your Web
Barrere, Paul
  Hangin' on to the Good Times
  Hate to Lose Your Lovin'
  Voices on the Wind
Barrett, Charles
  Stand or Fall
Barry, Jeff
  Christmas (Baby Please Come Home)
  Lie to You for Your Love
  River Deep, Mountain High

Lyricists & Composers Index

Lyricists & Composers Index

New Sensation
What You Need
Faulkner, Dave
  Good Times
  In the Middle of the Land
  Out That Door
  What's My Scene
Fearman, Eric
  Joystick
Fekaris, Dino
  I Pledge My Love
  I Will Survive
Feld, Marc
  Get It On (Bang a Gong)
Felder, Don
  Heavy Metal (Takin' a Ride)
Feldman, Jack
  I Made It Through the Rain
  Let Freedom Ring
Feldman, Richard
  D.C. Cab
Feldman, Rob
  I Want Candy
Feliciato, Phil *see* Cody, Phil
Feltenstein, George
  A Picture of Lisa
Fenderella
  Mr. D.J.
Fenn, Rick
  Family Man
Fenton, David
  Turning Japanese
  Waiting for the Weekend
Fenton, George
  Cry Freedom
Fequiere, Shaun
  Roxanne, Roxanne
Ferguson, Lloyd
  Pass the Dutchie
Ficca, William
  Square Pegs
Field, Robert
  Powerful Stuff
Fields, Philip
  Are You Single
Fields, Richard 'Dimples'
  If It Ain't One Thing It's Another

Finch, Richard
  Please Don't Go
Finer, Jem
  Fairytale of New York
  Tombstone
Finn, Neil
  Better Be Home Soon
  Don't Dream It's Over
  I Got You
  Something So Strong
  World Where You Live
Finn, William
  The Games I Play
  I Don't Want to Feel What I Feel
  I Never Wanted to Love You
  A Tight Knit Family
Fischer, Tony
  Good to Go
Fish
  Kayleigh
Fisher, Rob
  Promises, Promises
Fisher, Roger
  Room to Move
Fitzgerald, Alan
  When You Close Your Eyes
Fitzgerald, Francis
  Sentimental Street
Flack, Roberta
  Ballad for D
Fleming, George
  Freedom Overspill
Fleming, Kye
  I Was Country When Country Wasn't
    Cool
  I Wouldn't Have Missed It for the
    World
  Nobody
  Smokey Mountain Rain
  Years
Fleming, Rhonda
  Nobody Wants to Be Alone
Fletcher, E.
  The Message
Fletcher, Edward
  New York, New York
Flippin, John
  Backstrokin'

Lyricists & Composers Index

Lyricists & Composers Index

Everybody Dance
Jungle Love
Johnson, Larry *see* Starr, Maurice
Johnson, Louis
  Stomp
  Sweet Love
Johnson, Mark
  Love Radiates Around
Johnson, Matt
  The Beat(en) Generation
Johnson, Valerie
  Stomp
Johnson, William
  Relax
  Two Tribes
  Welcome to the Pleasure Dome
Johnston, Tom
  The Doctor
Johnstone, Davey
  Wrap Her Up
Johnstone, Phil
  Ship of Fools
  Tall Cool One
Jolicoeur, Dave
  Me Myself and I
Jolley, Steve
  Cruel Summer
Jones, Allen A.
  Freakshow on the Dancefloor
  Hit and Run
Jones, Booker T.
  To Be a Lover
Jones, Bucky
  Do You Wanna Go to Heaven
  Fewer Threads Than These
  Highway Robbery
  Living in the Promiseland
  Only One You
  War Is Hell (on the Homefront Too)
Jones, David
  Two Wrongs (Don't Make It Right)
Jones, David Lynn
  Bonnie Jean (Little Sister)
Jones, George Curtis
  Are You Single
  Make up Your Mind

Jones, Glenn
  We've Only Just Begun (The Romance
    Is Not Over)
Jones, Grace
  Vamp
Jones, Howard
  Everlasting Love
  Life in One Day
  No One Is to Blame
  Things Can Only Get Better
  You Know I Love You Don't You
Jones, Joe
  Iko-Iko
Jones, John Paul
  Fool in the Rain
Jones, Kacey
  I Thought He Was Mr. Right But He
    Left
  One Nite Stan
Jones, Kendall
  Q (Modern Industry)
Jones, Marylin
  Iko-Iko
Jones, Michael *see also* Kashif
  Train in Vain (Stand by Me)
Jones, Mick (The Clash)
  Rock the Casbah
  Wrong 'Em Boyo

Jones, Mick (Foreigner)
  Down on Love
  I Don't Want to Live without You
  I Want to Know What Love Is
  Juke Box Hero
  Say You Will
  That Was Yesterday
  Urgent
  Waiting for a Girl Like You

Jones, Paul H.
  I Wouldn't Change You If I Could
Jones, Paul Laurence *see* Laurence, Paul
Jones, Quincy
  Love Is in Control (Finger on the
    Trigger)
  Miss Celie's Blues (Sisters)
  P. Y. T. (Pretty Young Thing)
  Yah Mo B There

578

Lyricists & Composers Index

Medici, L.
New Orleans Ladies
Medley, Phil
Twist and Shout
Meher, T.
Century's End
Meier, Dieter
Oh Yeah
Meine, Klaus
Rhythm of Love
Rock You Like a Hurricane
Meisner, Randy
Deep Inside My Heart
Hearts on Fire
The Mekons
Only Darkness Has the Power
Melanie
The First Time I Loved Forever
Melcher, Terry
Getcha Back
Kokomo
Mellencamp, John *see also* Mellencamp,
John Cougar
Paper in Fire
Pop Singer
Mellencamp, John Cougar *see also*
Mellencamp, John
Ain't Even Done with the Night
The Authority Song
Check It Out
Cherry Bomb
Crumblin' Down
Hand to Hold Onto
Hurts So Good
Jack and Diane
Lonely Ol' Night
Pink Houses
Rock in the U.S.A. (A Salute to 60's
Rock)
Small Paradise
Small Town
Mellor, John *see* Strummer, Joe
Mellors, Joe *see* Strummer, Joe
Melrose, Ronald
Little H and Little G
Melton, Joe
Crying

Meltzer, Richard
Burnin' for You
Members, Jackie
Thin Line Between Love and Hate
Men Without Hats
Pop Goes the World
Mende, Gunther
The Power of Love (You Are My
Lady)
Menken, Alan
Feed Me
In the Cards
Kiss the Girl
Mean Green Monster from Outer Space
The Meek Shall Inherit
Somewhere That's Green
Suddenly Seymour
Under the Sea
Mercer, Kevin
Me Myself and I
Merchant, Natalie
Hey, Jack Kerouac
Poison in the Well
Trouble Me
Verdi Cries
Mercury, Freddie
Body Language
Merrill, Alan
I Love Rock and Roll
Merrill, Gary
How Will I Know
I Wanna Dance with Somebody (Who
Loves Me)
Waiting for a Star to Fall
Merrill, George
Simply Meant to Be
Messina, Jim
Call It Love
Your Mama Don't Dance
Metcalf, Gerald
Prisoner of Hope
Metheny, Pat
This Is Not America
Mevis, Alan R.
Fool Hearted Memory
Mevis, Blake
If You're Thinking You Want a

594

Lyricists & Composers Index

Lyricists & Composers Index

Lyricists & Composers Index

Payne, Harold
  I Wish He Didn't Trust Me So Much
Payne, Leon
  You've Still Got a Place in My Heart
Pearcy, Stephen
  Body Talk
  Round and Round
Pearl, Leslie
  You Never Gave up on Me
Pearson, Dernick
  Have You Had Your Love Today
Pearson, Michael
  Bottom of the Fifth
Peart, Neil
  Limelight
  New World Man
  The Spirit of Radio
  Tom Sawyer
Pebbles
  Mercedes Boy
Pedersen, Chris
  All Her Favorite Fruit
  Borderline
  (I Was Born in a) Laundromat
  When I Win the Lottery
Penniman, Richard
  Great Gosh a Mighty
Pennington, James P.
  Crazy for Your Love
  Give Me One More Chance
  I Can't Get Close Enough
  I Don't Wanna Be a Memory
  It'll Be Me
  Just in Case
  She's a Miracle
  She's Too Good to Be True
  Take Me Down
  Woke up in Love
Penny, Ed
  Somebody's Knockin'
Peoples, Alisa
  Don't Stop the Music
Percy, Michael
  Brand New Lover
  You Spin Me Round (Like a Record)
Perez, Louie
  The Hardest Time
  One Time One Night

River of Fools
Will the Wolf Survive
Perren, Chris
  A Little Bit of Love (Is All It Takes)
Perren, Freddy
  I Pledge My Love
Perry, Joe
  Dude (Looks Like a Lady)
  Love in an Elevator
  Rag Doll
  Walk This Way
Perry, Phil
  United Together
Perry, Steve
  After the Fall
  Any Way You Want It
  Be Good to Yourself
  Don't Fight It
  Don't Stop Believin'
  Foolish Heart
  Girl Can't Help It
  I'll Be Alright without You
  Oh, Sherrie
  Only the Young
  Open Arms
  Send Her My Love
  Separate Ways (World's Apart)
  Still They Ride
  Suzanne
  Who's Crying Now
Person
  Listen to Your Heart
Pert, Morris
  Family Man
Perven, Freddy
  I Will Survive
Pesce, Joseph
  Voices Carry
Pescetto, Jeffrey
  Lovin' on Next to Nothin'
  Spaceballs
Pessis, Andre
  New Shade of Blue
  Walking on a Thin Line
The Pet Shop Boys
  Always on My Mind
Peterik, Jim
  American Heartbeat

Lyricists & Composers Index

Pilson, Jeff
  Dream Warriors
Pinkard, Sandy
  Blessed Are the Believers
  I Can Tell by the Way You Dance
    (How You're Gonna Love Me
    Tonight)
  You're the Reason God Made
    Oklahoma
Pippin, Steve
  Better Love Next Time
Pirner, Dave
  Down on up to Me
  Endless Farewell
Pirroni, Marco
  Goody Two Shoes
Pistilli, Gene
  Too Gone Too Long
Pitchford, Dean
  After All (Love Theme from *Chances
    Are*)
  Almost Paradise... Love Theme from
    Footloose
  Birthday Suit
  Dancing in the Sheets
  Don't Call It Love
  Don't Fight It
  Fame
  Footloose
  Holding Out for a Hero
  Let's Hear It for the Boy
  Make Me Lose Control
  One Sunny Day
  Romance (Love Theme from *Sing*)
  Sing
  Somewhere I Belong
  You Should Hear How She Talks
    About You
Pitney, Gene
  Hello Mary Lou
Plant, Robert
  Big Log
  Fool in the Rain
  The Only One
  Ship of Fools
  Tall Cool One
Poindexter, Richard
  Thin Line Between Love and Hate

Poindexter, Robert
  Thin Line Between Love and Hate
Pointer, Anita
  I'm So Excited
Pointer, June
  I'm So Excited
Pointer, Ruth
  I'm So Excited
Pomeranz, David
  Far Away Lands
  The Old Songs
Pomus, Doc
  Hello Stranger
Ponger, Robert
  Der Kommissar
Poons, Larry
  Amnesia and Jealousy (Oh Lana)
Pop, Iggy
  China Girl
  1969
Porcaro, Jeffrey
  Africa
  Human Nature
Poree, Anita
  Going in Circles
Porter, David
  Soul Man
  Wrap It Up
Porter, Mike
  Tennessee Plates
Porter, Robbie
  It Ain't Cool to Be Crazy About You
Porter, Royce
  Ocean Front Property
  What's Going on in Your World
Portnoy, Gary
  Bring on the Loot
  Every Time I Turn Around
  Our Night
  People Like Us
  Theme from *Mr. Belvedere*
  We've Got Each Other
  Where Everybody Knows Your Name
Post, Mike
  The Theme from *Hill Street Blues*
  Theme from *Magnum P.I.*
  The Theme from *The Greatest
    American Hero*

606

Lyricists & Composers Index

Simmons, Bill
  Don't Rock the Boat
  Headlines
Simmons, Daryl
  Dial My Heart
  Don't Be Cruel
  It's No Crime
  Love Saw It
  The Lover in Me
  Lucky Charm
  On Our Own (From *Ghostbusters II*)
  Rock Wit'cha
  Secret Rendezvous
  Superwoman
  The Way You Love Me
Simmons, Gene
  A World Without Heroes
Simmons, Joseph
  Christmas in Hollis
Simmons, Joyce
  The Men All Pause
Simmons, Lonnie
  Beep a Freak
  Burn Rubber on Me
  Don't Stop the Music
  Early in the Morning
  Party Train
Simmons, Russell
  The Breaks
  Sleep Talk
Simmons, William
  Freak-a-Zoid
Simon, Bob
  What Am I Gonna Do About You
Simon, Carly
  Coming Around Again
  Jesse
  Let the River Run
  Menemsha
  The Stuff That Dreams Are Made Of
Simon, Dwayne
  I Need Love
  I'm That Type of Guy
Simon, Paul
  Ace in the Hole
  Allergies
  The Boy in the Bubble
  Diamonds on the Soles of Her Shoes

  Graceland
  Hazy Shade of Winter
  Homeless
  How the Heart Approaches What It
    Yearns
  The Late Great Johnny Ace
  Late in the Evening
  One Trick Pony
  Rene and Georgette Magritte with
    Their Dog After the War
  You Can Call Me Al
Simonon, Paul
  Rock the Casbah
Simple Minds
  Alive and Kicking
  Sanctify Yourself
Simpson, Fitzroy
  Pass the Dutchie
Simpson, Valerie
  Count Your Blessings
  I'll Be There for You
  Landlord
  Outta the World
  Solid
  Still Such a Thing
  Street Corner
  There's a Winner in You
Singletary, Larry
  Girl I Got My Eyes on You
Singleton, Charles
  Just Be Yourself
Singleton, Charlie
  She's Strange
  This Time
Singleton, Don
  Fool for Your Love
Singleton, Stephen
  The Look of Love
Sixx, Nikki
  Dr. Feelgood
  Girls, Girls, Girls
Sizemore, Arthur
  Right or Wrong
Skardina, Gary
  Jump (for My Love)
  (Come on) Shout
Skill, Mike
  Talking in Your Sleep

618

Lyricists & Composers Index

Lyricists & Composers Index

Torme, Mel
  The Christmas Song
Tosti, Blaise
  Affair of the Heart
Toussaint, Allen
  Shoo-Rah Shoo-Rah
  Working in the Coal Mine
Towers, Michael
  Nobody's Fool (Theme from
    Caddyshack II)
Townes, Jeff
  I Think I Can Beat Mike Tyson
  A Nightmare on My Street
  Parents Just Don't Understand
Townsend, David
  Closer Than Friends
  Don't Take It Personal
Townshend, David
  Happy
Townshend, Pete
  After the Fire
  Another Tricky Day
  Athena
  Don't Let Go the Coat
  Face the Face
  Let My Love Open the Door
  A Little Is Enough
  Rough Boys
  You Better You Bet
Tozzi, Umberto
  Gloria
Tramp, Mike
  Wait
  When the Children Cry
Traveling Wilburys
  Congratulations
  Handle with Care
  Not Alone Anymore
  Tweeter and the Monkey Man
Travers, Harry
  The Honey Thief
Travis, Chandler
  Discretion
Travis, Randy
  I Told You So
Troutman, Larry
  Dance Floor
  I Want to Be Your Man

Troutman, Roger
  Dance Floor
  More Bounce to the Ounce - Part 1
Trudeau, Garry
  I Can Have It All
True, Mark
  Too Many Lovers
Tubb, Glen
  Two Story House
Tubes
  Talk to Ya Later
Tuggle, Brent
  Just Like Paradise
Tullio, Jim
  Simple Things
Tuohy, Bill
  King of the New York Street
Turgon, Bruce
  Midnight Blue
Turi, John
  What a Thrill
Turner, Joe Lynn
  Stone Cold
Turner, Phil
  Thinking About Your Love
Turner, Raye
  Watching You
Tweel, Jeff
  Mornin' Ride
Twilley, Dwight
  Girls
Tyler, Adele
  Bobbie Sue
Tyler, Dan
  Baby's Got a New Baby
  Twenty Years Ago
Tyler, Daniel
  Bobbie Sue
  Modern Day Romance
Tyler, Steven
  Angel
  Dude (Looks Like a Lady)
  Love in an Elevator
  Rag Doll
  Walk This Way
Tyson, Ian
  The Gift

628

Waterson, Jack
Sorry Naomi
Watley, Jody
Don't You Want Me
Friends
Looking for a New Love
Real Love
Some Kind of Lover
Still a Thrill
Watson, Boaz
Operator
Rock Steady
Watson, Deek
(I Love You) For Sentimental Reasons
Watson, Jeff
Goodbye
Waybill, Fee
She's a Beauty
Wayne, Bernie
Blue Velvet
Weaktaar, Pal
Take on Me
Weatherly, Jim
A Lady Like You
Weaver, Blue
Hold on to My Love
Webb, Jim
Highwayman
The Moon Is a Harsh Mistress
Webb, Jimmy
Adios
In Cars
Lightning in a Bottle
Oklahoma Nights
Scissor Cut
She Moves, Eyes Follow
Still within the Sound of My Voice
Webster, Daniel
Watching You
Weidlin, Jane
Our Lips Are Sealed
Weil, Cynthia
All I Need to Know (Don't Know
Much)
All of You
He's So Shy
He's Sure the Man I Love
If Ever You're in My Arms Again

Just Once
Love Lives On
Love Will Conquer All
Never Gonna Let You Go
Running With the Night
So Far So Good
Somewhere down the Road
Somewhere Out There
Through the Fire
We're Going All the Way
You've Lost That Lovin' Feeling
Weill, Kurt
September Song
Weinstein, Bobby
It's Gonna Take a Miracle
Weir, Rusty
Don't It Make You Wanna Dance
Weiss, David see Was, David
Weiss, Donna
Bette Davis Eyes
Weiss, Elliot
Dungeons and Dragons
Mama Don't Cry
Our Favorite Restaurant
Weiss, George David
What a Wonderful World
Welch, Kevin
Fewer Threads Than These
Weller, Paul
My Ever Changing Moods
Set the House Ablaze
Wells, James Thomas
WKRP in Cincinnati
Wells, Kevin
Walking on a Thin Line
Wells, Robert
The Christmas Song
Werfel, Steve
I Live for Your Love
Werner, Fred
Flo's Yellow Rose
West, Kyle
Nite and Day
Off On Your Own (Girl)
Rescue Me
West-Oram, Jamie
Are We Ourselves
One Thing Leads to Another

Important Performances Index

Songs are listed under the works in which they were introduced or given significant renditions. The index is organized into major sections by performance medium: Album, Movie, Musical, Performer, Revue, Television Show.

Album

Abacab
  Man on the Corner
  No Reply at All
ABC in Alphabet City
  When Smokey Sings
About Last Night
  So Far So Good
About Love
  Landlord
Abracadabra
  Abracadabra
Absolute Torch and Twang
  Luck in My Eyes
Acadie
  Fisherman's Daughter
Across a Crowded Room
  She Twists the Knife Again
  When the Spell Is Broken
  You Don't Say
Act Naturally
  Act Naturally
Action Jackson
  Action Jackson
Action Replay
  No One Is to Blame

Actually
  It's a Sin
  What Have I Done to Deserve This
Adventures in Utopia
  Set Me Free
Affair
  Everything I Miss at Home
After Dark
  Desire
  I Can't Help It
After Eight
  Puttin' on the Ritz
After Midnight
  Shining Star
Afterburner
  Sleeping Bag
Against All Odds
  Against All Odds (Take a Look at Me
    Now)
Against the Wind
  Against the Wind
  Fire Lake
  You'll Accompany Me
The Age of Consent
  Small Town Boy
Agent Provocateur
  Down on Love

Important Performances Index — Album

As One
  Big Fun
As the Band Turns
  Secret Lovers
Asia
  Heat of the Moment
  Only Time Will Tell
Aspects of Love
  The First Man You Remember
At My Window
  For the Sake of the Song
At Yankee Stadium
  I Want You Bad
ATF
  Der Kommissar
Atlanta Blue
  Atlanta Blue
Attack of the Killer B's
  Amnesia and Jealousy (Oh Lana)
August
  Bad Influence
  Holy Mother
  It's in the Way You Use It
  Tearing Us Apart
Autoamerican
  Rapture
  The Tide Is High
The B-52's
  Rock Lobster
Baby Tonight
  Don't Go
Babylon and On
  Hourglass
Back for the Attack
  Dream Warriors
Back in Black
  Back in Black
  You Shook Me All Night Long
Back in the High Life
  Back in the High Life Again
  The Finer Things
  Freedom Overspill
  Higher Love
Back to Avalon
  Nobody's Fool (Theme from
    Caddyshack II)
Back to Basics
  A New England

Back to the Beach
  Surfin' Bird
Bad
  Bad
  Dirty Diana
  I Can't Stop Loving You
  Man in the Mirror
  Smooth Criminal
  The Way You Make Me Feel
Bad Animals
  Alone
  There's the Girl
  Who Will You Run To
Bad English
  When I See You Smile
Bagdad Cafe
  Calling You
Balance of Power
  Calling America
Balin
  Hearts
Bananarama
  Cruel Summer
Band of the Hand
  Band of the Hand (Hell Time Man!)
Barbara Mandrell Live
  I Was Country When Country Wasn't
    Cool
Barking at Airplanes
  Crazy in the Night (Barking at
    Airplanes)
Barry
  I Made It Through the Rain
Barry Manilow's Greatest Hits, Vol. II
  Read 'em and Weep
Based on a True Story
  Cheyene
  Judas Kiss
  Poem of the River
Batman
  Batdance (From Batman)
  Partyman
  Scandalous
Be a Winner
  Don't Waste Your Time
Be My Lover
  Lovelight

644

Important Performances Index

659

Important Performances Index

670

X-Static
  Wait for Me
Xanadu
  All over the World
  I'm Alive
  Magic
  Suddenly
  Xanadu
The Year 2000
  Girl, Don't Let It Get You Down
Years Ago
  Don't Wait on Me
  You'll Be Back Every Night in My
    Dreams
Yellow Moon
  Sister Rosa
Yentl
  Papa Can You Hear Me
  The Way He Makes Me Feel
Yes It's You Lady
  Tell Me Tomorrow
Yo Frankie
  King of the New York Street
  Serenade
Yo Yo
  I Don't Mind at All
You Again
  You Again
You Ain't Lovin' You Ain't Livin'
  Baby Blue
You Broke My Heart in 17 Places
  They Don't Know
You Could Have Been with Me
  You Could Have Been with Me
You Don't Know Me
  Lonely Nights
  Tears of the Lonely
  You Don't Know Me
You Look Marvelous
  You Look Marvelous
You, Me and He
  You, Me and He
Your Forever
  Touch a Four Leaf Clover
Your Move
  The Border
Your Wish Is My Command
  I Want to Hold Your Hand

The Youth of Today
  Pass the Dutchie
Youthquake
  You Spin Me Round (Like a Record)
You've Got a Good Love Comin'
  God Bless the U.S.A.
You've Still Got a Place in My Heart
  You've Still Got a Place in My Heart
The Zagora
  Slow Down
Zapp
  More Bounce to the Ounce - Part 1
Zapp II
  Dance Floor
Zebop
  Winning
Zenyatta Mondatta
  De Do Do Do, De Da Da Da
  Don't Stand So Close to Me
Zuma
  New Shade of Blue

Movie
About Last Night
  So Far So Good
Absolute Beginners
  Absolute Beginners
Action Jackson
  Action Jackson
Against All Odds
  Against All Odds (Take a Look at Me
    Now)
All the Right Moves
  All the Right Moves
American Anthem
  Take It Easy
American Gigolo
  Call Me
  The Seduction (Love Theme from
    American Gigolo)
An American Tail
  Somewhere Out There
Any Which Way You Can
  You're the Reason God Made
    Oklahoma
Armed and Dangerous
  Armed and Dangerous

Tin Men
  Good Thing
Tootsie
  It Might Be You
Top Gun
  Danger Zone
  Heaven in Your Eyes
  Take My Breath Away (Love Theme
    from *Top Gun*)
Tough Guys
  They Don't Make Them Like They
    Used To
  Tuff Enuff
Trouble Mind
  The Hawk (El Gavilan)
Twins
  Twins
Two of a Kind
  Twist of Fate
UHF
  UHF
Under the Cherry Moon
  Kiss
Up against It
  Parallel Lines
Urban Cowboy
  Could I Have This Dance
  Don't It Make You Wanna Dance
  Look What You Done to Me
Vamp
  Vamp
Vibes
  Hole in My Heart (All the Way to
    China)
Victor, Victoria
  Chicago, Illinois
  Crazy World
A View to a Kill
  A View to a Kill
Vision Quest
  Crazy for You
  Only the Young
Weird Science
  Weird Science
White Nights
  Say You, Say Me (Title Song from
    White Nights)

Separate Lives (Love Theme from
    White Nights)
Who's That Girl
  Causing a Commotion
  Who's That Girl
The Woman in Red
  I Just Called to Say I Love You
  Love Light in Flight
Working Girl
  Let the River Run
Xanadu
  All over the World
  I'm Alive
  Magic
  Suddenly
  Xanadu
Yentl
  Papa Can You Hear Me
Yes Giorgio
  If We Were in Love
Young Einstein
  Dumb Things

Musical

All Dogs Go to Heaven
  Love Survives
Amen Corner
  Rise and Stand Again
Annie Get Your Gun
  I Got Lost in Her Arms
Annie 2
  Changes
Aspects of Love
  The First Man You Remember
Attack of the Killer Revue
  A Picture of Lisa
Baby
  Easier to Love
  Fatherhood Blues
  I Want It All
  The Story Goes On
Ballroom
  I Love to Dance
Barnum
  The Colors of My Life
  Love Makes Such Fools of Us All

Big River
  Muddy Water
  River in the Rain
Bittersuite
  Dungeons and Dragons
  Mama Don't Cry
  Our Favorite Restaurant
Buzzsaw Berkeley
  That Demon Baby of Mine
  You Made Me Want to Sing
Cats
  Gus the Theatre Cat
  Memory
Charlie and Algernon
  Now
Chess
  The Arbiter (I Know the Score)
  Heaven Help My Heart
  I Know Him So Well
Chu Chem
  It Must Be Good for Me
City of Angels
  With Every Breath I Take
  You Can Always Count on Me
  You're Nothing without Me
A Day in Hollywood/A Night in the
    Ukraine
  Natasha
  Nelson
Diamonds
  Hundreds of Hats
  In the Cards
  What You'd Call a Dream
Doonesbury
  I Can Have It All
Dreamgirls
  And I Am Telling You I'm Not Going
  Cadillac Car
  One Night Only
The Fabulous Baker Boys
  Makin' Whoopee
Flora, The Red Menace
  The Kid Herself
The Gospel at Colonus
  How Shall I See You Through My
    Tears
  Lift Me Up (Like a Dove)
  Now Let the Weeping Cease

Grand Hotel
  Love Can't Happen
The Human Comedy
  Beautiful Music
  The Birds
Into the Woods
  Agony
  Ever After
  Hello Little Girl
  I Know Things Now
  No One Is Alone
Is There Life After High School
  Fran and Janie
  I'm Glad You Didn't Know Me
  Nothing Really Happened
  Second Thoughts
It's So Nice to Be Civilized
  I've Still Got My Bite
Juno
  I Wish It So
La Cage Au Folles
  The Best of Times
  I Am What I Am
  Look over There
  Song on the Sand
  With You on My Arm
Late Nite Comic
  Clara's Dancing School
  Late Nite Comic
Leader of the Pack
  Keep It Confidential
  River Deep, Mountain High
  Rock of Rages
  We're Gonna Make It (After All)
Legs Diamond
  The Music Went Out of My Life
Les Miserables
  Drink with Me to Days Gone By
  I Dreamed a Dream
  On My Own
The Little Rascals
  Where Did I Go Wrong
Little Shop of Horrors
  Feed Me
  Suddenly Seymour
Mail
  Crazy World
  It's Getting Harder to Love You

711

Important Performances Index — Musical

There Isn't Only One Girl
A Year from Today
Smile
  Disneyland
Song and Dance
  I Have Never Felt This Way Before
  Tell Me on a Sunday
  Unexpected Song
Starlight Express
  Only You
  Starlight Express
Starmites
  Hard to Be a Diva
  Superhero Girl
Sunday in the Park with George
  Beautiful
  Children and Art
  Finishing the Hat
  Move On
  Putting It Together
  Sunday

Swing
  Don't Come Inside My Head
  Twelve Rough Years
Taking My Turn
  Do You Remember
  This Is My Song
Tales of Tinseltown
  Jungle Fever
Teddy and Alice
  Battle Lines
  Can I Let Her Go
Tell Me on a Sunday
  Tell Me on a Sunday
Three Postcards
  She Was K.C. at Seven
Time
  Time Will Teach Us All
The Waltz of the Stork
  The Apple Stretching
Williams and Walker
  Nobody
The Wiz
  Home
Woman of the Year
  The Grass Is Always Greener

I Told You So
One of the Boys

Operetta
Magdelena
  The Broken Pianolita

Performer
a-ha
  The Living Daylights
  The Sun Always Shines on T.V.
  Take on Me
Abba
  The Winner Takes It All
Abbott, Gregory
  Shake You Down
ABC
  Be Near Me
  The Look of Love
  (How to Be a) Millionaire
  When Smokey Sings
Abdul, Paula
  Cold-Hearted
  Forever Your Girl
  Straight Up
  (It's Just) The Way That You Love Me
AC/DC
  Back in Black
  Who Made Who
  You Shook Me All Night Long
Adams, Bryan
  Hearts on Fire
  Heat of the Night
  Heaven
  It's Only Love
  One Night Love Affair
  Run to You
  Somebody
  Straight from the Heart
  Summer of '69
  This Time
Addotta, Kip
  Life in the Slaw Lane
Aerosmith
  Angel
  Dude (Looks Like a Lady)
  Love in an Elevator
  Rag Doll
Afrika Bambaata & The Soul Sonic Force
  Planet Rock

I Blinked Once
Romeo's Tune
Search Your Heart
Force M.D.'s
Itchin' for a Scratch
Love Is a House
Tender Love
Ford, Lita
Close My Eyes Forever
Kiss Me Deadly
Foreigner
Down on Love
I Don't Want to Live without You
I Want to Know What Love Is
Juke Box Hero
Say You Will
That Was Yesterday
Urgent
Waiting for a Girl Like You
Forester Sisters
I Fell in Love Again Last Night
Just in Case
Lonely Alone
Mama's Never Seen Those Eyes
Too Much Is Not Enough
You Again
Foster, David
And When She Danced (Love theme
from *Stealing Home*)
The Best of Me
Love Lights the World (Rendezvous)
Love Theme from *St. Elmo's Fire*
(Instrumental)
Winter Games
The Four Tops
When She Was My Girl
Clarence Fourtal and the Five Blind Boys
Lift Me Up (Like a Dove)
Fowler, Beth
Battle Lines
I Want It All
We've Got Each Other
Fox, Samantha
I Wanna Have Some Fun
Naughty Girls Need Love Too
Touch Me (I Want Your Body)
Franke & The Knockouts
Sweetheart

Frankie Goes to Hollywood
Relax
Two Tribes
Welcome to the Pleasure Dome
Franklin, Aretha
Freeway of Love
Get It Right
Gimme Your Love
I Knew You Were Waiting (for Me)
It Isn't, It Wasn't, It Ain't Never
Gonna Be
Jimmy Lee
Jump to It
Jumpin' Jack Flash
Just My Daydream
Sisters Are Doin' It for Themselves
Through the Storm
United Together
Who's Zoomin' Who
Franz, Joy
Dungeons and Dragons
Fraser, Wendy
She's Like the Wind
Frasier, Alison
Goodbye Emil
Parallel Lines
Fredericke, Jesse
As Days Go By
Everywhere You Look
Frehley, Ace
Do Ya
Fresh, Doug E.
The Show
Frey, Glenn
The Heat Is On
The One You Love
Sexy Girl
Smuggler's Blues
True Love
You Belong to the City
Fricke, Janie
Always Have Always Will
Don't Worry 'bout Me Baby
Down to My Last Broken Heart
He's a Heartache (Looking for a Place
to Happen)
Let's Stop Talkin' About It

Important Performances Index

You and I
You Never Gave up on Me
General Kane
Crack Killed Applejack
Generation X
Dancing with Myself
Genesis
In Too Deep
Invisible Touch
Land of Confusion
Man on the Corner
Misunderstanding
No Reply at All
That's All
Throwing It All Away
Tonight, Tonight, Tonight
George Thorogood & The Destroyers
Willie and the Hand Jive
Georgia Satellites
Battleship Chains
Hippy Hippy Shake
Keep Your Hands to Yourself
Getz, Mara
Crazy World
It's Getting Harder to Love You
Giant Steps
(You Don't Need) Another Lover
Gibb, Andy
All I Have to Do Is Dream
Desire
I Can't Help It
Time Is Time
Gibb, Barry
Guilty
What Kind of Fool
Gibbs, Terri
Somebody's Knockin'
Gibson, Debbie
Electric Youth
Foolish Beat
Lost in Your Eyes
No More Rhyme
Only in My Dreams
Out of the Blue
Shake Your Love
Gibson, Judy
Singin' a Song

Giles, Nancy
March of the Yuppies
Gilley, Mickey
Fool for Your Love
A Headache Tomorrow (or a Heartache Tonight)
Lonely Nights
Paradise Tonight
Stand by Me
Tears of the Lonely
That's All That Matters
True Love Ways
You Don't Know Me
Giuffria
I Must Be Dreaming
Gladys Knight & The Pips
Landlord
Glaser, Jim
You're Gettin' to Me Again
Glass Tiger
Someday
Glasser, Phillip
Somewhere Out There
Gloria Estefan & Miami Sound Machine
1-2-3
The Go-Go's
Head over Heels
Our Lips Are Sealed
Vacation
We Got the Beat
Go West
Call Me
The Godfathers
Birth, School, Work, Death
Godley and Creme
Cry
Golden Earring
Twilight Zone
Gooden, Dwight
Dr. K
Gordon, Robert
Fire
Someday, Someway
Gorka, John
I Saw a Stranger with Your Hair
Gosdin, Vern
Chiseled in Stone
I Can Tell by the Way You Dance

751

Important Performances Index — Performer

Girls Talk
Goodbye My Friend
How Do I Make You
Hurt So Bad
Mister Sandman
The Moon Is a Harsh Mistress
'Round Midnight
Somewhere Out There
Still within the Sound of My Voice
Talk to Me of Mendocino
Talking in the Dark
Telling Me Lies
To Know Him Is to Love Him
What's New
Wildflowers
Rooney, Jan
Love Is Being Loved
Roper, Skid
Debbie Gibson Is Pregnant (with My Two-Headed Love Child)
Elvis Is Everywhere
Legalize It
Ross, Diana
All of You
Endless Love
If We Hold on Together
I'm Coming Out
It's My Turn
Mirror Mirror
Missing You
Muscles
Swept Away
Upside Down
Why Do Fools Fall in Love
Workin' Overtime
Roth, David Lee
California Girls
Damn Good
I Ain't Got Nobody
Just a Gigolo
Just Like Paradise
Roxette
Dressed for Success
Listen to Your Heart
The Look
Royal, Billy Joe
Tell It Like It Is

The Royal Philharmonic Orchestra
Hooked on Classics
Ruffelle, Frances
On My Own
Ruffin, Jimmy
Hold on to My Love
Rufus
Ain't Nobody
Run D.M.C.
Christmas in Hollis
Walk This Way
Rundgren, Todd
Parallel Lines
Rupert, Michael
Crazy World
A Tight Knit Family
Rush
Limelight
New World Man
The Spirit of Radio
Tom Sawyer
Rush, Jennifer
Flames of Paradise
The Power of Love (You Are My Lady)
Rushen, Patrice
Feels So Real (Won't Let Go)
Forget Me Nots
Russell, Brenda
Piano in the Dark
Russell, Rebecca
Faith, Hope and Glory
Ryder, Nickie
The Pride Is Back
Sade
Never as Good as the First Time
Nothing Can Come Between Us
Paradise
Sally
Smooth Operator
The Sweetest Taboo
Safire
I Will Survive
Thinking of You
Saints
Just Like Fire Would
Salt-N-Pepa
Push It

Santana
  Hold On
  Winning
Sawyer Brown
  Step That Step
  This Missin' You Heart of Mine
  Used to Blue
Sayer, Leo
  More Than I Can Say
Scaggs, Boz
  Breakdown Dead Ahead
  JoJo
  Look What You Done to Me
  Miss Sun
Scaggs, Ricky
  Crying My Heart Out over You
Scandal
  All I Want
  Beat of a Heart
  Goodbye to You
  Love's Got a Line on You
  Maybe We Went Too Far
  Only the Young
  The Warrior
Scarbury, Joey
  The Theme from *The Greatest
    American Hero*
Scarlett and Black
  You Don't Know
Schmidt, Claudia
  Broken Glass
  Hard Love
Schmidt, Timothy B.
  Boys Night Out
Schneider, John
  Country Girls
  It's Now or Never
  I've Been Around Enough to Know
  Love, You Ain't Seen the Last of Me
  What's a Memory Like You (Doing in
    a Love Like This)
  You're the Last Thing I Needed
    Tonight
Schuyler, Knobloch & Overstreet
  American Me
  Baby's Got a New Baby

The Scorpions
  Rhythm of Love
  Rock You Like a Hurricane
Scott-Heron, Gil
  The Bottle
  Johannesburg
  The Revolution Will Not Be Televised
Screaming Blue Messiahs
  You're Gonna Change
Scritti Politti
  Perfect Way
Seals, Dan
  Addicted
  Big Wheels in the Moonlight
  Bop
  Everything That Glitters (Is Not Gold)
  I Will Be There
  Meet Me in Montana
  My Baby's Got Good Timing
  One Friend
  Three Time Loser
  You Still Move Me
Sedaka, Dara
  Should've Never Let You Go
Sedaka, Neil
  Should've Never Let You Go
Seduction
  Two to Make It Right
Bob Seger & The Silver Bullet Band
  American Storm
  Even Now
  Like a Rock
  Old Time Rock and Roll
  Shame on the Moon
  Understanding
Seger, Bob
  Against the Wind
  Boomtown Blues
  Fire Lake
  The Little Drummer Boy
  Makin' Thunderbirds
  Shakedown
  Trying to Live My Life Without You
  You'll Accompany Me
Sembello, Michael
  Gravity
  Maniac

765

Play

Revue

Television Show

Chronological Index

1981

Tom Sawyer
Tonight I'm Yours (Don't Hurt Me)
Too Much Time on My Hands
Touch Me When We're Dancing
Trouble
Trying to Live My Life Without You
Turn Your Love Around
Turning Japanese
Under One Banner
Under Pressure
Under the Covers
Urgent
Very Special
The Voice
The Waiting
Waiting for a Girl Like You
Waiting on a Friend
Walking on Thin Ice
We Got the Beat
What Are We Doin' in Love
What Cha Gonna Do for Me
Who's Crying Now
Wind Beneath My Wings
Winning
WKRP in Cincinnati
Woman
A Woman Needs Love
Woman's World
Working for the Weekend
Working in the Coal Mine
A World Without Heroes
Would You Catch a Falling Star
Yesterday's Songs
You Better You Bet
You Could Have Been with Me
You Don't Know Me
You Should Hear How She Talks About
    You
You Take Me for Granted
Young Turks
You're My Latest, My Greatest
    Inspiration
You've Got Another Thing Comin'

1982

Abracadabra

After the Fall
All This Love
All Through the Night
Always on My Mind
American Heartbeat
American Made
American Music
Another Honky Tonk Night on Broadway
Any Day Now
Athena
Atlantic City
Atomic Dog
(You're So Square) Baby, I Don't Care
Baby I Lied
Back on the Chain Gang
Be Italian
Beat It
The Beatles' Movie Medley
Big Fun
Big Log
Billie Jean
Blizzard of Lies
Blue Eyes
Blue Moon with Heartache
Blue Rider
Body Language
Boomtown Blues
Bottom of the Fifth
Boy with a Problem
Break It to Me Gently
Breaking Us in Two
Breathless
Broken Glass
Busted
Candy Girl
Can't Even Get the Blues
Cat People (Putting out Fire)
Caught up in You
Centerfold
Charlie's Medicine
Cheating in the Next Room
Circles
Come Back to Me
Come Go with Me
Come on Eileen
Crimson and Clover
Crying My Heart Out over You

787

1983

1984

1985

A Girls Night Out
Glory Days
The Glow
Good Friends
The Goonies 'R' Good Enough
Gotta Get You Home Tonight
Gravity
Hangin' on a String
Hanging on a Heartbeat
Have Mercy
Heart of the Country
The Heat Is On
Hello Mary Lou
Here I Am Again
Hero Takes a Fall
High Horse
High on You
High School Nights
Highwayman
Honor Bound
How Old Are You
How Soon Is Now
How'm I Doin'
I Ain't Got Nobody
I Don't Know Why You Don't Want Me
I Don't Mind the Thorns (If You're the
    Rose)
I Don't Think I'm Ready for You
I Don't Want to Do It
I Drink Alone
I Fell in Love Again Last Night
I Have Never Felt This Way Before
I Knew Him So Well
I Know the Way to You by Heart
I Miss You
I Need More of You
I Saw It on TV
I Sweat (Going Through the Motions)
I Told a Lie to My Heart
I Want to Know What Love Is
I Wish He Didn't Trust Me So Much
I Wonder If I Take You Home
If I Had a Rocket Launcher
If I Loved You
If You Love Somebody Set Them Free
I'll Keep It with Mine
I'll Never Stop Loving You

(No Matter How High I Get) I'll Still Be
    Lookin' up to You
I'm for Love
I'm Goin' Down
I'm Gonna Tear Your Playhouse Down
I'm on Fire
I'm Your Man
Impossible Dreamer
In a New York Minute
In Buddy's Eyes
In Love with the Flame
In My House
Invincible (Theme from *The Legend of
    Billie Jean*)
Itchin' for a Scratch
It's Only Love
Jesse
Jungle Fever
Jungle Love
Just a Gigolo
Just Another Night
Just As I Am
Just One of the Guys
Kayleigh
Keep It Confidential
Keeping the Faith
Knight Moves
Knocking at Your Back Door
Ladder of Success
The Ladies Who Lunch
A Lady Like You
Land of 1000 Dances
Lasso the Moon
The Last Dragon
Lay Down Your Weary Tune
Lay Your Hands on Me
Let Him Go
Let Me Dance for You
Let Me Down Easy
Lie to You for Your Love
Life in One Day
Lights of Downtown
Little Things, *see* Baby, It's the Little
    Things
Little Wild One (No. 5)
Lonely Ol' Night

Lost in the Fifties Tonight (In the Still of the Night)
Love Don't Care (Whose Heart It Breaks)
Love Is Alive
Love Is the Seventh Wave
Love Light in Flight
Love Radiates Around
Love Theme from *St. Elmo's Fire* (Instrumental)
Love to See You
Lover Boy
Lovergirl
Love's Calling
Lucky Girl
Make My Life with You
March of the Yuppies
Marlene on the Wall
Material Girl
Maureen, Maureen
Meat Is Murder
Meet Me in Montana
The Men All Pause
Men Without Shame
Method of Modern Love
Miami Vice Theme
Miracle Mile
Misled
Miss Celie's Blues (Sisters)
Missing You
Mr. Telephone Man
Modern Day Romance
Money for Nothing
Morning Desire
Mrs. Green
Muddy Water
Murphy's Romance
My Baby's Got Good Timing
My Elusive Dreams
My Girl
My Mind Is on You
My Only Love
My Toot Toot
My Tu Tu, *see* My Toot Toot
Mystery Lady
Name of the Game
Natural High
Neutron Dance

Never
Never Ending Story
Never Surrender
New Attitude
New Looks
The Night Spanish Eddie Cashed It In
Nightshift
19
Nobody Falls Like a Fool
Nobody Wants to Be Alone
Not Enough Love in the World
The Oak Tree
Obsession
Oh, Sheila
Old Hippie
The Old Man Down the Road
Once Bitten
One Clear Moment
One Lonely Night
One More Night
One Night in Bangkok
One Night Love Affair
One of the Living
One Owner Heart
One Silk Sheet
One Vision
One Way Love (Better Off Dead)
Only the Young
Operator
Outta the World
Part-Time Lover
Party All the Time
Peeping Tom
People Are People
People Get Ready
Percy's Song
Perfect Way
A Picture of Lisa
A Place to Fall Apart
Pop Life
Porn Wars
The Power of Love
Private Dancer
Putting It Together
? (Modern Industry)
Radio Heart
Rain Forest

1986

Like No Other Night
Listen Like Thieves
A Little Bit More
A Little Bit of Love (Is All It Takes)
Little Rock
Little Rock 'n' Roller
Live to Tell
Lives in the Balance
Living in America
Living in the Promiseland
Loco de Amor (Crazy for Love)
Lonely Alone
Longshot
Louisiana 1927
Lovable
Love Affair with Everyday Livin'
Love and Affection
Love at the Five and Dime
A Love Bizarre
Love Is Forever
Love Touch (Theme from *Legal Eagles*)
Love Walks In
Love Will Conquer All
Love Zone
Mad About You
Makin' up for Lost Time
Mama's Got a Lover
Mama's Never Seen Those Eyes
Man at the Top
Man Size Love
Mandolin Rain
Manic Monday
A Matter of Trust
Mean Green Monster from Outer Space
The Meek Shall Inherit
(How to Be a) Millionaire
Mind Your Own Business
Missionary Man
Modern Woman (from *Ruthless People*)
Moments Like This
Moonfall
Moonlighting
Morning Desire
Move Away
The Music of Goodbye
My Baby

My Brain Is Hanging Upside Down
   (Bonzo Goes to Bitburg)
My Father's House
My Home Town
Mystery
Nasty
Nearly in Love
Never as Good as the First Time
Never Be You
Never the Luck
The Next Time I Fall
Nikita
Nineteen Eighty-Two
No Money Down
No One Is to Blame
No Way to Treat a Lady
Nobody
Nobody in His Right Mind Would Have
   Left Her
Not Like You
Nothin' at All
Nothing in Common
Notorious
Now and Forever (You & Me)
Number One
On My Own
On the Other Hand
On the Western Skyline
Once in a Blue Moon
Once We Might Have Known
One Hundred Percent Chance of Rain
The One I Loved Back Then
One Love at a Time
One Simple Thing
One Sunny Day
Only One
Open Your Heart
Opportunities (Let's Make Lots of
   Money)
Our Love (Theme from *No Mercy*)
Papa Don't Preach
Perfect Strangers
Perfect World
Peter Gunn Theme
Pink Bedroom
The Power of Love (You Are My Lady)
The Pride Is Back

1987

1988

In Your Room
Iris
It Must Be Good for Me
It Would Take a Strong Strong Man
It's All Over Now Baby Blue
It's Money That Matters
It's Such a Small World
I've Been Lookin'
Joe Knows How to Live
Johnny B. Goode
Joy
Judas Kiss
Just Got Paid
Just Like Paradise
(Do You Love Me) Just Say Yes
Kiss Me Deadly
Kiss Me, Son of God
Kissing a Fool
Kokomo
L.A. County
Lakota
Late Nite Comic
Let the River Run
Letter in the Mail
Liar, Liar
Life Turned Her That Way
Lift Me Up (Like a Dove)
Lightning in a Bottle
Little April Shower
A Little Bit in Love
Little Love Affairs
Little Miss S
Little Walter
The Loco-Motion
Look Away
Look out Any Window
Loosey's Rap
Lost in You
Love and Mercy
Love Bites
Love Changes
Love Helps Those
Love Is My Decision (Theme from
    Arthur 2 On the Rocks)
Love Like We Do
Love Overboard
A Love Supreme

Love Will Find Its Way to You
Love Will Save the Day
Love Will Tear Us Apart
Love Wore a Halo (Back Before the
    War)
Lovin' on Next to Nothin'
Loving the Sinner, Hating the Sin
Madison Avenue Soul
Make It Last Forever
Make It Real
Make Me Lose Control
Mamacita
Man in the Mirror
Mandinka
Meet Me in My Dreams Tonight
Memories Can't Wait
Mercedes Boy
Missed Opportunity
Mr. Me
Mommy Daddy You and I
Monkey
More Than You'll Ever Know
Mountains O' Things
The Music Went Out of My Life
My Favorite Year
My Girl
My Prerogative
My Secret Place
Naughty Girls Need Love Too
Never Before
Never Die Young
Never Gonna Give You Up
Never Knew Love Like This
Never Mind
Never Tear Us Apart
New Orleans Wins the War
New Sensation
New Shade of Blue
Nice 'N' Slow
A Nightmare on My Street
Nite and Day
No Condom, No Sex
Nobody's Fool (Theme from *Caddyshack
    II*)
Not Alone Anymore
Nothin' But a Good Time
Nothing But Flowers

817

Pump up the Jam
Punk Rock Girl
Put Your Mouth on Me
Ready to Begin Again (Manya's Song)
Real Love
Realities
Reckless
Remember (The First Time)
Rhythm Nation
Right Here Waiting
Rock and a Hard Place
Rock On (From *Dream a Little Dream*)
Rock Wit'cha
Rocket
Rockin' in the Free World
Romance (Love Theme from *Sing*)
Roni
Room to Move
Rooms on Fire
(I Never Promised You a) Rose Garden, *see* I Beg Your Pardon
Rosemary
Runnin' down a Dream
Rush of Speed
Sacred Emotion
Sad and Lonely Child
Sad Sad Sad
Satellite
Satisfied
Save Me
Scandalous
Second Chance
Secret Rendezvous
See a Little Light
Self Destruction
Serenade
She Don't Love Nobody
She Drives Me Crazy
She Hates to Go Home
She Reminds Me of You
She Wants to Dance with Me
She Won't Talk to Me
She's Crazy for Leaving
She's Got a Single Thing in Mind
Shotgun down the Avalanche
Show and Tell
Shower Me with Your Love

Sincerely Yours
Sing
Sister Kate (Theme from the television show *Sister Kate*)
Sister Rosa
Sleep Talk
Sneaker Prison
So Alive
So Good
Sold Me Down the River
Soldier of Love
Somebody Loves You
Someplace Where Love Can't Find Me
Something in the Way (You Make Me Feel)
Something of a Dreamer
Something Real
Song of the South
Soul Corruption
Soul Provider
Sowing the Seeds of Love
Spend the Night (Ce Soir)
Spirit of the Forest
Stainsby Girls
Stand
Start of a Romance
Steel River
Still within the Sound of My Voice
Straight Up
Subcity
Summer of Love
Summerfly
Sunday in the South
Superhero Girl
Superwoman
Surrender to Me
Swing the Mood
Talent Show
The Ten Commandments of Love
Tender Lover
Tennessee Courage
That Demon Baby of Mine
There
There Isn't Only One Girl
There's a Tear in My Beer
They Want Money
Thing Called Love

821

Awards Index

A list of songs nominated for Academy Awards by the Academy of Motion Picture Arts and Sciences and Grammy Awards from the National Academy of Recording Arts and Sciences. Asterisks indicate the winners.

1980

Academy Award
  Fame
  9 to 5*
  On the Road Again
  Out Here on My Own
  People Alone
Grammy Award
  Drivin' My Life Away
  Fame
  Give Me the Night
  He Stopped Loving Her Today
  I Believe in You
  Lady
  Let's Get Serious
  Lookin' for Love
  Never Knew Love Like This Before*
  On the Road Again*
  The Rose
  Sailing*
  Shining Star
  Theme from *New York, New York*
  Woman in Love

Endless Love
The First Time It Happens
For Your Eyes Only
One More Hour
Grammy Award
  Ai No Corrida
  Arthur's Theme (The Best That You
    Can Do)
  Bette Davis Eyes*
  Elvira
  Endless Love
  I Was Country When Country Wasn't
    Cool
  Just the Two of Us
  Just the Two of Us*
  Lady (You Bring Me Up)
  9 to 5
  9 to 5*
  She's a Bad Mama Jama
  Somebody's Knockin'
  When She Was My Girl
  You're the Reason God Made
    Oklahoma

1981

Academy Award
  Arthur's Theme (The Best That You
    Can Do)*

1982

Academy Award
  Eye of the Tiger (The Theme from
    Rocky III)

How Do You Keep the Music Playing
If We Were in Love
It Might Be You
Up Where We Belong*
Grammy Award
Always on My Mind
Always on My Mind*
Chariots of Fire (Race to the End)
Do I Do
Ebony and Ivory
Eye of the Tiger (The Theme from
   Rocky III)
I. G. Y. (What a Beautiful World)
I'm Gonna Hire a Wino to Decorate
   Our Home
It's Gonna Take a Miracle
Let It Whip
Nobody
Ring on Her Finger, Time on Her
   Hands
Rosanna*
Rosanna
Sexual Healing
Steppin' Out
That Girl
Turn Your Love Around*

1983
Academy Award
Flashdance...What a Feeling*
Maniac
Over You
Papa Can You Hear Me
The Way He Makes Me Feel
Grammy Award
Ain't Nobody
All Night Long (All Night)
Baby I Lied
Beat It*
Beat It
Billie Jean
Billie Jean*
Electric Avenue
Every Breath You Take
Every Breath You Take*
Flashdance...What a Feeling
I.O.U.

Lady Down on Love
A Little Good News
Mama He's Crazy
Maniac
P. Y. T. (Pretty Young Thing)
Stranger in My House*
Wanna Be Startin' Something

1984
Academy Award
Against All Odds (Take a Look at Me
   Now)
Footloose
Ghostbusters
I Just Called to Say I Love You*
Let's Hear It for the Boy
Grammy Award
Against All Odds (Take a Look at Me
   Now)
All My Rowdy Friends Are Coming
   over Tonight
Caribbean Queen (No More Love on
   the Run)
City of New Orleans*
Dancing in the Dark
Dancing in the Sheets
Faithless Love
Girls Just Want to Have Fun
The Glamorous Life
God Bless the U.S.A.
Hard Habit to Break
The Heart of Rock and Roll
Hello
I Feel for You*
I Just Called to Say I Love You*
Time After Time
What's Love Got to Do with It
What's Love Got to Do with It*
Yah Mo B There

1985
Academy Award
Miss Celie's Blues (Sisters)
The Power of Love
Say You, Say Me (Title Song from
   White Nights)*

Separate Lives (Love Theme from *White Nights*)
Surprise Surprise
Grammy Award
  Baby's Got Her Blue Jeans On
  Born in the U.S.A.
  The Boys of Summer
  Desperados Waiting for a Train
  Every Time You Go Away
  40 Hour Week (for a Livin')
  Freeway of Love*
  Highwayman*
  I Don't Know Why You Don't Want Me
  I Want to Know What Love Is
  Lost in the Fifties Tonight (In the Still of the Night)
  Love Is Alive
  Money for Nothing
  New Attitude
  Nightshift
  The Power of Love
  Through the Fire
  We Are the World*
  You Give Good Love

1986

Academy Award
  Glory of Love (Theme from *The Karate Kid, Part 2*)
  Life in a Looking Glass
  Mean Green Monster from Outer Space
  Somewhere Out There
  Take My Breath Away (Love Theme from *Top Gun*)*
Country Music Association Award
  Bop*
  Grandpa (Tell Me 'Bout the Good Old Days)
  Nineteen Eighty-Two*
  On the Other Hand*
Grammy Award
  Addicted to Love
  Daddy's Hands
  Give Me the Reason
  Graceland
  Grandpa (Tell Me 'Bout the Good Old

Days)*
The Greatest Love of All
Guitar Town
Higher Love*
Higher Love
Kiss
Living in America
Sledgehammer
Sweet Love*
That's What Friends Are For*
That's What Friends Are For
What Have You Done for Me Lately
Whoever's in New England

1987

Academy Award
  Cry Freedom
  Nothing's Gonna Stop Us Now
  Shakedown
  Storybook Love
  (I've Had) The Time of My Life
Country Music Association Award
  Forever and Ever, Amen*
Grammy Award
  All My Ex's Live in Texas
  Back in the High Life Again
  Casanova
  Dance Little Sister*
  Didn't We Almost Have It All
  80's Ladies
  Forever and Ever, Amen*
  Graceland*
  I Still Haven't Found What I'm Looking For
  I'll Still Be Loving You
  Just to See Her
  La Bamba
  Lean on Me
  Luka
  Moonlighting (Theme)
  Nothing's Gonna Stop Us Now
  Skeletons
  Telling Me Lies
  (I've Had) The Time of My Life
  U Got the Look
  Who's That Girl

List of Publishers

A directory of publishers of the songs included in *Popular Music,* 1980-1989. Publishers that are members of the American Society of Composers, Authors, and Publishers or whose catalogs are available under ASCAP license are indicated by the designation (ASCAP). Publishers that have granted performing rights to Broadcast Music, Inc., are designated by the notation (BMI). Publishers whose catalogs are represented by The Society of Composers, Authors and Music Publishers of Canada, are indicated by the designation (SOCAN).

The addresses were gleaned from a variety of sources, including ASCAP, BMI, SOCAN, and *Billboard* magazine. As in any volatile industry, many of the addresses may become outdated quickly. In the interim between the book's completion and its subsequent publication, some publishers may have been consolidated into others or changed hands. This is a fact of life long endured by the music business and its constituents. The data collected here, and throughout the book, are as accurate as such circumstances allow.

A

Abacus Music (ASCAP)
see Chappell & Co., Inc.

ABC Circle (BMI)
1926 Broadway
New York, New York 10023

Abesongs USA (BMI)
see Almo Music Corp.

ABKCO Music Inc. (BMI)
1700 Broadway
New York, New York 10019

Acara (ASCAP)
see WB Music

Accabonac
see Cherry Lane Music Co.

Ackee Music Inc. (ASCAP)
see Polygram International

Across 110th Street Music (ASCAP)
636 Warren St.
Brooklyn, New York 11217

Acuff Rose Music (BMI)
65 Music Square West
Nashville, Tennessee 37203

Acuff-Rose Publications Inc. (BMI)
2510 Franklin Road
Nashville, Tennessee 37204

List of Publishers

Adams Communications, Inc. (BMI)
see Almo Music Corp.

Addax Music Co., Inc. (ASCAP)
c/o Famous Music Corp.
attn: Irwin Z. Robinson
15 Columbus Circle
New York, New York 10023

Addison Street Music (ASCAP)
c/o Sterling Music Co.
1200 Van Ness Ave., Ste. 201
San Francisco, California 94109

Adra Music (ASCAP)
c/o Fred Munao
175 Fifth Avenue
New York, New York 10010

A.D.T. Enterprises, Inc. (BMI)
c/o M. Warren Troob
4800 Gulf of Mexico Drive
Longboat Key, Florida 33548

Advanced Music Corp. (ASCAP)
488 Madison Avenue
New York, New York 10022

Aero Dynamic Music (ASCAP)
100 Jericho Quadrangle, Ste. 210
Jericho, New York 11753

Aerostation Corp. (ASCAP)
16214 Morrison Street
Encino, California 91436

AGF Music Ltd. (ASCAP)
30 W. 21st St.
7th Fl.
New York, New York 10010

Air Bear (BMI)
c/o Warner-Tamerlane
9000 Sunset Blvd.
Los Angeles, California 90069

Aixoise Music (ASCAP)
300 W 55th St.
New York, New York 10019

Alabama Band Music Co. (ASCAP)
PO Box 121192
Nashville, Tennessee 37212

Alamo Music, Inc. (ASCAP)
1619 Broadway, 11th Fl.
New York, New York 10019

J. Albert & Sons Music (ASCAP)
c/o Freddy Bienstock Ent.
1619 Broadway, 11th Fl.
New York, New York 10019

Albion Music Ltd. (ASCAP)
1706 E. 51st Street
Brooklyn, New York 11234

Alcor Music (BMI)
see EMI-April Music

Alessi Music
528 Cedar Swamp Road
Glen Head, New York 11545

Alexscar Music (BMI)
c/o William A. Cohen
2029 Century Park, E., Suite 1700
Los Angeles, California 90067

Algee Music Corp. (BMI)
see Al Gallico Music Corp.

Alibee Music (BMI)
The Entertainment Music Co.
1700 Broadway
New York, New York 10019

Alimony Music (BMI)
c/o Shapiro and Steinberg
315 S. Beverly Drive, Suite 210
Beverly Hills, California 90212

All Baker's Music (BMI)
804 N. Crescent Drive
Beverly Hills, California 90210

All Boys USA Music (BMI)
see Terrace Entertainment Corp.

All Nations Music (ASCAP)
8857 W. Olympic Blvd., Suite 200
Beverly Hills, California 90211

All Seeing Eye Music (ASCAP)
c/o Atlanta Artists Prod.
3423 Piedmont Rd. NE
Atlanta, Georgia 30305

Alley Music (BMI)
1619 Broadway, 11th Fl.
New York, New York 10019

Alligator Music (ASCAP)
Att: Randy Muller
2675th Ave., Ste. 801-50
New York, New York 10016

Almo/Irving Music (BMI)
1358 N La Brea
Los Angeles, California 90028

Almo Music Corp. (BMI)
360 N. La Cienega
Los Angeles, California 90048

Alpine One (BMI)
842 N. Mansfield, Rear House
Hollywood, California 90038

Alva Music (BMI)
3929 Kentucky Drive
Los Angeles, California 90068

Amachrist Music
P.O. Box 1770
Hendersonville, Tennessee 37077

Amadeus Music Co. (ASCAP)
c/o Franklin, Weinrib & Rudell
Att: Earl Rose
488 Madison Ave.
New York, New York 10022

Amanda-Lin Music (ASCAP)
P.O. Box 15871
Nashville, Tennessee 37215

Amazement Music (BMI)
805 Moraga
Lafayette, California 94549

American Broadcasting Music, Inc. (ASCAP)
30 W. 66th St.
New York, New York 10023

American Compass Music Corp. (ASCAP)
see Largo Music, Inc.

American Cowboy Music Co. (BMI)
14 Music Circle, E.
Nashville, Tennessee 37203

American Made Music (BMI)
c/o Little Big Town Music
803 18th Avenue, S.
Nashville, Tennessee 37203

AMR (ASCAP)
54 Music Sq. E.
Nashville, Tennessee 37203

John Anderson Music Co. Inc. (BMI)
c/o Al Gallico Music Corp.
344 E. 49th Street, Suite 1A B
New York, New York 10017

Angel Music Ltd. (ASCAP)
P.O. Box 1276
Great Neck, New York 11024

Angel Notes Music (ASCAP)
8787 Shoreham Dr., #802
West Hollywood, California 90069

Angela Music (ASCAP)
c/o Peter C. Bennett, Esq.
9060 Santa Monica Blvd., Suite 300
Los Angeles, California 90069

Judy Hart Angelo Music
see Entertainment Co. Music Group

Anidraks Music (ASCAP)
1018 2nd St.
Manhattan Beach, California 90266

Anta (ASCAP)
Address Unavailable

Anteater Music (ASCAP)
attn: Jay Davis
6624 Jocelyn Hallom Rd.
Nashville, Tennessee 37205

Anthrax Music (ASCAP)
see Island Music

Antisia Music Inc. (ASCAP)
183 Jonathan Dr.
Stamford, Connecticut 06903

Appian Music Co. (ASCAP)
737 Latimer Rd.
Santa Monica, California 90402

Applied Action (ASCAP)
Address Unavailable

Appogiatura Music Inc. (BMI)
see BMG Music

Arc Music (BMI)
c/o The Goodman Group
488 Madison Ave., 5th Fl.
New York, New York 10022

Arch Music Co., Inc. (ASCAP)
c/o A. Schroeder International,
Ltd.
1650 Broadway
New York, New York 10019

Arista Music, Inc.
8370 Wilshire Blvd.
Beverly Hills, California 90211

Arlon (ASCAP)
c/o Chappell & Co., Inc.
810 Seventh Avenue
New York, New York 10019

Arrival Music (BMI)
c/o Mietus Copyright Management
P.O. Box 432
2351 Laurana Road
Union, New Jersey 07083

Art Street Music (BMI)
c/o Fitzgerald Hartley Co.
7250 Beverly Blvd., Suite 200
Los Angeles, California 90036

Artwork Music Co., Inc. (ASCAP)
c/o Ivan Mogull Music Corp.
625 Madison Avenue
New York, New York 10022

Emil Ascher Inc.
630 Fifth Avenue
New York, New York 10020

Ashdale Music (BMI)
c/o David White
166 Ashdale Place
Bel Air, California 90049

Ashtray Music (BMI)
c/o Bobby Womack
2841 Firenze Place
Los Angeles, California 90046

Assorted Music (BMI)
Att: Earl Shelton
309 S. Broad Street
Philadelphia, Pennsylvania 19107

At Home Music (ASCAP)
Att: Wayne Henderson
P.O. Box 2682
Hollywood, California 90028

Atlantic-Gibron Music (BMI)
see MCA Music

Atlantic Music Corp. (BMI)
6124 Selma Avenue
Hollywood, California 90028

Attadoo (BMI)
c/o Bobby Emmons
Johnson Chapel Road
Brentwood, Tennessee 37027

ATV Music Corp. (BMI)
see MCA, Inc.

Audre Mae Music (BMI)
34 Dogwood Drive
Smithtown, New York 11787

August Dream Music Ltd. (BMI)
c/o Tom Eyen
41 Fifth Avenue
New York, New York 10003

R. L. August Music Co.
Att: Bonnie Blumenthal
40 W. 57th Street, Suite 1510
New York, New York 10019

Auspitz Music (ASCAP)
301 N. Canon Dr., Ste. 223
Beverly Hills, California 90210

Auto Tunes (BMI)
c/o Screen Gems-EMI
6255 Sunset Blvd., 12th Fl.
Hollywood, California 90028

Avant Garde Music Publishing, Inc. (ASCAP)
c/o Margo Matthews
Box 92004
Los Angeles, California 90009

Average Music (ASCAP)
47 Brookmere Drive
Fairfield, Connecticut 06430

Avid One Music (ASCAP)
see MCA Music

B

B. O'Cult Songs, Inc. (ASCAP)
c/o Robbins Speilman
Att: Bruce Slayton
1700 Broadway
New York, New York 10019

Ba-Ba-Do Music (ASCAP)
310 Greenwich Street, Apt. 36B
New York, New York 10013

Baby Fingers Music (ASCAP)
c/o Gary L. Gilbert Esq.
Blum, Bloom, Dekom, & Hercott
150 S Rodeo Dr.
Third Fl.
Beverly Hills, California 90212

Baby Love Music, Inc. (ASCAP)
c/o Fischbach & Fischbach, P.C.
1925 Century Park, E., No. 1260
Los Angeles, California 90067

Baby Shoes Music (BMI)
1358 N. La Brea
Los Angeles, California 90028

Backlash Enterprises (BMI)
P.O. Box 49217
Los Angeles, California 900490217

Backlog Music (BMI)
c/o Edward Pollack
P.O. Box 9711
Memphis, Tennessee 38109

Bad Ju Ju Music (ASCAP)
see Warner-Chappell Music

Tom Bahler (ASCAP)
see Yellow Brick Road Music

Bait and Beer (ASCAP)
PO Box 121681
Nashville, Tennessee 37212

Bakers Tune (BMI)
Address Unavailable

Bandier Family Music (ASCAP)
see EMI Music Publishing

Martin Bandier Music
see Entertainment Co. Music Group

Bangophile Music (BMI)
8033 Sunset Blvd., No. 853
Los Angeles, California 90046

Bantha Music (ASCAP)
c/o Lucasfilm Ltd.
P.O. Box 2009
San Rafael, California 94912

Bar Cee Music (BMI)
see Peso Music

Bar-Kay Music (BMI)
see WB Music

Bar-None Music (BMI)
c/o Bug Music
6777 Hollywood Blvd., 9th Fl.
Hollywood, California 90028

Baray Music Inc. (BMI)
49 Music Square, E.
Nashville, Tennessee 37203

List of Publishers

Barnwood Music (BMI)
see Singletree Music Co., Inc.

Denise Barry Music (ASCAP)
see Sony Tree Publishing

Basedown (BMI)
c/o Warner-Tamerlane
9000 Sunset Blvd.
Los Angeles, California 90069

Basically Gasp Music (ASCAP)
1401 Rugby Rd.
Charlottesville, Virginia 22903

Bayjun Beat (BMI)
see MCA Music

Beach Bum Music (BMI)
c/o Mason & Sloane
1299 Ocean Avenue
Santa Monica, California 90401

Beachhead Music (ASCAP)
4218 Waialae Ave., Ste. 201
Honolulu, California 96816

Beau Di O Do Music (BMI)
c/o Warner-Tamerlane Pub. Co.
9000 Sunset Blvd., Penthouse
Los Angeles, California 90069

Beckaroo (BMI)
P.O. Box 150272
Nashville, Tennessee 37215

Beechwood Music (BMI)
see EMI Music Publishing

Beeswing Music (BMI)
c/o Gary Stamler
2029 Century Park, E., Suite 1500
Los Angeles, California 90067

Beginner Music (ASCAP)
PO Box 50418
Nashville, Tennessee 37205

Begonia Melodies, Inc. (BMI)
c/o Unichappell Music Inc.
810 Seventh Avenue
New York, New York 10019

Belfast Music (BMI)
c/o Embassy Television
1901 Avenue of the Stars, Suite 666
Los Angeles, California 90067

Believe Us or Not Music (BMI)
811 18th Avenue, S.
Nashville, Tennessee 37203

Bellamy Brothers Music (ASCAP)
attn: David Bellamy
201 Restless Lane
Dade City, Florida 33525

Bellboy Music (BMI)
Att: Earl Shelton
309 S. Broad Street
Philadelphia, Pennsylvania 19107

Below the Surface Music (ASCAP)
c/o Brown & Co.
10 Bank St.
White Plains, New York 10606

Belwin-Mills Publishing Corp. (ASCAP)
see EMI Music Publishing

Bennie Benjamin Music, Inc. (ASCAP)
1619 Broadway
New York, New York 10019

Irving Berlin Music Corp. (ASCAP)
1290 Avenue of the Americas
New York, New York 10019

Bertam Music Co. (ASCAP)
see Jobete Music Co.

Bertus (BMI)
22723 Berdon Street
Woodland Hills, California 91367

Besame West Music
6202 Bluebell Avenue
North Hollywood, California 91606

Bethel Music (BMI)
see Hookem Music

Bethlehem Music (BMI)
see EMI Music Publishing

Better Days Music (BMI)
Moultrie Accountancy Corp.
Att: Fred S. Moultrie, C.P.A.
P.O. Box 5270
Beverly Hills, California 90210

John Bettis Music (ASCAP)
see WB Music

BGO Music (ASCAP)
3422 Falkirk Pl.
Atlanta, Georgia 30345

BHB Productions
Address Unavailable

Bibo Music Publishers (ASCAP)
see Polygram International

Bicameral Songs (BMI)
c/o Road Canon Music
Route 3, Box 447B
Vashon Island, Washington 98070

Bicycle Music (ASCAP)
8075 W. 3rd St.
Los Angeles, California 90048

Freddy Bienstock Music Co. (BMI)
c/o Hudson Bay Music Co.
1619 Broadway, 11th Fl.
New York, New York 10019

Bienstock Publishing Co. (ASCAP)
see Alley Music

Big Ears Music Inc. (ASCAP)
see Bughouse

Big Pig Music
see Warner-Chappell Music

Big Seven Music Corp. (BMI)
1790 Broadway, 18th Fl.
New York, New York 10019

Big Sky Music (ASCAP)
P.O. Box 860, Cooper Sta.
New York, New York 10276

Big Stick Music (BMI)
c/o Peter Beckett
7435 Kentland Ave.
West Hills, California 91307

Big Talk Music (BMI)
c/o Michael N. Miller, C.P.A.
9060 Santa Monica Blvd., Suite 305
Los Angeles, California 90069

Big Three Music Corp.
729 Seventh Avenue
New York, New York 10019

Big Thrilling Music (ASCAP)
7381 Beverly Blvd
Los Angeles, California 90036

Big Tooth Music Corp. (ASCAP)
see Chrysalis Music Group

Big Train Music Co. (ASCAP)
9110 Sunset Blvd., Suite 200
Los Angeles, California 90069

Big Tree Enterprises Ltd. (ASCAP)
Big Leaf Music Division
c/o Walden Music Inc.
Att: Diane Grassi
75 Rockefeller Plaza
New York, New York 10019

Big Wad/Famous Music Corp. (ASCAP)
261 A South Hamilton Dr.
Beverly Hills, California 90211

Bil-Kar (SESAC)
P.O. Box 25066
Nashville, Tennessee 37202

Billy Music (ASCAP)
c/o Kaufman & Bernstein, Inc.
1900 Avenue of the Stars, 22nd Fl.
Los Angeles, California 90067

Bilt (BMI)
see Bug Music

Bird Ankles Music
c/o Chris Williamson
Olivia Records
4400 Market Street
Oakland, California 94608

Stephen Bishop Music Publishing Co. (BMI)
c/o Segel & Goldman
9348 Santa Monica Blvd.
Beverly Hills, California 90210

Bittersuite Co.
Address Unavailable

Black Bull Music (BMI)
Att: Stevland Morris
4616 Magnolia Blvd.
Burbank, California 91505

Black Ice Music (BMI)
see Flyte Tyme Tunes

Black Impala Music (BMI)
c/o Austin Texas Sounds
3300 Hollywood
Austin, Texas 78722

Black Keys (BMI)
P.O. Box 3633
Thousand Oaks, California 91360

Black Lion (ASCAP)
6525 Sunset Blvd., 2nd Fl.
Hollywood, California 90028

Black Sheep Music Inc. (BMI)
see Screen Gems-EMI Music Inc.

Black Stallion County Publishing (BMI)
P.O. Box 368
Tujunga, California 91043-036

Black Tent Music (BMI)
c/o Bug Music
6777 Hollywood Blvd., 9th Fl.
Hollywood, California 90028

Blackmore Music Ltd. (ASCAP)
c/o Robbins Spielman Slayton & Half
on
888 7th Ave.
New York, New York 10106

Blackwell Publishing (ASCAP)
c/o C. Allen, Jr.
6914 S. Honore Street
Chicago, Illinois 60636

Bleu Disque Music (ASCAP)
see Warner-Chappell Music

Bleunig Music (ASCAP)
Att: Bill Withers
2600 Benedict Canyon Road
Beverly Hills, California 90210

Bludgeon Riffola Music (ASCAP)
see Zomba Music

Blue Book Music (BMI)
1225 N. Chester Avenue
Bakersfield, California 93308

Blue Drops (ASCAP)
P.O. Box 54
Fairview, Tennessee 37062

Blue Flute Music
Address Unavailable

Blue Gate Music (ASCAP)
see Bug Music

Blue Gator Music (ASCAP)
Gudvi Chapnick Co.
15250 Ventura Blvd., No. 900
Sherman Oaks, California 91403

Blue Horn Toad (BMI)
see Bug Music

Blue Lake Music (BMI)
see Terrace Entertainment Corp.

Blue Midnight Music (ASCAP)
c/o Padell
1775 Broadway
New York, New York 10019

Blue Moon Music (ASCAP)
see Zomba Music

Blue Network Music Inc.
Att: Dorothy A. Schwartz
c/o RCA Records
1133 Avenue of the Americas
New York, New York 10036

Blue Quill Music (ASCAP)
see MCA, Inc.

Blue Seas Music Inc. (ASCAP)
c/o Braunstein & Chernin
50 E. 42nd Street
New York, New York 10017

Blue Sky Rider Songs (BMI)
c/o Prager and Fenton
6363 Sunset Blvd., Suite 706
Los Angeles, California 90028

Blue Turtle
see Magnetic Music Publishing Co.

Blue Vision Music (BMI)
c/o Michael Miller
9060 Santa Monica Blvd., Suite 305
Los Angeles, California 90069

Blue Water (BMI)
Address Unavailable

Bluebear Waltzes
Address Unavailable

Hugh Blumenfeld (BMI)
Address Unavailable

BMG Music (ASCAP)
1540 Broadway
New York, New York 10036

BMG Songs Inc. (ASCAP)
8370 Wilshire Blvd.
Beverly Hills, California 90211

Bob-a-Lew Music (ASCAP)
P.O. Box 8649
11622 Valley Spring Lane
Universal City, California 91608

Bocephus Music Inc. (BMI)
see Singletree Music Co., Inc.

Body Electric Music (BMI)
see WB Music

Bon Jovi Publishing (ASCAP)
see Polygram Music Publishing Inc.

Bona Relations Music (BMI)
see Warner-Chappell Music

Boneidol Music (ASCAP)
Robbins & Speilman
1087 Cathedral Ave.
Franklin Square, New York 11010

Bonnie Bee Good Music (ASCAP)
1336 Grant Street
Santa Monica, California 90405

Bonnyview Music Corp. (ASCAP)
7120 W. Sunset Blvd.
Los Angeles, California 90046

Boo-Fant Tunes, Inc. (BMI)
c/o Zissu, Stein, Bergman,
Couture & Mosher
270 Madison Avenue, Suite 1410
New York, New York 10016

Boodle Music (BMI)
Address Unavailable

Boom Tat Music (ASCAP)
see Polygram International

Boone's Tunes (BMI)
c/o Richard Kaye Publications
13251 Ventura Blvd., Suite 3
Studio City, California 91604

Bootchute Music (BMI)
P.O. Box 12025
485 N. Hollywood
Memphis, Tennessee 38112

Boston International Music (ASCAP)
see EMI Music Publishing

Alain Boublil Music Ltd. (ASCAP)
c/o Stephen Tenenbaum & Co. Inc.
605 Third Ave.
New York, New York 10158

List of Publishers

Bouillabaisse Music (BMI)
see MCA, Inc.

Bourgeoise Zee (ASCAP)
Address Unavailable

The Bourne Co. (ASCAP)
5 W. 37th St.
New York, New York 10018

Bovina Music, Inc. (ASCAP)
c/o Mae Attaway
330 W. 56th Street, Apt. 12F
New York, New York 10019

Boy Meets Girl (BMI)
see Irving Music Inc.

Braintree Music (BMI)
c/o Segel & Goldman Inc.
9348 Santa Monica Blvd., No. 304
Beverly Hills, California 90210

Bramalea Music
see New Tandem Music Co.

Bramhall Publishing (BMI)
see Bug Music

Tom Brasfield Music (ASCAP)
c/o Chris Dodson Management
3002 Blakemore Avenue
Nashville, Tennessee 37212

Brassheart Music (BMI)
c/o Jeri K. Hull, Jr.
5970 Airdrome Street
Los Angeles, California 90035

Break Every Rule Music (ASCAP)
Breslauer, Jacobson, Rutman &
Chapman
10345 Olympic Blvd.
Los Angeles, California 90064

Break of Dawn Music Inc. (BMI)
c/o Real Records Inc.
P.O. Box 958
434 Avenue U
Bogalvsa, Louisiana 70427

Breeze (ASCAP)
Address Unavailable

Bregman, Vocco & Conn, Inc. (ASCAP)
1619 Broadway
New York, New York 10019

Brenee (BMI)
c/o Miller-Ward & Co.
9060 Santa Monica Blvd.
Los Angeles, California 90060

Briarpatch Music (BMI)
P.O. Box 140110
Donelson, Tennessee 37214

Brick Alley (ASCAP)
1704 Eighth Street
Irwin, Pennsylvania 15642

Brick Hithouse Music (BMI)
see Irving Music Inc.

Edie Brickell Songs (ASCAP)
see MCA, Inc.

Bricksongs (ASCAP)
470 General Washington Road
Wayne, Pennsylvania 19087

Bridgeport Music Inc. (BMI)
c/o Sam Peterer Music
530 E. 76th St.
New York, New York 10021

Bright Light Music (BMI)
231 West 58th Street
New York, New York 10019

Bright Sky Music (ASCAP)
c/o Gursey-Schneider & Co.
10351 Santa Monica Blvd., Suite 300
Los Angeles, California 90025

Brigitte Baby Publishing (BMI)
c/o Manatt, Phelps, Rothenberg
11355 W. Olympic Blvd.
Los Angeles, California 90064

Broadcast Music Inc. (BMI)
10 Music Square, E.
Nashville, Tennessee 37203

Brockman Enterprises Inc. (ASCAP)
5750 Wilshire Blvd.
Ste. 590
Los Angeles, California 90036

Brockman Music (ASCAP)
c/o Jess S. Morgan & Co., Inc.
5750 Wilshire Blvd.
Suite 590
Los Angeles, California 90036

Brogue Music (BMI)
see WB Music

Brojay Music (ASCAP)
see Warner-Chappell Music

Brooklyn Dust Music (ASCAP)
c/o Kenneth B. Anderson, Esq.
Loeb & Loeb
230 Park Ave.
New York, New York 10169

Broozertoones, Inc. (ASCAP)
c/o Karen Schauben Pub.
1555 Sherman Ave. #345.
Evanston, Illinois 60201

Brother Bill's Music (ASCAP)
3051 Clairmont Road, N.E.
Atlanta, Georgia 30329

Brouhaha Music (ASCAP)
c/o TVT Records
23 E. 4th St. 3rd Fl.
New York, New York 10003

Thomas Browne Publishing
Address Unavailable

Jocelyn Brown's Music
267 Grove Street
Jersey City, New Jersey 07302

Bruin Music Co. (BMI)
see Famous Music Corp.

Bruised Oranges (BMI)
4121 Wilshire Blvd., Ste. 5204
Los Angeles, California 10017

Peabo Bryson Enterprises, Inc. (ASCAP)
see Warner-Chappell Music

Buchu Music (ASCAP)
c/o Haber Corp.
16830 Ventura Blvd.
Encino, California 91436

Buckhorn Music Publishing Co., Inc. (BMI)
P.O. Box 120547
Nashville, Tennessee 37212

Budde Music (ASCAP)
see Warner-Chappell Music

Budson Music (BMI)
see Gopam Enterprises, Inc.

Bug Music (BMI)
Bug Music Group
6777 Hollywood Blvd., 9th Fl.
Hollywood, California 90028

Bug/Slimey Limey Music (BMI)
6777 Hollywood Blvd., 9th Fl.
Hollywood, California 90028

Bughouse (ASCAP)
c/o Bug Music Group
6777 Hollywood Blvd., 9th Floor
Hollywood, California 90028

Bugle Publishing (BMI)
c/o Bug Music Group
6777 Hollywood Blvd., 9th Floor
Hollywood, California 90028

Bullwhip Productions (ASCAP)
see Gedzerillo Music

Bumstead (SOCAN)
1616 W. 3rd Avenue
Vancouver, British Columbia V6J1K2
Canada

Bunch of Guys (BMI)
Address Unavailable

Bunch of Guys Music (BMI)
see WB Music

List of Publishers

Bungalow Music, N.V. (ASCAP)
see Polygram International

Burger Bits (ASCAP)
c/o Haber Corp.
16830 Ventura Blvd.
Encino, California 91436

Burn Em Up Music (BMI)
see Bug Music

Marie Burns (ASCAP)
Address Unavailable

Burthen Music Co., Inc. (ASCAP)
see Chappell & Co., Inc.

Bush Burnin' Music (ASCAP)
see MCA, Inc.

Bussy Music (BMI)
c/o Gary William Friedman
150 E. 72nd Street
New York, New York 10021

But For Music (ASCAP)
see EMI Music Publishing

Bill Butler Music (BMI)
1703 19th Street
Hondo, Texas 78861

Larry Butler Music Co. (ASCAP)
P.O. Box 121318
Nashville, Tennessee 37212

Butler's Bandits (ASCAP)
SBK Songs
810 Seventh Avenue
New York, New York 10019

Buttermilk Sky Music (BMI)
c/o Murray Deutsch
515 Madison Avenue
New York, New York 10022

Buy Rum (ASCAP)
see WB Music

Buzzherb Music (BMI)
c/o Scott Tutt Music
903 18th Avenue, S., 2nd Fl.
Nashville, Tennessee 37212

C

C & D (ASCAP)
c/o Chappell & Co., Inc.
810 Seventh Avenue
New York, New York 10019

Irving Caesar Music Corp. (ASCAP)
850 Seventh Avenue
New York, New York 10019

John Cafferty Music (BMI)
c/o Arnold Freedman
1200 Providence Hwy.
Sharon, Massachusetts 02067

Mark Cain Music
c/o Society of Composers, Authors,
& Publishers of Canada (SOCAN)
41 Valleybrook Dr.
Don Mills, Ontario
Canada

Cak Songs (ASCAP)
c/o Entertainment Music Co.
1700 Broadway, 41st Fl.
New York, New York 10019

Cal-Gene Music (BMI)
c/o Sound of New York Records
230 W. 230th Street, No. 1450
Bronx, New York 10463

Calhoun Street (BMI)
see Bug Music

California Phase Music (ASCAP)
c/o Gelfand, Rennert, O'Neil & Haga
man
1025 16th Ave. S.
Ste. 202
Nashville, Tennessee 37212

Calloco
Address Unavailable

Calypso Toonz (BMI)
see Irving Music Inc.

Camelback Mountain Music Corp. (ASCAP)
c/o Shapiro, Bernstein & Co., Inc.
10 E. 53rd Street
New York, New York 10022

Cameo Five Music (BMI)
Moultrie Accountancy Corp.
Att: Fred S. Moultrie, C.P.A.
P.O. Box 5270
Beverly Hills, California 90210

Camp Songs Music (BMI)
see BMG Music

Campbell-Connelly, Inc. (ASCAP)
565 Fifth Avenue
New York, New York 10017

Camper Van Beethoven Music
Address Unavailable

Canadiana-Morris (BMI)
c/o Chappell International-New York
810 Seventh Avenue
New York, New York 10019

Buddy Cannon Music (ASCAP)
see Polygram International

Captain Crystal Music (BMI)
7505 Jerez Court, No. E
Rancho La Costa, California 92008

James Car Publishing, Inc. (BMI)
c/o Freedman & Steinhorn
1 E. Lexington Street, Suite 500
Baltimore, Maryland 21202

Carbert Music Inc. (BMI)
1619 Broadway, Rm. 609
New York, New York 10019

Careers-BMG
see BMG Music

Careers Music Inc. (ASCAP)
see Arista Music, Inc.

Eric Carmen (BMI)
Address Unavailable

Carnelia Music (ASCAP)
149 W. 88th St.
New York, New York 10024

Carollon Music Co.
Att: Jay Warner
6351 Drexel Avenue
Los Angeles, California 90048

Carub Music (ASCAP)
c/o Cynthia J. Michaud, CPA
1990 Bundy Drive, #200
Los Angeles, California 90025

Casa David (ASCAP)
c/o Hal David
12711 Ventura Blvd.
Ste. 420
Studio City, California 91604

Caseyem Music (BMI)
c/o Mike Curb Productions Inc.
3300 Warner Blvd.
Burbank, California 91510

Cass County Music Co. (ASCAP)
c/o Breslauer, Jacobson & Rutman
10880 Wilshire Blvd., Suite 2110
Los Angeles, California 90024

Catpatch Music (BMI)
c/o Ken Weiss
5032 Lankershim Blvd., Suite 2
North Hollywood, California 91601

Cayman Music (ASCAP)
c/o David Steinberg Esq.p.
Rita Marley Music Div.
North American Bldg., 20th Fl.
121 Broad St.
Philadelphia, Pennsylvania 19107

CBS Inc. (ASCAP)
49 E. 52nd Street
New York, New York 10022

CBS Songs Ltd. (ASCAP)
see EMI April Canada

CBS Unart Catalog Inc. (BMI)
49 E. 52nd Street
New York, New York 10022

CC (ASCAP)
Address Unavailable

Cedarwood Publishing Co., Inc. (BMI)
39 Music Square, E.
Nashville, Tennessee 37203

Celann Music Co. (BMI)
c/o Pickwick Communications
36 Soundview Dr.
Port Washington, New York 11050

Cement Chicken Music (ASCAP)
13504 Contour Drive
Sherman Oaks, California 91423

Center City Music (ASCAP)
c/o Nick Ben-Meir
644 North Doheny Dr.
Los Angeles, California 90069

Ceros (BMI)
see Bug Music

C'est Music (ASCAP)
c/o Gelfand Rennert & Feldman
1880 Century Park E
Ste. 900
Los Angeles, California 90067

Champion Music (BMI)
1755 Broadway 8th Fl.
New York, New York 10019

Chances R Publishing (ASCAP)
240 Cedar Rock Circle
Sacramento, California 95823

Chapin Music (ASCAP)
83 Green St.
Huntington, New York 11743

Mike Chapman Publishing Enterprises
(ASCAP)
see All Nations Music

Chappell & Co., Inc. (ASCAP)
see Warner-Chappell Music

Chappell-Warner Brothers (ASCAP)
see Warner Brothers, Inc.

Chardax Music (BMI)
11337 Burbank Blvd.
North Hollywood, California 91601

Chariscourt Ltd. (ASCAP)
see Almo Music Corp.

Charisma Music Publishing Co., Ltd. (ASCAP)
see Charisma Music Publishing USA

Charisma Music Publishing USA (ASCAP)
1841 Broadway, Suite 411
New York, New York 10023

Charles Family Music (BMI)
1700 Broadway, 41st Fl.
New York, New York 10019

Chelcait Music (BMI)
6124 Selma Avenue
Hollywood, California 90028

Cherry Lane Music Co. (ASCAP)
110 Midland Avenue
Port Chester, New York 10573

Cherry Mountain (ASCAP)
see Cherry Lane Music Co.

Cheshire Music Inc. (BMI)
10 Columbus Circle
New York, New York 10019

Chi-Boy (ASCAP)
c/o Schwartz & Farquharson
9107 Wilshire Blvd., Suite 300
Beverly Hills, California 90216

Chic Music Inc. (BMI)
see WB Music

Chicago Brothers Music (BMI)
3612 Barnham Blvd.
Los Angeles, California 90028

Chiplin Music Co. (ASCAP)
c/o Edward J. Penney, Jr.
1318 Hildreth Drive
Nashville, Tennessee 37215

Chips Moman Music (BMI)
see Warner-Chappell Music

Choskee Bottom Music (ASCAP)
c/o Terrace Entertainment Group
PO Box 239
Las Vegas, New Mexico 87701

Chris-n-Ten Music (ASCAP)
Box 1809
Montclair, New Jersey 07042

Christian Burial (ASCAP)
c/o New York End Ltd.
143 W. 69th Street, Suite 2A
New York, New York 10023

Christian Burial Music (ASCAP)
c/o The New York End Ltd.
29 W. 65th St.
New York, New York 10023

Frank Christian Music (BMI)
c/o Michael Lessor
162 E. 64th St.
New York, New York 10021

Chriswald Music (ASCAP)
6255 Sunset Blvd., Suite 1911
Hollywood, California 90028

Chrome Willie Music (BMI)
c/o Don Bachrach, Esq.
Iglow & Bachrach
8601 Wilshire Blvd., Suite 1001
Los Angeles, California 90211

Chrysalis Music Group (ASCAP)
9255 Sunset Blvd., #319
Los Angeles, California 90069

Chubu (BMI)
c/o Iglow & Bachrach
1515 N. Crescent Heights Blvd.
Los Angeles, California 90046

Chung Music Ltd. (ASCAP)
Address unavailable

Circle L Publishing (ASCAP)
c/o Spectrum VII Music
Att: Otis Stokes
1635 N. Cahuenga Blvd., 6th Fl.
Hollywood, California 90028

City Girl Music (BMI)
see Bug Music

City Kidd Music (ASCAP)
c/o Manatt, Phelps & Phillips
11355 W. Olympic Blvd.
Los Angeles, California 90064

CL-2 (ASCAP)
see Cherry Lane Music Co.

William Claffey & Associates
see Screen Gems-EMI Music Inc.

Clair Audient (ASCAP)
Address Unavailable

Clarkee (BMI)
8501 Wilshire Blvd.
Beverly Hills, California 90211

Clean Sheets Music (BMI)
c/o Jess S. Morgan & Co., Inc.
6420 Wilshire Blvd., 19th Fl.
Los Angeles, California 90048

Cleveland International (ASCAP)
c/o International Records
1775 Broadway, 7th Fl.
New York, New York 10019

Cliofine (BMI)
see Hit & Run Music

Clita Music (BMI)
c/o Mietus Copyright Management
P.O. Box 432
2351 Laurana Road
Union, New Jersey 07083

CMI America (ASCAP)
1102 17th Ave. S.
Nashville, Tennessee 37212

Co-Heart Music (BMI)
1103 17th Avenue S.
Nashville, Tennessee 37212

Coal Dust West (BMI)
c/o Zifrin, Brittenham & Branca
2121 Avenue of the Stars
Los Angeles, California 90067

Coal Miner's Music Inc. (BMI)
7 Music Circle, N.
Nashville, Tennessee 37203

Cold Weather Music (BMI)
c/o Four Aces Music
P.O. Box 860, Cooper Sta.
New York, New York 10276

Colgems-EMI Music (ASCAP)
see EMI Music Publishing

Collins Court Music (ASCAP)
PO Box 121407
Nashville, Tennessee 37212

Tom Collins Music Corp. (BMI)
Box 121407
Nashville, Tennessee 37212

Phil Collins (ASCAP)
see Hit & Run Music

Colloco (ASCAP)
Address Unavailable

Colter Bay Music (BMI)
see Almo Music Corp.

Columbia Pictures Publications
16333 N.W. 54th Avenue
Hialeah, Florida 33014

Columbine Music Inc. (ASCAP)
see United Artists Music Co., Inc.

Combine Music Corp. (BMI)
see EMI Music Publishing

Commodores Entertainment Publishing Corp
(ASCAP)
c/o Benjamin Ashburn Associates
39 W. 55th Street
New York, New York 10019

Compelling Music (ASCAP)
12636 Beatrice St.
PO Box 66930
Los Angeles, California 90066

Congdon (BMI)
see Emil Ascher Inc.

Connie's Bank of Music (ASCAP)
6412 Dove St.
Norfolk, Virginia 23513

Conrad Music (ASCAP)
c/o The Goodman Group
488 Madison Ave., 5th Fl.
New York, New York 10022

Content Music, Inc. (BMI)
c/o Leo Graham, Jr.
124 Twin Oaks Drive
Oakbrook, Illinois 60521

Controversy Music (ASCAP)
c/o Ziffren Brittenham & Branca
2121 Ave. of the Stars
Los Angeles, California 90067

Conus Music (ASCAP)
c/o Robert H. Flax
65 E. 55th Street, Suite 604
New York, New York 10022

Roger Cook Music (BMI)
1204 16th Avenue, S.
Nashville, Tennessee 37212

Cookaway Music Inc. (ASCAP)
see Dick James Music Inc.

Cookhouse Music (BMI)
1204 16th Avenue, S.
Nashville, Tennessee 37212

Cookies Music (BMI)
see Zomba Music

Coolwell Music (ASCAP)
attn: Delda Sciurba
6124 Selma Ave.
Los Angeles, California 90028

Copyright Control (ASCAP)
see Bug Music

Copyright Service Bureau Ltd.
221 W. 57th Street
New York, New York 10019

Core Music Publishing (BMI)
c/o Oak Manor
Box 1000
Oak Ridges, Ontario
Canada

Corey Rock (ASCAP)
c/o Dennis Robbins
113 Karen Drive
Mount Joliet, Tennessee 37102

Cotillion Music Inc. (BMI)
75 Rockefeller Plaza, 2nd Fl.
New York, New York 10019

Cottonpatch Music (ASCAP)
c/o Mason and Sloane
1299 Ocean Avenue
Santa Monica, California 90401

Could Be Music (BMI)
see MCA Music

Country Road Music Inc. (BMI)
c/o Gelfand, Rennert & Feldman
Att: Babbie Green
1880 Century Park, E., No. 900
Los Angeles, California 90067

County Line (ASCAP)
c/o Zachary Glickman
PO Box 570815
Tarzana, California 91537

Crab Salad Music (BMI)
see Virgin Music

Robert Cray (BMI)
1315 Third Avenue W.
Seattle, Washington 98119

Crazy Crow Music (BMI)
see Siquomb Publishing Corp.

Crazy People Music/Almo Music Corp.
(ASCAP)
c/o Jesse W. Johnson
54 9th St., No. 353
Minneapolis, Minnesota 554402

Creative Bloc (ASCAP)
29 Greene Street
New York, New York 10013

Creeping Death Music (ASCAP)
c/o Manatt Phelps Rothenberg &
Tunney
11355 W. Olympic Blvd.
Los Angeles, California 90064

Cricket Pie Music (ASCAP)
c/o Bug Music Group
6777 Hollywood Blvd., 9th Fl.
Hollywood, California 90028

Crimsco Music (ASCAP)
c/o Almo Music Corp.
1416 N. La Brea Avenue
Hollywood, California 90028

Criterion Music Corp. (ASCAP)
6124 Selma Avenue
Hollywood, California 90028

Cross Keys Publishing Co., Inc. (ASCAP)
attn: Donna Hilley
PO Box 1273
Nashville, Tennessee 37202

Cross Under (ASCAP)
c/o Intuit Music Group
P.O. Box 121227
Nashville, Tennessee 37212

Crosstown (ASCAP)
c/o J. Hilliard
1427 N. Laurel Avenue
Hollywood, California 90046

Pablo Cruise Music (BMI)
see Irving Music Inc.

List of Publishers

Crush Club (BMI)
c/o David A. Braun
2029 Century Park E.
Suite 1900
Los Angeles, California 90067

Jan Crutchfield Music (BMI)
c/o Unichappell Music, Inc.
810 Seventh Avenue, 32nd Fl.
New York, New York 10019

Gretchen Cryer
see Zeitgeist Music Co.

Billy Crystal & Paul #Shaffer (ASCAP)
Address unavailable

Mike Curb Productions (BMI)
948 Tourmaline Dr.
Newbury Park, California 91220

Cal Curtis Music (BMI)
see EMI-Blackwood Music Inc.

Cutting Music (ASCAP)
c/o Norman Stollman
3720 Canterbury Way
Boca Raton, Florida 33434

D

D & D Music (ASCAP)
see Virgin Music

Dad Music (BMI)
see Hancock Music Co.

Daddy Oh Music
see Lipsync Music

Daksel Music Corp. (BMI)
see Warner-Chappell Music

Dan Daley Music (BMI)
c/o Dreena Music
80 Eighth Avenue, Suite 201
New York, New York 10011

Damusic (ASCAP)
c/o Michael B. Kent
598 Madison Ave.
New York, New York 10022

Dandelion (BMI)
see Jamie Music Publishing Co.

Dangling Participle (BMI)
c/o Rothman Business
P.O. Box 888503
Dunwoody, Georgia 30356

Danny Tunes (BMI)
c/o Iglow & Bachrach
1515 N. Crescent Heights Blvd.
Los Angeles, California 90046

Dare to Dream Music (ASCAP)
see Famous Music Corp.

Darjen Music (BMI)
c/o Blackwood Music Inc.
49 E. 52nd Street
New York, New York 10022

Dark Cloud Music (BMI)
373 Walnut Street
Englewood, New Jersey 07631

Dat Richfield Kat Music (BMI)
c/o Richard Fields
P.O. Box 36496
Los Angeles, California 90036

Mel Dav (ASCAP)
c/o Mr. Juan Molina
21241 Ventura Blvd.
Ste. 255
Woodland Hills, California 91364

Davince Music (ASCAP)
c/o Bug Music Group
6777 Hollywood Blvd., 9th Fl.
Hollywood, California 90028

Dawnbreaker Music Co. (BMI)
c/o Manatt, Phelps, Rothenberg &
Tunney
1888 Century Park, E., 21st Fl.
Los Angeles, California 90067

Day Ta Day (ASCAP)
c/o John Black
700 N. Mayslie Lane
Walnut, California 91789

Daywin Music (BMI)
see BMG Music

Dean of Music (BMI)
68 Water Street
Vancouver, British Columbia V68 1A4
Canada

Debdave Music Inc. (BMI)
P.O. Box 140110
Donnelson, Tennessee 37214

Deco Music (BMI)
see MCA, Inc.

Freddie Dee Music (BMI)
9766 Woodale Avenue
Arleta, California 91331

Deep Faith Music (ASCAP)
103 Marble Run
Williamsburg, Virginia 23185

Deertrack Music (BMI)
7563 Delongpre Avenue
Los Angeles, California 90046

Def American Songs (BMI)
16 W. 22nd St.
New York, New York 10010

Def Jam (ASCAP)
160 Varick St.
New York, New York 10013

Dejamus Inc. (ASCAP)
see Dick James Music Inc.

Del Sounds Music (BMI)
c/o Happy Valley Music
1 Camp Street
Cambridge, Massachusetts 02140

Dela Music (BMI)
see Charles Family Music

Delicate Music (ASCAP)
c/o Paul Glass, C.P.A.
Glass & Rosen
16530 Ventura Blvd., Suite 202
Encino, California 91436

Delightful Music Ltd. (BMI)
c/o Mr. Ted Eddy
200 W. 57th Street
New York, New York 10019

Demerie Music (ASCAP)
708 N. First Street
Minneapolis, Minnesota 55401

Depom Music (ASCAP)
see Jobete Music Co.

Deshufflin' Inc. (ASCAP)
38 Laurel Ledge Ct.
Stamford, Connecticut 06903

Desmobile Music Inc. (ASCAP)
c/o C. Winston Simone Mgmt.
1790 Broadway, 10th Fl.
New York, New York 10019

Desperate Music (BMI)
25671 Whittemore Drive
Calabasas, California 91302

DeSylva, Brown & Henderson, Inc. (ASCAP)
609 Fifth Avenue
New York, New York 10017

Deutsch/Berardi Music Corp. (ASCAP)
23 W. 76th Street, Suite 2A
New York, New York 10023

Devo Music (BMI)
c/o Unichappel Music Inc.
810 Seventh Avenue
New York, New York 10019

Devon Music (BMI)
see TRO-Cromwell Music Inc.

Diamond Dave Music (ASCAP)
c/o Gelfano, Rennert & Feldman
1880 Century Park East, #900
Los Angeles, California 90078

Diamond House
19208-8 Hamlin St.
Reseda, California 91335

Diamond Mine Music (ASCAP)
c/o Warner Brothers Music
9000 Sunset Blvd., Penthouse
Los Angeles, California 90069

Diamondback Music Co. (BMI)
see Columbia Pictures Publications

Diesel Music (BMI)
c/o J. Williams
701 Franklin Avenue
Brooklyn, New York 11238

Difficult Music (BMI)
c/o Beldock, Levine & Hoffman
565 Fifth Avenue
New York, New York 10017

Dillard (BMI)
c/o Gopam Enterprises
11 Riverside Drive
New York, New York 10023

Dionio Music (ASCAP)
c/o The Bug Music Group
6777 Hollywood Blvd., 9th Fl.
Beverly Hills, California 90028

Walt Disney Music (ASCAP)
500 S. Buena Vista Street
Burbank, California 91521

Diva One (ASCAP)
Gelfand, Rennert & Feldman
c/o Michael Bivens
1880 Century Park East, Ste. 900
Los Angeles, California 90067

Diva 1 Music (ASCAP)
see Avant Garde Music Publishing, Inc.

Dixie Stars Music (ASCAP)
see Hori Pro Entertainment Group

Dizzy Heights Music Publishing, Ltd.
(ASCAP)
Address Unavailable

DJO Music (BMI)
see Zomba Music

DJO Publishing Corp. (BMI)
6290 Sunset Blvd., Suite 916
Los Angeles, California 90028

DLE Music (ASCAP)
see EMI-April Music

Dr. Benway Music (BMI)
c/o Phillips, Mizer, Benjamin
& Krim
Att: Rosemary Carroll
40 W. 57th Street
New York, New York 10019

Dollar Clef Music (ASCAP)
1726 Dave Elliott Road
Saugerties, New York 12477

Donald Jay (ASCAP)
Address Unavailable

Donaldson Publishing Co. (ASCAP)
c/o Edward Traubner & Co., Inc.
1901 Avenue of the Stars, No. 880
Los Angeles, California 90067

Donna Music Publishing Co. (BMI)
c/o Artists Rights Enforcement Corp
New York, New York 10019

Donril (ASCAP)
Zomba House
1345 Lexington Avenue
New York, New York 10128

Donril Music (ASCAP)
225 W. 129th St.
New York, New York 10027

Don't You Know (ASCAP)
see Almo Music Corp.

Doolittle Music (BMI)
see WB Music

Dorff Songs (ASCAP)
see Warner-Chappell Music

Double Diamond Music (BMI)
c/o Blackwood Music Inc.
49 E. 52nd Street
New York, New York 10022

Double F Music (ASCAP)
see Delightful Music Ltd.

Downstairs Music, Inc. (BMI)
c/o Earl Shelton
309 S. Broad Street
Philadelphia, Pennsylvania 19107

DQ Music (ASCAP)
see WB Music

Dragnet Music (ASCAP)
2112 River Sound Drive
Knoxville, Tennessee 37922

Dick Dragon Music (BMI)
see Virgin Music

Dramatis Music Corp. (BMI)
see EMP Co.

Dream Dealers Music (ASCAP)
326 NE Ontario St.
Burbank, California 91505

Dreamette's Music (BMI)
The David Geffen Co.
9126 Sunset Blvd.
Los Angeles, California 90069

Dreamgirls Music (ASCAP)
9126 Sunset Blvd.
Los Angeles, California 90069

Dreena Music (BMI)
c/o Bradley Publications
80 Eighth Avenue, Suite 201
New York, New York 10011

Drunk Monkey Music (ASCAP)
see Bug Music

Druse Music Inc. (ASCAP)
c/o Meibach & Epstein
680 Fifth Avenue, Suite 500
New York, New York 10019

Dry Clam (BMI)
see Bug Music

Dub Notes
23 E. Lancaster Ave.
Ardmore, Pennsylvania 19003

Tim DuBois Music (ASCAP)
c/o Warner Brothers
9000 Sunset Blvd.
Los Angeles, California 90069

Duchess Music Corp. (BMI)
1755 Broadway, 8th Fl.
New York, New York 10019

Duck Songs (ASCAP)
P.O. Box 998
Lebanon, Tennessee 37087

Duke of Earle (ASCAP)
c/o Siegel, Feldstein & Duffin
1990 Bundy Dr., Ste. 200
Los Angeles, California 90025

Duke Reno Music (ASCAP)
Society of Composers, Authors & Publishers of Canada (Socan)
41 Valleybrook Dr.
Don Mills, Ontario M3B 2S6
Canada

Dum Di Dum (ASCAP)
see Polygram International

Dwarf Music Co., Inc. (ASCAP)
see Big Sky Music

Dyad Music, Ltd. (BMI)
c/o Mason & Co.
400 Park Ave.
New York, New York 10022

E

E/A Music (BMI)
75 Rockefeller Plaza
New York, New York 10019

E S P Management, Inc. (ASCAP)
Att: E. S. Prager
Evansong Ltd. Division
Crumpet Music Division
1790 Broadway
New York, New York 10019

Eaglewood Music (BMI)
c/o Irving Music, Inc.
1358 N. La Brea Avenue
Hollywood, California 90028

Earbourne Music (BMI)
812 N. McCadden Place
Los Angeles, California 90038

Earthly Delights (BMI)
c/o Gary Scruggs
774 Elysian Fields Road
Nashville, Tennessee 37204

East/Memphis Music Corp. (BMI)
8025 Melrose Avenue
Los Angeles, California 90046

Barry Eastmond Music (ASCAP)
see Zomba Music

Easy Action Music (ASCAP)
c/o Gabriel Markiz
4106 SW 43rd Ave.
Portland, Oregon 97221

Easy Listening Music Corp. (ASCAP)
344 E. 49th Street, Suite 1A/B
New York, New York 10017

Easy Money Music (ASCAP)
c/o Haber Corp.
16830 Ventura Blvd.
Encino, California 91436

Eat Your Heart Out Music (BMI)
c/o Vicki Wickham
130 W. 57th Street
New York, New York 10019

Ebbett's Field Music (ASCAP)
c/o David Robinson
David Robinson & Friends, Inc.
827 Folsom Street
San Francisco, California 94107

Eden Music, Inc. (BMI)
P.O. Box 325
Englewood, New Jersey 07631

Edge of Fluke (ASCAP)
c/o Fitzgerald Hartley Co.
50 W Main St.
Ventura, California 93001

Edition Sunrise Publishing, Inc. (BMI)
c/o Careers Music Inc.
8370 Wilshire Blvd.
Beverly Hills, California 90211

Edition Sunset Publishing Inc. (ASCAP)
c/o Merit Music Corp.
9229 Sunset Blvd.
Los Angeles, California 90069

EEG Music (ASCAP)
see Chappell & Co., Inc.

Eel Pie Music (ASCAP)
see Towser Tunes Inc.

E.G. Music (BMI)
9157 Sunset Blvd.
Los Angeles, California 90069

Eight/Twelve Music (BMI)
see Warner-Chappell Music

Eiseman Music Co., Inc. (BMI)
P.O. Box 900
Beverly Hills, California 90213

Eldorado Music Co. (BMI)
1717 N. Vine Street
Hollywood, California 90028

Eleksylum Music (BMI)
see Warner-Chappell Music

Elektra/Asylum Music Inc. (BMI)
  c/o Manatt, Phelps, Rothenburg
  & Tunney
  1888 Century Park, E., 21st Fl.
  Los Angeles, California 90067

Elettra Music
  see Braintree Music

E.L.F.
  Address Unavailable

Elliot Music Co., Inc. (ASCAP)
  P.O. Box 547
  Larkspur, California 94939

Edwin Ellis Music (BMI)
  c/o Nurk Twins Music
  1660 N. Queens Road
  Los Angeles, California 90069

Ellymax Music (BMI)
  see Zomba Music

Elorac Music (ASCAP)
  c/o Nick Ben Meir
  652 N Doheny Dr.
  Los Angeles s, California 90069

Emanuel Music (ASCAP)
  c/o Page Jenkins Financial
  |Service's Inc.
  433 N Camden Dr.
  Ste. 500
  Beverly Hills, California 90210

Embassy TV
  c/o Robin Rosenfeld
  1901 Avenue of the Stars
  Los Angeles, California 90067

Emboe (ASCAP)
  see EMI-April Music

Emergency Music Inc. (ASCAP)
  c/o AMRA
  attn: Patricia Benti
  333 S Tamiami Trail
  Ste. 295
  Venice, Florida 34285

EMI-Affiliated
  see EMI Music Publishing

EMI April Canada
  Address Unavailable

EMI-April Music (ASCAP)
  see EMI Music Publishing

EMI-Blackwood/Feist & April Music
  (ASCAP)
  see EMI Music Publishing

EMI-Blackwood Music Inc. (BMI)
  see EMI Music Publishing

EMI-Gold Horizon Music Corp. (BMI)
  see EMI Music Publishing

EMI Golden Torch Music (ASCAP)
  see EMI Music Publishing

EMI-Golden Torch Music Corp. (ASCAP)
  see EMI Music Publishing

EMI-Miller Catalogue
  see EMI Music Publishing

EMI Music Publishing
  810 Seventh Ave.
  New York, New York 10019

EMI U Catalogue (ASCAP)
  see EMI Music Publishing

EMI Unart Catalogue
  Address Unavailable

EMI Variety Catalog, Inc. (ASCAP)
  see EMI Music Publishing

EMI Variety Catalogue (ASCAP)
  see EMI Music Publishing

EMI-Virgin (ASCAP)
  see EMI Music Publishing

Emile Music
  509 Madison Avenue, Suite 1810
  New York, New York 10022

Emotional Rex Music (BMI)
  see Zomba Music

List of Publishers

EMP Co. (BMI)
The Entertainment Co.
40 W. 57th Street
New York, New York 10019

Empire Music (ASCAP)
see Emil Ascher Inc.

End of the Trail (ASCAP)
see Bug Music

Endless Frogs Music (ASCAP)
c/o Andre Pessis
PO Box 7072
Corte Madera, California 94976

Enlightened Kitty (ASCAP)
see MCA, Inc.

Ennes Productions, Ltd. (ASCAP)
Att: Nat Shapiro
157 W. 57th Street
New York, New York 10019

Ensign Music (BMI)
see Famous Music Corp.

Entente Music (BMI)
c/o Warner-Tamerlane Publishing Inc
9000 Sunset Blvd.
Los Angeles, California 90069

Entertainment Co. Music Group
40 W. 57th Street
New York, New York 10019

Enthralled (ASCAP)
Address Unavailable

Enz Music
c/o Grubman & Indursky
575 Madison Avenue
New York, New York 10022

Equestrian Music (ASCAP)
10 Columbus Circle
New York, New York 10019

Equinox Music (BMI)
c/o Raymond Harris
7060 Hollywood Blvd., Suite 1212
Hollywood, California 90028

ESP Management Inc. (BMI)
Att: E. S. Prager
1790 Broadway
New York, New York 10019

Essential Music (ASCAP)
see Warner-Chappell Music

Essex International Inc. (ASCAP)
see TRO-Cromwell Music Inc.

Essex Music, Inc.
see TRO-Essex Music, Inc.

Estus Music (BMI)
see EMI-Blackwood Music Inc.

Evanlee (BMI)
see Major Bob Music

Evesongs Inc. (ASCAP)
542 Valley View Rd.
Springfield, Pennsylvania 19064

Evie Music Inc. (ASCAP)
see Chappell & Co., Inc.

Evil Eye Music Inc. (BMI)
see Songways Service Inc.

Ewald Corp.
see Braintree Music

Exaskeletal (BMI)
see Warner-Chappell Music

Excalibur Lace Music (BMI)
600 Renaissance Center
Detroit, Michigan 48243

Excellorec Music Co., Inc. (BMI)
1011 Woodland Street
Nashville, Tennessee 37206

Eyedot Music (ASCAP)
1244 Brenner Dr.
Nashville, Tennessee 37221

Tom Eyen's Publishing Co. (BMI)
see Dreamgirls Music

Ezra (BMI)
Address Unavailable

Ezra Music Corp. (BMI)
  8600 Melrose Avenue
  Los Angeles, California 90069

F

F Sharp Productions (ASCAP)
  c/o Jim Di Giovanni
  157 W. 57th St.
  New York, New York 10019

Fab Bird (BMI)
  c/o Bug Music
  6777 Hollywood Blvd.
  Hollywood, California 90028

Face the Music (BMI)
  c/o Warner Brothers Music
  44 Music Square, W.
  Nashville, Tennessee 37203

Fall Line Orange Music (ASCAP)
  1880 Century Park E., No. 900
  Los Angeles, California 90067

Fall River Music Inc. (BMI)
  250 W. 57th Street, Suite 2017
  New York, New York 10019

Fallwater Music (BMI)
  see Hudson Bay Music

Fame Publishing Co., Inc. (BMI)
  Box 2527
  603 E. Avalon Avenue
  Muscle Shoals, Alabama 35660

Famous Monsters Music (BMI)
  140 E. Seventh Street
  New York, New York 10009

Famous Music Corp. (ASCAP)
  10635 Santa Monica Blvd.
  Ste. 300
  Los Angeles, California 90025

John Farrar Music (BMI)
  see Kidada Music Inc.

Fast Fade Music
  Att: James Thomas Wells
  8818 Noble Avenue
  Sepulveda, California 91343

Fast Folk Musical Magazine
  P.O. Box 938, Village Sta.
  New York, New York 10014

Fat Boys (ASCAP)
  Address Unavailable

Fat Jack the Second Music Publishing Co.
  (BMI)
  c/o Paul M. Jackson, Jr.
  P.O. Box 1113
  Gardena, California 90249

Fat Zach Music, Inc. (BMI)
  c/o Skinny Zach
  6430 Sunset Blvd., Suite 1531
  Hollywood, California 90028

Fate Music (ASCAP)
  1046 Carol Drive
  Los Angeles, California 90069

Father Music (BMI)
  c/o Bobby Hart
  7647 Woodrow Wilson Drive
  Los Angeles, California 90046

Fave Rave (BMI)
  Address Unavailable

Feat Music (ASCAP)
  c/o Loeb & Loeb
  10100 Santa Monica Blvd.
  Suite 2200
  Los Angeles, California 90067

Featherbed Music Inc. (BMI)
  see Unichappell Music Inc.

Fee Bee Music (BMI)
  4517 Wainwright Avenue
  Pittsburgh, Pennsylvania 15227

Leo Feist Inc. (ASCAP)
  see MCA Music

List of Publishers

Ferncliff (BMI)
c/o Harry J. Coombs
110112 Lantoga Road
Wayne, Pennsylvania 19087

Fever Music, Inc. (ASCAP)
Att: Jules Kurz, Esq.
161 W. 54th Street
New York, New York 10019

Fiction Music Inc. (BMI)
see Fourth Floor Music Inc./Fiction Music

Fiddleback (BMI)
see Valando Group

Fifth Floor Music Inc. (ASCAP)
Att: Martin Cohen
6430 Sunset Blvd., Suite 1500
Los Angeles, California 90028

Fifty Grand Music, Inc. (BMI)
50 Music Square, W., Suite 900
Nashville, Tennessee 37203

Finchley Music Corp. (ASCAP)
c/o Arrow, Edelstein & Gross, PC
32 E 57th St.
New York, New York 10022

Fingers Music (BMI)
c/o Breslauer, Jacobson & Rutman
10880 Wilshire Blvd., No. 2110
Los Angeles, California 90024

Fire and Water Songs (BMI)
9762 W. Olympic Blvd.
Beverly Hills, California 90212

Fire Mist (BMI)
2180 Stunt Road
Calabasas, California 90302

First Lady Songs, Inc. (BMI)
6 Music Circle, N.
Nashville, Tennessee 37203

First Release Music Publishing (BMI)
6124 Selma Avenue
Hollywood, California 90028

Fishin' Fool Music (BMI)
c/o Price, Elkins & Elkins
16130 Ventura Blvd., No. 210
Encino, California 91436

Five of a Kind, Inc. (BMI)
156 St. James Place
Brooklyn, New York 11238

Five Storks (ASCAP)
see MCA Music

Flames of Albion Music, Inc. (ASCAP)
Att: Stevens H. Weiss
34 Pheasant Run
Old Westbury, New York 11568

Flat Town Music (ASCAP)
Address unavailable

Fleedleedee Music (ASCAP)
c/o Jess Morgan & Co.
6420 Wilshire Blvd.
Los Angeles, California 90048

Fleetwood Mac Music Ltd. (BMI)
315 S. Beverly Drive, Suite 210
Beverly Hills, California 90212

Fleur Music (ASCAP)
see Columbia Pictures Publications

Flip 'n' Dog (BMI)
see MCA, Inc.

Flowering Stone Music (ASCAP)
2114 Pico Blvd.
Santa Monica, California 90405

Danny Flowers Music (BMI)
see Bug Music

Fly Girl Music (ASCAP)
188 Guardhill Road
Mt. Kisco, New York 10549

Flying Cloud Music Inc. (BMI)
c/o Copyright Management Inc.
50 Music Square, W., Suite 70
Nashville, Tennessee 37203

Flying Dutchman (BMI)
c/o Copyright Management Inc.
P.O. Box 110873
Nashville, Tennessee 37211

Flyte Tyme Tunes (ASCAP)
c/o Margo Matthews
Box 92004
Los Angeles, California 90009

Foghorn Music (ASCAP)
c/o Mizmo Entertainment
2106 W Magnolia
Burbank, California 91506

Folkswim
Address Unavailable

Forceful Music (BMI)
c/o Williston Music
P.O. Box 284
Brooklyn, New York 11203

Foreign Imported (BMI)
8921 S.W. Tenth Terrace
Miami, Florida 33174

Forerunner Music (ASCAP)
1308 16th Ave. S
Nashville, Tennessee 37212

Foreshadow Songs, Inc. (BMI)
P.O. Box 120657
Nashville, Tennessee 37212

Forest Music (ASCAP)
Address Unavailable

Foreverendeavor Music, Inc. (ASCAP)
Att: Arnold E. Tencer
5 Portsmouth Towne
Southfield, Michigan 48075

Forrest Hills Music Inc.
PO Box 120838
Nashville, Tennessee 37212

Forsythia Music (BMI)
4527 Old Belews Creek Road
Winston-Salem, North Carolina 27101

Fort Knox Music Co. (BMI)
1619 Broadway, 11th Fl.
New York, New York 10019

48/11 Music (ASCAP)
c/o MFC Management
1428 S. Sherbourne Drive
Los Angeles, California 90035

Fountain Square Music Publishing Co. Inc
(ASCAP)
c/o Signature Sound Inc.
655 Ave. of the Americas
New York, New York 10010

Four Buddies (ASCAP)
Att: William Campbell
541 S. Spring Street, No. 8
Los Angeles, California 90013

Four Kids Music
276 Fifth Avenue
New York, New York 10001

Four Knights Music Co. (BMI)
see MCA Music

Four Sons Music (ASCAP)
see Cross Keys Publishing Co., Inc.

Fourth Floor Music Inc./Fiction Music
(ASCAP)
Rte. 212
Wirrenberg Rd.
Bearsville, New York 12409

Fox Fanfare Music Inc.
see Twentieth Century-Fox Music Corp.

Fox Film Music Corp. (BMI)
c/o Twentieth Century Fox Film Corp
P.O. Box 900
Beverly Hills, California 90213

Foxborough Music (ASCAP)
Address Unavailable

Frank Music Co. (ASCAP)
see MPL Communications Inc.

Frankly Scarlett Music (BMI)
see MCA Music

List of Publishers

Franne Gee (ASCAP)
Address Unavailable

Frashon Music Co. (BMI)
c/o Frankie Smith
143 N. Dearborn Street
Philadelphia, Pennsylvania 19139

Len Freedman Music
123 El Paseo
Santa Barbara, California 93101

Freejunket Music (ASCAP)
c/o Salter Street Music
123 El Paseo
Santa Barbara, California 93101

Foster Frees Music Inc. (BMI)
c/o Shankman De Blasio
740 N. La Brea Ave.
Los Angeles, California 90038

French Surf Music (ASCAP)
c/o Joel S. Morse C.P.A.
824 Moaya Dr.
Los Angeles, California 90049

Frisco Kid Music (ASCAP)
c/o Cooper, Epstein, Hurewitz
9465 Wilshire Blvd., No. 800
Beverly Hills, California 90212

Front Burner Music (ASCAP)
PO Box 121274
Nashville, Tennessee 37212

Front Wheel Music, Inc. (BMI)
c/o Kim Guggenheim, Esq.
6255 Sunset Blvd., Suite 1226
Hollywood, California 90028

Frozen Butterfly Music Publishing (BMI)
c/o R. Lucas
260 Farragut Court
Teaneck, New Jersey 07666

Frozen Flame Music (ASCAP)
see Greg Guiffria Music

Full Armor Publishing Co. (BMI)
2828 Azalea Place
Nashville, Tennessee 37204

Full Keel Music (ASCAP)
9320 Wilshire Blvd., Suite 200
Beverly Hills, California 90212

Fullness Music Co. (BMI)
see EMI-Blackwood Music Inc.

Funk Groove Music Publisher Co. (ASCAP)
P.O. Box 72
South Ozone Park, New York 11420

Funzalo Music (BMI)
225 W. 57th Street
New York, New York 10019

Fust Buzza Music, Inc. (BMI)
Att: Shari Friedman
130 W. 57th Street, Suite 11B
New York, New York 10019

Future Furniture (ASCAP)
c/o Myman, Abell, Fineman &
Greenspan
11777 San Vicente Blvd., Ste. 880
Los Angeles, California 90049

G

Gabeson (BMI)
c/o Meitus Copyright
2851 Laurana Road
Union, New Jersey 07083

Galleon Music, Inc. (ASCAP)
344 E. 49th Street, Suite 1A/B
New York, New York 10017

Al Gallico Music Corp. (BMI)
9301 Wilshire, Ste. 311
Beverly Hills, California 90210

Gambi Music Inc. (BMI)
see Copyright Service Bureau Ltd.

David Gamson (ASCAP)
see WB Music

Gang Music Ltd. (BMI)
c/o TWM Management Services, Ltd.
641 Lexington Avenue
New York, New York 10022

Ganga Publishing Co. (BMI)
see Screen Gems-EMI Music Inc.

Garbo Music Division (ASCAP)
Gary Klein Productions Inc.
27 Broadlawn Avenue
Kings Point, New York 11024

Garden Court Music Co. (ASCAP)
Box 1098
Alexandria, Ontario K0C 1A0
Canada

Garden Rake Music, Inc. (BMI)
c/o Shankman De Blasio
185 Pier Avenue
Santa Monica, California 90405

Garwin Music Inc. (ASCAP)
c/o Irvin Bailey
1630 E 5th Ave.
Brooklyn, New York 11230

Gates Music Inc. (BMI)
c/o Chuck Mangione
1845 Clinton Avenue
Rochester, New York 14621

Larry Gatlin Music (BMI)
35 Music Square, E.
Nashville, Tennessee 37203

Gear Publishing (ASCAP)
Division of Hideout Productions
567 Purdy
Birmingham, Michigan 48009

Gedzerillo Music (ASCAP)
c/o Goetzman
14139 Valley Vista Blvd.
Sherman Oaks, California 91423

Geffen Again Music (BMI)
see Geffen Music

Geffen/Kaye Music (ASCAP)
see Warner-Chappell Music

Geffen Music (ASCAP)
see MCA, Inc.

Gemia Music (BMI)
see Irving Music Inc.

Gemrod Music, Inc. (BMI)
c/o Walter Hofer
221 W. 57th Street
New York, New York 10019

Genetic (ASCAP)
10 Church Road
Merchantville, New Jersey 08109

Genevieve Music (ASCAP)
c/o Wixen Music Publishing Inc.
PO Box 260317
Encino, California 91426

Gennaro (BMI)
4503 Dakota Avenue
Nashville, Tennessee 37209

Gentle General (ASCAP)
c/o Jobete Music
6255 Sunset Blvd.
Los Angeles, California 90028

Getarealjob Music (ASCAP)
see EMI Music Publishing

Gibb Brothers Music (BMI)
see BMG Music

Andy Gibb Music (BMI)
c/o Bruce Blitman
9050 Pines Blvd.
Ste. 450
Pembroke Pines, Florida 33024

Hugh & Barbara Gibb Music (BMI)
c/o Prager & Fenton
444 Madison Avenue
New York, New York 10022

G.I.D. Music (ASCAP)
PO Box 120249
Nashville, Tennessee 37212

Gil Music Corp. (BMI)
c/o George Pincus
1650 Broadway, Rm. 806
New York, New York 10019

Giraffe Tracks (SESAC)
Address Unavailable

Girl Productions (ASCAP)
Address unavailable

Girlsongs (ASCAP)
c/o Manatt, Phelps, Rothenberg &
Tunney
11355 W. Olympic Blvd.
Los Angeles, California 90064

Gladys Music (ASCAP)
see Hudson Bay Music

Glamour Music (ASCAP)
c/o Hayes & Hume
Att: Stuart Berton, Esq.
132 S. Rodeo Drive
Beverly Hills, California 90212

Glasco Music, Co. (ASCAP)
PO Box 8470
Universal City, California 91608

Glaser Holmes Publications (BMI)
916 19th Avenue, S.
Nashville, Tennessee 37212

Beverly Glen Publishing (ASCAP)
c/o Loeb and Loeb
Att: D. Thompson
10100 Santa Monica Blvd.
Suite 2200
Los Angeles, California 90067

Glenwood Music Corp. (ASCAP)
see EMI Music Publishing

Glory Music Co. (ASCAP)
8255 Sunset Blvd., Suite 104
Los Angeles, California 90046

GMPC (ASCAP)
see Giorgio Moroder Publishing Co.

Go Glow (ASCAP)
see Metro Goldwyn Mayer Inc.

Godhap Music (BMI)
see EMI Music Publishing

Bella Godiva Music (ASCAP)
see Chappell & Co., Inc.

Gold Hill Music, Inc. (ASCAP)
4985 N. Palm Ave., No. 905
Winter Park, Florida 32792

Goldcrest-Sullivan-Bluth Music (ASCAP)
Address Unavailable

Franne Golde Music Inc. (BMI)
8685 Lookout Mountain Ave.
Los Angeles, California 90046

Golden Bridge Music (BMI)
P.O. Box 121076
Nashville, Tennessee 37212

Golden Mountain Music Inc. (ASCAP)
c/o Freedman Snow & Co.
1092 Mount Pleasant Road
Toronto, Ontario M4P 2M6
Canada

Golden Spread Music
see WB Music

Goldline Music Inc. (ASCAP)
see Warner-Chappell Music

Goldpoint (ASCAP)
c/o Sound Stage Concepts
31 Girard Avenue
Bayshore, New York 11706

Goldrian Music (ASCAP)
1484 S Beverly Dr.
Los Angeles, California 90035

Julie Gold's Music (BMI)
see Irving Music Inc.

Bobby Goldsboro Music (ASCAP)
see Warner-Chappell Music

Michael H. Goldsen, Inc. (ASCAP)
6124 Selma Avenue
Hollywood, California 90028

Golf Pro Music (BMI)
see Bug Music

Gone Gator Music (ASCAP)
c/o Zeiderman, Oberman & Assoc.
500 Sepulveda Blvd., Ste. 500
Los Angeles, California 90049

Good Choice Music (BMI)
c/o Blane, Gilburne, Williams &
Johnson
Att: Bailey Spencer
1900 Ave. of the Stars, Suite 1200
Los Angeles, California 900674606

Gopam Enterprises, Inc.
11 Riverside Drive, No. 13C-W
New York, New York 10023

Gouda Music (ASCAP)
c/o Don Bachrach
1515 N. Crescent Heights Blvd.
Los Angeles, California 90046

Grabbitt Music (BMI)
Box 68
Bergenfield, New Jersey 07621

Grager Music (BMI)
c/o Merria Ross
8030 Via Pompeii
Burbank, California 91504

Granary Music (BMI)
c/o Linda Clark
P.O. Box 1304
Burbank, California 91507

Grand Alliance (ASCAP)
c/o Southern Grand Alliance Music
1710 Grand Avenue
Nashville, Tennessee 37212

Grand Canyon Music, Inc. (BMI)
c/o Mason & Co.
75 Rockefeller Plaza
New York, New York 10019

Grand Coalition (BMI)
1710 Grand Avenue
Nashville, Tennessee 37212

Grand Illusion Music (ASCAP)
see Almo Music Corp.

Grand Pasha (BMI)
c/o Spencer D. Proffer
5615 Melrose Avenue
Los Angeles, California 90038

Grandma Annie Music (BMI)
c/o Sy Miller, Esq.
18 E. 48th Street, Suite 1202
New York, New York 10017

Granite Music Corp. (ASCAP)
6124 Selma Avenue
Hollywood, California 90028

Gratitude Sky Music (ASCAP)
see Warner-Chappell Music

Gravel Bag Music (BMI)
see Bug Music

Gravity Raincoat Music (ASCAP)
see WB Music

Greasy King Music Inc. (BMI)
c/o Mr. Fogerty
P.O. Box 9245
Berkeley, California 94709

Great Lips Music (BMI)
see Virgin Music

Great Pyramid Music (BMI)
10 Waterville Street
San Francisco, California 94124

Al Green Music Inc (ASCAP)
see Hot Toddy Music

Green Skirt Music (BMI)
see Kear Music

Tim Green (BMI)
c/o Bug Music
6777 Hollywood Blvd.
Hollywood, California 90028

Steve Greenberg Music (ASCAP)
see Chappell & Co., Inc.

Gregorian Chance Music (ASCAP)
see Peer-Southern Organization

857

Grey Dog Music (ASCAP)
c/o Pryor, Cashman & Sherman
410 Park Avenue
New York, New York 10022

Groupie Music (BMI)
c/o Robert Nunn
7609 Faust Avenue
West Hills, California 91304

GSC Music (ASCAP)
see EMI April Canada

G3 (ASCAP)
Address Unavailable

Guerrilla Music (BMI)
c/o Warner Brothers Music
9000 Sunset Blvd.
Los Angeles, California 90069

Greg Guiffria Music (ASCAP)
111 Turnberg Rd.
Half Moon Bay, California 94019

Guns N' Roses (BMI)
1324 Wilshire Blvd.
Los Angeles, California 90025

Guns N' Roses Music (ASCAP)
c/o Prager and Fenton
1324 Wilshire Blvd.
Los Angeles, California 90025

H

Ha-Deb Music (ASCAP)
c/o Jane Stranch
Box 120011
Nashville, Tennessee 37212

Hall-Clement Publications (BMI)
see Welk Music Group

Rick Hall Music (ASCAP)
P.O. Box 2527
603 E. Avalon Avenue
Muscle Shoals, Alabama 35662

Hallowed Hall (BMI)
c/o Warner-Tamerlane
9000 Sunset Blvd.
Los Angeles, California 90069

Hammer & Nails Music (ASCAP)
see Almo Music Corp.

Albert Hammond Enterprises (ASCAP)
c/o Brenner & Glassbert
2049 Century Park E., #950
Los Angeles, California 90067

Hampshire House Publishing Corp. (ASCAP)
see TRO-Cromwell Music Inc.

Hamstein Music (BMI)
c/o Bill Ham
P.O. Box 19647
Houston, Texas 77024

Hancock Music Co. (BMI)
c/o David Rubinson & Friends Inc.
827 Folsom Street
San Francisco, California 94107

Hang Dog Music (BMI)
see Bug Music

Hanna Music (ASCAP)
see Brockman Enterprises Inc.

Hannah Rhodes Music (BMI)
c/o Copyright Management, Inc.
1102 17th Avenue, S., Suite 401
Nashville, Tennessee 37212

Happy Hooker Music Inc. (BMI)
c/o Alex J. Migliara
202 Adams Avenue
Memphis, Tennessee 38104

Happy Sack Music Ltd. (ASCAP)
Chillynipple Music Division
Att: Brian Ahern
2200 Younge Street, Suite 502
Toronto, Ontario M4S 2C6
Canada

Happy Trails (ASCAP)
6255 Sunset Blvd., Suite 1019
Hollywood, California 90028

Hard Ball Music (BMI)
3512 Central Avenue
Nashville, Tennessee 37202

Hard Fought (BMI)
c/o Rothman Business
P.O. Box 888503
Dunwoody, Georgia 30356

Jack Hardy Music (ASCAP)
see Fast Folk Musical Magazine

Hargreen Music (BMI)
c/o Shanks, Davis & Remer
888 Seventh Avenue
New York, New York 10106

Hargus McSneakerbottom Pub. (ASCAP)
c/o Tom Goodkind
385-2J South End Avenue
New York, New York 10280

Harnen (BMI)
see Emil Ascher Inc.

Harrick Music Inc. (BMI)
see Longitude Music

Joey Harris Music (BMI)
see Bug Music

Bobby Hart Music (ASCAP)
7647 Woodrow Wilson Dr.
Hollywood, California 90046

Hastings Music Corp. (BMI)
see United Artists Music Co., Inc.

Hat Band Music (BMI)
The Sound Seventy Suite
210 25th Avenue, N.
Nashville, Tennessee 37203

Edwin R. Hawkins Music Co. (ASCAP)
190 Moore St.
Ste. 306
Hackensack, New Jersey 07601

Haymaker Music (BMI)
c/o Dan Kavanaugh Management Inc.
6427 Sunset Blvd.
Hollywood, California 90028

Haynestorm Music (ASCAP)
c/o William A. Coben, Esq.
21390 Rambla Vista
Malibu, California 90265

Hear No Evil (BMI)
11684 Ventura Boulevard, Suite 509
Studio City, California 91604

Heart Wheel (BMI)
P.O. Box 50603
Nashville, Tennessee 37205

Heavy Nova Music (ASCAP)
Address Unavailable

Heavy Pedal (ASCAP)
c/o International Royalty Services
Inc.
214 E. 70th St.
New York, New York 10021

Hen-Al Publishing Co. (BMI)
c/o Mr. James E. Ingram
867 S. Muirfield Road
Los Angeles, California 90005

Henry SueMay Music (BMI)
see Mighty Three Music

Herald Square Music Co. (ASCAP)
attn: Freddy Bientetock
1619 Broadway
New York, New York 10019

Herds of Birds Music Inc. (ASCAP)
4421 Lankershim Blvd.
North Hollywood, California 91602

Keith Hermann Music
Address Unavailable

Heroic Music (ASCAP)
2037 Pine Street
Philadelphia, Pennsylvania 19103

Benny Hester Music (ASCAP)
c/o Klein & Co.
11812 San Vicente Blvd. Apt. 210
Los Angeles, California 90025

List of Publishers

Heumar Music (BMI)
see EMI-Blackwood Music Inc.

HG Music, Inc. (ASCAP)
c/o Angie Williams
Schultz & Gladstone
98 Cutter Mill Rd.
Great Neck, New York 10021

Hickory Grove Music (ASCAP)
see EMI-April Music

Hidden Lake (BMI)
Address Unavailable

Hidden Music (BMI)
see Hit & Run Music

Hidden Pun (BMI)
1841 Broadway
New York, New York 10023

Hide a Bone Music (ASCAP)
see Warner-Chappell Music

Hideaway Hits (ASCAP)
c/o Scholz Research & Development
Corp.
1560 Trapelo Road
Waltham, Massachusetts 02154

Hideout Records/Distributing Co. (ASCAP)
see Gear Publishing

High Falutin (ASCAP)
c/o Gene Pistilli
Box 121920
Nashville, Tennessee 37212

High Frontier (ASCAP)
c/o SBK Songs
1290 Avenue of the Americas
New York, New York 10019

High Varieties (ASCAP)
Address Unavailable

Robin Hill Music (ASCAP)
511 S. Serrano Avenue, No. 601
Los Angeles, California 90020

Hilmer Music Publishing Co. (ASCAP)
see EMI Music Publishing

Hip Chic (BMI)
c/o Carter Tuner
9229 Sunset Blvd.
Los Angeles, California 90069

Hip Hill Music Publishing Co. (BMI)
c/o Mira A. Smith
P.O. Box 17365
Nashville, Tennessee 37217

Hip-Trip Music Co. (BMI)
c/o Glen E. Davis
1635 N. Cahuenga Blvd., 6th Fl.
Hollywood, California 90028

Hiram (BMI)
c/o Rightsong
810 Seventh Avenue
New York, New York 10019

Hit & Run Music (ASCAP)
1841 Broadway, Suite 411
New York, New York 10023

Hitchings Music (ASCAP)
c/o William A. Coben, Esq.
Sklar & Coben Inc.
2029 Century Park, E., Suite 260
Los Angeles, California 90067

Hitwell (ASCAP)
Address Unavailable

Hobbler Music (ASCAP)
see WB Music

Holland Music
see Southern Music Publishing Co., Inc.

Hollysongs
Address Unavailable

Hollywood Boulevard Music (ASCAP)
3772 N. Calle Jazmin
Calabasas, California 91302

Holmes Line of Music (ASCAP)
228 W. 71st Street
New York, New York 10023

Holsapple (BMI)
see Criterion Music Corp.

Holy Moley Music (BMI)
2114 Pico Blvd.
Santa Monica, California 90405

Home Grown Music Inc. (BMI)
4852 Laurel Canyon Blvd.
North Hollywood, California 91607

Honest John Music (ASCAP)
15300 Ventura Blvd., Suite 202
Sherman Oaks, California 91403

Honey Look (ASCAP)
see Full Keel Music

Honey-Look Music (ASCAP)
see Full Keel Music

Hookem Music (ASCAP)
Terranceent Corp.
PO Box 239
Las Vegas, Nevada 87701

Hopi Sound Music (ASCAP)
c/o Chris De Walden
6255 Sunset Blvd., Suite 1911
Hollywood, California 90028

Hori Pro Entertainment Group (ASCAP)
1819 Broadway
Nashville, Tennessee 37203

Hot Cha Music Co. (BMI)
130 W. 57th St.
Ste. 12B
New York, New York 10019

Hot Corner (ASCAP)
c/o John Golden
5 Belvedere Path
Suffern, New York 10901

Hot Kitchen Music (ASCAP)
c/o James Jesse Winchester
2460 Chemin Corriveau
Canton Magog, Quebec J1X-5R9
Canada

Hot Toddy Music
Address Unavailable

Hotwire Music (BMI)
c/o Atlantic Music Corp.
6124 Selma Avenue
Hollywood, California 90028

House of Bryant Publications (BMI)
P.O. Box 570
Gatlinburg, Tennessee 37738

House of Cash Inc. (BMI)
c/o Reba Hancock
Box 508
Hendersonville, Tennessee 37077

House of Champions Music (ASCAP)
PO Box 2129
Upland, California 91785

House of Fun Music (BMI)
1348 Lexington Ave.
New York, New York 10128

House of Greed Music (ASCAP)
Address unavailable

Howlin' Hits Music (ASCAP)
P.O. Box 19647
Houston, Texas 77224

Hudmar Publishing Co., Inc. (BMI)
c/o Frances & Freedman Acct.
501 S. Beverly Dr.
Beverly Hills, California 90212

Hudson Bay Music (BMI)
1619 Broadway
New York, New York 10019

Huemar Music (BMI)
c/o Hubert Eaves
834 Jefferson Avenue
Brooklyn, New York 11221

Huevos Rancheros Music (ASCAP)
see Bug Music

Nancy Hughes
see Famous Music Corp.

Hulex Music (BMI)
P.O. Box 819
Mill Valley, California 94942

Human Boy Music (ASCAP)
see Warner-Chappell Music

Ian Hunter Music (ASCAP)
see EMI-April Music

Husker Music (BMI)
P.O. Box 8646
Minneapolis, Minnesota 55408

Hustlers Inc. (BMI)
c/o Alan Walden
5722 Kentucky Downs
Macon, Georgia 31210

Hygroton
1551 Filion Street, Apt. 504
St. Lambert, Quebec J4R 1W5
Canada

Hythefield Music (BMI)
1700 York Avenue, Apt. 9B
New York, New York 10028

I

I Before E Music Co. (ASCAP)
c/o Nick Ben-Meir
644 N. Doheny Drive
Los Angeles, California 90069

Ice Nine Publishing Co., Inc. (ASCAP)
P.O. Box 1073
San Rafael, California 94915

ID Music Ltd. (BMI)
see Bug Music

Ideola Music (ASCAP)
3521 Rosemary Avenue
Glendale, California 91208

Ides of March Music Division (ASCAP)
Wayfield Inc.
1136 Gateway Lane
Nashville, Tennessee 37220

If Eyes Inc. (ASCAP)
c/o Michael Smotherman
1122 N. Kings Road, No. 7
Los Angeles, California 90060

IJI (ASCAP)
c/o Chris Jasper
24 Birch Grove Drive
Armonk, New York 10540

Illegal Songs, Inc. (BMI)
c/o Beverly Martin
633 N. La Brea Avenue
Hollywood, California 90036

Impulsive Music (ASCAP)
Gelfand Rennert & Feldman
1301 Ave. of the Americas
New York, New York 10019

Index Music (ASCAP)
see Warner-Chappell Music

Inner Sanctum (BMI)
c/o D. L. Bryon
247 Grand Street
New York, New York 10002

Dave Innis Music (ASCAP)
attn: Dave Innis
8625 Fairfax
Roulett, Texas 75088

Inorbit Music, Inc. (BMI)
c/o Careers Music, Inc.
8370 Wilshire Blvd.
Beverly Hills, California 90211

Insoc Music (ASCAP)
496 LaGuardia Place, Box 155
New York, New York 10012

Interior Music (BMI)
c/o Margo Matthews
Box 92004
Los Angeles, California 90009

International Korwin Corp. (ASCAP)
60 W. 57th Street, Suite 14F
New York, New York 10019

Intersong, USA Inc. (ASCAP)
see Warner-Chappell Music

I.R.S. Music (BMI)
see First Release Music Publishing

Irving Music Inc. (BMI)
360 N. LaCienega Blvd.
Los Angeles, California 90048

Is Hot Music, Ltd. (ASCAP)
34 Pheasant Run
Old Westbury, New York 11568

Chris Isaak Music Publishing (ASCAP)
P.O. Box 547
Larkspur, California 94939

Island Music (BMI)
6525 Sunset Blvd.
Los Angeles, California 90028

Island Visual Arts (ASCAP)
see Island Music

Itasca Music (BMI)
c/o ATM Music
8732 Sunset Blvd., Suite 600
Los Angeles, California 90069

It's on Hold (ASCAP)
Bob Beckham Enterprises
824 19th Avenue, S.
Nashville, Tennessee 37203

I've Got the Music Co. (ASCAP)
Att: Terry Woodford
P.O. Box 2631
Muscle Shoals, Alabama 35662

Izzylumoe Music
c/o Financial Management
International
9200 Sunset Blvd., Suite 931
Los Angeles, California 90069

J

J. King IV (BMI)
Address Unavailable

J S H Music (ASCAP)
c/o Nigro-Karlin & Segal
10100 Santa Monica Blvd.
Suite 2460
Los Angeles, California 90067

Ja-Len Music Co/Intersong USA, Inc.
(ASCAP)
P.O. Box 50937
Nashville, Tennessee 37205

Jac Music Co., Inc. (ASCAP)
5253 Lankershim Blvd.
North Hollywood, California 91601

Jacobsen (ASCAP)
Address Unavailable

Jakota Music (ASCAP)
c/o Jerry G. Hludzik
430 E. Main Street
Dalton, Pennsylvania 18414

Jalma Music (ASCAP)
see Island Music

Dick James Music Inc. (BMI)
24 Music Square, E.
Nashville, Tennessee 37203

Tommy James Music Inc. (BMI)
Box 3073
Clifton, New Jersey 07012

Mickey James Music (ASCAP)
406 S.E. Caroline St.
Milton, Florida 32570

Jamie Music Publishing Co. (BMI)
2055 Richmond St.
Philadelphia, Pennsylvania 19125

Janiceps (BMI)
c/o SBK Entertainment
810 Seventh Avenue
New York, New York 10019

Al Jarreau Music (BMI)
9034 Sunset Blvd., Suite 250
Los Angeles, California 90069

List of Publishers

Jasper Stone (ASCAP)
c/o Warner Brothers
9000 Sunset Blvd.
Los Angeles, California 90069

Jasperilla Music Co. (ASCAP)
attn: James M. Messina
11377 W Olympic Blvd.
Los Angeles, California 90064

Jay-Boy Music Corp.
c/o Seymour Straus Herzog & Straus
155 E. 55th Street, Suite 300B
New York, New York 10022

Jay's Enterprises, Inc. (ASCAP)
c/o Chappell & Co. Inc.
10585 Santa Monica Blvd.
Los Angeles, California 90025

Jec Publishing Corp. (BMI)
c/o J. Cuoghi
308 Poplar Avenue
Memphis, Tennessee 38103

Jeddrah Music (ASCAP)
c/o Lopey & Gonzaley
attn: Ellen Burke
15250 Ventura Blvd.
Penthouse 1220
Sherman Oaks, California 91403

Jeff Who Music (ASCAP)
c/o Jeffrey R. Hanna
2410 Blair Blvd.
Nashville, Tennessee 37212

Jeffix Music Co. (ASCAP)
c/o William Jeffery
3571 Olympiad Dr.
Los Angeles, California 90043

Garland Jeffreys Music/April Music, Inc.
(ASCAP)
c/o Levine & Thall, PC
485 Madison Avenue
New York, New York 10022

Jen-Lee Music Co. (ASCAP)
5775 Peachtree Dunwoody Road, N.E.
Suite B-130
Atlanta, Georgia 30342

Jenn-a-Bug Music (ASCAP)
c/o Manatt, Phelps, Rothenberg
11355 W. Olympic Blvd.
Los Angeles, California 90064

Waylon Jennings Music (BMI)
1117 17th Avenue, S.
Nashville, Tennessee 37212

Jensong Music, Inc. (ASCAP)
P.O. Box 1273
Nashville, Tennessee 37202

Jent Music Inc. (BMI)
P.O. Box 1566
7 N. Mountain Avenue
Montclair, New Jersey 07042

Jerryco Music Co. (ASCAP)
MPL Communications, Inc.
c/o Eastman & Eastman
39 W. 54th Street
New York, New York 10019

Jessie Joe (BMI)
Address Unavailable

Jig-a-Watt Jams (BMI)
Division of New Day Publishing Co.
1948 Fullerton Drive
Cincinnati, Ohio 45240

Jim-Edd Music (BMI)
P.O. Box 78681
Los Angeles, California 90016

Jimmie Fun (BMI)
see EMI Music Publishing

Jim's Allisongs (BMI)
Address Unavailable

Jiru Music (ASCAP)
attn: Richard Gottehren
44 W 77th St.
New York, New York 10024

Jobete Music Co. (ASCAP)
attn: Denise Maurin
6255 Sunset Blvd.
Los Angeles, California 90028

Jodaway Music (ASCAP)
c/o Harris Management
PO Box 2098
Inglewood, California 90305

Joel (BMI)
c/o Maritime Music Inc.
200 W. 57th Street
New York, New York 10019

Joelsongs (BMI)
see EMI-April Music

Johnson Music (BMI)
Address Unavailable

Jolly Cheeks Music (BMI)
c/o Griesdorf, Chertkoff, Levitt &
Associates
2200 Younge Street, Suite 502
Toronto, Ontario M4S 2O6
Canada

Jonathan Three Music Co. (BMI)
c/o Lefrak Entertainment Co., Ltd.
40 W. 57th Street, Suite 1510
New York, New York 10019

Paul Laurence Jones, III (ASCAP)
Address unavailable

Jones Music Co.
c/o Dorothy Mae Rice Jones
1916 Portman Avenue
Cincinnati, Ohio 45237

Jonico Music Inc. (ASCAP)
31 W. 56th St., 4th Fl.
New York, New York 10019

Jonisongs (ASCAP)
2622 Fourth Street, Suite 10
Santa Monica, California 90405

JonoSongs (ASCAP)
3543 LWR Honoapilani Hwy.
B 408
Lehaina, Hawaii 96761

Jonware Music Corp. (BMI)
c/o Aleen Colitz, Esq.
578 Maitland Avenue
Teaneck, New Jersey 07666

Jouissance (ASCAP)
see WB Music

Jowcol (BMI)
Address Unavailable

Joy U.S.A. Music Co. (BMI)
c/o Robert B. Weiss
17208 Braxton St.
Granada Hills, California 91344

Julann Music (ASCAP)
c/o Laurence B. Gottlieb
333 E 45th St.
New York, New York 10017

Junior Music, Ltd.
Address Unavailable

Juters Publishing Co. (BMI)
c/o Funzalo Music
Att: Mike's Management
445 Park Avenue, 7th Fl.
New York, New York 10022

JVA Publishing Co. (ASCAP)
c/o John V. Anderson
384 Wildrose Ave.
Bergenfield, New Jersey 07621

K

Kadoc Music (BMI)
c/o Mrs. George
702 Lenox Road
Brooklyn, New York 11203

Irving Kahal Music, Inc. (ASCAP)
c/o A. Halsey Cowan, Esq.
1350 Avenue of the Americas
New York, New York 10019

Kalahari Music
Address Unavailable

Kamalar (ASCAP)
PO Box 411197
San Francisco, California 94141

Paul Kamanski Music (ASCAP)
see Bug Music

Kander & Ebb Inc. (BMI)
see Valando Group

Kieran Kane (ASCAP)
3607 Bellwood Drive
Nashville, Tennessee 37205

George Karaoglou Publishing (BMI)
28 Lakeside Ave.
Colts Neck, New Jersey 07722

Kashif Music (BMI)
c/o Minter & Associates Inc.
194 Lenox Road
Brooklyn, New York 11226

Kat and Mouse Music (BMI)
see EMI-April Music

Kaz Music Co. (ASCAP)
P.O. Box 38
Woodstock, New York 12498

Kazoom (ASCAP)
see MCA Music

Kear Music (BMI)
1635 N. Cahuenga Blvd.
Los Angeles, California 90028

Keejue (ASCAP)
Address Unavailable

Keishmack Music (BMI)
c/o Keith Mack
127 Lexington Avenue
New York, New York 10016

Kejoc Music (BMI)
c/o Shankman De Blasio
185 Pier Avenue
Santa Monica, California 90405

Rick Kelly (BMI)
4226 1/2 Gentry Avenue
Studio City, California 91604

Kemo Music Co. (BMI)
c/o Beechwood Music Corp.
6255 Sunset Blvd.
Hollywood, California 90028

King Kendrick Publishing (BMI)
Address unavailable

Kentucky Music, Inc. (BMI)
1619 Broadway, 11th Fl.
New York, New York 10019

Kentucky Sweetheart Music (BMI)
see Caseyem Music

Kentucky Wonder Music
Address Unavailable

Kenwon Music (BMI)
5032 Lankershim Blvd., Suite 2
North Hollywood, California 91601

Kermy (BMI)
Address Unavailable

Key West Inc. (ASCAP)
1252 E. Andreas Road
Palm Springs, California 92262

Gilbert Keyes Music Co. (ASCAP)
6223 Selma Avenue
Hollywood, California 90028

Keymen Music (BMI)
c/o Copyright Service Bureau, Ltd.
221 W. 57th Street
New York, New York 10019

Kid Bird Music (BMI)
c/o Ervin Cohen & Jessup
Att: Gregg Harrison, Esq.
9401 Wilshire Blvd., 9th Fl.
Beverly Hills, California 90212

Kidada Music Inc. (BMI)
see Warner-Chappell Music

Kiddio Music Co. (BMI)
c/o Martin Poll
919 Third Avenue
New York, New York 10022

Maxx Kidd's Music (ASCAP)
c/o Ackee Music Inc.
6525 Sunset Blvd.
Hollywood, California 90028

Kikiko Music Corp. (BMI)
see Jobete Music Co.

Kilauea Music (BMI)
c/o Jerry Swartz
9595 Wilshire Blvd.
Ste. 1020
Beverly Hills, California 90212

King Coal Music Inc. (ASCAP)
Attn: Lorene Allen
PO Box 120369
Nashville, Tennessee 37212

Jay King, IV (BMI)
c/o Mitchell Silberberg
11377 W. Olympic Blvd.
Los Angeles, California 90064

Kings Road Music (BMI)
1901 Avenue of the Stars
Suite 1240
Los Angeles, California 90067

Stephen A. Kipner Music (ASCAP)
Att: Stephen A. Kipner
19646 Valley View Drive
Topanga, California 90290

Kirshner/April Music Publishing (ASCAP)
see SBK Entertainment World

Don Kirshner Music Inc. (BMI)
see EMI-Blackwood Music Inc.

Kiss
Glickman/Marks Management Corp.
Att: Dolores Gatza
655 Madison Avenue
New York, New York 10021

Kissway Music, Inc. (BMI)
c/o Glickman Marks Management Corp.
655 Madison Avenue
New York, New York 10021

KJG Music (ASCAP)
6066 Summit Bridge Road
Townsend, Delaware 19734

Klenco (ASCAP)
c/o Richard Klender
P.O. Box 976
Simi Valley, California 93065

Klondike Enterprises Ltd.
c/o Randall Stewart
1785 W. Holmes Rd.
Memphis, Tennessee 38109

Klymaxx (ASCAP)
Address Unavailable

Bubba Knight Enterprises Ltd. (ASCAP)
c/o Seidenberg
1414 Sixth Ave.
New York, New York 10019

Knighty Knight (ASCAP)
see Arista Music, Inc.

Knockout Music Co. (ASCAP)
c/o Millennium Corp.
1619 Broadway, Suite 1209
New York, New York 10019

Know Music (ASCAP)
c/o VWC Management Inc.
13343 Bel Red Road, Suite 201
Bellevue, Washington 98005

Koala Music Inc. (ASCAP)
30 Highbrook Avenue
Pelham, New York 10803

Kokomo Music (ASCAP)
Att: Bonnie Raitt
P.O. Box 626
Los Angeles, California 90078

List of Publishers

Kool Koala (BMI)
c/o Richard Edward
45 E. 22nd Street
New York, New York 10010

Koppelman Family Music (ASCAP)
c/o Mason & Co.
400 Park Ave.
New York, New York 10022

Charles Koppelman Music
see Entertainment Co. Music Group

Kortchmar Music (ASCAP)
see WB Music

Kosher Dill Music (BMI)
162 Almonte Blvd.
Mill Valley, California 94941

Krell (BMI)
9255 Sunset Blvd.
Los Angeles, California 90069

Kris Publishing
P.O. Box 42218
San Francisco, California 94142

Kuwa Music (ASCAP)
c/o Bert Padell
1775 Broadway, 7th Fl.
New York, New York 10019

Kuzu Music (BMI)
see EMI Music Publishing

L

La Brea Music (ASCAP)
see Almo Music Corp.

A La Mode Music (ASCAP)
c/o Braun, Margolis, Ryan, Burrill
& Besse
attn: Malcolm Wiseman, ESQ
1900 Ave. of the Stars
Los Angeles, California 90067

La Rana (BMI)
1750 E. Holly Avenue
El Segundo, California 90245

Labor of Love Music (BMI)
c/o Randy Scruggs
2821 Bransford Avenue
Nashville, Tennessee 37204

Lacy Boulevard Music
see WB Music

Lady of the Lakes Music (ASCAP)
11067 Olallie Ln.
Bainbridge Island, Washington 98110

Lagunatic Music (ASCAP)
see Virgin Music

Lake Victoria Music (ASCAP)
104 MacDougal St.
Apt. 22
New York, New York 10012

Lamont Coward (BMI)
Address Unavailable

Land of Music Publishing (ASCAP)
1136 Gateway Lane
Nashville, Tennessee 37220

Jay Landers Music (ASCAP)
One E River Place
525 E 72nd St.
No. 281
New York, New York 10021

Lar-Bell Music Corp. (BMI)
9110 Sunset Blvd., Suite 140
Los Angeles, California 90069

Largo Music, Inc. (ASCAP)
425 Park Avenue
New York, New York 10022

Larry Junior Music (BMI)
1422 W. Peachtree Street
Atlanta, Georgia 30309

Lars (ASCAP)
Address Unavailable

Latin Songs (ASCAP)
Address unavailable

Lawyer's Daughter (BMI)
Homestead Road
Pottersville, New Jersey 07979

Lead Sheetland Music (BMI)
c/o Jess S. Morgan & Co., Inc.
6420 Wilshire Blvd., 19th Fl.
Los Angeles, California 90048

Otis Lee Music (ASCAP)
c/o Franklin, Weinrib, Rudell
488 Madison Avenue
New York, New York 10022

Leeds Music Corp. (ASCAP)
c/o Mr. John McKellen
445 Park Avenue
New York, New York 10022

Leesum Music, Inc. (BMI)
c/o James Bogard Associates
7608 Teel Way
Indianapolis, Indiana 46256

Leggs Four Publishing (BMI)
c/o Kim Guggenheim, Esq.
6255 Sunset Blvd., Suite 1214
Hollywood, California 90028

Legibus Music Co. (BMI)
c/o Peter Bennett, Esq.
9060 Santa Monica Blvd., Suite 300
Los Angeles, California 90069

Legs Music, Inc. (ASCAP)
c/o Abkco Music
1700 Broadway
New York, New York 10019

Jerry Leiber Music (ASCAP)
9000 Sunset Blvd.
Ste. 1107
Los Angeles, California 90069

Oliver Leiber Music (ASCAP)
see EMI Music Publishing

Lemon Tree Music, Inc. (ASCAP)
c/o Will Holt
9491 Readcrest Drive
Beverly Hills, California 90025

Lena May (ASCAP)
c/o SBK Songs
810 Seventh Avenue
New York, New York 10019

Lena Music, Inc. (BMI)
1619 Broadway, Suite 507
New York, New York 10019

Lenono Music (BMI)
The Studio
1 W. 72nd Street
New York, New York 10023

Leona (ASCAP)
Address Unavailable

Les Etoiles de la Musique (ASCAP)
21390 Rambla Vista
Malibu, California 90265

Let There Be Music Inc. (ASCAP)
attn: James E. Cason
2804 Azalea Place
Nashville, Tennessee 37204

Let's Have Lunch Music (ASCAP)
601 Miridian St.
Huntsville, Alabama 35801

Let's See Music (ASCAP)
see WB Music

Let's Shine (ASCAP)
PO Box 411197
San Francisco, California 94141

Levay (ASCAP)
see Giorgio Moroder Publishing Co.

Level 42 Songs (ASCAP)
Address Unavailable

Lew-Bob Songs (BMI)
P.O. Box 8031
Universal City, California 91608

Lexicon Music Inc. (ASCAP)
P.O. Box 296
Woodland Hills, California 91365

List of Publishers

LFR Music (ASCAP)
2541 Nicollett Ave. S.
Minneapolis, Minnesota 55404

Lido Music Inc. (BMI)
c/o Segel & Goldman Inc.
9348 Santa Monica Blvd.
Beverly Hills, California 90210

Liesse Publishing (ASCAP)
6265 Cote De Liesse, Suite 200
Montreal, Quebec
Canada

Lifo (BMI)
105-28 192nd Street
Hollis, New York 11412

Lijesrika Music Pub. (BMI)
see Irving Music Inc.

Likasa Music (BMI)
260 Farragut Court
Teaneck, New Jersey 07666

Likete Split Music (BMI)
see Lake Victoria Music

Lil Mama Music (BMI)
see MCA Music

Lillybilly
see Bug Music

Limerick Music Corp. (ASCAP)
c/o The Songwriters Guild
276 Fifth Avenue, 3rd Fl.
New York, New York 10001

Limited Funds Music (BMI)
c/o Mason, Sloane & Gilbert
1299 Ocean Avenue, Penthouse
Santa Monica, California 90401

Lincoln Pond Music (BMI)
3888 Alta Mesa Drive
Studio City, California 91604

Linda's Boys Music (BMI)
see WB Music

Dennis Linde Music (BMI)
35 Music Square E.
Nashville, Tennessee 37203

Linder Ltd. (BMI)
Address Unavailable

Lion Hearted Music (ASCAP)
35 Music Sq. East
Nashville, Tennessee 37215

Lionscub Music (BMI)
c/o Michael Gesas C.P.A.
Bash Gesas & Co.
9401 Wilshire Blvd., No. 700
Beverly Hills, California 90212

Lionsmate Music (ASCAP)
54 Music Sq. E
Nashville, Tennessee 37203

Lipsync Music (ASCAP)
c/o Nick Ben-Meir, C.P.A.
644 N. Doheny Drive
Los Angeles, California 90069

Lisabella Music (ASCAP)
see Cherry Lane Music Co.

Little Big Town Music (BMI)
see Jessie Joe

Little Birdie Music (BMI)
see Bug Music

Little Diva Music (BMI)
2029 Centry Park
Los Angeles, California 90067

Little Doggies Productions Inc. (ASCAP)
(Stray Notes Music Division)
c/o Dennis Katz, Esq.
845 Third Avenue
New York, New York 10022

Little Dragon Music (BMI)
c/o Mustola-Jorstad
One Harbor Drive, Suite 111
Sausalito, California 94965

Little Horn Music (ASCAP)
Address Unavailable

Little Laurel Music (BMI)
1406 Clayton Avenue
Nashville, Tennessee 37212

Little Life Music (ASCAP)
c/o Robert Friedman
217 E. 26th St.
New York, New York 10010

Little Mole Music (ASCAP)
c/o Lippman Kattane Entertainment
8265 Sunset Blvd., No. 104
Los Angeles, California 90046

A Little More Music Inc. (ASCAP)
P.O. Box 120555
Nashville, Tennessee 37212

Little Music (BMI)
Address Unavailable

Little Nemo (ASCAP)
see Almo Music Corp.

Little Shop of Morgansongs (BMI)
1102 17th Avenue S.
Nashville, Tennessee 37212

Little Steven Music (ASCAP)
Address Unavailable

Little Tanya (ASCAP)
see MCA Music

Liv Tunes (ASCAP)
see Lost Lake Arts Music

L.L. Cool J Music (ASCAP)
attn: James Todd Smith
PO Box 219
Elmont, New York 11003

Lla-Mann
c/o Chappell
9000 Sunset Blvd.
Los Angeles, California 90069

Llee Music (BMI)
see MPL Communications Inc.

Lo Pressor
705 Churchill Blvd., No. 202
St. Lambert, Quebec J4R 1M8
Canada

Lockhill-Selma Music (ASCAP)
see Rocksmith Music

Lois Publishing Co. (BMI)
1540 Brewster Avenue
Cincinnati, Ohio 45207

London (BMI)
Address Unavailable

Long Pond Music
see Revelation Music Publishing Corp.

Long Run Music Co., Inc. (BMI)
see WB Music

Long Tooth Music (BMI)
c/o Zeiderman, Oberman & Associates
Attn: Bernard H. Gudvi
500 S. Sepulveda, Suite 500
Los Angeles, California 90049

Longdog Music (ASCAP)
c/o Ned Doheny
136 El Camino Drive
Beverly Hills, California 90212

Longitude Music (BMI)
c/o Windswept Pacific Entertainment
Co.
9320 Wilshire Blvd., Ste. 200
Beverly Hills, California 91212

Looky Lou Music (BMI)
300 E. Washington Blvd.
Pasadena, California 91104

Lorimar Music Corp. (ASCAP)
see Warner-Chappell Music

Lorimar Music Publishing Co. (BMI)
P.O. Box 1340
Studio City, California 91604

Los Was Cosmipolitanos
Address Unavailable

List of Publishers

Lost Boys Music (BMI)
c/o Obsidian Productions, Inc.
Att: H Siegel
410 Park Avenue, 10th Fl.
New York, New York 10022

Lost in Music (ASCAP)
see House of Fun Music

Lost Lake Arts Music (ASCAP)
c/o Windham Hill Records
75 Willow Rd.
Menlo Park, California 94025

Love Wheel Music (BMI)
P.O. Box 110873
Nashville, Tennessee 37211

Lyle Lovett (ASCAP)
c/o Michael H. Goldsen Inc.
6124 Selma Avenue
Hollywood, California 90028

Low Noise America Music (BMI)
21 East Second Strett, Suite 37
New York, New York 10003

Lowery Music Co., Inc. (BMI)
3051 Clairmont Road, N.E.
Atlanta, Georgia 30329

Lu Ella (ASCAP)
see WB Music

Lucky Break (ASCAP)
16100 Bryant St.
North Hills, California 91343

Lucky Three Music Publishing Co. (BMI)
Division of Salsoul Record Corp.
c/o Larry Spier
401 Fifth Avenue
New York, New York 10016

Lucrative (BMI)
P.O. Box 90363
Nashville, Tennessee 37209

Ludlow Music Inc. (BMI)
10 Columbus Circle, Suite 1406
New York, New York 10019

Luna Mist Music (BMI)
c/o Laura Bianchini
Box 2865
Danbury, Connecticut 06813

Lunatunes Music (BMI)
2400 Fulton Street
San Francisco, California 94118

Lushmole Music (BMI)
see EMI Music Publishing

Lyon Farm Music Ltd.
626 W. Lyon Farm Road
Greenwich, Connecticut 06830

M

Mac Vac Alac Music Co. (ASCAP)
3646 Mt. Vernon Drive
Los Angeles, California 90008

Maclen Music Inc. (BMI)
see ATV Music Corp.

Macy Place Music (ASCAP)
see WB Music

Magic Castle Music, Inc. (ASCAP)
Att: Jerry Foster
P.O. Box 41147
Nashville, Tennessee 37204

Magicland Music (ASCAP)
c/o Madhouse Management
3101 E. Eisenhower, Suite 3
Ann Arbor, Michigan 48104

Magnetic Music Publishing Co. (ASCAP)
5 Jones St., Apt. 4
New York, New York 10014

Maizery Music (ASCAP)
295 E. Eighth Street, No. 1W
New York, New York 10009

Major Bob Music (ASCAP)
1109 17th Ave. S
Nashville, Tennessee 37212

Make Believus Music
109 Sanders Court
Franklin, Tennessee 37064

Make It Big (ASCAP)
c/o Jery Sunrty
9595 Wilshire Blvd.
#1020
Beverly Hills, California 90212

Makiki Publishing Co., Ltd. (ASCAP)
9350 Wilshire Blvd., Suite 323
Beverly Hills, California 90212

Making Betts Music (BMI)
c/o Warner-Tamerlane
Publications Corp.
9000 Sunset Blvd., Penthouse
Los Angeles, California 90049

Malbiz Publishing (BMI)
see EMI-Blackwood Music Inc.

Mallven Music (ASCAP)
c/o Mason & Sloane
P.O. Box 140110
Nashville, Tennessee 37214

Malvern Music Co. (ASCAP)
Chester County
Malvern, Pennsylvania 19355

Mambadaddi (BMI)
5606 Bennett Avenue
Austin, Texas 78751

Mammoth Spring Music (BMI)
c/o Rose Bridge Music, Inc.
1121 S. Glenstone
Springfield, Missouri 65804

Man-Ken Music Ltd. (BMI)
34 Pheasant Run
Old Westbury, New York 11568

Man Woman Together Now Music (BMI)
see Irving Music Inc.

Management Agency & Music Publishing
(BMI)
Att: Jon Devirian
10100 Santa Monica Blvd., Suite 205
Los Angeles, California 90067

Henry Mancini Enterprises (ASCAP)
see Chappell & Co., Inc.

Manitou-Champion (BMI)
c/o MCA, Inc.
445 Park Avenue
New York, New York 10022

Mann & Weil Songs Inc. (BMI)
see MCA, Inc.

Maplehill Music (BMI)
see Welk Music Group

Marc-Jean (BMI)
68 Summit Circle
Westmount, Quebec H3Y 1B5
Canada

March 9 Music (ASCAP)
see Almo Music Corp.

Marilor Music (ASCAP)
see Warner-Chappell Music

Mariposa Music Inc. (BMI)
713 18th Avenue, S.
Nashville, Tennessee 37204

Mark of Aries (ASCAP)
Address Unavailable

Marke Music Publishing Co., Inc. (ASCAP)
c/o The Songwriters Guild
276 Fifth Avenue, 3rd Fl.
New York, New York 10001

Markmeem Music
see Hudson Bay Music

E. B. Marks Music Corp. (BMI)
see Alley Music

Mick Mars (BMI)
9255 Sunset Blvd.
Los Angeles, California 90069

List of Publishers

Marsaint Music Inc. (BMI)
Att: Marshall E. Sehorn
3809 Clematis Avenue
New Orleans, Louisiana 70122

David Massengill Music
Box 938
Village Station
New York, New York 10014

Matak Music (ASCAP)
see MCA Music

Maypop Music (BMI)
Box 121192e Cavender
702 18th Ave.
Nashville, Tennessee 37212

Maz Appeal (ASCAP)
216 E. 10th Street, No. 5D
New York, New York 10003

MCA, Inc. (ASCAP)
1755 Broadway, 8th Fl.
New York, New York 10019

MCA Music (ASCAP)
1755 Broadway
New York, New York 10019

McBec Music (ASCAP)
54 Music Square East
Nashville, Tennessee 37203

Gene McFadden (BMI)
c/o Careers Music
8370 Wilshire Blvd.
Beverly Hills, California 90211

Earl McGrath Music (ASCAP)
123 El Paseo
Santa Barbara, California 93101

McKenzie Brothers
c/o Craig Fuller
P.O. Box 142
New Richmond, Ohio 45157

McNella Music (ASCAP)
5124 3/4 Colfax Avenue
North Hollywood, California 91601

McNoodle Music (BMI)
c/o Bernard Gudvi & Co., Inc.
6420 Wilshire Blvd., Suite 425
Los Angeles, California 90048

Medicine Hat Music (ASCAP)
see EMI Music Publishing

Megadude (ASCAP)
see WB Music

Mel-Bren Music Inc. (ASCAP)
c/o Loeb & Loeb
Att: John P. Mackey
10100 Santa Monica Blvd.
Suite 2200
Los Angeles, California 90067

Melder Publishing Co., Inc. (BMI)
c/o Joe Jones
10556 Arnwood Road
Lake View Terrace, California 91342

Mellow Music Publishing Co. (BMI)
1650 Broadway, Suite 305
New York, New York 10019

Menken Music (BMI)
c/o The Shukatt Co., Ltd.
340 W. 55th Street, Suite 1A
New York, New York 10019

Meow Baby (ASCAP)
c/o The Fitzgerald Hartley Co.
50 W Main St.
Ventura, California 93001

Mercury Shoes Music (BMI)
c/o Jesse Barish
2612 Pacific Avenue
Venice, California 90291

Merjoda Music, Inc.
see Warner-Chappell Music

Merovingian Music (BMI)
c/o Chris Butler
266 W. 11th Street
New York, New York 10014

Metal Machine Music (BMI)
see Oakfield Avenue Music Ltd.

Metered Music, Inc. (ASCAP)
Peter Matorin
c/o Beldock Levine & Hoffman
99 Park Ave.
New York, New York 10016

Metro Goldwyn Mayer Inc. (BMI)
10202 W. Washington Blvd.
Culver City, California 90230

Mevis Believus Music (ASCAP)
811 18th Ave. S.
Nashville, Tennessee 37203

MGM Affiliated Music, Inc. (BMI)
Address Unavailable

MGM/UA Music Inc. (ASCAP)
see Almo Music Corp.

MHC (ASCAP)
see Belwin-Mills Publishing Corp.

MHC Music (ASCAP)
c/o Michael Epstein
110 W 57th St., 7th Fl.
New York, New York 10019

Midnight Magnet (ASCAP)
see EMI Music Publishing

Midstar Music, Inc. (BMI)
1717 Section Road
Cincinnati, Ohio 45237

Midsummer Music (ASCAP)
1109 17th Ave. South
Nashville, Tennessee 37212

Mighty Mathieson Music (BMI)
c/o Shankman De Blasio, Inc.
185 Pier Avenue
Santa Monica, California 90405

Mighty Nice Music (BMI)
see Polygram Music Publishing Inc.

Mighty Three Music (BMI)
c/o Earl Shelton
309 S. Broad Street
Philadelphia, Pennsylvania 19107

Mijac Music (BMI)
see Warner-Chappell Music

Milene Music (ASCAP)
65 Music Square West
Nashville, Tennessee 37203

Milene Music Inc. (ASCAP)
65 Music Square West
Nashville, Tennessee 37203

Milk Money Music (ASCAP)
c/o Tribe Mgmt.
201 N. Robertson Blvd., Ste. A
Beverly Hills, California 90211

Roger Miller Music (BMI)
c/o Burn Management Co.
211 E. 51st Street, Suite 8E
New York, New York 10022

Mills Music Inc. (ASCAP)
see EMI Music Publishing

Milsap (BMI)
12 Music Circle, S.
Nashville, Tennessee 37203

Mine Music, Ltd. (ASCAP)
c/o S. Weintraub
271 Madison Avenue
New York, New York 10016

Miniature Music (ASCAP)
c/o Richard Barone
240 Waverly Pl.
New York, New York 10014

Minong Music (BMI)
P.O. Box 396
Palos Heights, Illinois 60463

Miraleste Music
8127 Elrita Dr.
Los Angeles, California 90046

Miserable Melodies (ASCAP)
c/o Mike's Artist Management
225 W. 57th Street, Suite 301
New York, New York 10019

List of Publishers

Misery Loves Co.
c/o Bearsville Record Co.
Wittenburg Road
Bearsville, New York 12409

Miss Bessie Music (ASCAP)
9247 Alden Drive
Los Angeles, California 90210

Missing Ball (BMI)
211 E. 57th Street
New York, New York 10022

Mr. Bolton's Music (BMI)
c/o David Feinstein
120 E. 34th Street, Suite 7F
New York, New York 10011

Mister Sunshine Music, Inc. (BMI)
c/o Patrick Armstrong
P.O. Box 7877, College Park Sta.
Orlando, Florida 32804

Stephen Mitchell Music (BMI)
Portchester Music, Inc.
121 S. Rossmore Avenue
Los Angeles, California 90004

Mochrie Music (ASCAP)
155 W. 131st Street
New York, New York 10027

Modern Love Songs (ASCAP)
c/o Joel S. Turtle
3210 21st St.
San Francisco, California 94110

Mokajumbi (ASCAP)
see Personal Music

Mole Hole Music (BMI)
see Bug Music

Mondo Spartacus Music (BMI)
see Criterion Music Corp.

Charlie Monk Music (ASCAP)
40 Music Square, E.
Nashville, Tennessee 37203

Monkeys, Dogs, Cattle, Ltd. (ASCAP)
see MCA, Inc.

Monosteri Music (ASCAP)
c/o Zachary Glickman Artist
Management
19301 Ventura Blvd., Suite 205
Tarzana, California 91356

Monster Music (ASCAP)
see Bob-a-Lew Music

Montage Music Inc. (ASCAP)
Address unavailable

Bob Montgomery Music Inc. (ASCAP)
P.O. Box 120967
Nashville, Tennessee 37212

Moolagenous (ASCAP)
334 3rd Ave. S
Franklin, Tennessee 37064

Moon & Stars Music (BMI)
see EMI Music Publishing

Moonwindow Music (ASCAP)
c/o David Ellingson
737 Latimer Road
Santa Monica, California 90402

Moore & Moore (BMI)
c/o Careers Music
8370 Wilshire Blvd.
Beverly Hills, California 90211

Mopage (BMI)
334 3rd Ave. Sn
Franklin, Tennessee 37064

More Cut Music (BMI)
see Hancock Music Co.

Morganactive Music (ASCAP)
c/o Dennis Morgan
1800 Grand Avenue
Nashville, Tennessee 37212

Moriel (BMI)
see Beverly Glen Publishing

Morning Crew (BMI)
see Irving Music Inc.

Morning Pictures Music (ASCAP)
c/o Al Kasha
337 El Camino Dr.
Beverly Hills, California 90212

Giorgio Moroder Publishing Co. (ASCAP)
Att: George Naschke
4162 Lankershim Blvd.
North Hollywood, California 91602

Edwin H. Morris
see MPL Communications Inc.

Dale Morris Music (BMI)
812 19th Avenue, S.
Nashville, Tennessee 37203

Gary Morris Music (ASCAP)
c/o Cooper, Epstein & Hurewitz
342 Maple Dr.
Beverly Hills, California 90210

Morris Music, Inc. (BMI)
c/o Unichappell Music, Inc.
810 Seventh Avenue, 32nd Fl.
New York, New York 10019

Bryan Morrison Music, Inc. (ASCAP)
c/o Cavalier Entainment Corp.
205 W. End Ave.
New York, New York 10023

Marvin Morrow Music (BMI)
see Famous Music Corp.

Mosquitos (ASCAP)
Address Unavailable

Mota Music (ASCAP)
P.O. Box 121227
Nashville, Tennessee 37212

Mother Bertha Music, Inc. (BMI)
686 S. Arroyo Pkwy.,
Penthouse Ste. 175
Pasadena, California 91105

Mother Fortune Inc. (BMI)
641 Lexington Avenue
New York, New York 10022

Mother Tongue Music (ASCAP)
see Roger Cook Music

Motley Crue (BMI)
see WB Music

Mount Shasta Music Inc. (BMI)
c/o Careers Music
8370 Wilshire Blvd.
Beverly Hills, California 90211

MPL Communications Inc. (ASCAP)
c/o Lee Eastman
39 W. 54th Street
New York, New York 10019

MRC Music Corp. (BMI)
see Management Agency & Music
Publishing

MTM Enterprises Inc. (ASCAP)
see Reno-Metz Music Inc.

Mtume Music Publishing (BMI)
54 Main Street
Danbury, Connecticut 06810

Muffin Stuffin (BMI)
3624 Fir
San Diego, California 92104

Multi Culler Music (ASCAP)
see Sony Tree Publishing

Mumbi Music (BMI)
c/o Satin Tenenbaum
Elcher Zimmerman
2049 Century Park, E., Suite 3700
Los Angeles, California 90067

Munchkin Music (ASCAP)
Att: Frank Zappa
P.O. Box 5265
North Hollywood, California 91616

Eddie Murphy Music (ASCAP)
c/o ML Management Associates Inc.
152 W. 57th St., 47th Fl.
New York, New York 10019

List of Publishers

Muscle Shoals Sound Publishing Co., Inc.
(BMI)
P.O. Box 915
Sheffield, Alabama 35660

Muscleman Music
c/o Super Ron Music
Loeb & Loeb
10100 Santa Monica Blvd.
Suite 2200
Los Angeles, California 90067

Music City Music (ASCAP)
see EMI Music Publishing

Music Corp. of America (BMI)
see MCA Music

Music Design Publishing (ASCAP)
c/o Elias Assoc.
attn: Jonathan Elias
6 W 20th St.
New York, New York 10011

Music of the World (BMI)
8857 W. Olympic Blvd.
Beverly Hills, California 90210

Music Sales Corp. (ASCAP)
257 Park Ave. S., 20th Fl.
New York, New York 10010

Music Theatre International
49 E. 52nd Street
New York, New York 10022

Mustaine Music (BMI)
see Screen Gems-EMI Music Inc.

Muy Bueno Music (BMI)
1000 18th Street, S.
Nashville, Tennessee 37212

My Dad's Songs (ASCAP)
Box 5184
Santa Monica, California 90405

My Gig Music (ASCAP)
see MCA Music

My My Music (ASCAP)
Address unavailable

My Own Music (BMI)
c/o Ellie Greenwich
315 W. 57th Street
New York, New York 10019

Mycenae Music Publishing Co. (ASCAP)
Martin Cohen
740 N. LaBrea Ave.
Los Angeles, California 90038

Mystery Man Music (BMI)
c/o Richard Wagner
414 Grenada Crescent
White Plains, New York 10603

N

NAH Music (ASCAP)
c/o Wernick Sanders & Co.
100 Jericho Quad
Jericho, New York 11753

Narrow Dude Music (ASCAP)
c/o J. Issac Personal Management
789 S.W. Underhill
Portland, Oregon 97219

Nashlon (BMI)
63 Music Square, E.
Nashville, Tennessee 37203

National League Music (BMI)
6255 Sunset Blvd., Suite 1126
Los Angeles, California 90028

Nebraska Music (ASCAP)
attn: Randy Meisner
c/o Moore & Co.
16055 Ventura Blvd.
Encino, California 91436

Nelana Music (BMI)
see MCA, Inc.

Willie Nelson Music Inc. (BMI)
225 Main Street
Danbury, Connecticut 06810

Nero Publishing (ASCAP)
505 Jocelyn Hollow Court
Nashville, Tennessee 37205

Neutral Gray Music (ASCAP)
405 W. 45th Street, No. 4D
New York, New York 10036

New & Used Music (ASCAP)
c/o Fischbach & Fischbach P.C.
1925 Century Park E., No. 1260
Los Angeles, California 90067

New Daddy Music (BMI)
c/o Unichappell Music, Inc.
810 Seventh Avenue, 32nd Fl.
New York, New York 10019

New East Music (ASCAP)
c/o The Fitzgerald Hartley Co.
50 W Main St.
Ventura, California 93001

New Envoy Music (ASCAP)
8730 Sunset Blvd., Ste. 485
Los Angeles, California 90069

New Generation Music (ASCAP)
Att: Gary D. Anderson
7046 Hollywood Blvd.
Hollywood, California 90028

New Hidden Valley Music Co. (ASCAP)
c/o Manatt, Phelps, Rothenberg
& Phillips
11355 W. Olympic Blvd.
Los Angeles, California 90064

New Jersey Underground
see Bon Jovi Publishing

New Media Music (ASCAP)
c/o Paul Tannen
1650 Broadway
New York, New York 10019

New Music Group (ASCAP)
c/o Walter R. Scott
P.O. Box 1518
Studio City, California 91604

New Tandem Music Co. (ASCAP)
c/o Tandem Productions
1901 Avenue of the Stars
Los Angeles, California 90067

New Version Music (BMI)
c/o William James E. Lee
165 Washington Park
Brooklyn, New York 11205

New World Music Corp. (NY) (ASCAP)
75 Rockefeller Plaza
New York, New York 10020

Randy Newman Music (ASCAP)
c/o Gelfand, Rennert & Feldman
1880 Century Park, E., Suite 900
Los Angeles, California 90067

Newton House Music (ASCAP)
c/o E.G. Music
9157 Sunset Blvd.
Los Angeles, California 90069

Next Decade
730 5th Ave.
New York, New York 10015

Next o Ken (BMI)
Route 4, New Hwy. 96W
Franklin, Tennessee 37064

Next Plateau Entertainment (ASCAP)
1650 Broadway
New York, New York 10019

Nick-O-Val Music (ASCAP)
254 W. 72nd Street, Suite 1A
New York, New York 10023

Night Garden Music (BMI)
see Warner-Chappell Music

Night Kitchen Music (ASCAP)
c/o Manatt, Phelps, Rothenberg
& Phillips
11355 W Olympic Blvd.
Los Angeles, California 90064

Night River Publishing (ASCAP)
c/o Jack Tempchin
103 N. Highway 101, Apt. 1013
Encinatas, California 92024

Niji Music (BMI)
5315 Laurel Canyon Blvd.
N. Hollywood, California 91607

List of Publishers

No Cal Music (BMI)
Address Unavailable

No Ears Music (ASCAP)
4153 Woodman Ave.
Sherman Oaks, California 91423

No K. O. Music (ASCAP)
c/o Bug Music Group
6777 Hollywood Blvd., 9th Fl.
Hollywood, California 90028

No Pain, No Gain (ASCAP)
c/o Danny Sembello
1234 Third St., #286
Santa Monica, California 10401

No Surrender (BMI)
c/o Warner-Tamerlane
9000 Sunset Blvd.
Hollywood, California 90069

Nonpariel Music (ASCAP)
c/o Beldock Levine & Hoffman
99 Park Ave., Ste. 1600
New York, New York 10016

Norbud (BMI)
see New Tandem Music Co.

Northern Music Co.
Address Unavailable

Northern Music Corp. (ASCAP)
c/o MCA Music
445 Park Avenue
New York, New York 10022

Northridge Music, Inc. (ASCAP)
8370 Wilshire Blvd.
Beverly Hills, California 90211

Notable Music Co., Inc. (ASCAP)
Cy Coleman Enterprises
200 W. 54th Street
New York, New York 10019

Nottsongs
c/o Careers Music, Inc.
Att: Billy Meshel
8370 Wilshire Blvd.
Beverly Hills, California 90211

November Nights (ASCAP)
555 S. Barrington Ave.
Los Angeles, California 90049

Now & Future (ASCAP)
1800 S Robertson Blvd.
Los Angeles, California 90035

Now Sounds Music (BMI)
c/o Gelfand Rennert & Feldman
1880 Century Park E., Ste. 900
Los Angeles, California 90067

Noyb Music (BMI)
c/o Gary Corbett
2164 82nd Street
Brooklyn, New York 11214

N2D Publishing (ASCAP)
PO Box 121682
Nashville, Tennessee 37212

Nuages Artists Music Ltd. (ASCAP)
see Almo Music Corp.

Nurk Twins Music (BMI)
1660 N. Queens Road
Los Angeles, California 90069

Nymph Music (BMI)
90 University Place
New York, New York 10003

O

Oakfield Avenue Music Ltd. (BMI)
c/o David Gotterer
Mason & Co.
75 Rockefeller Plaza, Suite 1800
New York, New York 10019

Michael O'Connor Music (BMI)
P.O. Box 1869
Studio City, California 91604

Kenny O'Dell Music (BMI)
P.O. Box 43
Nolensville, Tennessee 37135

Of the Fire Music (ASCAP)
19 Bethune St.
New York, New York 10014

Off Backstreet Music (BMI)
90 Universal City Plaza
Universal City, California 91608

Oh-Ber (ASCAP)
Address Unavailable

O'Hara Music (BMI)
see MCA Music

Oil Slick Music (ASCAP)
2705 Glendoer Avenue
Los Angeles, California 90027

Old Brompton Road Pub. (ASCAP)
c/o Gwen Fuqua
279 S. Beverly Dr., Ste. 1058
Beverly Hills, California 90212

Old Fashion Music (ASCAP)
c/o Catherine Tiffany and Assoc.
9420 Reseda Blvd.
Ste. 827
Northridge, California 91324

Old Friends Music (BMI)
P.O. Box 121076
1225 16th Avenue, S.
Nashville, Tennessee 37212

Old Wolf Music (BMI)
c/o Little Big Town Music
803 18th Avenue, S.
Nashville, Tennessee 37203

Olga Music (BMI)
c/o Delores Jabara
135 79th Street
Brooklyn, New York 11209

Ollie Brown Sugar Music, Inc. (ASCAP)
attn: Margo Matthews
c/o Avant Garde Music
PO Box 92004
Los Angeles, California 90009

Olrap Publishing Co., Inc. (BMI)
c/o George R. Davis, Jr.
206 Vanderbilt Avenue
Brooklyn, New York 11205

O'Lyric Music (BMI)
c/o Jim O'Loughlin
1837 11th St., Ste. 1
Santa Monica, California 90404

Oman Kahalil (BMI)
Address Unavailable

On the Boardwalk Music (BMI)
888 Seventh Avenue
New York, New York 10106

On the Move
Address Unavailable

On the Note (BMI)
c/o Bug Music
6777 Hollywood Blvd.
Hollywood, California 90028

On the Trail Music
c/o Southern Melody Music
P.O. Box 4040, Duke Sta.
Durham, North Carolina 27706

One For Three (BMI)
see Warner-Chappell Music

One Song Publishing (BMI)
c/o Dave White
8250 Lankershim Blvd., No. 6 Pine
North Hollywood, California 91605

Onid Music (BMI)
see Island Music

OPC (ASCAP)
see Next Decade

Oppornockity Tunes (BMI)
see Zomba Music

Walter Orange Music (ASCAP)
c/o Grand & Tani Inc.
9100 Wilshire Blvd.
Beverly Hills, California 90212

List of Publishers

Orbisongs (ASCAP)
see EMI-April Music

James Osterberg Music
c/o Bug Music Group
6777 Hollywood Blvd., 9th Fl.
Hollywood, California 90028

Otherwise Publishing (ASCAP)
c/o Mark Tanner
9595 Wilshire Blvd.
Beverly Hills, California 90212

Out Time Music (ASCAP)
c/o Fitzgerald & Hartley
50 West Main St.
Ventura, California 93001

Oval Music Co. (BMI)
c/o Murray Wizzell
15 Central Park, W.
New York, New York 10023

Overboard Music
3432 La Sombra Drive
Los Angeles, California 90068

Overdue Music (ASCAP)
c/o Fitzgerald Hartley Co.
50 W Main St.
Ventura, California 93001

P

Pacific Island Music (BMI)
see Arista Music, Inc.

Martin Page Music (ASCAP)
see EMI Music Publishing

Paige by Paige Music (BMI)
see Cherry Lane Music Co.

Pal-Park Music (ASCAP)
c/o Mitchell-Silberberg-Knupp
11377 W. Olympic Blvd., Suite 900
Los Angeles, California 90064

Palancar Music (BMI)
see Chappell & Co., Inc.

Pamalybo (BMI)
see Irving Music Inc.

Panchin (BMI)
c/o Alan N. Skiena
200 W. 57th Street
New York, New York 10019

Pants Down Music (BMI)
c/o William Richard Cuomo
19815 Big Pines Hwy.
Valyermo, California 93563

Paper Boy Publishing (BMI)
Attn: Lorrin C. Bates
8674 Falmouth Avenue, No. 304
Playa del Rey, California 90293

Paperwaite Music (BMI)
c/o Twin Management Services Ltd.
641 Lexington Avenue
New York, New York 10022

Paradox Music
Address Unavailable

Pardini
Address Unavailable

Parker Music (BMI)
Tenth & Parker Streets
Berkeley, California 94710

Park's Music
see MCA Music

Parody Publishing (BMI)
c/o Mr. Don Bowman
1538 N. Grand Oaks
Pasadena, California 91104

Parquet Music (BMI)
111 W. 57th Street, Suite 1120
New York, New York 10019

Participation Music, Inc. (ASCAP)
c/o Zomba House
1348 Lexington Avenue
New York, New York 10128

Partner (BMI)
see Polygram Music Publishing Inc.

Party Music (USA) (BMI)
c/o Tim Berne
P.O. Box 1230
Canal Street Sta.
New York, New York 10013

Joe Pasquale Music (ASCAP)
c/o Des-Dawn Inc.
10608 Culver Blvd.
Culver City, California 90232

Pass It On Music (ASCAP)
see Pea Pod Music

Patchwork Music (ASCAP)
c/o David Loggins
P.O. Box 120475
Nashville, Tennessee 37212

Patricia Music Publishing Corp. (BMI)
c/o Big Seven Music Corp.
1790 Broadway, 18th Fl.
New York, New York 10023

Paul & Jonathan (BMI)
Route 2, Box 129
Kingston Springs, Tennessee 37082

Paulanne Music Inc. (BMI)
c/o Feinman & Krasilovsky
Att: Andrew J. Feinman, Esq.
424 Madison Avenue
New York, New York 10017

Paytons (BMI)
c/o Irving Music
1358 N. La Brea Avenue
Los Angeles, California 90028

P.B.T.W. Music (ASCAP)
7848 Ben Avenue
North Hollywood, California 91605

Pea Pod Music (ASCAP)
930 Brett St.
Inglewood, California 90302

Pebbitone Music (ASCAP)
see Diva One

Peer International Corp. (BMI)
see Peer-Southern Organization

Peer-Southern Organization (ASCAP)
810 7th Ave.
New York, New York 10019

Peg Music Co. (BMI)
c/o Earl S. Shuman
111 E. 88th Street
New York, New York 10028

Penrod & Higgins (ASCAP)
95 Hathaway St.
Providence, Rhode Island 02907

Pentagon Music Co. (BMI)
c/o Harold B. Lipsius
919 N. Broad Street
Philadelphia, Pennsylvania 19123

Penzafire Music (ASCAP)
see EMI Music Publishing

Perceptive (ASCAP)
c/o Jerry Green
25 Forest Hills Dr.
Farmington, Connecticut 06032

Perfect Pinch Music (BMI)
c/o Stephen Lunt
207 E. 37th Street, No. 4K
New York, New York 10016

Perfect Ten Music (ASCAP)
6255 Sunset Blvd., Ste. 705
Att: Donna Ross
Hollywood, California 90028

Perk's Music, Inc. (BMI)
c/o Duchess Music Corp.
MCA Music
445 Park Avenue
New York, New York 10022

Perren Vibes Music, Inc. (ASCAP)
Att: Christine Perren
4028 Colfax Avenue
Studio City, California 91604

Personal Music (ASCAP)
see BMG Music

883

Peso Music (BMI)
6255 Sunset Blvd., Suite 1019
Hollywood, California 90028

Petwolf Music (ASCAP)
c/o Savitsky Satin & Giebelson
1901 Ave. of the Stars
Ste 1450
Los Angeles, California 90067

PGP Music (ASCAP)
see Warner-Chappell Music

Philly World Music Co. (BMI)
2001 W. Moyamensing Avenue
Philadelphia, Pennsylvania 19145

Phivin International Enterprises
see Geffen/Kaye Music

Phosphene Music (BMI)
c/o Craig Krampf
4249 Rhodes Avenue
Studio City, California 91604

Pi-Gem Music Publishing Co., Inc. (BMI)
Address Unavailable

Piano (BMI)
c/o Connie Heigler
309 W. Broad Street
Philadelphia, Pennsylvania 19107

Pine Barrens Music (BMI)
c/o Fred Small
80 Aberdeen Avenue
Cambridge, Massachusetts 02138

Pink Pig Music (BMI)
Box 1770y But Music
153-155 Sanders Ferry Rd.
Hendersonville, Tennessee 37077

Pitchford (BMI)
1880 Century Park
Los Angeles, California 90067

Placa Music (BMI)
see Bug Music

Plain & Simple Music Corp. (ASCAP)
see Hudson Bay Music

Planet Dallas Music (ASCAP)
see WB Music

Playhard Music (ASCAP)
2434 Main Street
Santa Monica, California 90405

Pods Publishing (BMI)
c/o Law Financial
1 Gate Six Road, Suite E
Sausalito, California 94965

Poetical License (ASCAP)
c/o Socan
41 Valleybrook Dr.
Don Mills, Ontario M3B 2S6
Canada

Poetlord Music (ASCAP)
c/o John Mason, Esq.
Mason & Sloane
1299 Ocean Avenue
Penthouse
Santa Monica, California 90401

Buster Poindexter, Inc. (BMI)
c/o Blue Sky Records, Inc.
745 Fifth Avenue
New York, New York 10022

Point Music Ltd. (ASCAP)
see Cherry Lane Music Co.

Anita Pointer Publishing (BMI)
1901 Ave. of the Stars
Ste. 1450
Los Angeles, California 90067

Ruth Pointer Publishing (BMI)
Box 6588
Malibu, California 90265

Poison Brisket Music (BMI)
see Bug Music

Poison Oak Music (ASCAP)
c/o Goldman, Grant & Tani Inc.
10960 Wilshire Blvd.
Ste. 938
Los Angeles, California 90024

Pokazuka (ASCAP)
see Alamo Music, Inc.

Polifer Music (BMI)
c/o Manatt, Phelps, Rothenberg
11355 W. Olympic Blvd.
Los Angeles, California 90064

Polite Music (ASCAP)
Att: Crystal Zevon
6420 Wilshire Blvd., 19th Fl.
Los Angeles, California 90048

Polo Grounds Music (BMI)
Div. of David Rubinson & Friends
827 Folsom Street
San Francisco, California 94107

Polygram International (ASCAP)
1416 N. LaBrea Ave.
Los Angeles, California 90028

Polygram Music Publishing Inc. (ASCAP)
Att: Brian Kelleher
c/o Polygram Records Inc.
810 Seventh Avenue
New York, New York 10019

PolyGram Records Inc. (ASCAP)
810 Seventh Avenue
New York, New York 10019

Polygram Songs (BMI)
810 Seventh Avenue
New York, New York 10019

Ponder Heart Music (BMI)
see Almo Music Corp.

Poolside (BMI)
c/o Warner-Tamerlane
9000 Sunset Blvd.
Los Angeles, California 90069

Poopys (ASCAP)
see WB Music

Poperetta (BMI)
c/o Delores Jabara
12 Windy Hill Road
Westport, Connecticut 06880

Poppy-Due (BMI)
9570 Wilshire Blvd.
Beverly Hills, California 90212

Poppy's Music (ASCAP)
c/o Murphy & Kreff
1925 Century Park, Suite 920
Los Angeles, California 90067

Porcara Music (ASCAP)
c/o Fitzgerald Hartley Co.
7250 Beverly Blvd., Suite 200
Los Angeles, California 90036

Porpete Music (BMI)
P.O. Box 777
Hollywood, California 90028

Port St. Joe (BMI)
41 Music Square, E.
Nashville, Tennessee 37203

Portal Music (BMI)
c/o Mitchell, Silberberg & Knupp
1800 Century Park, E.
Los Angeles, California 90067

Portrait/Solar Songs Inc. (ASCAP)
c/o Sony Tunes
8 Music Square West
Nashville, Tennessee 37203

Posey Publishing (BMI)
412 Oakleigh Hill
Nashville, Tennessee 37215

Possibilities Publishing (ASCAP)
300 Main Street, Ste. 201
Huntington, New York 11743

Mike Post Productions, Inc. (ASCAP)
Darla Music Division
11846 Ventura Blvd., Suite 202
Studio City, California 91604

Postvalda Music (ASCAP)
c/o Bjerre & Miller
1800 Century Park E., No. 300
Los Angeles, California 90067

885

Raybeats Music (ASCAP)
  c/o Pat Irvin
  45-17 21st St. #4A
  Long Island City, New York 11101

Raydiola Music (ASCAP)
  PO Box 7819
  Northridge, California 91327

Razaf Music (ASCAP)
  c/o The Songwriters Guild
  276 Fifth Avenue, 3rd Fl.
  New York, New York 10001

Ready for the World Music (BMI)
  600 Renaissance Center
  Detroit, Michigan 48243

The Really Useful Group (ASCAP)
  c/o Eastman & Eastman
  3910 54th St.
  New York, New York 10019

Really Useful Music (ASCAP)
  c/o Eastman & Eastman
  39 W. 54th St.
  New York, New York 10019

Realsongs (ASCAP)
  Attn: Diane Warren
  6363 Sunset Blvd., Ste. 810
  Hollywood, California 90028

Receive Music (BMI)
  P.O. Box 3420
  Nashville, Tennessee 37219

Red Aurra Publishing (BMI)
  641 Lexington Avenue
  New York, New York 10022

Red Bullet Music (ASCAP)
  see Warner-Chappell Music

Red Cloud Music Co. (ASCAP)
  15250 Ventura Blvd.
  Penthouse 1220
  Sherman Oaks, California 91403

Red House Music (BMI)
  c/o Red House Records
  317 Main Avenue
  Norwalk, Connecticut 068516103

Red Instructional Music (ASCAP)
  c/o David B. Cole
  134 Ninth Avenue, No. 5F
  New York, New York 10011

Red Label (BMI)
  980 N. Michigan Avenue
  Chicago, Illinois 60611

Red Network Music (BMI)
  c/o RCA Records
  Att: Dorothy Schwartz
  1133 Avenue of the Americas
  New York, New York 10037

Red Sky
  Address Unavailable

Red Snapper
  see Fleetwood Mac Music Ltd.

Van Ross Redding Music
  see Carollon Music Co.

Redeye Music Publishing Co. (ASCAP)
  c/o Michael Mainieri
  275 W 10th St.
  New York, New York 10014

Reformation Publishing USA
  c/o Robbins Spielman Slayton & Co.
  1700 Broadway
  New York, New York 10019

Refuge Music, Inc. (ASCAP)
  see WB Music

Reganesque Music Co. (BMI)
  c/o The Songwriters Guild
  Att: Lewis M. Bachman
  276 Fifth Avenue, 3rd Fl.
  New York, New York 10001

Regent Music (BMI)
  110 E. 59th Street
  New York, New York 10022

Reggatta Music, Ltd.
c/o Phillips Gold & Co.
1140 Avenue of the Americas
New York, New York 10036

Rella Music Corp. (BMI)
see Warner-Chappell Music

Renjack Music (BMI)
see Mijac Music

Reno-Metz Music Inc. (ASCAP)
9000 Sunset Blvd.
Los Angeles, California 90210

Resaca Music Publishing Co. (BMI)
811 16th Avenue, S.
Nashville, Tennessee 37203

Reswick-Werfel (ASCAP)
6202 Bluebell Avenue
North Hollywood, California 91606

Revelation Music Publishing Corp. (ASCAP)
444 Madison Ave.
Ste. 2904
New York, New York 10022

Rewind Music, Inc. (ASCAP)
10201 W. Pico Blvd.
Los Angeles, California 90035

Reynsong Music (BMI)
215 E. Wentworth Avenue
West St. Paul, Minnesota 55118

Rhyme Syndicate Music (ASCAP)
c/o Myman, Abell, Fineman
& Greenspan
11777 Vicente Blvd., Ste. 600
Los Angeles, California 90049

Rhythm Ranch Music (ASCAP)
212 Robin Hill Road
Nashville, Tennessee 37205

Rich McBitch Music (BMI)
see Virgin Music

Rich Way Music, Inc. (BMI)
1117 17th Avenue, S.
Nashville, Tennessee 37212

Regina Richards (ASCAP)
197 10th Ave.
New York, New York 10011

Richer Music (ASCAP)
216 Chatsworth Drive
San Fernando, California 91340

Rickim (ASCAP)
Address Unavailable

Rick's Music Inc. (BMI)
see Warner-Chappell Music

Rightsong Music (BMI)
see Warner-Chappell Music

Rilting Music Inc. (ASCAP)
1270 Ave. of the Americas
Ste. 2110
New York, New York 10020

Ring Inc. (ASCAP)
see National League Music

Rising Storm Music (ASCAP)
c/o Fitzgerald Hartley Co.
50 West Main St.
Ventura, California 93001

Rit of Habeas (ASCAP)
c/o Fran Amiten
6520 Selma Ave.
Hollywood, California 90028

Riva Music Ltd. (ASCAP)
see Arista Music, Inc.

River House (BMI)
c/o Willie Nile
257 Kenview Blvd.
Buffalo, New York 14215

Riverstone Music, Inc. (ASCAP)
2910 Poston Ave.
Nashville, Tennessee 37203

R.K.S. (ASCAP)
see Jobete Music Co.

Roaring Fork Music
Address Unavailable

List of Publishers

Robertson Publishing (ASCAP)
Address Unavailable

Robin Hood Music Co. (BMI)
c/o John Marascalco
5531 Tuxedo Terrace
Hollywood, California 90028

Roland Robinson Music (BMI)
see Hitchings Music

Rock Dog Music (ASCAP)
c/o Carolina Bagnarol
526 43rd Avenue
San Francisco, California 94121

Rockin Leprechaun (ASCAP)
PO Box 278
Smartsville, California 95977

Rocknocker Music Co. (ASCAP)
c/o R2O Inc.
110 W 57th St.
New York, New York 10019

Rockomatic Music (BMI)
830 Warren Avenue
Venice, California 90291

Rocksmith Music (ASCAP)
c/o Trust Music Management
6255 Sunset Blvd., Suite 705
Hollywood, California 90028

Rockwood Music (BMI)
see Virgin Music

Rodsongs (ASCAP)
see Almo Music Corp.

Rok-Mil Music (BMI)
see EMI-Blackwood Music Inc.

Roliram Lorimar Music (BMI)
see Lorimar Music Publishing Co.

Rolling Tide Music (ASCAP)
c/o Holly Yellen Mgmt.
79 Main St.
Nyack, New York 10960

Rondor Music Inc. (ASCAP)
see Almo Music Corp.

Roosevelt Music Co., Inc. (BMI)
711 Fifth Avenue
New York, New York 10022

Rose Bridge Music Inc. (BMI)
1121 S. Glenstone
Springfield, Missouri 65804

Fred Rose Music, Inc. (BMI)
P.O. Box 40427
Nashville, Tennessee 37204

Roseynotes Music (BMI)
c/o Martin Wolff Associates
P.O. Box 4217
North Hollywood, California 91607

Rosstown Music (ASCAP)
c/o Loeb & Loeb
Att: John T. Frankenheimer
10100 Santa Monica Blvd.
Suite 2200
Los Angeles, California 90067

Rosy Publishing Inc. (ASCAP)
c/o Martin Cohen esq, Cohen
 & Luckenbacker
740 N. La Brea Ave.
Los Angeles, California 90038

Rough Play (BMI)
c/o Bruch Cohn
P.O. Box 878
Sonoma, California 95476

Round Wound Sound (BMI)
see Bug Music

Rounder Music (ASCAP)
Address Unavailable

Roundhead (BMI)
1900 Avenue of the Stars
Los Angeles, California 90067

Rowdy Boy Music (ASCAP)
640 N La Jolla
Los Angeles, California 90048

Royalhaven Music, Inc. (BMI)
P.O. Box 120249
Nashville, Tennessee 37212

R.U. Cerious (ASCAP)
Address Unavailable

Rubber Band Music, Inc. (BMI)
c/o Gelfand, Breslaver, Rennert
and Feldman
1800 Century Park, E., Suite 900
Los Angeles, California 90067

Rubicon Music (BMI)
8321 Lankershim Blvd.
North Hollywood, California 91605

Rude Music (BMI)
c/o Margolis Burrill & Besser
1901 Avenue of the Stars, No. 888
Los Angeles, California 90067

Ruff Mix Music (BMI)
Address Unavailable

Rugged Music Ltd. (ASCAP)
45 E. Putnam Avenue
Greenwich, Connecticut 06830

Ruler Music Co., Inc. (BMI)
P.O. Box 422
Trussville, Alabama 35173

Rumble Seat (BMI)
c/o Randy Sharp
14321 Valerio Street
Van Nuys, California 91405

Todd Rundgren (BMI)
see Fiction Music Inc.

Rush Groove Music (ASCAP)
1133 Broadway, Ste. 404
New York, New York 10010

Rust Enterprises, Inc. (ASCAP)
c/o Laurie Publishing Group
20-F Robert Pitt Drive
Monsey, New York 10952

Michael Rutherford Music (ASCAP)
see Hit & Run Music

Rutland Road (ASCAP)
see WB Music

Rye-Boy Music (ASCAP)
c/o Joel S. Turtle
3210 21st St.
San Francisco, California 94110

S

S J C Music (ASCAP)
c/o Jess S. Morgan & Co., Inc.
Att: John E. Rigney
6420 Wilshire Blvd., 19th Fl.
Los Angeles, California 90048

Sabal Music, Inc. (ASCAP)
1416 N La Brea Ave.
Los Angeles, California 90028

Sac-Boy (ASCAP)
c/o Robert F. Brookings
6201 Sunset Blvd.
Hollywood, California 90028

Safespace Music (BMI)
see WB Music

Carole Bayer Sager Music (BMI)
c/o Segel, Goldman & Macnow Inc.
9348 Santa Monica Blvd.
Beverly Hills, California 90210

Saggifire Music (ASCAP)
c/o April Music, Inc.
49 E. 52nd Street
New York, New York 10022

Sailmaker Music (ASCAP)
Att: Robert M. Millsap
PO Box 1028
Hot Springs, Arizona 71902

Sailor Music (ASCAP)
Box 4127
Bellevue, Washington 98009

Saja Music Co. (BMI)
see Warner-Chappell Music

List of Publishers

Saloon Songs, Inc.
see Sergeant Music Co.

Sanpan Music Inc. (ASCAP)
c/o Barnett & Assoc. Inc.
PO Box 246
Scottsdale, Arizona 85252

Kevin Savigar (ASCAP)
see Peer-Southern Organization

Sawgrass Music (BMI)
1722 West End Avenue
Nashville, Tennessee 37203

SBK Entertainment World (ASCAP)
1290 Avenue of the Americas
New York, New York 10019

Ricky Scaggs (BMI)
c/o Hall-Clement
1299 Ocean Avenue, Suite 800
Santa Monica, California 90401

Scaramanga Music (ASCAP)
c/o William A. Coben, Esq.
2029 Century Park, E., No. 2600
Los Angeles, California 90067

Scarlet Moon Music (BMI)
see CMI America

Don Schlitz Music (ASCAP)
PO Box 120594
Nashville, Tennessee 37212

Schwartz Music Co., Inc. (ASCAP)
Laurie Publishing Group
20-F Robert Pitt Drive
Monsey, New York 10952

Science Lab (ASCAP)
see EMI April Canada

Scoop (ASCAP)
Address Unavailable

Andrew Scott Inc. (ASCAP)
150 W. 56th St., Ste. 4005
New York, New York 10019

Scred Songs
see AGF Music Ltd.

Screen Gems-EMI Music Inc. (BMI)
6255 Sunset Blvd., 12th Fl.
Hollywood, California 90028

Sea Foam Music Co. (BMI)
200 W. 58th Street, #5E
New York, New York 10019

Seabreeze (ASCAP)
see WB Music

Seagrape Music Inc. (BMI)
c/o Jess S. Morgan & Co.
5750 Wilshire Blvd., Ste. 590
Los Angeles, California 90036

Sebanine (BMI)
see EMI Music Publishing

Sebastian Music (ASCAP)
see Word Music

Second Decade Music (BMI)
c/o TWM Management
641 Lexington Avenue
New York, New York 10022

Second Nature Music Inc. (ASCAP)
81 Clinton Avenue
Westport, Connecticut 06880

Security Hogg Music (ASCAP)
c/o Gudri, Chapnick & Co.
Sumatome Bank Bldg.
15250 Ventura Blvd.
Ste. 900
Sherman Oaks, California 91403

Seesquared Music (BMI)
1266 Stanyan Street, Suite 1
San Francisco, California 94117

Selessongs (ASCAP)
9710 Zelzah Avenue, No. 101
Northridge, California 91325

Semper Fi Music
attn: Mr. David Weiss
11031 White Oak Ave.
Granada Hills, California 91344

Senor Music (ASCAP)
Rte. 2 Box 94 B
Rope City, Texas 75189

Sergeant Music Co. (ASCAP)
c/o Sinatra Enterprises
1041 N. Formosa Avenue
Hollywood, California 90046

Seventh Son Music (ASCAP)
Box 158717
Nashville, Tennessee 37215

Sextunes Music (ASCAP)
see Unicity Music, Inc.

Terry Shaddick Music (BMI)
c/o Terry Shaddick
21219 Lopez Street
Woodland Hills, California 91364

Shade Tree Music Inc. (BMI)
c/o Merle Haggard
P.O. Box 500
Bella Vista, California 96008

Shakeji (ASCAP)
3221 La Mirada
Las Vegas, Nevada 89120

Shakin Baker Music, Inc. (BMI)
c/o Howard Comart, C.P.A.
1775 Broadway, Rm. 532
New York, New York 10019

Shaman Drum Music (BMI)
152-18 Union Turnpike, Apt. 125
Flushing, New York 11367

Shapiro, Bernstein & Co., Inc. (ASCAP)
Att: Leon Brettler
640 5th Ave.
New York, New York 10019

Sharp Circle (ASCAP)
P.O. Box 121227
Nashville, Tennessee 37212

Eddie Shaw Music Co. (ASCAP)
9128 Sunset Blvd.
Los Angeles, California 90069

Sheddhouse Music (ASCAP)
1710 Roy Acuff Place
Nashville, Tennessee 37203

Sheer Music (ASCAP)
1915 Interlaken Drive, E.
Seattle, Washington 98112

Shel Sounds Music (BMI)
see Irving Music Inc.

Sherlyn Publishing Co., Inc. (BMI)
see Big Seven Music Corp.

Shipwreck (BMI)
c/o Ellen Shipley
55 Third Place
Brooklyn, New York 11231

Shobi Music (BMI)
c/o DeBarris Music
1107 17th Avenue S.
Nashville, Tennessee 37212

Shop Talk (ASCAP)
c/o WB Music
9000 Sunset Blvd.
Los Angeles, California 90069

Short Order (ASCAP)
see MCA Music

Short Trip Music (BMI)
see Bug Music

Sikki Nixx (BMI)
9255 Sunset Blvd.
Los Angeles, California 90069

Silver Angel Music (ASCAP)
see Playhard Music

Silver Dollar Music (ASCAP)
see Bug Music

Silver Fiddle (ASCAP)
c/o Segel & Goldman Inc.
9200 Sunset Blvd., Suite 1000
Los Angeles, California 90069

Silver Nightingale Music (ASCAP)
Att: Ms. Joan Nemour
10861 Moorpark, #208
North Hollywood, California 91602

Silver Sun Music (ASCAP)
see Warner-Chappell Music

Silver Sun Publishers (ASCAP)
see BMG Songs Inc.

Silverline Music, Inc. (BMI)
329 Rockland Road
Hendersonville, Tennessee 37075

Sid Sim Publishing (BMI)
2112 Elder Street
Lake Charles, Louisiana 70601

Simile Music, Inc. (BMI)
see Famous Music Corp.

Paul Simon Music (BMI)
1619 Broadway
New York, New York 10019

Simonton (BMI)
c/o Sound Seventy Management
210 25th Avenue, N.
Nashville, Tennessee 37203

Sin Drome (BMI)
c/o SBK Entertainment
810 Seventh Avenue
New York, New York 10019

Sing a Song Publishing Co. (BMI)
R.R. 8, Box 532
Athens, Alabama 35611

Singing Ink Music (BMI)
P.O. Drawer 1300
Trinidad, California 95570

Singletree Music Co., Inc. (BMI)
815 18th Avenue, S.
Nashville, Tennessee 37213

Siquomb Publishing Corp. (BMI)
c/o Segel & Goldman Inc.
9348 Santa Monica Blvd.
Beverly Hills, California 90210

Sir & Trini Music (ASCAP)
Taylor & Lieberman
10866 Wilshire Blvd.
Los Angeles, California 90024

Siren Songs (BMI)
c/o Gelfand, Rennert & Feldman
Att: Babbie Green
1880 Century Park, E., No. 900
Los Angeles, California 90067

Sister Fate Music (ASCAP)
PO Box 763
Excelsior, Minnesota 55331

Sister John Music, Inc. (BMI)
c/o Publishers Licensing Corp.
94 Grand Avenue
Englewood, New Jersey 07631

Sitting Pretty (ASCAP)
see WB Music

Six Continents Music (BMI)
see Warner-Chappell Music

Six Pictures Music (BMI)
c/o Gelfand, Rennert & Feldman
1880 Century Park, E., No. 900
Los Angeles, California 90067

Sixty Ninth Street Music (BMI)
c/o Joey Carbone
13142 Weddington Street
Van Nuys, California 91401

Sizzling Blue Music (BMI)
19983 Ruston Road
Woodland Hills, California 91364

Skinny Zach Music Inc. (ASCAP)
PO Box 57815
Tarzana, California 91357

Skintrade (ASCAP)
Address Unavailable

Skull Music (BMI)
c/o Mac Rebennack
1995 Broadway
New York, New York 10023

Skunk DeVille (BMI)
Address Unavailable

Skyhill Publishing Co., Inc. (BMI)
see Island Music

Slam City (ASCAP)
attn: Alvin Moody
1285 Sunny Ridge Rd.
Mohegan Lake, New York 10547

Slam Dunk Music (ASCAP)
1046 Carol Drive
Los Angeles, California 90069

Slapshot Music (BMI)
c/o Shankman De Blasio
185 Pier
Santa Monica, California 90405

Slavetone Music (ASCAP)
3527 Wonderview Drive
Los Angeles, California 90068

Sleepy Hollow Music (ASCAP)
P.O. Box 7
Swannanda, South Carolina 28778

Slick Fork Music (ASCAP)
see Bug Music

Sloopus (BMI)
c/o Gold Horizon Music
Columbia Plaza, S.
Burbank, California 91505

Small Hope Music (BMI)
see Virgin Music

Smokin' Dog (BMI)
Address Unavailable

Sneaker Songs (BMI)
468 S. Aldenville
Covina, California 91723

Snow Music
c/o Jess Morgan & Co., Inc.
6420 Wilshire Blvd., 19th Fl.
Los Angeles, California 90048

Phoebe Snow Music (ASCAP)
1450 Palisade Ave.
Fort Lee, New Jersey 07024

Snow Songs (ASCAP)
c/o Snow Music
8809 Appian Way
Los Angeles, California 90046

Snowden Music (ASCAP)
Box 11512th Street
Purdys, New York 10578

Soft Music (BMI)
c/o Randall Oda
2023 Tamalpais Avenue
El Cerrito, California 94530

Soft Summer Songs (BMI)
1299 Ocean Avenue
Santa Monica, California 90401

Solar (BMI)
see Sony Songs

Solid Smash Music Publishing Co., Inc.
(ASCAP)
see EMI Music Publishing

Solidarity (ASCAP)
Address unavailable

Some Other Music
see Lipsync Music

Somerset Songs Publishing, Inc. (ASCAP)
c/o Int'l Royalty Services Inc.
attn: Michele Bourgerie
214 E 70th St.
New York, New York 10021

Song of Cash Inc. (ASCAP)
see House of Cash Inc.

Song Painter Music (BMI)
see Screen Gems-EMI Music Inc.

List of Publishers

Song Tailors Music Co. (ASCAP)
P.O. Box 2631
Muscle Shoals, Alabama 35660

Songmedia (BMI)
c/o Multimedia Entertainment
of Tennessee, Inc.
3401 West End Avenue, No. 185
Nashville, Tennessee 37203

Songs Can Sing (ASCAP)
P.O. Box 36496
Los Angeles, California 90046

Songs of Jennifer (ASCAP)
c/o Entertainment Music Co.
1700 Broadway, 41st Fl.
New York, New York 10019

Songs of Manhattan Island Music Co. (BMI)
see House of Cash Inc.

Songs of Polygram (BMI)
see Polygram International

Songs of the Knight (BMI)
136 E. 57th Street
New York, New York 10001

Songways Service Inc.
10 Columbus Circle, Suite 1406
New York, New York 10019

Sony Music (ASCAP)
550 Madison Ave.
New York, New York 10022

Sony Songs (BMI)
see Sony Music

Sony Tree Publishing (BMI)
1111 16th Ave. S.
Nashville, Tennessee 37212

Sony Tunes (ASCAP)
see Sony Tree Publishing

Sordid Songs (ASCAP)
c/o Socan
41 Valleybrook Dr.
Don Mills, Ontario M3B 2S6
Canada

Southern Melody Music
P.O. Box 4040, Duke Sta.
Durham, North Carolina 27706

Southern Music Publishing Co., Inc. (ASCAP)
see Peer-Southern Organization

Southern Nights Music Co. (ASCAP)
35 Music Square, E.
Nashville, Tennessee 37203

Southern Soul Music (BMI)
see Tree Publishing Co., Inc.

Southwind Music, Inc. (BMI)
c/o John M. Weaver
739 E. Main Street
Ventura, California 93001

Southwing (ASCAP)
1300 Division, Suite 202
Nashville, Tennessee 37203

Spaced Hands Music (BMI)
see Beverly Glen Publishing

Special Rider Music (ASCAP)
P.O. Box 860, Cooper Sta.
New York, New York 10276

Spectrum VII (ASCAP)
1635 Cahuenga Blvd., 6th Fl.
Hollywood, California 90028

Spelling Venture Music (BMI)
Att: Martie Long
1041 N. Formosa Avenue
Hollywood, California 90046

Larry Spier, Inc. (ASCAP)
928 Broadway, Ste. 205
New York, New York 10010

Spinning Avenue Music (BMI)
c/o Bug Music
6777 Hollywood Blvd.
Hollywood, California 90028

Spoondevil (BMI)
see Bug Music

Bruce Springsteen Publishing (ASCAP)
  c/o Jon Landau Management, Inc.
  Att: Barbara Carr
  136 E. 57th Street, No. 1202
  New York, New York 10021

Springtime Music Inc. (BMI)
  c/o Andrew Feinman
  424 Madison Avenue
  New York, New York 10017

Sprint (BMI)
  Address Unavailable

Sprocket Music, Inc. (BMI)
  10201 W. Pico Blvd.
  Los Angeles, California 90035

Sputnick Adventure (ASCAP)
  1485 Bayshore Blvd.
  San Francisco, California 94124

Stage & Screen Music Inc. (BMI)
  see Unichappell Music Inc.

Stark Raving (BMI)
  c/o Rothman Business
  P.O. Box 888503
  Dunwoody, Georgia 30356

Maurice Starr (ASCAP)
  c/o SBK Songs
  1290 Avenue of the Americas
  New York, New York 10019

Maurice Starr Music (ASCAP)
  see EMI-April Music

State of the Artless
  Address Unavailable

State of the Arts Music (ASCAP)
  c/o Quincy Jones Music Publishing
  3800 Barham Blvd., #503
  Los Angeles, California 90068

Statler Brothers Music (BMI)
  c/o Copyright Management Inc.
  50 Music Square, W.
  Nashville, Tennessee 37203

Stay Straight Music (BMI)
  c/o E.G. Music
  9157 Sunset Boulevard
  Los Angeles, California 90069

Stazybo Music (BMI)
  c/o Will Bratton
  611 Broadway, Ste. 422
  New York, New York 10012

Steeple Chase Music (ASCAP)
  c/o Segel and Goldman
  9348 Santa Monica Blvd., Suite 306
  Beverly Hills, California 90210

Billy Steinberg Music (ASCAP)
  see Sony Tree Publishing

Stephen Cannell Music
  see EMI-April Music

Sterling Music Co. (ASCAP)
  8150 Beverly Blvd., Suite 202
  Los Angeles, California 90048

Stevie Ray Songs (ASCAP)
  see Bug Music

Rod Stewart (ASCAP)
  c/o Armstrong Hendler & Hirsch
  Att: Barry W. Tyerman
  1888 Century Park, E., Suite 1888
  Los Angeles, California 90067

Stigwood Music Inc. (BMI)
  see Warner-Chappell Music

Still Life (BMI)
  c/o Warner-Tamerlane
  9000 Sunset Blvd.
  Los Angeles, California 90069

Jerry Stoller (ASCAP)
  Address Unavailable

Mike Stoller Music (ASCAP)
  9000 Sunset Blvd.
  Ste. 1107
  Los Angeles, California 90069

Stone Agate Music (ASCAP)
  see Jobete Music Co.

Stone and Muffin Music (BMI)
608 River Ridge
Nashville, Tennessee 37221

Stone City Music (ASCAP)
c/o Gary Michael Walters
8205 Santa Monica Blvd.
Ste. 1-122
Los Angeles, California 90046

Stone Diamond Music (BMI)
see Jobete Music Co.

Stonebridge Music (ASCAP)
see Bicycle Music

Storky Music (BMI)
see MCA Music

Strange Euphoria Music (ASCAP)
c/o VWC Management, Inc.
Att: Ann Wilson
13343 Bel-Red Road, Suite 201
Bellevue, Washington 98005

Strange Mind Productions (ASCAP)
see MCA, Inc.

Stranger Music Inc. (BMI)
c/o Machat & Kronfeld
1501 Broadway, 30th Fl.
New York, New York 10036

Stratium Music Inc. (ASCAP)
c/o Meibach & Epstein
680 Fifth Avenue, Suite 500
New York, New York 10019

Straw Songs (BMI)
see Unichappell Music Inc.

Streamline Moderne (BMI)
see Warner-Chappell Music

Street Talk Tunes
Manatt, Phelps, Rothenberg &
Tunney
11355 W. Olympic Blvd.
Los Angeles, California 90064

Streetwise Music (ASCAP)
5644 Tyrone Ave.
Van Nuys, California 91401

Charles Strouse Music (ASCAP)
see Big Three Music Corp.

Stygian Songs (ASCAP)
see Almo Music Corp.

Stymie Music (ASCAP)
Address Unavailable

Su-Ma Publishing Co., Inc. (BMI)
P.O. Box 1125
Shreveport, Louisiana 71163

Succubus Music (ASCAP)
see Warner-Chappell Music

Sugar Hill Music Publishing, Ltd.
96 West Street
Englewood, New Jersey 07631

Sugar Song Publications (BMI)
c/o Dutchess Music Corp.
Att: John McKellen
445 Park Avenue
New York, New York 10022

Sugartown Music (BMI)
see EMI-Blackwood Music Inc.

Sunflower County Songs (ASCAP)
P.O. Drawer 37
Hendersonville, Tennessee 37075

Sunset Burgundy Music, Inc. (ASCAP)
see Thriller Miller Music

Al B. Sure (ASCAP)
P.O. Box 8075
Englewood, New Jersey 07631

SVO Music
c/o Aaron Spelling Productions
Att: Marvin Katz
1041 N. Formosa Avenue
Los Angeles, California 90046

Swag Song Music (ASCAP)
5 Bigelow Street
Cambridge, Massachusetts 02129

Swallow Turn Music (ASCAP)
c/o Manatt, Phelps, Rothenberg & Ph
illips
11355 W. Olympic Blvd.
Los Angeles, California 90064

Swanee Bravo Music (BMI)
c/o Marty Panzer
500 E. 77th Street, Apt. 1627
New York, New York 10162

Keith Sweat Publishing (ASCAP)
c/o Gelfano, Rennert & Feldman
1301 Avenue of the Americas, 8th Fl

New York, New York 10019

Sweet Angel Music (ASCAP)
see EMI Music Publishing

Sweet Baby Music (BMI)
35 Music Square E.
Nashville, Tennessee 37203

Sweet Cyanide (BMI)
see Willesden Music, Inc.

Sweet Jelly Roll Music, Inc. (ASCAP)
P.O. Box 9109
San Rafael, California 94912

Sweet Karol Music (ASCAP)
c/o Music Umbrella
P.O. Box 1067
Santa Monica, California 90406

Sweet Summer Night Music (ASCAP)
100 Wilshire Blvd.
Ste. 2040, 20th Fl.
Santa Monica, California 90401

Sweet Talk Music Co. (ASCAP)
c/o Raen Nalli
A & R Consultants Inc.
219 S Main St.
Ann Arbor, Michigan 48104

Sweet Tater Tunes (ASCAP)
809 18th Ave. S.
Nashville, Tennessee 37203

Swiftwater Music (ASCAP)
Att: David L. Frishberg
6053 Burralo Avenue
Van Nuys, California 91401

Swindle Music (ASCAP)
c/o Joseph Minkes & Assoc.
2740 W. Magnolia Blvd.
Burbank, California 91505

Swing Tet Publishing (BMI)
c/o Dave Roberts
Box 153
2520 N. Lincoln
Chicago, Illinois 60614

Swirling Vortex (ASCAP)
Address Unavailable

Sy Vy Music (ASCAP)
Box 2264
Hollywood, California 90078

Sycamore Valley Music Inc. (BMI)
2 Music Circle, S.
Nashville, Tennessee 37203

T

T-Boy Music (ASCAP)
c/o Lipservices
1841 Broadway
Ste. 411
New York, New York 10023

T-Man (BMI)
Address Unavailable

Taco Tunes Inc. (ASCAP)
c/o Overland Productions
1775 Broadway
New York, New York 10019

Talk Dirty Music (BMI)
c/o The Bug Music Group
6777 Hollywood Blvd., 9th Fl.
Hollywood, California 90028

Talk Time Music, Inc. (ASCAP)
35 Lake Shore Drive
Copake, New York 12516

Tallyrand Music (ASCAP)
see Bicycle Music

Talmont Music Co. (BMI)
c/o Pickwick International
1370 Avenue of the Americas
Suite 603
New York, New York 10019

Tamir Music (ASCAP)
c/o Philip Springer
P.O. Box 1174
Pacific Palisades, California 90272

Tammi Music Ltd. (BMI)
c/o Zolt and Loomis
60 E. 42nd Street, Suite f1442
New York, New York 10017

Tan Division Music Publishing (ASCAP)
c/o Cheryl Lynn
8033 Sunset Blvd.
Los Angeles, California 90046

Tangerine Music Corp. (BMI)
Att: Joe Adams
2107 W. Washington Blvd.
Los Angeles, California 90018

Tapadero Music (BMI)
815 18th Avenue S.
Nashville, Tennessee 37203

Tarka Music Co. (ASCAP)
see Island Music

Tauripin Tunes (ASCAP)
c/o The Doobro Corp.
Att: Kathy Nelson
P.O. Box 359
Sonoma, California 95476

TCF (ASCAP)
see WB Music

Ted-On Music (BMI)
Gladwyne Postal
P.O. Box 376
Gladwyne, Pennsylvania 19035

Tee Girl Music (BMI)
see Tommy Boy Music

Teenie Bopper Music Publishers (ASCAP)
c/o A. Schroeder International,
Ltd.
200 W. 51st Street
New York, New York 10019

Teete (BMI)
c/o Bob Lieberman
825 N. San Vicente
Los Angeles, California 91608

Telephone Pole Music Publishing Co. (BMI)
P.O. Box 232
Marblehead, Massachusetts 01945

Temp Co. (BMI)
Att: Rochelle Mackabee
1800 N. Argyle, Suite 302A
Hollywood, California 90028

Tempo Music (ASCAP)
c/o Alexandria House
P.O. Box 300
Alexandria, Indiana 46001

Ten-East Music (BMI)
c/o L. Lee Phillips
Mitchell, Silberberg & Knupp
1800 Century Park, E.
Los Angeles, California 90067

10 Music (ASCAP)
Address Unavailable

10/10 (BMI)
c/o Careers Music, Inc.
8370 Wilshire Blvd.
Beverly Hills, California 90211

Tenacity Music (ASCAP)
Address Unavailable

Tender Tunes Music Co., Inc. (BMI)
c/o Werner Hintzen
United Artists Music Co., Inc.
6753 Hollywood Blvd.
Los Angeles, California 90028

Termite Music (ASCAP)
c/o Michael Woody
127 Holly Forest
Nashville, Tennessee 37221

Terrace Entertainment Corp. (BMI)
Box 239
Las Vegas, Nevada 87701

Terraform Music (ASCAP)
see Warner-Chappell Music

Texas City (BMI)
c/o Backstreet
90 Universal City
Universal City, California 91608

Texican Music Co. (ASCAP)
P.O. Box 22614
Nashville, Tennessee 37202

Thames Talent Publishing, Ltd. (ASCAP)
626 Lyon Farm Road
Greenwich, Connecticut 06830

Theory Music (BMI)
see Screen Gems-EMI Music Inc.

They Might Be Giants Music (ASCAP)
232 N. Fifth Street
Brooklyn, New York 11211

Thickouit Music (BMI)
c/o Alan Thicke
15431 Dickens Street
Sherman Oaks, California 91403

Bob Thiele Music, Ltd. (ASCAP)
1414 Avenue of the Americas
New York, New York 10019

Thirty-Four Music (ASCAP)
see Eddie Shaw Music Co.

This Is Art (BMI)
c/o Careers Music
8370 Wilshire Blvd.
Beverly Hills, California 90211

William Thomas (BMI)
Address Unavailable

Thornwall (ASCAP)
c/o Warner Brothers
9000 Sunset Blvd.
Los Angeles, California 90069

Three Knights, Ltd.
Address Unavailable

Three Story (ASCAP)
Address Unavailable

Threesome Music Co.
6100 Wilshire Blvd.
Ste. 1500
Los Angeles, California 90048

Thriller Miller Music (ASCAP)
9034 Sunset Blvd., Suite 250
Los Angeles, California 90069

Thunderkat (ASCAP)
Address Unavailable

Thursday Music Corp. (BMI)
c/o Fred Ahlert, Jr.
8150 Beverly Blvd., Suite 202
Los Angeles, California 90048

Tickson Music (BMI)
see Len Freedman Music

Tiger Bay Music (BMI)
1012 Fair Oaks, Suite 370
South Pasadena, California 91030

Tiger Shards
Address Unavailable

Tigertrax (BMI)
Address Unavailable

Tight List Music Inc. (ASCAP)
PO Box 742495
Dallas, Texas 75374

List of Publishers

Tika Tunes (ASCAP)
see Famous Music Corp.

'Til Tunes Associates (ASCAP)
c/o Symmetry Management
234 W. 56th Street
New York, New York 10019

Timberwolf Music (BMI)
2520 Cedar Elm Lane
Plano, Texas 75075

Time Coast Music (BMI)
6253 Hollywood Blvd., No. 1128
Hollywood, California 90028

Times Square Music Publications Co. (BMI)
1619 Broadway, 11th Fl.
New York, New York 10019

Timic (ASCAP)
Address Unavailable

Tintagel Music, Inc. (ASCAP)
c/o Earle Enterprises
Att: Linda Wortman
160 W. 88th Street
New York, New York 10024

Tiny Tunes (ASCAP)
attn: Roy Marinell
719 Harms Rd.
Glenview, Illinois 60025

Tioaga Street Music (BMI)
11684 Ventura Boulevard, Suite 509
Studio City, California 91604

Tionna Music
see Controversy Music

Tobago Music Co.
Address Unavailable

George Tobin (BMI)
c/o Studio Sound
11337 Burbank Blvd.
North Hollywood, California 91601

Tol (ASCAP)
Address Unavailable

Tomata du Plenti (ASCAP)
attn: Michael Lembo
594 broadway
New York, New York 10012

TomJon Music (BMI)
see Nero Publishing

Tommy Boy Music (BMI)
902 Broadway
New York, New York 10010

Tommy Jymi, Inc. (BMI)
c/o Dennis Katz, Esq.
845 Third Avenue
New York, New York 10022

Toneman Music Inc. (BMI)
6603 Lincoln Avenue
Carmichael, California 95608

Tongerland (BMI)
see Bug Music

Too Tall Music (BMI)
see EMI-Blackwood Music Inc.

Tools (BMI)
c/o Jim Tullio
405 N. Wabash
Chicago, Illinois 60611

Toosie (ASCAP)
Address Unavailable

Total X Publishing Co. (ASCAP)
see Tempo Music

Townsway Music (BMI)
c/o Mr. Garry Kief
P.O. Box 69180
Hollywood, California 90069

Towser Tunes Inc. (BMI)
c/o Ina Lea Meibach
Meibach & Epstein
680 5th Ave.
New York, New York 10019

Tranquility Base Songs (ASCAP)
see Warner-Chappell Music

Tree Publishing Co., Inc. (BMI)
see Sony Tree Publishing

Trevcor Music (ASCAP)
113 Karen Drive
Mt. Juliet, Tennessee 37122

Tri-Chappell Music Inc. (ASCAP)
see Chappell & Co., Inc.

Trinifold Music (ASCAP)
see Virgin Music

Trio Music Co., Inc. (BMI)
c/o Leiber & Stoller
9000 Sunset Blvd., Ste. 1107
Los Angeles, California 90069

Triple Star Music (BMI)
see EMI Music Publishing

Trixie Lou Music (BMI)
14234 Grandmont
Detroit, Michigan 48227

TRO-Cromwell Music Inc. (ASCAP)
11 W. 19th St.
New York, New York 10010

TRO-Essex Music, Inc. (ASCAP)
10 Columbus Circle, Suite 1460
New York, New York 10019

TRO-Hollis Music, Inc. (BMI)
10 Columbus Circle, Suite 1460
New York, New York 10019

Troph
Address Unavailable

Tropicbird (BMI)
P.O. Box 2605
Nashville, Tennessee 37219

Troutman's Music (BMI)
c/o Larry Troutman
2010 Salem Avenue
Dayton, Ohio 45406

Trumar Music (BMI)
c/o Prelude Records
200 W. 57th Street
New York, New York 10019

Trumpet Blast Music (BMI)
see Bug Music

Trunksong Music (BMI)
c/o The Shokatt Company, Ltd.
340 W. 55th Street, Suite 1A
New York, New York 10019

Trycep Publishing Co. (BMI)
c/o John P. Kellog, Esq.
33 Public Square, No. 810
Cleveland, Ohio 44113

Trycet (BMI)
Address Unavailable

TSP Music, Inc.
1875 Century Park, E., Suite 700
Los Angeles, California 90067

Tubbs Hill Music (BMI)
Division of Maple Hill Productions
P.O. Box 16
Hillsboro, New Jersey 03244

Tuggle Tunes Music (ASCAP)
c/o Gerald F. Rosenblatt, Esq.
100 Wilshire Blvd., Ste. 2040
Santa Monica, California 90401

Tunaday Songs (ASCAP)
1660 Orchard Dr., Apt. B
Placenita, California 92670

Tuneworks Music (BMI)
5061 Woodley Avenue
Encino, California 91436

Turnout Brothers Publishing Co. (ASCAP)
c/o Lawrence Lighter, Esq.
3 E. 54th Street, Suite 1200
New York, New York 10022

Turnpike Tom Music (ASCAP)
see United Artists Music Co., Inc.

List of Publishers

Turtle Music (BMI)
  c/o Theodore Glasser
  5229 Balboa Blvd., No. 17
  Encino, California 91316

Tutone-Keller Music (BMI)
  see New Daddy Music

Twentieth Century-Fox Music Corp. (ASCAP)
  Att: Herbert N. Eiseman
  P.O. Box 900
  Beverly Hills, California 90213

Twentieth Century Music Corp. (ASCAP)
  see Warner-Chappell Music

Twice As Nice Music
  c/o Gelfard, Rennert & Feldman
  1880 Century Park East
  Los Angeles, California 90067

Twin Duck Music (BMI)
  see Bug Music

Twist & Shout Music (ASCAP)
  c/o Hemming Morse Inc.
  650 California St.
  San Francisco, California 94108

Two-Sons Music (ASCAP)
  see WB Music

Two Tuff-Enuff Music (BMI)
  see Almo Music Corp.

Tyrell-Mann Music Corp. (ASCAP)
  Address unavailable

U

U/A Music, Inc. (ASCAP)
  c/o MGM
  Attn: Music Dept.
  2500 Broadway St.
  Ste. 3021
  Santa Monica, California 90404

Ujima Music (ASCAP)
  c/o Hall, Dickler, Lawler, Kent
    & Friedman
  2029 Century Park, E., Ste. 3590
  Los Angeles, California 90067

Ultrawave (ASCAP)
  see EMI Music Publishing

Unami Music (ASCAP)
  505 N 5th St.
  Att: Jimmy Ibbotson
  Aspen, Colorado 81611

Unart Music Corp. (BMI)
  see United Artists Music Co., Inc.

Unart-Unart (BMI)
  c/o Werner Hintzen
  United Artists Music Co., Inc.
  6753 Hollywood Blvd.
  Los Angeles, California 90028

Uncle Artie (ASCAP)
  Address Unavailable

Uncle Beave Music (ASCAP)
  see WB Music

Uncle Ronnie's Music (ASCAP)
  c/o Padell, nadell, Fine,
    Weinburger & Co.
  1775 Broadway
  New York, New York 10019

Under Cut Music Publishing Co., Inc. (BMI)
  c/o Robert Casper
  1780 Broadway
  New York, New York 10019

Underdog (BMI)
  P.O. Box 1517
  Key Largo, Florida 33037

Unearthly Music Inc. (BMI)
  see Fiction Music Inc.

Unforgettable Songs (BMI)
  see Fox Film Music Corp.

Unichappell Music Inc. (BMI)
  see Warner-Chappell Music

Unicity Music, Inc. (ASCAP)
see MCA, Inc.

United Artists Music Co., Inc.
6753 Hollywood Blvd.
Los Angeles, California 90028

United Lion Music Inc. (BMI)
c/o United Artists Corp.
729 Seventh Avenue
New York, New York 10019

Upward Spiral
see WB Music

Upward Spiral Music (ASCAP)
see WB Music

Urban Noise Music (ASCAP)
251 W. 89th Street, No. 2EE
New York, New York 10024

Urge Music (BMI)
c/o Blackwood Music, Inc.
49 E. 52nd Street
New York, New York 10022

USA Exotica (ASCAP)
7707 Sunset Blvd., Ste. 104
Los Angeles, California 90046

USA for Africa
5670 Wilshire Blvd.
Los Agneles, California 90036

U2 Music (ASCAP)
see Warner-Chappell Music

V

Vabritmar (BMI)
15445 Ventura Blvd.
Sherman Oaks, California 91413

Val-ie Joe Music (BMI)
c/o Shelton, Kalcheim and Cotnoir
79 W. Monroe Street, Suite 1305
Chicago, Illinois 60603

Valando Group (BMI)
1233 Avenue of the Americas
New York, New York 10036

Valgovino Music (BMI)
c/o Jess Morgan & Co.
Att: John Rigney
6420 Wilshire Blvd., 19th Fl.
Los Angeles, California 90048

Valley Music Ltd.
Address Unavailable

Van Halen Music (ASCAP)
c/o Nigro-Karlin & Segal
10100 Santa Monica Blvd., Ste. 2460
Los Angeles, California 90067

Van Hoy Music (BMI)
c/o Unichappell Music, Inc.
810 Seventh Avenue
New York, New York 10019

Vandorf Songs Co. (ASCAP)
15625 Vandorf Place
Encino, California 91436

Varry White Music (ASCAP)
6607 Sunset Blvd.
Los Angeles, California 90028

Vavoom (ASCAP)
c/o Warner Brothers
9000 Sunset Blvd.
Los Angeles, California 90069

Vavoom Music (ASCAP)
6224 15th Avenue, 2nd Fl.
Brooklyn, New York 11219

Velvet Apple Music (BMI)
c/o Gelfand
1880 Century Park E., Ste. 900
Los Angeles, California 90067

Venus Three Music (BMI)
c/o Ralph Hawkins
3429 Country Club Drive
Los Angeles, California 90019

List of Publishers

Vera Cruz Music Co. (ASCAP)
c/o Manatt Phelps & Phillips
11355 W. Olyumpic Blvd.
Los Angeles, California 90064

Verseau Music (BMI)
see Virgin Music

Very Every Music, Inc. (ASCAP)
c/o Roberta Flack
One W. 72nd Street
New York, New York 10023

Vibemeister (BMI)
Address Unavailable

Victunes (BMI)
c/o John Victor
100 Richmond West, No. 320
Toronto, Ontario M5H 3K6
Canada

Vine Street Music
Att: George Tipton
12249 Shetland Ln.
Los Angeles, California 90049

Vintertainment (ASCAP)
Address Unavailable

Virgin Music (ASCAP)
see EMI Music Publishing

Virgin Music Ltd. (ASCAP)
see Chappell & Co., Inc.

Virgin Nymph (BMI)
90 University Place
New York, New York 10003

Virgin Songs (BMI)
see EMI Music Publishing

Visa Music (ASCAP)
c/o Happy Sack Music
Att: Franny Parrish
5102 Vineland Avenue
North Hollywood, California 91601

Viva Music, Inc. (BMI)
c/o Warner-Tamerlane
Publishing Corp.
9200 Sunset Blvd.
Los Angeles, California 90069

Jerry Vogel Music Co., Inc. (ASCAP)
501 Fifth Avenue, 15th Fl.
New York, New York 10017

Vogue Music (BMI)
see Welk Music Group

W

Waifersongs (ASCAP)
see Warner-Chappell Music

Walden Music, Inc. (ASCAP)
see Warner-Chappell Music

Walk on Moon Music (ASCAP)
Address unavailable

Walkin Music (BMI)
Ziffren Brittenham Gullent & Ingber
2049 Century Park, E., Suite 2350
Los Angeles, California 90067

Wall to Wall Music (ASCAP)
8008 Stallion Ct.
Nashville, Tennessee 37221

Wallet Music (BMI)
1900 Avenue of the Stars
Suite 2270
Los Angeles, California 90067

Steve Wariner (BMI)
c/o Siren Songs
Gelfand, Rennert & Feldman
1880 Century Park, E., No. 900
Los Angeles, California 90067

Warlock Music (ASCAP)
see Island Music

Warm Springs (ASCAP)
c/o Ross T. Schwartz
9107 Wilshire Blvd., Suite 300
Beverly Hills, California 90210

Warner Brothers, Inc. (ASCAP)
  9000 Sunset Blvd.
  Los Angeles, California 90069

Warner Brothers-Seven Arts Music (ASCAP)
  9000 Sunset Blvd.
  Los Angeles, California 90069

Warner-Chappell Music (ASCAP)
  10585 Santa Monica Blvd.
  Los Angeles, California 90025

Warner/Elektra/Asylum Music (BMI)
  see Warner-Chappell Music

Warner House of Music (BMI)
  9000 Sunset Blvd., Penthouse
  Los Angeles, California 90069

Warner-Refuge Music Inc. (BMI)
  see Warner-Chappell Music

Warner-Tamerlane Music (BMI)
  see Warner-Chappell Music

Warneractive Songs (ASCAP)
  see Warner-Chappell Music

Warnerbuilt
  see Warner-Chappell Music

Warning Tracks Inc. (ASCAP)
  see MCA, Inc.

Watch Hill Music (BMI)
  c/o Unichappell Music, Inc.
  810 Seventh Avenue, 32nd Fl.
  New York, New York 10019

Wavemaker Music Group Inc. (ASCAP)
  c/o Lipservices
  1841 Broadway
  Ste. 411
  New York, New York 10023

WB Gold Music Corp. (ASCAP)
  c/o Warner Brothers Music
  10585 Santa Monica Blvd.
  Los Angeles, California 90025

WB Music (ASCAP)
  10585 Santa Monica Blvd.
  Los Angeles, California 90025

W.B.M. Music (SESAC)
  see Warner-Chappell Music

Web 4 Music Inc. (BMI)
  2107 Faulkner Road, N.E.
  Atlanta, Georgia 30324

Webo Girl (ASCAP)
  see House of Fun Music

Wedot Music (ASCAP)
  Att: Joseph E. Webb
  809 E. Sixth Street
  New York, New York 10009

Wee B Music (ASCAP)
  Route 2, Box 466-B
  Ash Street
  Central City, Kentucky 42330

Weed High Nightmare Music (BMI)
  c/o Screen Gens-Emi Music, Inc.
  6920 Sunset Blvd.
  Hollywood, California 90028

Welbeck Music
  see Cherry Lane Music Co.

Welbeck Music Corp. (ASCAP)
  see MCA, Inc.

Welk Music Group
  1299 Ocean Avenue, Suite 800
  Santa Monica, California 90401

Well Received Music (ASCAP)
  c/o Joel S. Turtle, Esq.
  1032 Broadway
  Russian Hill
  San Francisco, California 94133

Welsh Witch Publishing (BMI)
  c/o Gelfand, Breslauer, Rennert &
  Feldman
  1880 Century Park, E., Suite 900
  Los Angeles, California 90067

List of Publishers

Wenaha Music Co. (ASCAP)
P.O. Box 9245
Berkeley, California 94709

Wenkewa Music (ASCAP)
c/o Fitzgerald-Hartley Co.
7250 Beverly Blvd., Suite 200
Los Angeles, California 90036

WEP (BMI)
c/o Irving Music
1358 N. La Brea
Hollywood, California 90028

Lauren Wesley Music (BMI)
see Screen Gems-EMI Music Inc.

Westminster Music, Ltd. (ASCAP)
Address Unavailable

Billy Edd Wheeler
see Sleepy Hollow Music

Cheryl Wheeler Music (ASCAP)
see Bug Music

When Worlds Collide (ASCAP)
326 Panoramic Hwy.
Mill Valley, California 94941

Whiskey Drinkin' Music (BMI)
see Bug Music

White Cottage Music (ASCAP)
see Cross Keys Publishing Co., Inc.

Tony Joe White Music (BMI)
see Screen Gems-EMI Music Inc.

White Oak Songs (ASCAP)
156 5th Ave., Ste. 916
New York, New York 10010

Bobby Whiteside Ltd. (ASCAP)
Teapot Products Division
100 E Walton St.
Chicago, Illinois 60611

Whitesnake (ASCAP)
Address Unavailable

Whitsett Churchill Music (BMI)
c/o Tim Whitsett
4033 Manhattan Drive
Jackson, Mississippi 39206

Wicked Stepmother Music Publishing Corp.
(ASCAP)
1790 Broadway
New York, New York 10019

Wide Music (BMI)
c/o Segel & Goldman Inc.
9348 Santa Monica, Suite 304
Los Angeles, California 90210

Wild Gator Music (ASCAP)
Gudui Chapnick & Co.
Sumitome Bank Bldg.
15250 Ventural Blvd.
Sherman Oaks, California 91403

Willarie Publishing Co. (ASCAP)
see EMI Music Publishing

Willesden Music, Inc. (BMI)
c/o Zomba House
1348 Lexington Avenue
New York, New York 10028

William V (ASCAP)
see Welk Music Group

Dootsie Williams, Inc. (BMI)
PO Box 431217
Los Angeles, California 90043

Williamson Music (ASCAP)
see Warner-Chappell Music

Willin' David (BMI)
1205 16th Avenue, S.
Nashville, Tennessee 37212

Wimot Music Publishing (BMI)
c/o Alan Rubens
1307 Vine Street
Philadelphia, Pennsylvania 19107

Win or Lose Publishing (BMI)
see Walden Music, Inc.

Wind and Sand Music (ASCAP)
P.O. Box 324
Bearsville, New York 12409

Windecar Music (BMI)
see EMI-Blackwood Music Inc.

Window Music Publishing Inc. (BMI)
809 18th Avenue, S.
Nashville, Tennessee 37203

Wing & Wheel Music (BMI)
see Almo Music Corp.

Wing It
Address Unavailable

With Any Luck Music (BMI)
c/o Randy Sharp
14321 Valerio Street
Van Nuys, California 91405

Withrow Publishing (ASCAP)
see MCA, Inc.

M. Witmark & Sons (ASCAP)
see WB Music

WM Music
see Almo/Irving Music

Elliott Wolff Music (ASCAP)
Address Unavailable

Wolftoons Music (ASCAP)
68430 Perlita Rd.
Cathedral City, California 92234

Won Ton Music (ASCAP)
see Almo Music Corp.

Wonderland Music (BMI)
see Walt Disney Music

Wood Hall Publishing Co. (BMI)
1025 17th Avenue, S.
Nashville, Tennessee 37212

Wood Monkey Music (ASCAP)
c/o Barry Bergman
350 E. 30th St., Ste. 4D
New York, New York 10016

Wood Street Music, Inc. (BMI)
21051 Costanso Street
Woodland Hills, California 91364

Wooden Wonder (SESAC)
Address Unavailable

Woody Creek Music (ASCAP)
c/o Kaufman & Co.
1201 Alta Loma Road
Los Angeles, California 90069

Woolnough Music Inc. (BMI)
1550 Neptune
Leucadia, California 92024

Word Music (ASCAP)
Attn: Lu Ann Inman
5221 N O'Connor Blvd., Ste. 1000
Irvin, Texas 75039

Words & Wings Songs (BMI)
164 S. Kingsley Drive
Los Angeles, California 90004

World Song Publishing, Inc. (ASCAP)
see Warner-Chappell Music

Wow and Flutter Music Publishing (ASCAP)
5750 Wilshire Blvd., Ste. 590
Los Angeles, California 90036

Wren Music Co., Inc. (BMI)
c/o MPL Communications, Inc.
39 W. 54th Street
New York, New York 10019

Wrensong (ASCAP)
1229 17th Avenue S.
Nashville, Tennessee 37212

Writer's Group Music (BMI)
P.O. Box 120555
Nashville, Tennessee 37212

Writers House Music Inc. (BMI)
c/o Warner-Tamerlane
9000 Sunset Blvd.
Los Angeles, California 90069

List of Publishers

Wyoming Flesh (ASCAP)
    c/o Mitchell Froom
    1965 Canyon Dr.
    Los Angeles, California 90068

Y

Yadsirrom Music (ASCAP)
    see Warner Brothers, Inc.

Yanina Music (ASCAP)
    c/o Booker
    176 W. 87th Street, Apt. 6B
    New York, New York 10024

Yeah Inc. (ASCAP)
    Mr. Melvin Van Peebles
    353 W. 56th St.
    New York, New York 10019

Yellow Brick Road Music (ASCAP)
    see WB Music

Yessup Music Co. (ASCAP)
    10100 Santa Monica Blvd., Ste. 2340
    Los Angeles, California 90067

Yeston Music, Ltd.
    c/o Maury Yeston
    21 Pine Ridge Road
    Woodbridge, Connecticut 06525

Yiggy (ASCAP)
    see Irving Music Inc.

Yonder (ASCAP)
    see WB Music

Yontrop Music
    see Entertainment Co. Music Group

You and I Music (ASCAP)
    1800 Grand Avenue
    Nashville, Tennessee 37212

Yougoulei Music (ASCAP)
    c/o Fitzgerald-Hartley Co.
    7250 Beverly Blvd., No. 200
    Los Angeles, California 90036

Young Beau Music (BMI)
    66 Music Square W.
    Nashville, Tennessee 37203

Young Man Moving Music (ASCAP)
    c/o Turner & Irvine
    6500 Wilshire Blvd.
    Suite 2040
    Los Angeles, California 90048

Young Millionaires Club (BMI)
    see MCA Music

Young Terrence
    Virgin Music
    827 N. Hilldale Avenue
    West Hollywood, California 90069

Johnny Yuma (BMI)
    c/o Fitzgerald Hartley Co.
    7250 Beverly Blvd.
    Los Angeles, California 90036

Z

Zama Lama Music (BMI)
    c/o Copyright Management, Inc.
    1102 17th Avenue, S., Suite 401
    Nashville, Tennessee 37212

Zappo Music (ASCAP)
    see Bob-a-Lew Music

Zavion (SOCAN)
    1948 Sasamat Place
    Vancouver, British Columbia V6R4A3
    Canada

Ze'ev Music
    see Pal-Park Music

Zeitgeist Music Co. (BMI)
    c/o Gretchen Cryer
    885 West End Avenue
    New York, New York 10025

Zen of Iniquity (ASCAP)
    see Almo Music Corp.

Zero Productions (BMI)
c/o Clog Holdings
3300 Warner Blvd.
Burbank, California 91501

Zevon Music Inc. (BMI)
c/o Jess Morgan & Co., Inc.
6420 Wilshire Blvd., 19th Fl.
Los Angeles, California 90048

Ziggy (ASCAP)
see EMI Music Publishing

Zomba House (ASCAP)
137-139 W. 25th St, 8th Floor
New York, New York 10001

Zomba Music (ASCAP)
137-139 W. 25th St., 8th Fl.
New York, New York 10001

Zookini (ASCAP)
32670 Christian Way
Coburg, Oregon 97408

Zubaida Music (ASCAP)
see Arista Music, Inc.

ISBN 0-7876-0205-1

90000

9 780787 602055